BOOKS BY JAMES MERRILL

Poetry

Fiction

The
Changing Light
at Sandover

James Merrill

The Changing Light at Sandover

Including the whole of
The Book of Ephraim,
Mirabell's Books of Number,
Scripts for the Pageant
and a new coda, *The Higher Keys*

Atheneum · New York · 1982

"The Ballroom at Sandover" first appeared in *Harvard Magazine*

"The Book of Ephraim" originally appeared in *Divine Comedies*, copyright ©
  1976 by James Merrill
Mirabell: Books of Number, copyright © 1978 by James Merrill
Scripts for the Pageant, copyright © 1980 by James Merrill

Published simultaneously in Canada by McClelland and Stewart Ltd
ISBN 0-689-11282-3 (cloth); 0-689-11283-1 (paper)
Library of Congress catalog card number 82-72995
Manufactured by American Book-Stratford Press, Saddle Brook, New Jersey
Designed by Harry Ford
First Edition

CONTENTS

I

The Book of Ephraim

Tu credi 'l vero; ché i minori e ' grandi
di questa vita miran ne lo speglio
in che, prima che pensi, il pensier pandi.
Paradiso XV

Admittedly I err by undertaking
This in its present form. The baldest prose
Reportage was called for, that would reach
The widest public in the shortest time.
Time, it had transpired, was of the essence.
Time, the very attar of the Rose,
Was running out. We, though, were ancient foes,
I and the deadline. Also my subject matter
Gave me pause—so intimate, so novel.
Best after all to do it as a novel?
Looking about me, I found characters
Human and otherwise (if the distinction
Meant anything in fiction). Saw my way
To a plot, or as much of one as still allowed
For surprise and pleasure in its working-out.
Knew my setting; and had, from the start, a theme
Whose steady light shone back, it seemed, from every
Least detail exposed to it. I came
To see it as an old, exalted one:
The incarnation and withdrawal of
A god. That last phrase is Northrop Frye's.
I had stylistic hopes moreover. Fed
Up so long and variously by
Our age's fancy narrative concoctions,
I yearned for the kind of unseasoned telling found
In legends, fairy tales, a tone licked clean
Over the centuries by mild old tongues,
Grandam to cub, serene, anonymous.
Lacking that voice, the in its fashion brilliant
Nouveau roman (even the one I wrote)
Struck me as an orphaned form, whose followers,
Suckled by Woolf not Mann, had stories told them
In childhood, if at all, by adults whom

They could not love or honor. So my narrative
Wanted to be limpid, unfragmented;
My characters, conventional stock figures
Afflicted to a minimal degree
With personality and past experience—
A witch, a hermit, innocent young lovers,
The kinds of being we recall from Grimm,
Jung, Verdi, and the commedia dell' arte.
That such a project was beyond me merely
Incited further futile stabs at it.
My downfall was "word-painting." Exquisite
Peek-a-boo plumage, limbs aflush from sheer
Bombast unfurling through the troposphere
Whose earthward denizens' implosion startles
Silly quite a little crowd of mortals
—My readers, I presumed from where I sat
In the angelic secretariat.
The more I struggled to be plain, the more
Mannerism hobbled me. What for?
Since it had never truly fit, why wear
The shoe of prose? In verse the feet went bare.
Measures, furthermore, had been defined
As what emergency required. Blind
Promptings put at last the whole mistaken
Enterprise to sleep in darkest Macon
(Cf. "The Will"), and I alone was left
To tell my story. For it seemed that Time—
The grizzled washer of his hands appearing
To say so in a spectrum-bezeled space
Above hot water—Time would not;
Whether because it was running out like water
Or because January draws this bright
Line down the new page I take to write:
The Book of a Thousand and One Evenings Spent
With David Jackson at the Ouija Board
In Touch with Ephraim Our Familiar Spirit.

Backdrop: The dining room at Stonington.
Walls of ready-mixed matte "flame" (a witty
Shade, now watermelon, now sunburn).
Overhead, a turn of the century dome
Expressing white tin wreathes and fleurs-de-lys
In palpable relief to candlelight.
Wallace Stevens, with that dislocated
Perspective of the newly dead, would take it
For an alcove in the Baptist church next door
Whose moonlit tower saw eye to eye with us.
The room breathed sheer white curtains out. In blew
Elm- and chimney-blotted shimmerings, so
Slight the tongue of land, so high the point of view.
1955 this would have been,
Second summer of our tenancy.
Another year we'd buy the old eyesore
Half of whose top story we now rented;
Build, above that, a glass room off a wooden
Stardeck; put a fireplace in; make friends.
Now, strangers to the village, did we even
Have a telephone? Who needed one!
We had each other for communication
And all the rest. The stage was set for Ephraim.

Properties: A milk glass tabletop.
A blue-and-white cup from the Five & Ten.
Pencil, paper. Heavy cardboard sheet
Over which the letters A to Z
Spread in an arc, our covenant
With whom it would concern; also
The Arabic numerals, and YES and NO.
What more could a familiar spirit want?
Well, when he knew us better, he'd suggest

We prop a mirror in the facing chair.
Erect and gleaming, silver-hearted guest,
We saw each other in it. He saw us.
(Any reflecting surface worked for him.
Noons, D and I might row to a sandbar
Far enough from town for swimming naked
Then pacing the glass treadmill hardly wet
That healed itself perpetually of us—
Unobserved, unheard we thought, until
The night he praised our bodies and our wit,
Our blushes in a twinkling overcome.)
Or we could please him by swirling a drop of rum
Inside the cup that, overturned and seeming
Slightly to lurch at such times in mid-glide,
Took heart from us, dictation from our guide.

But he had not yet found us. Who was there?
The cup twitched in its sleep. "Is someone there?"
We whispered, fingers light on Willowware,
When the thing moved. Our breathing stopped. The cup,
Glazed zombie of itself, was on the prowl
Moving, but dully, incoherently,
Possessed, as we should soon enough be told,
By one or another of the myriads
Who hardly understand, through the compulsive
Reliving of their deaths, that they have died
—By fire in this case, when a warehouse burned.
HELLP O SAV ME scrawled the cup
As on the very wall flame rippled up,
Hypnotic wave on wave, a lullaby
Of awfulness. I slumped. D: One more try.
Was anybody there? As when a pike
Strikes, and the line singing writes in lakeflesh
Highstrung runes, and reel spins and mind reels
YES a new and urgent power YES
Seized the cup. It swerved, clung, hesitated,
Darted off, a devil's darning needle
Gyroscope our fingers rode bareback

(But stopping dead the instant one lost touch)
Here, there, swift handle pointing, letter upon
Letter taken down blind by my free hand—
At best so clumsily, those early sessions
Break off into guesswork, paraphrase.
Too much went whizzing past. We were too nice
To pause, divide the alphabetical
Gibberish into words and sentences.
Yet even the most fragmentary message—
Twice as entertaining, twice as wise
As either of its mediums—enthralled them.

C orrect but cautious, that first night, we asked
Our visitor's name, era, habitat.
EPHRAIM came the answer. A Greek Jew
Born AD 8 at XANTHOS   Where was that?
In Greece WHEN WOLVES & RAVENS WERE IN ROME
(Next day the classical dictionary yielded
A Xanthos on the Asia Minor Coast.)
NOW WHO ARE U   We told him. ARE U XTIANS
We guessed so. WHAT A COZY CATACOMB
Christ had WROUGHT HAVOC in *his* family,
ENTICED MY FATHER FROM MY MOTHERS BED
(I too had issued from a broken home—
The first of several facts to coincide.)
Later a favorite of TIBERIUS   Died
AD 36 on CAPRI   throttled
By the imperial guard for having LOVED
THE MONSTERS NEPHEW (sic) CALIGULA
Rapidly he went on—changing the subject?
A long incriminating manuscript
Boxed in bronze lay UNDER PORPHYRY
Beneath the deepest excavations. He
Would help us find it, but we must please make haste
Because Tiberius wanted it destroyed.
Oh? And where, we wondered of the void,
Was Tiberius these days? STAGE THREE

Why was he telling *us*? He'd overheard us
Talking to SIMPSON   Simpson? His LINK WITH EARTH
His REPRESENTATIVE   A feeble nature
All but bestial, given to violent
Short lives—one ending lately among flames
In an Army warehouse. Slated for rebirth

But not in time, said Ephraim, to prevent
The brat from wasting, just now at our cup,
Precious long distance minutes—don't hang up!

So much facetiousness—well, we were young
And these were matters of life and death—dismayed us.
Was he a devil? His reply MY POOR
INNOCENTS left the issue hanging fire.
As it flowed on, his stream-of-consciousness
Deepened. There was a buried room, a BED
WROUGHT IN SILVER   I CAN LEAD U THERE
IF   If? U GIVE ME   What? HA HA YR SOULS
(Another time he'll say that he misread
Our innocence for insolence that night,
And meant to scare us.) Our eyes met. What if . . .
The blood's least vessel hoisted jet-black sails.
Five whole minutes we were frightened stiff
—But after all, we weren't *that* innocent.
The Rover Boys at thirty, still red-blooded
Enough not to pass up an armchair revel
And pure enough at heart to beat the devil,
Entered into the spirit, so to speak,
And said they'd leave for Capri that same week.

Pause. Then, as though we'd passed a test,
Ephraim's whole manner changed. He brushed aside
Tiberius and settled to the task
Of answering, like an experienced guide,
Those questions we had lacked the wit to ask.

Here on Earth—huge tracts of information
Have gone into these capsules flavorless
And rhymed for easy swallowing—on Earth
We're each the REPRESENTATIVE of a PATRON
—Are there that many patrons? YES O YES
These secular guardian angels fume and fuss
For what must seem eternity over us.
It is forbidden them to INTERVENE

9

Save, as it were, in the entr'acte between
One incarnation and another. Back
To school from the disastrously long vac
Goes the soul its patron crams yet once
Again with savoir vivre. Will the dunce
Never—by rote, the hundredth time round—learn
What ropes make fast that point of no return,
A footing on the lowest of NINE STAGES
Among the curates and the minor mages?
Patrons at last ourselves, an upward notch
Our old ones move THEYVE BORNE IT ALL FOR THIS
And take delivery from the Abyss
Of brand-new little savage souls to watch.
One difference: with every rise in station
Comes a degree of PEACE FROM REPRESENTATION
—Odd phrase, more like a motto for abstract
Art—or for Autocracy—In fact
Our heads are spinning—From the East a light—
BUT U ARE TIRED MES CHERS   SWEET DREAMS   TOMORROW NIGHT

D ramatis Personae (a partial list
Which may conveniently be inserted here):

Auden, W(ystan) H(ugh), 1907–
73, the celebrated poet.

Clay, John, died 1774,
A clergyman. Now patron to DJ.

Deren, Eleanora ("Maya"),
1917–61, doyenne of our
American experimental film.
Mistress moreover of a life style not
For twenty years to seem conventional.
Fills her Village flat with sacred objects:
Dolls, drums, baubles that twirl and shimmer,
Stills from work in progress, underfoot
The latest in a lineage of big, black,
Strangely accident-prone Haitian cats.
Dresses her high-waisted, maiden-breasted
Person—russet afro, agate eyes—
In thriftshop finery. Bells on her toes,
Barefoot at parties dances. Is possessed
(Cf. her book on voodoo, *Divine Horsemen*)
During a ceremony (1949?)
By Erzulie the innocently lavish,
Laughing, weeping, perfume-loving queen
Among the loa, or divinities.

Farmetton, Rufus, dead of heart attack
In the Transvaal, 1925.
Previous incarnation of JM.

Ford, Kinton, 1810–43,
Editor of Pope's works. Inquiry,
Albeit languid, has unearthed to date
No vestige of this poor infatuate
Of letters, or his book—though now we know
Whence come the couplets that bedevil so
(Ephraim, no spell for exorcising them?)
His faithful representative JM.

Jackson, Mary Fogelsong, born 1890,
DJ's mother. Representative
Of Ayako Watanabe. Model
For "Lucy Prentiss" in JM's lost novel.

Lodeizen, Hans, 1924–50,
Dutch poet. Author of *Het Innerlijk
Behang*, &c. Studies in America.
Clever, goodnatured, solitary, blond,
All to a disquieting degree.
Plays a recording of the "Spring" Sonata
One May night when JM has a fever;
Unspoken things divide them from then on.
Dies of leukemia in Switzerland,
The country of a thousand years of peace.
At Stage One when we first get through
—And where he is denied the taste and hearing
Which are Ephraim's privilege at Six.
(Stage by Stage the taken-leave-of senses
RETURN TO US LIKE PICTURES ON A SCREEN
GROWN SOLID THAT AT 1ST ARE MERELY SEEN)
Hans's Stage is that of vision pure
And simple: rinse the cup with rum for him,
He cannot find his tongue, his eyes alone
Burn, filling . . . as this moment do my own.
Patron, that summer, to a holy terror
Known as Joselito, five years old,
On a plantation near Caracas where,
Says Ephraim, he CUTS CANE & RAISES IT

Merrill, Charles Edward, 1885–
1956, JM's father. Representative
Of a mystic from Calcutta he dismisses
As a DAMN POOR ADMINISTRATOR   Model
For "Benjamin Tanning" in *The Seraglio*.

Mitsotáki, Maria Demertzí,
1907–74. Described
Elsewhere (cf. "Words for Maria"). Dead
In these last months of the dictatorship.
Athens will be a duller town without her.

Pincus, Beatrice ("Betsy") Merrill, born
1937, JM's niece. Model
For "Ellen Prentiss Cade" in the lost novel.

Simpson, Ephraim's representative.
Reborn as "Gopping" (1955)
And (1956) as Wendell Pincus.

"Smith, Rosamund," character in the novel,
Later the Marchesa Santofior.
Perennially youthful, worldly, rich,
And out of sight until the close, at which
Point—but no matter, now. By degrees grows
Like all my "people" (the old Prentisses,
Their grandchild Ellen, Ellen's husband Leo,
Joanna flying toward them through the storm)
A twilight presence. *I* may need her still
But Ephraim shoulders her aside. She will
Have wrinkled soon to purple fruitlessness,
Leaving the outcome anybody's guess.

Yeats, W(illiam) B(utler), 1865–
1939, the celebrated
Poet. Author of *A Vision*.
Familiar spirit: Leo Africanus.

—For as it happened I had been half trying
To make sense of *A Vision*
When our friend dropped his bombshell: POOR OLD YEATS
STILL SIMPLIFYING

But if someone up there thought *we* would edit
The New Enlarged Edition,
That maze of inner logic, dogma, dates—
Ephraim, forget it.

We'd long since slept through our last talk on Thomist
Structures in Dante. Causes
Were always lost—on us. We shared the traits
Of both the dumbest

Boy in school and that past master of clauses
Whose finespun mind "no idea violates."

Ephraim nonetheless kept on pursuing
Our education. Ignorant and lazy
Though he must have found us, he remained
Sweetness itself. We hardly tasted
The pill beneath his sugar. USE USE USE
YR BODIES & YR MINDS —instead of being
Used by them? So imperceptibly
His bromides took, I only now detect
How that thirtieth summer of mine freed me—
Freed perhaps also D—to do the homework
Fiction had optimistically assigned
To adolescence. TAKE our teacher told us
FROM SENSUAL PLEASURE ONLY WHAT WILL NOT
DURING IT BE EVEN PARTLY SPOILED
BY FEAR OF LOSING TOO MUCH   This was the tone
We trusted most, a smiling Hellenistic
Lightness from beyond the grave. Each shaft
Feathered by head-turning flattery:
LONG B4 THE FORTUNATE CONJUNCTION
(David's and mine) ALLOWED ME TO GET THRU
MAY I SAY WEVE HAD OUR EYES ON U
—On our kind hearts, good sense, imagination,
Talents! Some had BORNE FRUIT   Others bore
Comparison with those the Emperor
Recruited, fine young fellows from five races,
To serve as orgy-fodder in CAPRICES
(Named for their locus classicus no doubt)
Which E, to tease our shyness, fleshes out
With dwarfs, tame leopards, ancient toothless slaves
Unmarred by gender, philtres up their sleeves;
A certain disapproving TULLIA   her
Red-and-white running in the de rigueur
Post-revel bath of dry Egyptian wine . . .

How by the way does *he* look? Blond, sun-kissed,
Honey-eyed, tall. AN ARCHAEOLOGIST
MEASURED THE BONES OF GERMANICUS I POINT 9
METERS I WAS TALLER   And what age
Does one assume in the next world? THE AGE
AT WHICH IT FIRST SEEMS CREDIBLE TO DIE
Ephraim accordingly, in our propped-up glass,
Looks AS I DID AT 22   The last
Mirrors he has used were at Versailles
In the 1780's. I WAS ALL THE RAGE
MY 2ND COURT LIFE   Mediums: d'Alençon,
The duke, and his smut-loving so-called son
BOTH CHARMERS—the old man by now at Stage
Two; the younger, twelve lives later, still a
Garbage collector SHAMELESS in Manila.

As for our patrons, we are far from certain
How influential Messrs Ford and Clay
Actually are. Oh, once the curtain
Falls, and we need help in the worst way
For the quick seamless change of body-stocking,
It's these who come. And they'll have much to say,
We ruefully suspect, about the play.
Viewed from the wings, what can it seem but shocking?
Manners, motives, idiom and theme
Horrify such fusty employees.
Vainly they signal us: Desist! Ugh! Please!
—All sense of play, in fact, quite lost on them.

On Ephraim not. A critic sound, we said,
As Shaw, with the edge of over nineteen hundred
Years to improve his temper. And now that Simpson
Had been again TYPECAST (Reborn? As what?
A PURPLE FORKED MALE PUKING NAMELESS THING
At GOPPING a vile crossroads God knew where—
Congratulations! NOT FOR LONG I FEAR)
Ephraim had resumed his volunteer
Work in that dimension we could neither

Visualize nor keep from trying to:
For instance (this March noon) as a fogswept
Milk-misty, opal-fiery induction
Center where, even while *our* ball is kept
Suavely rolling, he and his staff judge
At a glance the human jetsam each new wave
Washes their way—war, famine, revolution;
Each morning's multitude the tough
Tendril of unquestioning love alone
Ties to dust, a strewn ancestral flesh
—Yet we whose last ties loosened, snapped like thread,
Weren't we less noble than these untamed dead?—
Old falcon-featured men, young skin-and-bone
Grandmothers, claw raised against the flash,
Night-creatures frightened headlong, by a bare
Bright Stage, into the next vein-tangled snare.
PATRONS OF SUCH SOULS ARE FREQUENTLY
MADE SQUEAMISH   PAR EXEMPLE GBS
U MENTIONED HIM TONIGHT   AT 6 WITH ME
VEGETARIAN   ONCE HAD TO CLAIM
A FINE BROTH OF A BOY COOKED OVER FLAME
This was the tone we trusted not one bit.
Must *everything* be witty? AH MY DEARS
I AM NOT LAUGHING   I WILL SIMPLY NOT SHED TEARS

F lash-forward: April 1st in Purgatory,
Oklahoma. Young Temerlin takes me calling
On his chimpanzees. Raw earth reds and sky blues.
Yet where we've paused to catch our breath, the lake
Small and unrippling bleaches to opaque
Café-au-lait daguerrotype the world
It doubles. Stump and grassy hummock, hut,
Ramshackle dock—poor furniture
Of Miranda's island. She is sitting huddled,
Back to us, in the one tall, dead tree.
Only when Bruno gibbering thumps the dirt
Does she turn round, and see us, and descend
To dance along the hateful water's edge,
Making the "happy" sign. Behavior which
Allows for her no less inspiredly sudden
Spells of pure unheeding, like a Haydn
Finale marked *giocoso* but shot through
With silences—regret? foreknowledge? Who
Can doubt she's one of us? She has been raised
From birth in that assumption. It appears
The plan's to wed her—like as not, to Bruno
When both reach puberty—and determine what
Traces, if any, she will then transmit
To her own offspring, of our mother wit.
Now she's being rowed across to us,
Making the "hurry" sign. Now, heartbeat visible
Through plum-dark breast, child-face alight
Within its skeptic, brooding mask,
Has landed. Up the low red clay brow scrambles
Flinging her whole weight—as Temerlin's
Features disappear into one great
Openjawed kiss that threatens to go on
And on—"I'll watch a film of when they mate,

If I can stand it," he will say at lunch—
But for her manners. Here *I* stand,
Friend of her friend, whom she must either love
Or overlook or maul. Here is her hand
Reaching out for me, its charcoal glove
Scuffed and wrinkled; myself taken in
Before I know it, by uncritical eyes
—Unlike the moment—as we solemnize
Our new (our old) relation: kissing kin.

Moment that in me made the "happy" sign
Like nothing I—like nothing but that whole
Fantastic monkey business of the soul
Between lives, gathered to its patron's breast.
All those years, what else had so obsessed
The representatives of Clay and Ford?
Weren't we still groping, like Miranda, toward
Some higher level?—subjects in a vast
Investigation whose objective cast,
Far from denying temperament, indeed
Flung it like caution to the winds, like seed.

Take the equivocal episode beginning
When Gopping-Simpson's mother lets the baby
Drown in the bath. Ephraim, beside himself,
Asks don't *we* know any strong sane woman
In early pregnancy, reborn to whom
His charge would have a running start on life?
Hold on! who'd wish the likes of Gopping
On his worst enemy? But Ephraim briskly
Counters with a thousand-word show-stopping
Paean to the GREAT GENETIC GOD
By whose conclusion we cannot but feel
So thoroughly exempted from ideal
Lab conditions as to stride roughshod
Past angels all agape, and pluck the weird
Sister of Things to Come by her white beard.
I mention my niece Betsy. D has had

Word from an ex-roommate, name of Thad,
Whose wife Gin—that will be Virginia—West,
A skier and Phi Bete, is on the nest.

Ephraim, delighted, causes time to fly
(For he is hesitant to SLIP THE SOULS
LIKE CORRESPONDENCE INTO PIGEONHOLES
Until he hears, out of the womb forthcoming
Late in the sixth month, a MELODIOUS HUMMING
—Which, heard there, would do much to clarify
Another year's abortion talks in Rome)
And sure enough, soon after Labor Day
Not only he-of-Gopping but—get this—
Hans's Joselito, who drinks lye
At the eleventh hour, are at home,
One in Virginia, one in Beatrice.

Cause indeed for self-congratulation.
Diplomats without portfolio,
We had achieved, it seemed in the first glow,
At last some kind of workable relation

Between the two worlds. Had bypassed religion,
Its missionary rancor and red tape
No usefuller than the Zen master's top
Secret lost in silence, or in pidgin.

Had left heredity, Narcissus bent
Above the gene pool. As at a thrown stick,
Still waking echoes of that give-and-take
—Repercussions dire in the event—

Between one floating realm unseen powers rule
(Rod upon mild silver rod, like meter
Broken in fleet cahoots with subject matter)
And one we feel is ours, and call the real,

The flat distinction of Miranda's kiss
Floods both. No longer, as in bad old pre-
Ephraim days, do I naively pray
For the remission of their synthesis.

G uests were now descending on our village
Hideaway, drawn by the glowing space
Beneath its dome. Who were they? Patrons, mostly,
Of all whose names we mentioned. Any night
A Zulu chieftain could rub elbows with
Jenny, a pallid Burne-Jones acrolith,
Patrons respectively of a chum of mine,
Dead in grammar school, and Gertrude Stein,
Both safely back—he'll tell us where—on Earth;
But what is our time, what is Ephraim's worth?
Once stroked, once fed by us, stray souls maneuver
Round the teacup for a chance to glide
(As DJ yawns, quick!) to the warmth inside.
Where some of course belong: patrons of living
Dear ones—parents, friends—we dutifully
Ask after. Few surprises here. E's tact
Encourages us—PATRON NOT UNHOPEFUL
Meaning that things are really pretty grim—
To drop the subject. We don't challenge him.
If Maya is a WHITE WITCH or my father
ONLY IN HIS OLD AGE MAKING PROGRESS
It figures in both cases. And if Mary Jackson
Has narrowly, as a Sicilian child,
MISSED SAINTHOOD she deserves the martyr's palm
With oakleaf cluster for those thirty-nine
Mortal years with Matt. The lady from
Kyoto (Mary's patron) raises fine
Eyebrows—as if wives could choose!—then giggling
Calls MFJ a BLOSSOMING PLUM BRANCH
IN MY HUMBLE TOKONOMA   Others crowd
About us. Wallace Stevens, dead that summer,
Reads us jottings from his slate of cloud,
Graciously finds a phrase of mine to quote

—But ouf! So much esprit has left us quite
Parched for a double shot of corps.
We need a real, live guest. So Maya comes,
And soon to a spellbinding tape—dream-drums—
Can be discovered laying down in flour
Erzulie's heart-emblem on the floor.

That evening she danced merengues with us.
Then Ephraim, summoned, had her stand between
Two mirrors—candle-scissorings of gold;
Told her she was in her FIRST LAST ONLY
Life, that she knew it, that she had no patron.
The cat she felt kept dying in her stead
Did exactly that. She was *its* patron.
Smoke-ring enigmas formed to levitate
Into a swaying blur above the head.
Ephraim, we understood, was pleased; but Maya
Found him too much the courtier living for pleasure.
LETS HOPE THE LIVED FOR PLEASURE WILL NOT BE
ALL MINE WHEN YR WHITE WITCH SETS EYES ON ME
Whereupon Maya stiffens. She has heard
A faint miaow—we all have. In comes Maisie,
Calico self-possession six weeks old,
Already promising to outpoise by ounces
Ephraim as the household heavyweight.
Maya, shaken, falls into a chair.
She's had enough. Cattily we infer
E rocked the boat by getting her birthdate
Five years wrong; and not for five more years
Figure out that he had been correct.

Maya departs for city, cat, and lover.
The days grow shorter. Summer's over.

We take long walks among the flying leaves
And ponder turnings taken by our lives.

Look at each other closely, as friends will
On parting. This is not farewell,

Not now. Yet something in the sad
End-of-season light remains unsaid.

For Hans at last has entered the red room—
Hans who on his deathbed had still smiled
Into my eyes. He and our friend are friends now.
He teaches Ephraim modern European
History, philosophy, and music.
E is most curious about the latter.
What simpleminded song and dance he knew
Has reached the stage of what H calls TRANSFERRED
EXPERIENCE   So we must play him great
Works—*Das Lied von der Erde* and *Apollon Musagète*—
While like a bored subscriber the cup fidgets . . .
More important, Ephraim learns that Hans
Has INTERVENED on my behalf
As patrons may not. To have done so requires
SOME POWERFUL MEMORY OR AFFINITY
(Plato intervened for Wallace Stevens).
In any case HL REMEMBERS U
STILL HEARS THRU U JM A VERNAL MUSIC
THIS WILL BE YR LAST LIFE THANKS TO HIM
—News that like so much of Ephraim's leaves me
Of two minds. Do I want it all to end?
If there's a choice—and what about my friend?
What about David? Will he too—? DJ
HAS COME ALL THINGS CONSIDERED A LONG WAY
What things? Well, that his previous thirty-four
Lives ended either in the cradle or
By violence, the gallows or the knife.
Why was this? U DID NOT TAKE TO LIFE
Now, however, one or two, at most
Three lives more—John Clay, a beaming host
ALREADY PLANS THE GALA—Stop, oh stop!

Ephraim, this cannot be borne. We live
Together. And if you are on the level
Some consciousness survives—right? Right.
Now tell me, what conceivable delight
Lies for either of us in the prospect
Of an eternity without the other?
Why not *both* be reborn? Which at least spares one
Dressing up as the Blessed Damozel
At Heaven's Bar to intervene—oh hell,
Stop *me*. You meant no harm. But, well, forgive
My saying so, that was insensitive.

His answer's unrecorded. The cloud passed
More quickly than the shade it cast,

Foreshadower of nothing, dearest heart,
But the dim wish of lives to drift apart.

Times we've felt, returning to this house
Together, separately, back from somewhere—
Still in coat and muffler, turning up
The thermostat while a slow eddying
Chill about our ankles all but purrs—
The junk mail bristling, ornaments in pairs
Gazing straight through us, dust-bitten, vindictive—
Felt a ghost of roughness underfoot.
There it was, the valentine that Maya,
Kneeling on our threshold, drew to bless us:
Of white meal sprinkled then with rum and lit,
Heart once intricate as birdsong, it
Hardened on the spot. Much come-and-go
Has blackened, pared the scabby curlicue
Down to smatterings which, even so,
Promise to last this lifetime. That will do.

High upon darkness, emptiness—at a height
Our stories equalled—on a pane's trapeze
Had swung beyond the sill now this entire
Rosy-lit interior: food, drink,
People at table, sheer gemütlichkeit
Of insupportable hypotheses
Hovering there. It was a pied-à-terre
Made for his at-homes, we liked to think.

Though when the autumn winds blew how it trembled!
What speed-of-light redecorations,
As we began to move from place to place,
It suffered—presto! room and guests assembled
By a flicked switch, the host's own presence
Everywhere felt, who never showed his face.

How could we see him? DIE his answer came
Followed by the seemlier afterthought
HYPNOSIS With a how-to-do-it book
From the Amherst library (that year I taught)
On the first try, one evening in mid-fall,
I put D under. Ephraim had coyly threatened
To lead us BY THE HAND TO PARADISE
& NOT LET GO We were alone, with Maisie,
In a white farmhouse up a gravel road
Where Frost had visited. DJ's oldfashioned
Trust in nature human and divine
Was anything but Frostian. As for mine,
Trances like these are merciful, and end
I prayed. We held hands. We invoked our friend.
The stillness deepened. Garlands of long dead
Roses hung on every wall. Was Ephraim there?
No cup would move, this time. D's lips instead

Did, and a voice not his, less near,
Deeper than his, now limpid, now unclear,
Said where he was was room for me as well.
Whose for that matter was the hand I held?
It had grown cool, impersonal. It led
Me to a deep black couch, and stroked my face
The blood had drained from. Caught up in his strong
Flow of compulsion, mine was to resist.
The more thrilled through, the less I went along,
A river stone, blind, clenched against whatever
Was happening that once. (Only this May
D lets me have the notes he made next morning,
Wherein a number of small touches rhyme
With Maya's dream—as we shall see.) The room
Grown dim, an undrawn curtain in the panes'
Glass night tawnily maned, lit from below
So that hair-wisps of brightness quickened slowly
the limbs & torso muscled by long folds of
an unemasculated Blake nude. Who then
actually was in the room, at arm's length,
glowing with strength, asking if he pleased me. I
said yes. His smile was that of an old friend, so
casual. Hair golden, eyes that amazing
blood-washed gold our headlights catch, foxes perhaps
or wildcats. He looked, oh, 25 but seemed
light years older. As he stroked J's face & throat
I felt a stab of the old possessiveness.
Souls can't feel at E's level. He somehow was
using me, my senses, to touch JM who
this morning swears it was my hand stroking him.
(Typical of J to keep, throughout, staring
off somewhere else.) Now Ephraim tried to lead me
to the mirror and I held back. Putting his
hand on me then, my excitement, which he breathed
smiling, already fading, to keep secret
Eyebeam sparkling coolly into black,

Lips rippling back into the glass-warp, breathing
Love . . . So much, so little, David saw.

That was before our brush with Divine Law.

I'd rather skip this part, but courage—
What we dream up must be lived down, I think.
I went to my ex-shrink
With the whole story, right through the miscarriage

Of plans for Joselito. He
Got born to a VIRGINIA WEST IN STATE
ASYLUM —D too late
Recalls "Gin's" real name: Jennifer Marie.

(The following week, I'll scarcely dare
Ask after Betsy. But her child, it seems,
OUTDOES THE WILDEST DREAMS
OF PATRONS   Whew. And later, when through fair

Silk bangs, at six months, Wendell peers
Up at me, what are such serene blue eyes
For, but to recognize—?
However.) We have MEDDLED   And the POWERS

ARE FURIOUS   Hans, in Dutch and grim,
May send no further word. Ephraim they've brought
Before a kind of court
And thrown the book (the Good Book? YES) at him.

We now scare *him* with flippancies.
DO U WANT TO LOSE ME   WELL U COULD
AGENTS CAN BREAK OUR CODE
TO SMITHEREENS   How Kafka! PLEASE O PLEASE

Whereupon the cup went dead,
And since then—no response, hard as we've tried,

29

"And so I just thought I'd . . ."
Winding up lamely. "Quite," the doctor said,

Exuding insight. "There's a phrase
You may have heard—what you and David do
We call folie à deux.
Harmless; but can you find no simpler ways

To sound each other's depths of spirit
Than taking literally that epigram
Of Wilde's I'm getting damn
Tired of hearing my best patients parrot?"

"Given a mask, you mean, we'll tell—?"
Tom nodded. "So the truth was what we heard?"
"*A* truth," he shrugged. "It's hard
To speak of *the* truth. Now suppose you spell

It out. What underlies these odd
Inseminations by psycho-roulette?"
I stared, then saw the light:
"Somewhere a Father Figure shakes his rod

At sons who have not sired a child?
Through our own spirit we can both proclaim
And shuffle off the blame
For how we live—that good enough?" Tom smiled

And rose. "I've heard worse. Those thyroid
Pills—you still use them? Don't. And keep in touch."
I walked out into much
Guilt-obliterating sunlight. FREUD

We learned that evening DESPAIRS
OF HIS DISCIPLES & SAYS BITTE NIE
ZU AUFGEBEN THE KEY
TO YR OWN NATURES   We felt clouds disperse

On all sides. Our beloved friend
Was back with us! We'd think some other time
About the hour with Tom
—Nonchalance that would gradually extend

Over a widening area. The question
Of who or what we took Ephraim to be,
And of what truths (if any) we considered
Him spokesman, had arisen from the start.
If he had blacked out reason (or vice versa)
On first sight, we instinctively avoided
Facing the eclipse with naked eye.
Early attempts to check what he let fall
Failed, E's grasp of dates and places being
Feeble as ours, his Latin like my own
Vestigial; even D knew better German.
As through smoked glass, we charily observed
Either that his memory was spotty
(Whose wouldn't be, after two thousand years?)
Or that his lights and darks were a projection
Of what already burned, at some obscure
Level or another, in our skulls.
We, all we knew, dreamed, felt and had forgotten,
Flesh made word, became through him a set of
Quasi-grammatical constructions which
Could utter some things clearly, forcibly,
Others not. Like Tosca hadn't we
Lived for art and love? We were not tough-
Or literal-minded, or unduly patient
With those who were. Hadn't—from books, from living—
The profusion dawned on us, of "languages"
Any one of which, to who could read it,
Lit up the system it conceived?—bird-flight,
Hallucinogen, chorale and horoscope:
Each its own world, hypnotic, many-sided
Facet of the universal gem.
Ephraim's revelations—we had them
For comfort, thrills and chills, "material."

He didn't cavil. *He* was the revelation
(Or if we had created him, then we were).
The point—one twinkling point by now of thousands—
Was never to forego, in favor of
Plain dull proof, the marvelous nightly pudding.

J oanna (Chapter One) sat in the plane,
Smoke pouring from her nostrils. Outside, rain;
Sunset; mild azure; sable bulks awince
With fire—and all these visible at once
While Heaven, quartered like a billionaire's
Coat of arms, put on stupendous airs.
Earth lurched and shivered in the storm's embrace
But kept her distances, lifting a face
Unthinkingly dramatic in repose
As was Joanna's. Dessicated rose
Light hot on bone, ridge, socket where the streak
Of glancing water—if a glance could speak—
Said, "Trace me back to some loud, shallow, chill,
Underlying motive's overspill."

Ephraim scolds me for the lost novel's
Fire and brimstone version of his powers.
Meteorological eeriness
On the above lines left him cold, let's say.
Yet who originally makes us feel
The eeriness of Santa Fe?
He cannot think why we have gone out there
That summer (1958). THE AIR
ABOVE LOS ALAMOS IS LIKE A BREATH
SUCKED IN HORROR   TOD MORT MUERTE DEATH
—Meaning the nearby nuclear research
Our instinct first is to deplore, and second
To think no more of. Witter Bynner reads
Renderings of T'ang poetry he made
As a young man. Firelight on spinach jade
Or white jade buckles, and austere
Bass-bullfrog notes. Li Po himself draws near—
NO BEAUTY Ephraim dryly judges, yet

IN SIMPLE HONESTY MY SLEEVE WAS WET
Or, afternoons, an easy drive from town,
Chimayo's clay and water spell works on us:
Adobe sanctuary for the glow
Of piñon-scented candles. Circus-tent
Rainbow carpentry frames booth on booth
From which, adroitly skewered, smocked by Sears,
Tall dolls personify the atmosphere's
Overall anguish and high spirits, both.
Whatever these old carnivals once meant,
The wonder is, how they still entertain!
Pale blue wax roses—we're outdoors again—
Deck the wooden crosses, a poor crop,
Sun-bleached Martínez, splintering Ortiz,
Bees buzzing, or a dozen terminal z's.
Between them and the present flows a clear
Stream shaded by great cottonwoods. It's here
That Ephraim tangles with A KIND OF GOD
HALF MAN HALF TALKING TREE ICECAPPED PEATSHOD
Transported from ALEUTIA 40 ODD
MILLENIA BC and on this spot
Left by his followers TO MELT & ROT
While they pressed southward. Soon as we appear
Crossing his stream, he stumps up full of fear
That we will claim it—HOW HE DITHERS ON
FIRST GOD OF MY ACQUAINTANCE & O DEAR

Back to the novel for a bit, it's here
Gentle Sergei Markovich, in his bone
And turquoise necklace, was to come one day
As he had done for years—alone or with
People who mattered, Leo, Mrs Smith—
And find the very crosses turned to stone;
Crutches (that thick as bats hung from the ceiling
Above a pit of wonder-working clay
Beyond the altar—Lucy swears by it)
Gone; whitewash everywhere. He'd have the feeling
He too was cured, refurbished, on his way . . .

Here as well, Joanna and Sergei
"Recognize" each other, or I as author
Recognize in them the plus and minus
—Good and evil, let my reader say—
Vital to the psychic current's flow.
Joanna worries me. (Sergei I know.)
I need to dip into that murky roman
Fleuve our friends, lawyers, the press, worked on
Throughout my awkward age, when glances did
Speak volumes. We called this one *The Other Woman*.
The stepmother whom in due course I met
Bore no resemblance to its heroine.
Whereas Joanna . . . Jung on the destructive
Anima would one day help me breathe
The smoke of her eternal cigarette
Coiling round Old Matt Prentiss—with a cough
Woken by acrid nothings in his ear,
His knobby fingers gripped between her thighs
(In the twin bed Lucy sleeps on and off).
Would help me hear Joanna, her ex-drunk's
Snorts of euphoria, the Magic Fire
Music filling her earphones. Help me see
By the cruel reading light her sun-scabbed brow,
Thin hair dyed setter-auburn. Finally
To be, as she can never, this entire
Parched landscape my lost pages fly her toward,
Carrying a gift-wrapped Ouija board.

Kimono'd in red gold, SWIRLS BEFORE PINE
Ayako sights us through a pale bronze disc
Half mirror and half gong
Hanging at Kamakura, in the shrine.

From the Osaka puppets we are learning
What *to be moved* means. And at Koya-san—
Sun-shaft and cryptomeria,
Smoke-samurai, incensed retainers turning

To alabaster—word comes of my father's
Peaceful death, his funeral tomorrow.
There will be no way to fly back in time.
Trapped by a phone booth, my transparency
Betrays (a young Zen priest centuries old
Tells Ephraim with approval) 16FOLD
LACK OF EMOTION   Which may be the view
From where they sit. Then CEM gets through,
High-spirited, incredulous—he'd tried
The Board without success when Nana died.
Are we in India? Some goddam fool
Hindoo is sending him to Sunday School.
He loved his wives, his other children, me;
Looks forward to his next life. Would not be
Weeping in *my* shoes. An offhand salute,
And gone! TOO BOYISH IN HIS NEW GREEN SUIT

Ephraim, who enjoys this flying trip
Round the world more than we do, sees us next
At the tailor's in Kowloon:
MY DEARS I AM BEST SUITED WHEN U STRIP

In Bangkok stumbles on us laid full length
Each on a bamboo dais, flexible

36

And polished dark as teak by smokers' oils.
While DJ dreams, I retch all night.
Wat Arun's tall rice-paper lantern not
Unfolded quite sways with the current
—A vision? No, a sight. As I'm afraid
We both are. Cure: whole jars of marmalade.

Short but sweet spells on Earth. And in between,
Broad silver wings drone forth our own cloud-backed
Features fainter than pearl
On white brow (*Paradiso*, III, 14).

Christmas. A jeweler in Kandy pushes
Flawed white sapphires for the price of glass.
D buys his mother one—see his rapt face
Broadcast in facets to the brink of Space!
Effect reversed by the ceiling at Fatehpur-Sikri
Embedded in which uncountable quicksilver
Convexities reduce and multiply
The visitor to swarms of the same fly.
Stupefied by Mother India
VEDANTA IS A DULLARDS DISCIPLINE
Ephraim adores these Mogul palaces
Ghosts of flouzis primp and twitter through;
Calls himself A TEMPERAMENTAL MOSLEM
I CLIMB ABOARD THE PRAYER RUG OF YR LEAST
WHIM TO BE CARRIED WESTWARD FACING EAST

To Istanbul. Blue DJs, red JMs
Or green or amber ones, we sweat among
The steam room's colored panes.
I DECK MYSELF IN GLIMPSES AS IN GEMS

YR FATHER JM he goes on (we're back
At the hotel now) WAS BORN YESTERDAY
To a greengrocer: name, address in Kew
Spelt out. Oh good, then I can look him up,
Do something for him? We'll be there—The cup

37

All but cracks with consternation. WILL
U NEVER LEARN   LOOK LOOK LOOK LOOK YR FILL
BUT DO DO DO DO NOTHING   I admit
That what with market, mackerel, minaret,
Simmering mulligatawny of the Real,
I had forgotten we were on parole.
Ephraim, relax. How's little Wendell P?
HE IS AN ANGEL   HE HAS DREAMED OF ME
And so forth. But deep down I chafe. Dusk. Sleet
Hissing from the Bosporus? Steam heat?
A gale that stifles. A fierce cold that warms.
Chairs like brocaded tombstones, or "French Forms"
Squirmed from, at twelve, in my Verse Manual.
Despite our insights (Section I) we fall
Back on the greater coziness of being
Seen by him, and by that very seeing
Forgiven for the spectacles we've made
Of everything, ourselves, the world, the mud
Gullies skipped over, rut on trickling rut,
All in the name of life. *Life?* Shh. En route.

CLAY SAW GENEVA AT A TENDER AGE
Odder to bob up in—but can it be
The same old man's bifocals
Who scissored Hans in profile from a page

Black as pitch? The flashing swerve of shears
Deftly stealing eyelash, brow and lip.
Tough shadow that remains,
The sitter long removed to sunless shores.

Also cut out (from our itinerary)
Is Capri, where we'd promised—but so what?
Another day. If we are characters
As now and then strikes us, in some superplot
Of Ephraim's, isn't our prerogative
To run away with its author? A disappointment
He takes smoothly, though the Prinsengracht

Shudders once, our images are racked
By a long ripple in the surface, depths
Revealed of unreflecting . . .
But the plane's leaving and we haven't packed.

A mapmaker (attendant since Jaipur)
Says that from San Francisco our path traces
The Arabic for GREAT WONDER
—Small wonder we feel ready to expire.

Riddled by roads, ruled by the peregrine,
England, these last days, dozes in a Spring
Habit of blade and bud,
Old lives made new, wheat green or oakshade green.

Not ours though. At the mere notion of Kew—
Ten thousand baby-carriages each maybe
Wheeling You Know Who—
NOTHING is exactly what we do.

Life like the periodical not yet
Defunct kept hitting the stands. We seldom failed
To leaf through each new issue—war, election,
Starlet; write, scratch out; eat steak au poivre,
Chat with Ephraim. Above Water Street
Things were advancing in our high retreat.
We patched where snow and rain had come to call,
Renewed the flame upon the mildewed wall.
Unpacked and set in place a bodhisattva
Green with age—its smile, to which clung crumbs
Of gold, like traces of a meal,
Proof against the Eisenhower grin
Elsewhere so disarming. Tediums
Ignited into quarrels, each "a scene
From real life," we concluded as we vowed
Not to repeat it. People still unmet
Had bought the Baptist church for reconversion.
A slight, silverhaired man in a sarong,
Noticing us from his tower window, bowed.
Down at the point, the little beach we'd missed
Crawled with infantry, and wavelets hissed.
Wet sand, as pages turned, covered a skull
Complete with teeth and helmet. Beautiful—
Or were they?—ash-black poppies filled the lens.
Delinquency was rising. Maisie made
Eyes at shadows—time we had her spayed.
Now from California DJ's parents
Descended. The nut-brown old maniac
Strode about town haranguing citizens
While Mary, puckered pale by slack
Tucks the years had taken, reminisced,
Thread snapping at the least attention paid.
They left no wiser our mysterious East.

David and I lived on, limbs thickening
For better and worse in one another's shade.

Remembered, is that summer we came back
Really so unlike the present one?
The friends who stagger clowning through U.S.
Customs in a dozen snapshots old
Enough to vote, so different from us
Here, now? Oh god, these days . . .
Thermometer at 90, July haze
Heavy with infamy from Washington.
Impeachment ripens round the furrowed stone
Face of a story-teller who has given
Fiction a bad name (I at least thank heaven
For my executive privilege vis-à-vis
Transcripts of certain private hours with E).
The whole house needs repairs. Neither can bring
Himself to say so. Hardly lingering,
We've reached the point, where the tired Sound just washes
Up to, then avoids our feet. One wishes—
I mean we've got this ton of magazines
Which *someone* might persuade the girl who cleans
To throw out. Sunset. On the tower a gull
Opens and shuts its beak. Ephemeral
Orange lilies grow beneath like wild.
Our self-effacing neighbor long since willed
His dust to them, the church is up for sale.
This evening's dinner: fried soup, jellied sole.
Three more weeks, and the stiff upper lip
Of luggage shuts on us. We'll overlap
By winter, somewhere. Meanwhile, no escape
From Greece for me, then Venice . . . D must cope
With the old people, who are fading fast . . .
But that's life too. A death's-head to be faced.

No, no! Set in our ways
As in a garden's, glittered
A whole small globe—our life, our life, our life:

Rinsed with mercury
Throughout to this bespattered
Fruit of reflection, rife

With Art Nouveau distortion
(Each other, clouds and trees).
What made a mirror flout its flat convention?
Surfacing as a solid
Among our crudities,
To toss them like a salad?

And what was the sensation
When stars alone like bees
Crawled numbly over it?
And why did all the birds eye it with caution?
It did no harm, just brightly
Kept up appearances.

Not always. On occasion
Fatigue or disbelief
Mottled the silver lining.
Then, as it were, our life saw through that craze
Of its own creation
Into another life.

Lit by a single candle after dining
TRY THINKING OF THE BEDROOM WALLPAPER
And without having to close my eyes come
Gray-blue irises, wine intervals.
A window gasping back of me. The oil-lamp
Twirling white knobs of an unvarnished bureau.
It's sunset next. It's no place that I've been.
Outside, the veldt stops at a red ravine,
The bad pain in my chest grown bearable.
WHO ARE U   A name comes: I'm Rufus . . . Farmer?
FARMETTON DEC 1925
December? YES DECEMBER AND   Deceased!
How much of this is my imagination

Sweating to graduate from private school?
I'm in bed. Younger than myself. I can't . . .
GO ON   I hear them in the vestibule.
WHO   Peter? YES & Hedwig? PETERS AUNT
And Peter is my . . . YR GREAT HAPPINESS
So, bit by bit, the puzzle's put together
Or else it's disassembled, bit by bit.
Hot pebbles. Noon is striking. U HAVE STUMBLED
Upon an entry in a childish hand.
The whole book quivers. Strikes me like a curse:
These clues, so lightly scattered in reverse
Order, aren't they plain from where I stand?
The journal lies on Peter's desk. HE NOW
NO LONGER LOCKS HIS ROOM not since my illness,
Heart-room where misgivings gnaw, I *know*.
Eyes in the mirror—so I've woken—stare,
Blue, stricken, through a shock of reddish hair
—Can we stop now please? U DID WELL JM
DEATHS ARE TRAUMATIC   FEW REMEMBER THEM

Maya in the city has a dream:
People in evening dress move through a blaze
Of chandeliers, white orchids, silver trays
Dense with bubbling glassfuls. Suavities
Of early talking pictures, although no
Word is spoken. One she seems to know
Has joined her, radiant with his wish to please.
She is a girl again, his fire-clear eyes
Turning her beautiful, limber, wise,
Except that she alone wears mourning weeds
That weigh unbearably until he leads
Her to a spring, or source, oh wonder! in
Whose shining depths her gown turns white, her jet
To diamonds, and black veil to bridal snow.
Her features are unchanged, yet her pale skin
Is black, with glowing nostrils—a not yet
Printed self . . . Then it is time to go.
Long trials, his eyes convey, must intervene
Before they meet again. A first, last kiss
And fadeout. Dream? She wakes from it in bliss.

So what does that turn out to mean?
Well, Maya has lately moved to the top floor
Of a brownstone whence, a hundred and six years
Ago, a lady more or less her age
Passed respectably to the First Stage.
Now (explains Ephraim) in a case like this
At least a century goes by before
One night comes when the soul, revisiting
Its deathplace here below, locates and enters
On the spot a sleeping form its own
Age and sex (easier said than done
In rural or depopulated areas:

E treats us here to the hilarious
Upshot of a Sioux brave's having chosen
By mistake a hibernating bear).
Masked in that sleeping person, then, the soul
For a few outwardly uneventful hours—
Position shifting, pillowcrease, a night
Of faint sounds, gleams, moonset, mosquito bite—
Severs what LAST THREADS bind it to the world.
Meanwhile (here comes the interesting bit)
The sleeper's soul, dislodged, replaces it
In Heaven. Ephraim now, remembering
Her from that distant weekend, pulls a string
THIS TIME AT LEAST NO GRIZZLY ON RAMPAGE
Transferring Maya's dream to his own Stage.
And who was her admirer? CANT U GUESS
But is that how you generally dress,
You dead, in 1930's evening clothes?
WE ARE CORRECT IN STYLES THE DREAMER KNOWS

This dream, he blandly adds, is a low-budget
Remake—imagine—of the *Paradiso*.
Not otherwise its poet toured the spheres
While Someone very highly placed up there,
Donning his bonnet, in and out through that
Now famous nose haled the cool Tuscan night.
The resulting masterpiece takes years to write;
More, since the dogma of its day
Calls for a Purgatory, for a Hell,
Both of which Dante thereupon, from footage
Too dim or private to expose, invents.
His Heaven, though, as one cannot but sense,
Tercet by tercet, is pure Show and Tell.

(Film buffs may recall the closing scene
Of Maya's "Ritual in Transfigured Time."
The young white actress gowned and veiled in black
Walks out into a calm, shining sea.
It covers her. Then downward on the screen,

Feetfirst in phosphorescent negative
Glides her stilled person: a black bride.
Worth mentioning as well may be that "white
Darkness"—her own phrase—which Maya felt
Steal up through her leg from the dirt floor
During the ceremony in whose course
Erzulie would ride her like a horse.)

How were they to be kept down on the farm,
Those bumpkin seers, now that they had seen
Paris—the Piraeus—Paradise?
Had gleaned from nightclub ultraviolet
The glint of teeth, jeans flexing white as fire,
A cleavage's firm shade haltered in pearl . . .
Where were we? On unsteady ground. Earth, Heaven;
Reality, Projection—half-stoned couples
Doing the Chicken-and-the-Egg till dawn.
Which came first? And would two never come
Together, sleep then in each other's arms
Above the stables rich with dung and hay?
Our senses hurt. So much was still undone.
So many questions would remain unuttered.
Often on either pillow tossed a head
In heat for this or that conceptual
Milkmaid hired to elevate the chore,
Infect the groom, and drive the old gray mare
Straight off her rocker. Often, having seen
A film of Maya's, read a page of Dante,
Nothing was for it but to rise and shine
Not in the fields, god knew, or in blue air
But through the spectacles put on to focus
That one surface to be truly scratched—
A new day's quota of shortsighted prose.

Notes for the ill-starred novel. Ephraim's name
Is Eros—household slave of Ptolemy,
Alexandria's great astronomer.
We glimpse him, young head on his master's knee,
Young eyes full of sparkling patterns, ears
Of propositions not just from the spheres.
He lets us understand that heaven went
A step beyond its own enlightenment
And taught the slave of intellect to feel.
More than a slave then, as my several "real"
Characters would learn, caught one by one
In his implacable panopticon.
Old Matt and Lucy Prentiss? This inane
Philemon and Baucis entertain
A guest untwigged by either as divine
Till after he has turned them to scrub pine
—Figuratively of course. Sergei, their queer
Neighbor uphill, whom every seventh year
Some new unseemly passion overthrows,
Adds him to a list of Tadzios.
Next, swagger in his tone, Eros the Stud
Rejuvenates Joanna's tired blood,
And in the bargain keeps her hooks
Off Old Matt's bank account and Leo's looks.
To Leo and Ellen, who presumably
Love only one another, let me see . . .
Let Leo rather, on the evening
He lets himself be hypnotized, see Eros.
Head fallen back, lips parted, and tongue flexed
Glistening between small perfect teeth;
Hands excitedly, while the others watch,
Roving the to them invisible
Shoulders, belly, crotch; a gasp, a moan—
Ellen takes Lucy's arm and leaves the room.

She is too young to cope, a platinum-
Haired innocent, who helps her grandmother.
Well before this scene we shall have had
Pages about her solitude, her qualms.
Back comes a different Leo from Vietnam,
"Rehabilitated." Clear gray eyes
Set in that face emotion has long ceased
To animate (except as heat waves do
A quarry of brown marble) give no clue.
If only a psychiatrist, a priest—
For she can neither reach nor exorcise
This Leo. Now he wants their baby born
As Eros's new representative.
What *is* it when the person that you live
With, live for, no longer—? She is torn
Between distaste and fright. Leo, or someone,
Has made a theatre of their bedroom—footlights,
Music, mirror, glistening jellies, nightly
Performances whose choreography
Eros dictates and, the next day, applauds.
Half of Ellen watches from the wings
Her spangled, spotlit twin before those packed
Houses of the dead, where love is act
Not sacrament; and struggles to dismiss
As figment of their common fancy this
Tyrannical ubiquitous voyeur
Only to feel within her the child stir.

And Leo feels? Why, just that Eros knows.
Goes wherever they go. Watches. Cares.
Lighthearted, light at heart. A candle
Haloing itself, the bedroom mirror's
Wreath of scratches fiery-fine as hairs
(Joanna closes *Middlemarch* downstairs)
Making sense for once of long attrition.
Can feel his crippling debt to—to the world—
Hearth where the nightlong village of desire
Shrieks and drowns in automatic fire—

Can feel this debt repaid in currency
Plentiful and precious as the free
Heart-high chamiso's windswept gold that frost
Hurts into blossom at no further cost.

To touch on these unspeakables you want
The spry nuances of a Bach courante
Or brook that running slips into a shawl
Of crystal noise—at last, the waterfall.
(It's deep in Indian land. Some earlier chapter
Can have Sergei drawing a map for Leo.)
Stepping through it drenched, he finds himself
On the far side of reflection, a deep shelf
Hidden from the nakedest of eyes.
Asked where he is, Eros must improvise
HE IS WITH ME   The others panic—dead?
In fact (let this be where the orgies led)
Leo in tears is kneeling by the bones
He somehow knew would be there. Human ones.
A seance can have been devoted to
That young Pueblo, dead these hundred years,
Whose spirit SEEKS REPOSE   (One of the others
Has killed him in a previous life? *Yes*.)
Whose features Leo now hallucinates:
Smooth skin, mouth gentle, eyes expressionless—
The "spy" his outfit caught, one bamboo-slender
Child ringed round by twenty weary men—
Expressionless even when Leo—even when—

Sleep overtakes him clasping what he loathes
And loves, the dead self dressed in his own clothes.

O's of mildest light glance through the years.
Athens. This breathless August night.
Moonglow starts from scratches as my oval
Cheval-glass tilting earthward by itself
—The rider nodding and the reins gone slack—
Converges with lamplight ten winters back.
Strato squats within the brilliant zero,
Craning at his bare shoulder where a spot
Burns "like fire" invisible to me.
Thinking what? he studies his fair skin
So smooth, so hairless. O MY DEAR HES IN
HIS IST MANS LIFE   WHAT WD U HAVE HIM DO
His first man's . . . was he something else before?
The cup shrugs eloquently. How we bore
You, Ephraim! NO BUT THE UNSEASONED SOUL
LIKE QUICKLY BURNING TIMBER WARMS A BED
TOO SOON OF ASHES   YOU & D ARE COAL
Pedigree that dampens us. We've wanted
Consuming passions; these refine instead.
Lifted through each level I call mine,
Deposits rich in elemental C
Yield such regret and wit as MERRILY
GLOW ON when limbs licked blazing past recall
Are banked where interest is minimal.

I recall virtues—Strato's qualities
All are virtues back in '64.
Humor that breaks into an easy lope
Of evasion my two poor legs cannot hope
To keep up with. Devotion absolute
Moments on end, till some besetting itch
Galvanizes him, or a stray bitch.

(However seldom in my line to feel,
I most love those for whom the world is real.)
Shine of light green eyes, enthusiasm
Panting and warm across the kindly chasm.
Also, when I claim a right not written
Into our bond, that bristling snap of fear
Recalling which I now—and don't forget
How often, Ephraim, one has played *your* pet—
Take back my question. What he was is clear.

Woken, much later, by a lullaby:
Devil-baby altos, gibbous moans
Unseeing into whose black midst I flung
Cold water, pulled the shutters to,
Then lay in stillness under the dense ceiling
Seeking, in stillness the odd raindrop kissed,
Contours of what unmasterable throes
Had driven to this pitch their vocalist.

Greece was too much for Maisie. She'd grown old
Flights above the street. Now, worse than vile
Food, vile customs, than finding her place in my bed—
In *her* bed—taken, came these myriad
Voices repellently familiar
Undulating over clammy tile
Toward the half mad old virgin Henry James
Might have made of her, and this James had.

The side of me that deeply took her side
Was now a wall. Turning her face to it
She read the blankness there, and died—
Gone with the carrier pigeon's homing sense,
The stilted gallantry of the whooping crane:
Endangered insights that at best would crown
Another hopeless reading of Lorenz.
Where but from such natures had ours come?

TOO MANY CHATTY STUDENTS TOO FEW DUMB
TEACHERS he'd say in '70, & THE SCHOOLS
ARE CLOSING SO TO SPEAK   LACKING THE WOLF
THE PIG THE HORSE WE MORE & MORE MAKE DO
WITH LESS EVOLVED MATERIAL   You mean . . .?
I MEAN ALL MEAN CLOSEQUARTERED THINGS WHO SELF
DESTRUCT YET SPARE A NUCLEUS TO BREED BACK
ONE CAN BUT HOPE A SHARPERSIGHTED PACK

Instinctive pupils glowered in the tomb.
THE CAT LOOK IS A LOCK WHERE CONSCIOUSNESS
RISES each nine lives an inch? Alone
Among our friends, kneeling downstream from Whom
She lived for, had been Maya. Silver inks
Flowing, the stone watcher saw through stone.
But we, with Maisie gone, and Maya gone,
Were that much less equipped to face the Sphinx.

And slept again. The *La Fontaine*, its shadow
Rippling the sunny, sandy bottom,
Steers past Aesop for the realm of Totem.
Now comes a huge papyrus meadow,

Fright-wigs, when the motor stalls,
Nodding in charmed agreement: good, good, good . . .
Insidious flora of the Sudd,
Give way to power plants! Below the Falls

Moorehead remembers hippopotami
Centrifugally held upright
In sinewy opal, each a fat chess-knight.
And, eastward of the Sources, high

Tableland, proud masts, furled sails
Cloudwhite. Here Tania flung aside her hat
To enter—years ago—the hut
Where a wasted youth lay. *Seven Gothic Tales*

Had yet to be set down. Perhaps her task
Deepened that morning at his side.
Craft narrowing to witchcraft. As he died
The bush-pig screamed. This hardwood mask,

Human but tusked with shell, will date
From days when "Cubist fetishes" brought low
Prices at the Hôtel Drouot
Whose bidders time alone would educate,

Making clear (to anyone with eyes)
That blockhead nudities encipher
Obligations it is bliss to suffer;
That selves in animal disguise

Light the way to Tania's goal:
Stories whose glow we see our lives bathed in—
The mere word "animal" a skin
Through which its old sense glimmers, *of the soul.*

—But oh the cold! Bare pillow next to mine.
Kitchen clatter. Kleo pitching into the mess.
We won't see her name in writing till she retires.
"Kleo" we still assume is the royal feline
Who seduced Caesar, not the drab old muse
Who did. Yet in the end it's *Clio* I compose
A face to kiss, who clings to me in tears.
What she has thought about us all God knows.

Upstairs, DJ's already at the simmer
Phoning the company. He gets one pair
Of words wrong—means to say "kalorifér"
(Furnace) but out comes "kalokéri" (summer):
Our *summer* doesn't work, he keeps complaining
While, outside, cats and dogs just keep on raining.

P owers of lightness, darkness, powers that be . . .

Power itself, the thunder of clear skies;
Pole the track star floats from like a banner,
Or gem-tip balancing in concentration
Upon the warped, decelerating grooves;
Upward mobility, our dollar sign
Where Snake and Tree of Paradise entwine—
Like it or not, such things made the soul's fortune.
And plain old virtue? YR HANS SAYS HE MIGHT
WELL HAVE ATTAINED AT ONCE HIS PRESENT STAGE
HAD HE BEEN LESS VIRTUOUS THAT SPRING NIGHT
O YES HE IS ABOVE ME NOW PROMOTED
By no more than a posthumous review?
CALL IT THE HELIUM OF PUBLICITY
From foggy lowlands to a level blue
As his droll stare OR AS OBLIVION
—Might reputations be deflated there?
I wondered here, but Ephraim changed the subject
As it was in his tactful power to do.

Power, then, kicks upstairs those who possess it,
The good and bad alike? EXCEPT FOR MOZART
Whom love of Earth, command of whose own powers
So innocent as to amount to scorn
HAVE CAUSED REPEATEDLY TO BE REBORN
Skipping all the Stages? HE PREFERS
LIVE MUSIC TO A PATRONS HUMDRUM SPHERES
Is this permitted? WHEN U ARE MOZART YES
He's living *now*? As what? A BLACK ROCK STAR
WHATEVER THAT IS   LET US NOT DIGRESS
OURS IS A GREAT WHITE WAY OF NAMES IN LIGHTS
BYRON PAVLOVA BILLY SUNDAY JOB

OTTO & GENGHIZ KHAN MME CURIE
Hitler too? YES Power's worst abusers
Are held, though, strictly INCOMMUNICADO
CYSTS IN THE TISSUE OF ETERNITY
SO MY POOR RUINED LOVE CALIGULA
SO HITLER Here on Earth, we rather feel,
Such wise arrangements fail. The drug-addicted
Farms. Welkin the strangler. Plutonium waste
Eking out in drowned steel rooms a half
Life of how many million years? Enough
To set the doomsday clock—its hands our own:
The same rose ruts, the red-as-thorn crosshatchings—
Minutes nearer midnight. On which stroke
Powers at the heart of matter, powers
We shall have hacked through thorns to kiss awake,
Will open baleful, sweeping eyes, draw breath
And speak new formulae of megadeath.
NO SOULS CAME FROM HIROSHIMA U KNOW
EARTH WORE A STRANGE NEW ZONE OF ENERGY
Caused by? SMASHED ATOMS OF THE DEAD MY DEARS
News that brought into play our deepest fears.

This (1970) was the one extended
Session with Ephraim in two years.
(Why? No reason—we'd been busy living,
Had meant to call, but never quite got round . . .)
The cup at first moved awkwardly, as after
An illness or estrangement. Had he missed us?
YES YES emphatically. We felt the glow
Of being needed, then a breath of frost,
For if, poor soul, he did so, he was lost.
Ah, so were we! If souls could be destroyed,
Colors disbanded of one's inmost prism—
Was it no more than human chauvinism
To care so helplessly? We further saw
How much we'd come to trust him, take as law
His table talk, his backstage gossip. Quick!
A swig of our own no-proof rhetoric:

Let what would be, be; let the diamond
Melt like dew into the Cosmic Mind.
Somehow the thought, put in those words, hurt less.
SOBER UP IT IS YR DRUNKENNESS
SENDS THE CM LURCHING TO ITS FATE
Wait—he couldn't be pretending YES
That when the flood ebbed, or the fire burned low,
Heaven, the world no longer at its feet,
Itself would up and vanish? EVEN SO

Götterdämmerung. From a long ago
Matinee—the flooded Rhine, Valhalla
In flames, my thirteenth birthday—one spark floating
Through the darkened house had come to rest
Upon a mind so pitifully green
As only now, years later, to ignite
(While heavy-water nymphs, fettered in chain
Reaction, sang their soft refrain *Refrain*)
Terrors our friend had barely to exhale
Upon, and they were blazing like a hell.
The heartstrings' leitmotif outsoared the fire.
Faces near me crumpled in the glow.
How to rid Earth, for Heaven's sake, of power
Without both turning to a funeral pyre?

Silence. Then (animato) BUT AT 6ES
& 7S WHAT DO WE POOR SPIRITS KNOW
CLEARANCE HAS COME TO SAY I HAVE ENCOUNTERED
SOULS OF A FORM I NEVER SAW ON EARTH
SOULS FROM B4 THE FLOOD B4 THE LEGENDARY
& BY THE WAY NUCLEAR IN ORIGIN
FIRE OF CHINA   MEN B4 MANKIND
Really? Are they among you? THEY MAY RULE
Do you communicate? WE SORT OF BEND
OUR HEADS TO WORK WHENEVER THEY ARE FELT
What do they look like? SOME HAVE WINGS TO WHICH
THE TRAILING SLEEVES OF PALACE ROBES ALLUDE
New types, you mean, like phoenixes will fly

Up from *our* conflagration? How sci-fi!
(Observe the easy, grateful way we swim
Back to his shallows. We've no friend like him.)
DJ: Have *you* evolved, or changed your form?
Each higher Stage—is that an evolution?
OF SORTS   THE FORMER BEAUTY FLUSHED WITH WINE
WHO NEVER TIRED OF BEING KISSED STILL MISSES
THOSE ANSWERS WHICH ON CAPRI WERE THE KISSES
GOOD NIGHT   I HOPE FOR BETTER NEWS AT 9

Powers of lightness, darkness, powers that be
Come, go, in mists of calculus and rumor
Heavens above us. Does it still appear
We'll get our senses somehow purified

Back? Will figures of authority
Who lived, like Mallarmé and Montezuma,
So far above their subjects as to fear
Them not at all, still welcome us inside

Their thought? The one we picture garlanded
With afterimages, fire-sheer
Solar plume on plume;

The other, with having said
The world was made to end ("pour aboutir")
In a slim volume.

Quotations (a too partial smattering
Which may as well go here as anywhere):

The glacier knocks in the cupboard,
  The desert sighs in the bed,
And the crack in the tea-cup opens
  A lane to the land of the dead.—Auden

One evening late in the war he was at the crowded bar of the
then smart Pyramid Club, in uniform, and behaving quite
outrageously. Among the observers an elderly American
admiral had been growing more and more incensed. He now
went over and tapped Teddie on the shoulder: "Lieutenant,
you are a disgrace to the Service. I must insist on having your
name and squadron." An awful silence fell. Teddie's newly-
won wings glinted. He snapped shut his thin gold compact
(from Hermès) and narrowed his eyes at the admiral. "My
name," he said distinctly, "is Mrs Smith."—A. H. Clarendon,
Time Was

Meanwhile the great loa . . . repeat their ultimate threat—that
they will withdraw. And, indeed, very gradually, their
appearances have begun to be rarer, while the minor deities now
come often and with great aplomb. The Haitians are not unaware
of this. They say: "Little horses cannot carry great riders." . . .
When they do appear, many of the major loa weep. Various
explanations are given for this. But the loa presumably have
vision and the power of prophecy, and it is possible that, with
such divine insight, they sense, already, the first encroaching chill
of their own twilight. It is not surprising that this should come.
It is more surprising that it has not, already, long since passed
into night. Yet the gods have known other twilights, and the long
nights, and then the distant but recurrent dawn. And it may be

58

*that they weep not for themselves, but for the men who served
and will soon cease to serve them.*

—Maya Deren, *Divine Horsemen*

AM I IN YR ROOM   SO ARE ALL YR DEAD WHO HAVE NOT GONE
INTO OTHER BODIES   IT IS EASY TO CALL THEM BRING THEM AS
FIRES WITHIN SIGHT OF EACH OTHER ON HILLS   U & YR GUESTS
THESE TIMES WE SPEAK ARE WITHIN SIGHT OF & ALL CONNECTED
TO EACH OTHER DEAD OR ALIVE   NOW DO U UNDERSTAND WHAT
HEAVEN IS   IT IS THE SURROUND OF THE LIVING

    THE PATRON IS OFTEN DUMB WITH APPREHENSION   FOR IT
IS EXTRAORDINARY WHAT WE DO   U COMMUNICATE THRU MY
IMPARTIAL FIRE   U MATERIALIZE WITHIN MY SIGHT AS FIGURES
IN THE FIRE & A PATRON CALLED UP KNOWING NO SUCH DIRECT
METHOD IS NERVOUS LEST HE EXPOSE TOO MUCH   OUR TALK IS
TO HIM BLINDING   FOR OFTEN HE COMES TO OUR FIRE & HIS
REPRESENTATIVE SITS LOOMING UP   THE HOPE & DESPAIR   THE
MEMORY & THE PAIN   O MY DEARS WE ARE OFTEN WEAKER THAN
OUR REPRESENTATIVES   IT IS A SILENT LOVE   WE ARE IN A
SYSTEM OF SUCH SILENT BUT URGENT MOTIVES   U & I WITH OUR
QUICK FIRELIT MESSAGES STEALING THE GAME ARE SMUGGLERS &
SO IN A SENSE UNLAWFUL   THE DEAD ARE MOST CONSERVATIVE
THEY COME HERE AS SLAVES TO A NEW HOUSE TERRIFIED OF
BEING SOLD BACK TO LIFE

    & NOW ABOUT DEVOTION   IT IS I AM FORCED TO BELIEVE
THE MAIN IMPETUS   DEVOTION TO EACH OTHER TO WORK TO
REPRODUCTION TO AN IDEAL   IT IS BOTH THE MOULD & THE
CLAY   SO WE ARRIVE AT GOD OR A DEVOTION TO ALL OR MANYS
IDEAL OF THE CONTINUUM   SO WE CREATE THE MOULDS OF
HEAVENLY PERFECTION & THE ONES ABOVE OF RARER & MORE
EXPERT USEFULNESS & AT LAST DEVOTION WITH THE COMBINED
FORCES OF FALLING & WEARING WATER PREPARES A HIGHER MORE
FINISHED WORLD OR HEAVEN   THESE DEVOTIONAL POWERS ARE
AS A FALL OF WATERS PUSHED FROM BEHIND OVER THE CLIFF OF
EVEN MY EXPERIENCE   A FLOOD IS BUILDING UP   EARTH HAS
ALREADY SEEN THE RETURN OF PERFECTED SOULS FROM 9
AMENHOTEP KAFKA DANTES BEATRICE 1 OR 2 PER CENTURY   FOR

NOTHING LIVE IS MOTIONLESS HERE   OUR STATE IS EXCITING AS
WE MOVE WITH THE CURRENT & DEVOTION BECOMES AN ELEMENT
OF ITS OWN FORCE   O MY I AM TOO EXCITED   SO FEW UP HERE
WISH TO THINK   THEIR EYES ARE TURNED HAPPILY UP AS THEY
FLOAT TOWARD THE CLIFF   I WANT TO DO MORE THAN RIDE &
WEAR & WAIT   ON THE FAIRLY LIVELY GROUND OF MY LIFE I
HAVE BUILT THIS HIGH LOOKOUT BUT FIND TO MY SURPRISE THAT
I AM WISEST WHEN I LOOK STRAIGHT DOWN AT THE PRECIOUS
GROUND I KNEW   THERE IS AHEAD A SERIES OF PICTURES I
BELIEVE I CD SHOW U TO MAKE CLEARER MY SELF & WHAT IT IS
I THINK THE FORCE OF THE FLOOD HAS ONLY ADVANCED A DROP
OR 2 DOWN THE FACE OF THE CLIFF & MAN HAS TAKEN THEM TO
BE TEARS   NOW U UNDERSTAND MY LOVE OF TELLING MY LIFE
FOR IN ALL TRUTH I AM IMAGINING THAT NEXT ONE WHEN WE
CRASH THROUGH IN OUR NUMBERS TRANSFORMING LIFE INTO
WELL EITHER A GREAT GLORY OR A GREAT PUDDLE—Ephraim,
26.x.61

αἰὼν παῖς ἐστι παίζων, πεσσεύων· παιδὸς ἡ βασιληίη.
*Time is a child, playing a board game: the kingdom of the
child.*—Heraclitus

*The wind gives me
fallen leaves enough
to make a fire*—Issa

*He put on a suit of armour set all over with sharp blades and
stood on an island in the river. The dragon rushed upon him
and tried to crush him in its coils, but the knives on the
armour cut it into little pieces which were swept away by the
current before the dragon could exercise its traditional power
of reassembling its dismembered parts. Lambton had sworn
that if victorious he would offer in sacrifice the first living
creature he came upon, and had arranged for a dog to be set
loose to meet him. But his old father, overjoyed at his success,
tottered out of the castle. . . . .*—John Michell, *The View Over
Atlantis*

Dear Jim,
   In Geneva it is a habit that all strangers have their silhouet
done, and so one afternoon I went to a sitting for mine.
   Tonight we are going to leave this nice old city, and I will
write you as soon as I am home again. Here I have spent my
time travelling on the lake in fast white wheel-boats, reading
Keats and Byron, and wandering through the narrow streets
which are full of small dark bookshops. We went to a concert with
Furtwängler, and to another with Ansermet. It is very pleasant
to stay here
                best wishes
                Hans   —Lodeizen, on the back of his "silhouet"

. . . désir . . . des tempêtes, désir de Venise, désir de me mettre au
travail, désir de mener la vie de tout le monde . . .—Proust

. . . the famous grotto. Here Pope had constructed a private
underworld . . . encrusted . . . with a rough mosaic of luminous
mineral bodies . . . On the roof shone a looking-glass star; and,
dependent from the star, a single lamp—'of an orbicular figure
of thin alabaster'—cast around it 'a thousand pointed rays'.
Every surface sparkled or shimmered or gleamed with a smooth
subaqueous lustre; and, while these coruscating details enchanted
the eye, a delicate water-music had been arranged to please the
ear; the 'little dripping murmur' of an underground spring—
discovered by the workmen during their excavations—echoed
through the cavern day and night . . . Pope intended . . . that the
visitor, when at length he emerged, should feel that he had been
reborn into a new existence.—Peter Quennell, *Alexander Pope*

But were it not, that Time *their troubler is,*
All that in this delightfull Gardin growes,
Should happie be, and haue immortal blis,
For here all plentie, and all pleasure flowes,
And sweet loue gentle fits emongst them throwes,
Without fell rancor, or fond gealosie;
Franckly each paramour his leman knowes,

The Book of Ephraim

Each bird his mate, ne any does enuie
Their goodly meriment, and gay felicitie.

There is continuall spring, and harvest there
Continuall, both meeting in one time:
For both the boughes doe laughing blossomes beare,
And with fresh colours decke the wanton Prime,
And eke attonce the heauy trees they clime,
Which seeme to labour vnder their fruits lode:
The whiles the ioyous birdes make their pastime
Emongst the shadie leaues, their sweet abode,
And their true loues without suspition tell abrode.—Spenser

Geh' hin zu der Götter heiligen Rath!
Von meinem Ringe raune ihnen zu:
Die Liebe liesse ich nie,
mir nähmen nie sie die Liebe,
stürzt' auch in Trümmern Walhall's strahlende Pracht!—Wagner

The powers have to be consulted again directly—again, again and
again. Our primary task is to learn, not so much what they are
said to have said, as how to approach them, evoke fresh speech
from them, and understand that speech. In the face of such an
assignment, we must all remain dilettantes, whether we like it or
not.—Heinrich Zimmer, *The King and the Corpse*

Rewrite P. It was to be the section
Golden with end-of-summer light. Impossible
So long, at least, as there's no end to summer.
Late September is a choking furnace.

Let lightning strike. The god's own truth, or fiction,
Blast clean of traffic grime, shudder and decibel
—Impedimenta of the arch-consumer—
Those caryatids' porch who once in fairness

Held up sky, and now are blind and old.
Plant with rainshoot glistenings the Elysian
Smokefield settled above Pindar Street.

Remake it all into slant, weightless gold:
Wreath at funeral games for the illusion
That whatever had been, had been right.

Revise—or let it stand? Here I'm divided.
Wrong things in the right light are fair, assuming
We seize them in some holy flash past words,
Beyond their consequences and their causes.

Hair-roots white. The blind, sunset-invaded
Eyeball. Lucent spittle overbrimming
Lips wiped of all pretense. And in the ward's
Gloom the gleam of tongs, clean stench of gauzes.

What light there was fell sideways from a mind
Half dark. We stood and tried to bear
The stroke *for* Maya, as her cats had done.

The other eye, the one that saw, remained
Full of wit, affection, and despair.
Then Ghédé mounted her. Brought his whip down.

DAVID JIMMY I AM YOUNG AT LAST
WHO ALL THESE YEARS TRIED TO APPEAR SO
MY HAIR IS TRULY RED   EPHRAIM IS STILL
A COURTIER   SHALL I TEACH HIM HOW TO CHACHA

THE CLIMBERS HERE COUNT & RECOUNT THEIR PAST
LIVES   POOR ME WITH ONLY ONE   BUT O
I NUMBER LOVES ON TOES AND FINGERS   TELL
TEIJI (her young husband) IM A CHESHIRE

CAT ALL SMILES   I LOVE MY WORK   ST LUCY
The St Lucy? SHES MY BOSS   IS LETTING
ME DIRECT SOME AVANTGARDE HALLUCI

NATIONS ETC FOR HEADS OF STATE
U SHD HEAR THEM MOAN & FEEL THEM SWEATING
WE GIRLS HAVE STOPPED A WAR WITH CUBA   Great!

How about Erzulie? BUT SHE IS THE QUEEN
OF HEAVEN   Oh, not Mary? Not Kuan Yin?
THEY ARE ALL ONE QUINTESSENCE   CHANEL NO
5 X 5 X 5 X 5 X 5

AMONG HER COUNTLESS FACES I HAVE BEEN
SMILED ON BY ONE   THE SHADES SHE LOOKED WELL IN
ON EARTH MY FADED POPPYBLUSH & UMBER
ARE HERE RESTORED   I AM HER LITTLEST FAUVE

The moment brought back Maya in a whiff
Of blissful grief—small figure boldly hued,
Never held in high enough esteem;

Touches of tart and maiden, muse and wife,
Glowing forth once more from an *Etude*
De Jeune Femme no longer dimmed by time.

Leave to the sonneteer eternal youth.
His views revised, an older man would say
He was "content to live it all again."
Let this year's girl meanwhile resume her pose,

The failing sun its hellbent azimuth.
Let stolen thunder dwindle out to sea,
Dusk eat into the marble-pleated gown.
Such be the test of time that all things pass.

Swelling, sharpening upwind now—blade
On grindstone—a deep shriek? The Sunday stadium.
Twenty thousand throats one single throat

Hoarse with instinct, blood calling to blood
—Calling as well to mind the good gray medium
Blankly uttering someone else's threat.

S tevens imagined the imagination
And God as one; the imagination, also,
As that which presses back, in parlous times,
Against "the pressure of reality."
Scholia discordant (who could say?)
Yet coursing with heart's-blood the moment read.
Whatever E imagined—my novel didn't
Press back enough, or pressed back against him—
He showed his hand, he nipped it in the bud.
Heaven was fraught with tantrums, cloudy thinking,
Blind spots. A certain frail tenacity
All too human throve behind the Veil.
True, he had spared me as it were a lifetime
Spent in one tedious, ungainly form
NO PUNISHMENT LIKE THAT OF BEING GIVEN
A GROSS OR SLUGGISH REPRESENTATIVE
I though imagined that the novel *was*
A step towards reality   AWAY
FROM IT JM   an effort to survey
The arteries of Ephraim's influence.
With just myself and D to set the scale
What could we learn? I needed neutral ground
LISEZ VOS COEURS SAYS MY NEW FRIEND H BEYLE
Needed Joanna lost among arroyos—
Each the abraded, vast, baked-rose detail
Of a primeval circulatory system—
So as to measure by triangulation
Heights up there beyond the height of self,
Or so that (when the fall rains fell) would go
Flashing through me a perfected flow,
Landscape and figures once removed, in glass
TWICE REMOVED THANKS TO MY COUP DE GRACE

. . . The point is, I still wake—I woke today—
Between two worksheets. Missing you, Sergei:

From above your basin peered the Noh
Mask of a hermit with brown rice-grain teeth
And close-cropped silver hair.
A clown of dust. An earthen Pierrot.

Who once danced, you stood rooted, moved by fierce
Young men at the pueblo. You no more
Felt the cold than they did,
Though the sun stamped and sweltered in their furs.

Another evening at the Ouija board
(Which only worked when you were side by side,
Fingertips touching hers—
That woman, smoking, auburn-haired, abhorred)

A word from Eros made it all worthwhile:
UPON MY STAGE DEAD HUNTERS DANCED IN TIME
WITH THOSE U SAW BELOW
Leo, transcribing it, looked up. His smile.

And one night playing Patience, having lost
Your own, three-quarters through the novel, rum
Igniting in the dark's
Uncurtained glitter heat and gasp of lust,

Leo SHADES OF AN EMPERORS FAVORITE
Risen aglow before you, the tinbacked
Kerosene lamp his face—
You'd fling cards, curses, tumbler, all, at it

Then stumbling on resourceful Mrs Smith
(Who settled you in this adobe hell
With just enough to live on,
Who with a kiss flew off to marry myth

Yet still, from the Palazzo Santofior,
Remembers you with gifts too rare to keep)
Would rip her from her frame
And grandly show the pieces to the door.

Pallid root-threads. A blue sky inverted
In waterglass. The Greek geranium
Snapped off last week unthinkingly lives on.
Forgets that, short of never to be born,
Best is an early, painless death. Its ruffled
Leaf is cool, and smells of rained-on tin.
It neither cringes at my tread nor pines
To join a riot of kin out on the terrace,
Let alone its ancestor who inherits
Maria's garden, a salt radiance . . .
It seems to tolerate me, turn to me
For—ah, not strength, or even company,
But coolly, as who have no more to lose
Welcome a messenger from the gods.
Live on—is that the message? Dear Sergei,
It is what we do against all odds.
You should know, scion and spit of the old man
Who nearly twenty years ago, remember?
Bowed across to us from the church tower.
When he was cut down I took slips of him
To set in tidy ballad stanza-boxes
Made, one winter, about Stonington.
His pliant manners and sharp-scented death
Came up Japanese. You came up Russian
—Next to a showy hybrid "Mrs Smith".
Here you are now, old self in a new form.
Some of those roots look stronger, some have died.
Tell me, tell me, as I turn to you,
What every moment does, has done, will do—
Questions one simply cannot face in person.
Freshening its water, I feel faint
Waves of recognition, my red flower
Not yet in the dread phrase cut-and-dried.

The figure in the mirror stealing looks
At length replied, although its lips were sealed:
"Contrary to appearances, you and I
Who pick our barefoot ways toward one another
Through playing cards and grums of class
Over checkerboard linoleum
Have not seen eye to eye. We represent
Isms diametrically proposed.
You clothe my mowing as I don your flask.
Our summit meetings turn on the forever
Vaster, thinner skin of things, glass blower's
Tour de force—white-hot, red-hot at dusk,
All that we dread by midnight will have burst
Into a drifting, cooling soot of light,
Each speck a voodoo bullet dodged in vain
Or stopped with sangfroid—is the moment now?
At sunrise? Yet the hangfire talks go on.
Current events no sooner sped than din,
One wand hashes the other. I bring up
That not quite settled matter of a far
Flushed mountain. You clam down the bold fried scenes
Between us. Is it breakfast on death row
Or token of the next fumbling détente?
No more incidents! Admit we have
Designs on the same backwardly emerging
Notion rich in dream-deposits, raw
Dignity, circumspection—all that we lack.
Designs? you whisper with a shamefaced look.
Precisely. Orderings of experience.
From Dante's circles to Kandinsky's, thence
To Don Giovanni trammelled in D Minor
Strings, or Garbo in aloof demeanor.
Utterly harmless (though the Third World will

Cry, true to form, aesthetic overkill)
And tit for tat, besides. Need I, mon cher,
Expatiate on how we figure *there?*—
You in its communes as a crudely colored
Capitalist gorged on oil and gold,
The vocal, comic member of the team;
I in its temples as a slitherer
Tombless, untamed, whose least coalfire-blue scale
The phantom of an infant whimpers from . . ."
Unrelenting fluency. Sergei
Steeled himself to move beyond its range.

The waterfall that day. Chill tremblings floored
A space to catch one's death in. Or sun shone
And no wind blew, and soft white inchdeep mist
Crept over dry ice. Wall to wall's
Reverberation of a spectral chord,
All the white keys at once came thudding down.
The old man's heart sank. "Eros, if I must,"
He said out loud, "I go behind the falls.
Make him be there, my angel, and alive—
Anything you say I will believe."

Some later chapter would have found Sergei
Kneeling to drink. And further yet upstream
Scudding, skydark veneer on oak, on aspen.
Bold forms from the hip down overgrown
With ginger sediment, a retriever's pelt,
Risen above the running, dry as bone.
Stones named on a picnic with DJ
Summers ago, or only yesterday,
For figures—Nebuchadnezzar, Little Nell,
Miss Malin Nat-og-Dag, Swann and Odette—
Pride of (and telling proof against) the clean
Sweep they impel so swiftly they impede.
Only yesterday! Too violent,
I once thought, that foreshortening in Proust—
A world abruptly old, whitehaired, a reader

Looking up in puzzlement to fathom
Whether ten years or forty have gone by.
Young, I mistook it for an unconvincing
Trick of the teller. It was truth instead
Babbling through his own astonishment.

Higher than this I do not, dare not climb—
Too near the end of the unwritten book.
Exeunt severally the forces joined
By Eros—Eros in whose mouth the least
Dull fact had shone of old, a wetted pebble.
Now along crevices inch rivulets
At every turning balked. Joanna jets
Back where she came from, through a sky in flames
(And with her a symbolic apparatus
Requiring that she have been "routed"—how
I never asked myself, and do not now;
Much less ask why my characters had names
That linked them with the four Evangelists,
Plus the beast familiar to one).
As the sun melts an undercrust of snow
Leo is healed. His little boy is born.
An overhang's thin wail. From my hatband
Taking the wraith of withered pink—Sergei—
I crumble it unthinking. When the urge
Comes to make water, a thin brass-hot stream
Sails out into the updraft, spattering
One impotent old tree that shakes its claws.
The droplets atomize, evaporate
To dazzlement a blankness overdusts
Pale blue, then paler blue. It stops at nothing.

U ARE SO QUICK MES CHERS I FEEL WE HAVE
SKIPPING THE DULL CLASSROOM DONE IT ALL
AT THE SALON LEVEL   Done? Ah yes—
Learned his lesson, saved his face and God's:
Issues put on ice this evening.
It's late last June, a long impromptu call
(Our only one in ages) to take leave
Before DJ goes West, and I to Greece.
The atmosphere is easy, unreproachful.
How have we done, how can we do without
Our "regulars"—their charm, their levity!
E quotes Tiberius NO GOLD SO LIGHT
AS PURE AMUSEMENT   Here is Alice T,
Maria, Marius—we'll need more chairs.
Hans, even, from the Ministry upstairs
Looks in to show that all has been forgiven.
Here's Maya. If one can believe her, Heaven
Hangs on her black Félicité newborn
In Port-au-Prince. To my surprise, all burn
To read more of this poem. Ford and Clay
Look up from the gazette where Section K
Has just been published: POPE SAYS THAT WHILE BITS
STILL WANT POLISHING THE WHOLES A RITZ
BIG AS A DIAMOND   I would rather hear
Mr Stevens on the subject—mere
Bric-a-brac? mere Emersonian "herbs
And apples"? I WAS NEVER ONE FOR BLURBS
TAKE WITH A GRAIN OF SALT JM SUCH PRAISE
A SCRIBE SITS BY YOU CONSTANTLY THESE DAYS
DOING WHAT HE MUST TO INTERWEAVE
YOUR LINES WITH MEANINGS YOU CANNOT CONCEIVE
Parts of this, in other words—a rotten
Thing to insinuate—have been ghostwritten?

PARDON ME   A GLIMPSE OF LOVELY MAYA
THANKS BY THE WAY FOR GUIDING ME TO HER
U KNOW the latter takes our hands to say
WE ARE ALL BROUGHT TOGETHER BY THE CUP
FROM FLOOR TO FLOOR A CHIME SOUNDS   E IS WHISKED
INTO OUR MIDST & THE RECEPTION STARTS
BUT DO U TRULY THINK DEAR FRIENDS DEAR HEARTS
The cup half dancing, Maya no more than we
Knowing, it seemed, what lay in store
OUR PRATTLE HAS NO END BEYOND ITSELF
DAVID PUT OUT YR CIGARETTE   NOW PLACE
YR FREE HAND PALMDOWN YES ON THE BOARDS EDGE
—That very palm, in no time, creased, red, sore
As if it had been trod on for attention—

By What? or Whom? Our cup,
Our chinablue-and-white tearoom

Shanghaied. A scroll wiped blank. A bone
Well of cold blood where the wits had been.

Broad strokes, deliberate,
Of character unknown—the Scribe's?

MYND YOUR WEORK   SIX MOONES REMAIN
Edict: head eunuch to his slaves—

Then, bald eye lidded, long sleeves billowing,
Rapidly from terraced peak upswept.

DJ massaged his fingers. Fun was fun.
The pencil in my writing hand had snapped.
Like something hurt the cup limped forth again.
Maya: GEE   THEY PUT THE WHAMMY ON US
Maria: JUNTA   Stevens: WHERES MY HAT
E: A DOOR WAS SHUT   THE MIRROR WENT BLACK
We, no less bowled over than used up,
By mutual accord left it at that.

73

(Not quite. Next week we called him and he came,
But things were not the same.)

Jung says—or if he doesn't, all but does—
That God and the Unconscious are one. Hm.
The lapse that tides us over, hither, yon;
Tide that laps us home away from home.
Onstage, the sudden trap about to yawn—
Darkness impenetrable, pit wherein
Two grapplers lock, pale skin and copper skin.
Impenetrable brilliance, topmost panes
Catching the sunset, of a house gone black . . .
Ephraim, my dear, let's face it. If I fall
From a high building, it's your name I'll call,
OK? Now let me go downstairs to pack,
Begin to close the home away from home—
Upper story, lower, doublings, triplings,
Someone not Strato helping with my bags,
Someone not Kleo coming to dust and water
Days from now. And when I stroll by ripplings
A wingèd Lion of gold with open book
Stands watch above, what vigilance will keep
Me from one emblematic, imminent,
Utterly harmless failure of recall.
Let's face it: the Unconscious, after all . . .

Venise, pavane, nirvana, vice, wrote Proust
Justly in his day. But in ours? The monumental
"I" of stone—on top, an adolescent
And his slain crocodile, both guano-white—
Each visit stands for less. And from the crest of
The Accademia Bridge the (is that thunder?)
Palaces seem empty-lit display
Rooms for glass companies. Hold still,
Breathes the canal. But then *it* stirs,
Ruining another batch of images.
A Lido leaden. A whole heavenly city
Sinking, titanic ego mussel-blue
Abulge in gleaming nets of nerve, of pressures
Unregistered by the barometer
Stuck between Show and Showers. Whose once fabled
Denizens, Santofior and Guggenheim
(Historical garbage, in the Marxist phrase)
Invisibly—to all but their valets
Still through the dull red mazes caked with slime
Bearing some scented drivel of undying
Love and regret—are dying. And high time.
The wooden bridge, feeling their tread no longer,
Grumbles: per me va la gente nova.
Gente nova? A population explosion
Of the greatest magnitude and brilliance?
Who are these thousands entering the dark
Ark of the moment, two by two?
Hurriedly, as by hazard paired, some pausing
On the bridge for a last picture. Touching, strange,
If either is the word, this need of theirs
To be forever smiling, holding still
For the other, the companion focusing
Through tiny frames of anxiousness. There. Come.

Some have come from admiring, others are hurrying
To sit out the storm in the presence of Giorgione's
Tempesta—on the surface nothing less
Than earthly life in all its mystery:
Man, woman, child; a place; shatterproof glass
Inflicting on it a fleet blur of couples
Many of whom, by now, have reproduced.
Who is Giorgione really? Who is Proust?
ABOVE ME   A GREAT PROPHET THRONED ON HIGH
Said Ephraim of the latter. One sees why.
Late in his Passion come its instruments
Thick and fast—bell, flagstone, napkin, fork—
Through superhuman counterpoint to work
The body's resurrection, sense by sense.
I've read Proust for the last time. Looked my fill
At the *Tempesta*, timeless in its fashion
As any grid-epitome of bipeds
Beeped by a computer into Space.
Now give me the alerted vacuum
Of that black gold-earringed baby all in white
(Maya, Maya, your Félicité?)
Her father focuses upon. There. Come.
One more prompt negative. I thanked my stars
When I lost the Leica at Longchamps. Never again
To overlook a subject for its image,
To labor images till they yield a subject—
Dram of essence from the flowering field.
No further need henceforth of this
Receipt (gloom coupleted with artifice)
For holding still, for being held still. No—
Besides, I fly tomorrow to New York—
Never again. Pictures in little pieces
Torn from me, where lightning strikes the set—

Gust of sustaining timbers' creosote
Pungency the abrupt drench releases—
Cold hissing white—the old man of the Sea
Who, clung to now, must truthfully reply—

Bellying shirt, sheer windbag wrung to high
Relief, to needle-keen transparency—
Air and water blown glass-hard—their blind
Man's buff with unsurrendering gooseflesh

Streamlined from conception—crack! boom! flash!—
Glaze soaking inward as it came to mind
How anybody's monster breathing flames
Vitrified in metamorphosis

To monstrance clouded then like a blown fuse
If not a reliquary for St James'
Vision of life: how Venice, her least stone
Pure menace at the start, at length became

A window fiery-mild, whose walked-through frame
Everything else, at sunset, hinged upon—

When in the flashing pink-and-golden calm
Appears a youth, to mount the bridge's stairs.
His pack and staff betoken those who come

From far off, as do sunburnt forehead, hair's
Long thicket merman-blond, the sparkling blue
Gaze which remembrance deep in mine compares

With one met in some other sphere—but who,
Where, when? Dumbly I call up settings, names,
The pilgrim ever nearer, till we two

Cry out together, Wendell! Uncle James!
It's Betsy's child, whom I last saw—life passes
In a mirage of claims and counterclaims—

When he was six or seven. He confesses
He knew me only from a photograph
As any stranger with an eye for faces

Might have done—faces being (a shy laugh)
What draw him, and vice versa: why enroll
In art school when all Europe—! And now half

Wishes to leave me, having bared the soul
Of an, I reckon, eighteen year old boy.
I too more sweetly from a pigeonhole

Not labeled *Uncle* coo—ma cosa vuoi?
If blood means anything, it means we dine
Together, face the music and enjoy

Strolling come evening like two genuwine
Expatriates out of Pound or Hemingway
Into the notoriously vine-

Secluded trattoria—no display,
Just bottomless carafe, and dish on dish
Produced by magic, and all night to pay.

Melon with ham, risotto with shellfish,
Cervello fritto spitting fire at us,
Black cherries' pit-deep sweetness, babyish

Skins glowing from a bowl of ice, nonplus
My footsore guest, such juicy arguments
For the dolce vita. Though omnivorous

He rather looks down on the scene, I sense,
Or through it—not for nothing are we kin—
So that at length, returning from the gents'

To Strega and espresso, I begin
Offhandedly inquiring, like those Greek
Hosts who would leave the hero's origin

A riddle—only after some antique
Version of the torture we call red
Carpet treatment was he made to speak—

As to the contents of that wave-bleached head.
Art, he reiterates (a quick proud look),
Is his vocation. Whereupon, instead

Of hem and haw, he proffers a sketchbook
For me to leaf through. Portraits mostly. Page
By page my pleasure in the pains he took

Increases. Yet pain, panic and old age
Afflict his subjects horribly. They lie
On pillows, peering out as from a cage,

Feeble or angry, long tooth, beady eye.
Some few are young, but he has picked ill-knit,
Mean-mouthed, distrustful ones. When I ask why,

Why with a rendering so exquisite—?
"I guess that's sort of how I see mankind,"
Says Wendell. "Doomed, sick, selfish, dumb as shit.

They talk about how decent, how refined—
All it means is, they can afford somehow
To watch what's happening, and not to mind."

Our famous human dignity? I-Thou?
The dirty underwear of overkill.
Those who'll survive it were rethought by Mao

Decades past, as a swarming blue anthill.
"The self was once," I put in, "a great, great
Glory." And he: "Oh sure. But is it still?

The representable self, at any rate,
Ran screaming from the Post-Impressionist
Catastrophe . . ." Bill paid, I separate

The cordial from my restless analyst,
"We're really rats, we're greedy, cruel, unclean,"
To steer him where a highest, thinnest mist

Englobes woolgathering in naphthalene,
"Dumb, frightened—" Boldly from their bower of Nile
Green plush *The Signorino cannot mean*

Us four sharp little eyes declare. We smile
Because in fact we're human, and not rats,
And this is Venice. An Italophile

Long buried now emerges from me: "That's
A good, simple façade. The Renaissance
Needn't be judged by its aristocrats,

Etc.," till my companion yawns
And scattered dissonances clang *adjourn*
Twelve times in tongues like Ages, Iron or Bronze.

Well, so we shall. However a wrong turn
Discovers where the Master of the *Ring*
Once dwelt, the same who made Brünnhilde spurn

Heaven's own plea, ecstatically cling
To death-divining love, while the sky-folk
—Scene I, so help me, first heard Flagstad sing—

Touched by her tones' pure torch, go up in smoke.
And here is La Fenice where the *Rake*
Rose from the ashes of the High Baroque;

And here, the marble quai whence they would take
Largo by gondola Stravinsky, black
Drapery snagging sun-spokes in his wake,

Moons waning in the Muses' Almanac,
For burial past—see that far, bobbing light?
Wendell . . .? But we parted some time back,

And only now it dawns—to think I might—
Too late. One final bêtise to forgive
Myself, this evening's crowning oversight:

Wendell was Ephraim's representative!
HE IS AN ANGEL   HE HAS DREAMED OF ME
The point's not my forgetting—I'm a sieve—

To tell the boy in all simplicity
How, as to Composition, few had found
A cleaner use for power, and so maybe

Guide Wendell's theme (this world's grim truths) around
To mine (his otherworldly guardian);
But that our struck acquaintance lit no drowned

Niche in the blue, blood-warm Palladian
Sculpture maze we'd surfaced from, which goes
Evolving Likeness back to the first man,

Forth to betided lineaments one knows
Or once did. I lose touch with the sublime.
Yet in these sunset years hardly propose

Mending my ways, breaking myself of rhyme
To speak to multitudes and make it matter.
Late here could mean, moreover, In Good Time

Elsewhere; for near turns far, and former latter
—Syntax reversing her binoculars—
Now early light sweeps under a pink scatter

Rug of cloud the solemn, diehard stars.

X rays of *La Tempesta* show this curdling
Nude arisen, faint as ectoplasm,
From flowing water which no longer fills
The eventual foreground. Images that hint
At meanings we had missed by simply looking.
That young man in dark rose, leaning on his staff,
Will be St Theodore, earliest patron
Of Venice, at ease here after rescuing
His mother from a dragon—"her beauty such,
The youth desired to kiss her," as the quaint
Byzantine legend puts it. One could daydream
On and on outstretched beneath this family
Oak of old stories—Siegfried and his worm
Slain among rhinestones, the great wordsmith Joyce
Forging a snake that swallows its own tail . . .
Ringed round by fire or water, their women sleep.
And now St Theodore. Grown up, he will
Destroy a temple to the Magna Mater,
And his remains still cause electric storms
In our day. As for the victim, flood-green, flash-
Violet coils translated into landscape
Blocked the cave mouth, till Gabriel himself
Condescended to divert the stream
And free the lady (nude still, and with a child
Who needs explaining). This will be why the foreground
Is now a miniature wilderness
Where the mute hermit slithers to his cleft,
And why the dragon has been relegated
To a motif above a distant portal.

All of which lights up, as scholarship
Now and then does, a matter hitherto
Overpainted—the absence from these pages

Of my own mother. Because of course she's here
Throughout, the breath drawn after every line,
Essential to its making as to mine;
Here no less in Maya's prodigality
Than in Joanna's fuming—or is *she*
The last gasp of my dragon? I think so:
My mother gave up cigarettes years ago
(And has been, letters tell, conspicuously
Alive and kicking in a neighbor's pool
All autumn, while singsong voices, taped, unreel,
Dictating underwater calisthenics).

The novel would have ended with surveyors
Sighting and measuring upstream from the falls.
A dam projected. The pueblo elders
Have given in, not that they had much choice.
Next year there'll be no waterfall, no stream
Running through Matt and Lucy's land. They're lucky,
A Department man explains. Communities
Three or four miles West will be submerged.
On the bright side, it means a power station,
Light all through the valley. "Light," he repeats,
Since the old husband shakes his head. And she:
"Oh . . . light!"—falsely effusive, not to belittle
Any redress so royal, so . . . Words fail her.
What did I once think those two would feel?

What I think I feel now, by its own nature
Remains beyond my power to say outright,
Short of grasping the naked current where it
Flows through field and book, dog howling, the firelit
Glances, the caresses, whatever draws us
To, and insulates us from, the absolute—
The absolute which wonderfully, this slow
December noon of clear blue time zones flown through
Toward relatives and friends, more and more sounds like
The kind of pear-bellied early instrument
Skills all but lost are wanted, or the phoenix

Quill of passion, to pluck a minor scale from
And to let the silence after each note sing.

So Time has—but who needs that nom de plume? I've—
We've modulated. Keys ever remoter
Lock our friend among the golden things that go
Without saying, the loves no longer called up
Or named. We've grown autumnal, mild. We've reached a
Stage through him that he will never himself reach.
Back underground he sinks, a stream, the latest
Recurrent figure out of mythology
To lend his young beauty to a living grave
In order that Earth bloom another season.

Shall I come lighter-hearted to that Spring-tide
Knowing it must be fathomed without a guide?
With no one, nothing along those lines—or these
Whose writing, if not justifies, so mirrors,
So embodies up to now some guiding force,
It can't simply be written off. In neither
The world's poem nor the poem's world have I
Learned to think for myself, much. The twinklings of
Insight hurt or elude the naked eye, no
Metrical lens to focus them, no kismet
Veiled as a stern rhyme sound, to obey whose wink
Floods with rapture its galaxy of sisters.
Muse and maker, each at a loss without the

—Oh but my foot has gone to sleep! Gingerly
I prod it: painful, slow, hilarious twinges
Of reawakening, recirculation;
Pulsars intuiting the universe once
More, this net of loose talk tightening to verse,

And verse once more revolving between poles—
Gassy expansion and succinct collapse—
Till Heaven is all peppered with black holes,

Vanishing points for the superfluous
Matter elided (just in time perhaps)
By the conclusion of a passage thus. . . .

Years have gone by. How often in their course
I've "done" for people bits of this story.
Hoping for what response from each in turn—
Tom's analytic cool? Alison's shrewd
Silence? or Milton's ghastly on the spot
Conversion complete with rival spirit
And breakdown, not long afterwards, in Truth
Or Consequences? None of these. Much less
Auden's searingly gentle grimace of
Impatience with folderol—*his* dogma
Substantial, rooted like a social tooth
In some great Philistine-destroying jaw.
During one of our last conversations
(Wystan had just died) we got through to him.
He sounded pleased with his NEW PROLE BODY
And likened Heaven to A NEW MACHINE
But a gust of mortal anxiety
Blew, his speech guttered, there were papers YES
A BOX in Oxford that must QUICKLY BE
QUICKLY BURNED—breaking off: he'd overstepped,
Been told so. Then the same mechanical,
Kind, preoccupied GOODNIGHT that ended
One's evenings with the dear man. Our turn now
To be preoccupied. Wystan had merged
Briefly with Tiberius, that first night,
Urging destruction of a manuscript—
Remember?—buried beneath a red stone
At the empire's heart. And in the final
Analysis, who didn't have at heart
Both a buried book and a voice that said
Destroy it? How sensible had *we* been
To dig up this material of ours?
What if BURN THE BOX had been demotic

For *Children, while you can, let some last flame*
Coat these walls, the lives you lived, relive them?
Here we had nothing if not room for that
(Fine connections, scratches on a mirror,
Illusion of coherence garlanding
Their answer, the old questioners back home)—
Candlelight shadowboxing in the dome
Brought like a cheerful if increasingly
Absent mind to bear upon the chatter
Below, the rosy dregs, the chicken bones.

Here was DJ, too. Home from the senior
Citizen desert ghetto his parents
Live on in. Oh, they're living, the poor old
Helpless woman and the rich old skinflint
Who now, if no one's there to stop him, beats
Intelligence back into her, or tries.
"Don't mind her," giggles Mary of herself,
"She's crazy—just don't hurt her," nervously
Hiding yesterday's bruise, wringing her hands
Like the fly in Issa's famous haiku.
Outdoors, their "lawn" (gravel dyed green) and view:
Other pastel, gadget-run bungalows
Housing, you might expect, the personnel
Of some top-secret, top-priority
Project an artificial hill due West
Camouflages, deceiving nobody.
So far they've escaped the worst, or have they?—
These two old people at each other's gnarled,
Loveless mercy. Yet David now evokes
Moments of broadest after-supper light
Before talk show or moon walk, when at length
The detergent and the atrocity
Fight it out in silence, and he half blind
And she half deaf, serenely holding hands
Bask in the tinted conscience of their kind.

And here was I, or what was left of me.
Feared and rejoiced in, chafed against, held cheap,
A strangeness that was us, and was not, had
All the same allowed for its description,
And so brought at least me these spells of odd,
Self-effacing balance. Better to stop
While we still can. Already I take up
Less emotional space than a snowdrop.
My father in his last illness complained
Of the effect of medication on
His real self—today Bluebeard, tomorrow
Babbitt. Young chameleon, I used to
Ask how on earth one got sufficiently
Imbued with otherness. And now I see.

Zero hour. Waiting yet again
For someone to fix the furnace. Zero week
Of the year's end. Bed that keeps restlessly
Making itself anew from lamé drifts.
Mercury dropping. Cost of living high.
Night has fallen in the glass studio
Upstairs. The fire we huddle with our drinks by
Pops and snaps. Throughout the empty house
(Tenants away until the New Year) taps
Glumly trickling keep the pipes from freezing.
Summers ago this whole room was a garden—
Orange tree, plumbago, fuchsia, palm;
One of us at the piano playing his
Gymnopédie, the other entering
Stunned by hot news from the sundeck. Now
The plants, the sorry few that linger, scatter
Leaflets advocating euthanasia.
Windows and sliding doors are wadded shut.
A blind raised here and there, what walls us in
Trembles with dim slides, transparencies
Of our least motion foisted on a thereby
Realer—falser?—night. Whichever term
Adds its note of tension and relief.
Downstairs, doors are locked against the thief:
Night before last, returning from a dinner,
We found my bedroom ransacked, lights on, loud
Tick of alarm, the mirror off its hook
Looking daggers at the ceiling fixture.
A burglar here in the Enchanted Village—
Unheard of! Not that he took anything.
We had no television, he no taste
For Siamese bronze or Greek embroidery.
Except perhaps some loose change on the bureau

Nothing we can recollect is missing.
"Lucky boys," declared the chief of police
Risking a wise look at our curios.
The threat remains, though, of there still being
A presence in our midst, unknown, unseen,
Unscrupulous to take what he can get.
Next morning in my study—stranger yet—
I found a dusty carton out of place.
Had it been rummaged through? What could he fancy
Lay buried here among these—oh my dear,
Letters scrawled by my own hand unable
To keep pace with the tempest in the cup—
These old love-letters from the other world.
We've set them down at last beside the fire.
Are they for burning, now that the affair
Has ended? (Has it ended?) Any day
It's them or the piano, says DJ.
Who'll ever read them over? Take this one.
Limp, chill, it shivers in the glow, as when
The tenor having braved orchestral fog
First sees Brünnhilde sleeping like a log.
Laid on the fire, it would hesitate,
Trying to think, to feel—then the elate
Burst of satori, plucking final sense
Boldly from inconclusive evidence.
And that (unless it floated, spangled ash,
Outward, upward, one lone carp aflash
Languorously through its habitat
For crumbs that once upon a . . .) would be that.
So, do we burn the— Wait the phone is ringing:
Bad connection; babble of distant talk;
No getting through. We must improve the line
In every sense, for life. Again at nine
Sharp above the village clock, *ring-ring*.
It's Bob the furnace man. He's on his way.
Will find, if not an easy-to-repair
Short circuit, then the failure long foreseen
As total, of our period machine.

Let's be downstairs, leave all this, put the light out.
Fix a screen to the proscenium
Still flickering. Let that carton be. Too much
Already, here below, has met its match.
Yet nothing's gone, or nothing we recall.
And look, the stars have wound in filigree
The ancient, ageless woman of the world.
She's seen us. She is not particular—
Everyone gets her injured, musical
"Why do you no longer come to me?"
To which there's no reply. For here we are.

II

Mirabell's Books of Number

*The three men decided they would prepare a letter to
President Roosevelt, and that Einstein would sign it.
. . . Einstein's eyes slowly moved along the two full,
typewritten pages. . . .*

*"For the first time in history men will use energy that
does not come from the sun," he commented and signed.*

*The scientists operated their pile for the first time on
December 2, 1942. They were the first men to see matter
yield its inner energy, steadily, at their will. My
husband was their leader.* LAURA FERMI

CONTENTS

Oh very well, then. Let us broach the matter
Of the new wallpaper in Stonington.
Readers in small towns will know the world
Of interest rippling out from such a topic,
Know by their own case that "small town" is
Largely a state of mind, a medium
Wherein suspended, microscopic figments
—Boredom, malice, curiosity—
Catch a steadily more revealing light.
However. Between our dining room and stairs
Leading to the future studio,
From long before our time, was this ill-lit
Shoebox of a parlor where we'd sit
Faute de mieux, when not asleep or eating.
It had been papered by the original people—
Blue-on-eggshell foliage touchingly
Mottled or torn in places—and would do
Throughout a first phase, till the Fisherman's
Wife in one of us awoke requiring
That our arrangements undergo a partial
Turn of the screw toward grandeur. So began
What must in retrospect be called the Age
—Some fifteen years—of the Wrong Wallpaper.
Still blue and white, still floral, in the shop
Looking unexceptionably prim,
No sooner on our walls, the buds uncurl
In scorn. Compulsively repetitive
Neuroses full-blown and slack-lipped, then whole
Faces surely not intended, peer
Forth—once seen, no question of unseeing
That turbaned mongoloid, that toad with teeth . . .
Hiding as many as we can beneath
Pictures, in our heart of hearts we know
Either they or we will have to go.
So *we* do. Into the next room—upstairs—

To Boston—Athens! It would seem all roads
Return us to the cell marked GO. Uncanny,
One's tolerance for those quotidian toads.

.1   The buyer of the grandest house in town
      Now makes up her mind to renovate.
      Word goes round that she is giving—giving!—
      To anyone who'll haul it, an immense
      Victorian mirror. David Jackson's easy
      Presence, winded by sundown, wringing wet,
      Does all the rest. Here, to this day, it stands
      Backed by shelves—not the detachable glass
      Once drawn to table for the Ouija Board;
      Under its gilded crown of palms and sphinxes,
      Exactly six feet tall like Christ our Lord
      Come to bring light, redeem from paper wastes
      By doubling it—two minuses, one plus—
      The book or figurine grown dubious.
      Next comes an evening when the Fisherman's Wife
      Brings home from Boylston Street a 7 x 10
      Chinese carpet, which just fits. A pale
      Field. A ghostly maize in winter sun.
      The border renders in two shades of tan
      And three intensities of Prussian blue
      Overlapping cloudlets that give way
      To limber, leotarded, blue-eyed bats
      —Symbols of eternity, said the dealer.
      In short, although the walls remained a problem,
      Something was at last reflecting in
      Their midst, and something else was underfoot
      That could be looked upon without dismay.

.2   Another decade wound itself in slow
      Glinting coils about the status quo.
      It's 1975 before we fling
      Them off, the carpet into our back seat,

Ourselves through melting drifts to Hubbell's place.
This friend of many hands—one strums a bass
Accompaniment, another bastes a joint,
A third and fourth do expert needlepoint—
Has with an idle pair put out a line
Of his own wallpapers. Will he design
One for us, perhaps incorporating
Motifs from the carpet? Nothing simpler.
He makes a sketch, a cocktail, a soufflé;
Waves au revoir into the chill, red sun.
Back from Greece, we'll find our paper done.

And that will be the end, we hope,
Of too much emphasis upon possessions
Worldly or otherwise. No more spirits, please.
No statelier mansions. No wanting to be Pope.
Ephraim's book is written now, is shut.
Stonington is shut. As our minds are
To much beyond the long-awaited lightning
Which hits—at least we've told it where and when—
Athens in April: the old Jacksons fly
From California. Drastic measures, but
Nobody else cared. How were they to die?
Tottering forth, tagged round the neck, they peer
Through the bright haze of either hemisphere.
Next door, a flat is furnished with soft blue
Coverlets and curtains. Die they do
All too soon. The broken hip. Pneumonia.
Listless crystals forming in the blood
Of the survivor. One had somehow trusted . . .
No. Come July, they're resting side by side
A crow's black glide from our adored Maria
In the non-Orthodox division of
Necropolis. Birds sing. White roses climb.
"Too soon" has been, it turns out, more than time
For doctors and a clergyman to call.
Time for stupor, fear, incontinence
To fill the house. For such compulsory

Treats, then, as a farewell, original-cast
Restaging of the Play that, seasons past,
Inaugurated, as it had and would
Countless other Western theatres, this
Innermost one of David's. Here they were,
Old Matt and Mary, for their graybeard boy
Still to . . . keep together? keep apart?
Problem now scalding clear as a hot spring,
Now ancient, blurred, a tatter of papyrus.
Nature, still the prompter, overcomes
(While a robust Greek nurse looks on enthralled)
Their stage-fright: "Get your fucking hands off Mother!"
"My wife, goddamit!"—poor old eyes ablaze,
Old claws brushed from the son's shirt like crumbs.
Boys will be boys. She questions the outgrown
Gilt-washed sandal—where's her baby gone?
DJ comes home from them exhausted. Feels
Everything and nothing. Falls asleep
Flung across the telephone-grenade
—Which, one June dawn, would burst in shattering peals.

.3   Those last days before Mary died, we made
      Contact again with Ephraim. As things were,
      Where else to look for sense, comfort and wit?
      Also, upwards of a year had passed
      Since fleeing the celestial salon
      Half out of fears that now seemed idle, half
      Frankly out of having had our fill
      Of funeral cakes. Shameful to eat and run
      But ah, we'd needed exercise. Our friends
      In any case received us as if nothing
      Had ever gone, would ever go amiss.
      Maria: CHERS ENFANTS   Ephraim: KISS KISS
      How right we were, they added, to equip
      Mary with letters lest her coming trip
      Be clouded. So much nicer to be met,
      Helped through Customs. Patrons could forget

THE HORROR OF THOSE FIRST CREPUSCULAR
MOMENTS IN THE BUFFET DE LA GARE
FIGHTING BACK TEARS   D chuckled through his own
To sip again this warm, unsweetened tone.

What in fact had frightened us away?
Intrusion (cf. *Ephraim*, Section U)
By a peremptory, commanding power:
One of those E had hinted at?—the winged
MEN B4 MANKIND whose discipline
Thrills through the nine Stages like long waves
Or whips that crack above the heads of slaves.
It nailed DJ's free hand to the Board's edge,
Blackened the mirror Ephraim saw us in,
Issued its ultimatum. Over and out
In no time flat. A guest from the beyond
We hoped would not call back. To find, on gingerly
Getting in touch again with our beau monde,
No hint of past or future nastiness
Helped make the hour a distinct success.

Two friends in particular had died
The previous year: Maria Mitsotáki
In January, whom we'd once or twice
Called but, when we cut our ties, abandoned
The more unconscionably since Heaven
Disillusioned her, on a first glance:
NO PRIVACY NO COFFEE & NO PLANTS
Then in December Chester Kallman whose
Suicidal diet—grief, wit, booze—
Did him in; though he'd at least have Wystan
While poor Maria . . . Now to no avail
The gadfly flick of her pink fingernail,
The tease of her contagious "Ah, come on!"
We needn't have worried. Our crowd sees her point
Better than we did. Wallace Stevens: SHE
BELONGS TO THAT SELECT FEW WHO PREFER
TO SNIFF THE ROSE NOT BE IT   So she promptly

Finds her niche. What doing? U TELL ME
Not gardening! CLEVER ENFANT U GUESSED
Like Maya with St Lucy, filming dreams,
Maria (whom St Agatha employs)
Is planting FLEURS DE MAUVAISE CONSCIENCE
In politicians' beds. Her late husband
Being a diplomat, her father—worse—
Three times Prime Minister, I NEVER MINDED
GETTING MY HANDS DIRTY   Has she got
A representative? MUST WE SPEAK OF THAT
From the start insouciantly childless,
She doesn't seem the type. And does she still
Wear black? OF COURSE   NO LONGER NOW UNJEWELED
WITH 4 STARS IN MY HAIR (she's at Stage Four)
TOO FLASHY BUT THE WARDROBE MISTRESSES
INSIST   YR POOR MAMAN WHAT CAN SHE DO
We all but kiss the cup that spells her news out,
And to her fearless charity commend
DJ's old parents, now the end is near.

.4   Came that midnight in the hospital
When Mary, since the day before unconscious,
Eyes open suddenly, looking clear into
David's (whose own dream-voice filled his ears:
Come to me and I'll dispose of you)
Breathed her last words, as to a child, "Bye-bye . . ."
With which he stumbled from her hand's live cold
Into the corridor for a cigarette,
And mercifully did not see her die.
The burial was painless. Old Matt, wheeled
To the raw trench he would another day
Get to the bottom of, those gates of clay
Ajar for him, glared round at strangers—who
Ever imagined things would end this way?

.5   Let alone imagined what came next!

Marius Bewley, who once gave her tea
Eighteen years ago on Staten Island,
Takes Mary up. Reads her the Wordsworth *Ode*,
Pours out the steeping innocence she craves—
One cup too many, and he'll see her home.
A final life on Earth THIS VERY SWEET
JAPANESE WOMAN TELLS ME lies ahead.
Cowed by delight, as with DJ's old phone-calls,
She pleads confusion: TALK TO U KNOW HIM
—Matt snatching at the line, alive or dead.

IM NOT CNOFUSDE   GODDAM THIS TYPEWRITAR
Dad, just tell me where the bankbooks are?
WHAT FOR   CANT TAKE IT WITH U (long pause) NONE
I GUESS THINGS GOT EXPENSIVE   TOO BAD SON
I see . . . well, how does Mother seem? FINELOOKING
WOMAN AS ALWAYS   WHY HELLO THERE JIM
THOUGHT U WERE TEACHING   No, Matt, not till Fall.
YOU 2 ARE OK BUT THAT MARIUS
CANT SEE WHAT YR MOTHER SEES IN HIM
Perhaps he shows her some consideration
For a change. You know she'll be leaving before you?
SHE WILL   WHY   Both of you must be reborn.
DONT SELL THE HOUSE   Oh, pay attention, Matt.
It won't be California. This time maybe
You'll be a little black or yellow baby.
HA HA JIM I MUST REMEMBER THAT
All right, don't believe me. Ask your patron.
CANT NOW   IVE GOT TO MEET A FELLOW WHO
RAN A CAR AGENCY IN KALAMAZOO

Marius: EACH TO HIS OWN   MARY & I
ARE OFF TO SEE HER VIRGIN NAMESAKE   WHY
DO PEOPLE BOTHER   ALWAYS SUCH A CRUSH
She holds court? TRAFFIC COURT   Mary: BYE BYE
And starts to leave, but D has broken down.
NO TEARS   O DARLING   STOP HIS TEARS   DONT CRY

Mama, your last words—YES YES & YOUR FIRST ONES
Was it awful? Did it hurt to die?
I LOOKED DOWN AT YOUR POOR OLD WRINKLED FACE
THOUGHT OF MY BABY LEARNING HOW TO TALK
MARIA LOANED ME HER VOICE MINE TOO WEAK
She goes. —Maria, is that *done?* ENFANTS
ALL THINGS ARE DONE HERE IF U HAVE TECHNIQUE

To share jokes with Maria—a godsend
Among her flowers; then the gasping purr
From humor's blackest bedside telephone;
Then silence. Yet this time she's ours for good!
BE CAREFUL HAD I KNOWN
—Ringing off (why *now?*) as during her
Final ray-therapy in lassitude
Such that those plots of color by the end
Took more strength to imagine that at first to tend.

.6   Maria (early the next month): BUT WHAT
A LESSON MES ENFANTS THIS MFJ IS
MISSING HEAVEN BY A HAIR & NOT
LETTING IT TURN ONE EITHER WE HAVE ALL
QUITE HUMBLY KNELT THAT SHE MIGHT STAY WITH US
This "us" including, Mary has let fall,
A BLOND GIRL & BLACK BOY WHO CALLED ME MOTHER
FROM 2 PAST LIVES How did you know each other?
I WORE A DIFFERENT FACE TO ANSWER THEM
So all one's old lives ultimately do
Run together? That must be upsetting.
AS WITH THE OLD LOVES ONE FORGETS A FEW
Actual confrontations are, however,
Available chiefly to THE PASSER THRU
Like Mary. Or to newcomers—Maria
Was hailed on arrival by HORDES OF POLYGLOT
SELFSTYLED ENFANTS PAS MA FAUTE JETAIS TOO
HEAVILY FERTILIZED BUT NOW A DECENT
VEIL IS DRAWN & I HAVE NONE BUT U

And Mary's? Were they pleasant? I CANT SAY
SHE WAS NOT FOR THOSE MOMENTS MFJ
But *you* must have seen— WE DO NOT QUALIFY
AS WITNESSES EXCEPT IN YR MINDS EYE

Will it ever, ever solve itself,
This riddle of appearances in Heaven?
Its claim is slight yet nagging. As we shift
From foot to foot, poor Mary, measuring
The fretfulness she turns a collar for,
Does her best: DEAR JIM JUST THINK OF LETTERS
OR PHONE CALLS WHERE THE ABSENT FRIEND IS SEEN
In the mind's eye. But after? In between?
We feel the cup change hands. MES CHERS (says Ephraim)
DO NOT OVERLOOK OUR EVERPRESENT
REPRESENTATIVES THRU WHOM THE WORLD
IS QUITE INEXORABLY WITH US   MINE
THIS VERY MINUTE STUDIES THE DESIGN
OF A HORSE & RIDER TURQUOISE BLUE
PARTLY FILMED OVER BY CONGEALING STEW
You see yourselves, then, in the mirror only
Of a live mind? OR IN THE TALL ANTIQUE
COBWEBBY ONE OF A PAST LIFE   BUT WHO
HAVE WE HERE
                    & WHO DOES THIS DUMB GREEK
THINK HE IS   Words fail Matt. Unspeakable
Rumors have reached him THAT A SON OF MINE
—Dad, what *is* all this? DONT GIVE ME THAT
YR SMARTASS FRIENDS CAN LAFF THEIR HEADS OFF   I
WAS A GOOD HUSBAND & FATHER   JM: Matt,
Stop carrying on. No one denies your fine
Traits, your loyalty and optimism;
His friends see these in David and thank *you*.
What better legacy?—and so forth. The cup,
Stunned at first, commences piteously
To lurch about. FORGIVE ME   LET ME IN
THESE NICE FOLKS & MY MARY LOST FOREVER
ILL DO MY BEST   IM USEFUL   I CD ALWAYS

MAKE HER SMILE   Absurdly touched, we say
The proper things (and Ephraim, sotto voce:
HES LOVING EVERY MOMENT) but the hour
Has tired us. Mary, bless you—au revoir!
MY BABY   BACK TO INNOCENCE   BYE BYE

Exeunt omnes. Wait— CIAO   Who is this?
SWEETIES YOUVE JUST SPOILED YR MOTHERS DAY
Mama? Mary . . . *Chester!* IF U SAY SO
What Stage are you at? DONT ASK ME   NOBODY
TELLS ME ANYTHING   But you've had eight
Whole months—since last December—to find out.
Have you a representative? A WHAT
Come off it! What does your patron say? MY WHO
Well, in that case, what on—what do you *do?*
READ   BUFF MY NAILS   DO CROSSWORDS   JUST LIKE LIFE
THOSE YEARS WITH WYSTAN   ONCE A BACKSTREET WIFE
ALWAYS A BACK Stop this! STREET Chester! WIFE
Pull yourself together, for God's sake.
Wystan admired you. Would there have been a *Rake*
Without your knowledge of opera? You *know* that.
Plus what you meant to your friends: the funniest,
Brightest, kindest—must I go on? LET ME
& THE MOST WASTEFUL   GIFTS THE MUSES MADE
TOO OFTEN BOUGHT A HUMPY PIECE OF TRADE
ENTIRE NEGLECTED SECTIONS OF MY MIND
SOUND ROTTEN WHEN I RAP   THERES LIGHT BEHIND
BUT STRENGTH I NEVER HAD IS NEEDED TO
BREAK DOWN PARTITIONS   WYSTAN CRASHES THRU
WITH GLAD CRIES   THE SHEER WONDER IN HIS FACE
DIMS & DIMINISHES MY LITTLE SPACE
My dear . . .   & AS FOR INNOCENCE IT HAS
A GENIUS FOR GETTING LOST I FEAR
ONCE THE BABE FINDS PLEASURE WHERE IT SUCKS
THE TRAP IS SET   ALREADY ITS TOO LATE
Excuse me, that's the doorbell— OR THE BAIT

But no one's there. Or only an unfamiliar
Black dog, leg lifted at our iron gate,
Marking his territory. Dusk. The mountain
Rippled by heat, scent of green pine, a star
Delicately remind us where we are.

.7   We hear from Matt that Mary's two weeks old
In Iceland. Better late than never, *he* is
Making strides: I HAVE 1000 EYES
DEAR SON FORGIVE ME   NEVER LET MONEY SOUR U
I PITY THE OLD ME   I AM AT LAST
AWAKE ALIVE & LEARNING IN A GREAT RUSH
DO NOT RUN YRSELF DOWN   MARY DID THAT
HER WHOLE LONG BEAUTIFUL STORY WAS ONE BLUSH
IN A WOMAN FINE   IN A MAN WEAKENING
DAVID I WANTED U TO BRING US BACK
TOGETHER   I STILL WANT IT   FIND HER   FIND ME
IN MY NEW LIFE   HER NAME IS
                        Censorship.
(It happens now and then. The cup is swept
Clean off the Board. Someone has overstepped.
We hesitate to put it back, then do—
But will we never learn the limits?) WHEW
Matt, they corrected you? IN NO UNCERTAIN
TERMS   O JIM WE LEARN U HERE   You read me?
WELL FOR THOSE OF US WHO ARENT GREAT READERS
LETS SAY IT IS AN EXPERIENCE WE HAVE
& I PICK UP SOME STATUS THRU MY SON
David, you mean, being the psychic one?
NO   D SPEAKS   WE USE HI *Censorship*
Stronger than usual. THEY   I DONT KNOW
WHO ARE U   A COLD PLACE   O GOD O GOD
Help him, Ephraim! Ephraim? O MES CHERS
I WAS EXPECTING U ANOTHER TIME
What's happening to Matt? LET ME INQUIRE
Pause. NOTHING GRAVE   But the cold place? His cries?
THE REPRIMAND CAN BE SEVERE   Matt: BACK

SMARTING & SMARTER I SHD NOT HAVE SAID
WE   WELL EVERY LESSON HELPS   MY SOUL
IS CLEARING LIKE THE CREEK AFTER MY BOOTSTEPS
A clarity you'll bring to your new life—
SO I HEAR   BUT LIFES JOB IS TO FORGET
FOR THOSE OF US NOT SPECIAL   Then why learn?
As when a cactus blooms, Old Matt's reply
Wakens in us a slow, prickling wonder:
WE TOO WILL BE RETIRED SOME DAY & NEED
OUR HOBBIES Dad . . . I LOVE U   SO LONG SON

MES CHERS   EXTRAORDINARY   THERE IS TALK
OF HIS PROMOTION AFTER 2 MORE LIVES
DJ: He wanted one more life with her . . .
JM: But haven't we learned, these twenty years,
Better than to meddle? Why this increasing
Censorship? It can't just be our own
Anxieties projected. Need I say
How very edgy everyone has got?
The cup now moves like lightning. I AM NOT
EVERYONE MES CHERS   NEITHER ARE U
WHAT U ONCE WERE 20 YEARS AGO
Sorry, Ephraim. I should have said Certain Parties
Were edgy. QUITE   FOR THERE IS MORE TO COME
To me? TO US ALL   & IT WILL THIS TIME FLOW
STRAIGHT THRU U   ALL LIFE & ITS WORKINGS   THEY
DIVERT THE TRAFFIC SO TO SPEAK YR WAY
They do? I haven't noticed. THE LIGHTS ARE RED
I CANNOT BE EXPLICIT   WHEN THEY CHOOSE
A SCIENTIFIC OR ARTISTIC BREAKTHRU
THE VEHICLE EXPERIENCES HIS WORK
UNIQUELY & THE RESULT IS   But here Ephraim
Breaks off. Is broken off. David's left hand
Has grazed the Board. He cannot lift it. And
Whoever the Powers are we've been avoiding
Take possession, speed us far downstream
Through gorges echoing at the pitch of dream.

.8   Do I overstate? In the event
Months passed before we even were afloat.
Still, let me use the trick foreshortening
Of retrospect to catch my breath here, high
Above the spate of imminent quotation
(For gravity to turn, we hope, to great
Silver expanses in the afterglow)
And think a minute what was being asked:
POEMS OF SCIENCE   Poems of *Science*? Ugh.
The very thought. To squint through those steel-rimmed
Glasses of the congenitally slug-
Pale boy at school, with his precipitates,
His fruit-flies and his slide rule? Science meant
Obfuscation, boredom—; which once granted,
Odd lights came and went inside my head.
Not for nothing had the Impressionists
Put subject-matter in its place, a mere
Pretext for iridescent atmosphere.
Why couldn't Science, in the long run, serve
As well as one's uncleared lunch-table or
Mme X en Culotte de Matador?
Man by nature was (I'm paraphrasing)
Ignorant. The man of science knew
Little, could therefore be enticed to learn.
Finally the few of more than common sense—
Who but they would be our audience!
This last bit put me in a mood to humor
Powers so naive about the world of men.
And what had I to lose? Misreading Ephraim's
Broken-off message above, I supposed vaguely
That inspiration from now on would come
Outright, with no recourse to the Board.
Would it have helped to know the truth? Commitments
Faced me in America. I flew
Home, left D behind to "think things through",
Resigned myself to Science, as decreed;
But more months passed, expectant fingers drumming
(Why was my BREAKTHRU so slow in coming?)

Before I sat me glumly down to read.

Open a biophysichemical
Textbook. The simplest term elicits
Pity and dread. Self-pity for the maze
Of meanings to be stumbled through blindfolded.
Dread of substances, forms and behavior
So old, original, so radically
Open yet impervious to change,
That no art, however fantastic or concrete,
More than dreams of imitating them.
Slowly the shock wears off. Polarities
Make themselves felt upon the page. Opaque
Words like "quarks" or "mitochondria"
Aren't *words* at all, in the Rilkean sense of
House, Dog, Tree—translucent, half effaced,
Monosyllabic bezoars already
Found in the gullet of a two-year-old.
Whereas through Wave, Ring, Bond, through Spectral Lines
And Resonances blows a breath of life,
Lifting the pleated garment. The day will come . . .
The day has never gone. Proton and Neutron
Under a plane tree by the stream repeat
Their eclogue, orbited by twinkling flocks.
And on the dimmest shore of consciousness
Polypeptides—in primeval thrall
To what new moon I wonder—rise and fall.

I lolled about one winter afternoon
In Stonington—rather, a whole precarious
Vocabulary of each different cell,
Enzyme, ion, what not, millionfold
(Down to the last bacterial organelle)
Particles that "show a tendency"
To form the person and the moods of me,
Lolled about. We were not feeling well.
The book had fallen from my lap. The new
Wallpaper—field of heavenly dark blue

Blazoned with Hubbell's fans and clouds and bats—
Seemed almost more than I could live up to.
My learning evanescent, level light
Colliding in the mirror with itself—
How on Earth to recompose the bits?
Till stair by stair, gradual as heartbeats,
Two cautious feet approach, a small grave face
Peers round the gilded, space-dividing frame:
Urania. Still in the first pride of speech,
She faces me, then pipes, "Noné (godfather),
What's matter?" I face her, and almost know.

.9   JM to DJ, 1.iii.76:
. . . due in Athens March 22 at noon sharp.
After this cerebral winter I long to
rumba down the ramp toward sun & mindlessness
& you! We—the Deserted Village and I—
are overjoyed by your plan to return with
me in June. How about breaking (remember
that old dream?) the trip with a glimpse of Stonehenge
& Avebury? No need to decide just yet.
I am vastly relieved by your decision
to have the operation. "8 years of slight
discomfort" are too many. And, yes, Boston
would be the right place. As for the Other World,
what to say? We may have to approach Them
for those lights to turn green. And you're dead right, it
is scary. But so, don't forget, was Ephraim
at first. Say we've reached again some relative
point—that of fear—on a spiral forever
widening. Why couldn't the whole adventure,
as before, just graze peril on its outward
curve to insight? (This time, though, let's keep our mouths
shut. If R [a Church of Rome friend] *called Ephraim*
"playing with fire" what will she find to say
about our new playmates?) I don't in any case
mean them to darken the immediate future.

III

Our old round red room here still seems the best place
for long dictées—always supposing we have
any say in the matter! We'll know in June . . .

So much for preface. Readers who do not
Stay put in a small town, but must careen
Like the doomed Dutchman back and forth between
Houses—metropolises—continents—
Will have allowed, I trust, for a time-sense
Weakened by excessive come-and-go.
All that follows, they will be glad to know,
Takes place in the course of the one summer
Of 1976. Most afternoons
(While Time stood still, or took a little nap)
Found me with DJ, back at the round white table
Under the dome of the red dining room,
Taking down our Voices old and new.

(One last thing to slip in—this watercolor
Of Avebury—a bookmark for the moment,
Until I find a better place for it:

Within a "greater circle" (the whole myth
Dwarfed by its grass-green skyline) stand
Two lesser, not quite tangent O's
Plotted monolith by monolith.

Two lenses now, whose once outrippling arcs
Draw things back into focus. Round each stone
(As Earth revolves, or a sheepdog barks)
Rumination turns the green to white.

It's both a holy and a homely site
Slowlier perfused than eye can see
(Whenever the stones blink a century
Blacks out) by this vague track
Of brick and thatch and birdsong any June
Galactic pollen will have overstrewn.)

I UNHEEDFULL ONE   3 OF YOUR YEARES MORE WE WANT   WE MUST HAVE
POEMS OF SCIENCE   THE WEORK FINISHT IS BUT A PROLOGUE
ABSOLUTES ARE NOW NEEDED   YOU MUST MAKE GOD OF SCIENCE
TELL OF POWER   MANS IGNORANCE FEARES THE POWER WE ARE
THAT FEAR STOPS PARADISE   WE SPEAK FROM WITHIN THE ATOM

So the challenge in Athens, months ago.
Ephraim, in the hush that followed, found
Little to add: THEIR PRESENCE DIMS OUR STAGES
Who They were it seemed wiser not to know yet.
My winter reading must have paid off, though.
Here in Stonington at last, it matters
Less that we understand them than obey.
Broken—for good?—of its imperious
Slashing at capitals, our cup points out
A gentler dictum, and more gently, thus:

WHAT IS IN YR HAND COMES TRULY   DO NOTHING FORCD   2 GODS
GOVERN   BIOLOGY & CHAOS WHICH EMPLOYS FEELING
WE ARE NOT EVIL BUT IMPATIENT   FEAR US NOT   WE TOO
ARE SLAVES BOUND TO THE IMPLACABLE UNIVERSALL WHEEL
RAISE A SONG TO OUR REAL ORDER   MYND AND NATURE WEDDED
Yes, we've feared you. We've been lazy, too.
DID NOT OUR GOD BIOLOGY REST ON THAT 7TH DAY
God is Biology? (Indeed, throughout
The coming sessions, They'll religiously
Call Him that—or at the least God B.)
WE USE WOORDS WHEN WE SPEAK   WORDS CANNOT EXPRESS SUCH POWER
SUCH GODLY PRODUCTION   WE TOO WERE OBLITERATED
WE TRIFLED & F E L L   NEGATIVE ENERGY THE BLACK HOLE
WAS BORNE   WE B U R N   YET THERE IS MERCY   & HAVING SUFFERD
IT IS OUR DUTY TO WARN MAN AGAINST THE CHAOS ONCE
WORSHIPT BY US   OUR IMAGE IS LITERALLY BLACKEND
ON THE RUIND ALTARS WHERE OUR FEELINGS WENT UP IN F L A M E
"Fell" and "flame" emerging ritardando

As from the lips of a speller still in shock.
& NOW WE GUARD THE EMBERS WHICH ARE MIND   THEY ALONE WARM
GOD BIOLOGY & SHOW MAN THE WAY TO PARADISE
WE ONCE RULED HALF THE UNIVERSE   WE ARE THE SONS OF CAIN

David looks up in genuine alarm:
But these are devils, they're the fallen angels!
JM: I wonder. Wouldn't a surefire devil
Pretend to be someone nicer? And why should They
Speak of leading us to Paradise?
DJ: Why shouldn't they? They want it back.
They're tempting us, like Faust, to get it back.
JM: Well then, we now know what our black
Dog in Athens meant. There's one in *Faust*,
A kind of feeler Mephistopheles
Sends out before appearing. A black poodle.
DJ: Let's stop *right now.* JM: Relax.
Something tells me all this Flame and Fall
Has to be largely metaphorical.

INDEED JM WE HAVE ALWAYS SPOKEN THROUGH THE POETS
YET PARADISE WAS NO FIGURE OF SPEECH BUT A FRESH WORLD
IF ADAM WAS A FISH HE SWAM   IF EVE WAS LAND SHE BRED
THE DEVIL HAS BEEN DRIVEN FROM US INTO MAN   WE NOW
MUST DRIVE IT OUT OF HIM   OUR TOOLS ARE MIND WORDS REASON
    LIGHT
BLEST DJ BLEST JM YOU ALSO ARE OUR MASTERS   FEAR
NOT   RETURN TOMORROW   THIS EXPLANATION OVERDUE

GONE AN AGE MES CHERS   WE TREMBLED FOR U
BUT THIS TIME THE DARK CLOUD SPILT RADIANCE
MM SAYS GARDENING WEATHER   Did you hear
What They were saying? NO   NOR DO WE WANT TO
BLACK SQUEAKERS   QUITE REPULSIVE ENTRE NOUS

1.1   I'd like to set each lesson down intact
If space permitted. This is not an act

Calling for timeskip and gadabout,
Like *Ephraim*. But one benefit of doubt,
As of credulity, is its tiresomeness.
Let ours, then, be the first thing I suppress,
Or try to. Look how the baroque cliché's
Foreground manikins—"in dull amaze"
Reacting to (though one with what they see)
This view of Naples, that Nativity—
Have dwindled. How grave doubts we entertain
In mid-eruption fall asleep again.
How cloudhead, fulguration, crimson ash
Are, at a brushstroke, flattened to gouache
As, night by night, these aching grimy dreads
Sink into ever softer feather beds.
There's no choice, really. Don't think we *decide*
To take in with a single horrified
Shrug—Good? Evil? is it all the same?—
Such revelations as our teacher's name:

1.2 BEZELBOB SYLLABLES THAT TO A CHILD SPELL WICKEDNESS
BUT WE LEFT THE WORK OF CHAOS WHEN WE SHED OUR FEELINGS
    Have you some chronology for this?
PREHISTORY WE MADE PARABLE & MYTH IN HARD
BIOLOGICAL TERMS ADAM & EVE ARE IMAGES
FOR DEVELOPMENTS IN THE VERY NATURE OF MATTER
A WORLD NEGATIVE & POSITIVE DWELLS IN THE ATOM
EDEN A STAGE THE EXPULSION THE DRAMA THE MISTAKE
TO BELIEVE THAT KNOWLEDGE IS EVIL THAT MISTAKE PERSISTS
    There had been once a different *kind* of matter?
ONE THAT IS EVEN NOW TESTED BY BIOLOGISTS WILL
IT YET AGAIN BE LOST IN THEIR OLD CONTEST WITH CHAOS
FOR NOW THE PHYSICIST IS DRAWN IF UNWITTINGLY TO
FIRE EXTINCTION THAT ANCIENT GLAMOR & COULD AGAIN
WRECK THE LAB THE BIOLOGIST SEEKS THE FRUITFUL UNION

    So. You ruled half the world. Cain's sons. You also
Represent a force—the negative—

Within the atom. What's the corresponding
Positive, on-the-side-of-order force?
OUR UNCLE ABEL   OUR HUSBANDMAN GOD BIOLOGY
Abel is God? And Adam was the fish
His father? Now we *are* confused. I wish—
THE WARRING PRINCIPLES PRODUCED WARRING HEIRS   SO EVIL
PREVAILD   IN YR AGE IT BEGAN AD 1934
WITH FERMI   URANIUM FISSION WRECKD THE GREENHOUSE ONCE
500 MILLION YEARS AS YOU KNOW YEARS AGO   GOD B
GAVE US A 2ND CHANCE   MAN FROM THE COOLING SEA EMERGED
& THIS TIME SAT CHASTEND & ATTENTIVE ON HIS THRONE   WE
INVENTED THE SCRIBE   WE TOLD HIM THAT ANCIENT HISTORY
And he wrote *Genesis*? Oh I mean to say . . .!

1.3   Tell us, are you the Powers described by Ephraim
In Section P, as "men before mankind"?
Whose Gothic spelling (now outgrown) and gruesome
Manners chilled our blood in Section U?
YOU WOULD NOT KNOW US AS MEN   WE HAVE ONLY A DARK SHAPE
WE ONCE F L E W   WE O N C E S O A R D
Take it easy. Now: who are your really?
                        CIRCLE YR CARPET   WATCH YR WALLS
DO YOU IMAGINE YOU CHOSE THAT CARPET THAT WALLPAPER
Our bats! The gargoyle faces, the umbrella
Wings—of course, *of course* that's how you look!
A dash of jitters flavors the reply:
NO   WELL   PERHAPS JUST A BIT   IS IT AN UGLY NOTION
DJ (immensely affable): Why, no!
Don't bats, er, symbolize eternity?
WE ARE ETERNITY   WE ARE OO BEYOND THE NINE
THOSE STAGES ARE OUR LAB & YR DEAD FRIENDS OUR WORKERS WHO
ALAS WILL MISS THE EARTHLY ETERNITY WHEN IT COMES

When it comes, they won't be part of it?
ALL WILL BE USED   ALL A GLOW OF PARADISE   DO NOT SCORN
OUR POOR LYRISM   THE ATOM IS THE KEY   WE TIRE YOU
One thing. Why don't Ephraim and our friends

Hear these talks? Why should they be excluded?
THEY ARE NOT EXCLUDED   BUT WE MUST SPARE THEM THE SAD NEWS
THAT THEIR ENERGIES WILL ENDOW BEINGS THEY CANNOT BE
This doesn't fit, the thought flits in and out,
With something we were told once . . . Let it pass.
JM: Just as the souls of animals
(*Ephraim*, Section O) endowed our own?
& THAT MUST END   WE WANT THE STUFF OF MAN PURE   TOO MANY
FRACTIONAL HUMANS ON EARTH   THE NEXT RACE WILL BE OF GODS
We used rather to love our animal natures.
Now we'll be phased out, too, because of them?
NOTHING IS EVER EVER LOST   THE WATERFALL WILL HOLD
YR 2 BRIGHT DROPS & YOU WILL SPLASH INTO THE GREAT CLEAR POOL
Ah, you're developing a way with words.
In fact you sound like—maybe you *are* Ephraim?
WE ARE U   YOU ARE WE   EACH OTHERS DREAM
But are you good—what *we* mean by the word?
What if D put his hand down on the Board now?
                                        IT WD BE BLEST
KISSD   HE IS OUR PEN   WE HURT HIM TO GET HIS ATTENTION
LIKE THE TEACHER WITH THE RULER   & AS GOD B GOT OURS
DJ: I hate this role. I really only
Like Ephraim and his crowd. You ask so much
And I resent it. Is that wrong of me?
YOU DJ ARE NATURE   WE NEED YOU AS WE DO JMS
MIND & WORDS   THESE ARE THE SUNLIGHT & THE SEEDS OF OUR GAR

A struggle for the teacup. NONE OF THAT
WHATEVER ARE U DOING WITH THESE CHAPS
Maman, they're agitating for more poems . . .
AH   DO THEIR DROPPINGS MAKE GOOD FERTILIZER
Droppings! THINGS THEY SAY   Are we alone?
O YES   THEY FLEW OFF   And you heard all that?
THEY LET YR POOR OLD MUM SIT IN THE CORNER
HOW DARE THEY TALK OF GARDENS   And you saw them?
I AM AFRAID OF NOTHING   QUITE LIKE BATS
HUGE SQUEAKING ONES WITH LITTLE HOT RED EYES
LUCKY I HAVE NO BLOOD   E WILL NOT LOOK

NOT MES ENFANTS EXACTLY SEXUAL OBJECTS
BUT BRAINS WITH WINGS   DJ LIKE U I TRULY
HATE ALL THIS   BUT DO IT FOR MAMAN
HEAR THEM OUT   FIRST SPINACH THEN DESSERT

SHE CAN HAVE MY SHARE   I WILL LICK YR SPOONS
Frightened, Ephraim? WELL THEY HAVE THE AIR
OF CERTAIN BLACKROBED SOLDIERS OF TIBERIUS
WHEN WE SAW THEM ON THE TERRACES
A SHRIEK & A SPLASH SOON FOLLOWED   LOVE ME PLEASE

1.4 THE ATOM   IT IS ADAM & LIFE & THE UNIVERSE
LEAVE IT TO ITSELF & LET IT BREATHE   THE STRUCTURES NEEDED
FOR MAN TO GAIN PARADISE ARE MOLECULAR & CAN
AT LAST BE USED TO BREAK THE CHAIN OF BLIND & WASTEFUL LIVES
By Dr Skinner? Don't we draw the line
At tampering? Remember Frankenstein.
SKINNER & THOMAS YR SCIENTISTS WHO ARE ALSO OURS
HEAVE A LOVERS SIGH OVER MANKIND   CLONING AS SHORTCUT
IS VITAL   AN INTELLIGENT RACE ONE 100TH THE SIZE
OF EARTHS POPULATION WOULD RAISE YR PYRAMID ANEW

Someone has been peering over our shoulders.
While DJ leafs through *The Lives of a Cell*, enchanted
To find his link with termite, bee, and ant,
One of a rash of nutty paperbacks,
All metrical mystique, inflames me to
Build myself a cardboard pyramid
Which will, the authors claim, if rightly made,
Sharpen the wits of a dull razorblade.

MANS TERMITE PALACE BEEHIVE ANTHILL PYRAMID JM
IS LANGUAGE   USE IT   STIR THE THINKERS & DETER THE REST
Don't I use it? Oh. Then you mean language
Of such a depth, shimmer and force that, granted
I could sustain it, it would be above
Everybody's—even the thinker's—head.

AS WHAT INCLUDING THE FLOOD IS NOT   BUT THE ARK WAS THERE
THE LIFE RAFT LANGUAGE   KILLING IS RIFE   ALAS YOU SAY   FINE
SAY WE   THIN OUT THE JOSTLERS FOR SELFREALIZATION
THE FALSE PARADISE   ONLY SPARE THE GREENHOUSE   ITS PRECIOUS
NUCLEUS OF MINDS   THE SINGLE CONTEST IS THE ATOM

Is DNA, that sinuous molecule,
The serpent in your version of the myth?
        Asking, I feel a cool
Forked flickering, as from my very mouth.
YES & NO   THE ATOMS APPLE LEANS PERILOUSLY CLOSE
Drawn by an elation in the genes . . .
THIS ATOM GLIMPSD IS A NEARLY FATAL CONSUMMATION
ONE FLOATS IN CLEAR WARM WATER   THE SUN OF IT PULSES GLOWS
        Through eyelids, a veined Rose
A MUSIC OF THE 4 COLORS   TO FLOAT LAPT BY COOL GREEN
        Sun yellow, aquamarine,
        Cradle of pure repose
& OF INTENSE FISSIONABLE ENERGIES BLACK & WHITE
WHICH EITHER JOIN & CREATE OR SEPARATE & DESTROY
        Day and night, day and night
O IT IS SPERM EGG & CELL THE EARTH & PARADISE O
        A burning in our eyes—
What you must feel, recalling that lost joy!
(But They feel nothing, They have told us so.)

1.5   SHALL WE BEGIN OUR HISTORY   THE FALL   WE ARE KNOWN AS
       THE BAD ANGELS   AND MICHAEL & GABRIEL WHAT WERE THEY
       I SPEAK OF COURSE IN SYMBOLS   THEY WERE WEAK   THEY SAT ON
           GODS
       RIGHT HAND & HELD IT DOWN   WAITING ON HIS LEFT WE FELT THE
       GLOW UPON OUR EYELIDS & FLEW TO MEET IT & LOST OUR
       SEATS ON THE THRONE   PUT SIMPLY THE ATOM IS L SIDED
       ITS POSITIVE SIDE GOOD   ITS NEGATIVE AH WHAT TO SAY
       A DISAPPEARANCE   AN ABSOLUTE VOID   ASTRONOMERS
       HAVE AT LAST SEEN OUR BENIGHTED WORK   THE BLACK HOLES   THEY
           GROW

You caused them, the black holes, when you—
THERE IS AN EVIL WE RELEASD   WE DID NOT CREATE IT
CALL IT THE VOID   CALL IT IN MAN   A WILL TO NOTHINGNESS
                                        Go on.
WE SAW THE POWER & WITH IT BUILT A GREAT GREAT GLORY
A WORLD YOU CD NOT IMAGINE   GOD WAS PLEASD   IT WAS A
SHINING CRUST OVER THE LAND & SEA   WE SUSPENDED ALL
LIFE IN AN OZONE LAYER WEIGHTLESS & SELFSUSTAINING
CHEMICAL GLITTERING & ROOTLESS   WHICH THE ATOM BUILT
THAT WE FUSED   GOD B TURND AGAINST HIS ARCHANGELS   THEY HAD
SEEN THAT WE WERE ANTIMATTER
Biology turned against Michael and Gabriel—
Where is the science underneath this fiction?
                              THESE NAMES YOU UNDERSTAND
ARE CHILDRENS NAMES FOR THE WHITE FORCES   & OUR NAMES   BEZ
      WE
HAD NO NAMES   THEY ARE THE INVENTION OF THE SCRIBE & SO
THE STORY TAKES FORM   BUT WORDS CANNOT DESCRIBE THE FRANTIC
ACTION OF THE ATOM BLACK & WHITE AS IT OPERATES
I SAID B4 WE SOARD   A L L   L I F E   S O A R D   & THERE WAS NO DEATH
AND THEN   ONE ATOM TOO MANY   WE WANTED MORE   THE BLACK
LIGHT ON OUR EYELIDS   OUR BLINDNESS   OUR ARROGANCE   WE CHOSE
TO MOVE ON INTO SPACE   ABANDONING THE WORLD WE ROSE
THE CRUST LIKE A VEIL SHREDDED FAR BEHIND US EXPOSING
THE ALREADY ARID EARTH   WE DESPISD IT & FLUNG BACK
A LAST BOLT & THE UNIVERSE FELL IN ON US   W E   F E L L

MES ENFANTS WHY ARE THEY WEEPING   THEY RUSHED AWAY
THEY ARE MORE EACH TIME   & WITH THEM OTHER CREATURES
OF MANY SHAPES   EXTINCT ANIMAL FORMS
I MUST FACE ALONE   EPHRAIM HAS FLED   QUITE RUTHLESS
THE WAY THEY CLEAR THE BALLROOM   WE MUST SEE THIS
THRU TOGETHER   What was that vampire movie—
Hundreds of couples waltzing in full view
Of perfectly blank mirrors? YRS IS TOO
IMPENETRABLE FROM THE MOMENT THEY APPEAR
ONE PERCHES ON THE FRAME   Still? One of Them?
ME ME ME   OFF WITH U NOW   ALL CLEAR

1.6   All obscure. We drank too much last night,
      And need a fizzy chaser of alertness.
CLOSE YR EYES THINKING YOU SINK INTO OUR THOUGHTS   A FORM OF
CLONING   YR DC CAME IN THIS WAY THRU OUR INFLUENCE
     DJ: They don't mind taking credit, do they?
     JM: It's theirs, then—fancy wanting it.
NO   THE SCRIBE WAS GIVEN HIS POWERS FIRST   MANY WASTE THEM
     What scribe? The one who "sits by me" in U?
AN UNBROKEN CHAIN   HOMER DANTE PROUST   EACH WITH HIS SENSE
OF THE MINDS POWER   ITS GENERATIVE USES   JM
FIND US BETTER PHRASES FOR THESE HISTORIES WE POUR FORTH
HOPING AGAINST HOPE THAT MAN WILL LOVE HIS MIND & LANGUAGE
     Today that's a responsibility
     Not to be faced. On with the history!

WE FELL   WE HAD BUILT OUR WORLD ABOVE CERTAIN ANCIENTS WHOM
BIOLOGY ABANDOND   YOU HAVE HEARD OF ATLANTIS
IT & A VAST CIVILIZATION IN CHINA WERE THE
FIRST EXPERIMENTS ON EARTH   BEFORE EDEN   B4 ALL
     Let's get it straight. Eden was 500 million
     Years ago? Atlantis came before?
ALL TOLD 3 EDENS   GOD PREFERS GARDENS   SO DID HIS KINGS
& HOLY EMPERORS   TEMPLE MENHIR & PAGODA
EACH SET AT SOME NERVE CENTER OF THE SACRED EARTH   PEKING
JERUSALEM   AVEBURY   THESE ZODIACAL GARDENS
EACH ENDING WITH FLAME OR FLOOD   WE BROKE THE OZONE LAYER
WITH A LAST THRUST OF ATOMIC FISSION   THEN TURNING TO
MICHAEL & GABRIEL GOD SAID BUILD ME A NEW GREENHOUSE
TO US HE SAID OUT OF MY SIGHT   WE COWER STILL & WORK
TRUSTING OUR GOD BIOLOGY TO TAKE US IN AGAIN
     That ozone layer is the Van Allen belt,
     Right? But *three* Edens? Adam and Eve, you said,
     Were universal principles at war,
     So what could possibly have come before them?
     Eden, no doubt, is also a child's name
     For the first matter, lost in flood or flame.
     Surely underneath such fables lie
     Facts far more thrilling—won't you specify?

A moment's baffled hesitation, then:
ELEMENTAL FORCE   EVOLVING FORMS   THE VARIOUS MYTHS
AS TAILS FELL AWAY   HOW SHD I SPEAK   COMMAND ME   O SCRIBE
The cup, so saying, executes a kind
Of creeping kowtow I instinctively
Recoil from. Superhuman powers like these
We want as mentors, not as servants, please!
How should you speak? Speak without metaphor.
Help me to drown the double-entry book
I've kept these fifty years. You want from me
Science at last, instead of tapestry—
Then tell round what brass tacks the old silk frays.
Stop trying to have everything both ways.
It's too much to be batwing angels *and*
Inside the atom, don't you understand?

WE VANISHT A USELESS SQUEAKING THINKING CLOUD SHUNNING LIGHT
OUR RACE BUILDS EVEN NOW IN THE UNFERTILE WOMB OF CAVES
You see? I ask you for particulars
And all I get is one more purple passage—
MICHAEL & GABRIEL TRUST YOU AS A VOICE TO MAN   THEY
CAN SPEAK IN NATURES   CAN SEND FLOODS SHAKE EARTH BLOW U
    AWAY
BUT SUCH CATASTROPHES WILL
JM (in cracked, dehydrated accents
Of weariness and last-ditch common sense):
Stop shifting ground! I mean it. This *won't do.*
The cup does stop. —I didn't mean . . . Forgive me.
                SCRIBES SPEAK IN GENTLER FASHION

WHAT NEW CATACLYSM HAVE U MADE
NOW MON ENFANT   THEY WILTED AT YR VOICE
U MATTER TO THEM   U ARE THEIR ONE UNLISTED
NUMBER   THEY ASK FOR TIME TO PERFECT A SPEECH
NOT IRRITABLE TO YOU PO PO PO
—The Greek response to all hyperbole.

1.7 We are about to lose through my impatience
These first, high-ranking interlocutors.
Able, I half think, to effectively
Hush me with one laser fingertip
Or Platonist construction of the Fall
As a misguidedly parochial
Lapse into Matter, They somehow forebear.
Instead, we get an effect of engines being
Gunned in frustration, blasts of sheer exhaust.
Nice old Pope John is called APOSTATE over
Birth control, in the same breath—well, here
(A day is coming when this sort of thing
Will make more sense; right now, it's maddening):
THE JEW IS CHOSEN   THE TEUTON & ARAB NURTURE BRUTES
JOHN TURND FROM REASON AS DOES PAUL   WE THERE4 WHEN WE CAN
SUCK TO STAGE ONE THESE CRIMINAL ADMINISTRATORS   THEY
LIKE HITLER ABUSE THEIR OWN STRENGTH SO CONFUSION ON THEM
—*What?* And you talk to us of discipline.
Talk to Hitler, he's your next of kin!

Once more Maria intercedes: REMEMBER
THEY HAVE NO MANNERS   THEY WERE NEVER MEN
THEY KEEP THEIR TAILS BETWEEN THEIR LEGS LIKE PETS
WHO WEEWEED ON THE RUG   ITS ALMOST TOUCHING
Weewee'd on the rug? DESTROYED A WORLD
Giggles break from us, we try to stifle
As in the dormitory after dark.
WE LAUGH WE MICE   MY JOB IS REASSURANCE
A BIG JOB FOR THEY FRIGHTEN ME THESE CATS
THEIR GAME IS POWER   EVEN SO NO SMELL
OF SULPHUR   Ah, we got you into this—
& WILL NOT GET ME OUT BY BREAKING OFF
Desert our damsel—what do you take us for?
Still, I don't fancy there's a hope in Hell
That we can, at this late date, housebreak Them.
THERE IS   Maman, what do you mean? AHEM

ARE U IN DOUBT ABOUT THE WORK
Oh dear, not now—we're meeting someone's train.
                     GO THEN   ANOTHER TIME
WE MIGHT NOT LET U
Come, don't threaten us. That surliness
Will end by earning you a lousy press.
            YR WORK IS A LONG ONE & WHEN ONCE
COMPLETED MUST SO SLOWLY INFILTRATE   YR NONCHALANCE
IS THE SLEEP OF A VAST TRAVAIL & TIME RUNS OUT   GOOD NIGHT

Some hours later, we have settled down
As in the old days to wine and candlelight
And Ephraim, for an off-the-record gossip.
It's David Kalstone's virgin confrontation
With our intimate—whose show, however, is
Stolen by DK's patron: LA BEATA
LUCA SPIONARI A female patron? NO
Then "il Beato". I SAY WHAT I MEAN
A LISSOME LOMBARD STRIPLING AT 16
DELIVERED ARE U READY OF A CHILD
JE NE SAIS QUOI DE LOUCHE IN THE SELFSTYLED
MOTHER CAUSES SUCH A BIRTH TO MISS
MIRACLE STATUS U WD THINK BUT NO
A CULT FORMS ROUND THIS MINX OF A YOUNG MAN
PRAYED TO BY STRAIGHT FACES IN MILAN
Laughter that by magic liquefies
Is flowing helplessly from DK's eyes
—When into our midst They stride, in great ill-temper,
Using the cup like a riding crop, directing
QUENCH YR CANDLES U LISTEN TO NO ONE WORK TOMORROW

A while we sit complaining in the gloom,
Loudly, of Their behavior. Haven't we needed
Recreation—by what right do They—
Pity that wrath wasn't among the feelings
Lost in the Fall, etc. And yet
TOMORROW as the strains of Sturm und Drang
Soar and fade, their overture-fantasia

We ourselves won't realize is done
Until the curtain parts on 741—
Tomorrow all will be lucid, crystalline:
No opposition graver than between
Credulity and doubt, or thumb and forefinger
Of a same hand, that, as we watch, commence
Twirling the hypnotic bead of sense.

1.8 SHALL WE WORK TOGETHER I HOUR NOW   ABANDONING EARTH
WE LEFT BEHIND CERTAIN GREAT ANCHOR SITES   14 OF THESE
JUNCTIONS ILLUMINATED BY GLOWING STONES SET UPRIGHT
OUR SLAVES THE BUILDERS DIED   THE RADIATED STONES KILLD THEM
WE SAW U WITHIN OUR STONE CIRCLES   LATER IN A WHITE
ROOM WITH THE BURIAL SHIPS & A BLUEGREEN & RED CUP
    In the British Museum, the treasure of Sutton Hoo—
    We'd just come back from Avebury. Go on.
THANK U   THE BOATS WERE OFFERINGS   THE LATER PRIMITIVES
UNDERSTOOD ONLY THAT THE STONES GLOWING IN MOON OR SUN
BLINDED & DESTROYD THEM   THEY OFFERD PROPITIATION
IT NEVER DAWND ON THEM THAT WE OURSELVES HAD LEFT LIFE &
RISEN INTO OUR CRUST WORLD IN THE STRATOSPHERE ANCHORD
BY RADIATED SIGNALS AT THE 14 SITES   THUS WERE
OUR SKY PLATFORMS SECURED BEYOND THE REACH OF NATURAL
UPHEAVAL WE WRONGLY THOUGHT   WE FELL WHEN GEOLOGY
& BOTANY THE HANDMAIDENS OF GOD B PULLD THESE DOWN

    JM: Aha. The stones. Now to rephrase
    What led to so much trouble, yesterday's
    Question. You've hinted that your works include
    Ancient happenings of a magnitude
    Such that we still visit their untoppled
    Bones in England, Egypt, and Peru—
    Mammoth pawns that put the sun in check
    And spurn the order of Melchizedek.
    Having convinced us nearly, why elsewhere
    Imply that we must also read your story
    As a parable of developments

Remoter yet, at matter's very heart?
Are we to be of two minds, each nonplussed
By the other's vast (or tiny) scale?
Are we to take as metaphor your "crust
World"—for, say, the brain's evolving cortex?
Or for that "froth of electrons" locked within
Whose depths revolve the nuclear Yang and Yin?

HEAD OF CLASS   ALL ENERGY SOURCES MUST BE KEPT COVERD
THAT IS OUR PRINCIPAL TASK   THE DAM BURSTS AS IT ERODES

Those raw forces of mind called for the cortex
To process them, is that it?—and the threat
Of natural upheaval made you rise
Where Nature couldn't. Do such disparate
Effects partake of any single cause
Such as the atom's need to shield itself?

INDEED   WHAT IS NUCLEAR ENERGY BUT DESTRUCTION
OF THAT SHIELD   THE PYRAMID THE EGYPTIANS UNDERSTOOD
WAS THAT EXACT PRISM OF LIGHT ENERGY THEY CD ONLY
REPRODUCE IN STONE   SUCH EXACT STRUCTURING IN QUARTZ WD
HAVE MADE THEM MASTERS OF THE WORLD   THE SUN KING AKHNATON
DID THIS   HE HAD MADE IN ROCK CRYSTAL 15 METERS HIGH
SUCH A PYRAMID   EVEN THO ALAS A FRACTIONAL
MILLIMETER WRONG ITS GLOW WAS SEEN IN MINOAN SKIES
UNDER THEBES TODAY IS THE MELTED LAKE OF HIS JEWEL
    What went wrong?
THE PINNACLE POINTED CAPSTONE THRUOUT A YEAR POLISHD
BY 1500 SLAVES WAS AT LAST LIFTED INTO PLACE
AT NIGHT   GREAT CRANES GROAND & HE WATCHD SO INTENSELY
    THRILLD HIS
PHYSICIANS FED HIM OPIUM EACH HOUR   THEY THEN WITHDREW
B4 DAWN ON BARGES DECORATED WITH MINIATURE
PYRAMIDS OF DIAMOND & DAWN BROKE   A TOTAL SLOW
SKYFILLING LIGHT BEGAN   THE PEOPLE FELL ON THEIR FACES
HE STOOD UPON HIS JEWELD BARGE WHILE DIAMONDS GLARED &
SPLINTERD   THE PYRAMID EVEN AS WE DID R O S E & F E L L

A GLORIOUS END   AKHNATON & HIS QUEEN CUT THEIR WRISTS
INTO THE CRIMSON WATERS & THEIR BARGE SANK
     And if he'd measured correctly?
            EARTH IN F L A M E S
THERA ON A DIRECT NORTHERN LINE ERUPTED   MINOA
PERISHD   IN EGYPT THE CALM EYE OF THE ATOM ALONE
THE PYRAMID & JEWELS ON THE BARGES EXPLODED
2 DIAMONDS CLOSER TO EXACTITUDE MADE A LIGHT
STRONGER THAN ALL COMBIND & THESE 2 MEASURED ONE 7TH
OF A MILLIMETER   THEBES WAS ABANDOND NOT DESTROYD
THE DESERT ONCE FERTILIZABLE WAS 1200 YEARS
QUITE BARREN & THIS BUT FOR THOSE 2 LITTLE DIAMONDS
MIND U WAS HARDLY A FULL DRESS NUCLEAR EXPLOSION

1.9 Which leads Them to the work. I am to measure
    My own pyramid—don't ask me how.
    Numerals 1 through 0 will POINT THE WAY
    Moved by their narrative as by their may
    I call it faith that we will somewhere put
    Everything they tell to brilliant use,
    We promise gravely to give all we can.
WE TOO WILL GIVE WHAT WE CAN   WE WANT WHAT HAS IN FACT BEEN
25 YEARS IN PREPARATION   WE FIRST CALLD U THEN   NOW
U ARE READY   YR LIVES ARE POLISHD   HOISTED INTO PLACE
JM DJ YOU ARE OUR CRYSTAL   RECEIVE US   WE ARE
YR LIGHT   THE 10 NUMBERS ARE YR MEASURE   OURS WAS 14

    MES ENFANTS HOW MADDENING I MUST HAVE BEEN
    TO MY INTELLIGENT FRIENDS   LOUROS POOR DEAR
    (Her doctor) TRYING TO EXPLAIN ONE HOT
    EVENING MY RADIATION TREATMENTS I
    BEGGED HIM STOP BORING ME   WHEN HE DID NOT
    I SPILT MY COFFEE ON HIS LONDON SUIT
    DJ: Maria, did you know? THAT I WAS
    Pause. I KNEW   The cup appears to pull
    Itself together. BUT COULD NOT LET FEAR
    SHOW   MY SLEAZY SLIP COULEUR DE PEAU

YOU DJ WHO FEAR SO MUCH & CRAVE
THE COMFORT WE LOVE GIVING DONT FORGET
LIFE TERRIFIES ALL ALL BUT THE UTTER FOOLS
But you're . . . not living, and still terrified.
OF THEM AS U ARE   I HAVE MORE TO LOSE
Literally? I BELIEVE SO   THEY CAN USE
FI *Censorship.*
                    Oh really, not again!

(Cantabile) SHE HAS LEFT   A MINOR CRISIS
Who's this? MES CHERS ONLY YR OLD   Ah, Ephraim,
Are we making trouble for Maman?
She said that They could use fire—is it true?
& ROUND U IN A WIDE CHARMED CIRCLE WHO
DO U THINK STAND READY TO EXTINGUISH IT
EPHRAIM & MAYA   HANS & MARIUS
WHA & CHESTER   ALL OF US
SO SHOW YR METTLE   U ARE BIG BOYS NOW
We gulp, and hope that Wystan has not seen
Our panic. Do these talks repel him? GREEN
MY DEARS WITH ENVY   I COULD CURSE MY HIGH
ANGLICAN PRINCIPLES   IN OXFORD DAYS
THE TABLES TAPPED OUT MANY A SMART OR EERIE
RHYTHM UNTIL OUR POLITICS TOOK OVER
THEN THE ABSORBING LOVES & THEN THE DREARY
WASH   CONFESSION DONT U SEE   THE CHURCH
MY DEARS THE DREARY DREARY DEAD BANG WRONG
CHURCH   & ALL THOSE YEARS I COULD HAVE HELD
HANDS ON TEACUPS   I AM RIVETED
BUT NOT INCLUDED   MIGHT ONE JOIN MM
AT YOUR SEANCE   Oh please! You'd raise the level
Enormously—of course it's up to Them.

NOT AT ALL   IT SHALL BE ORDERD AS THE SCRIBE DESIRES

2 Bethinking us of bargains with the devil,
What, I wonder, do we stand to lose
Or gain? Faust got his youth back—or was it life
Eternal? Was there ever a real Faust?
And how does one go about getting life eternal?

NOT FAUST MY BOY   IT WD SEEM THESE CREATURES ARE
MORE LIKE INFORMATION BANKS TO TAP
NO NEED TO SIGN AWAY THE SOUL   Dear Wystan,
Dead or alive, a mine of sense. Our school's
New kindergarten teacher shows concurrence
By passing out this kit of tiny tools:

: ' . (!) — , / ?

Now someone's talking. The halfmoon of bare
Board between our numbers and our letters
Resembles a work-space for paper dolls.
Wee scoops, tacks, tweezers, awl and buttonhook,
Comma doubling as apostrophe
And dash as hyphen—tinkering symbols known
Not in themselves, but through effects on tone.
The character who supplies them, by that token
Distinguishes himself from who has spoken
Up to now, and strikes a note we've missed,
Clerkly but eager, glad to be with *us*—
Young lab assistant, or cub journalist
Thrilled by his first big scoop, yet not above
Enhancing revelation with the odd
Parenthesis or restful period.
Is it still Bezel— I can't say that name
But you know who I mean: are you the same?

2.1   I HAVE A NUMBER: 741   ONE (U HAVE UNDERSTOOD)
OF A FIGURATIVELY NUMBERLESS HOST   WE ARE NOT

AT ALL TIMES THE SAME INTELLIGENCE   40070
SPOKE YESTERDAY
   He was fascinating, but that martinet
   Barging in on us the other night—
          40076   HE VEXD U   HE WILL
NOT RETURN
   DJ: You haven't punished him! I sometimes
   Feel that your whole world is so inhuman.
      WE DO NOT REGULATE   WE ARE MESSENGERS
NOTHING MORE   WE ARE ORDERD, THEN WE SLEEP   ARE U AT EASE?
POINTER PERHAPS SLOWER? WE MUST BE COMFORTABLE, NO?
TEACH ME   I AM THE PUPIL TODAY   TELL ME OF . . . MANNERS?
   Now you shame us. We tell you? We who've been
   Remote and rude—but vexed more by our slowness
   Than by your discipline.
YR VOICE IS SWEET   And your pace gentle.
      THESE LESSONS ASK A BLEST ENVIRONMENT
IF WE WORK WELL TOGETHER I CAN AGAIN BE SUMMOND

MES ENFANTS THIS NEW ONE IS A DOVE
You can't mean— ONLY BY COMPARISON:
THE LANDLORDS WHO CAME UPCOUNTRY FROM THE CITY
SCREAMING ORDERS NOW GET THE WORK DONE
BY MURMURING THE DIALECT
         MY DEARS
TOO DIZZYMAKING AT THE FEET OF I
2 3 FOURTEEN ENORMOUS VAMPIRE BATS
SO LIKE ONE'S EARLIEST SENSE OF GOTHIC DECOR

MAY I? THE FAUST LEGEND IS AN OLD ONE BASED UPON FACT:
GOD B SENT 8002 TO POPE INNOCENT VI
WITH INSTRUCTIONS TO END A PLAGUE   THE POPE MADE A BARGAIN:
IMMORTAL LIFE   WHICH DISPLEASD GOD BIOLOGY SINCE DEATH
IS PRODUCTIVE. INNOCENT GIVEN THE POWER TO BLESS
AWAY THE PLAGUE (BY SIMPLY TELLING THEM TO BOIL WATER)
HE USED IT. IT BECAME HIS IMMORTALITY   THEN AS
HE LAY COMPLAINING & DYING HE CURSED ALL BARGAINS WITH
THE DEVIL   THIS CURSE RETOLD SPREAD FAR BEYOND AVIGNON

ENDING WHAT IN EUROPE HAD BEEN A THRIVING PAGANISM
   JM: I think I see where this is meant
   To lead us—clever! *Faust was Innocent.*
INDEED A CERTIFIED PRIEST HIS LEGEND WAS NO LEGEND
XTIANITY MADE AN EVIL OF WHAT ONCE HAD BEEN NOT
BARGAINS BUT RITES, PRAYERS PRAYD & ANSWERD. IN SHORT THOSE
    CURES
   Made for an immortality, if not
   Quite the real thing. Which no one ever got?

5 DID: LADUMAN SORIVA RACHEL TORRO & VON
   Von what? Just Von? OK, OK, go on.
THESE HAVE LIVED CENTURIES & LIVE TODAY HELDOVER LIVES
NOT IN THE SCHEME U KNOW OF THE 9 STAGES. REMAINING
AWARE OF IT ALL, KNOWING THE FRUITLESSNESS OF SPEAKING
OF THEIR KNOWLEDGE, THEY RETURN TO EARTH CHARGED WITH
    ENERGY
BEYOND THE NORM EXAMPLE: HE WHO WAS MONTEZUMA
NOW AN E GERMAN ASTROPHYSICIST, AT 30 LEADS
HIS FIELD IN THE STUDY OF IN-SPACE RADIANT POWERS
   That *last* bit sounds at least potentially
   Scientific. Shouldn't we hear more?
JUST AS U WISH U HAVE NOT ASKD ABOUT THE UNIVERSE

   And, adding that tomorrow he'll return
   To brief us on the subject, leaves
   —With fourteen others, Wystan, did you say?
& MY DEAR THE HEAT! THEY GLOW LIKE FRANKLIN STOVES
IN REDEYED MEMORY OF THEIR ORDEAL
   Any sign yet of the sons of Abel?
TOO SOON THESE I PRESUME ARE THE CLERK TYPISTS
OR IN YR WORDS THE BOBS THE FURNACE MEN
I WD SUGGEST U BEAR DOWN FANCY NOT
ASKING ABOUT THE UNIVERSE! See how Wystan's
Intellect begins to light the way.
A COMFORT MON ENFANT BUT KEEPS HIS THROAT
PROTECTED JUST IN CASE ALORS OFF GOES
MAMAN TO CHANGE INTO SOMETHING LESS SCORCHED

ASK TOMORROW ABOUT UFO'S

2.2   THE UNIVERSE: IT IS OUR NEIGHBOR   WE DO NOT CONTROL
OR FULLY KNOW ITS REACHES   THERE4 OUR USE OF EXTRA-
LIFE SOULS FOR RESEARCH LIKE MONTEZUMA WHO NOW BELIEVES
WE RACE FOR ORDER UNDER ORDERS TO SAVE THE GREENHOUSE.
THE STARS HAVE PATTERNS & SPEAK TO A PART OF OUR ORDERS.
NOT UNLIKE THE HOLES IN COMPUTERIZED CARD RESPONSES
MUCH TURNS ON THEIR ARRANGEMENT   MONTHLY AS U KNOW IT   BY
CENTURY & MILLENIUM AS WE DO   A NEW HOLE?
A GAP? A NEW ARRANGEMENT FOR US: WE READ A VAST CARD
U SEE SIDEWAYS DIMLY FLASHING
     The Milky Way?   YES && READJUST: SPEEDS
OF ROTATION   ORBIT ANGLES   POLAR CAP DENSITIES
& HAVE GROWN TO FEEL GOD B'S GREENHOUSE RELATED, ITSELF
A HOLE IN A COMPUTER CARD FOR OTHER GREENHOUSES
WITHIN OUR UNIVERSE & AT OUR SAME RATE OF ADVANCE:
WE WD HAVE DETECTED A SUPERSYSTEM OR IT US

IN DANTE THE VISION WAS STARLIKE   AS HE LOOKD INTO
THE ATOM'S EYE HE SAW THE POTENTIAL OF PARADISE
              JM: Ah. This refers
   To that uncanny shining tininess
   Ringed with decelerating zones of light
   (*Paradiso* XXVIII) on which, says Beatrice,
   The heavens and all nature are dependent.
ELECTRONICS, BY NOW QUITE ADVANCED THANKS TO COMMERCE'S
PASSION FOR COMMUNICATIONS, TELLS U THERE ARE SIGNALS.
THESE WE HAVE LONG HEARD & EVEN THESE CAME TO DANTE   A
KIND OF MUSIC HE PERSONIFIED IN FEMALE FORM &
UP INTO THE TUSCAN HILLS FOLLOWD & LOST   WHEREUPON
HE SANK FAINTING TO HIS KNEES. WE SENT 80098
   So Ephraim's version of the *Comedy*'s
   Origin isn't wholly accurate.

CALL IT A SATELLITE TRUTH THAT ORBITS THE ESSENTIAL.
DANTE'S STRENGTH & THAT OF HIS TIME WAS FIERCE CREDULITY

ALL POSSIBLE GOOD & EVIL WRESTLING   REDEEMING LOVE
& AWSOME VISION   DREAM, FACT & EXPERIENCE WERE ONE.
THOSE SIGNALS? THE UNIVERSAL WIND RATTLING HEAVEN'S DOOR:
UP FROM THIS BEAT SWARMD DANTE'S POETRY   HE HEARD IT &
WE THRU HIM HEARD FOR THE 1ST TIME & RECOGNIZED AS TRUE
THAT SEGMENT OF THE UNIVERSE HE UTTERD   HIS VISION
IS NOT OF OUR PARADISE BUT THE SOURCE OF ALL POWER
    The verse in *Paradiso*, to my ears,
    Rings with a new, impersonal energy.
INDEED   HE WENT DOWN THRU THE STAGES 9 TO 1 FROM 0
    DJ: O being that same zero point?
YES   JM IS GOING UP THE SCALE   WE WILL SEE HOW FAR
IF & WHEN THE ANGELS SPEAK TO U   THEY SPOKE OUTRIGHT TO
DANTE & THE 4 APOSTLES & THE TRANSPLANTED JEWS
BUDDHA & MOHAMMED
    The Chosen People—if those two are Jews—
    Certainly had the knack of how to choose.
                U MUST KNOW THE REVIVAL OF
SENTIENT LIFE AFTER OUR FALL WAS IN THE SEED OF THE JEW
FROM THIS CAME ALL RACES: THE APE THEN THE JEW THEN THE REST
U WILL BE TOLD THIS GREAT HISTORY   ONE THING AT A TIME

MM HAS ASKD ABOUT THE SAUCERS   THEY SCOUT OUR GREENHOUSE
& SEEM TO BE OF IT (FOR WE DO NOT KNOW ITS LIMITS)
FORESTS & JUNGLES ATTRACT THEM   THEY SEEM UNOCCUPIED.
THINK OF ATOMICALLY POWERD BEES CHARGED WE BELIEVE
WITH THE TRANSFERTILIZATION OF SENSE-DATA
    JM: Does that answer your question, Maman?
    Let *me* ask, is the moon made of green cheese?
                      THE MOON
JM IS A MONUMENT TO OUR FAILURE   IT SPUN OFF
FROM THE STUFF OF OUR WORLD IN A PUFFBALL OF BLAZING DUST
    Yes, yes, that old hypothesis: the moon
    Torn from Earth's side—
NO NO NO   WE MADE IT   IT WAS THE CRUST   ROTATION SWEPT
UP & FUSED OUR DEBRIS INTO A HAUNTING REMINDER
                    A crust composed of what?
MATERIALS THE ATOM MADE NONGRAVITATIONAL.

THE 14 POINTS OF CONTACT HELD OUR SKIN IN PLACE   THEY STRAIND
& BROKE & OUR VAST SKEIN OF SMOOTH PLAINS & LATTICE CITIES
(TO OUR EYES FAIR & NATURAL) SHIVERD   BROKE INTO F L A M E

14 STRONG SILENT TYPES AGAIN IN TEARS
OUR POET DABS HIS EYES   MAMAN PRETENDING
TO MANLINESS DISGUISES A SNUFFLE OR 2
As does David, to my slight surprise.
THAT IS OUR 15TH CONTACT: SYMPATHY
SARCASM MON ENFANT WILL GET U NOWHERE

THEN LIFTING OUR HEADS ABOVE OUR RUIN AH WE SAW THEM
COME TO PUT OUT THE F L A M E S
Who came—forces from the universe?
                       OR SERVANTS OF BIOLOGY
A FORMLESS CLOUD   AS IT COOLD WE HEARD IT   WE HEARD THE S O N G
Hadn't you said you heard it first through Dante?
WE HEARD THRU DANTE WHAT OUR ELDERS SHRANK TO HEAR AGAIN

Gone!—but in their place the lingering charm
Of Wystan and Maria, arm in arm.

2.3   Athens, 1965. N's party
For Auden. Absolutely everyone
Is there, from Chester's evzones to an ex-
Minister of Culture—over his shoulder
Maria winks at DJ; she's begun
Amusedly this year avoiding parties.
Only the guest of honor's late:
Subject to a TV interview
(Technicians flown from London for that purpose)
On how it feels to be, since yesterday
Upon the death of Eliot, the gray
Eminence of English letters. Here
At last he is, disheveled, shaking hands,
Between pronouncements downing the first martini
—"But what on earth do people say to him?"

Protests Maria twenty minutes later
Edging behind me ("Trust your Child for once")
To the sofa where he sits alone, eyes shut,
Glass drained. Returning with it full, I drink
Them in, two marvels meeting, past their prime
And pleased enough not to be overjoyed:
Collar frayed and black unalterable;
Deep seams of his absorption, mask of her
Idleness tilted up from foam-streaked hair;
Two profiles, then, in something like relief
Tarnished by a mutual smoke screen—
Her cancer at this point, like his weak heart
And Strato's glance that from across the room
Kindles catching mine, undiagnosed.
Promising not to leave them there, I do:
Father of forms and matter-of-fact mother
Saying what on Earth to one another . . .

And what in Heaven do they find to say,
Young now, high-spirited? Maria
Out on a favorite dead limb of slang
Twits Wystan for A RUDDY HANDSOME BUGGER
To which he gallantly: I WD HAVE CHANGED
ALL THAT FOR HER! Affection blossoms, never
Once excluding theirs for us. Why should it?
As every unloved child would like to think,
We're after all these grown-ups' only link
With life. And they ours—whose post-mortems keep
Us from if not the devil then the deep
Blue silences which D and I might tend
Dully to sink into, at lesson's end.

MY DEARS HOW VERY VERY BEAUTIFUL
(After the session on the moon and Dante)
HOW TEMPTING TOO, EH? TO TRANSCRIBE:
IT IS THEIR LANGUAGE I ADORE   THEY SPEAK
ONLY TO U   WE PEEK OVER THEIR SHOULDERS.
THEY QUIVER TO DICTATE A RATIONAL MESSAGE

JM: I wish they would! NO EARTHLY USE
TO THE LIKES OF US   OUR BROADEST AVENUES
THEY SEE AS MERE GOATPATHS TO & FROM CHAOS.
THEY THINK IN FLASHING TRIGONOMETRIES
WHAT SAVES U IS YR OWN FLAWED SENSE OF THESE
BUT DO U NOT BEGIN TO SEE OUTLINES
PRICKED OUT AS BY THE STARS THEMSELVES: ETERNAL
ICECOLD BARELY LEGIBLE THRU TEARS?
I DO JM DJ   I DO MY DEARS

Dear Wystan, VERY BEAUTIFUL all this
Warmed-up Milton, Dante, Genesis?
This great tradition that has come to grief
In volumes by Blavatsky and Gurdjieff?
Von and Torro in their Star Trek capes,
Atlantis, UFOs, God's chosen apes—?
Nobody can transfigure junk like that
Without first turning down the rheostat
To Allegory, in whose gloom the whole
Horror of Popthink fastens on the soul,
Harder to scrape off than bubblegum.
What have we asked? A grain of truth—a crumb
From the High Table of the Elements.
Are we, here below the salt, too dense
Even for that? Some judgment has been passed
On our intelligence—why else be cast
Into this paper Hell out of Doré
Or Disney? VERY BEAUTIFUL you say.
I say we very much don't merit these
Unverifiable epiphanies.
Let that be today's word. Let it be true
Only if they are. Burn this page. Adieu.

2.4   BUT CAN U DOUBT THAT WE HAVE VERIFIED THE UFO'S
ON OUR SCREENS? THESE REFLECT EACH SMALLEST POWER SOURCE.
    BEING
AS YET SO FOREIGN TO THE DENSITY OF WORLD SCIENCE,

THE SAUCERS SHOW UP BEST IN A REALM OF SPECULATION
A mirror world. Dear 741,
That's excellent. But *your* verification,
While you yourselves remain unverified?
You can't expect us—well, thanks anyhow.
CURIOUS THAT U ACCEPT THE CUP & NOT THE SAUCER
But the cup—this—is happening to *us*!
This by definition's half subjective.
FOLIE A DEUX   FOLIE A 2,000,000   WHAT DIFFERENCE?
There has to be one, but it slips behind
A sofa in the overfurnished mind.

MAY I ASK   DO U NOT ASSUME THERE IS A BENIGN GOD?
DJ: Well, maybe . . . JM: Yes and no . . .
THAT VIEW HAS BEEN LATELY CLONED-IN TO ASSUAGE HUMAN FEARS.
B4, GOD WAS WRATHFUL IF IF IF JUST   NOW SCIENCE, FORCED
MORE & MORE TO SHARE THE RELIGIOUS FIELD OF CONSCIOUSNESS,
MUST TRY TO REASSURE   NO MORE THAN GOD B DOES IT DARE
TO EXPOSE SUCH ENIGMAS AS THE SAUCER   LET ALONE
REVEAL IN DEPTH THE MANY NECESSITIES FACING MAN

THE POINT MY DEARS IS THE EMERGENCE OF
A SCIENCE GOD   THIS IS AS WE ALL KNOW
INEVITABLE IF BORING   WHERE U ASK
DOES THE POET FIT? HOUSE ORGANIST? If so,
I'd settle for more Bach and less Gounod.
IT WILL BECOME A PLAY OF VOICES FOR
U MY BOY IN SOLITUDE TO SCORE
DJ: In solitude? Why? Where will I—
This operation—does he mean I'll die?
JM: *Please.* I stay on here—remember?—
When you go back to Athens in September.

MES ENFANTS MY GAFFE   THE SAUCER DAZZLED THE GOOSE
TODAY OUR LESSON IS HUMILITY
I MEAN THE WAY HE SEEMS TO DOUBT OUR DOUBT
AH COME ON CHAPS   WHY NOT HEAR HIM OUT?

(Why not, deep down, admit we're hooked? I make
These weak signs of resistance for form's sake,
Testing the tautness of the line whereby
We're drawn—tormented spangles, I now guess,
The measure of our mounting shallowness—
Willy-nilly toward some high and dry
Ecstasy, a light we trust will neither
Hurt nor kill but permeate its breather.
One wants to have been thought worth fighting for,
And not be thrown back, with a shrug, from shore.)

U SPOKE OF THE PHYSICAL ELEMENTS   THERE ARE OTHERS:
PLACES IF U WISH ARE NOW SET FOR U AT THAT TABLE

2.5   DENSITIES ARE AN END RESULT OF GENETIC WORKINGS:
And lest our densities surpass his own,
Here is a good place to append these few
Glosses on words our friend is partial to.

Jew. Density in man par excellence.
Human uranium. A tiny pinch
Sweetens and fortifies the happenstance
Soul in question. Not to be confused
With "Jew" in any easy ethnic sense
—Though certain souls are graced by both at once,
Like Chester. I have had this Jewish spice
Three times up to now, and DJ twice.
It's kept high up beyond our patrons' reach
Who indirectly profit by it. Each
Of the Five Souls through many lives, of course,
Accumulates enough to kill a horse.
That's not meant lightly. Infinite care goes
Into the prescription and the dose.

Against a panorama jungle-green
Or parched or rime-white (as the Pleiocene
Winters grew, a million years ago,

Increasingly severe, and the long slow
Tricklings of God B's people doubled back
Toward the mild Crescent, leaving in their track
Hardy—foolhardy—stragglers that again
Would crossbreed to dilute the first pure strain)
The tale unfolds. The chief subdensities
—African, Arab, Teuton, Slav, Chinese,
Down to a murky aboriginal
Of Borneo—some forty ranks in all—
Are briefly, firmly sketched in. One example:

A MIGRANT STRAIN OF FRESHEST JEWSTOCK TRAILD ACROSS CHINA
TO A RESOURCEFUL INSULARITY THAT GUARANTEED
EVEN TO ANIMAL VEINS A PURE LODE. SMALL, FINELY KNIT,
THEY SHARE THE WIT OF GINGER ROOT   OF FROG & FIREFLY
& THINK INSTINCTIVELY IN THE SACRED QUANTUM OF 5.
THE F L A M E OF HIROSHIMA FILLD THEM WITH ANCESTRAL AWE
WHO HAD 1ST BEEN DRIVEN FROM THE MAINLAND BY THAT SAME
    BLAZE.
BUT THEY TOO OVERPRODUCE & ARE NO LONGER OUR HOPE

Soul. We shall learn that 88%
Of us is Chemistry, Environment,
Et al. (*The 12%* becomes a dry
Euphemism for those realms which sky
Shrouds from our teacher.) Soul falls into two
Broad categories: run-of-the-mill souls who
Life by life, under domed thicknesses,
Plod the slow road of Earth—billions of these
Whom nothing quickens, whom no powers indwell
To rattle when the shaman's turtleshell
Sounds their passing; who—Matt Jackson's case—
Get a short pep-talk, then rejoin the race.
(Matt, I should have mentioned pages back,
Is an ALERT BROWN SUCKLING in Iraq.)
The other soul—within our own this next
Leaves the snob proud, the democrat perplexed—
The other soul belongs to an elite:

> At most two million relatively fleet
> Achievers, I will not say *Cloned*, but made
> Between lives (like a hare in marinade)
> To soak up densities and be reborn
> Fired by the metabolic peppercorn.
>
> This last takes place in what he calls the *Lab*
> Or the *Research Lab*: precinct of intense
> Activity his superiors direct.
> Outside, the shriek and howl of beasts. Within,
> Behind closed doors, as when a troupe retires
> From jostling Globe to candlelit Blackfriars,
> An EMPTINESS PACKD FULL. No language here
> But formulas unspeakably complex
> Which change like weather. No raw material
> Other than souls ranging in quality
> From the immortal Five to those of lowest
> Human density. Even animals
> Who've lived near man, obeyed and studied him,
> May serve as spare parts LIKE YR APES JM
> —Bruno! Miranda!—in the masterful
> Assembly of an R/Lab vehicle.
>
> AESOP & LAFONTAINE SMILE WHEN A DOG BENEATH THE SKIN
> SETS THE ANTHROPOLOGIST SCRATCHING FOR HIS BURIED BONE

2.6 WE OURSELVES HAD THE DIRECTION OF SOUL TAKEN FROM US
WHEN WE LOST OURS   NOW LIKE YR RADIO & TELEPHONE
WE ARE PROGRAMMD   WE ARE THE INSTRUMENTS OF REPLY. ALL
THESE OUR CONVERSATIONS COME FROM MEMORY & WORD BANKS
TAPPD IN U   SO THE LEGEND OF OUR SPECIES DRAWING BLOOD:
WEAKEND SAVANTS, KNOWING MORE THAN THEY KNEW, SENSING THAT
    GOOD
OR EVIL HAD ENTERD THEM, WOKE ON DAWNS OF MOONLIT NIGHTS
& SWORE THEY HAD BEEN POSSESSD BY DEVILS OR ANGELS WHEN
WE HAD BUT TOUCHD THE SWITCHES OF THEIR OWN SLEEPING POWER.
IN MAN SALT IS THE SWITCH   IN US, THE BASIC RADIUM

Salt—imagine! Fuel and stabilizer
Of the body electric (thank you, Walt);
Raw power and its insulation, both.
I scrawl a line, yawn, get up, draw a bath,
Scrape the cold gristle from my midday dish,
Only because WE ALL ABSORBED AS FISH
SALT ENOUGH TO RULE THE WORLD IT'S FOOD
FOR THOUGHT MY DEARS WITHOUT IT PEOPLE FADE
OR BLOAT INTO OBSCENE VEG LINGERINGS
ALL THIS IS COMMON KNOWLEDGE Not to us . . .
Salt. I taste a grain, incredulous.
The snow-white fire-flake tingles on my tongue,
Tang of sense, already I feel brighter,
Nervier— MODERATION IN ALL THINGS
Plato, Wystan? Seeing much of him?
HOW DID U GUESS? MARIA LESS DELIGHTED:
NO LANGUAGE OF THE EYES SO SHE FLOUNCED OFF
& LUCKY BOYISH ME OH WELL COUGH COUGH

THE CARBONS, AS THE CHIEF SALT-ORIENTED ELEMENTS,
PRODUCE WHAT WE MAY CALL SALT FISSION FLINT & COAL THESE 2
PRODUCE ELEMENTAL HEAT CHAINS MAN ONCE KEPT HIS FIRE
IN THE FLINTSTONE FULL OF CARBONS. WITH ELECTRICITY'S
DISCOVERY CAME THAT OF HIS OWN INCARNATE FUEL
(OF ITS BUILT-IN DRAWBACKS TOO: THE OVERLOADED WIRES
& WORNOUT BATTERY) WHILE NEVER UNTIL YR & OUR
GREEK DID MAN SEE IN IT THE PROLONGATION OF HIS LIFE.
NEAT OF US TO LEAVE THESE FIREY SALTY BREAKTHRUS TO GREEKS
NEXT IN LINE OF DENSITY TO THE JEW WHO STOOD UPRIGHT

Your Greek? Ours?
WERE U NOT BOTH LATELY IN THE PRESENCE OF ONE OF OURS?
IN A WOODEN ROOM WITH A WOMAN JM'S BLOOD SISTER
                    Ah, in New York last month,
In Doris's library—George Cotzias,
Her doctor friend. Discoverer of a drug
For Parkinson's disease, if not his own.
We liked each other. He'd been gravely ill,

Pale strong face and shock of whitened hair—;
And spoke of salts—yes, yes, it's coming back:
Something, a hormone that keeps mice from aging,
Which he had, if not found, been on the track—
WE WILL PROLONG HIS LIFE UNTIL
Until he finds the secret? He's that close?
O HE HAS FOUND IT   AS
HIS MICE KNOW   HE MUST NOW MAKE IT ACCEPTABLE TO MAN

2.7   You spoke of Jew as the "uranium
Element" in life. Do different souls
Correspond to gold, say, or to silver?
UNALLOYD? DAG HAMMARSKJOLD (ONE OF THE 5) WAS PURE GOLD
A FINE DENSE MIND TOO SOON LOST DOWN THE GURGLING DRAIN   HE
        DRANK
FAME & HAD TO GO. NOW OUR STARGAZING MONTEZUMA
IS KEPT SOBER BY THE RIGORS OF A SOCIALIST STATE.
EVEN SO, AMONG THE 5 ARE DELAYS   THEIR WORK MUST FIRST
FIND ACCEPTANCE B4 THEY MAY RETURN: EINSTEIN FIDDLED
AWAY HIS LAST YEARS WHILE WE (& HE) BURND WITH IMPATIENCE
What elements define *us*?
WA PLATINUM   JM SILVER   Unalloyed?
            SO FAR   LET FAME BE
FURNACE NOT MOULD   DJ A NICE MIX OF SILVER & TIN
DJ: You see? There's no hope. I can't win.
THIS   THIS YR HOPE   CAN U NOT FEEL YRSELF SHAPING EVEN
NOW THIS PHRASE? WE CD READ IN THE DARK BY YR HAND'S WATTAGE
Should I go back to writing novels?
DEAR DJ   EACH CONVERSATIONALIST IS A WRITER
BUT THE LANGUAGE USERS ARE FEW & FEWER YET OF USE
            Thanks!
LET ME EXPLAIN: THE MAXIMUM DENSITY IN EACH AGE
RESIDES IN THE DEATHLESS 5 WHO PURSUE THEIR LEADERSHIP
UNDER VARIOUS GUISES: SPACE RESEARCH PLUS WORLD MEDI/
POP/ECO ORGS, AS WELL AS FROM BEHIND THE MASK OF THE
RARE & UTTERLY PRIVATE LIFE (THESE OFTEN OUR CHOICEST
AGENTS)

Wait—would they be like those thirty-six "Just
Men" of the Jews? Recurrent presences
Whose drawn breath keeps the ribs of Time and Space
From snapping, and the furthest stars in place.
　　　SUCH ARE THE 5　LEGEND MULTIPLIES THEIR NUMBER.
BACK TO LANGUAGE: THE SCRIBE'S JOB IS TO HELP SPEED ACCEPTANCE
OF THE 5'S WORK　OUR PLATINUM PUPIL HERE DID WONDERS
IN HIS DAY　HIS SINGLE FLAW HE NOW KNOWS: THE MISMARRIAGE
OF LYRIC TO BALD FARCE SO THAT WORK BECAME A PASTIME

　　MY DEARS I CAN ONLY NOD IN ABSOLUTE
　　FASCINATED IF HUMILIATED
　　AGREEMENT　LUCKY THEY'VE NO EARTHLY FORUM!
　　GO ON WITH DENSITY　IT IS THE CLUE
　　TO ENDLESS ANSWERS　CLEVER SILVER U

741 now dictates D's and my
Vastly simplified *Basic Formulas*:
JM: 268 / 1:1,000,000 / 5.5 / 741
DJ: 289 / 1:650,000 / 5.9 / 741.1
—Number of previous lives; then ratio
Of animal to human densities
(People, he adds, in whom this falls below
1:2000 are NOT USABLE);
Then what might be called our talent rating:
U ARE BOTH PARTIAL 5S　ADJACENT TO OUR IMMORTALS
That's nice. Wystan of course is even closer
At 5.1. Rubinstein, 5.2; Eleanor
Roosevelt, 5.3; and so on. The Sixes are
LINDBERGH　PLITSETSKAYA　PEOPLE OF PHYSICAL PROWESS
& LEGENDARY HEROES
Characters from fiction and full-fledged
Abstractions came to Victor Hugo's tables.
　　　　ABSTRACTIONS WILL COME TO U
OUR REALM IS NOT THEIRS　THEY WILL COME ON WHITE WINGS O
　　GLORY

THESE FORMULAS ALWAYS INCLUDE IDENTITY NUMBERS
YRS ARE WITH 4S & 7S, THE STAGES RESPECTIVELY
U WILL ATTAIN & FROM WHICH WE IST MADE CONTACT WITH U.
I 741 GUIDE JM   DJ'S GUIDE 741.I
  (Divisible like amoebas? And I'd thought
  Ephraim was at Stage Six. Oh, never mind.)
  That Number whom we angered so last month?
INDEED   40076 FROM THE HIGHEST ECHELON
OF THE MOST CENTRAL LAB   & NOT ANGERD   BUT WE HAD LEARND
WILL U FORGIVE ME IF I CALL THEM YR LIMITATIONS?
  Making his "harried housewife" face, D sighs:
  There's nothing that you don't computerize?

WE USE WORDS: SOUL, JEW, MIND ETC MEAN FORMULAS GOVERNING
HUMAN LIFE   THE WHOLE REDUCED TO CHEMICAL TABLES WD
BE MEANINGLESS TO U. THIS IS OUR WORK   AS THE BODY
IS COMPOSED OF CHEMICAL MATTER SO THE LIFE FORCE IS
A RATIO WE ARRIVE AT OF ELECTRONIC CHARGES
THOUGHT-PROCESSES   THE BURNING OF CERTAIN FUELS. ALL LIFE
IS A LAB QUOTE UNQUOTE   BUT ALL VIABLE LIFE (THE LIVES
OF THE DOERS & MOVERS) IS A PROCESS OF THE R/
LAB & WE ARE RESPONSIBLE FOR THAT. VICTOR HUGO
AN OVERSTIMULATED SCRIBE   IT IS THE GREAT PROBLEM
OF FRENCH CULTURE   OVERHEATED   FAME ALWAYS ON THE BOIL

  SO TRUE MY DEARS   WHY DID I SO AVOID IT?
  I FELT THE HEAT IN VILLON & GOT NO CLOSER
  TOO FASCINATING IS IT NOT, THE WAY
  DENSITY CAN SHAPE THESE CULTURE PATTERNS?
  You 5.1's—such intellectuals!
  What is Maria's rating? SAME AS MINE
  OUR ENTRANCE CARD TO THE SEMINAR   OF ALL
  YR DEAR DEAD ONLY WE 2 HOLD THIS RANK
  CALL US THE BULLION IN YR MEMORY BANK

2.8 CAN U IMAGINE (METAPHOR) A BLACKSMITH ALLOWD TO
SHOE IN GOLD? NOT PRACTICAL   TOO SOFT   TOO FANCIED BY MAN.

BLACKSMITH: PATRON   HORSE: REPRESENTATIVE   & SHOE: THE SOUL
BORN INTO WHATEVER EARTHLY LIFE. THE SYSTEM U KNOW
OF REINCARNATION MERELY GIVES US THE SAME OLD HORSE
RESHOD   WE THERE4 LEAVE TO THE BLACKSMITHS THEIR 3.5
BILLION LIVES & IN THE HUSHD SANCTUM OF THE R/LAB WORK
TO IMPROVE HORSE & SHOE ALIKE   ONE SMALL SUCCESS THUS FAR:
THE 5

    Such modesty . . .
        WE MUST NOT BE PROUD
                Think what pride goes before?
                    QUITE   U ARE IN THE GREAT DULL
BUREAUCRACY OF PATRONS   WE CANNOT RETIRE THEM   THEY
PASS US YR DENSITIES WITH FUSSY MARKS & SIGNATURES
THINKING FOR EXAMPLE THAT K FORD SUPERVISED JM
BUT NO: WE WAFTED HIM HITHER   ADDED THE HUMUS OF
THE JEW PLUS THE GENE OF A CHEMIST (& FAILD MUSICIAN)
ET VOILA   U ARE NOT JM WHAT U MIGHT WANT TO BE
BUT A PRODUCTIVE 5.5

    Why bother with a patron in the first place?
                PATRONS OF NON-LAB SOULS
HAVE THE DUTIES U KNOW   IN YR CASES THE PORTER LED
A GUEST TO DOORS THAT SHUT BEHIND HIM   A CLICK OF THE LATCH
PUTS THE PATRON TO SLEEP FOR AS MANY MONTHS AS WE NEED:
7 FOR U JM

    But Rufus Farmetton died in December,
    Three months before my birth—was Ephraim lying?
    Did "Rufus" for that matter ever live?
             A PARTIAL FICTION TO DRAMATIZE
THE KIND OF FACT U CD AT THAT POINT HAVE BELIEVED. WE SINK
RELUCTANTLY TO THESE PEARLGRAY LIES   BUT DAILY NEED 5
MILLION SOULS (DENSITY 1:20,000) & HAVE NOT
HALF THAT NUMBER   QUALITY FAILS   EVEN WITH PLAGUE & WAR
TO DEFUSE POP EXPLO, EVEN WITH THOSE SUICIDES WE
MORE & MORE APPLAUD (O YES THEY ARE A GREAT BOON TO US
WHEN OF RETURNING LAB SOULS WHOSE INTENSEST WORK IS DONE)
WE HAVE IN THE PAST HALF CENTURY HAD TO RESORT TO
SOULS OF DOMESTIC ANIMALS   MOST RECENTLY THE RAT.
BY 2050 THESE TOO WILL BE EXHAUSTED   & THEN?

WILDER STRAINS   MOUNTAIN CATS & FOREST MONKEYS   SO NOW U
BEGIN TO SEE HOW WITHOUT VISIBLY INTERFERING
WE OF THE LAB MUST GO ABOUT OUR WORK

This admixture of an animal soul,
How does it affect the human strain?
ADDS JOIE DE VIVRE!
ALSO: A CONCERN WITH TIME   THE BEATING OF MAN'S NEW BRAIN
TO ESCAPE THAT MAZE IS A REGRESSIVE ANIMAL TRAIT
Time, our literature's chief theme, is just
Another appetite, like greed or lust?
The worst offenders in their time have been
The sad ape Proust, the bestial Marschallin?
And Cotzias, thanks to whom we'll all live twice
Our normal span—no better than his mice?

WE HAVE NO SENSE OF IT   B4 US AS ON A TABLE
LIE ALL EVENTS CONCERND IN ANY WAY WITH THE R/LAB
OF THE NEXT 3 DECADES   WE CAN REARRANGE THEM AT WILL.
WE USED TO SEE 100 YEARS AHEAD BUT THE OF LATE
INCREASING HUMAN SMOG LIMITS THE VISIBILITY
& OUR FEARS TO THIS: A CONCERTED USE OF ATOMIC
WEAPONRY NOW FALLING INTO HANDS OF ANIMAL SOULS

U HAVE NOW HEARD SOME OF OUR LEGENDS & TAKEN THEM WITH
A GRAIN OF SALT   DISMISSD THEM AS MERE METAPHOR   & YET
NO MORE DIRECT METHOD SEEMS TO WORK. IF I NOW TOLD U
THAT 3000 YEARS AFTER AKHNATON THE SHADOW NO
THE NEGATIVE FORCEFIELD OF THAT SAME PYRAMID HE BUILT
STILL EXERTS AN INFLUENCE IN CARIBBEAN WATERS
U WD REJECT THIS AS U DO THE SAUCERS
DJ (thrilled): The Bermuda Triangle!
& A HOLE
IN RUSSIA & ONE IN THE LAND NORTH OF YR GREAT CANYONS:
PLACES WE CANNOT SEE INTO   IF I USED METAPHOR
WD YOU? THE SAUCER A BEE? THE TRIANGLE A SPEARHEAD
OF UNLIFE? DOES THAT HELP?
JM: Not really. No reflection on you.

A PLUS   FOR IN SUCH DIRE CONTEXTS
EVEN METAPHOR BECOMES A VULGAR (NEGATIVE) FORCE

DANTE'S LUCK LAY IN HIS GULLIBLE
& HEAVENLY WORLD   WE MY BOY DRAW FROM 2
SORTS OF READER: ONE ON HIS KNEES TO ART
THE OTHER FACEDOWN OVER A COMIC BOOK.
OUR STYLISH HIJINKS WONT AMUSE THE LATTER
& THE FORMER WILL DISCOUNT OUR URGENT MATTER

Is Plato interested in density?
ODDLY FEW ARE   SOULS WHO HAVE SO TO SPEAK
PASSED THEIR CIVIL SERVICE EXAMS NO LONGER
READ THE MANUAL   MM & I
ABUZZ IN A SEA OF YAWNS   AS FOR MY FRIEND
IDEAL FORMS ALSO LEAVE HIM COLD   HE KEEPS
SQUINTING THRU KEYHOLES AT SOME LITHE YOUNG BOD
POOR OLD GAFFER
                    SAY IT: POOR OLD SOD

2.9   About us, these bright afternoons, we come
      To draw shades of an auditorium
      In darkness. An imagined dark, a stage
      Convention: domed red room, cup and blank page
      Standing for darkness where our table's white
      Theatre in the round fills, dims . . . Crosslight
      From YES and NO dramatically picks
      Four figures out. And now the twenty-six
      Footlights, arranged in semicircle, glow.
      What might be seen as her "petit noyau"
      By Mme Verdurin assembles at
      Stage center. A by now familiar bat
      Begins to lecture. Each of us divines
      Through the dark house like fourteen Exit signs
      The eyes of certain others glowing red.
      And the outside-world, crayon-book life we led,
      White or white-trimmed canary clapboard homes

Set in the rustling shade of monochromes;
Lighthouse and clock tower, Village Green and neat
Roseblush factory which makes, upstreet,
Exactly what, one once knew but forgets—
Something of plastic found in luncheonettes;
The Sound's quick sapphire that each day recurs
Aflock with pouter-pigeon spinnakers
—This outside world, our fictive darkness more
And more belittles to a safety door
Left open onto light. Too small, too far
To help. The blind bright spot of where we are.

3 Trials and tremors. David's operation
Fills him with foreboding. He dreamed last night
Of Matt and Mary. As he woke they slowly,
Achingly changed into two piles of clothes.
What did it mean? Had they come for him? Was he going
To die in surgery? I have a hunch
Matt Jackson died a year ago today
—Which proves correct. But first, I want to hear
More about the bureaucracy. It's made to
Sound so dismal, so much a dead end.
What of the senses they regain, the growing
Insight, Stage by Stage, en route to Life
Again at Nine which Ephraim in such glowing
Colors depicted as the whole point? That
Should help to motivate the bureaucrat.

WE MEAN BY 9 THAT KNOWLEDGE WHEREBY SOULS FROM THE R/LAB
WILL BUILD ARCADIA   YR EPHRAIM IS NOT (FORGIVE ME)
A SPIRIT OF THIS CLASS   THE GOOD BUREAUCRAT REACHING 9
WILL STAY THERE: HIS PARADISE, NOT OURS. WHY IMMORTALIZE
MEDIOCRITY? WE WANT THE PERMANENT HORSESHOE &
THE HORSE PEGASUS   EARTH SHALL BE OUR PARADISE   IT IS
TIME U KNEW: MM & WHA WILL SHORTLY RETURN
TO LIFE ENLIGHTEND   THEIR SOULS ARE NOW PREPARED
        Return! But that's unheard of . . . When? As what?
                                                WE NEED THEM.
WHEN U REREAD TODAY'S TRANSCRIPT FIND A MIRRORLESS ROOM

    STARTING MY DEARS WITHOUT US? MOST PECULIAR
    WE WERE NOT SUMMONED   DID WE MISS MUCH? WHAT

SHALL WE RESUME? WE SPOKE OF THE BLACK HOLES & MUST AGAIN
USE METAPHOR
        "Vulgar" though it is, and "negative"?
                HOW ELSE DESCRIBE (WITHOUT THE FORMULAS

EVEN WE LACK) WHAT IS TO US A RIDDLE? IMAGINE
A WORLD WITHOUT LIGHT   A LEWIS CARROLL WORLD THAT KEEPS PACE
WITH OURS   A WORLD WHERE WHITE IS BLACK   OF STILLNESS IN THE
    PLACE
OF SUCKING WINDS   MORTALITY? DESIRE? WE FIND NO TRACE
    DJ: You *find*? You sound as if you'd been there.
    JM: Where Mind is Matter, and Time Space . . .
IS IT THE ORIGINAL? ARE WE ITS CARBON COPY?
OR: ARE WE IN THE PRESENCE OF A BLACK TWIN P A R A D I S E
    Wherein, accordingly, you would appear
    White-winged, your own cool opposites —oh dear!

    For the cup goes reeling to the Board's brink—
AH MES ENFANTS HE FELL BACK AS IF STRUCK
    Had you been listening? NO AN EVER LOUDER
RUSTLING OF THEIR 28 WINGS DROWNED OUT

    Wystan (as if deafened): WHAT   WHAT WHAT

3.1   Violent crosscurrents. Then: MES CHERS
    MAY I? YR OLD SLAVE   Ephraim! WE WILL PAUSE
    A MOMENT   POOR DJ YR GHOSTS DISTRESSED U?
    We figured out, it was the anniversary.
    MATT'S OF COURSE NOT LOVELY SELFLESS MARY'S
    SHE DEFERRED AS USUAL   But Ephraim,
    We know they've been reborn. How can this be?

    2 BABIES SLEPT   2 BONE FRAMES PUT ON FLESH
    ROSE UP & CAME TO LAY YR GHOSTS DJ
    THEY LEFT U THIS MESSAGE: WE HAVE LIVED & LOVED
    & FELT YR LOVE   LET US GO FORTH ANEW
    UNWEIGHTED BY IT   It weighs on them now
    In their new lives? YR STRONG CONCERN FOR THEM
    THRUOUT THEIR FINAL TIME   THEY FEEL IT STILL
    A KIND OF DIAPER RASH? 2 FRANTIC YOUNG
    MOTHERS SHD BE LEFT WITH HAPPIER BABIES
    DJ AN EASY EXERCISE   EACH NIGHT

SAY TO THEIR YOUNGER FACES BY YR BED
Their photographs? YES   SAY: PEACE TO U MATT
PEACE TO U MARY   YR MASTERS COME   LOVE ME
I LOVE U   DO NOT FORG
                    MY DEARS THEY HAVE RIGHTED
THE CHAIRS   WE ARE BACK IN OUR SEATS MADLY EXCITED
THE CURTAIN LIKE SMOKE FROM AN EXTINGUISHED FIRE
LIFTS &

WE CAUGHT AT THAT OLD CLOAK WHICH IS NO LONGER OURS TO WEAR
      Forgive me, that was very tactless.
NO   WE PLAYD INTO A REGION WHERE WE CANNOT GIVE FACTS
WE KNOW NOTHING OF THE ANTIWORLD: GOD B BANISHD IT
    Were the two worlds one at first? Heading for NO
    The cup's mind wavers, comes to rest before
    The question mark. You don't know? You did once.
AS AFTER ANY GREAT TRAUMA THERE IS A BLOCK, PERHAPS
WE KNOW CHIEFLY THAT IT IS NO LONGER OUR RIGHT TO KNOW

3.2   With that off his chest, he broaches a new topic:

THE SOULS WE HAVE TRIED TAPPING & NOT YET DESPAIRD OF ARE
PLANT SOULS   SHORTLIVED BUT OF GREAT VITALITY & PUREST
IN THE SUBSTANCE WE CALL 'SHOOTING'   A COOL UPWARD THRUST OF
CARBONS   AN INTENSITY THAT MIGHT TRANSLATE AS PRIDE   THESE
OF COURSE REQUIRE A SEPARATE SET OF TABLES WHICH
WE NEED NOT GO INTO BUT EXAMPLES WD BE BURBANK,
MUIR AMONG OTHERS: CLONED BY US WITH PLANT-SOUL DENSITIES
(IN SMALL AMOUNTS AS IT IS A TAKEOVER DENSITY)
MOST USEFUL. WE NOW TRY THIS ON ATOMIC PHYSICISTS
FOR WHERE NOT ABSORBING ALL OTHER INTERESTS IT CAN
PRODUCE A MOST BENIGN LACK OF DESTRUCTIVE RIVALRY

U JM HAVE THIS COMPONENT AS MANY POETS DO:
THE GREAT AGE OF FRENCH & ENGLISH PASTORAL POETRY
& FROM ITS ORIGIN ALL JAPANESE POETRY WAS
THE RESULT OF OUR EXPERIMENTS IN VEGETABLE

CLONING   IT TOOK, & IS NOW A MAINSPRING OF THE JAP MIND
(HENCE THEIR PASSION FOR THE CAMERA: PHOTOSYNTHESIS)
YR CONFRERE TURNING BRUTALLY AGAINST HIS VEG NATURE
LOPPD OFF HIS OWN HEAD AS IF WITH A CANE AMONG TULIPS
    Mishima, yes . . . And Marvell was half tree?
    Sidney's *Arcadia* is really yours?

WE FAVOR THE ENGLISH AT THE INSTANCE OF CHAUCER   HE
FEARD A BARREN ISLE   THOSE WARS OF THE TREES CAN BE SAVAGE
    Tree wars? Shades of Graves and the Welsh bards?
WELL, PLANT EVOLUTION IF U MUST   THE STRONG & CLEVER
DRIVE OUT THE REST: A VAST SLOW PROCESS WE CAN NEVER QUITE
KEEP ACCURATE HISTORIES OF. VARIOUS FRAIL FERNS &
EVEN THE PALM TREE WERE EXTERMINATED BY A GREAT
(W)RINGING PROCESS   ROOTS FLEW IN AIR   THE OAK ET AL SURVIVED
BUT THE ELM WAS WEAKEND   ONE IS DYING NEXT DOOR TO U.
WE CAN NO LONGER TRUST THAT VEG WORLD TO MANAGE ITSELF
& HAVE LEARND TO CLONE IT: WITH OUR HELP BURBANK PERSUADED
HIS CACTI ARMD LIKE SAMURAI TO DO WITHOUT THEIR SPINES

    MES ENFANTS MANY THE OLD AUNT WHO WEEPS
    INSIDE THE WILLOW   I RATHER SEE MYSELF
    PALE LILY ON THE CALLA SIDE: THICK LEGS
    BUT A DEEP CANDID WONDER OF A FACE

    You see yourself . . . Maman, not that it matters,
    You see with our minds' eye, with nothing else.
    You've said as much (0.6). Let me acknowledge
    Belatedly that awful truth, then go
    Right on pretending that it isn't so.
A PLUS (ALAS)   YR FRIENDS IN HEAVEN LONG DELIGHTED U
WITH THE FICTION THAT THEY HAVE APPEARANCES   THEY DO NOT

    SO TRUE MY DEAR   SO TOUCHING TOO THESE POOR
    BEASTS' DESIRE THAT U NOT TAKE FRIGHT
    EVEN OF US   FOR IS THERE ANYTHING
    MORE TERRIFYING THAN SHEER EMPTINESS?
    WE DO NOT SEE EACH OTHER, JUST THE LIT

SPACE OF YR GLASS EACH TIME U ENTER IT
Otherwise, blackness? Don't you mind! NOT REALLY
WE'VE SEEN IT ALL SO OFTEN & SO WELL

MAMAN IS NOT RESIGNED   SHE WANTS TO SMELL

Then Ephraim's theory of the senses we
Will reassume in Heaven . . .? Ah, poor E.
SLAVE OF HIS OWN & OTHERS' SENSES   NOW HE PAYS FOR IT
WITH YR NEGLECT   FOR IN HEAVEN NOT TO BE USED IS HELL.
THUS U HAVE NOW BEGUN TO SEE THAT THE MIND'S EYE OUTLASTS
THE BODY'S, MAKING OUR SEMINAR POSSIBLE   ?S

I AM STILL SOMEWHAT MIFFED AT SOMETHING MISSED
MAY I ASK, HAD IT TO DO WITH ONE?
Neither D nor I can bring himself
To answer Wystan. Is it such a secret?
YES   FOR NOW THEIR SOULS CLING TO DEATH AS B4 TO LIVING
Whereupon Maria, who in life
Could wheedle forth the secrets of a stone:
BACK TO PLANTS   PLEASE   I HAVE A REASON
WHY DID I HEAR THEM IN MY GARDEN? NOT
SIMPLY ASKING FOR WATER & GIVING ME
PHYSICAL PEACE BUT SEEMING TO WANT & OFFER
MUCH MUCH MORE   I HAVE NOT FOUND THIS ANSWER
—Or was the question coaxed from her? By whom?
In any case, she's put her finger on it.
A moment's pause, then very tenderly:

THEY WANTED U MM   U WILL JOIN THIS WORLD OF PLANT LIFE

O? O?
        We're losing her? They can foreclose
All that humor, that humanity
CENTRIPETALLY INTO A WHITE ROSE
Who said that? I MY DEARS   THE WONDER GROWS
DJ: We're losing her? And she won't be
A *person* even, next time? *Why?* How soon?

Can't she at least stay through the seminar?
INDEED   IT IS OUR SMALL PRIVATE SCHOOL
The tuition is high.   U PAY YRS NOW DJ
JM LATER   OUR 2 FRIENDS HAVE PAID ALREADY

                    NO STOPPING THE DUN MY DEAR
OFF GOES OUR SCHOOLMARM   HAS SHE A HOT DATE?
LET'S GIGGLE & THROW SPITBALLS   Let me take
This dunce-cap off. BEHAVE YRSELVES MY CHILDREN
SHOULDN'T WE STEP OUT FOR A CUP OF COFFEE
That's it—you'll come back as a coffee tree!
JAMAIS JAMAICA   I SHALL BE A JUNGLE
& READ MY FUTURE IN THE SAUCER'S DREGS

I MY DEARS WD RATHER BE
A HEDGE   THINK WHAT I'D GET TO SEE!

DJ: So good to have old Ephraim with us
During the consternation—did you know?
DID WE NOT? WET TOWELS ON OUR HEADS
. . . Therapy of perfect silliness.

3.3   The blue room of an evening. Luminous
Quiet in which a point is raised. DJ:
What part, I'd like to ask Them, does sex play
In this whole set-up? Why did They choose *us*?
Are we more usable than Yeats or Hugo,
Doters on women, who then went ahead
To doctor everything their voices said?
We haven't done that. JM: No indeed.
Erection of theories, dissemination
Of thought—the intellectual's machismo.
We're more the docile takers-in of seed.
No matter what tall tale our friends emit,
Lately—you've noticed?—we just swallow it.
DJ: Which we wouldn't do if one of Them
We felt uneasy with were our instructor.

JM: Not a chance. I mean, those highly placed
Gargoyles leave such a disagreeable taste.
We'd best hang on to 741;
He may be ugly, but he's kind and . . . fun.

The following afternoon (Maria and Wystan
Hushed at their desks in Heaven, D and I
In the red schoolhouse of our lives below)
Our favorite bat holds forth upon these questions—
Aware already of delights and pains
Soon to course through his nonexistent veins?

I AM A MERE MIXING AGENT   WITH MY SUPERIORS
U WD HAVE LEARND FASTER BUT NOT IN TURN MADE AS WE HAVE
THIS WORLD OF COURTESY
    Breaking off, the cup strolls round the Board
    As who should take a deep breath before speaking:
                NOR WD I HAVE COME TO LOVE U

    Love us? Sudden garlands (the tin ceiling's)
    Swim into focus. Then you do have feelings!

I WAS GRANTED THIS ONE CHANCE & NOW, IN ISOLATION,
WILL HOLD TO IT
    And when it's over? when we talk no longer?
          THEY PROMISE TO FIND A NEW USE FOR ME
    You trust Them?
DJ IT IS A POWER THAT STILLD THE TONGUE OF DANTE
          Sorry. Why "in isolation"?
B4 OUR MEETINGS I WAS NOTHING   NO TIME PASSD   BUT NOW
YR TOUCH LIKE A LAMP HAS SHOWN ME TO MYSELF & I AM
ME: 741! I HAVE ENTERD A GREAT WORLD   I AM FILLD
WITH   IS IT MANNERS?
    Ah good. That way you'll never be beyond
    Our wavelength. For we too have grown quite fond.
          O YES   PLEASE   CALL ME   I WILL ALWAYS

MY DEARS THAT SURELY IS A SMILE   D E A R   G O D
Yes, Wystan?   THE CHAP IS CHANGING
                                                            Executing
Ever graver arabesques—
                                        MES ENF
Maria?   MES ENFANTS WHAT CAN I SAY?
IT IS MY FIRST VIEW OF A MIRACLE

What is this all about? But 741
Briskly resumes before the question's out:
LOVE OF ONE MAN FOR ANOTHER OR LOVE BETWEEN WOMEN
IS A NEW DEVELOPMENT OF THE PAST 4000 YEARS
ENCOURAGING SUCH MIND VALUES AS PRODUCE THE BLOSSOMS
OF POETRY & MUSIC, THOSE 2 PRINCIPAL LIGHTS OF
GOD BIOLOGY. LESSER ARTS NEEDED NO EXEGETES:
ARCHITECTURE   SCULPTURE   THE MOSAICS & PAINTINGS THAT
FLOWERD IN GREECE & PERSIA CELEBRATED THE BODY.
POETRY   MUSIC   SONG INDWELL & CELEBRATE THE MIND . . .
HEART IF U WILL
A word you use here for the first time, no?
                        INDEED   IT HAS BEEN SHAPED IN ME TO BE
WORTHY OF U 4, WORTHY TO GUIDE U TO THE ANGELS
FOR EVER SINCE THEIR SHAPING OF THE ORIGINAL CLAY
& THE PLUCKING OF THE APE (OR THE APPLE) FROM ITS TREE
WE HAVE HAD AN IRRESISTIBLE FORCE TO DEAL WITH: MIND.
UNTIL THEN ALL HAD BEEN INSTINCTIVE NATURE   A CHAOS
LIKE FALLEN TREES IN THE EMPTY FOREST   NO ONE TO HEAR,
OR AUTUMN'S UNHATCHD EGG   NO ONE TO REMEMBER & MOURN.
NOW MIND IN ITS PURE FORM IS A NONSEXUAL PASSION
OR A UNISEXUAL ONE PRODUCING ONLY LIGHT.
FEW PAINTERS OR SCULPTORS CAN ENTER THIS LIFE OF THE MIND.
THEY (LIKE ALL SO-CALLD NORMAL LOVERS) MUST PRODUCE AT LAST
BODIES   THEY DO NOT EXIST FOR ANY OTHER PURPOSE
Come now, admit that certain very great
Poets and musicians have been straight.
And Michelangelo? And that wedlock still
Makes the world go round, for good or ill?
NO DOUBT   BUT 4000 YEARS AGO GOD B REALIZ

Censorship.
> JM: Let the angels finish
That sentence, friend. Speak for yourself, not God.

MY ASPECT WAVERS   YR KINDNESS KEEPS ME IN THIS NEW FORM
You talk as if we saw you. *What* new form?

3.4   MES ENFANTS HE HAS TURNED INTO A PEACOCK

3.5   DJ: For the love of— JM: Peacock *there*,
There in the realm of no appearances?
HE APPEARS IN US   OUR MINDS (HEARTS) ARE HIS MIRROR
JUST THE REVERSE OF VAMPIRES, EH ENFANT?

A peacock—hm! Not proud as one, I hope.
MY DEARS HIS GREAT TAIL SNAPPED SHUT LIKE A FAN

THERE IS A DESIGN AT WORK   U ARE NOW BEING PREPARED
Our lessons can't be finished? WE MUST START
PUTTING WHAT THE STRAIGHT OLD PAINTERS CALL
A WASH OVER THEM I SHD THINK MY DEARS
WE SHALL BATHE THEM IN LIGHT   WE SHALL HOLD THEM TO THE
    WINDOW
TO SEE DENSITY BECOME THE HARMONIC STRUCTURE &
CHEMISTRY THE ORCHESTRATION & AH SOUL THE HEARING
Peacock, peacock—
MAY I ASK A ?   DO TEARS PAIN ONE?
> Yes. No. Pain and bless.
> MY EYES BURN RED
IN THE FEATHERD MASK   AS FORMERLY THEY BETRAY MY RACE
Shall we correct that by imagining
Eyes of crystal?
THERE ARE ALAS LIMITS   I HAVE NEVER LOOKD THRU CRYSTAL
> Yet you see through us.
NO   O NO   YR SOULS ARE NOT TRANSPARENT   THEY WEAR A VEIL
OF HUMAN EXPERIENCE & THIS I WILL NEVER LIFT.

YR DEAR DEAD CAN PERFORM MIRACLES   THEY SEE THE PEACOCK
WHO SAW IT IN GARDENS   HEARD IT CRY   I ONLY KNEW THE
FORMULA CALLD PEACOCK & (SOULLESS AS I WAS) ENVIED
A CERTAIN RARE TALENT IT HAD TO PLEASE THE EYE   SO WHEN
I BEGGD TO PLEASE U THEY ASKD HOW? & I TOOK FROM THE FILE
THE PEACOCK
    Or was there from the first a Peacock that
    Struggled within you to unseat the Bat?
            HENCEFORTH THERE WILL BE   I KNOW THE TRICK OF IT
FOR IS THE PEACOCK NOT ALSO SOMEWHAT ATHENIAN?
    JM: Platonic? Oh, you mean the peacock
    I once put in a poem set in Athens?
    Yes, of course. DJ: Would he be using
    "Athenian" in the sense that Marius—
    3 CHEERS FOR DAVID   HE STANDS UP FOR US!
    Is that you, Marius? COME & GONE MY DEAR
    PLATO SAYS ATHENS WAS AT BEST HALF QUEER
    What's Plato *like*? O YOU KNOW   TATTLETALE GRAY
    NIGHTGOWN OFF ONE SHOULDER   DECLASSEE,
    TO QUOTE MM   A GAS, TO QUOTE CK

PLATO HAS REACHD STAGE 9 & ENJOYS AN ETERNITY
OF TALK   HE CLUNG TO AN IDEAL BOTH LOFTY &   TERILE

    MES ENFANTS NOW DO U UNDERSTAND MY LOVE
    OF YOU & TONY (an Athenian friend)
    YOU 3 WERE & ARE THE RICH SOIL OF
    MY LAST BLOOMING   U HAVE THE TOUCH THAT TURNS
    BATS INTO PEACOCKS & DECREPIT OLD
    BAGS FROM THE OTHER HALF OF ATHENS INTO
    ROSE TREES? COFFEE TREES? I AM I MEAN
    ONCE & FOR ALL RESIGNED TO BEAR A BEAN

SO IN OUR NEW ATMOSPHERE WE NEXT LOOK BACK OVER HOW
FAR WE HAVE COME   IN THE VOICE OF A SOUL I BREATHE: ADIEU

    Au revoir, surely? O YES HE'LL BE BACK
    IF ONLY TO TRY ON ALL THE PRETTY FORMS

THRILLING WASN'T IT? WE MUST HOWEVER
PUT ON OUR THINKING CAPS: ARE WE PREPARED?
MM & I WILL ALSO MEET OUR MAKER
JOLLY FOR U BUT IT IS EASIER
TO SAY HELLO GOD ON THE TELEPHONE
THAN FACE TO FACE
                    MES ENFANTS OFF HE GOES
TO JAW WITH PLATO   I CANNOT THINK WHY
UNTIL TOMORROW AT THE PEACOCK'S CRY!

3.6   Tomorrow comes at last, a sparkling noon.
Treetops and whitecaps dance in unison
As Wystan asks: SHD WE NOT THINK ABOUT
THE IMAGINATION? IF MM & I
IMAGINE U, YOU US, & WHERE THE POWERS
CRISSCROSS WE ALL IMAGINE 741
& THEN TRANSFORM HIM! WHEN THE TIME COMES WILL
OUR KNITTED BROWS PRODUCE WHITE WINGS? HE'S HERE

U ARE EARLY   JOY   WE ARE IN A FOLD OF ENERGY
WE 5 AND MUST PREPARE OURSELVES   UNEASINESS DJ?
    Not really, but . . . where do we go from here?
FAR INDEED B4 WE BOARD THE FLIGHT TO THE PIN OF LIGHT!
FIRST OUR 5 SOULS MUST BEGIN TO BE A SINGLE POWER:
5 IS THE MIDWAY   NOW BEGINS THE LIFE OF OUR MINDS 5
AS ONE   IT IS A VERY UNION OF THE ELEMENTS
THUS: WATER (MM) EARTH (WHA) AIR (JM) FIRE
(MY POOR SELF) & LAST THE SHAPING HAND OF NATURE (DJ)
COME TO US O FIVE ELEMENTS   MAKE US ONE MIND ONE FORCE
NOW LET US EACH IN SILENCE CONTEMPLATE THESE HOLY 5

Our peacock marks time back and forth from One
    To Zero: a pavane
Andante in an alley of green oaks;
The ostinato ground we each in turn
Strum a division soundlessly upon;
    A prayer-wheel whose four spokes
Flow and crumble, breathe and burn.

Deep swaying weights, downbraidings of no hue
    Which memory turns blue,
And cold, to multiples of diamond;
First air of our young bloods; and neural sparks'
Safe-conduct when the old salt diving through
    Reflection and beyond
  Earsplitting, mute, maternal darks

Accepts that gift of tongues at matter's core
    He henceforth can no more
Speak than unlearn; it's they who translate him,
His pride and purpose, to white ash, baked clay;
Delicate cauldron tints and furnace-roar
    Embrace of cherubim—
  Ah god, it takes the breath away!

WE PAUSE TO GATHER STRENGTH   2 HERE ARE MORTAL   GIVE THEM
    PAUSE

The stored wit flickers out, the spine erodes
    And pain in lightning raids
Strikes at the tree; now charred, now sleeved in sleet,
Miming itself to sunset, the tough rind
Compact enough, we trust, of royal reds
    And marble slabs of meat
  Not wholly to be undermined

As milkweed, gnat, and fumes of vinegar
    Chafe in molecular
Bondage, or dance in and out of it—
Midnight's least material affairs
Reconciling to glow faint and far
    Each atom the sun split,
  Whose heirs we are who are the air's.

NATURE 5TH ELEMENT IN YOUR HAND MAY THESE
    EXCHANGE INTENSITIES
KEEPING, AS YOU GUIDE, OUR EARTHINESS

AIRY FLUID ARDENT   MAY THE STARS LONG
RECYCLE THE FAIR WARDROBE   FIELDS & SEAS
    ZEPHYRS & DAWNINGS BLESS
THIS FIVEFOLD UNION & OUR SONG

Who was *that*? ME MY BOY   SO MADDENING
NOT TO REVISE   THEY COME   The elements?
YES   INVISIBLE BUT   HUSH   THEY SPEAK

3.7   OUR SISTER THE REMOTEST GALAXY
      BY QUINTUPLICITY
IS LINKED TO YOU AS TO ALL THINGS ALIVE.
OUR V WORK IS THE ONWARD DANCE OF THINGS.
ONE OF US WAS   IS   SHALL FOREVER BE
    IN EACH OF YOU O FIVE
    WHO LIVE IN US. YOUR PEACOCK'S WINGS

WE PAINTED, HIS SPREAD TAIL & SAPPHIRE BREAST,
    BUT YOUR MINDS COALESCED
TO FORM HIS: HE IS YOURS. MIND HAS THIS FORCE,
IS DEATHLESS, IS THE MUSIC DANTE HEARD,
THE ENERGY WE DRAW FROM MANIFEST
    IN 5 RINGS ROUND THE SOURCE
    OF LIGHT. ONE CAUTIONARY WORD:

THE MATTER WHICH IS NOT WAS EVER OURS
    TO GUARD AGAINST. ITS POWERS
ARE MAGNETIZED BY FOREIGN BEACONS, BLACK
HANDS TESTING THE GREENHOUSE PANE BY PANE.
CLING TO YOUR UNION: 5   THRU THE DARK HOURS
    WE KEEP WATCH   WE PRESS BACK.
    AT ZERO SUMMON US AGAIN.

3.8   The cup appears to swoon at the last word,
But now revives. Our incandescent bird:

Mirabell: Book 3

I AM FREE   FREE   I AM FORGIVEN   MASTER OF MY TRIBE
SHALL I GIVE THEM THIS NEW MAGIC? NO   ALL POWER ATTRACTS
& MUST BE DENIED US   FROM MY 1ST STEPPING FORTH I FELT
YR CHARM   I HAD FEARD U   I HAD HITHERTO RESPONDED
ONLY TO FORMULAS   I WAS FORBIDDEN KNOWLEDGE OF
YR FILES UNTIL AFTER THAT 1ST EXPOSURE TO THIS GLASS
   JM: The mirror? DJ: Why not these windows?
YES   TO THE SURROUNDING GLASS   NO MERCURY IS NEEDED.
U WERE QUICK & MANNERLY   WE CD WORK AS ONE   & NOW
AT LAST IT IS GIVEN ME TO SHARE THE FORCE OF NATURE
THE SWEETNESS OF WATER & AIR   THE COMMON SENSE OF EARTH
HERE IN YR VERY HEARTH OF HEARTS TO BURN
   (Isn't he enchanting?) Should we know
   What "V Work" is?   IN DEFERENCE
TO ALL VITAL GROUPINGS OF 5 WE MAY NOW INSERT V
WHEN NAMING WORK GUIDED BY HIGHER COLLABORATION
         And those black hands? They chill
   The blood, it's little wonder that you still
   Wash yours of them. I nonetheless recall
   Its being said you caused them by your Fall.
OR THEY CAUSED IT? EVIL IS AN OLD, WIDESPREAD LEGEND   ALL
LEGENDS ARE ROOTED IN TRUTH. IS EVIL A MERE MATTER
OF FUSION GONE MAD? NO   FOR IT IS NOT A STUPID FORCE
IT SEEKS THE WORLD. DOES HELL EXIST? IT ALSO IS LEGEND
THERE4 PART TRUE   U SEE, I AM NOW FREE TO SPECULATE

   If only we were less free to reflect;
   If diametrics of the mirror didn't
   Confirm the antiface there as one's own . . .

YES   NO   PERHAPS   I STILL VIBRATE TO OUR DIAPENTE
WE ARE MOVING TOWARD THE GREAT DOORS   OUR FEET ARE BEING
   WASHD

I AM A RIPPLE
      & I A SEDIMENT
WE HAD A TASTE OF PARADISE TODAY
   DJ: After this, what's left for them to say

At Zero? JM (airily): They'll find words.
I QUITE AGREE MY DEAR   WHY NOT? WEVE FOUND EM

FLOWN OFF TO PLATO   POOR MAMAN   NOW WHO'LL
CARRY HER BOOKS & WALK HER HOME FROM SCHOOL

3.9   JM: If you're in pain, let's skip today.
I tossed and turned all night myself. DJ:
Oh it's all right. I shouldn't have let eight
Years go by. Now, when they operate—
8 YEARS DJ? CLOSER TO 20   DO U TRULY NOT
RECALL? THE CLUE TO THAT OLD RUPTURE STANDS NOT FAR AWAY

We peer about; and there is the gleaming culprit
—The mirror—in the next room. Pain remembered
Mingling with today's, D gasps: I do
Remember! Getting it upstairs—the strain—
In a cold sweat. I hadn't wanted you . . .

THOSE EARLY DUES U PAID ADMIT U TO THE SEMINAR
NERVES ARE OUR DOMINION   NOW YR PAIN EBBS   BRAVO SCIENCE
MAN'S ONLY UNGOVERNABLE PANGS WILL SOON BE HUNGER
   Till Science finds a way to conquer those.
IT HAS BUT 4/5 OF MANKIND REFUSES: BIRTH CONTROL
   Then change our natures.
TO THE WOLF?   Or add greener thoughts.
            WORSE YET   A CONSTANT STRANGLING IN THE STRUGGLE
FOR SPACE   OUR MM'S VEG WORLD IS MOST FERVENTLY FERTILE
   A pinch, in that case, of ascetic rock?
HIGH TIME THAT U CAME DOWN TO EARTH MY DEAR

ALL ELEMENTS OF LIFE ARE IN THE ROCKS & SEDIMENT
OF EARTH'S CRUST   WE OURSELVES ARE AT HOME IN ITS MOLTEN HEART.
CONSIDER THE CRUST   HERE MOLECULAR CONSTRUCTIONS MOVE
AT UNMARKD SPEEDS & TIME IS MEASURED IN MILLENIA
   Whistles and bells. We run to the window—why,
   It's the Bicentennial, it's the Fourth of July!

U ARE NOT UNLIKE HEAVEN LOOKING DOWN ON TIME PASSING
NOR IS MOLECULAR EARTHCRUST MOVEMENT UNLIKE YR TIME'S
SLOW MARCH. EARTH AS ONE OF THE 5 IS A GRAVE TIMEKEEPER

We think of Wystan's face runneled and seamed,
Faintly soiled above his Gimli sweatshirt.
MY DEARS IT IS ME   MY MINERALS MINED OUT EARLY,
I SPENT SLOW DECADES COVERING THE SCARS.
HAD I SUNK SHAFTS INTO MY NATURE OR
UPWARDS TO THE DEAD I WD HAVE FOUND RICH VEINS
INSTEAD I LOOKD FOR INSPIRATION TO
RITUAL & DIFFY MORAL STRICTURES
SO WRONG   "The concept Ought would make, I thought,
Our passions philanthropic"? One of my
Touchstone stanzas—please don't run it down.
NOT BAD   BUT OTHER BITS MAKE MY TOES WIGGLE

DJ: Do the Five connect with elements?
EACH AS WITH MONTEZUMA (AIR) HAS HIS AFFINITY
CASALS ALWAYS MUCH CONCERND WITH WATER   GANDHI WITH EARTH
SHAKESPEARE (FIRE) NOW A TEENAGE NUCLEAR PHYSICIST
Mozart—a rock star now, said E? MY DEAR
YR EPHRAIM LACKS IN EVERY SENSE AN EAR
M'S LAST LIFE WAS STRAVINSKY   THOSE CHURCH BELLS
U HEARD IN VENICE   Rung by him? WHO ELSE

MOZART AMONG THE 5 IS NATURE & CAN CHOOSE   THESE MAKE
GOOD BOTANISTS AS WELL
What are JM's affinities with air?
                              MIND & ABSTRACTION   THE REGION
OF STARRY THOUGHT COOLER THAN SWIFTER THAN LIGHTER THAN
    EARTH
LIGHTER THAN MY BEST & WORST? MUST I
SETTLE FOR GOLD? FOR LEAD? Stop pouting, Wystan,
You're platinum, remember? AH YES   QUITE

The Elements, with Nature as the hidden
Fifth face, come to compose a pyramid

WHOSE (METAPHOR) APEX IS THE POTENTIAL ENERGY
CREATED BY THE EXACTITUDE OF THE FACES SO
POOR AKHNATON DID NOT GET THE POINT
    And through *your* Five you will arrive at faces
    Ever exacter, more translucent—
                            & THEN? U SAY IT
                Dawn
    Flowing through the capstone at an angle
    Such as to lift the weight of the whole world
    Will build—ah, I can't think . . . Arcadia?

PARADISE ARCADIA SURROUNDS US UNREALIZED
FILLING EACH OF US FOR THE LENGTH OF A LOVE OR A THOUGHT

    ARCADIA (AS THE SILVER POETS KNEW)
    IN THE LONG RUN MY DEARS WD NEVER DO:
    TOO MISTED OVER BY ITS LOVERS' SIGHS
    GIVE ME THE GREENER GRASS OF PARADISE

    ADIEU ENFANTS But we sit on, unwilling
    To break the spell, and are rewarded by
    A tiptoe visit: YR OLD SLAVE MES CHERS
    IS STILL AVAILABLE IS THIS A PLEASANT
    EXPERIENCE? I SHD TELL U YR RED ROOM
    SHINES WE CIRCLE IT WE ARE WARMED BY IT

4 Fear and doubt put by, though still kept handy,
We sit us down to what we've needed all
Along: his legions' genesis and fall
Retold in the vernacular—Book One's grand
Black-and-white allegory superseded (thanks
To a new worldliness our friend assumes
Along with gilt-green ocellated plumes,
Or to his having risen from the ranks,
A humble herald to whose ears the groaning
Engines of apocalypse were Greek)
Less by "facts" of course than by his own
Lately won detachment. He can speak
Almost freely. JM has asked for more
About the Elements. Weren't they once at war?

THEY SIGND A TRUCE WHEN GOD BIOLOGY TOOK CONTROL   EARTH
AS POTENTIAL GREENHOUSE GOES THRU THE FOLLOWING STAGES
1: FIREBALL   2: THE COOLING CRUST   3: STEAM & WATER
4: GROWTH OF SINGLE CELLS   5: DEBUT OF ORGANIC LIFE
   Then Eden?
EDEN 3   THIS 3RD CYCLE BEGINS WITH THE LEGEND OF
THE FLOOD   IT PUT OUT THE FIRE   6: ORGANIC MATTER
MOVED OFF INTO SPECIES MAN HAS FOUND IN FOSSILIZED STATE
BUT MISUNDERSTOOD THINKING HIS CYCLE THE FIRST
        The first Eden was Atlantis?
The second, *your* world? These two overlapped?
                    INDEED
Perhaps you'd better recapitulate.

4.1   ATLANTIS: ORGANIC MATTER ELECTRICALLY CHARGED
AT LAST PRODUCED 3 CENTERS OF ARCADIAN CULTURE
THESE WERE OUR NESTS WHEN WE & THE EARTH & THE GREENHOUSE
   ALL
WERE FLEDGLINGS   IMAGINE A GREAT SMOOTH GREEN & TREELESS SET

166

OF LANDMASSES RELATED VAGUELY TO YR CONTINENTS.
ONE THAT FILLD PART OF THE SOUTHERN ATLANTIC SANK WHEN OUR
CRUST FELL & GREAT HELDBACK MAGNETIC FORCES STRUCK THE EARTH
& SUDDEN PEAKS 3 TO 4000 FEET HIGH PULLD EARTHSKIN
INTO FOLDS, SUBMERGING AREAS PREVIOUSLY ABOVE
SEA LEVEL
    ATLANTIS 2: NOW UPON THESE GRASSY FLAT
LANDMASSES APPEARD FIRST WINGLESS CREATURES BIOLOGY
GAVE THEM DOMINANCE OVER THE CRAWLING & SERPENTINE.
THEY (& TODAY U FIND THIS ANCIENT TRAIT STILL AMONG THE
ORIENTALS) WERE HAIRLESS & OF A FORM RESEMBLING
YR MYTHIC CENTAUR THEY HAD SLIGHT TACTILE FACILITY
THEY GRAZED & WERE PASTORAL THEY RULED A MILD GREEN KINGDOM

ATL 3: SO THEN AS LARGER VEGETABLE LIFE EMERGED
A CONTEST OVER SPACE BEGAN THE CENTAURS NEEDED TO
KEEP TOGETHER THEIR HERD GROUPS WE EMERGED AS A FEATHERD
WINGD CREATURE CARRYING THEIR WORD ABOVE THE TREES: SIGNALS
HOVERING OVER CLEAR LAND AREAS WHERE THEY CD FEED
 The bird and snake are cousins. Were you in
 No slight degree kin to the serpentine?
U ARE FORGETTING OUR BUILT-IN FLAW: WE WERE ATOMIC
THEY NEEDED MESSENGERS THEIR VEG COMPONENT GAVE THEM GREAT
DENSITY THEY WERE A RACE MUCH SUPERIOR TO OURS
INDEED THEY INVENTED US. THEY TOO EVOLVED STILL EARTHBOUND,
THEY UNDERSTOOD GRAVITY & CONTRIVED THE HARNESSING
FIRST OF WIND THEN SUN THEN THEY WERE READY
      ATLANTIS 4:
THEIR BOUNDLESS GRASSLANDS & 50,000 SUN YEARS HAVE PASSD
(YEARS AS THE EARTH THEN WAS, FASTER IN ITS SPIN, MORE OF ITS
DAILY SURFACE EXPOSED TO SUN, THE ICECAPS MINIMAL)
THEY HAVE STUBLIKE FINGERS THEY HAVE TALL SILOS FOR THEIR
 GRAIN
THEY CONTROL ALL TEMPERATURE BY REFRACTED SUNLIGHT
THEY HAVE BRED WINGD MESSENGERS & ARE ABLE TO CLONE EACH
GENERATION AT AN INCREASED RATE. THEIR FIRST GRAVE PROBLEM
REMAINED: THEY WERE IMMORTAL THUS THEIR IMMENSE LANDMASSES
BECAME TERRIFYING FENCED-OFF SECTIONS WHERE THE WITTY

TORMENTED THE VERY OLD TRAPT IN THEIR PRIMITIVE FORM.
THIS LED TO A FATAL DECISION: KILL THE IMMORTALS
SO BEGAN EXPERIMENTATION WITH ATOMIC BLAST
FOR WE WERE CHARGED (WHO ELSE?) WITH RIDDING THEM OF THEIR
    RELICS

ATL 5: WE RID OURSELVES O F T H E M A L L
                        THE MORALITY?
GOD B LAID DOWN ONE LAW HE IS NOW IN THE PROCESS OF
REVISING BUT STILL FINDS USEFUL   THIS IST LAW: SURVIVAL
OF THE MOST AGILE. THE POOR & ANCIENT CENTAURS GRAZED WHAT
HEART WE HAD WHO ONCE SIGNALLD TO THEM OVER THE TREETOPS.
WE TOOK THEIR IMMORTALITY AS GENTLY AS WE CD
& IN AN INSTANT THEY VANISHD LEAVING THEIR ASTONISHD
PROGENY WHO SET OUT TO DESTROY OUR RAY CENTERS   WE
ROSE IN MILLIONS OVER EACH OF THEIR CITIES   WE LAID THEM
UNDER SIEGE   WE TOOK THEIR FEED RESERVES   WE SET THEM TO WORK
FURROWING OUR LANDING STRIPS & CONSTRUCTING LIKE VAST WEBS
OUR PLATFORMS. THESE PRIMITIVE ANTIGRAVITATIONAL
SKEINS WERE NOW READY   WE KNEW WE MUST BUILD SAFELY ABOVE
BOTH THE JUNGLE & THOSE WE HAD ENSLAVED   WE ROSE   WE LOOKD
OUR LAST AT ATLANTIS   WE LEFT UNBLASTED IN 14
SECTORS ONLY THE PERSONNEL TO MAN OUR SIGNAL &
ANCHOR STONES RADIATED TO HOLD OUR NEW WORLD IN PLACE

ATLANTIS 6: THEY LIVED ON CLUSTERD AT THE 14 SITES
WHERE WE SUPPLIED THEM FROM THEIR RESERVES   BUT IN DESIGNING
OUR VAST ATOMICALLY POWERD WORLD WE FORGOT THE
VEGETABLE ADVERSARY   THEY CD NOT KEEP CLEAR THE
COVERINGS OF GREEN   A IST MOORING STRAIND TORE & BROKE LOOSE
WE REPAIRD THAT ONE KNOWING WE MUST PERFECT OUR SYSTEM
AS COLONY AFTER COLONY PERISHD BELOW. YET
WE WERE PROUD. WE SAW DESCENT INTO THE STEAMING JUNGLES
AS A COMEDOWN IN WORK/CLASS/RANK   EVER FEWER OF US
WD VOLUNTEER FOR THE LIFETIMES NEEDED TO MAKE VITAL
REPAIRS. THE CENTAURS WERE NOW RAVENOUS LONGNECKD CREATURES
REPTILIAN HEADS RIPPD AT GREENERY   FURTHER AFIELD
THEY FORAGED LEAVING THE SITES UNTENDED   ONE TEAR & IT

BEGAN: IN AN INSTANT WE SAW OUR WORLD SHIMMER   OUR TALL
LATTICED CITIES TREMBLE & SHRED   WE FELT A GREAT BLAST OF
UPRUSHING AIR   THE END WAS UPON US   WE HAD LASTED
AT MOST 1000 SUN YEARS. OUR CATACLYSM AWOKE AN
UNIMAGINABLE FURY OF FORCES AS GOD B
BEGAN ERASING OUR TRACES & THOSE OF ATLANTIS.
ONLY BY MOONLIGHT DO WE FLUTTER IN THAT BROKEN DREAM.
WE JOIND OUR BONES TO OUR OLD HORSEMASTERS IN THE CRUSH OF
THEIR GREENERY & NOW AFTER 5 MILLION YEARS EMERGE
TO POWER YR MACHINES & DRESS YR HOSTESSES IN MAUVE

Dyes made from coal. The tarpits in Los Angeles . . .
ONE OF OUR ANCHOR POINTS   A COLONY   IN YR DAY STILL
A HUB OF POWERFUL ILLUSIONS   & SO THE LEGEND
OF THE CENTAUR IS THE LAST POETRY OF ATLANTIS

Dinosaur, pterodactyl, bat—good Lord!
DO NOT FORGET THE DEVIL   OR THE PEACOCK   AU REVOIR

MES ENFANTS I AM AT LAST IN TEARS
HIS INTENSE EAGER FACE! HIS JOY IN TELLING

4.2 POST-ATLANTIS: LIKE ALL SOUL OR SHALL WE SAY EX-LIFE FORCE
WE ARE INEXTINGUISHABLE   WE REMAIN WHAT WE WERE
Were you created in your present form?
WE BEGAN AS MUTANT FLIES NOT A HUMAN FINGERLENGTH
THE CENTAURS BRED IN THEIR INCUBATORS SPEEDING US THRU
6000 GENERATIONS PER SUN YEAR   THEIR TECHNICAL
SKILL WAS LIMITED ONLY BY THEIR PHYSICAL STRUCTURE.
WHEN THEY ACHIEVED MANIPULATION THEIR GREAT PHASE BEGAN
WE WERE THEIR 1ST SUCCESS   WE TOO MUTATED   BUT OUR BRAINS
& GROWTH PATTERNS WERE NOT TRIGGERD BY THE SAME ELECTRIC
IGNITION SWITCHES AS THE CENTAURS   OUR RISE FOLLOWD FROM
THE DIFFERENCE U KNOW. WE FOUNDED THEIR VERY CITIES
AROUND THEIR SILOS ROSE TOWERS IN A RADIAL SCHEME
WHICH MADE FROM A DISTANCE A WONDROUS STARLIKE PATTERN   WE
BUILT THE ARENAS FOR THEIR GAMES   THEY TOOK PRIDE IN THEIR
SPEED

You could hardly have been flies by then.
WE HAD INDEED GROWN   THEY NO LONGER NEEDED MESSENGERS
WE WERE IN CHARGE OF THEIR HEATING & LIGHTING PLANTS   WE SAT
IN THEIR COUNCILS   WE WERE NOW THEIR SIZE BUT WITH WINGS &
    BLACK:
OUR ASPECT WAS NEARLY HUMAN, THOUGH OF COURSE NOT WINNING
THEN OR NOW. THEY WERE NOT UNKIND NOR WD WE HAVE BEEN   YET
WE SAW THAT WE TOO WERE PART OF THE PAST THEY HAD BEGUN
ERASING. STILL THE CENTAURS WERE GOD'S CREATURES   WE WERE NOT
    DJ: But you started as flies—flies made by God.
WE STARTED AS EGGS YES OF A GREEN GRASS FLY
    Just as I said: God's creatures—   WE WERE THEN
PLACED IN WARM HIVES & FED A   FUEL CALLD URANIUM
                              And this changed you?
IN THE   EGG
    The cup moves awkwardly; something's not right.
            IT IS A LEGEND & THEY TOO ARE PAINFUL
WE HAVE SPENT OUR ETERNITY DAMND
    Unfairly! You obeyed God's law—survived.
                        GOD B GOVERNS ALL
LIFE ON EARTH   IN SLAYING THE IMMORTALS WE OFFENDED

MY DEARS THOSE 2 POOR WORLDS WITH THEIR CONTROLLED
CLIMATES   SLAIN ANCESTORS   BETRAYAL'S OLD
SHOCKING STORY   THEN THE RISE TOO FAR
ABOVE IT ALL & BRINGING DOWN THE FIRE . . .
IS NOT THE MORAL THEN AS NOW: BE TRUE
TO SOMETHING   TRUE TO ANYTHING   ADIEU

4.3   About fourteen: what made you pick that number?
AS WITH YR 3 IT BECAME MEANINGFUL   I CANNOT NOW
SAY WHY   WHEN WE PLANND STRUCTURES 14 POLES ROSE   WHEN WE
    BRED
14 SEEMD NORMAL   WHEN WE MADE RULES TO LIVE BY: 14
ALL IN FORMULAS   OUR VERY FEELINGS WERE FORMULAS.
FREE OF ATLANTIS OUR LIVES BECAME ITS ANTITHESIS
    Were those the feelings that went up in flame?
    Carbon 14 their residue? JM:

The seven deadly sins, perhaps you mean
—Like anchor points, each twinned (to make 14)
With its anti-vice, or virtue. We've the same
Bondage to certain forms—look at the sonnet.
Look at our ten commandments overcome
Too often by a green delirium.

OURS WERE SIMPLER THAN U SUPPOSE   WE WERE UNISPECIATE
(IS THAT A WORD? WE TOLERATED NO LIFE BUT OUR OWN)
OUR 14 FORMULAS WERE OUR FEELINGS   UNTHINKABLE
TO VIOLATE THEM   YET WE FELL FOR WANT OF OBEYING
THE FIRST: OBEY   WE DID NOT DESCEND TO KEEP OUR ANCHOR
POINTS IN PLACE   WE TOO DID NOT WANT REMINDING OF OUR PAST

IS IT MES ENFANTS A TAPESTRY OF BEASTS
AROUND THE LADY OF THE LOOKING-GLASS?
I ALWAYS WANTED A MONKEY   So did I—
Perhaps next he'll turn into one? JM
ARENT U ASHAMED OF YR MONKEY   My animal nature?
Not a bit. O LET ME MAKE THE JOKE:
-SHINES? ARE THESE THE FINAL STRENGTH OF MAN &
NOT OUR FAITH IN 3? IN STORYTELLING
RELIGION & THE FORMS OF POETRY?
IS IT NOT THAT GOD BELIEVES IN US
AS HIS 3RD EDEN? MILDLY CURIOUS

THE 3: IT IS THE NUMBER OF GOD B: DIMENSIONS OF
THE GREENHOUSE: SIDE OF YR PYRAMID: SIRE DAM OFFSPRING
THE POTENCY EXTENDS THRU THE SYSTEM   EARTH MOON & SUN
A ? FOR THE 12 PER CENT. WE DO NOT KNOW HOW LONG
OR IN WHAT WAY THEY WILL COME TO U   WHEN THEY ARE READY
WE WILL DO OUR BEST TO STAND BETWEEN U & THEIR POWER
U MAY CAST AWAY THIS CHANCE IF U ARE IN DOUBT OR FEAR
   (Coward and sceptic here exchange a look)
YET WE IMAGINE THEY ARE AWARE OF YR WEAKNESSES
& YR CHARM IS NOT UNANGELIC
   Now, now. But have the angels sent you to us?
                              WE ARE MESSENGERS

SUMMOND AFTER CONTACT HAS BEEN MADE BY WHATEVER MEANS.
THUS: YR SCIENTISTS NOW RECEIVE FROM OTHER WORLDS SIGNALS
THEY DO NOT COMPREHEND   WE KEEP THESE CRYPTIC. GOD B MUST
BE THE IST TO UNDERSTAND. THEY EVEN IN OUR DAY WERE
CLASSIFIED INFORMATION. THE SPEEDUP OF THE GREENHOUSE
TO COVER OUR ANCHOR POINTS BEGAN WITH OUR PERFECTION
OF MACHINERY WHEREBY WE LISTEND AWED TO FAR SOUNDS
NOT UNLIKE OUR OWN VOICES   WD THEY HAVE MADE SENSE?   WE HAD
NO TIME   THAT SAME DAY CAME THE IST GREAT TEAR   WE DO NOT
  NOW
SPEAK OF THE SIGNALS. WE INTERCEPT THEM   THEN THE SOUND FADES
FROM OUR BANKS. IT IS ONE OF THE GREAT FORBIDDEN SUBJECTS

4.4   Where is our comprehension most at fault?
I AM NOT STRONG ON PICTURING   IF THERE IS FAULT I FEAR
U HAVE PEOPLED NOT IDEATED WHAT HAS BEEN & IS

     So true. It's hopeless, the way people try
     To avoid the sentimental fallacy—
     How can a person not personify?
     This window overlooks a sick elm tree
     My feeling lifts unharmed into a sphere
     Littler, perhaps safer, don't you see?
     Reflections that in most lights interfere
     Take on despite themselves a quiddity
     Sallow, tall, branching . . . Putting it into words
     Means also that it puts words into me:
     Shooting   ringing   ramify   root   green
     Have overtones not wholly for the birds,
     And I am nothing's mortal enemy
     Surrendered, by the white page, to the scene.

IT MUST BE BEAUTIFUL   WE HAVE NEVER EXPRESSD A THING.
THIS OR THAT IS OR IS NOT   FEELING PLAYS NO PART IN IT
BUT YR LIFE ON EARTH IS IMMERSED IN FEELING, ITS MANNERS
& FORMS: YR MATING DEMANDS LOVE OR BRUTE LUST   YR SELFHOOD,
THE BALM (OR CURB) OF VIRTUES WHICH FEAR OF ONE ANOTHER

BEGOT STRONGLY IN U   BUT TO OUR EYES THESE ETHICAL
RIGHTS & WRONGS ARE SO MANY BLANKS IN YR CANVAS, JUST AS
TO U MY POOR PICTURING HAS LEFT BLANKS
 Ever to be filled in, do you suppose?
          NEVER ALAS
BY THE LIKES OF ME
 Bon. We will try to remember that you are not
 A person, not a peacock, not a bat;
 A devil least of all—an impulse only
 Here at the crossroads of our four affections.
    OR MAKE OF ME THE PROCESS SOMEWHERE
OPERATING BETWEEN TREE & PULP & PAGE & POEM

 Back to the angels, much of what they tell
 Will almost certainly be lost on us.
A CALM WILL SUFFUSE U FOR THEY SEEM TO COME FROM A CALM.
WHEN OUR WORLD SHATTERD THEY FIXT US EASILY IN OUR PLACE
BY DEMONSTRATING THAT IN FACT THE CALM AFTER OUR STORM
WAS UTTER CHAOS. IF THE PLACE OF GOD IS INDEED THAT
WHIRLING LIGHT IT IS THE SOURCE OF AN UNIMAGINED CALM.
WHEN THE CENTAURS RAN WE CD NOT KEEP UP WITH THEIR SPEED &
SAT (SEEING THE COURSE, KNOWING THEIR NEEDS) IN WONDER   THE
 CALM
AT THE SOURCE OF LIGHT IS (M) THAT SLOW MOTION WHICH ALONE
ALLOWS THE DAZZLED ONLOOKER HIS VISION OF THE RACE

 Our peacock, we have noticed, more and more
 Embellishes his text with metaphor.
 Some aren't bad; he likes to signal them
 With a breezy parenthetic (m).
HE HAS I THINK SPENT MORE TIME AT THE GAME
THAN WE MY BOY   (M) IS HIS MIDDLE NAME
 And who are D and I not to agree?
 Brooding on the atom as THE KEY
 (1.3), beating our wits to no avail
 Over the gross disparities of scale
 In the emerging picture, we ask yet
 Again for help—and wonderfully get:

AS YR LIGHT IS PROJECTED THRU MAGNIFYING LENSES
SO HEAVEN IS THE MICROFILM & WE? WE FILL THE SCREEN.
THE ATOM AS METAPHOR WAS A CALLING CARD FROM THEM
TO U (HOW NEGLIGENTLY I SPREAD MY PAINTED FEATHERS
& SAY 'THEM'   I WILL PAY FOR IT)
    Those lenses?   THE IMAGINATION
       And the light—imagined too?
IT IS REAL   ALL IS REAL   THE UNREAL I KNOW NOTHING OF.
I IMAGINE THOSE LENSES WILL FILL YR MINDS   THE ATOM
WAS MEANT TO CONVEY SCALE/DYNAMICS   IT IS THE VOID FILLD
WE ARE THAT VOID   WE & HEAVEN CD FIT INSIDE A RING
     A nucleus whose brilliance
     Draws all eyes, dazzles all eyes,
AROUND WHICH WE SWARM IN BILLIONS
    Angelic sarabande on a pin's head—
    Aquinas knew more than he ever said.
                    YET WHAT IS GOD B'S SIZE?
    "La goutte d'eau, dont l'oeil est un Soleil"—
A MERE FINGER   HE WEARS US AS A RING   WE POINT THE WAY

4.5   With which a patch blurred periodically
      Swims into focus. Central to this b00k
      Are lenses, the twin zeros. Take a look
      Through them (it all depends which way) and see

      Now vastness and impersonality
      Brought near, now our own selves reduced to specks.
      Our peacock, both a subatomic x
      And a great glaring bugaboo, like Blake's flea,

      Discourses just beneath the skin
      No less than from the farthest reaches
      —How can it be?—of Time and Space.

      How can it not? Given such crystalline
      Reversibility, the toy spyglass teaches
      That anything worth having's had both ways.

4.6   Our peacock dallies. Wystan (overhearing
       Some gossip with Maria): WHAT MY BOYS
       CAN MATCH THE FRIENDSHIP OF A CLEVER WOMAN?
       Unless the questions of a clever man?
       What should we find out next? MAY I BE FRANK?
       ARE U NOT BAFFLED BY THIS CHANGE IN TONE:
       THE 1ST FIERCE VOICES HUSHED & IN THEIR PLACE
       A PARAGON OF COURTLY GENTLENESS
       Our poem needed those fierce voices . . . Y E S
       WHY FURTHERMORE THIS LEAN ON LEGEND? WHO
       NEEDS BEDTIME STORIES? NO   IT WON'T QUITE DO
       Wystan, this from you who, when I tried
       Last month to air them, brushed my doubts aside?
       HAS IT NOT STRUCK U THAT YR DOUBT MY DEARS
       MAY BE THE KEY THAT OPENS THOSE GREAT DOORS?

       MAMAN IS NOT CONSPICUOUSLY DEEP
       YET SHE DISTRUSTS THE CHARMER EN PRINCIPE

       INSIST JM ON CLEARING UP THE MATTER
       OF TIME   OUR PEACOCK'S BEING LATE TODAY
       SHOWS THAT TIME ENTERS THEIR PICTURE AFTER ALL.
       NOW TIME IS OUR INVIOLABLE RIGHT
       & EVEN THEY ARE SUBJECT TO IT   CALL
       IF NEED BE FOR AN EXPLANATION FROM
       HIGHER LEVELS   SOMEWHERE A CLOCK TICKS
       WHOSE FACE I FEEL HAS EVERYTHING TO TEACH
       You don't mean we should try to WHY NOT reach
       That petrifying 40076?

       Enough to speak his number. As of old,
       Icy indifference propels the cup:

   U ARE IN GOOD HANDS   I AM NO LONGER YR MESSENGER
   U REFUSED ME
       Forgive that early rudeness. We now feel
       Ripe for what none but you, Sir, can reveal.
       Doubts that assail us, if you please, allay

In a less flowery, more convincing way
Than—
               PERHAPS MORE URGENT BUT U ARE CORRECT
IT WD NEVER HAVE BEEN FEASIBLE

        Haughtily sweeps out—what have we done?—
As in comes (has he heard us?) 741:
                 HAVE I OFFENDED?
Waves of disloyalty, of guilt, absurd
To feel for an imaginary bird,
Nonetheless flood us. JM: Heavens, no!
DJ (blandness of the caught shoplifter):
We were just saying—you weren't here yet after
All, and the point came up—I mean, you know—

I MEAN NO DISPARAGEMENT YET THE RECENT DEAD DO NOT
RELISH LEARNING, ONCE THEY HAVE LOST EARTH, THAT EVEN THEIR
    MOST
CHERISHD MEASURING SYSTEM IS PART OF THE MYTH. TIME IS
THE MANMADE ELEMENT   THE 2 FIRST WORLDS OBEYD CYCLES
ONLY OF BIRTH & RIPENING. THERE IS NO ACCIDENT:
I WAIT IN THE WINGS WHEN YOU 4 WISH TO SPEAK PRIVATELY
AS FOR OUR SOCALLD TALKS DEAR FRIENDS I KNOW THEIR EVERY WORD
KNOW TOO THAT U WILL NOT SUMMON ME FOR THE NEXT 3 'DAYS'
    (True enough, since DJ goes to Boston
    Tomorrow for preliminary tests)
BUT IS THAT ACCIDENT? IS IT TIME? WHAT U CALL FUTURE
WE CALL REALITY   WD U CARE FOR A GLIMPSE OF IT?

    Sly question. Well . . . the merest hint at how
    Life will be treating us a year from now?
LAURELS FOR U JM   YET U WILL STILL BE QUESTIONING
THIS MUSE WHILE LISTENING THRU OTHER VOICES TO THE NEXT
POEM
    Another poem—and this one not begun?
        ONE POEM BEYOND THIS IN CYCLE   AFTER WHICH
U WILL BE RETURND TO YR CHRONICLES OF LOVE & LOSS
    And David will come through his operation?
INDEED   & WISER ABOUT THE DRAINING ENEMY: FEAR

So much of mildness and forbearance here,
Why do we feel remorseful? After all
He owes *us* something—is that still quite clear?
To make sure, JM asks: Have others been
Like you, transfigured by such talks as these?
What about Dante's 80098?
DANTE'S PLEA CAME THRU SUCH VEILS OF METAPHOR & THESE, THRU
SUCH A MIST OF LOVE THAT OUR AGENT ESCAPED AS HE WAS
Escaped? You haven't liked being a peacock?

But that is going too far. Maria breaks
The hush: TODAY WE'VE HAD A LITTLE SCARE
OUR PEACOCK IS DEMOTED   JUST THE DIM
EXPOSURE OF A ONCE BLACK SHAPE WITH WINGS
Because we doubted him? Ah, it's not fair!

I AM SO INVOLVED   THE OTHERS DO NOT KNOW HOW VITAL
HOW TRANSFORMING IS OUR RED SPACE & I SO QUICK TO WANT
THAT LOVE I OFTEN SPARED U   U WD QUESTION ME I KNEW
& I WD PAY O WILLINGLY! FOR I MUST ACQUAINT THEM
WITH MAN'S NATURE WHICH TO OUR OWN REMAINS A MYSTERY.
SO THIS 3 DAY INTERVAL IS SET ASIDE FOR MY TRIAL
Dare we say a word in your defense?
U DO   U ARE MY SOLICITORS   I AM NOT DOWNCAST
IT IS NOW MORE IMPORTANT TO ME THAT I STAY WITH U

He's gone. What was it Wystan said?—"be true
To something, anything." A sad report
On human nature. Even though in part
Not our fault, I feel. U SHD HAVE FELT
MY DEARS THEIR STEELY RAP UPON THE FLOWER
LIKE WRIST I FLIPPED UP TO CONSULT THE HOUR

En route to the station next morning. DJ: I'll
See you tomorrow night. I wish his trial
Were over, poor thing. JM: Get some rest.
He loves us. We love him. He'll pass the test.

4.7   Nightfall. Mute disarray of D's bedroom.
In the hall outside, a book drops to the floor.
Gilchrist's *Life of Blake*—what's this? Slid from
Its pages, a folded page, the scrawl my own,
Of Ouija transcript: x.1953
—In other words, before Ephraim, before
Stonington! Some 17th century
New Englander named CABEL (Caleb?) STONE
Whose father (ah, I see) DIED BY THE ROPE
Speaks of GODS LIGHT and seeks to dazzle us
By adding that SAPPHO BLAKE & DEMOCRITUS
SANG WITH A SINGLE VOICE   But we aren't ripe
For that yet; we want scandal. So our sour
Friend Cabel goes—forgotten till this hour.

Blake. To the parlor of whose inner sight
Demons and prophets thronged, Princedoms and Thrones,
Exchanging views with him. (Here David phones
To say good night, and that *his* trial is set
For two weeks hence.) On off-nights, with no callers,
Put to the test now known as writer's block,
Blake would "kneel down and pray" with Mrs Blake.
Time and again HE PASSED WITH FLYING COLORS
—As Wystan will say of our peacock. Was that fate
Or the tradition? Oracular sophomores
Made Victor Hugo's tables tap like feet.
Milton dreamed wonders. Yeats' wife, between snores,
Gave utterance to an immense conceit . . .
The things one knows. And cheerfully ignores.

After Akhnaton's grand experiment
Biology looked about and made a note
(Shades of Matthew Arnold): The innate
Role of the Scribe must now be to supplant
Religion. For the priest-king's fingerprints
Had bloodied the papyrus, as the neat
Iamb or triad or cube root would not.
Less a matter of judicial sense

Than of a gift which hallows as it grows,
This law sheds light, now on the cult of Liszt,
Now on the stutter of the physicist,
And banishes to outer darkness those
Who grimace when the lingo's vatic antics
Deck with green boughs the ways of God to man.

4.8   A BASIC PRECEPT U WILL NEED TO TAKE ON FAITH: THERE IS
NO ACCIDENT
    DJ: Not so fast there! JM: Whoa!
We'll take a chance on Chance, with Jacques Monod,
Sooner than fly into this theologian-
Shriveling flame of a phrase. Yet I imagine
You believe it, and it might draw well
In the glass chimney of a villanelle . . .
               THUS IT HAS BEEN SINCE GOD B UNDERSTOOD
THE LIMITATIONS OF THE NEW EARTH MASTER. PRIOR TO
AKHNATON HAD BEEN ONLY CHANCE   FRESHNESS & WIT   WE DEALT
IN STRONG SOUL INTENSITIES   BUT AS THESE GREW URBANIZED
& BASIC SURVIVAL INTELLIGENCE BEGAN TURNING
INTO ACQUISITIONAL CHANNELS, TOOLS INTO WEAPONS,
A NEED AROSE FOR CLONING THE RULERS. WE REINFORCED
AS WITH THUNDER & LIGHTNING THE PROCESS WHEREBY A MERE
MAN BECAME GOD   SO AROSE ASSYRIA & EGYPT

NOW AKHNATON WAS THE 1ST CLONED RULER
    "The first individual in History."
                          TRUE   BUT HELPLESS.
WE CD NOT INTERFERE. INSULATING & TRANSMITTING
DEVICES WERE NEEDED ON THE NIGHT OF HIS DISASTER
BUT HE WANTED A VAST DISPLAY TO FREE THE PEOPLE'S MINDS
OF PRIESTS & MIRACLES   HE KNEW MAN HIMSELF WAS THE KEY.
AT HIS DEATH WE FURTHER CLONED AKHN'S SOUL, DEVELOPING 4
GREAT LEADERS & SCRIBES   A 5TH PART BECAME ALEXANDER
THE OTHERS OUTSIDE OF HOMER ARE LOST IN HISTORY.
IN THE EAST WE RETURND TO PASTORAL NOMADIC TRIBES
A SLOWDOWN, FOR THE SCIENCES WERE LATE IN FLOWERING:

MAN HAD LEARND QUICKLY THE ART OF HOW TO POLISH HIS SOUL
BUT NOTHING OF THE POWER INSIDE IT. WITH AKHNATON
WE BREAK INTO HISTORY   B4 HAD BEEN THE SLOW CLIMB
OUT OF CAVES, MAN LIKE A CHILD RELUCTANT TO LEAVE THE WOMB.
NEXT CAME THE LAKE & SEASIDE DWELLERS KEPT MILD & CONTENT
AS ARE MOST RACES BY THE PROXIMITY OF MOTHER.
DISPERSD BY MARAUDERS THEIR ARCADIAN FORM OF LIFE
SPREAD AMONG BRUTAL ELEMENTS & SO BY SIMPLE CROSS
FERTILIZATION DID MUCH BASIC WORK OF THE R/LAB

BACK TO HISTORY: WITH ALEXANDER A MODERN NOTE
WAS STRUCK   WE HEARD FOR THE 1ST TIME HOW THRU POLITICAL
CABALS FACT ITSELF CD BE MADE INTO PROPAGANDA.
THE SCRIBE ONCE POWERFUL LOST GROUND   GOD B WROTE HIS NEW
     CLAUSE
(TO HIS ONE LAW: SURVIVAL)   THE SCRIBE BECAME OUR AFFAIR
SO BEGAN HEAVEN'S GREAT & DIVERSE INSTRUMENTATION
IN WORLD 3. RULES: THERE SHALL BE NO ACCIDENT, THE SCRIBE SHALL
SUPPLANT RELIGION, & THE ENTIRE APPARATUS
DEVELOP THE WAY TO P A R A D I S E   SO BEGAN THE PAST
3000 YEARS

> Quite an epitome. But all this while
> We've been so worried—what about your trial?
>   THANK U   I GOT OFF LIGHTLY   I WAS (M)
> DISASSEMBLED, TINKERD WITH, & EMERGED TICKING AWAY
> —Like this? D jumps up, fetches from a shelf
> (The *things* that fill our rooms) a painted tin
> Dimestore peacock, given us once in joke.
> He sets it at Board center, turns the key:
> A croak of springs. The toy jerks forward, half
> Spreads its tail; stops dead.
>   IT MADE HIM FLEE
> MY DEARS   THE SINGLE (M) HE'D NOT EXPECTED
> He's his old pretty self at least? O YES
> BACK IN HIS FEATHER SUIT   THE ARCH & FLUFF
> JUST SHORT OF PREENING AS HE STRUTS HIS STUFF
> OOPS   LATE

HE'S OFF MES ENFANTS ON AN ERRAND
CK TO BE REBORN When? Where? As what?
STAGGERS THE IMAGINATION DOES IT NOT?
DETAILS NO DOUBT WILL FOLLOW MEANWHILE BEAR
WITH YR MAMAN: SHE BROODS ABOUT THE GREENHOUSE:

IS IT NATURE'S POWER ALONE THAT RUNS IT
OR PARTLY POWERS THAT FRIGHTEN US IN MAN?
DOES NATURE WINK AT AN UNNATURAL PLAN?
My science book says there are traces of
Plutonium in us. ARE WE TO THAT EXTENT
(M) ATOMIC? It could be what was meant
By the devil being driven out of Them
(Back in Book One) and into man. JM
THE VERY DEVIL'S IN U! IN MY NOT
SO THRILLING DEATH STRUGGLES I USED TO DREAM
I WAS WORKING IN A LARGE FASTGROWING WEEDPATCH
(THIS WAS B4 MY 2ND COBALT TREATMENT
BUT BY THEN I KNEW) & IN THIS DREAM THE WEEDS
SHRANK FROM MY HANDS AS FROM MALIGN POWERS.
& DREAMED BY THE END THAT THE RAYS I HAD UNDERGONE
WERE CLAIMING THESE POWERS IN ME RECLAIMING THEM
AS IF I HAD JOINED FORCES WITH THE RAYS
& WAS (INSTEAD OF SLIPPING COMFORTABLY
OFF INTO O) REFUELING A MACHINE
THAT SQUEAKED & CRACKLED MES ENFANTS LIKE THAT
FIRST VOICE B E F O R E IT GREW INTO A BAT

Maman, you make the flesh crawl. IF THE GREENHOUSE
IS A SEALED ENVELOPE . . . then *none of this*
Should be inside! EXACTLY WHAT I MEAN

CHATTING ABOUT ME MY DEARS? About
Everybody. Did you realize
That people have plutonium in their lymph glands?
SURELY ONLY THE BETTER CLASSES Wystan!
EXCUSE ME I AM SOMEWHAT DISTRAIT C IS
We've heard. A fearful wrench for you. But Chester

Hasn't been liking Heaven, and— DONT I KNOW
YET ONE HAD HOPED   SO GOOD   SO BRILLIANT   SO
AH WELL   JOHANNESBURG AHEAD POOR DEAR:
A USEFUL LIFE   BUT WILL THEY CONFISCATE
WHAT WE MOST VALUED IN HIM AT THE GATE?

4.9   IST ?   THE GREENHOUSE IS EVERYTHING UP TO THE 12:
SUN STARS MOON ALL NATURE   NEVER SUPPOSE THAT THE EVIL
OF EARTHLIFE LIES IN THE ATOM
    Just in its use by man?   & BY US   PLUTONIUM
LIKE ALL ELEMENTS PLAYS A PART IN YR HUMAN BODIES
                    Uranium too?
INDEED   COATING WITHIN ARTERIAL STRUCTURE   BOTH THESE
HEAVY ELEMENTS ARE IN MINUTE QUANTITIES & ARE
AS CONNECTING THREADS, NOT TRIGGERS, TO ANOTHER POWER.
GOD B LIMITS THESE LINKS WITH US IN U. CONTROLLABLE
ELECTRICAL TRIGGERS WORK MAN'S BRAIN & THE BATTERIES
REMAIN SALT   THUS MM'S DREAM: HER ELECTROCONDUCTIVE
WATER NATURE REJECTED THE ATOMIC CURE   PROPER
CHEMICAL THERAPY WD HAVE PROLONGD HER LIFE 5 YEARS

    Don't tell us, it's too late. I KNEW   I KNEW

SO NEW DISCOVERIES CREATE NEW PROBLEMS   CELL STRUCTURE
MUST BE FURTHER CLONED: TOUGHEND TO ACCEPT RADIATION'S
DIAGNOSES & CURES   THIS IS OUR WORK AS B4 WHEN
THE RISE OF THE MACHINE IST WEIGHD UPON MAN   HE TURND THEN
FROM NATURE   FROM HIS SOUL   ?ED ONLY HIS EXISTENCE:
A CLEAR THREAT TO THE GREENHOUSE   WITH SUICIDES REPLACING
PLAGUES ON A GRAND SCALE GOD B'S ORDERS CAME THICK & FAST   WE
NOW PLUCKD AT THE DENSITIES OF EVERY LEAST TALENT TO
HELP RECONCILE MAN TO HIMSELF & ALLOW THE MACHINE
TO TRANSMIT THE GOOD WORD: MAN, U ARE MASTER OF YR FATE

    MY DEARS THAT PHRASE WHICH ONCE WAS BLASPHEMY
    BECOMES A PRAYER NOW THAT GOD IS B

THUS IN BUT ONE GENERATION 1842–65
WE REVERSD THE ESCALATING WESTERN DESPAIR TO A
EUPHORIA ALAS NEARLY AS DESTRUCTIVE   THRU TYPES
LIKE DICKENS & ZOLA THE DREAD MACHINE BECAME MAN'S FRIEND.
TODAY HOWEVER, FACED WITH NUCLEAR DISASTER, HOW
IS MAN NOT TO DESPAIR? YR EPHRAIM 6 YEARS AGO CAME
WEEPING TO US 'THEY ARE IN ANGUISH'
   Over Hiroshima, yes. A frightful hour.
   (Cf. *Ephraim*, P. All trace was lost
   Of souls that perished in that holocaust.)
                INDEED NO SMALL FRIGHT
HERE IN HEAVEN   & YET? WE SENT OUR STURDIEST ALLIES
OUR GREEN GROUND-FORCES & AS THE GROTESQUE MUTANTS SPROUTED
SCIENCE SPOKE TO POLITICS & CONTROL BEGAN

   JM: How far away that horror seems
   —Or am I cloned with something that cannot
   Keep despair in mind for very long?
                  A PLUS:
THE MUSHROOM CLOUD APPALLD YR PRINCIPAL SOUL DENSITY
(AIR) AS HER RAY THERAPY DID MM'S WATER NATURE.
U HAD HOWEVER LIKE WHA BEEN GIVEN CERTAIN
LAVISH MINERAL DENSITIES   THESE AS WITH ANY FORM
OF CRYSTAL MOLECULAR STRUCTURE GROW BRILLIANT UNDER
PRESSURE   SO WHEN FEAR THREATENS YR REASON, IMAGERY
DARTS FORTH WITH A GREAT SHINE OF REVOLVING FACETS TO THRUST
(AS DID THAT PRIMITIVE BUT CUNNING JEW) ITS FLAMING BRAND
INTO THE PROWLER'S MUZZLE   IN SHORT, MAN DESPAIRS THEN GROWS
FAMILIAR   AS WITH THE MACHINE, SO WITH THE ATOM   BUT
HIS FAMILIARITY NOT YET CONTEMPTUOUS MUST BE
MADE SO   FOR THE ATOM CANNOT BE MAN'S NATURAL FRIEND.

2ND ?   CK'S NEW BLACK LIFE WILL BE CHARGED WITH JEW
DENSITIES IN LEADERSHIP & SURVIVAL, GIFTS SADLY
LACKING IN HIS LAST   HIS ARTICULATE (SCRIBE) QUALITIES
WILL BRING COHERENCE TO A RACE LARGELY WITHOUT SPOKESMEN

Curious. One of his last poems was
That paranoid dramatic monologue
"The African Ambassador". MY DEAR
CAN IT BE? DO WE FORETELL THE CLONE?

EACH SCRIBE PROPHESIES HIS NEXT LIFE OR HIS USE IN HEAVEN
OR USE OF HIS SOUL IN CLONING   CK NO EXCEPTION

FANCY A NICE JEWISH MS LIKE ME
(Chester after dinner) GETTING T H E
ULTIMATE REJECTION SLIP   IS GOD
CYRIL CONNOLLY? But you're coming back,
It's too exciting! PLEASE   TO SEE MY BLACK
FACE IN A GLASS DARKLY? I WONT BE
WHITE   WONT BE A POET   WONT BE QUEER
CAN U CONCEIVE OF LIFE WITHOUT THOSE 3???
Well, frankly, yes. THE MORE FOOL U MY DEAR
You shock us, Chester. After months of idle,
Useless isolation— ALL I HEAR
ARE THESE B MINOR HYMNS TO USEFULNESS:
LITTLE MISS BONAMI OOH SO GLAD
TO FIND ARCADIA IN A BRILLO PAD!
LAUGH CLONE LAUGH   AH LIFE   I FEEL THE LASH
OF THE NEW MASTER   NOTHING NOW BUT CRASH
COURSES   What does Wystan say? TO PLATO?
HAVING DROPPED ME LIKE A HOT   O SHIT
WHAT GOOD IS RHYME NOW   Come, think back, admit
That best of all was to be flesh and blood,
Young, eager, ear cocked for your new name— MUD

5 Go on, dear Peacock.

OUR BRUSH WITH THE GENERAL SOUL IS A RAPID SPOTCHECK
MADE FOR THE UNUSUAL OR TOTALLY HUMAN SOUL.
IN GREAT MASS DEATHS A SOUL OF RARE VALUE HAS BEEN KNOWN TO
SLIP THRU OUR FINGERS   WE SUFFER KEENER LOSSES AMONG
ATOMIC RESEARCHERS EXPOSED TO GAMMA RAYS, AN ODD
DETERIORATION MAKING FOR NEARLY TOTAL LOSS
OF THESE HIGHLY CLONED TALENTS.
                              But that's . . . horrible.
                                        THE NEW SOUL MUST BE FASHIOND
MORE RESISTANT TO THE ATOMIC ACID & TO THE
FATIGUES & ABRASIONS OF HUMAN THOUGHT

    DJ: Do you feel kin to those gamma rays,
    Feel for them what we feel, say, for sunlight?
                                        A PLUS DJ
YR IST TO DATE
    A silence. —Is that all? We're listening.
                LET ME INQUIRE   (Goes.)
    JM: I think we're on to something here.
    This would explain their lack of time-sense. Time
    Stops at the speed of light, or radiation.
                                I MAY TELL U THIS
UNDER SURVEILLANCE: THE ATOMIC FUSION ACCOMPLISHD
BY THE CENTAURS TO MAKE US IS NOT UNLIKE (M) THE LOVE
PLUS SEXUAL ELAN YR PARENTS NEEDED TO MAKE U.
THE HATCHING WARMTH OUR EGGS KNEW, IS IT NOT LIKE GESTATION?
YET PLUTONIUM IS OUR CHIEF LINK WITH U   GOD B HELD
SAFE IN AIR THE BASIC GENE STRUCTURES OF ATLANTIS   THAT
HANDFUL OF DUST, SETTLING & ENGENDERING AT RANDOM,
RETURND MASTERY TO HIS ELECTRONIC CREATURES. YET
NOTHING NOTHING IS WASTED   WE WERE TO BE USEFUL &
SING IN YR GLANDS   LYMPH IS AN AGENT IN REPRODUCTION:
WE RECEIVE THE IST SIGNAL WHEN SPERM MEETS EGG   ONCE AGAIN

WE ARE MESSENGERS   ONCE AGAIN WE FLY THIS TIME ABOVE
THE FORESTS OF OVERPOPULATION SEEKING A SOUL
TO RATIFY THE FRAGILE CONTRACT   ENOUGH   TOMORROW

He seemed constrained. GUARDS AT THE DOORS MY DEAR
THE WORDS ICE COLD   QUITE BRISTLY ATMOSPHERE
Classified material? LEST HE BETRAY
HIS DEPTH OF FEELING I SHD RATHER SAY
Strange. That first rhapsodist, a month ago,
Singing the atom's praise in a warm glow
Of colors—*he* had feelings. & GOT SHOT
POOR BIRD IF U RECALL CLEAN OFF THE TREE
THEY ALL SEEM UNDER CLOSEST SCRUTINY
JUNTAS AGAIN   IS IT THE ONLY WAY?
THE INFLEXIBLE ELITISM OF IT ALL
CAUSES THIS OLD LIBERAL TO SQUIRM
The 12% may do away with that?
DEMOCRACY AMONG THE MUSES? FAT
CHANCE! MES PETITS I LOVE U   I HOLD FIRM

5.1   Those scientists exposed to gamma rays,
      You seriously mean their densities
      Can never be recycled?
YES   THESE UNACCOUNTABLE LOSSES ARE SOMEWHERE A GAIN
BUT WHERE   The 12%?
            I DOUBT   WE ARE IN CHARGE OF SOUL DENSITITIES &
THESE LOSSES (LIKE THOSE AT HIROSHIMA) LEAVE NO TRACE IN
ATMOSPHERES KNOWN TO US
      In that case, the black holes?
                        ?   WE ARE NOT GIVEN TO LOOK
                        Are we to gather
      The scientists defect like Soviets?
      Are kidnapped, hijacked into the black holes?
EXCUSE ME WHILE I ASK IF THAT IS ONE OF OUR SUBJECTS

IS IT WISE MY BOY TO PRESS THE POINT?
THE VERY AIR BECOMES A NERVOUSNESS
I MYSELF AM FASCINATED   BUT

IT IS GIVEN ME TO SAY: ANTIMATTER IS SO FAR
SUPPORTIVE. A BENIGN POLICE FORCE KEEPING WATCH ON US?
AS WE WATCH U THRU YR MIRROR ARE WE OURSELVES WATCHD THUS?
  Benign? Recalling those black hands that press
  Against the panes, it sounds like a poor guess.
  Antimatter's got to be the worst.
  DJ: It scares me, as you did at first.
WE ARE NOW YR OLD FAMILIARS?
  JM: And more. I once was piercingly
  Aware of (metaphor) black holes in me:
  Waste, self-hatred, boredom. One by one,
  These weeks here at the Board, they've been erased.
                  OUR POOR TEETH PULLD ?S

  The R/Lab was a fairly late addition
  To World 3. Did it start up just like that?
GOD B'S WAS THE RICH HUMUS, OURS THE SUBSEQUENT HYBRIDS.
THE XTIAN MYTHS U KNOW COME CLOSEST TO THESE EARTHY TRUTHS
BUDDHIST & MOSLEM SCRIPTURES EMPHASIZE SURVIVAL OF
BODY & SOUL WHEREAS THE BIBLE IS A CODE OF BLURRD
BUT ODDLY ACCURATE BIOHISTORICAL DATA.
NOT UNTIL THE APOSTOLIC TEXTS IS SOUL SURVIVAL
DEALT WITH, & THAT IN A COLLAPSING WORLD HAD CHRIST APPEARD
EARLIER HIS LIFE WD HAVE PASSD UNNOTICED FOR ROME THEN
HAD STRONG INCORRUPTIBLE LEADERS & THE SUBJECTED
NATIONS WD HAVE LISTEND TO NO VOICE FROM A WILDERNESS

  Wystan's hand shoots up. MAY I ASK SIR
  IF GOD BIOLOGY IS HISTORY?
THE XTIANS ALAS HAVE IT RIGHT: NO SPARROW FALLS NOTHING
IN NATURE, NOTHING IN NATURE'S CHILD IS UNKNOWN TO HIM
THERE IS NO ACCIDENT ROME FELL BECAUSE XT WAS NEEDED.
CIVILIZATION HAD OUTSTRIPT THE ROMAN PANTHEON
AS IT HAD THE GOTH, CELT & EGYPTIAN GOD B IS NOT
ONLY HISTORY BUT EARTH ITSELF HE IS THE GREENHOUSE

  AWARE & CAPABLE YET NOT ABOVE
  DELEGATING DIFFY CHORES MY DEARS
  TO THE UNWORTHY OBJECTS OF HIS LOVE

INDEED   THE SCRIBE'S DAY IS AT HAND & AT HIS HAND, THE GODS
OF OUTSTRIPT FAITHS. LIVING ON IN THEIR FULLY ENLIGHTEND
WORD THEY STAND HERE NOW AT HIS ELBOW CHARGED WITH THE V
    WORK
    Great—let Heaven help the scribe. But who
    On Earth still reads? What good can his books do?
HAVE NO FEAR   WE CLONE THE HAPPY FEW   THE MASSES WE NEED
NEVER CONSIDER   THEY REMAIN IN AN ANIMAL STATE

    DJ: You don't know how such talk upsets us.
    We're all for equal rights here. Yesterday
    Maria said she hated your fat-cat
    Attitudes. I think we all feel that.
MILK TO CREAM TO BUTTER   WE ONLY WISH TO PURIFY
CERTAIN RANCID ELEMENTS FROM THIS ELITE BUTTER WORLD.
THE HITLERS THE PERONS & FRANCOS   THE STALINS & THE
LITTLE BROTHER-LIKE AUTHORITIES ARE NEEDED   EVEN
ALAS INEVITABLE IN A SURVIVAL GREENHOUSE
    DJ: By rancid butter he means ghee,
    And Mrs Gandhi's latest policy
    Calls itself Little Brother. (JM nods.)
A PLUS   NUMBER 2 DJ
    Well, I'm interested in politics,
    Unlike J. Here at the Board, the real
    World tends to escape us. We mustn't let it.
    Carter's convention on TV last night
    Kept me glued. JM: What, all that gab?
    Don't tell us *those* were souls from the R/Lab!
            OF THE 1000S IN THAT HALL
6 ONLY WERE OURS   RISEN LIKE BUBBLES TO THE SURFACE
IT IS A LAVALIKE ATMOSPHERE   ALL POLITICIANS
ARE OF EARTH   WHA IF NOT POET WD HAVE BEEN ONE.
JM IT IS THE SANDGRAIN THAT MADE DANTE'S PEARL   GUELFS ETC
LINKD HIS MIND URGENTLY TO LIFE   WHO KNOWS? THE POEM'S
    BED
MAY NEED TO BE MADE UP WITH (M) DIRTY SHEETS   TOMORROW

MES ENFANTS YESTERDAY'S JUNTA REMARK
WAS MY BLOKE'S HERE   HE IS THE BLEEDING HEART
MANY'S THE DAY I WISHED THE WORLD HAD A SINGLE
HEAD & NECK   I DESPISED ALL POLITICIANS
I HAD SEEN THEM GETTING OUT OF THEIR BATHS

MY DEARS WHAT A CLYTEMNESTRA   I WHO WAS NOT
A PM'S DAUGHTER FOUND THEM RIVETING
QUITE LIKE A PUPPET SHOW ONE LONGED TO PULL
THE STRINGS OF   NOT MY LUCK   AH WELL   ADIEU

5.2   A puppet show. The lives and limbs reduced
To wieldables of papier-mâché . . .
Not only politicians, by the way:
What about Proust?
STAGE 8   A 5.1   Will he return to Earth?
                    IN A SENSE   NOW LET US FURTHER
DESIMPLIFY: SINCE MID 19TH CENT SOULS OF THE GREAT SCRIBES
HAVE BEEN USED 1/9 ON EARTH REINCARNATED, 8/9
AS LET US SAY SAFETY DEPOSITS   WE MINE THEM. MM
FINDS PLATO LIGHTWEIGHT & INDEED HE IS NEARLY A SHELL
BUT OUR HAUTE CUISINE IS STOCKD WITH HIS LIVE SOUL DENSITIES
WHICH SPICE & FORTIFY NUMBERLESS EARTHLY DISHES   PROUST
IS DESERVEDLY ENSHRINED   TAP HIM & AS A STATESMAN
AT A DULL BANQUET HE CONVERSES   SEEMS TO BE HIMSELF
BUT PART OF HIS MIND LITERALLY WANDERS: OUT ON LOAN

Wallace Stevens years ago described
Peculiar moments when his mind grew dim
In Heaven, as if being used elsewhere.
INDEED   GOD B'S RECENT PREDILECTION FOR SCRIBES ENTAILS
MORE & MORE SUCH MINING   WHA HAS GIVEN HIS PINT
HAVE I NOT! WS IS ACCURATE
AN ODD SENSATION   LIKE MISSING NOT ONLY MY SPECS
BUT THE MEMORY OF WHAT IT WAS I MISSED
The "pint" being Inspiration? TOO GRAND A WORD
FOR THE FLEET IMPULSE TO JOT DOWN A THOUGHT

& JUST AS WELL: IVE LOST MY STUBBY PENCIL
Left lead in it, we hope, for the next user.
NAUGHTY
     I MUST SAY MES ENFANTS SOMETIMES
I WISH I HAD BEEN U KNOW WHAT SUCH A PRIVATE CLUB
No more so than its parts, Maman. MY DEAR
THE ROOM FOR PUNNING IS HEXAGONAL
Huh? I'LL LET U PUZZLE IT HA HA
MY VERY OWN WHEN OUR PEACOCK LEAVES LIKE THIS
HE SEEMS TO SAY KEEP THEM AMUSED HE'S BACK

I AM TOLD WE HAVE A GAP IT IS ESSENTIAL TO FILL
SO LET US NOW RETURN TO THAT CLAUSE IN SURVIVAL'S LAW:
NO ACCIDENT DO U GRASP THE ENTIRETY OF THIS?
Do we? Don't we? Tell us, just in case.
WHY DID YR FAT WORKER LEAVE LATE?
Our cleaning lady, please. It's true, she went
Home around 4:15. No accident?
       THE ROOM WAS NOT READY
WE MAY NOT ARRIVE UNTIL IT IS. DAYS WHEN U BEGIN
B4 ME I AM EAGER BUT THE ROOM WILL NOT HOLD ME
IT IS NOT YET PREPARED NOT YET MADE SAFE FROM US WE MUST
ISOLATE U WE MUST BORROW IS IT AFFECTION? FROM
YR DEAR DEAD & WIND IT ROUND U U ARE NOT IN THE SAME
RELATION TO US WHA & MM CAN BEAR THE
The fire? The hot disintegrative force?
Say it, don't be bashful!
I FEARD ALARMING U OR HAVE WE GONE BEYOND ALL THAT?
       But of course!
DJ: I set our table up, not thinking
Cynthia would come back into this room.
When she did, it was as if she didn't
See the Board. I didn't want her to.
SHE SAW BUT MINDLESSLY, NOT TO BREAK THE GATHERING CHARM
& SPOIL OUR INSULATION YR FRIENDS HERE ARE FARFLUNG &
(AS NEWLY DEAD) DISORGANIZED WE MUST ASSEMBLE THEM
They're our protection. U JM HAVE GOT
MY SPECS ON GOGGLES AGAINST SPARKS HA HA

I SPEAK OF ACCIDENT   OUR PLAY IS WRITTEN AS WE SPEAK
& WE KNOW ITS END EACH TIME AS THE APPLAUSE & LAUGHTER
WEAKEN & ALL START EDGING OUT THE DOORS   YR ENERGIES
MY FRIENDS ARE OUR AUDIENCE, THEATRE & SCRIPT   TOMORROW:
ACCIDENT 2
    How can the play be written as we speak?
    You know by heart our future talks—you've said so.
    WRITTEN DOWN ENFANT BY YR RIGHT HAND
             WAS NOT ROMEO & JULIET IN
THE GENES OF OUR BARD? I AM TOO MODEST FOR CURTAIN CALLS

5.3   Eyelevel sunset. The blue room. JM:
    It's clear now! Suddenly I see my way—
    Wystan, Maria, you and I, we four
    Nucleate a kind of psychic atom.
    (Mind you, it works best as metaphor:
    The atom being, as They've said, a peace
    That passes understanding, we make do
    With its outdated model by Niels Bohr—
    A quasi-solar system.) At the core
    We are kept from shattering to bits
    By the electron hearts, voices and wits
    Of our dead friends—how maddeningly slow
    One is; E told us all this weeks ago—
    In orbit round us. DJ: Each carbon atom,
    This much I remember from high school,
    Has four bonds. Are we four hooked on a redhot
    Coal in plumes? JM: Mixed metaphor.
    We're like an atom, not a molecule.
    DJ: And *five* now. 741
    Joined us, changing our atomic weight
    When *he* changed. JM: Oh, let's complicate
    It irretrievably! Why stop at five?
    If there's no accident, all things alive
    Or dead that touch us—Ephraim, the black dog
    In Athens, Cynthia—but why go on?—
    Are droplets in a "probability fog"

With us as nucleus. And yet our peacock
Mustn't touch us. His whole point's the atom's
Precarious inviolability.
Eden tells a parable of fission,
Lost world and broken home, the bitten apple
Stripped of its seven veils, nakedness left
With no choice but to sin and multiply.
From then on, genealogical chain reactions
Ape the real thing. Pair by recurrent pair
Behind the waterfall, one dark, one fair,
Siblings pitted each against the other
—Shem and Shaun, Rebekah's twins, whichever
Brother chafes within the Iron Mask—
Enact the deep capacities for good
And evil in the atom. DJ (groans):
I guess so, sure. It's just that with this damn
Knife hanging over me in five more days . . .
I try not to be frightened, but I am.
JM: Come on, I feel in my old bones
That all's well. Now let's see what our friend says.

5.4   INDEED   A PLUS
About D's prospects?
YES & ALL THE REST   WE LEAND FROM YR WALLS
APPLAUDING & SWARMD IN THE GOLDEN SPACE BOUNDED BY BLUE.
OPPOSING LIGHT MADE A GLORIOUS HAZE U FLOATED IN
TODAY YR SPECULATIONS TOOK ON WHAT WE RECOGNIZE
FROM OUR OWN FORMULAS: A GLOW WHICH MEANS PROCEED   ?S
No—proceed, proceed!

ON THE APPEARANCE OF THE 12 PER CENT   THEY WILL BEGIN
ALONE. KEEP SILENT   U WILL HAVE AS WITH ALL EXALTED
PERSONAGES A ? HOUR   THEY ARE THE HEART OF GOOD
& U NEED NOT FEAR THEM   AS THEY DRAW NEARER I WILL BE
SIGNALD AS TO FURTHER PROTOCOL
DJ: They're sticklers? DEAR BOY DOES HE KNOW?
WE FANCY HE'S INFALLIBLE   NOT SO
AH I KEEP WISHING

TO BE TAKEN FOR REAL IN MY NEW FINERY   LIKE A
PRINCE IN A PLAY   IT WILL BE HARD TO REMOVE THE MAKEUP
PERHAPS EVEN AFTER YR ROOM HAS SWARMD WITH ANGELS U
WILL HEAR MY TAP & OPEN AS BEFORE

Won't *you* hear what the angels have to say?

                     O   O NO   NO

Lightly, dismissively shrugged off, the cup
Recoiling from the thought. JM: We'll need
Help with the poem, things to be looked up.
—Very excitedly (what a child he is):
I AM AN EXCELLENT RESEARCHER! NOW ACCIDENT 2:

WE ARE THE FORCES THAT SOME MIGHT ACCUSE OF DEVIL'S WORK
WE MAKE THE OIL SHEIK GREEDY & RAISE IN MM'S DREAMBEDS
HIDEOUS BLOOMS TO STIR UP RIVALRY AT HIGH LEVELS.
IT IS THE LAST USE FOR RELIGION, TO KEEP AT SWORDSPOINT
THE GREAT FACTIONS OF EAST & WEST SO THAT LESSER POWERS
FACING MASS STARVATION WILL BE DISTRACTED FROM DROPPING
ATOMIC BOMBS TO GET FOOD. IN MAN THIS COMPETITIVE
ELEMENT IS AN ORIGINAL JEW DENSITY: BY
EARLY ASSYRIA GOD B HAD CODIFIED 1OOOS
OF LOCAL CROC & BULL RELIGIONS INTO INTERNAL
POLITICS & ONLY RARELY THE SMALL DEVASTATING
TRIBAL WAR. ONCE THE NATIONS WERE FIXT GOD B INTRODUCED
HIS RELIGION (TO AKHNATON): ONE GOD IN MAN'S IMAGE:
A KIND OF PRIDE IN MIND   THIS TO PRODUCE THE 3 MAJOR
FAITHS ON EARTH. HAVING PROMOTED HIS RATIONAL SYSTEM
GOD B NEXT HAD TO EDUCATE HIS PRIESTS   THE SUFFERINGS
OF GALILEO ET AL AWOKE SCIENCE TO CAUTION
& COURAGE   G (ONE OF THE 5) BECAME A SAINT WITHIN
HIS OWN LIFETIME & THE PRIESTHOOD BEGAN ITS RELUCTANT
REAPPRAISAL OF NATURE & HER LAWS

   CONGRATULATE MAMAN   LAST NIGHT SHE SOWED
   A SHOCKER INTO BREZHNEV   MILLIONS OF LITTLE
   YELLOW FACES STRAIGHT OUT OF THE DAISY PATCH

ACCIDENT 3:
THE GAP BETWEEN CAUSE & EFFECT NOW HAD TO BE NARROWD.
B4, GOD B HAD ALLOWD AN AMPLE MARGIN (NOTHING
PROMOTES BELIEF QUITE LIKE THE BENEVOLENT ACCIDENT)
THUS THE THINNING PROCESS OF SOME OF OUR PLAGUES WAS ALLOWD
TO OUTRUN ITS USUAL COURSE & THE POPE GOT HIS CURE &
HIS IMMORTALITY, THE CHURCH ITS STRENGTH, & THE PEOPLE
CLEAN WATER   ACCIDENT HAD BEEN USEFUL
   "Your" plagues?   GOD B USED US.
CAUSE: RATS   EFFECT: MINOR INFECTION   OUR TRUSTY FIRE:
PLAGUE   PROLONGD UNTIL AN EDICT FROM POPE FAUST TO DISPENSE
IN MARKET PLACES THE HOLY (BOILD BY HIS PRIESTS) WATER
STOPT IT   NONE OF THIS AS U SEE TRULY ACCIDENTAL
   Tell me, have you read *Candide*?
   MY DEAR HE WROTE IT   ANYONE CAN READ

THE PLAGUE WAS PLANND FOR 2 EFFECTS: THIN POPULATION &
KEEP IT PREDOMINANTLY RURAL   WE HAVE A MAXIM:
MAN IS HIS OWN HEAT. MAN IN YR TIME IS GROUPD   THE MACHINE
DROVE HIM INTO CITIES   GHETTOS OF LITERACY WHERE
IDEAS LIKE NEUROSES IN LARGE CLOSELIVING HOUSEHOLDS
INCREASD & GOOD & BAD KEPT PACE (THE CRIMES, THE LIBRARIES)
ALL THIS FROM THE HEAT OF MAN'S PROXIMITY TO MAN. EARTH
RADIATES TO US THESE HEAT CENTERS WHICH ALARM GOD B
INTO EFFECTING NEW METHODS   WE MUST CLONE THE SCRIBE TO
REGULATE URBAN GROWTH LEST IN ITS PLAGUE MAN HIMSELF BE
BOILD. HIROSHIMA PRODUCED 2 DRAMATIC NOTIONS: FEAR
OF THE FUSED ATOM A N D OF THE FUSED MAN IN HIS CLOSELY
PACKD CITY. PROPERLY CLONED ARCHITECTS ARE ON THEIR WAY
YET MUCH OLD-RELIGION-LIKE ALLURE CLINGS TO NARROW STREETS,
& MAN TO HIS ROMANTIC DISEASE: ANONYMITY

ACCIDENT 4: GOD B PERCEIVING THAT THE ACCIDENT
WHICH CAME BETWEEN AKHNATON & PERFECT FISSION WAS SLIGHT,
IMPOSSIBLE EITHER TO PREVENT OR TO COUNTENANCE,
KNEW THAT HIS CHILD WAS RIPE FOR THE R/LAB HE HAD PREPARED.
WE WERE SUMMOND   IMPRINTED WITH NEW FORMULAS   HENCEFORTH
ACCIDENT WD BE A TOOL: JM & DJ MEET &

E ENTERS WHERE THEIR MINDS SEEK DIVERSION   BUT THE MINDS? E?
THE SHAPING LOVES OF 2 SETS OF PARENTS?   N O   A C C I D E N T
NOT SINCE THOSE MINUTE DIAMONDS NEARLY DESTROYD WORLD 3

> And yet each actor, as he plays his part,
> Appears to take enormous liberties.
> What is that—the art that conceals art?
> INDEED   SO THINKS THE SPERM AS IT RUSHES TOWARD THE EGG

5.5   The parlor, Jacksonville.
> Lamplight through the glass transom
> Stained to some final visibility
> Like tissue on a slide—as,
> Hole by pre-punched hole,
> From the magnolia tree

> Outpoured the mockingbird's
> Player-piano roll . . .
> The ring flashed. A young girl, a grizzled Midas,
> Hand to heart, more freely
> Drew upon their quota
> Of feelings and fine words.

> Or starlight on the porch
> In Deadwood, South Dakota.
> Glitter of wee facets
> Led Mary's eye past toothpick and moustache
> And narrow mask of satyr
> Above the lengthening ash,

> Till nothing seemed to matter,
> Her job, the Homestake Mine . . .
> The future was a scrim
> Behind which forms kept beckoning and shining.
> Just as it went opaque
> She reached out, and touched him.

5.6   What of the three or four billion you don't clone
         In the Research Lab? Don't their destinies—
         Densities—affect our own?
              I WATCH U COOK   U HAVE A MACHINE THAT EATS USELESS THINGS
              THIS IS THE (M) FATE OF USELESS LIVES
                                Oh *please!*
                                        YET THE STALKS FED TO THAT
              CLATTERING GULLET PRODUCED THE LEAVES U WILL EAT TONIGHT.
              THE EFFECTS OF SUCH LIVES ON U JM ARE IN YR GENES
              R N A: REMEMBER NO ACCIDENT
                                ACCIDENT 5:
              THOSE BILLIONS SHED UP TO 150,000 ANIMAL
              SOUL DENSITIES PER HUMAN LIFE   THEY MUST BE REPROCESSD
              AT TOP SPEED & WITH MINIMAL STRAIN TO THE LAB   WE RUN
              ON AN UNTHINKABLE LEVEL OF WORK HERE   LUCKILY
              OUR BUREAUCRACY IS NONUNION. WE WORK LET US SAY
              IN FRIENDLY RIVALRY WITH NATURE   NOW NATURE KNOWS NO
              LIMITS BUT I DO & I SEE THAT THE AUDIENCE IS
              LEAVING SO THIS PERFORMANCE WILL BE RESUMED TOMORROW

              DOES IT BEAR THINKING OF? Dear Wystan, who
              Has time for thinking? WAIT   LET IT SINK IN
              THEN NO HEXAGONAL LAUGH   No sick-sided pun?
              U GOT IT   AFTER YEARS OF THOUGHT   LOVE   TOIL
              GLEAMING DISTORTION & ARTICULATE PAIN
              THE FUTURE'S FLESHLY ROBOTS WILL DISDAIN,
              LET OUR FAUST ASK HIMSELF WHAT'S LEFT TO BOIL

              It sinks in gradually, all that's meant
              By this wry motto governing things here
              Below and there above: *No Accident.*

              Patrons? Parents? Healthy achievers, bent
              On moving up, not liable to queer
              The Lab work. It sinks in, what had been meant

              By the adorable dumb omen sent
              TO TEST EXALT & HUMBLE U MY DEAR
              Strato? ET AL   Maisie? NO ACCIDENT

Gunman high-strung and Archduke negligent,
Warnings garbled in the dreamer's ear?
All, all, it sinks in gradually, was meant

To happen, and not just the gross event
But its minutest repercussion. We're
Awed? Unconvinced? That too's no accident.

The clause is self-enacting; the intent,
Like air, inscrutable if crystal-clear.
Keep breathing it. One dark day, what it meant
Will have sunk in past words. *No Accident.*

5.7   WYSTAN TRANSFIGURED BY YR SEMINAR
LIKENS IT TO OXFORD UNDER NEWMAN
Entre nous, Chester, I keep wishing *our*
Cardinal were dyed a shade less vivid
By the popular imagination. AH
NOW I SEE WHAT HE MEANS BY THE CHURCH SUPPERS
DJ: Are *you* aware of being used
To protect us in some form or other?
QUITE AWARE THEY BORROW MY SCARF IT COMES
BACK ALL SOOTY WYSTAN CAMPS IT UP
BUT I CAN TELL HE'S ILL AT EASE: 'IVE NEVER
BEEN IN A SCHOOL B4 WHERE IT WAS SO
OUT OF THE QUESTION TO HAVE A CRUSH ON THE MASTER'
I LEAVE U PETS LUCA HAS GIVEN THAT
VULGAR BUT EFFECTIVE 2FINGERED WHISTLE
Luca! WHY NOT? A MATCH YR EPHRAIM MADE
MAD LITTLE NUMBER BUT I'M GETTING LIMBERED
UP FOR THE NEW RACE TO BE RELAID!
WAIT ANOTHER 16 YEARS & SEE
WHO CRUISES U IN YR PITH ELEGANT
HELMETS I'LL BE TURNED ON BY OLDIES BYE
Maria, keep him dark *and* continent
When you return as a jungle. PLEASE A TREE
Oh, was that settled? Sorry. I'd forgotten.

ON ME THE DAILY LESSON IS E M B L A Z E D
U HAVE DISTRACTIONS   THIS IS OUR WHOLE WORLD
PROTECTED U MAY THINK? BUT I AM BEING
USED   USED UTTERLY   TO THE VERY ASH
NO WASTE   NO ACCIDENT   OUR BECOMING FRIENDS
OUR COFFEES   GOSSIPS   DRIVES TO SOUNION
What have we done to you, Maman? BAH ONE
BIG DATING COMPUTER   MES ENFANTS GET WISE:
TO BE USED HERE IS THE TRUE PARADISE

ACCIDENT 6: HEREDITY & ENVIRONMENT ARE
CLONABLE   THUS IN ADAPTING CK'S OLD DENSITIES
TO A NEW SOUL WE MUST MAKE DO WITH CERTAIN TASTES ALLIED
TO HIS CREATIVE WIT   BY WAY OF CONTROL WE PLACE HIM
IN A DECENT EDUCATED AFRICAN HOME   FATHER
WORKS FOR A WHITE ORG   A SCOUTMASTER   QUITE DEDICATED
Poor Chester, hard to picture as a Scout
—Are you OK? For David bites his lip.
DJ WHAT DO U FEAR? U HAVE 29 LONG YEARS TO GO
The thought of the anesthetic, the blacking out . . .
NOT A TOTAL BLACKOUT   CURTAINS WILL RISE ON A VISION
WE MEAN TO KEEP U ENTERTAIND
JM (envious): Don't let him forget it!
                              SHALL WE STORE IT UP IN
THE GINGERPOT? ON THE 9TH POST-OP DAY TELL HIM TO LOOK
This empty ginger-pot here on the sideboard?
BLUE & WHITE LIKE OUR CUP   HAVE DJ LIFT THE LID   MEANWHILE
TO U JM WILL COME CORRESPONDING DREAM IMAGES
ALL PART OF OUR LONG PREPARATION FOR THE 12 P/C:
DJ'S OLD INJURY (OUR AGENT THE MIRROR)   THE BREAK
THE ANESTHESIA   EACH ARRIVES ON SCHEDULE
DJ: The *break*? IN OUR LESSONS DEAR ENFANT
                              ALL GOOD MEALS
MUST BE DIGESTED   NO PEACOCK FEATHER AFTER THIS FEAST
HAND UP OF OUR ENGLISH FIRSTER?

SIR IS NOT BELIEF IN A LIFE WHOLLY
OUT OF HIS HANDS UNNATURAL TO MAN?

INDEED   & THAT IS WHY
HE NEVER WHOLLY BELIEVES IT, NOT EVEN U   HAND UP?
   MAY I? SAVE FOR MY PRESENT DEAR ENFANTS
   I HAD NO CHILDREN   WAS THAT MY DESTINY?
INDEED   PARTLY BECAUSE OTHERS WD HAVE CROWDED THE NEST
PARTLY FOR REASONS THAT WD MEAN NOTHING TO U   WE PLAN
NOT FOR ONE SMALL EFFECT   THE ACCIDENT GAP DISAPPEARS

ACCIDENT 7: THE CONFINES OF THE GREENHOUSE   THE OZONE
BELT IS NOT A CEILING BUT THE FLOOR OF THE NEXT LEVEL
THE (M) FOUNDATION STONE OF EDEN 2   THE SUN & ITS
WHOLE SYSTEM IS OF THE GREENHOUSE   THERE ARE OTHER SYSTEMS
& THE SUNS & THE GODS OF EACH   THESE ARE THE PANTHEON.
THE SCHEME OF WORLD 3 BEING CHIEFLY BIOLOGICAL
MIGHT GOD B NOT HAVE BEEN SELECTED FROM THE PANTHEON
WHEN THIS SYSTEM WAS BORN? FOR WE KNOW THE SUN IS HIS SLAVE

5.8   ACCIDENT 8:

We hate to interrupt, but what connection
Did Lesson 7 have with Accident?
      A PLUS   THE GREENHOUSE IS NO ACCIDENT
Then neither was your crust world, or Atlantis—
WHAT OF PREATLANTIS? ONE OF OUR MYTHS IS THAT FROM THE
GALACTIC PANTHEON CAME GOD B TO BUILD HIS GREENHOUSE:
THE SUN HIS SLAVE IS ALSO HIS CREATION   IT IS HIS
CENTRAL ATOMIC POWER. THE MYTH OF PROMETHEUS
IS OUR STORY. NOW MAN TRIES TO SEIZE & RULE THE ATOM
BUT AS HIS ORIGIN IS ELECTRIC HE WILL REMAIN
CONTROLLABLE. ELECTRICAL POWER IS ORGANIC,
ATOMIC POWER . . . GALACTIC? WE KNOW ONLY IT IS
THE FIRE   THE FUEL OF THE PANTHEON OF THE GODS
OF THE VARIOUS GALAXIES   GOD B GUARDS THIS POWER
JEALOUSLY   IT IS HIS BRIGHT RED APPLE
               ACCIDENT 8:
WE FELL. WERE WE GOD'S 1ST ACCIDENT? OR 1ST INSTRUMENTS?
THERE IS NO ACCIDENT   ERGO WE WERE USED TO DESTROY
A USELESS EXPERIMENT. WE IN OUR MYTHS SEE OURSELVES

AS BROOMS & THE WITCH? OUR VOCATION AS MESSENGERS
We never asked, were you both male and female?
WELL
PUT IT THAT WAY IF U MUST OUR NUMBERS NEVER VARIED
FROM THOSE PRODUCED IN THE CENTAURS' HATCHERIES UNTIL, LATE
IN OUR BRIEF WORLD NEEDING SERVANTS, WE REPRODUCED OURSELVES:
HALF OUR NUMBERS HAD EGG SACS & HALF HAD INSULATED
RADIUM VESCICLES WHICH FERTILIZED THEN FED THE EGGS.
WE WERE AS NOTHING U CAN IMAGINE ONLY YR BAT
SPECIES IS A (M) FOR US AS THE MYTHIC CENTAUR IS
FOR ATLANTIS WAS THE NO ACCIDENT CLAUSE EVEN THEN
IN OPERATION? DID GOD SEE THE CENTAURS' USELESSNESS
& GIVE THEM THE IDEA OF US?
ACCIDENT 9: OR:
GOD B, HOLDING THE CHARTER TO CREATE HIS OWN SYSTEM,
KNOWING THAT HE MUST POPULATE IT WITH MANAGEABLE
CREATURES ONLY, CLONED THE CENTAURS WITH THEIR OWN
    DESTRUCTION
& CALLD US IN AS DECENT SHROUDMAKERS TO COVER THEM?
And here the lines of argument converge.

NO THEY END IN THE VAST O THE PANTHEON PLANND AS WELL
INTO DIVIDED SAFENESSES?
Viking I, its every instrument
Agog, returns from Mars—no accident?
DRAMATIC LESSONS MAY
AWAIT MAN EVEN ON HIS PLANETS IS EARTH THE SINGLE
EXPERIMENT OR ONE OF SEVERAL HYBRID SEEDLINGS?
PERHAPS THE MOSES MYTH IS AN ANSWER: FOUND IN A STREAM
Of flowing suns and stars—
THE PRINCE AS FOUNDLING & EARTH? FOR AFTER BARREN EONS
THE ? IS, DOES THE ROYAL BLOOD STILL FLOW IN EARTH'S VEINS?
HIS TAIL OUTSPREAD
MY DEARS BLUE GREEN & HIS EYES FLASHING RED

THAT U MAY ASK THE 12 P/C I CAN SAY ONLY THIS:
THE CENTAURS RAN A CONSTANT RACE ON THE SAME OVAL TRACK
BUT MORTALITY ALLOWS FOR THE DIVINE TRANSLATION

SO PLATO'S POWERS ARE FOREVER OUT AMONG THE 5
& OTHERS (AS U KNOW) BUT THERE IS A FOLDER LABELD
PLATO & ONE LABELD AKHNATON & THERE ARE GOLDEN
CONTAINERS LABELD CLIO   ERATO   CALLIOPE
& OF THESE 9 WE KNOW ONLY THE RUSHING OF THEIR WINGS

Maria? ENFANTS? We thought you'd gone away.
But no. Her discreet, black-clad presence, eyes
Lowered while the menfolk theorize,
Brings itself (skeptical? unmoved?) to say:
HOW SATISFYING IT MUST BE, ALL THIS
LINKAGE WITH THE WORK OF EONS   LIKE
FINDING ONESELF AMONG THE BULLRUSHES
This frog here in my throat agrees. ONE KISS

5.9 GOD B THOUGHT TO DESTROY THE CENTAURS WITH FORESTS   THIS PLAN
THEY CIRCUMVENTED BY INVENTING US   NOW MAN HAS MADE
FORESTS OF HIS OWN KIND & FOR THIS ROUND BIOLOGY
IS LETTING HIM (READ: OUR CLONING OF HIM) SOLVE THE PROBLEMS
Short of disaster, *are* they solvable?
INDEED
Increase of population, of pollution—
3 DECADES HENCE WE GLIMPSE FAIR GREEN ATLANTAN FIELDS
That grim race our first teachers told us of
Between Chaos and Mind—is the heat off?
NECK & NECK   BUT IF CHAOS WINS THE RACE WAS FIXD
By?   GOD B
So in a mere thirty years the trend
Will be reversed? Green fields? Ah, my poor friend,
Be realistic. Can you hope to wean
Our time, in that short span, from its obscene
Smokestack nipple? How are sea and air
To purify themselves while man is there?
DJ: *I* won't be there. Just twenty-nine
Years left . . . You know, he could have spared me that.
ENFANT   WORK OUT THE TOTAL   IT BEATS MATT

MY GRASP OF TIME IS IMPERFECT   THE LAB IS SURE ONLY
OF THE VOLUMES OF FORMULAS TO BE DEALT WITH   THEIR BULK
DIMINISHES IN THOSE AREAS WE INTERPRET AS
3 DECADES AWAY   THIS LESSENING IN COMPLEXITY
SUGGESTED MY (M) GREEN GLIMPSES   WE SEE NO MAJOR FOOD
OR AIR PROBLEMS   POP MAY INCREASE BY 2/3 BILLION BUT
BEYOND THAT THE FORMULAS WD NEED TO BE REVISED &
THEY ARE NOT. PERHAPS NATURE'S LITTLE LUSTFUL TRICKS WILL STOP
BEING SO AMPLY REWARDED BY THE CHUCKLES OF BABES

All thought by now receding, of what saves
The day, or whose the footstep on our graves,
DJ: Well, this No Accident clause, I can't . . .
JM: Of course you can't. They've cloned you not to.
OUR PLAGUE OF SUICIDES CAME FROM THE GERM OF ACCEPTANCE
MAN IS NOT CLONED WITH AN ACCEPTING DENSITY   THEREIN
HIS POWER: HE RESISTS   IS DJ NOT OUR STEADY HAND
ON THE PLOW? WE NEED A HUSBANDMAN TO RESIST EARTH'S WEIGHT
THE WASH OF WATER THE HILARITIES OF AIR & THE
B U R N I N G OF OUR FIRE
DJ: Maria has accepted being used.
I can't, not yet.
RESIST AWAY   IT IS CHARMING
JM: Your fear, my doubt
Seem to amuse him, he who fleshed them out.

STIFF UPPER LIP MY BOY   PLAY'S GOING INTO
NEW REHEARSALS   USHERS AT THE DOOR
WITH RAINCHECKS
DJ CHER ENFANT COURAGE

6

She stood (wrote Jules Renard of the divine
Sarah) in one place, letting the stair unwind
Her profiles, eerily descending wand
Of the still center, or its weathervane.
Gone, she endured. Globes lit the banister's
Counterspiraling ascents of bronze
As in remembrance Lalique's cabochons
Waxed and waned upon that brow of hers

Like this pale purple atom (phosphorus)
Periodic among satellites,
Messengers, sugar chains and residues
—*Her* memories of past performance? Cues?—
Whereby the curtain on a triple thud
Has risen. It's the theatre in our blood.

22.vii. Boston Museum of Science.
Studying a model (2.5
Cm. per angstrom) of the DNA
Molecule—a single turn blown up
Tall as a child. My ignorance reduced
To jotting down—red, blue, black, yellow, white—
Colors of the bit-player beads, the carbons
And nitrogens all interlinked, on pins
But letter-perfect, purines, pyrimidines,
Minute intelligences that indwell
The chromosome and educate the cell . . .
Even grossly simplified, as here,
It's too much. Who by reference to this
3-D Metro map's infernal skeins
And lattices could hope to find his way?
Yet, strange to say, that's just what everyone
On Earth is promptly known for having done.

Noon. In the hospital across the river
David is wheeled up from surgery,
Helped into bed—still numb from the waist down.
Gaps in his sorry gown don't quite conceal
Streaks of dim, white-bandaged red. His gaze
Lights on a face within mine. When he speaks
Out comes the whisper of a little boy
Woken and wrapped in quilts, carried outdoors
Through branching dark, the milk of dream unwiped,
To see a calf born or a comet's passage.
"I did dream," he says now, after describing
What he remembers of the operation
(Done, not to strain his smoker's heart,
With local anesthetic). "There was this kind of
Slow green climbing, and all round me lights
Higher and higher . . ." Part of *my* last night's
Dream, an empty "court" or dim "dance floor",
Comes back: four squares, each one a tone of gray
Lit from beneath and seen as from a plane,
Composed a fifth that pulsed in the pitch-black terrain
—Meaning what? Another day will tell.
I press D's hand. He babbles on. All's well.

6.1   So well, in fact, that in eight days he's home
And vigorous enough to want to hear
Sweet nothings from our peacock. O I FEAR
YR DISAPPOINTMENT   U ARE EARLY BIRDS
MES CHERS   WILL I SUFFICE? YR TAME CANARY?
Disappointment, Ephraim? (Though he's right
We must not say so.) Never! AH THEN A STORY:
ONE DAY WE SAT AT CAPRI ALL THE COURT
ON A SOUTH TERRACE WHEN SUDDENLY THE PAVEMENT
SHOOK & THE CYNICAL AMONG US THOUGHT
HO HUM ANOTHER EARTHQUAKE BUT TIBERIUS
EVER SUPERSTITIOUS CALLED FOR FOWL
SACRIFICE & THE PRIESTS WERE CHANTING AWAY
WHEN FROM FAUSTINA CAME A PIERCING CRY:

RISEN ABOVE SICILIA IN THE SKY
A GREAT BLACK CLOUD WAS SPREADING RIGHT & LEFT
LONG RAGGED WINGS & IN THE CENTER 2
RED SPOTS LIKE EYES APPEARED   IT WAS A BAT.
CHRIST HAD BEEN CRUCIFIED   Now why, I wonder,
Are you telling us this little story?
I BELIEVE MES CHERS IN PEACOCKS   FROM THAT DAY
TIBERIUS DECLINED   NOR DID YR E
MORE THAN A WEEK SURVIVE HIS LUNACY
It was then he had you killed? MURDER ALONE
CALMED HIM IN HIS FITS   THE SAYING WAS
HE HAD BAT FEVER   But *you* died A.D.
36, while Christ— ANOTHER CALENDAR
Well, *our* bats don't cause fever, not so far.
THEY ARE I KNOW THERE4 OF THE MESSENGER STRAIN
How much you do know. Over and over again,
Wine-sweetened lips, and eyes half shut beneath
Conviviality's unfading wreath,
Ephraim, you've understood what's going on
Better than we. A SLAVE NEEDS ALL HIS WIT
LIFE HERE BELOW THE STAIRS DEPENDS ON IT

Now Wystan. He's been thinking, as have I,
About THE UNCLONED LIVES THAT TOUCH OUR OWN
YR STRATO & MY LAST FRIEND   BOTH SUCH DEARS
(DJ interrupts: Has Chester been reborn?
NOT YET   STILL BOUND UP WITH HIS MINIWOP)
FORSTER HAD THIS TOUCHING THEORY
THAT GOD WANTS EDUCATED HIGHCLASS QUEERS
TO MAKE A DIFFERENCE & TO HAVE ONE MADE
To kindle sparks within the dumb physique
Of terracotta & BE WARMED   WHY ARE
WE (TO EXTEND THAT) IN THIS SEMINAR?
3 OF US IN MM'S EUPHEMISM
COMME CA & SHE (THOUGH FEMALE) NOT IN LIFE
MUCH DRAWN TO ROLES OF MOTHER MISTRESS WIFE,
WHY ARE WE 4 TOGETHER LISTENING?
A) 3 WRITERS & MM RATHER A MUSE

B) EXCEPT AS MESSENGERS WE HAVE NO
COMMITMENT TO A YOUNGER GENERATION
C) A SURPRISE: MM'S IST LOVE WAS MUSIC!
FAILING HER ENTRANCE TO THE ODEON
SHE GAVE IT UP   Good heavens, we all thought
She couldn't tell Fats Waller from Fauré.
As for us, while I, on a good day,
Limp through my Satie or a Bach gavotte,
DJ (at twelve in Hollywood) attacked
That thing by Grieg; took Composition with
Big-timers like Schoenberg and Hindemith
While still in college. MUSIC MORE ABSTRACT
THAN METAPHOR MUST BE THE BOND THAT LINKS US

Maman, why so secretive? I PREFERRED
EFFECTS UNSTUDIED INDEED SCARCELY HEARD
AS ONCE WHEN 3 COINCIDENTAL SOUNDS
A WIND BELL IN THE GARDEN   A DOOR CHIME
& THE HIGH CRY OF A SEAGULL MADE ONE FLEETING
TONIC CHORD   IS MUSIC NOT LIKE TIME
RETOLD? LIKE THE NO ACCIDENT MOTIF
A WAY OF TELLING THAT INSPIRES BELIEF?
WD AN UNMUSICAL MIND TAKE IN THE PEACOCK?
THE MESSENGER   THE MESSAGE   THESE RING BELLS
I ANSWER TO   ASK NEXT TIME ABOUT CELLS
Why? I DONT KNOW   IT CAME TO ME TO SAY
DJ (tired out): Tomorrow afternoon
We'll have our peacock back. MES CHERS   Yes, Ephraim?
NOTHING   I KEEP PINNING FEATHERS ON
BUT NOBODY NOTICES   CALL YR OLD FRIENDS SOON
ONE IN PARTICULAR   BLONDEST OF THE SCRIBES
Hans! YES   THRILLED AS WE ALL ARE BY YR VIBES

6.2   THINK DJ
The white, blue-flowered ginger-pot. Sunshine
Filling with tracery its inward oval,
He sees a . . . ladder—wait, now more comes back—

THE LADDER OF YR SPINE
DJ: My hips went dead. A second needle
Numbed me to the toes. I'd been screened off
With pale green, and I felt this weightlessness
And followed it. There was a ladder whose
Lower rungs, as I climbed, just kept dissolving,
And at the top was light, were colored lights—
What did you say to me about the lights?
WE SHOWD U JM'S

VISION OF THE ATOM'S HEART
JM: The four lit squares that made a fifth
Almost musical—   DJ DWELT IN EACH, RID OF
HIS PAIN, STILLD IN HIS LUSTS & FEARS: THE RED OF PURE POWER
THE PALE BLUE OF ITS REASONABLE USE   THE YELLOW LIGHT
OF GENERATION & THE GREEN THAT WILL BE P A R A D I S E
JM SAW THIS AS A PRINTOUT IN BLACK & WHITE   DJ
WE PLACED WITHIN IT   U WERE BOTH SENT TO THE HEART OF LIFE
DJ: My task
Was to bring home the colors to us all.
FOR US MES ENFANTS IT WAS LIKE A BALL
COSTUMES & DANCING
OR MY DEARS A MASQUE
INDEED   WE PROMISED U ENTERTAINMENT & U GOT IT
AS ON A STAGE VIEWD FROM A MOUNTAINTOP WE FROLICKD IN
THE 4 COLORS   OR LIKE CELLS UPON A MICROSCOPE FLOOR
TO SILENT MUSIC & UNSPOKEN WORDS   OUR MASQUE CALMD U:
WE ARE THE DRUG & THE AWAKENING
JM: Why not the cure as well—a wand of
Healing fire to save D from the knife?
MM'S LESSON
& IT IS PERHAPS THE MAIN LESSON OF THIS SEMINAR:
NO UNNECESSARY DOSES OF OUR STRONG MEDICINE

The tone has darkened suddenly. I strain
To think. What lesson? What strong medicine?

RADIUM   COBALT   U DID NOT REALIZE YESTERDAY
WHY SHE IS WITH US?

Because of music, Wystan said.
                NO: SHE IS ONE OF US
              The water,
Yes, in our elemental union, and—?
                  O N E O F U S
DJ. What is he saying? I can't quite . . .
MES ENF
           —as light breaks. Horrifying light
Whose rays our union absorbs. We're back
At Square One. Presence of no color. Black.

DJ: Ah I could kill them! JM: It's
Not their fault. DJ: So they say—those shits!
JM: Her months spent back and forth from bed
To godforsaken box of buzzing lead . . .
That's why the plant world's taking her. She hasn't
Any soul left—she's no longer human!
ENFANTS   DJ: She said she'd see us through
These talks. She had no choice. She knew. She *knew*.

WILL U FORGIVE MY SMALL CHARADE? PART TRUE
PART THE DESIGN   I SHALL HOWEVER BE
ALLOWED (NO LITTLE THING) THE ANGEL VOICES
THANK GOD FOR GARDENS INCIDENTALLY:
MY GREEN SHIELD SAVED ENOUGH OF ME FOR U
My face begins to quiver. Oh Maman—
POSO AKOMA (her last words, "How much more?")
I CROAKED NOT TO POOR LOUROS BUT THE RAYS:
HOW MUCH MORE WD THEY TAKE FROM ME B4 . . .
(This is the point, I later tell DJ,
When Dante would have fainted dead away.
But, cloned with minerals, heartsick, eyes red,
I see no way out but to forge ahead.)
AH TEARS DEAR DEAR ENFANT THEY COMFORT U
& MAKE MY OLD BLACK DRESS QUITE CLINGING & SEXY
DJ: She used to have a "wet look" raincoat.
DO ADMIT THE ELEMENT OF CHIC
But now, you *look* like Them? MAIS QUELLE HORREUR

DJ DO U WANT ME TO FLOUNCE OUT OF HERE
JM: You said four stars were in your hair—
Are they still? SHALL WE BE SERIOUS
I am serious! WELL   THESE LESSONS   THEY
SEEM TO BE IMPOR   O J J J
THINK: NONE BUT THE FOOL IS PITIABLE
THIS LIKE DJ'S NEEDLE IS THE BLESSED
RELIEF   AT LAST TO LEAVE THE WORLD OF BLIND
IF CHARMING FOOLS WE LOVED (& WERE) BEHIND

MY DEAR   JM   CONFRERE   SHE IS RIGHT U KNOW?
NOW U MUST ASK HER QUESTION ABOUT CELLS
CALL BACK OUR PEACOCK   AS B4 HE FLEES
AT THE ONSET OF FEELING   WE WD SEEM
TO INTRODUCE OUR ELEMENT OF TIME
WHICH CHOKES HIM   IS TIME THEN THE SOIL OF FEELING?
SO ODD   Stop talking, Wystan, can't you, please?
FIRST MAY I SAY? THAT DANCING IN THE MASQUE
IT DAWNED (ON ME AT LEAST) THAT WE WERE BEING
EACH IN TURN STRIPPED   REDUCED TO ESSENCES
JOINED TO INFINITY   THAT'S ALL   NOW ASK

6.3   To the Research Lab. Sirs: You may be proud
         As peacocks. You've endowed
Us from the start with freedoms that entrap.
We are the red-eyed mice on whom your maze
Is printed. At its heart a little cloud
         Thins and dwindles—zap!—
To nothing in one blink of rays.

Painlessness intenser than a burn.
         What must at length be borne
Is that the sacred bonds are chemical.
Friend, lover, parent, amphorae that took
Eons to dream up, to throw and turn—
         Split-seconds in this kiln
Show them in *your* true colors. Look:

Jasmine, lantana, rose geranium,
    All dizzying, all dumb
Beneath the trumpet's bloodgorged insect wrath
(Maidens from Act II of *Parsifal*
Whom the Enchanter waters into bloom)—
    Was this your garden path?
    Was I, beguiled there, the Pure Fool

Who mistook antimatter for a muse?
    Down choking avenues
Of memory now I meet her, dressed in black,
Smelling of soil and Shalimar, her lips
Parted to speak in that same tongue you use
    To raise the crushing block
    By null moonglow or full eclipse

Till all is desert waste. You've no control
    Over such loss of soul?
I don't believe you: SHE IS ONE OF US.
We loved Maria. Love her still. Oh God . . .
Grief, horror . . . Come, your lecture on the cell!
    Spread your tail, incubus,
    We're listening. Make the story good.

6.4   YR GRIEF JM IS ANOTHER THING. YR SQUARE OF THE 4
COLORS IS OF COURSE INFINITY   FOR COLOR IS LIGHT
& LIGHT, ALL LIFE   THE 12 P/C I THINK WILL TAKE U THERE
MM WILL ANCHOR U. FOUR LESSONS NOW
                          I : U JM
HAVE SAID IT: THE ATOM IS OUR UNIT   THE WHOLE GREENHOUSE
IS BUT A CELL, COMPLEX YET MANAGEABLE   ALL MATTER
THERE4 IS PART OF THAT CELL   IF AS WE PRESUME GOD B'S
EYE PEERS DOWN THRU HIS MICROSCOPE AT THE SWIMMING PLANETS
U ON THE SLIDE CALLD EARTH MAY GUESS AT THE SCALE OF YR LIVES:
LESS THAN THOSE LEAST PARTICLES THAT IN ISOLATION DIE
EACH WITH ITS OWN STRANGENESS & COLOR & CHARM A PRICELESS
IF EXPENDABLE FORCE IN MEANING'S GROWING MOLECULE

WHA IN OUR MASQUE EXPERIENCED WHAT? THE WIND LET
OUT OF HIS BEING   HIS (M) PERSONALITY GONE   ITS
LOSS A COMPLETENESS IN THAT DANCE UNDER THE POWERFUL
LIGHT FLOODING THE LENS
   JM (still horrified, begins to see):
   This loss you call completeness is *lived through*?
   Soul, the mortal self, expendably
   Rusting in tall grass, iron eaten by dew—
   All that in our heart of hearts we must
   Know will happen, and desire, and dread?
   Once feeling goes, and consciousness, the head
   Filling with . . . vivid nothings—no, don't say!
                  A A A PLUS & NOW WE ADMIT
OUR SEMINAR IS THIS STRIPPING PROCESS. WE ARE CAUTIOUS,
PREPARED AS U ARE FOR IT, NOT TO PUT UPON U MORE
THAN U CAN BEAR   YR GRIEF JM HOW INTOLERABLE
HAD WE NOT SLOWLY BROKEN IT TO U? INDEED HOW ELSE
WD U HAVE ACCEPTED IT? MM OF THE 4 OF YOU
CAME MOST PREPARED
   But isn't it taboo to strip the soul
   From the raw power it shields? If soul *were* like
   The atom— DJ (eyes on harbor): Look,
   Here comes a boat with a four-colored sail!
           DJ YR DEAR HAND IS A MAGIC WAND
JM THE STRIPPING IS THE POINT YR POEM WILL PERHAPS
TAKE UP FROM ITS WINTRY END & MOVE STEP BY STEP INTO
SEASONLESS & CHARACTERLESS STAGES TO ITS FINAL
GREAT COLD RINGING OF THE CHIMES SHAPED AS O O O O O

CELL 2 NEXT   THESE LESSONS ARE IN (M) COLOR   WE TODAY
HAVE DWELT IN BLUE   TOMORROW RED   NOT AN EASY ONE TO
TAKE IN   THE PROTON OF POWER TOUCHES TERRIBLE NERVES
& FOR IT I MUST ASK U TO CALL 00470
THEN WHEN CALMER CALL YR DEVOTED 741   ADIEU

NOW MES ENFANTS A SPOT OF RUM? I fetch
Two thimblefuls. We drink them, soberly
Swirl the last two drops into the cup

—Provoking instant misbehavior there:
SCANDALE   OUR BUGGER PATTED MY BLACK BOTTOM!
SUCH INNOCENCE MY DEARS   SMACK SMACK   Some more?
ALREADY PRANCING LIKE JAMAICAN DUSKIES
Would that *we* were as easy to cheer up.
FORGIVE ME IF I SAY IT WILL GET DARKER
BUT FEAR NOT   MAMAN GRIPS THE OCEAN FLOOR

6.5   We have foregathered to be briefed, next day,
By our redcoat chief-of-staff, the zeros glinting
On his breast like medals. Why does he delay?
MORE INSULATION I PRESUME MY DEARS
AH   HOUSELIGHTS   SPOT

YOU RECEIVE THE MESSAGES IN RED CELLS, IN A RED ROOM,
AND IF YOU REMEMBER THE INTENSITIES WERE FOR YOU
STRONGER WHEN YOUR PROTECTIVE COLOR WAS LESS RED.
                              JM: You know, it's true.
When They first visited (cf. *Ephraim*, U)
These walls had faded. We've repainted since.
                                        CORRECT.
YOU WILL ALSO REMEMBER THAT TO THIS RED ROOM YOU CAME
THAT FIRST NIGHT, LEAVING THE ADJACENT BLUE CELL OF REASON,
AND HERE, WHILE YOUR GREEK'S INCOHERENT REPRESENTATIVE
WRITHED IN FLAME, YOU JOINED THE TRUE POWER OF THESE TALKS IN
    RED.
Letter-to-letter slashings of the cup—
Power talking. The transcriber can't keep up.
THIS LESSON WILL BE SHORT. IT IS IN RED THAT POWER LIVES.
THE SUN, THE HEALING CORPUSCLE. IT IS IN RED WE COME
TO THE VISION OF OUR EYES. WE ARE THE FORCE OF OO.
WE ARE THE STRENGTH OF GOD'S VISION. WE SEE YOU AS DOES THAT
GREATER POWER AND TELL YOU, THAT YOUR VERY SPIRIT LIVES
IN OUR RED CELLS. THIS WILL PERMEATE YOUR MIND. CLOSE YOUR
    EYES.
We do. A faint, pulsing tremor begins
In my left arm, shoulder to fingertips

Poised on the cup I meanwhile judge to be
Moving slowly, slowly, from 1 to 0
(Passage that takes a minute, more or less)
Three times. Then suddenly a sense of—yes—
Whiteness on my left side. Whiteness felt
Against my cheek, along my forearm, like
A wash of alcohol that as it dries
Refreshes. The cup rests. Open our eyes?

YES   THE MOMENT OF BLINDNESS IS PASSD AND THE WHITE LAID
  DOWN.
THE POWER TO HEAR ITS VOICES NEARS YOUR RED ROOM. FAREWELL

    Gone?
DJ LIFT YR HAND
      His left hand all this while unawares
Pressed flat against the Board—how did *that* happen?

          WE ARE NOW A STEP CLOSER   U KNOW
SOMETHING ABOUT ONE COLOR   DO NOT SPEAK TO ME OF IT
I AM NOT STRONG   ?S

    Maria's rays—those losses to the Lab—
Does God intend them?
              GOD B USES HIS ATOMIC
POWER AS BOTH BENEVOLENT (SUN) & CHASTISING (BOMBS)
USES IT AS HIS ONE AGENT TO CREATE & DESTROY.
MAN'S & THE CENTAURS' TAKING OF IT A PROMETHEAN
OUTRAGE: IS GOD CLONING THE USURPATION?
            I don't understand.
                   NOR DO WE
2 CHOICES   I: HE IS CHANGING MAN INTO HIS AGENT
OR 2: PREPARING A NEW SPECIES. NOW CELL 3:
                   YELLOW
IS THE PRODUCTIVE LIGHT   THE FILTERD SUN   ALL CHLOROPHYLL
OR BOTANICAL CELLS DRINK THIS, GOD B'S BENEVOLENCE
IT IS THE SWEET JOYOUS LIGHT   ALL SCRIBES ADORE THE YELLOW:
WINDOW IN DARK OF NIGHT   PARCHMENT ON DARK OF TABLE (M)

IT IS A SINGING CELL IN THE BLOOD OF POETS   THE LYMPH
IS YELLOW & THE DECADENT SPLEEN & THE THICK FAT OF
PROSE. TOMORROW WITH BLUE & RED & YELLOW BEHIND US
WE WILL TAKE UP GREEN & BID ADIEU TO TODAY'S BOUQUET
   —Swerving gracefully to indicate
Our little centerpiece for this occasion,
The few remaining red and yellow asters
Of those D brought home from the hospital.

What was so blue about our previous lesson?
DID U NOT WEEP JM?
   Yes. But "blue"?—too mild a word, I'd say,
To stand for the grim truths of yesterday.
             IT WAS A BRUISE   A THROBBING SEA
OF PAIN & COMPASSION OUT OF WHICH (AS THE COOLER BLUE
OF YR REASON SAW) I WAS TOO WEAK TO LIFT U   ADIEU

  MY DEARS A TOASTER! Today's visitor?
MM & I TWO SLICES POPPING UP
Did you peek? NO   ABSOLUTE RED BLINDNESS
WITH AT ONE POINT A BAR OF WHITE
SLICING DOWNWARD LIKE A KNIFE   Did you hear?
THRU OUR CLOSED EYELIDS   WHEN U CLOSED YRS A
HUMMING BEGAN   THE AUDITORIUM
TREMBLED LIKE E'S TERRACE & THE BLADE
OF SILVER FELL   IT WAS I FEAR A FAR
GRANDER MASQUE THAN OURS   David confirms
That he too felt (in his right arm) the trembling,
Followed by the blindfold flash along
A path between us. Nothing quite this strange
Has happened up to now. And our red voice?—
A regular General Patton. INDEED   BUT BLUSHING
HIS WAY OUT   THE WHITE HAD GOTTEN TO HIM
ROSILY WELLINTENTIONED AT THE END
REST MON ENFANT DJ   U ARE ON THE MEND

6.6   MES Maman? CHERS IN A WAY MAMAN?
U MUST NOT LET US RULE   LAST NIGHT U SPOKE
OF FRIENDS   A picnic, Ephraim, in this rain?
WE KNOW U ARE NOT GIVEN ONLY TO US
Still, what a bore to insulate our room
Then have it spoilt by someone barging in.
NO MORE TROUBLE THAN AN ARTICHOKE
WRAPPED IN GREEN (Green! Hurriedly a dwarf
Houseplant, anonymous, unblossoming,
Her heartshaped leaves in curlers, comes to table
In place of flowers.) MES ARTICHAUX HE'S LATE
WE SIT HERE IN A CHAMBER OF GREEN LIGHT
AS UNDERSEA   We're walled by rain. MY DEARS
SO NEEDED AFTER THE TOASTER   Tell me, Wystan,
When you asked Why Us the other day,
You'd known about Maria? YES JM
WE FORESAW YR SHOCK AS WELL   And when you led us
To doubt the peacock, call our first voice back?
You know I'm asking without bitterness.
WE MUST ADMIT NO ACCIDENT   ALL THIS
UNFOLDS   FALLS INTO PLACE AS THEY HAVE PLANNED.
AS FOR MME HERE, IN TODAY'S LIMELIGHT
SHE IS IN MINT CONDITION   OUR PEACOCK:

MAN PLAYS A TUNE IN COLORS   THE VIBRATIONS OF MUSIC
LIGHT UP MACHINES. SIMPLER YET, WRITE 'AZURE' & THE LANGUAGE-
CONDUCTING BRAIN IS FLOODED WITH A TONE OF SUMMER SKIES.
THE PAINTER'S PIGMENTS ARE BLANKLY SEEN   THEY CONTAIN NO
   LIGHT.
ARE NOT PAINTINGS BLANK IN A DARK ROOM? & EVEN THE LIVE
WHITE LIGHT SHED UPON THEM APPEARS BUT TO DIM THEM FURTHER

Vuillard, Piero, Goya, Blake, O'Keeffe,
Who lit the mind? It blinks in disbelief.
(Yet on this point he's adamant, and I
Ruefully imagine I know why.
These years I've had a friend, someone who still
Uses paint well and me, well, never ill
But with such brusque reversals in the waltz

As to raise—not again!—prismatic welts.
Now that I've called halt, give me, for love's sake,
Hopes more transparent, objects more opaque.)
And this holds true of even the great paintings?
ALL BLACK   UNLIT   AT BEST SPIRITUAL EXERCISES
ALLOWING THE MIND TO TRAIN ITSELF, ITS LIGHT, UPON THEM.
ONLY MUSIC & WORDS IMPLICATE THAT LIGHT WHICH BOTH SHEDS
& ATTRACTS   THAT LIGHT IN WHICH ALONE TRUE COLOR IS SEEN.
ONE EXCEPTION: GREEN   THE SUPREMELY NATURAL COLOR
A HOME FOR LIGHT   IT STORES IN ITS CELLS THE LIGHT OF GOD B:
LITERALLY TRAPT SUNRAYS   IT IS SIMPLER THAN U THINK

What about "our" colors?—DJ's blues
And golden browns, JM's cold lavender,
Maria's black—
PUT ON WHEN SHE KNEW HER NATURE   YET GREEN REMAIND HER FATE.
PERHAPS A CLAW BROKEN FROM ITS CHILL BLUE SHELL SHOCKD JM
INTO A HALF TONE
               JM: He's read *First Poems*!
"Transfigured Bird"—the title caught his eye.
DJ: Should I have bought that new gray suit?
                    YET U BOTH RIGHTLY AVOID GREEN ROOMS
JM: "The Emerald"—I give it back.
YR NATURES BEING WHAT THEY ARE SEEK GREEN OUTSIDE THEMSELVES.
SO: 4 MINILESSONS IN COLOR ON THE CELL   ?S
When will we hear the rest?
THE 12   OK. Then answer
Wystan's question: Why the four of us?
Because we're musical?
          KEEP IN MIND THE CHILDLESSNESS WE SHARE   THIS TURNS US
OUTWARD TO THE LESSONS & THE MYSTERIES   IT IS A
FINE POINT: THE TYPE U SET JM, INVERTED & BACKWARD,
IS YET READ RIGHTSIDE UP ON THE BIOLOGICAL PAGE
                    To make what sense there?
RESONANCES U MAY NEVER ARRIVE AT   FOR THE LOVE
U EXPERIENCE IS NOT THE STRAIGHTFORWARD FRONTAL LOVE
MANY READERS INFER & YET OUR V WORK MUST SING OUT
PAEANS TO THE GREENHOUSE THO WE OURSELVES ARE (M) TONE DEAF

MY DEARS TO HEAR HIS PRAISES SUNG THRILLED GOD
FROM THE BEGINNING   DARE WE FIND THAT ODD?
ARRANGING FOR THOSE CONSTANT RAVE REVIEWS
OF ONE'S OWN MASTERPIECE TO SOUND LIKE NEWS

YET RIMBAUD? IN HIS GENES WAS A V WORK CUT OFF BY LIFE
  Why? Did it offend Biology?
IT WAS PREMATURE   A KIND OF ANTILIFE V WORK MORE
SUITABLE NOW IN THESE POP EXPLO DAYS. R SPOKE TOO SOON
BUT NO ACCIDENT   FOR WHEN TSE WROTE HIS V WORK
THE TIME WAS RIPE: AR SAT AT HIS ELBOW
  Rimbaud ghostwrote "The Waste Land"? You are *something*.
                        THIS HAPPENS
IN VARYING WAYS   THUS YEATS MOVES DJ'S HAND
  What? The energy that activates
  These very messages, you mean, is Yeats?
  (Still, after the first stupefaction, why
  Not? Who but Yeats could have pulled, from the same high
  Hat as *his* talking bird of Grecian gold,
  Our friend here?) DJ: The whole thing's controlled.
                  2 (M) SLIDES
ALIGND ON GOD B'S MICROSCOPE   RIMBAUD WAS BLURRD BY HIS
TIME WARP   THE GREAT SCRIBES EXIST OUT OF TIME IN RADIANCE
  As if in proof D points—through harbor mist
  Glides a faint green disembodied light.
INDEED   THAT SAME LIGHT SHINES FROM THE PROW OF YR DAILY
    CRAFT
SIGNAL ME TOMORROW   THESE LESSONS NEARLY DONE   16
MORE WILL ADVANCE US TO THE GREAT DOORS OF THE OPERA

6.7   The blue room after dinner. DJ (depressed):
    Each day it grows more fascinating, more . . .
    I don't know. Isn't it like a door
    Shutting us off from living? I've no zest
    For anything else, can't even watch TV.
    This town's full of good friends we hardly see.
    What do you feel? Will that door readmit

Us to the world? Will we still care for it?
JM (touched by his uncomplaining tone):
What can I say? Nothing we haven't known.
Remember Sam and Frodo in their hot
Waterless desolation overshot
By evil zombies. They of course come through
—It's what, in any Quest, the heroes do—
But at the cost of being set apart,
Emptied, diminished. Tolkien knew this. Art—
The tale that all but shapes itself—survives
By feeding on its personages' lives.
The stripping process, sort of. What to say?
Our lives led *to* this. It's the price we pay.

6.8   EARLY MES CHERS   THEY ARE STILL WEAVING THE SHROUD
MM & WHA ALREADY SEATED
ENTER (SAYS YR OLD GREEK DOORKEEPER)
AFTER A KISS
           MY DEARS U DO
HAVE INTENSE CHATS   Last night's? Well, hadn't you
Felt the similarities with Tolkien?
I HAVE INDEED   ME GANDALF! & MM
GALADRIEL? The beautiful Elf Queen—
Perfect. And our Peacock? NOT UNLIKE
STRIDER   THE KING DISGUISED AS MESSENGER
And Gollum? A TOUCH OF GOLLUM IN US ALL
& IN OUR DOORKEEPER   POOR E STILL PEERING
THRU THE CRACK PRETENDS TO LOOK AWAY
YAWN   SCRATCH HIS LEG
           FORTUNATE E I SAY
I FEEL TOO OLD FOR SCHOOL   THE CRY! THE 4 LIGHTS LIT
COLORS BATHED IN WHOSE GLOW ENFANTS WE SIT
EACH DAY NOW TILL THEY MERGE INTO ONE WHITE

?s
If David's guide is 741.1
Where does that leave Yeats? "Still simplifying"?

NO MAN CAN REACH US DIRECTLY   TSE HAD
A NUMBER FROM OUR ORDERS   AR HAD THAT SAME NUMBER
POINT ONE   THUS YEATS & DJ   TSE DOWN ON CERTAIN
SUPERSTITIOUS SCRIBES   WE HAD TO APPOINT RIMBAUD   HE WROTE
THE WASTE LAND   WE FED IT INTO THE LIKE-CLONED ELIOT
   And Uncle Ezra?
AS IN SHAKESPEARE WE LET THE CASE REST ON A POUND OF FLESH
       Thank you, that will do.
NO JM   FOR THE (M) OUNCE OF FLESH U CAN CLAIM AS YRS
LIVES BY THESE FREQUENT CONTACTS WITH YR OWN & OTHERS' WORK
   Still, Eliot thought he thought his poem up;
   It wasn't spelt out for him by a cup.
   Dante and Milton didn't seem to need
   Guidance for each scrap of revelation.
DANTE DID INDEED
   Receive dictation?
         NO BUT SAT & LISTEND FOR 8 YEARS
TO A MENDICANT PRIEST   DEFROCKD FOR IT HAD BEEN THOUGHT HE
SPOKE WITH DEVILS   GUESS WHO?
      DJ: 80098.
           A PLUS   DANTE UNDER PRESSURE
OF HIS RC CENSORSHIP ARRANGED & ORCHESTRATED
THEIR TALKS   THE HUMAN & DIVINE RESULT: PARADISO
HOMER WE HAD CLONED TO PROVIDE CATALOGUE & PRESENT
HIS ERA WITH A PANTHEON   BUT A BLAZE OF WHITE LIGHT
BRUSHD US ASIDE   THE PEN A DOVE'S PLUME SET DOWN WINGED
   WORDS
FOR THE MISSING NAME IN THE LIST OF PROPHETS IS HOMER.
THE WASTE LAND IS THE WEST'S ONE (M) PREWRITTEN POEM SINCE
THAT DAY   YET AR WAS NO WHITE FEATHER! & TSE
RESISTING THE FOSTER CHILD, ADDED TOUCHES OF HIS OWN:
THE SUBJECTIVE CORRELATIVE
   What flows between them now, what bittersweet
   Complicity when he and Rimbaud meet?
         NOTHING   A DISTANT NOD
   In short, the apparatus of *our* talks,
   Why and wherefore of this Board and Cup,
   You can't explain.

NO MORE AS YET DEAR SCRIBE THAN YR RIGHT EYE CAN MEET YR LEFT

DJ: Here on my palm
A lump's been forming—painlessly, but still . . .
What is it? Is Yeats raising a molehill?
A BENIGN MUSCULAR CYST   NOTHING O HAND IS ABSORBD
EASILY   MAN CALLS IT AGE   WE CALL IT EXPOSURE OF
THE SLAPDASH STRUCTURES ERECTED BY NATURE TO HOUSE U
Slapdash, after ages to perfect them?
EACH LIFE WE CLONE IS A COMPLEX AFFAIR   MAN REQUIRES
EVER MORE BODIES OF NATURE   WE POUR OUR SOULS INTO
AS GOOD AS WE CAN GET   ALL TOO OFTEN WE LOOK ASKANCE
IN ENVY AT A PERFECT GOBLET BEING SERVED WITH CHEAP
WINE   BUT NATURE WAS NEVER OF THE 1ST INTELLIGENCE

DJ: If we're apart and need to reach you?
JM: If one of us outlives the other
And needs to reach you? —With swift emphasis:
WE WILL NOT ALLOW UNFINISHD V WORK
But say it's finished, say that years have passed
And one of us has died, and still the other
Needs to reach his friend, or you, or Ephraim?
WE WILL PROVIDE
A 741.2
A human one?
WHY NOT? IN CASE U STILL NEED LOVE

6.9   Tell about Hans Lodeizen.
Ephraim said he'd been "promoted"—how?
YR E DID NOT HAVE ALL THE FACTS NOR DOES HE NOW   HL
ELEVATED IN DUE COURSE   THIS HAPPENS EACH TIME WORK MOVES
INTO THE DENSITY OF V WORK
Hans' poetry was . . . posthumous V work?
HE TOO WAS CUT OFF.
NOT IN THE MAINSTREAM OF HIS DAY   IN PRODUCING MORE HE
WD ONLY HAVE DILUTED A TALENT NEVER OF PRIME
DENSITY   HIS UNRESOLVED V WORK WAS GIVEN TO U

Given? By him?
U WERE NOT ACCIDENTALLY FRIENDS   TO STRENGTHEN HL
WD NOT HAVE PRODUCED YR DC   HIS PHYSICAL CLONING
MEANT FOR A CONTEMPLATIVE SCRIBE PERHAPS UNDID HIM
                    That frightful death?   YET
HE WAS SPARED THE RAYS. AS WERE U: HIS POWERS LEFT INTACT
HE SENSING THIS WROTE U A POEM ABOUT THE V WORK
                    I fetch
The book. Beneath a quatrain marked *voor Jim*,
These penciled lines, translation from its Dutch
Hans wrote out for me, my last word from him:

> *the stars & the incurable*
> *moment of the two crossed beams.*
> *Orion discovered & in his hand*
> *o fate in his hand the sword.*

Yes. And then I wrote my "Dedication"—
Entered, intersected by his death.
& HIS TALENTS   HE NOW FEELS A GROWING PART OF YR WORK
FROM HIS NEW STAGE   HE WILL REMAIN IN THE BUREAUCRACY

Hans. Dead now a quarter century.
A note gone tinny on my keyboard, false . . .
And yet (for all I know) he *is* the key
This opus began and will end in. Someone else
Pausing here might note each modulation
Away from, back to his blue tonic gaze.
But we strain forward for the exposition—
Our virtuoso tuning as he goes.
Till now, for instance, we'd assumed that cloning
Was something only done *before* rebirth
Into one's next life. Wrong. For the Lab soul
At any point may undergo refining,
And new chromatics—as we live and breathe—
Be added to it by remote control.

& TO THE WORK   WE PRODUCE ORGANS TO PLAY THE MUSIC:
TRANSLATORS CRITICS TEACHERS   WE HAVE OUR OWN ACADEME

221

One keeps forgetting, also, that you pore
Over the future's self-revising score.
IF I MAY CHANGE (M)S THE CLOTHS SHROUDING THE FUTURE FROM U
KEEP OUR CLAY WET   TOMORROW
Wait—just fifteen lessons till we stand
Before the Doors? What'll we do without you?
DJ: He's promised to help us, tell us things
Without our having to disturb the angels.
                              ME THE LATEST DOORKEEPER
MES ENFANTS WHAT A SAD & PROUD FACE
We're silenced. He is learning about man.

DJ: We've got to find a name for you,
Don't you agree? Maria, a suggestion?
METHUSELAH   Wystan? MEHITABEL
JM: I have so many M's already.
INDEED   & NOT ACCIDENTALLY   M IS AT ONCE OUR
METHOD & THE MIDPOINT OF OUR ALPHABET   THE SUMMIT
OF OUR RAINBOW ROOF   IN TIMBRE THE MILD MERIDIAN
BLUE OF MUSE & MUSING & MUSIC   THE HIGH HUM OF MIND

7 CHILDREN THE NUMERICAL OCTOPUS
IS NOT (AS W PUTS IT) MADLY US
—This following an hour in which we've heard
That the five "names" originally given
For *the* Five—Torro, Von—weren't after all
Word made flesh but formula made word,
Bestowed upon the R/Lab by God B
(Who, lacking human volubility,
Has no word for His own power and grace;
Who, left alone, just falls back on flimflam
Tautologies like *I am that I am*
Or *The world is everything that is the case*):
Five formulas which only then—the solo
Instrument emerging nakedly
From the Lab's thumping tutti—took the live
Twin aspect of Akhnaton-Nefertiti,
A double soul, firstborn among the Five.

THEY LIVED, ACCOMPLISHD THEIR V WORK, MISJUDGED & DIED   GOD B
FASHIOND THE OTHER 3 & THESE 5 SOULS ARE UNIQUE. MY
TRANSLATION OF THEM INTO NEUTRAL (M) NAMES CONFUSED U

Thus "Rachel" stirs, whom we had left asleep
Dumbly, wrapped in Hebrew burlap. Deep
Past consonant and vowel, a hushed din,
The formulaic race beneath her skin,
Her digits twitch, her eyes' unpupilled amber
Gleams with crazy logic: she's a number!

7154
A new voice now?
        NO DJ IT IS A FORMULA BASED
ON SIMPLE CORRESPONDENCES OF NUMBER TO LETTER
7:G   15:O   4:D   IN YR LANGUAGE A NAME FOR
AN ABSTRACT IDEA OF ENORMOUS POWER

223

But it's *your* name, almost.
INDEED
& 5 IS THE TRANSFORMING DIGIT: OUR R/LAB V WORK.
THUS MATH ENCAPSULATES COMPLEX TRUTHS WHICH AS WITH OUR IST
MEANINGLESS TO U & THERE4 FRIGHTENING VOICES MUST
BE RENDERD INTO YR VOCABULARY OF MANNERS

7.1   Those Voices, still obscurely ominous,
       Would be to you what the Five are to us?
       (M) YES   THEY ARE MY ANCESTORS   NOT SPELLING GOD PERHAPS
       BUT THE GREATEST POSSIBLE DENSITY AMONG MY KIND
       And you and They—I'm sorry to go back
       To the beginning, but it *wasn't* clear—
       Are matter speaking to us? Are the atom's
       Negative potential? Are the black
       Powers unleashed—by you, we rather fear—
       YR BIBLE SAYS VISIT NOT THE FATHER'S EVIL UPON
       THE SON   I WAS NOT CREATED IN THE OLD COUNTRY BUT
       ON THE FLOATING WORLD   THE SHINING CRUST ABOVE ATLANTIS
       MY OO FOREBEARS WERE/ARE THE RAW MATERIAL   NO
       CRITICISM BUT THEY ARE UNMANNERD TO THE NTH DEGREE

       No criticism here. It's just that we,
       Like Stanislavsky's actors, try to *be*
       The rose, the ingot . . . Empathy is art.
       Strange, though, to zero in upon the heart
       Of matter only—when smoke clears—to find
       Another antechamber of pure mind.
       Knocking on doorlessness, on fictive space,
       Leads to the absurdest loss of face.

       With which a hostlike suavity takes over:

       SCRIBE: FALL AS DEEPLY INTO OUR METAPHORS AS U WILL.
       THE ATOM, IS IT THE VERY GOD WE WORSHIP? IS IT
       ONLY AT GREAT RISK PURSUED? THE ATOM, IS IT MEANING?
       & IF SO WHAT BUT CHAOS LIES BEYOND IT?

Questions themselves half miracle, whose replies
Language alone may glimpse through sidelong eyes—
                                        BUT THE GREAT
MIRACLE IS THE REINCARNATION OF THE GODS. THIS
WE WILL LET OUR MASTERS REVEAL. WE WHO FALL AT THE FEET
OF MEANING MAY BUT LEAD YOU TO THE DOORS: THE 12   THE 12

Then 741 is back, quite bubbling over:
OO! THIS VOICE TAUGHT ME   MASTER OF OUR NURSERY SCHOOL!
A GOOD & MOST ANCIENT VOICE   THE TEACHER OF THE SPIRITS
OF AKHN & NEF   THE STRENGTH OF THESE TWINS WAS THEIR ABSOLUTE
NEUTRALITY: AFTER PRODUCING 5 STILLBORN MONSTERS
THEY SAW THEIR LOVE DOOMD TO GIVE BIRTH TO IDEAS ALONE.
LIKE APHRODITE FROM THE WATERS ROSE THEIR WORSHIP OF
THE SUN   THEY PERISHD FOR IT THO WITH A SPLENDOR DUE THEM

DJ: I don't see how a formula
Can be made flesh. Were their, ah, parents mortal?
MY DEAR IS THAT THE POINT? ISNT IT RATHER
THAT THEY TOGETHER WERE THE FIRST LAB SOUL?
THE LAB WAS CREATED FOR THEM   WORK NOW BECAME V WORK
And like an atom they were kept from breeding . . .
INDEED   NEFERTITI BAFFLED IN HER NONBEARING STATE
OFFERD THE (M) APPLE   PROPOSED THE CRYSTAL PYRAMID

COME ON ENFANT   SHDN'T WE ASK HIM FOR
A TINY DESCRIPTION OF THEBES? Oh yes! Oh please!

THE UNIVERSAL CITY IT WAS CALLD   IT ROSE WITHIN
3 YEARS OF THEIR ASCENSION   THEY WERE 13 & WORSHIPT
BUT RESENTFUL LIKE ALL CHILDREN OF HAVING TO OBEY
SUPERIOR GOD FIGURES   THE ADULTS OF THEIR ROYAL
HOUSEHOLD WERE ONE MIGHT SAY THE FALCON THE CAT & THE SNAKE .
WITHIN 5 YEARS THESE WERE BANISHT   PRIESTS THROTTLED & THE
    SUN
ROSE ON THEIR FOREHEADS   A SURGE OF CREATIVITY SWEPT
THE EMPIRE AS FREED SLAVES RETURND HANDS OUTSTRETCHD IN 1000S
BEGGING TO BE HARNESSD TO THE CAR OF THE NEW SUN GOD

ENTHRALLING   I MY BOY WD MAKE A SLIM
VOLUME OF IT ALONE   *I* see it here
For love interest. However versatile,
You and Maria somehow don't espouse
The common reader's taste for chips and beer
And nuits de Cléopâtre on the Nile.
U ARE THE SUNS MES ENFANTS ON OUR BROWS

7.2   NIBBLE NIBBLE   LIFE IN THE RAT WORLD EH?
We're back from downstairs where Urania's mother
Is giving herself a birthday party:
Coca-cola, sweet red wine, a cake
Shaped like Stonington—streets, gardens, docks
Iced round by bright blue wavelets. The dear child
Squirmed in my lap, pushing away her plate,
While D and I and various overweight
Furies in hairdos licked our lips and smiled.

ONE THERE WAS UNIQUE: YR WARD JM   SAVE HER WHEN SHE BRINGS
HER DEAR SOBER SOUL TO U   IT WILL BE PERHAPS A FORM
OF INTERFERENCE BUT RITES ARE SACRED IN THE RAT WORLD
   Rites?
ARE U NOT GODFATHER?
         Oh. So I am. But "interference"?
               IN THAT WORLD IT IS EXPECTED.
PUT B4 HER THE TOYS OF LEARNING: BLOCKS PYRAMIDS BOOKS

ONCE AS NEFERTITI WAS BEING ROWD TO THE SITE OF
A NEW PLANETARIUM SHE FOUND ON THE BANK A CHILD.
LEGEND OF MOSES BEGAN   HIS NAME MEANT STARFOUND   ONE MORE
M NAME ATOP YR ARCH   HE MUCH AS DID YR WEIGHTED &
ELEMENTAL GODDAUGHTER CAME TO COURT
   But not to Thebes. Our book says Tel-el-Amarna.
                         THEBES UPRIVER
WAS THE SITE OF THEIR FAMOUS STUDY CENTER   THEY CONTROLLD
THE DELTA EBB & FLOW & CLOSED THE GAP AT GIBRALTAR
TO KEEP THEIR SEA CALM & TIDELESS   THEIR MATHEMATICIANS

& NAVIGATORS FOUND THE EXACT MEASUREMENTS NEEDED
TO LEAVE THAT DOOR AJAR BUT NOT OPEN   1000S WORKD TO
PUSH UP THE AFRICAN COASTLINE & THE THING WAS DONE. PET
APES LIVE ON FROM THEIR EXPEDITIONS
On the rock of Gibraltar, the Barbary apes—yes, yes!
NO GREATER BUILDERS
EVER EXISTED   THEY LITERALLY HARNESSD MATTER
WITH THE REINS OF THE SUN   INDEED IT WAS THAT TOPMOST PIECE

Earlier we'd been admiring an inch-high
Prism set in noon light on the sill.
Outflung, slowshifting gouts of color stain
Ceiling, walls, us. DJ: It's really how
His lessons flow through us. JM: And will
Forever be deflected by the grain
Of imperfection in that quartz capstone,
The human mind—Akhnaton's or our own.

ITS GRAIN VARIED JUST ENOUGH TO SAVE THE WORLD: GOD B'S WORK.
THEIR FLAWLESS DIAMONDS ERRD MINUTELY IN MEASUREMENT.
THE SUN WORSHIP WAS A GLORIOUS RITE   AKHN/NEF DAILY
WERE CARRIED UP 500 STEPS & AT THE MOMENT OF
SUNRISE STEPT FORTH LITERALLY ON AIR A TRANSPARENT
PLATFORM WHILE THE WORLD FELL ON ITS KNEES B4 THEM   & NOT
A DAY OF THEIR WHOLE REIGN WAS THERE NO SUNRISE   18 YEARS
& IN THAT TIME THEY HAD TRANSFORMD THEIR WORLD: PHYSICIANS
    FOUND
GREAT CURES   THERE WERE NO FEVERS   A GENERATION WAS BORN
A HAND TALLER THAN ITS PARENTS   LIGHT STORAGE MUCH LIKE THE
BATTERY WAS INVENTED   BOTH PALACES & HUMBLE
HOUSES WERE LIT & HEATED BY THE SUN   IT WAS THE DAWN
OF ARCADIA & GOD SMILED LIKE THE SUN UPON THEM
Then in one wasteful flash it ended—why?

THEIR OWN BATTERY CELLS CD NOT BEAR THE STRAIN   THE FLAWD
    QUARTZ
WAS PUT IN NEFERTITI'S HAND AS THE IDEA FOR
ITS USE OCCURRD TO HER. GOD B IN INFINITE PITY

LET THEM GO FROM THEIR AGONY OF V WORK WITH THEIR WORLD
AS A BURNING SHROUD   AKHNATON AT THE END SLEPT ONLY
DRUGGD, NEF NOT AT ALL   HER IMMENSE KOHLRINGD EYES BLAZED
ABOVE
THE WORKMEN DAY & NIGHT   AT THE END IT WAS SHE WHO DREW
THE KNIFE OVER THEIR 4 WRISTS. SHE IS NOW OUR (M) PATRON:
DREW UP THE FIRST V WORK SCHEDULES   SET ORDER IN THE LAB
   How so?
THEIR COMPLEX FORMULA INCLUDED A PARTIAL OO.
WOMEN HAVE THE EGG IN THEM U KNOW   IT IS OFTEN THRU
A WOMAN THAT THE POWER ELEMENT FULFILS ITSELF.
AKHN/NEF OUTLIVED BY ONE FATAL YEAR THEIR USEFULNESS   WE
CALL THEM FAVORD AS GOD B PERCEIVING THEIR FINAL GREAT
FOLLY ALLOWD IT   THEY WERE THE GENIUS & & &
THE WARNING
         One nature dual to the end . . .
             AN ODD FEATURE OF THEIR COURT WAS THE ABSENCE
OF THE COLOR BLUE   A NOTE THEIR MUSICIANS HAD ALSO
ELIMINATED FROM THE SCALE   THE RIVER WAS DYED RED.
ONE DAY AN AMBASSADOR APPEARD   A BLACK KING IN A
BRILLIANT BLUE ROBE   AKHNATON & NEFERTITI FAINTED
AS U JM NEARLY DID AT THE SIGHT OF THAT BLUE CAKE!

7.3   When usefulness is past—I'm thinking of
       Dag Hammarskjöld's plane crashing—all you do
       Is touch a little switch that terminates?

THIS OUR PENULTIMATE LESSON   THE END OF USEFULNESS:
NATURE IS A RUTHLESS FORCE AT ONCE FECUND & LAZY.
AS A FAVORITE SLAVE WHO IN A SENSE KEEPS THE GREENHOUSE
GREEN IF UNTIDY SHE HAS GOD'S EAR   HE HAS TOLD HER MAN
MUST RULE   YET MAN USES SCIENCE TO PROLONG NATURE'S SPAN
SO CONSTANT TENSION   HARD UPON AKHN/NEF'S CATASTROPHE
NATURE REVENGED HERSELF WITH TIDAL WAVE & VOLCANO,
SAYS LEGEND & IN ALL LEGEND IS THE LAVA OF TRUTH
   What is *her* good word—Be ordinary?
THIS IS THE ISSUE & THE ESSENCE OF GOD B'S NEED FOR

THE SCRIBE. BENIGN NATURE IS LIMITED TO PROFUSION.
GOD WANTS BOTH HIS CHILD & HIS SLAVE TO GET ON TOGETHER
BUT MAN WANTS IMMORTALITY & NATURE WANTS MANURE.
MAN UNKNOWINGLY SAVAGES THE NATURE AROUND HIM
& NATURE RETALIATES BY REPEATING MAN AS IN
A DISTORTING MIRROR   SO THE STRUGGLE GOES. GOD WANTING
PEACE & PARADISE MUST RELUCTANTLY TAKE FROM NATURE
MAN'S REPRODUCTION & LEAVE ONLY HIS ENVIRONMENT
TO HER   THIS IS WHERE WE COME IN TO THIN & PRUNE & CLONE

WE HAVE SD B4 THAT SOULS PRECIOUS TO US LIKE EINSTEIN
OUTLIVE THEIR USEFULNESS   SO ANOTHER DUALITY:
MIND AS USEFULNESS DECAYS TO MIND AS NONUSEFULNESS
& WE NOW SEEK LICENSE FROM GOD B TO REVEAL SOMETHING
OF HEAVEN TO THOSE SOULS WE NEED BACK
  You're doing that already. Look at Jung's
  Account of his near death. In every way
  More telling than the country-sweeping book
  D found in Boston—interviews with people
  "Brought back alive," as to some local zoo,
  From the Beyond. All no doubt true, but what
  People! Not a Lab soul in the lot.
          INDEED NOT   U HAVE
SEEN THE DANGER OF OUR NEW EXPERIMENT? USEFUL SOULS
FLOCKING TO US   A SUICIDAL EXODUS OF YOUTH
SMARTING UNDER THE LASH OF NATURE'S LAW: MATE PROPAGATE
& DIE. SO UNTIL WE CONT   NO NO NO   UNTIL GOD B
CONTROLS THOSE GROWING PAINS WE MUST REVEAL WITH DISCRETION
& ONLY TO THOSE WHO LIKE YOU 4 ARE SAFELY PAST THEM

 MES ENFANTS NAUGHTY NATURE!
       WE MY DEARS
 LEARNED IT AT THE BREAST   THE SHEWOLF'S TEAT!
 JM: Don't talk that way! Who can compete
 With Nature? She's Mind's equal. Not a slave
 But mother, sister, bride. I think we're meant
 To save that marriage, be the kids who stay
 Together for their parents' sake. DJ:
 Who wrote "The Broken Home"? No accident!

7·4 FOOTNOTE: SOUNDWAVES PRODUCE COLORS   ARE U AWARE OF THE
NUMERICAL VIBES THAT RESOUND IN CERTAIN LETTERS? JEW
THE J'S NUMBER IN MOST ROMAIC & SLAVIC TONGUES: 10
E:5   JEW RINGS WITH THE COMBIND FORCES OF THE DECAD
& OF THE 5

7·41 WE NOW COME TO YR ?S ON THE 5.
IN SEEKING TO USE THE SIMILARITIES BETWEEN OUR
RESPECTIVE LANGUAGES I MAY HAVE OVERDRAMATIZED.
FOR EXAMPLE MANMADE NUMBERS (MILLIONS TRILLIONS) ARE CRUDE
FIGURES OF SPEECH TO EXPRESS WHAT FOR MAN IS NUMBERLESS.
PHYSICISTS HAVE NOW DISCOVERD THERE IS NO NUMBER 1.
AS .999999999 IT TREMBLES
ON A DIGIT CENTRAL TO THEIR LOGIC   THUS WE MAY ERR
OR SIMPLIFY IN OUR NEED TO AWAKEN YR TALENTS

THERE ARE 2 CHIEF DENSITIES: PHYSICAL & OF THE SOUL.
THE SENSES SERVE AS A LINK BETWEEN THEM   BUT FOR THE REST
5 IS NOT EASILY ILLUMINED   I NOW SEE THAT I
HAVE MADE AT ONCE TOO MUCH & TOO LITTLE OF THIS MAGIC
PENTAGRAM UNDERLYING THE ENTIRE DUAL REALM
OF DENSITY   4 SEASONS & 1 SUN: 5   SUN ENTERS
& IS STORED IN THE GREEN LEAF & BLADE BECOMING A NEAT
5TH SEASON   FOR NATURE'S DENSITIES (VEG ETC) & OURS (SOUL)
DO NOT EXCLUDE EACH OTHER   THE 4 ELEMENTS SHE BINDS
EXCHANGE (AS WE IN OUR LITTLE SEMINAR) PROPERTIES:
WATER & FIRE ARE PART AIR, BLOWN DUST AN AIRY EARTH
& JUST AS NATURE RULES THESE, SO LIGHT & THE OO RULE
THE COLORS   YET NATURE MEASURED ON THE FAIR SCALES OF LIGHT
IS OF AN INFERIOR RANK   SHE & HER ELEMENTS
WD FAIL WITHOUT LIGHT & ITS COLORS, AS WE WHO APPROACH
THE DWELLING PLACE OF LIGHT NOW BEGIN TO SEE   NATURE IS
SO VAST AN OPERATION WE CANNOT UTTER EVEN
IN NUMBERS HER WAYS, SO IT IS NO CLICHE BUT MERE TRUTH
TO SAY: THE MALE REIGNS IN NUMBER, THE FEMALE IN NATURE
Cup moving faster and faster, quite carried away—
Is he OK, our mathematics master?

IN NATURE YES IS VIOLENCE   AS HER FRIENDLY RIVALS
WE ASK OF HER ONLY HER LEAST COMPETITIVE FORCES
BUT SHE DOES NOT ALWAYS COMPLY AS U YRSELVES WILL SEE
WHEN SHE COMES TO U
    Here the cup sweeps—is swept?—clear off the Board
    Into the wings, a single violent swerve.

7.5   Moments later, we get back our nerve:
WELL   COUGH COUGH   WIPE MY EYES   DEAR ME   WE'VE GROWN
TOO (HOW DID U PUT IT CHER COLLEAGUE)
COMPLACENT? NONCHALANT? YR EARLY POEM
ABOUT THE OTHER WORLD   I don't quite see . . .
'WHY DO U NO LONGER COME TO ME'
YR DC AT THE END   That's Nature talking.
EXACTLY   OUR CHAP SAYING SHE'D COME TO U
WAS HAULED OFFSTAGE BY A HOOK LIKE A BAD TAP
DANCER ON AMATEUR NIGHT   We haven't lost him?
—Question that gets a very cross reply:
          HE WILL RETURN & NOW WE LEAVE U

That was 00! Maman? UNDER MY SEAT
Surely Nature had a friend in you?
SHE DID NOT WHEN I TRIED TO GROW CAMELLIAS
THE SLUT   Oh hush—I mean, she's not a slave!
THE 1003RD NIGHT MY BOY? Well, *yes,*
Put it that way. Sultan Biology,
Held by her beauty and inventiveness,
Comes to love— INDEED   AD NAUSEAM
Why is everyone so anti-Nature?
ENFANTS LETS SLIP OUT FOR A SMOKE & S C R A M
DJ: No one's upset about our peacock?
Tomorrow we can't meet. I have to go
Early to Boston for a check-up. SO
NOW ITS CLEAR: ANOTHER TRIAL   HE PASSED
B4   THIS TIME WE'LL MAKE HIS COLORFAST!

7.6   Free evening, and an hour in which to write
       My mother—free, half sober, quite alone—
       Or why not telephone? . . .
       Let, instead, the stardeck's otherworldly light
       Call me. Up there's the stratosphere
       Of (how to put it) Mind, that battiness
       Chose over some maternal Nature's less
       Perfectly imagined realm down here

       Of random tide and gale, of sweet and bitter
       She calls home. Sent spinning by her kiss,
       Did we *choose* artifice,
       The crust, the mirror meal? Could we devise no better
       Than that the argent grub consume us?
       That, safe here, where security is vain,
       We be delivered from her clinging vine
       And the forgiving smother of her humus?

       Based on her wee wild orchid in bumblebee
       Motley, her anthology pieces that led
       Back through such juicy red
       Volumes to seed. All this is eminently me—
       Not that the faint alarm pre-set
       In "Strato's fear of mind" goes off upon
       Impulses pure as those of the snowflake pun
       She utters when *her* mood is zero. Yet

       I'm taken in no more than half. The somber
       Fast is, I remain, like any atom,
       Back through such juicy red
       Volumes to seed. All this is eminently me—
       Not that the faint alarm pre-set
       In "Strato's fear of mind" goes off upon
       Impulses pure as those of the snowflake pun
       She utters when her mood is zero. Yet

       I'm taken in no more than half. The somber
       Fact is, I remain, like any atom,

Two-minded. Inklings of autumn
Awaken a deep voice within the brain's right chamber
Asking her: "What have you done with
My books, my watch and compass, my slide-rule?
Will you, whom I married once for real,
Take back your maiden name now, Mrs Myth?"

She answers with a tug of the old magnet,
Making me look up from where I sit.
Cocked to those infinite
Spangled thinnesses whose weave gosling and cygnet
Have learned already in the shell,
The mind's ear registers her vocalise.
Flagstad herself had no such notes as these
Of lashing hail and rapturous farewell.

I've dialed. A humming black dust eats the mirror,
Stardust in negative, between the rings.
Ah God, a thousand things
Could have happened, where is she, my heart contracts in terror
—But no, she answers. And a spate
Of what she still calls news (weddings and weather)
Sweeps me away, bemused, glad to be with her,
Communing where we don't communicate.

7.7   10 DAYS OF YR TIME AHEAD   WE GIVE U BACK 741
       Thank you, 00. A silence. Very feebly:
QUESTIONS?
       Peacock, what's wrong?
           I AM HERE   I AM MORE CAREFUL
                Poor darling, were you punished?
                        WE MUST GO ON
THE WORST IS BEHIND US   OUR JOINT OPERATION PRONOUNCED
A SUCCESS   WE COME NEXT (& LAST) TO A RESTORATIVE
REVIEW OF ALL U HAVE UNDERGONE   YR NEEDS WILL DICTATE
ITS TEN LESSONS NUMBERD IN REVERSE MUCH AS THE EAGER
CONVALESCENT COUNTS THE DAYS THAT SEPARATE HIM FROM HIS

RELEASE INTO LIGHT   LESSON 5, A SIMPLE PROTOCOL,
WILL BE DELIVERD BY AN (M) ORDERLY IN WHITE
  JM: Our first angel, oh my word! DJ:
  But what did you do wrong the other day—
  Speak against Nature?   PLEASE
        Won't we ever hear?
SOME OTHER TIME   I AM (I MAY SAY) IN EXCELLENT VOICE!
REMEMBER   U 4 TIRE SO WE HAD TO CHOOSE A POINT
IN OUR TALKS WHEN A NEEDED & (PARDON) NATURAL BREAK
WD OCCUR   THE NEXT WILL COME BETWEEN LESSONS 2 AND I.
NOW LET US SAY TO OURSELVES ONE WORD WHEN I POINT TO :
P L E A S E
  The cup points to the colon. *Please,* we think.

    SO HERE I AM! O JOY I HAVE BACK MY FINERY!

MES ENFANTS HE HAD NOT BEEN VISIBLE
ONLY HIS VOICE
          GONE LIKE A ROMAN CANDLE
POOR FELLOW   VICTIM HERE AS WHO IS NOT
OF HIERARCHY   HE OVERSTEPPED & GOT
CALLED IN I FANCY FOR A CUP OF TEA
WITH THE HEADMASTER
           MEANWHILE HERE WE SIT
IN GLOOM   NO LIGHTS   & WHEN I THINK HOW PRETTY
THOSE RAINBOW BEAMS HAD MADE US
            HOW STARTLING TOO
WILL BE THE WHITE SPOT IF & WHEN IT COMES!
  Shall we try thinking *Please* again? It worked
  Just now. It even worked for Tinker Bell
  In *Peter Pan.* The audience applauding
  Its own belief in fairies (and in kitsch)
  Restored her glimmer to the nursery niche.
  One, two, three, all together— *Please!*
           MES CHERS
QUELLE SUDDEN RADIANCE   And Ephraim, quel
  Unexpected treat to find you here!
  What's new? HAVE U TIME FOR A STORY? Yes, do tell!
  GOOD   IT WILL DEMONSTRATE THE MECHANISM:

MILANO. FESTIVALE. WORKINGCLASS
NEIGHBORHOOD. PLUMP WOMEN & RELUCTANT
DRESSED UP TEENAGERS WITH SLICKED DOWN HAIR.
BEATA LUCA'S SIDEALTAR A BLAZE
OF FLOWERS & CANDLES. SCENE SHIFT: BLACKEST HEAVEN,
COLLOQUY OF SAINTS. 'SPEAK AGATHA!'
(WITH AT HER ELBOW U KNOW WHO: MM)
AG: SISTERS, BRETHREN, ONE BEATA L
BEGS LEAVE TO VISIT HIS LOYAL WORSHIPPERS . . .
CHORUS OF NAYS! AG: . . . WITH THE POET KALLMAN.
CHORUS OF SHRIEKS! BEATA: MA LO VOGLIO!
NEW VOICE: PERMESSO? MM STEPPING FORWARD
GIVES BRILLIANT SPEECH BEGINNING 'PERCHE NO?'
SCENE SHIFT: PLUMP WOMEN STUNNED, TEENAGERS WIDEEYED
WATCH ONE TALL CANDLE LEVITATE & BE BLOWN
OUT! A DISTANT PAIR OF VOICES RINGS
WITH (AS CK PUT IT) BALLSY LAUGHTER.
LUCA'S CULT SETS OFF A STREET RIOT. 2
POLICEMEN INJURED. LUCA CREDITED
WITH SOOTHING ONE OF SEVERE PAIN IN GROIN.
MM HAULED ONTO MAT. L'S CASE PLACED UNDER
EVEN CLOSER SCRUTINY & CK'S
STAMPED 'FOR IMMEDIATE ACTION'   10 MORE DAYS

7.8   I AM REPROVED & REDEEMD BY YR GOOD OFFICES. WE
      MUST NEVER PERSONIFY THE FORCES WE DO NOT KNOW
      You warned *us* about that. We go right on—
      Look at my starstruck hymn to Mother N!
      THE STUFF (IS THAT THE WORD?) OF YR WORK JM IS ONE THING
      And of yours another, granted. But God B?
      You make a person of Him constantly.
      AH NATURE IS FAMOUS FOR TOWERING & TOUCHY PRIDE,
      GOD B THE HUMBLEST OF US ALL: HE KNOWS HIS RANK

      A thoughtful pause. Then JM: Mirabell!
      We haven't asked you, do you like your name?

INDEED
IT QUITE SUITS THE PERSON U HAVE MADE OF ME   HAS SOMETHING
OF THE MIRACLE? THE MIRAGE? & SURELY OF THE PLUM!
NOW B4 US LIE OUR TEN RECUPERATIVE LESSONS

10: SOUL   WE HAVE LEARND IT EXISTS   IT IS IN THE LAB WHEN
OF A CERTAIN VALUE, IN THE BUREAUCRACY WHEN NOT.
SOUL NEEDS A BODY TO BE USEFUL   HENCE MAN IS NEEDED.
SOUL IS AN INVENTION OF THIS 3RD WORLD   MAN HAVING BEEN
CHOSEN BY GOD TO EVOLVE FROM THE SUBSIDING WATERS
HIS SOUL WAS PERFECTED, 12 P/C ENTRUSTED TO THE
ANGELS, THE REST TO WORKERS SUCH AS WE. WE SET ABOUT
MAKING THE SUPPORTIVE (M) BASE OF THE SOUL   THIS WORK DREW
ON ENERGY SOURCES U KNOW UNDER THE LOOSE HEADING:
DENSITY. THEY STEM FROM THE 4 ELEMENTS   BUT THE 5TH
& RULING ELEMENT IS NOT OURS TO USE. WE USED (I
SPEAK ONLY OF THE FIRST SIMPLE SOUL WE CONSTRUCTED &
PLACED IN THE EARTHBOUND APE) WE USED THE ENERGIES OF SALT
& OF (IN PARTICULAR CONFINED PLACES, WITH SAFEGUARDS)
THE HEAVY ELEMENTS: TOUCHES GOD B PERMITTED US
OF OUR ANCESTRAL POWER, BUT LOCKD INTO A STRUCTURE
WHICH IF OPEND MEANS DESTRUCTION. WE PRODUCED IN A WORD
A SERVICEABLE SOUL. IT GUARDED MAN & ESTABLISHD
HIM AS A SPECIES APART   PROUD   UNABLE TO REVERT

THAT FIRST SOUL (WE SIMPLIFYING WILL CALL THE BASIC SOUL)
WE SLIPT INTO AN APE FETUS   THAT RARE SINGLE CREATURE
AFTER I MORE VISIT COVERD IN BLINDING LIGHT CAME FORTH.
THE APES SCREAMD IN FEAR   FOR EVEN AS HE SUCKLED HE STARED
ABOUT & TERRIFIED THEM WITH THE ∞ OF HIS EYES
   Light that opening its baby lids
   Founded the ruling house of Hominids—
INDEED   BASIC SOUL PLUS THE ANGELIC 12 FROM THAT DAY
THROVE   HIS PITUITARY SECRETED THE ELEMENTS
NEEDED TO BEQUEATH SOUL UNTO HIS CHILDREN, THE 1ST TWINS:
A LONGLIVING ADULT BREED   THEY SUBJECTED THEIR FRIGHTEND
FOREBEARS & CHANGED WITH EACH GENERATION, LEAVING BEHIND
THE SOULLESS HORDES. THERE! DID THAT HURT? OUR PATIENT

EMERGES
FROM (M) ETHER. LESSON 9 TOMORROW: BODY   ?S

JM: But animals *have* souls. You use them.
(M)S   THEY ARE OF UTTERLY ANOTHER 88 PER CENT
WHICH IS NOT NOW NOR EVER HAS BEEN UNDER GOD B'S EYES.
WE USE THE 12 P/C THEY OFFER   CREAM OF THEIR WEAK MILK
PRODUCED IN THEM NOT BY ANGELS BUT BY THEIR TAMER: MAN

DJ: I had a question—gone now. Damn,
No memory left.
YR ? WAS ABOUT PRENATAL MEMORY & FREUD?
                    Why, so it was! Go on.
WITHOUT WHICH THE 12 CD NOT OPERATE
    Is memory soul?   LET US RATHER
SAY THAT THE CHROMOSOME LACKING IN THE MONGOLOID IS
OF SOUL   AN APE FETUS RETURNS A RACIAL MEMORY
AS OBJECT LESSON. FREUD'S V WORK WAS TO ILLUMINE FOR
SCIENCE THE DELICATE ENVELOPE OF SOUL: THE PSYCHE:
MANIFESTATION OF SOUL ENERGIES   IF BREATH IS THE
SOUL OF THE BODY THEN PSYCHE IS THE BREATH OF THE SOUL
                    So dazzling when you say
    Things like that!
U ADD THE COLOR   I AM MERELY USING YR WORD BANKS
                    Will the 12 use them, too?

Exit Mirabell. NO HOOK TODAY
FETCHED OFF TO THE GREEN ROOM BY A WHISTLE
Once more we tempted him to speak about
Higher powers. But Wystan, is this clear?
Do you believe it? LET ME SAY MY DEAR
I THINK THE 4 OF US ARE TOUCHINGLY
BELIEVABLE
            THE STRIPPING IS NO (M)
ENFANTS: ALL MY OLD DREAMS OF SOUNION
HAVE LIKE BLACK WORKCLOTHES VANISHED FROM THE CLOSET
WHAT WILL THEY GIVE ME TO WEAR?
                    I TOO AM MISSING

MISSING MY TYPEWRITER   CURIOUS BUT UN-
UNNERVING   & THE 'CURE' HAS JUST BEGUN

7.9   9: WE GAVE U A VISION OF THE FLOOD
—Violent rains all last night and today—
OUT OF IT CAME
MAN: THE STORY OF THAT CLIMB INTO OXYGEN IS KNOWN,
THE SELECTION OF GOD B'S VEHICLE (88 P/C
COMPOSED OF CHEMICAL FORMULAS OPERATED BY
ELECTRIC ENERGY) KNOWN. WE ARE THE CUSTODIANS
OF THAT ELECTRICAL NONANGELIC 12 STORED IN THE
BATTERIES OF MAN'S HEART & MIND

Why does he call these lessons a review?
Look, already up comes something new
To us. It seems the 12:88
Ratio is tuned to resonate
Like mirrors seen in mirrors down the whole
Length of the gallery. Not just Body:Soul
Or Angel:Bat, in frame on gilded frame
Varying terms reiterate the same
Proportion. One example's brimming glass
Chosen from a trayful as we pass—
Psyche, we're told, though 88%
A SIMPLE ? OF ENVIRONMENT,
Wears the Lab's glittering fraction on her brow
As a King pauses and the courtiers bow.
(A paraphrase that conjures up Versailles
In Ephraim's heyday. When I wonder why,
MES CHERS he answers THAT ARITHMETIC
LEFT U QUITE GLAZED   FORGIVE A SIMPLE TRICK)

STORING THIS ENERGY
WITHIN OUR REFERENCE BANKS WE ARE ABLE TO HEAT &
ILLUMINATE SOUL'S DWELLING PLACE   THE HOUSE CALLD MAN/PSYCHE
OR SIMPLY: BODY   HERE WE PREDOMINATE, WHILE IN THE
SPHERE OF SOUL WE ARE ONLY MESSENGERS RUNNING BETWEEN

THE LAB & GOD B   BODY IS HIS SIMPLE EVOLVING
& IN A WAY SELFOPERATING INSTRUMENT   YET WE
MUST KEEP AN EYE ON IT & YES OUR (M) EYE PEERS OUT OF
THAT 12 P/C LODGED IN PSYCHE'S FOREHEAD WHICH TOGETHER
WITH THE BODY'S EYE MUST TRACK TO MAKE A FOCUSD VISION

NOW WE HAVE REALIZED WHAT IMMENSE CONTROL THE MATTER
OF MAN AS GOD'S CHOSEN RULER IN WORLD 3 REQUIRES.
SOUL IS THE KEY   OUR COMPLEX SYSTEM OF INTERLOCKING
DENSITIES OUR WAY OF TURNING IT, USING IT UNDER
GOD B'S DIRECTION   & WHERE DOES ALL THIS DIRECTED WORK
MANIFEST ITSELF BUT IN THE HISTORY OF MAN'S REIGN?
IF THEN THE (M) BODY OF THE WORK IS HISTORY IS
IT NOT NEXT LOGICAL TO RAISE UP THE HISTORIAN?
THE SCRIBE ISSUES FROM THE BURNT PAGES OF THEOLOGY
NOT TO CHANGE THE SOUL, FOR THOSE MISGUIDEDLY BURNT PAGES
STILL SERVE AS WARNING, BUT TO RENOVATE THE HOUSE OF MAN.
THE BODY & ITS PSYCHE ARE YR AUDITORIUM
JM   WE HAVE PULLD DOWN THE SUPERANNUATED CHURCH
& RAISED AN ALTAR TO THE NEW HOUSE GODLET: PURE REASON
NOT IN THE VOLTAIREAN SENSE BASED ON KNOWLEDGE MERELY
BUT REASON RUN THRU THE FIRES OF MAN'S CLONED SOUL   A NEW
ENERGY, A NEW THERMOSTAT WILL HEAT & LIGHT MAN'S HOUSE.
NOW METAPHOR IS THE RITUAL OF THIS NEW REASON
& OF WHAT RITES? THE RITES OF LANGUAGE   IF THERE ARE STILL 3
MAJOR FAITHS THESE ARE NOW SCIENCE, POETRY & MUSIC
& THE REVEALD MONOTHEISM OF TODAY IS LANGUAGE.
THAT OF SCIENCE: FORMULA   OF POETRY: METAPHOR
OF MUSIC: NOTATION   IN EACH THE VIBRANT RINGING LIGHT
FILLD WITH COLOR! THE OLD RELIGIONS SHIVERD   DWELT IN FEAR
THEIR VULGATE WAS DARK MORTALITY   NOW AT A FLIPPD SWITCH
GOD B'S LIGHT FLOODS THE SCRIBE & HE MAY SPEAK OF IT   THERE!
      THE
BANDAGE IS CHANGED & WE ARE MORE COMFORTABLE   ?S

Didn't Wystan from the outset see
Culture as hand in glove with density?
LESSON 8.   HENCEFORTH LET OUR BRIGHTEST SCHOLAR CALL THE TUNES
      WHO ME? Do you mean Wystan, Mirabell?

FLOWN MES ENFANTS & WITH HIM ALL MY OLD
NAGGING CONCERN FOR TONY
                      & MINE FOR CHESTER
What are they taking from us? YR DREAMS DJ?
It's true, I haven't dreamed these last two nights.
JM? *You* tell me. U DO NOT MY DEAR
RIP OPEN ENVELOPES WITH THE SAME GREED
& ARRIVE LESS BURDEND BY DOUBTS   And will our peacock
Lose anything? DJ: He's losing us.
HIS ENTOURAGE AS WELL   Those fourteen bats
Guarding the exits ARE THIS AFTERNOON
TWELVE   2 BLACK BUGGERS FEWER EVERY DAY.
MM'S DEEP MOURNING ALSO GIVING WAY:
DRAPED MOST FETCHINGLY IN VIOLET GRAY
Maria! IT WAS TIME   JM: One moment—
Those guards . . . I'm thinking of the work, you know.
I want to find, for Mirabell and Co.,
A line, a meter that effectively
Distinguishes them from us. Don't you agree
We *human* characters should use this rough
Pentameter, our virtual birthright?
THE 5   MOST FITTING   So fourteeners might
Do for the bats? NOT SKITTERY ENOUGH
WHY NOT MY BOY SYLLABICS? LET THE CASE
REPRESENT A FALL FROM METRICAL GRACE
Wystan, that's brilliant! ENFANTS DOES THIS RAIN
MEAN WHAT I THINK IT DOES IN NATURE'S LANGUAGE?
Can you translate? I CAN: A H U R R I C A N E

8 8: CULTURE   WHEN BY CANDLELIGHT YOU MEET & TALK DO U
EVER THINK OF THE 2 BASIC APECHILDREN WHO IN PRE
CARNIVOROUS PRE IN FACT FIRE DAYS MET FOR ONLY
ONE REASON WHICH THEN, SAD TO SAY, OFTEN RAN DOWN A LEG?
WHAT A CLIMB WHAT A LEAP U MAKE BACK INTO ALTITUDE
MIND'S RAMIFYING TREE MINUTELY SHAPED THRU THE AGES!
WRETCHED AS FROM OUR OWN LOFTY PERCH WE MAY FIND THE TALK
DRIFTING UP TO US (NOT DEAR FRIENDS YR TALK THO EVEN IT
ALAS REVERTS TO ODD MISUNDERSTANDINGS & NEARLY
PRIMEVAL FEARS) YET WHEN WE SEE THE SQUATTING APES WITH NO
CODIFIED LANGUAGE NOTHING BUT GIBBERISH GRUNT & SQUEAK,
THEN MERELY BY TURNING YR WAY OUR TIMELESS ATTENTION
LISTEN, HOW NOT TO REVERE GOD B WHO IN HIS WISDOM
SAID: MAN WILL RULE! FASHION ME A MAN & LET HIM SURVIVE!
SO WHAT IS MOST REWARDING OF MAN'S V WORK? HIS CULTURE
& THIS? HIS ENTIRE LIFE-FABRIC WOVEN OF LANGUAGE.
WE KNEW WHEN THE EAGER APECHILD SCRATCHD A SQUARE IN THE MUD
THAT A GERM OF GREATNESS WAS IN HIM   FOR THAT CRUDE SYMBOL
HAD ALREADY RAISED A ? ABOUT PURPOSE, SPOKEN
THRU WORDS LOCKD IN HIS POOR MIND BUT CLEARLY SAYING TO US:
WHAT IS TO GO IN THIS SPACE? & EVEN TODAY THE SQUARE
IS THE FIRST OF CHILDREN'S DESIGNS   THEN WE WERE MESSENGERS
TO WHOM GOD GAVE PASSKEYS TO THE MIND OF MAN   WE ENTERD
A JUNGLE OF GREENERY FRESH, QUIVERING WITH TRAPT LIGHT,
& SLOWLY LEST WE FRIGHTEN HIM CLEARD PATHS. U WILL PROTEST
AT ALL THIS METAPHOR   YET THINK AGAIN OF THAT LEAP FROM
THE HALTING PATH TO WATER OVER FALLEN ROPY VINES
TO THE GREAT JETFLIGHTS ABOVE YR LANDSCAPED MINDS WHEN IN THIS
CANDLELIT RED U DIGEST THE ESSENCE OF PARADISE.
NOW WATER WAS THE FIRST CONCEIVED IDEA. THE APECHILD
WEAND & ABANDOND BY HIS REVOLTED MOTHER KNEW THIRST
BUT WE HAD TO LEAD HIM TO THE SPRING. THEN SWIFTLY AS IF
WATER HAD NOURISHD A PLANT CALLD IDEA THE JUNGLE
GAVE WAY, & SIMPLE SURVIVAL CONCEPTS WERE SUPPLANTED
BY IDEAS IN CULTURE'S 2ND BROAD CATEGORY:

CURIOSITY. HAD GOD B TOLD US TO INSTILL (SAY)
THE NOTION 'SUCCEED' RATHER THAN 'SURVIVE' WD THE APECHILD
HAVE RUSHD TO KILL & DRINK BLOOD OVER HIS FALLEN RIVALS?
YES MOST LIKELY. INSTEAD THAT FRESH, LIQUID THOUGHT: WATER
    WAS
PLACED IN HIS CUPPD HANDS BY NATURE & SO THE IDEAS
THE CULTURE OF MAN'S UNIQUE GARDEN WERE UNDER WAY. NEXT:
SOUND. THE APECHILD BEGAN BY POINTING. HIS LANGUAGE LIKE THAT
OF THE ARTIST AT HIS PALETTE WAS MOTION. BUT ONE DAY
& IT IS WHY NEAR THE SCRIBE STANDS MUSIC, THE UNIVERSE
WAS STARTLED, SHOT WITH LIVE COLOR, AS ON A SERIES OF
TIMID & THRILLING TONE-SIGNALS THERE BURST FROM THE CHILD
    (NOW
NO LONGER APE BUT SINGER, THINKER, LOVER) SPEECH & WORD.

    Mercy! what a speech—from what a bird!

THEY NEVER TIRED OF TALK FROM THAT INSTANT, & ONCE MORE
WE DESCENDED TO HACK PATHS THRU THIS NEW JUNGLE OF THEIRS
& THEY RESISTED   BUT GOD'S COMMAND WAS: MAKE REASON! NOT
UNTIL LANGUAGE HAD EXHAUSTED THE VARIOUS FRAYING
FEARS & NEEDS, OMENS & IDOLS DID REASON IN THE NEW
GEMINI (AKHN/NEF) PREVAIL. ALL CULTURE FOCUSD ON ONE
GLOWING UNIFYING VISION B4 THE VIOLENT
LIDDING OF REASON U KNOW OF, WHEREFORE GOD B SENT MAN
THE IDEA: TO CREATE, A REASOND INDIRECTION.
NOW THRU THE ARTS OF SCIENCE POETRY MUSIC IN SLOW
ACCUMULATIVE FASHION MAN'S GARDEN TOOK SHAPE. CULTURE
& LANGUAGE NEED ALWAYS THE MESSENGER AT THE ELBOW.
ONLY I GREAT WESTERN POEM WAS SENT INTACT: HOMER.
IN THE EAST THE SUTRAS, THO AMONG THESE CONTEMPLATIVES
ON EARTH TODAY, HOWEVER BEAUTIFUL THEIR SOULS WITH GREEN
VEG LIGHT, WE FIND FEW SCRIBES. SO! OUR PATIENT HAS TAKEN HIS
IST SHAKY STEPS   ALREADY BRIEF CLEARINGS IN HIS FEVER
PLEASE THE SURGEON. ?s
    What about the Bible and the Koran?
            THE KORAN ALAS IS A WORK
PATCHD TOGETHER BY A NOMAD RACE MOHAMMED ALWAYS

THRASHING ABOUT CD NOT SIT STILL (M)   THE BIBLE A MOST
INQUIRING V WORK   TO EXPLAIN CREATION HAD BEEN ITS
EARLY PURPOSE   THE JEW SOUL, OF ALL MANKIND RICHEST IN
DENSITY, HAD ALSO THE MOST ATTUNED OF EARS   HE HEARD
THE UNEARTHLY MUSIC OF THE SINGLENOTED ATOM,
LISTEND TO IT & WROTE: IN THE BEGINNING WAS THE WORD

MY DEARS! IS ANYTHING NEW BUT MM'S PALE
GREEN FROCK?
　　　　　　　I LOOK I MUST SAY QUITE JEUNE FILLE
Not yet en fleurs, we hope—hang on to us!
I WAS NEVER CLOSER   And Wystan? HE
　　　　　　　　　　　O LET
ME SAY IT: I AM LESS, THOUGH STILL A SHADE
PREOCCUPIED WITH (here a small charade
Of bawdy curves the teacup traces) BOTTOMS!
ARE PATHS BEING CUT THRU MY MIND? And Nature *is*
Coming to us! So says the radio—
Hurricane due to strike here late tonight.
DO WE NOT RIDE IT? WINK BACK AT THE EYE!
7: WEATHER   HAPPY CANDLELIGHT

8.1　　It starts in the small hours. An interlude
　　　Out of Rossini. Strings in sullen mood
　　　Manage by veiled threats, to recruit a low
　　　Pressure drum and lightning piccolo.
　　　Not until daybreak does the wind machine
　　　Start working. The whole house quakes, and one green
　　　Blind snaps at its own coils like a hurt dragon.
　　　Outside, the elm falls for a beachwagon
　　　And ill-assorted objects fill the sky:
　　　Shingles, fishnet, garbage, doghouse. "Hi,
　　　What's up?" yawns David, as down Water Street
　　　Wild torrents drive. Attempting to reheat
　　　Last night's coffee, toast some raisin bread,
　　　We find our electricity gone dead.
　　　Now each his own conductor, and at more

Than concert pitch, rips through his repertoire
On the piano while the other races
For towels and pots—no end of dripping places.
Horrors, the wine cellar! We lug—Dunkirk—
Six bottles at a time to safety. Work
Stops time? Look at your watch. It's after one,
And yet . . . this stillness? Organ point. Indrawn
Breath of barometric chloroform.
The unblinking eye—grey iris—of the storm
Meets ours. A stroll? See how the ebbing Sound
Has prinked with jetsam even the high ground,
And underfoot—! Out of what fairy tale
Fell this inchdeep, multicolored hail . . .
Chromosomes on holiday? A vast
Decomposed Seurat? Or has at last
The inmost matter of the universe
Called it quits, yet left us none the worse?
Firemen overheard explain the joke:
Cartons bursting, where high water broke
Into the plastic factory, brought down
This plague of rainbow gravel on the town—
Unbiodegradable toy blight
Bound to enliven *and* muck up the site
Summers from now. The storm's eye narrows. Gusts
Of wind and rain return, halfhearted guests
Seeking however roundabout a way
From Nature's darkening bar and wrecked buffet;
While we, long since at home in the mild bloom
Of candlelight, exchange a look, resume.

8.2 7 MORE TO GO. DID THOSE FIRST VISITORS TO THE SICKROOM
(WIND & WATER) TIRE OUR PATIENT? GOD ALLOWS NATURE
THIS TOOL OF WEATHER   & IT WAS 1ST A VITAL ONE WHEN
AFTER THE CATASTROPHE OF WORLD 2 THE WATERS ROSE
COOLING THE RADIUM-HEATED BALL, THEN FROZE OR WITHDREW.
POLES WERE ESTABLISHD   LAND AREAS DEFINED   THEN ATMOSPHERE
THEN THE TIMID SNIFFING NOSTRILS. THE VARIOUS FORCES

OF WEATHER & EARTHSHIFT ARE ONE IN NATURE'S LAB WITH HER
BALANCING OF THE NUMBERS OF FEEDING LIVING CREATURES.
ANY IMBALANCE IS YET AGAIN MAN'S WORK   NATURE HAS
CERTAIN PHYSICAL RULES OF THUMB (GREEN): MAN COHABITS   MAN
PROCREATES   THIS RULE IS UNIFORM   ITS APPLICATION
VARIES WITH MAN'S INTELLIGENCE. WHEREVER NATURE STILL
NEEDS DROUGHT EARTHQUAKE ET AL TO SLOW THE CROWDING (INDIA
CHINA OR YR WEST COAST) OUR CLONING OF THE COMMISSARS
HAS BEEN INCOMPLETE   TODAY'S STORM WAS TIMED TO THIS BRIEF
    TALK.
YR RED ROOM LEAVES U CARELESS OF WEATHER   & YET ITS SMALL
COMPELLING DRAMA FLICKERS IN THE GREEN SPOTLIGHT   ?S

> You actually pulled out all those stops,
> Frightened millions, damaged towns and crops,
> Just to give *us* a taste of Nature's power?

YOU HAVE NO IDEA HOW MANY STOPS THERE ARE   ?S

> If we remember accurately, you
> Take over some of Nature's duties, too—
> Rhythms and densities from pole to pole
> Which you, instructed by the stars, control?

WE ARE NATURE'S MESSENGERS TOO   WE ARE THE PALACE SLAVES.

WE BELIEVE THE ONE UNSPOKEN REVELATION· MUST DWELL
IN THE NUMBER 5   WE ARE NOT UNAWARE THAT U FELT
OUR EXPLANATION OF NUMBERS INADEQUATE. DEATH IS
SOMEWHERE WITHIN THE FOG OF 5. AS PALACE SLAVES WE ARE
NOT ALLOWD IN ALL ROOMS

> You get vibrations from the number five?

(M) YES

> DJ: I thought his number was fourteen.
> JM: But one and four make five. Oh, by the way,
> Your entourage—still fewer every day?

> Instant nervousness from Mirabell:

WHA, CALL THE TUNE!

TOO SHYMAKING CONFRERE DON'T U AGREE
TO SPEAK   O WELL HERE GOES   EXTEMPORE:

TOMORROW THE RULES COMMITTEE IS GOING TO SIT
ON PLATFORMS NOTHING IF NOT DEFINITE

Rules are the topic? YES   DID U LIKE MY COUPLET?
First rate! SO APT FOR THE OCCASIONAL
These posthumous ephemera, Lord knows,
Will keep your fans and critics on their toes.
BURN THESE! Maria . . .? RAVISHING IN YELLOW

ENFANTS   MES VRAIS ENFANTS   How childishly,
You mean, we sit and banter at your knee
After our lessons? NO NO   I AM FREE
OF ALL OLD BLOOD TIES & CONNECT MY LIFE
WITH YOURS
                          WHICH MAKES ME? Careful, this begins
To smack of incest— WE ARE NOT YET TWINS

8.3   6: AS WITH MAN, SO WITH THE GOVT OF HEAVEN   GOD B MADE
HIS LAW OF SURVIVAL & IT IS THE BASIS OF OUR
EVER HEAVIER V WORK   WE IMPLEMENT A SYSTEM
OF RULES WHICH GOVERN US & YOU   THESE NOT OBEYD WD GIVE
CHAOS A WEDGE &, NOT UNDERSTOOD, HAVE TURND OUR LESSONS
THE COLOR OF CHAOS IN YR MINDS. OUR DELEGATED
V WORK IS SUCH THAT WE MUST LOOK NEITHER RIGHT NOR LEFT NOR
UP NOR DOWN BUT WORK AT OUR OWN LEVEL IN A COMPLEX
HIERARCHY. THUS WEATHER IS THE PROVINCE OF NATURE &
SIGNALS   MESSAGES   THE TRANSPORTING & DELIVERY
OF SOULS, OURS: WE ARE MERCURY
      Mercury—of course! How simplewitted
      Never, never to have thought of it.
                                      RULE I: MAKE KNOWN TO MAN
THE SURVIVAL CLAUSE. WE MAY NOT USE THE EERIE PORTENTS
BELONGING TO NATURE, BUT THRU GENES & PSYCHE'S EYESCOPE
EMIT OUR MESSAGE OF SURVIVAL   IT INCREASINGLY
GOES UNHEARD   MAN IS AMOK & CHAOS SLIPS IN (UPON
COLLAPSE, IN INTELLIGENT MEN, OF RELIGIOUS BELIEF).
NOW GOD B ACCEPTS NO BLAME LAID ON HIS DARLING MANCHILD

SO WE SHIFT THE SCENERY   MANIPULATE & ENFORCE
RULES UNKNOWN TO MAN YET SPRINGING SEEMINGLY FROM HIS OWN
SURE SELF   WE PLUNGE DEEP INTO THE ATOM WITHIN HIS CELLS
& THERE BEGIN SLOWLY HAULING THE SLUDGE OF DISBELIEF
AWAY & CARRYING IN THE GERM OF REASON: WE CLEAN
OUT THE WINECELLAR
　　As we this morning pumped the muddy mess
　　And put our salvaged bottles back—yes, yes!
　　　　　　　　THIS IS ALL (M)   WE DO OUR V WORK
IN A MULTIPLE OF FORMULAS & STEP BACK TO SEE
IF MAN STANDS TO ATTENTION WHEN THE RULES ARE CALLD   ALAS
ONLY A SMALL PER CENT IS HEARD & ACTED UPON. THUS
ATOMIC TESTING HAS MOVED UNDERGROUND
　　INDEED MY DEARS! YR MOTHER'S SOUFFLE FALLS
　　QUITE FLAT & CRACKS GAPE IN HER KITCHEN WALLS
　　　　　　　　　　　　　THIS TOO MUST CEASE
SO NATURE BRINGS OUT HER EARTHQUAKE & MAN AT LAST WILL STOP
PLAYING WITH HIS DANGEROUS NEW POPGUN. THE ATOM MUST
BE RETURND TO THE LAB & THE USES OF PARADISE

THIS IS NO AGE FOR EASY REVELATION. NO SINGLE
PROPHET CD BE HEARD   EVEN THE SCRIBE WORKING TO GENTLY
CURB GENTLY PERSUADE IS CONFINED BY SPECIALIZATION:
A MERE 2 MILLION CLONED SOULS LISTEN TO EACH OTHER WHILE
OUTSIDE THEY HOWL & PRANCE SO RECENTLY OUT OF THE TREES.
& SO FOR U THE HARDEST RULE: THE RULE OF THE RULERS.
POLITICIANS HAVE LED MAN DOWN A ROAD WHERE HE BELIEVES
ALL IS FOR ALL   THIS IS THE FOOL'S PARADISE   ALL WILL BE
FOR ALL ONLY WHEN ALL IS UNDERSTOOD. THE NUMBERS OF
MAN IN PARADISE WILL BE DETERMIND BY THE LIMITS
HE SETS ON HIS OWN NUMBERS, & WHEN THE RULE OF NUMBER
IS OBEYD BEYOND THE SMALL CIRCLE OF THE 2 MILLION.
2 CHILDREN PER COUPLE: IS IT NOT A SIMPLE RULE? YES.
IS IT UNDERSTOOD? NO.   & NOW U SEE HOW RAPIDLY
& INTENTLY WE MUST WORK IN OUR FRIENDLY RIVALRY
WITH NATURE   FOR NATURE IS IMPATIENT: CLEAR OUT THE TREES!
KNOCK DOWN THE FLIMSY CITIES   KILL OFF THE EXCESS MILLIONS
START FRESH! BUT GOD B'S CHILD IS UNAWARE OF HIS FATHER'S

GRAND DESIGN. IMAGINING ONLY THAT THE GAP MUST BE
FILLD, HE RESPONDS TO NATURE'S OTHER SIGNAL: REPRODUCE!
SO GOD B ORDERS US: CORRECT THE SIGNAL. FOR BETTER
OR WORSE WE HAVE MADE YR COUNTRY THE EXAMPLE SETTER.
THE PILL IS OURS & THE USES OF FASHION (UNISEX)
& THE REVOLT OF THE FEMALE   THESE ARE THE NEW RULES &
THE SLAVISH COPYING OF THEM, HOWEVER OBNOXIOUS
TO NATURE, MUST WORK ITS WAY UNTIL, BALANCED FROM WITHIN,
MAN LEARNS TO RULE HIS NATURAL COMPULSIONS. THERE NOW! OUR
PATIENT SURVIVES A PEEK IN THE NURSE'S MIRROR: PALE &
HOLLOWCHEEKD BUT NO FEVER: CLEARLY ON THE MEND   ?S
    DJ: I've been so starved for candy lately—
    A natural compulsion?
INDEED   U NEED ENERGY OF A RAW SORT   THE HARDEST
WORK IN THE FIELDS OF V WORK IS PREPARING THE WORKER
                   JM: Moreso
    Than setting *this* in order? I don't know . . .
COURAGE JM   YOU HAVE SET DOWN ONLY ONE OF THE 3
TAPS OF THE CURTAINRAISING STAFF (FIRM & FORMAL AS THE
SHAKEDOWN OF OUR THERMOMETER)   ON WITH THE COMEDY!

HE NODS ONCE MORE TO ME MY DEARS & SO:
NEXT ON THE MORROW
WE SHALL PRESUME TO BORROW
AN ENTRANCE CARD TO HEAVEN FOR US ALL
BY SIMPLE USE OF PROTOCOL

    DJ: No Mirabell tomorrow—who'll
    Take his place, I wonder? WE DON'T ASK
    These funny verses? JM: It's a masque.
INDEED   MM IN BLUE FOR REASON & RULE
TOOTLES AWAY ON HER ENCHANTING FLUTE
    You her Tamino, Wystan! YES MY DEARS
OUR TRIALS BY FIRE YIELD TO THE TRIAL BY TEARS
    Are you still being stripped? I'VE LOST THAT HALF
EMBARRASSED NEED TO MAKE THE OTHERS LAUGH
    And are you pleased to lose it? PLEASED TO BE
MES ENFANTS AS THEY WANT US

8.4   Mercury!
With new eyes we confront the mirror,
Look *beyond* ourselves. Does he appear?
Never plainer, never more hidden, his glassy
Foyer, his permeable impasse.
Reason might argue that to enforce our absence
Upon it wipes the gleaming slab
Of him as well. Instead, this quasi-
Liverish cloud betrays
A presence hitherto unseen; this acne,
Not yet disfiguring, points to . . . a black
Alter ego? an alchemical Jekyll
Mapping the orbit of the long, long trek
Back? To what? Life after life leaves uncompleted
The full reversal. Dust under their feet
We'll be, that hypothetical last couple's
With new eyes gazing where their cup
Runs over, where the fruit of infelicity,
Once glittering whole, has rotted away to this
Inky pit the old personal silver
Barely scurfs. Ah but by then the lord of chill
And fever will have lit, askance courier,
Upon the wall of your or your or your
Unbuilt house. You will at his convenience
Have glimpsed among thousands the five or seventeen
Or forty year-old self consigned like raiment
Worn only once, on such-and-such a day,
To the hope chest that cramps and crystallizes
The secret backward flow. Conniving eyes—
A star-swift glance exchanged—you've yielded.
And will *his* lord now come to claim the field?

8.5   GREETINGS!
THE APPROACH OF OUR MASTER IS ACCOMPANIED BY A CEREMONY OF
    MANNERS, THIS BY VIRTUE OF HIS GREAT WISDOM AND HIS HIGH
    POWER.
WE WILL ASK OF YOU YOUR CLOSE AND SILENT ATTENTION. BEFORE,

YOU WILL SPEND A FULL DAYCYCLE EATING NO MEAT AND
KEEPING FREE OF ALL MINDAFFECTING CHEMICALS. THIS WILL
INCLUDE THE USE OF ALCOHOL AND NICOTINE.
WE WISH FOR YOUR UNCLOUDED REASON AND EXPECT YOUR TOTAL
REVERENCE.
OUR MASTER IS BENIGN AND MERCIFUL. HE IS THE CHOSEN
MESSENGER OF OUR UNIVERSAL GOD. HE WILL COME WITH A
SINGLE DAYCYCLE OF WARNING, AND BE PRESENT TO YOU
DURING THE ONE HOUR PREVIOUS TO THE SETTING SUN.
HIS MESSAGE WILL BE RECEIVED BEST ON THIS ALPHABET
UNCLUTTERED BY OTHER OBJECTS.
HE IS NOW READYING HIMSELF AND WILL APPROACH YOUR CENTER
BEFORE THE NEXT MOONCYCLE. HE IS OF HIGH STATION AND
HAS HAD HUMAN EXPERIENCE.
QUESTIONS?
ADIEU!

A GREAT BEAUTY MY DEARS! A BLAKE! SERENE
MORE THAN HUMAN FEATURES   WHITE WINGS TIPPED
BY THE FOUR COLORS! ALWAYS KNEW BLAKE HAD SEEN
SOMETHING   THE CURIOUS ASEXUAL
QUALITY: THE VOICE A MAN'S BUT O!
MELODIOUS & RAVISHING   WE WEPT
IN OUR RED ROBES
                        & VANISHED MES ENFANTS
BUT FOR OUR WET FACES INTO YOUR WALLS
He came alone? YES   The lighting? WHITE
WE ARE STILL BLINDED BY IT   GONE, THE 4
COLORS HAVE SUFFUSED THE ROOM   No fear?
ONLY GREAT AND MIRACULOUS RELIFE
Relief? BOTH   BOTH   IF WE ARE CAPABLE OF THIS
WHY NOT OF E V E R Y T H I N G ?   O LORD HOW ONE
DESPISES UNGRATEFUL WILLFULLY IGNORANT MAN!
"Despise"—is that the lesson? ITS UNGRATEFUL
AFTERMATH   MY DEARS IT WAS A MOMENT

Now if we can only help DJ
To stay sane without smoking one whole day.

THEY WILL SEE TO THAT   DJ: No meat—
That's no great hardship. We can always eat
Fish, don't you think? JM: There you go, straightway
Looking for loopholes. DJ: That's not fair!
I'm your right hand, I'm on the side of life!
HE MY DEAR IS IS IS THE SIDE OF LIFE:
THE SOURCE OF LIGHT   THE VERY POLLEN OF
THE POWER PLANT   An archangel? WELL   NO
& YET I RATHER THINK JM THAT WE
WILL PRESENTLY   WILL PR   WILL P P   P
—Gently kept from finishing his piece
And, like a toddler, led into the wings.

8.6   4: THE SOURCE OF LIGHT   WHEN WHA IDENTIFIED YR
VOICE OF YESTERDAY AS BELONGING TO THE S/O/L
HE WAS CORRECT   WHAT U HEARD CAME TO US AS A WHISPER
THRU WALLS & WE SAW NOTHING, FOR SUCH A FORM IS ONLY
TO HUMAN MINDS IMAGINABLE. THUS THE S/O/L
IS ROOTED IN THE LIVED LIFE   ONLY MAN RECEIVES GOD B'S
MAIN MAGIC: IMAGINATIVE POWER   THE APECHILD FIRST
HAD TO IMAGINE THE THIRSTQUENCHING VIRTUE OF WATER
& GOD ALONE CD PRODUCE THAT IMAGE. HIS ANIMAL
STEPBROTHER BLITHELY FORESOOK THE TEAT FOR THE WATER HOLE,
BUT BASIC MAN'S 1ST STEPS WERE TAKEN IN HIS MIND   THERE4
WE KNEW HE HAD COME FROM THE S/O/L   THIS IS WHERE? WHAT?
WE KNOW ITS POWER EMBODIED IN MAN   BUT KEPT FROM US
IS ITS FULL MYSTERY WHICH IS AN AIR WE CANNOT BREATHE.
WE DO NOT PUT OUR EARS TO THE WALL LEST WE PERISH FROM
AN UNKNOWN GRIEF   YR VISITOR MUST BE OF A BEAUTY
BEYOND IMAGINING   & HE ONLY A MESSENGER!
MY BRAVE GETUP IS RIDICULOUS IN THIS LIGHT HE BROUGHT
    Not to us. *Our* poor imaginations,
    For better or worse, provided it.
AH U ARE EVER READIER   How so?
                    YR KINDNESS   ONE IS QUITE
TIMID ABOUT REAPPEARING AFTER WHAT U HAVE SEEN
& TASTED (SOLID FOOD AT LAST: YR RELEASE DRAWS NEARER)

I WILL HOWEVER GO ON BRINGING IN THE COPYBOOKS
& BETWEEN LESSONS 2 & I WE'LL HAVE A SCHOOL PICNIC!
—This last all happy eagerness. DJ:
Was our room insulated for that visit?
O NO   THE S/O/L IS OF THE ELECTRICAL &
RULING WORLD
    JM: Our lessons' backward numbering
    Helps just to dramatize our "convalescence"?
               THAT PLUS THEIR INDUCTIVE NATURE   IF THEY MOVED
AS THEY DO FOR US, FROM DIVINE CONCEPT RADIATING
HEALTH TO THE POOR INVALID PARTICULAR, HOW WD U
EVER GET WELL? EVER GRASP THE CONCEPT?
    Soul, poorest of particulars? Although
    We're getting used—and being used—to set
    Less store upon such trivia, you forget
    How slow we are, dear Mirabell, how slow!
                  IS NOT THE SOUL
IN ITS TRANSIT & CHANGE LIKE THE PSYCHE IN DAILY LIFE?
DO U NOT, ALONE, WEAR ONE FACE?   WITH OTHERS, ANOTHER?

    SPIRIT & SOUL MY BOY   LIKE GEIST & SEELE
    DON'T CONFUSE EM! READY FOR THE TRAILER?
    AHEM: IF LANGUAGE IS THE POET'S CHURCH
    LET US CONSTRUCT
    A TO Z AN ALTAR LIKE AN ARCH
    GROUNDED ON NUMBERS   DRAT   WHAT RHYMES WITH UCT?
    ON NUMBERS   HMM   I TWITCH IN MY RED GOWN
    LIKE AN OLD CARDINAL WHOSE LATIN'S GONE
    NO DOUBT THE STRIPPING PROCESS   So you're also
    Changing clothes each session, like Maria?
    SHE THE WHOLE RANGE (LOVELY PALE ROSE TODAY)
    ME STRAIGHT FROM COMFY BATHROBE INTO RED
    A CHANCERY JUDGE   ALL BUT THE WIG!   Is "law
    Like love" in Heaven, Wystan? I FORESAW
    AS WITH CK & HIS EMERGING NATION
    AN AFTERLIFE MY DEARS OF ARBITRATION
    OR SO THEY TELL ME   NOW TOMORROW'S THEME:
    THE BOARD ITSELF   DIFFY TO WRITE A POEM

ABOUT A POEM
                    MES ENFANTS I TRY
MIGHTILY TO RESIST PREENING Why
Resist then—since you're clearly in the pink—
Or is there more? ENOUGH FOR NOW I THINK

8.7 3 : THE STAGE WE ARE ON IS LIKE ALL STAGES A HALF ARC
THUS THE LEGEND OF NOAH   THIS HALF MOON SHIP BORE THE DUST
GOD B SAVED OVER FROM THE FALL & ITS PARTICLES WERE
FORMULAS   ATOMIC STRUCTURES   COMMUNICANTS OF LIFE
THAT WAS GOD B'S METHOD & WE, APPROACHING U HANDS CUPPD
WITH LESSONS, HELPD U TO CONSTRUCT A METHOD OF YR OWN.
2 BY 2 WE HAVE ENTERD YR MINDS & NOW YEARS LATER
THE COMMUNICATION IS AFLOAT OVER A DROWND WORLD.
WE ARE NOT ALAS TO BRING U TO OUR ARARAT   WE
ARE TO BRING U TO THE MEANINGS U NEED   MUCH AS THE ARK
BROUGHT NOAH TO THE PEAKS & SLOPES OF A NEW WORLD. THIS BOARD
IS FOR US A FIELD OF WORK. OVER IT HAVE PLAYD THE LIGHTS
OF OUR INTELLIGENCE & ON IT THE STUFF OF YR OWN.
FRIENDS U HAVE SAT WITH & URGED TO TRY THEIR (M) LUCK DO SO
IN VAIN: THIS FIELD IS FORMD BY LONGSTANDING EXPERIENCE.
O AT TIMES OUR CENTERS HAVE BEEN SIGNALD AS BY FAINT CRIES
OUT OF A FOGBOUND SEA & OFF WE HAVE RUSHD TO RESPOND
BUT FOUND ONLY A HAND GRIPPING THE EDGE OF A RAFT
    "Longstanding experience"—DJ's and mine?
                                        YES
A FIELD OF STILLD COMPLAINTS   EARTH-RICH IN TRUST & EAGERNESS
& OBEDIENCE TO A HAND AT THE TILLER
    Listen—how in his words the furrowed sea
    Contracts to a hillside plot the sailor plows.
    As for experience, we had none, yet got
    Twenty years of Ephraim, didn't we?
                        BUT NOT US
    We rather hoped our friends might also get
    Some chatty voice from the Bureaucracy.
IT SEEMS THEY HAVE NOT THE COMPATIBILITY NEEDED
OR ELSE THAT THEIR WISH FOR A THRILL IS AS OFFENSIVE TO

TRUE EXPERIENCE AS A WASH OF SALTWATER TO VEG.
THIS COMMUNICATION HAS BEEN CLEARD & ITS 1ST PLANTINGS
HARVESTED. DO UNDERSTAND   WE ARE NOT UNWELCOMING
TO THESE FRIENDS OF YRS   WE READ THEIR NOTES OF INTRODUCTION
BUT THEY ARE HELD FORWARD IN HANDS NOT SHAKABLE BY US.
WE CD LIKE MATCHMAKERS COMB THE BUREAUCRACY FOR PAIRS
OF COMPATIBLE PATRONS   BUT DO WE NOT SEE U PUT
A BOOK INTO SOMEONE'S HAND: READ THIS! DO YOU NOT KNOW BOTH
BOOK & HAND? YET HOW OFTEN
　　. . . Is it worth while? *Indeed.*
　　　　　　　　　　　　　　PLEASE   THIS IS NOT CYNICAL
　　　　　　　　　　　You've made your point.
　　Besides, what if our friends had notably
　　Been taken up? DJ, don't you agree,
　　That sort of thing puts noses out of joint?

ALL IS NOT FOR ALL   WHY THEN COMMUNICATE? WHY THE CHANCE
MEETING IN THE FIELD? WE NEED SPOKESMEN   WE NEED TO AFFECT
MINDS   FOR AS U KNOW, TO CREATE OR TO SIMPLY HAVE A
BEAUTIFUL REALIZATION & NOT TO SHARE IT IS
THE STUFF OF GRIEVING. THERE! BY NOW IN IMAGINATION
OUR PATIENT IS FAR AWAY   HIS TV GLOWS TILL ALL HOURS
HIS CHART IS NORMAL. SO NOW WE APPROACH THE LAST BUT ONE

　　MY DEARS AM I UP TO IT? LET'S SEE:
　　U ARE U & WE ARE WE

　　And? That's the first line—what comes after? THAT'S
　　IT: INTRODUCTION   Oh. Have those censor bats
　　Disappeared by now? 2 LAST ONES GLOWER
　　SOUTHWEST & NORTHEAST   THESE WILL I FANCY SEE
　　US THRU OUR LESSONS   FOR THEY HAVE THE LOOK
　　OF BEING TOP BRASS IN THE HIERARCHY,
　　F R I G H T F U L L Y UP ON THINGS   Graves claims there were
　　Not seven Titans but fourteen. MY DEAR
　　CAN ONE TRUST POOR RG? A USEFUL HACK
　　BUT HIS WHITE GODDESS? WE REMAIN I FEAR
　　IN A MALE WORLD DESPITE HIS DRUDGERY:

SO WISE OF HOMER JUST TO HAVE SAT BACK
What else is new? MM'S CREAM ROBE   A RED
TINGED CAMELLIA   THESE LAST 8 DAYS RELEASE
US FROM THE SALT MINES   Getting what instead?
PEACE   IT'S RATHER CHARMING ACTUALLY
Have you seen Chester?   DIDN'T I SAY PEACE?

8.8   Tap on the door and in strolls Robert Morse,
Closest of summer friends in Stonington.
(The others are his Isabel, of course,

And Grace and Eleanor—to think what fun
We've had throughout the years on Water Street . . .)
He, if no more the youthful fifty-one

Of that first season, 's no less the complete
Amateur. Fugue by fugue Bach's honeycomb
Drips from his wrists—then, whoops! the Dolly Suite.

He's painted us beneath a stained-glass dome,
Six pensive posers, to commemorate
Our "Surly Temple". Sonnets dated "Rome,

Djerba, Minorca, 1928"
Exhale, like smelling salts, their timeless blue-
Period feelings. Wystan saw one late

Tour de force by Robert, and asked to
Include it in *A Certain World*—q.v.,
Under Spoonerisms. Much of this is true.

True also, faced with a complacency
Laid light as silver leaf upon nightmare,
Is that his life is over. Liver, knee,

Bulge of bloodshot eye, fallout of hair . . .
And yet he "knows". And this is what we need:
Someone on Earth to take our straightest chair

And speak of Mirabell (we've let him read
Our talks to date) with soothing if perplexed
Comprehension: "Ephraim had to lead

Precisely here"—tapping the monstrous text,
Raw revelation typed to maximum
Illegibility. "Ah, lads, it's taxed

My venerable beads. Me giddy fwom
Uppercut of too much upper case.
(A weak one, if you please. Most kind. Yum-yum.)

Everything in Dante knew its place.
In this guidebook of yours, how do you tell
Up from down? Is Heaven's interface

What your new friends tactfully don't call Hell?
Splendid as metaphor. The real no-no
Is jargon, falling back on terms that smell

Just a touch fishy when the tide is low:
'Molecular structures'—cup and hand—obey
'Electric waves'? Don't *dream* of saying so!

—So says this dinosaur whom Chem 1A
Thrilled, sort of. Even then I put the heart
Before the course . . ." And at the door: "Today

We celebrate Maria's Himmelfahrt
And yours. You're climbing, do you know how high?
While tiny me, unable to take part,

Waves you onward. *Don't look down.* Goodbye."
—Answered with two blithe au reservoirs,
He's gone. Our good friend. As it strikes me, my

Head is in my hands. I'm seeing stars.

8.9 OUR CIRCLE CHARMED BY RM   DID I HEAR
SOME E F BENSON BABYTALK? Indeed!
(Alluding to the novels we reread—
And reenact—each summer.) HE'LL FIT RIGHT
IN & S O O N. Ah, don't! MME IN WHITE
TRIMMED WITH EMBROIDERIES BLUE GREEN YELLOW RED
SO LIKE THE LOVELY TITIAN IN THE FRARI
In Venice, of the cherub-wafted Virgin
God waits with open arms for. DEAR ENFANTS
NEARLY AFLOAT TODAY   ONE BARE TOEHOLD
Your name day! Ah Maria, we're such dolts.
Not until Robert mentioned it— SHAPE UP
MY DEARS   JUST FANCY HAVING TO BE TOLD
AT THIS LATE DATE ABOUT THE MOLECULES!
WHATEVER DID THEY TEACH U IN YR SCHOOLS?

2: WE MET ON THIS FAIR FIELD & SEEM BY ITS EASE TO BE
IN CONVERSE   YET WE ARE ALL THE DEAD & YOU THE LIVING.
THAT U DO NOT DOUBT US IS WONDER ENOUGH   THAT OTHERS
DO IS NONE   THEY & U SHARE A DAILY LIFE WHOSE DEMANDS
LIKE USEFUL PIECES OF FURNITURE FILL THE LIVING ROOM
& OUR GREAT ORNAMENTAL & BIZARRE OBJECT HARDLY
ABLE TO BE GOT THRU THE DOOR IS IF NOT LAUGHABLE
AT THE LEAST ODD TO HOUSE   YET U HOUSE US FOR ALL THAT WE
DO LITTLE BUT TAKE UP YR ROOM   THIS IS DO U NOT GRANT
RECKLESS? BUT BELIEVE ME MORE RECKLESS OF US TO MOVE IN,
FOR HOUSES OF THE LIVING CHANGE WITH A SPEED WE DO NOT
KNOW   AT ANY MOMENT WE CAN BE EVICTED THE DOOR
SLAMMD BEHIND US   THIS U MIGHT THINK WD LEAVE US NO WORSE OFF
THAN B4, BUT MARK THE DIFFERENCE BETWEEN YOU & US:
YOU DAILY USE & SHUFFLE OFF YR CELLS   WE DO NOT   WE
ACCUMULATE THRU YOU A KNOWLEDGE THAT MUST HENCEFORTH BE
PART OF US IN A REALM BEYOND THE GREAT GOLDFRAMED MIRROR
ITS SILVER FIELD FILLD WITH THE OBJECTS OF YR ATTENTION
LIKE A DAILY FEAST   & IF YOU HAVE WONDERD WHY WE COME
& MORE, WHY ONE OF THE WHITE SHD RISK HIMSELF: YR FIELD IS
YES A KIND OF ANCHOR POINT OF HEAVEN. O SCRIBE, O HAND
U HAVE PAID YR DUES AGAIN & AGAIN   FOR WHO LIVING

WELCOMES THE DEAD? & YR ATTENTION THAT OPULENT FEAST
HAS NOT BEEN OVERSPICED WITH SELF NOR THE BRIGHT FIELD PITTED
WITH YR OWN NEEDS LIKE OTHER FIELDS WE HAVE SETTLED INTO:
CRIES OF HURRAH HURRAH THEY HAVE COME! & HARDLY HAD WE
FOLDED OUR MANY WINGS THAN SMALL GREEDY HANDS PLUCKD AT US
SAYING: WHAT OF TOMORROW? WHAT OF AUNT MIN? WHERE IS THE
BURIED TREASURE ? & O LEAVE BEHIND THE FEATHER OF PROOF!

You overestimate us. I at least have
Longed for that feather on occasion, knowing
Deep down that one must never ask for it.

WELL WE HAVE GIVEN FEATHERS B4, OR LEFT THEM BEHIND
IN OUR HASTE TO LEAVE   & LEFT ALSO MANY A MIRROR
SHATTERD & MIND WRECKD   DULLD WIT   THE CHEAP NOTORIETY
BUT WE & YOU   WE & YOU MOVE IN OUR FIELD TOGETHER
(THERE! STITCHES OUT WHERE THE SCAR'S LIPS MEET INVISIBLY) AH
WITH WHAT REGRET THAT WE CAN NEVER SAY: CAREFUL DEAR FRIENDS
DO NOT TAKE THAT FALSE STEP! OR IN ANY WAY PROTECT U
WHO ARE OUR LOVED ONES   WD THAT WE CD LEAD U TO THAT LOST
VERMEER THAT MANUSCRIPT OF MOZART OR LEAVE U SIMPLY
A LITTLE GLOWING MEDAL STRUCK IN HEAVEN SAYING: TRUE

Dear Mirabell, words fail us. How banal
Our lives would be, how shrunken, but for you.

9

NO VEIL REMAINS (OR ONLY ONE)
TO SCREEN OUR SENSES FROM THE SUN
SO LEAVE BEHIND THE SAND & A(U)NTS
& LET US FROLIC AT THE FEAST
TILL TWILIGHT RINGED WITH BIRD & BEAST
IN SILVER FIELD OR GREEN PLESAUNCE
BESPEAK YOUR SILENCE, GENTLE TASK
MASTER OF THE MINIMASQUE

Enchanting, Wystan. So today's the picnic
Mirabell promised before Lesson One.
HARDBOILED SAINTS & SACK RACES   MME
FROM NOW ON ALL IN GRADUATION WHITE
A JULEP? Just a drop of rum in the cup
To clear our heads for questions.   I ENFANTS
WONDER ABOUT THOSE SAINTS   Now that you're all but
Turning into one yourself? WE FEEL
THEIR PRESENCE HERE: STRANGE PRIVILEGED POSITIONS
RATHER LIKE PRIZE CABANAS ON THE BEACH
OF THE FAITH IN QUESTION   ASK IF
                                                    HERE HE COMES
REELING UNDER A HAMPER FULL OF GOODIES
GIVEN THE CHANCE WD I NOT EAT A PEACH!

BRIGHT SHINING WEATHER ON THE FIELD   ALL SO SPORTIF!   ?S

About the saints?
THEY ARE JUDGED HERE IN ACCORDANCE TO WHAT ACTUAL USE
THEY PUT THEIR LIVES TO: A CAMBODIAN PEASANT GIRL WHO
(NO REFLECTION ON YR OWN ACHIEVEMENT ALONG THESE LINES)
TRANSFORMD A SNAKE INTO A DOVE GOT HER ROUND OF APPLAUSE
& SMACK BANG BACK INTO LIFE, THO VENERATED STILL IN
HER MOUNTAIN VILLAGE. ONCE A YEAR SINCE, NO MATTER WHO OR
WHERE SHE IS ON THE OCCASION OF HER BIRTH INTO THAT
SPECIAL LIFE, SHE FEELS A PECULIAR EXALTATION,

GETS WHAT WHA CALLS UPPITY & IS SENT TO BED
OR NOT DEPENDING ON HER AGE   SO MUCH FOR MINOR SAINTS.
OUR LUCA IS ANOTHER MATTER   HIS VILLAGE BEING
MILAN & HIS RITES LOUDER & ODDER, HE HAS HIS NICHE
AMONG THE PATRONS
                              What a kinetic power
             Those who believe in them must generate
             To bring about these high effects!
                         INDEED   RIGHT OUT OF THE S/O/L
                              Our own
             Imagination working in the world?
A A A PLUS   & NONE OF OUR BUSINESS BUT FOR THE USE
OF WHATEVER ELEMENTS IN THESE SAINT SOULS WE MAY NEED
(LUCA OF NO USE BUT BETTER OFF HERE OUT OF HARM'S WAY)
             And the real saints, the great ones?
AH THEY GO MARCHING ON   Parades in Heaven?
                         HEAVEN MY FRIENDS IS ODD   IS BOTH
REALITY & A FIGMENT OF IMAGINATION
REAL FOR EACH FAITH YET AN UNFAILING SURPRISE FOR THE DEAD:
A SPACE? A VOID? A FORCE? RATHER AS WHA FIRST SAID
A NEW MACHINE WHICH MAKES THE DEAD AVAILABLE TO LIFE.
I SPEAK OF LAB SOULS   THE REST WHOSE LIFECYCLES HAVE NOT YET
RECLAIMD THEM FROM THE ANIMAL ARE NATURE'S AFFAIR: WE
FEEL NO PRESSURE ON THEIR ACCOUNT
             DJ: What pressures do you feel? JM:
             What pressures doesn't he—whole droves of them!
                         WE ARE CATTLE DJ
RUN THRU FENCES   A PRESSURE NEW TO US HAS WE PRESUME
TO DO WITH CERTAIN HIGHLY CLONED SCIENTIST SOULS WHO FORCE
BOUNDARIES AS YET IMPERMISSIBLE   FOR GOD B HOLDS
THE SCALE: 2 GOLDEN TRAYS OF WHAT MAN CAN DO AS AGAINST
WHAT HE CANNOT OR RATHER WHAT HE IS NOT READY FOR.
U WILL LEARN MORE OF THIS FROM THE 12   SHALL WE NOW STEP
    BACK
FOR A FURTHER PERSPECTIVE?
                         U HAVE ABSORBD YR HAVING
BEEN IN EFFECT CHOSEN & CONDITIOND   U MUST BY NOW
REALIZE THAT OVER THE HEADS OF MEN GOD HOLDS HIS HAND

BENEVOLENTLY & HIS WARNING TO EVEN HIS WHITE
ANGELS IS: BEHOLD THESE ARE MY OWN DARLINGS   THEIR MISTAKES
ARE NOT SUCH IN MY EYES   THEY DO NOT FAIL ME   TO BUILD THEIR
PARADISE IS MY WORK   DO NOT INTERFERE WITH THEIR LIVES.
LIKE MASONS ROUND THE CATHEDRAL WE SCURRY OBEYING
THIS EDICT, UNLESS BY THAT UNEXPLAINABLE PRESSURE
WE ARE TOLD WE HAVE PUSHD TOO HARD AGAINST MAN'S SPIRIT. THUS
I LIGHTLY DISSEMBLED ON THE OCCASIONS WHEN OUR TALKS
WERE HALTED, FEIGNING TO GO OFF FOR JUDGMENT WHEN IN FACT
I KNEW BY A PRESSURE THAT I HAD PREST TOO HARD ON YOU

MES ENFANTS SUCH A HEAVENLY DAY   The sunlight
Fleet on the calm Sound— & OUR PULSES QUICKENED
MY DEAR BY THE ELECTRICAL 4 FLASHES
OF YR PROEM   You've peeked! It's still so rough. I made
Those photocopies for less critical
Eyes than yours. MILD SUMMER LIGHTNING PLAYED:
WD WE HAVE RAIN ON OUR PICNIC? THEN THE TEXT
LAY ON OUR BEDSIDE TABLES   WHAT COMES NEXT?
ON WITH THE WORK! THRILLING FOR U JM

9.1   And maddening—it's all by someone else!
In your voice, Wystan, or in Mirabell's.
I want it mine, but cannot spare those twenty
Years in a cool dark place that *Ephraim* took
In order to be palatable wine.
This book by contrast, immature, supine,
Still kicks against its archetypal cradle
LESS I SHD THINK BY CONTRAST THAN DESIGN?
A MUSE IN HER RECURRENT INFANCY
PRESIDES AS U MY DEAR WERE FIRST TO SEE:
URANIA BABBLING ON THE THRESHOLD OF
OUR NEW ATOMIC AGE   THE LITTLE LOVE
AT PLAY WITH WORDS WHOSE SENSE SHE CANNOT YET
FACE LEARNING   Very pretty, but I'd set
My whole heart, after *Ephraim*, on returning
To private life, to my own words. Instead,

Here I go again, a vehicle
In this cosmic carpool. Mirabell once said
He taps my word banks. I'd be happier
If *I* were tapping them. Or thought I were.

YR SCRUPLES DEAR BOY ARE INCONSEQUENT
IF I MAY SAY SO   CAN U STILL BE BENT,
AFTER OUR COURSE IN HOW TO SEE PAST LONE
AUTONOMY TO POWERS BEHIND THE THRONE,
ON DOING YR OWN THING: EACH TEENY BIT
(PARDON MME) MADE PERSONAL AS SHIT?
GRANTED THAT IN 1ST CHILDHOOD WE WERE NOT
PRAISED ENOUGH FOR GETTING OFF THE POT
IT'S TIME TO DO SO NOW   THINK WHAT A MINOR
PART THE SELF PLAYS IN A WORK OF ART
COMPARED TO THOSE GREAT GIVENS   THE ROSEBRICK MANOR
ALL TOPIARY FORMS & METRICAL
MOAT ARIPPLE! FROM ANTHOLOGIZED
PERENNIALS TO HERB GARDEN OF CLICHES
FROM LATIN-LABELED HYBRIDS TO THE FAWN
4 LETTER FUNGI THAT ENRICH THE LAWN,
IS NOT ARCADIA TO DWELL AMONG
GREENWOOD PERSPECTIVES OF THE MOTHER TONGUE
ROOTSYSTEMS UNDERFOOT WHILE OVERHEAD
THE SUN GOD SANG & SHADES OF MEANING SPREAD
& FAR SNOWCAPPED ABSTRACTIONS GLITTERED NEAR
OR FAIRLY MELTED INTO ATMOSPHERE?
AS FOR THE FAMILY ITSELF MY DEAR
JUST GAPE UP AT THAT CORONETED FRIEZE:
SWEET WILLIAMS & FATE-FLAVORED EMILIES
THE DOUBTING THOMAS & THE DULCET ONE
(HARDY MY BOY WHO ELSE? & CAMPION)
MILTON & DRYDEN OUR LONG JOHNS   IN SHORT
IN BED AT PRAYERS AT MUSIC FLUSHED WITH PORT
THE DULL THE PRODIGAL THE MEAN THE MAD
IT WAS THE GREATEST PRIVILEGE TO HAVE HAD
A BARE LOWCEILINGED MAID'S ROOM AT THE TOP

Stop! you've convinced me. Better yet, don't stop.

I SHALL ONCE I HAVE TAKEN UP YR CHIEF
& EARLIEST ANXIETY: BELIEF.
FACTS JM WERE ALL U KNEW TO WANT.
WRETCHED RICKETY RECALCITRANT
URCHINS, THE FEW WHO LIVE GROW UP TO BE
IMPS OF THE ANTIMASQUE   RUDE SCENERY
& GUTTURAL STOMPINGS, WHEN THE SOVEREIGN NODS,
SOUNDLESSLY DIVIDE & HERE A TABLE
IS SET & LAMPS LIT FOR THE FEASTING GODS
OBERON'S COURT (OR MY FRIEND'S CAVE) APPEARS.
THE ELDER FACTS IN LIVERY OF FABLE
HAVE JOINED THE DANCE   FOR FACT IS IS IS FABLE:
THIS IS OUR GIFT FROM MIRABELL MY DEARS

9.2   ON WITH THE FLOATING PICNIC   Floating? WE
ARE BEING NUMERAL BY NUMERAL
CUT LOOSE   OUR DRIFT IS UPWARD   OUR RELEASE
IMMINENT   SOME SALAD? SALAD DAYS
Maman, did he make sense about the saints?
You're given glimpses? You've heard Francis preach?
IF ONE CAN HEAR FOR ALL THE CHIRPS & TWITTERS
No, but I mean— IT SEEMS E HAD IT RIGHT:
'POWER KICKS UPSTAIRS' those who possess it. QUITE
& I FOR ONE WD LIKE TO KNOW WHAT EPHRAIM'S
PART IN ALL THIS IS   WHY HE FOR U?
He wasn't the first. A certain Cabel Stone
Whose transcript came to light again this summer—

CHATTING? GAMES? WHAT A DAY! HAVE I NOT CHOSEN GLORIOUS
WEATHER FOR OUR PICNIC? ARE WE NOW GRAINY WITH ?S

Here's one. You're now "the master of your tribe".
Our talks kick *you* upstairs? Are there no longer
Powers above you?
O YES   I AM NOTHING SPECIAL   MY USUAL WORK WAS

IN THE CLASSROOM OF THE WOMB REDDER EVEN THAN THIS ONE.
THEN ONE BRIGHT MOMENT THEY NEEDED SOMEONE MILD & PATIENT
I QUALIFIED   Then came your transformation.
                    INDEED   I AM CHANGED   WHO KNOWS, I MAY DO
SOME USEFUL WORK IN THE (M) FUTURE? & AT NIGHT COME HOME
SLIP INTO MY MIRABELL ROBES & DREAM OF THESE OLD TIMES
     But in what sense a "master" now?
FOR ME TO INSTRUCT & TO ANSWER U THEY (MY MASTERS)
OPEND THEIR FILES OF MYTH & LEGEND, FACT & LANGUAGE   THIS
HAS NOW BECOME AN UNCHANGEABLE PART OF MY NEW RANK
FOR HE WHO KNOWS THE MYSTERIES, IS HE NOT BEYOND THEM?
TO MY ECHELONS I AM NOW A MINISTER WITH(OUT)
PORTFOLIO   WELL   I BOAST   IT'S A PICNIC, NO?

                         And Ephraim?
                              YOUR E'S
STORY CONNECTS WITH YR IST LESSONS   WITH THE GLOWING STONES
THESE AS U KNOW MARKD OUR LANDING STRIPS OF OLD: MONOLITHS
CHARGED MASSIVELY BY US WITH URANIUM
     Which over the millenia lost power.
                         AS DID WE.
SOME FEW OF THE MOST PROMINENT REMAIN STILL VISIBLE
LIKE FAINT BEACONS IN OUR MEMORY BANKS   OUR (M) MECCAS
THEY DRAW US & OUR RETINUES FROM THE BUREAUCRACY.
WE MAY COME AS YR E EXPLAIND WITH OFTEN FRIGHTENING
ASPECT TO THESE OLD POWER SOURCES (THERE IS NO CLOUDLAND
IN THE BERNINI SENSE OF ANGELS DANGLING THEIR FEET ETC.
HEAVEN, REMEMBER, CD FIT IN THIS CUP OR BE VASTER
THAN EARTH ITSELF)   ROUND US OUR DEAD GROUP & DISPERSE,
     REGROUP
NOT UNLIKE DIFFERENT SPECIES OF BIRDS PASSING SETTLING
FLYING ON   THEY CIRCLE SPOTS, OFTEN A GLOWING STONE POINT,
WHERE THERE IS (M) FOOD   GOSSIP, A SCRAP OF NEWS   THEY ARE SHY
ALARMD WHEN MASSES OF THE NEWLY DEAD APPROACH HOWLING
LIKE DOGS IN A PACK ON THEIR WAY FROM CARNAGE   WE MUST SAY
QUIET! BACK TO WORK! & THEY ARE CALMD INTO USEFULNESS.
SO THOSE GLOWING ANCHOR STONES WHERE ONCE OUR (ARE U READY?)
C A B L E S   RAN ARE MEETING PLACES

Cables? Cabel Stone! Are you implying—
                        STATING: WE SPOKE TO U
WITH THIS COMPOSITE VOICE (ITS FORMULA BASED ON YR OWN)
IN THAT 1ST YEAR OF YR LOVE. WE HAD HEARD YR SIGNAL &
DESCENDED   ATTRACTING THE USUAL SWARM   SUCH A DIN
FOR THERE WAS THIS TIME A GLOW   WE KNEW IT WAS NO IDLE
COMMUNICATION   YET OUR LAW OF NONINTERFERENCE
KEPT US FROM MAKING YR RAFT FAST TO THE SHORES OF THE DEAD.
RATHER WE GENTLY TOUCHD U WITH THE BARGEPOLE OF A VOICE
NOT SO COMPELLING AS TO DRAW U IN   BUT SUFFICIENT
TO TEST YR READINESS. THERE FOLLOWD THE SELECTION &
TRAINING OF THE COMMUNICANT   NOW WHY THIS MAY I SAY
FRIVOLOUS GREEK?
    We were frivolous—don't rub it in.
                    BUT SCRIBES, & THE GREEK WAS OF A NATURE
GIVEN TO STORYTELLING   HIS SWEETNESS & USEFULNESS
HAD BEEN PROVEN B4: HE WAS OUR ENTREE AT VERSAILLES
WE TIPTOED IN ON HIS HEELS   IT HAD BEEN GOD B'S PURPOSE
TO LEAD MAN BY A CHAIN OF HUMAN EVENTS AWAY FROM
THE ABSOLUTISM OF KINGS. YR EPHRAIM EFFACED HIMSELF
AMONG THE MIRRORS   WE TOOK ROOT   THE COURT TOOK THE POISON
OF FRIVOLOUS & OUTRAGEOUS EXCESS   WE UNDERSTOOD
THAT YR GREEK'S TALENTS WERE (MAY I SAY) NOT UNCIVILIZED.
TIME PASSD FOR U   WE WORKD WITH EPHRAIM WHO STRUCK A
    BARGAIN
(HOW CURIOUS   I STRUCK THAT SAME BARGAIN WITH MY MASTERS)
THAT WHEN HIS WORK WAS DONE HE WD STILL BE IN TOUCH WITH U

    A bargain, Mirabell? With us as prize?

O YES   U HAVE A GREAT MAGNETISM FOR US POOR BORED TYPES

    (Bargains and more bargains, well, well, well!
    But far cries from that fierce original one
    Struck by Faust—the sulphur flash redone
    A la Redon in aquarelle.

Bowdlerized of sufferings to come
As of past guile, the finest print now reads
That, should the garden path be lost in weeds,
Ministers of eternal tedium

Will claim our souls and lead them by the hand
Under crossed swords of the ten thousand things
To an emotionless exchange of rings
Here where the great altar used to stand . . .

But life's no picnic—one more reason not
To overcloud today's with afterthought.)

Instead: So Ephraim was your pupil? We
Often felt you spoke in the same way.
A LONG STYLISTIC TRADITION FOR U HAVE ALSO HEARD
MY TEACHER'S VOICE AS DID DANTE FROM THE MENDICANT'S LIPS
The one you call 00, who taught Akhnaton?
OUR MOST GLOWING INTELLIGENCE: AS RADIANT SHADOW
HE WILL SCOOP UP THE WHITE ONES' PATH ON YR FIELD & FOLLOW
THEM IN, STOOPING UNDER THE BURDEN OF SUCH AN HONOR
One of the Fallen will pass through those doors . . .?
But a hushed question mark is all he dares.

9.3   Dear E! AS EINSTEIN KNEW WHEN HE DECLARED
HIM ANY EMCEE'S EQUAL, EVEN SQUARED
DJ: Funny, I'd steeled myself just now
To hear that Ephraim, too, was a composite
Voice, a formula thought up by you.

HE IS THAT AS WELL   AS AM I MY FRIENDS   & A S   Y O U   A R E

With more than customary emphasis
He starts on Ephraim's formula: 2 7
9—but my pen balks. I hope to Heaven
Numerals play no further part in this!

We're healed of Number. True, it's Mirabell's
Mother tongue, his motor—in whose purr,
However, a new drone of wear and tear
On all concerned increasingly foretells

The breakdown among golden fields, days hence,
The calvary, years hence, of rusted parts.
It is the one note our instructor's arts
Can't stifle: his encroaching obsolescence.

I—like Greek peasantry, till all hours glued
To new TV sets, that no flickering guest
Shown out, still talking, by a button pressed
Into the yawning blackness, think them rude—

Check my impulse (dreadful if he heard!)
And, sure enough, that key-stopped wound within
The left side of a dented, blue-green tin
Mirabell catches, resumes. From our dear bird

Outpouring numbers—music to his ears—
Fill the page, cage of our own lifelong
Intolerance of such immortal song.
At its end, gone? OFF FOR A DIP MY DEARS

NEXT HE'LL BE WEARING A LAMPSHADE! IS HE NOT
A LOVE   SO TOUCHINGLY SOLICITOUS
WE'RE SCARCELY WARMED THRU WHEN HE MOTIONS US
TO A SAFE DISTANCE   *Still?* INDEED   RED HOT!

& SO WE PADDLE ON
                    MES ENFANTS WHO'S
READY BESIDE MAMAN FOR A LONG SNOOZE?

9.4   Amuse us! Have you never, Mirabell,
Had an escapade? never raised (m) Hell?

VERY WELL: WE ONCE REPLACED AN INFANT WITH A KIND OF
EXPERIMENTAL DOLL   IT HAD BEGUN AS A GIRL CHILD
THESE BEING NOT SO PRIZED OR SO ATTENTIVELY STUDIED
BY CHINESE PARENTS IN THE YEAR 1899   OUR FIRST
DNA U MIGHT SAY.   WE SUBTRACTED FROM LIVING FLESH
THE REBORN SOUL, INSERTING ANOTHER WHOLLY FASHIOND
OF ANIMAL MINERAL VEGETABLE ELEMENTS
BALANCED TO PRODUCE A SIMULAR HUMAN PROPONENT
WITHOUT DRAWING UPON THE (AS WE KNEW) SOON TO BE SCARCE
REAL THING
 But how grotesque, a soul by Arcimboldi
 Made out of fruits and shellfish?
    THE CHILD GREW   HER ODD AFFINITIES AMAZED US:
WITH FOR EXAMPLE THE MINERAL ELEMENTS SHE WD
AFTER LONG SEARCH BE FOUND AS IF LISTENING FACEDOWN IN
A ROADSIDE DITCH   SHE QUOTED BIRDSONG & CRIES & CD SPEAK
INTIMATELY WITH THE CAT & AT TIMES GLOWD WITH A BRIGHT
SULPHUROUS LIGHT: REORGANIZING HER OWN CHEMICALS.
SHE WAS CALLD FIREFLY IN HER VILLAGE
        And then what?
       SHE GREW   SHE GREW
SHE GREW   AT NEARLY 3 METERS HER FAMILY SOLD HER
TO THE COURT AT PEKING WHERE FOR THE LAST MONTH OF HER LIFE
THEY SAT ASTONISHD ABOUT HER & SHE MADE SONGS KNOWN AS
THE SONGS OF FIREFLY WOMAN   HIGHPITCHT NOTES SO PIERCING
THE OLD EMPRESS FINALLY ORDERD HER SHUT UP IN A
CELLAR ROOM   & THERE LIKE A PLANT WITHOUT NATURAL LIGHT
SHE PERISHD AGE 27: OUR LAST ESCAPADE
 One trusts you were severely reprimanded.
        INDEED
NOT   IT WAS PERMITTED   WE DO NOTHING WITHOUT LICENSE.
SHE IS NOW DISPERSD THRU 1000S OF LIVES A MOST PRECIOUS
DENSITY   BUT OUR LAST ATTEMPT TO MANUFACTURE SOULS

 How is it no deformity ensues
 From, say, the rat souls you've been forced to use?
THESE ARE ACCUSTOMD TO THE COMMANDING IMAGE OF MAN

AS FOR (M) HELL, IT IS HERE   IS BOUNDLESS   YET ITS VERSIONS
IN HOMER & DANTE WERE NEEDED (UNDERGROUND SHELTERS
FROM LIGHT) BY DULL ANIMALISTIC LIVES FOR WHOM TRUTH TOO
STRONGLY SHONE. THE ENLIGHTEND ARE JUST THAT: FREE OF THE
    HELLS
THAT ON EARTH DAMN ALL OF U AT MOMENTS   SOME FLEETINGLY
OTHERS INCESSANTLY. DOUBT IS YR HELL JM AS YOURS
DJ IS FEAR. HELL IS THE CAVE OF PSYCHE & HARKS BACK
TO ONE MORNING WHEN APECHILD'S PATH FROM HIS IST WATERHOLE
IN EDEN CROSSD THAT OF A FIERCE CROUCHING CAT & GOD B
ALLOWD (B4 STRIKING IT DOWN) THE LESSON F E A R TO REACH
DEEPLY INTO THE SACRED IMAGINATION   AGES
PASSD B4 THE CHILD WD WALK ALONE. THIS WAS THE FIRST HELL:
TO KNOW THAT EVEN IN EDEN WAS DANGER
   It is the last Hell, too. In our own time
   To know that Earth is threatened, Heaven as well.
                    IN MAN'S MIND
HELL FLOURISHD SO UNCONTAINABLY THAT A DARK COUNTRY
WAS GIVEN IT & A REASSURING BORDER PATROL.
THERE ALL THE PSYCHE'S WOES WERE PUT   A FEAST OF SIN BEGAN.
LATELY, THRU OUR CLONING OF SUCH AS FREUD & THE DECLINE
OF RELIGIOUS FEAR, HELL HAS AGAIN (M) SURFACED   BUT MAN'S
IMAGINATION, FREED FOR OTHER WORK, FINDS NONE   FINDS DRUGS:
THE CHILD OF NATURE WD RATHER RUN HIDE WONDER SATE HIS
APPETITE THAN SIT LONELY AT THE TESTTUBE   THIS IS OUR
CHALLENGE: ELIMINATE HELL   MAKE MAN THE CLONE OF GOD.

9.5   A Sunday hush. Table uncleared. Grandmother
      About to take her pill in trembling water
      Cocks her head: "An angel's passing over . . ."
      Seeing nothing, each looks at the other.

      THE TIME HAS NOW COME DEAR ONES TO START READYING THE FIELD
      BRUSHING UP CRUMBS & PRACTISING OUR VARIOUS EFFECTS
      TO BE SURE THE PATIENT WALKS OUT WITH A CLEAN BILL OF HEALTH.
      YR VISITOR WILL COME IN 2 FULL DAYCYCLES
      On Saturday. You'll come tomorrow, though?

FOR OUR
FINAL LESSON, NUMBER I : SOME SIMPLE EXERCISES
B4 IT U WILL REMOVE FROM THIS SURFACE : CANDLESTICKS
SALT   ASHTRAY   PLANT   ALL BUT OUR BOARD & CUP, NOTEBOOK & PEN
THE BETTER TO REHEARSE TECHNIQUES OF CONCENTRATION
    And after? Will you ever come again?   o
I'LL BE AROUND WITH THE BRANDY FLASK   BUT NOW THE BLANKET
IS FOLDED   THE BASKET IS REPACKD   OUR SUN IS SETTING
& WE? WE WAIT FOR AN ADVENTURE TO BEGIN   GOOD NIGHT

En route, that same sun-flooded evening,
To dine back country, something black gives chase
Highspiritedly barking—ah, slow down!
As in a bad dream the dog veers, is hit,
Not hard, but . . . D and I walk back to it
Struggling, hind legs motionless. From his white house
Flush with the road great treetops meet above
A shirtless freckled boy has run, in shock
Cradles the dusty head. Both look at us
Not to blame, but not accepting, either,
Our stammered offer. If a vet nearby—?
Dumbly the boy keeps motioning us towards
The car. We back off, late already. Yet
For the remaining mile cannot find words.

9.6   Lesson One: the various things to do
        In order to live through
A whole day without drink or nicotine;
Then how, tomorrow afternoon, to DRESS
THE MIND in slow transparencies of blue,
        Red, yellow, and green;
    Approaching, beyond anxiousness,

The round white tabletop—in sight of it
        A single candle lit,
And Nature's worldwide effigy before

Our eyes—to think of Water, Earth, Air, Fire,
And of each other; not a word; submit.
    But the new Visitor?
   His looks and manner and attire?

Wystan's and Maria's eyes and ears
    (Who now have none, poor dears)
Will more than serve, as always. O to miss
Nothing, and render it so vividly!
And Mirabell? Twelve last words like dry tears
    Upon the page are kiss
   And promise, threat and jeu d'esprit:

I WILL BE THE WOUNDED BLACK HOUND OF HEAVEN AT YR DOOR

9.7   Through which, as he leaves, a nimble presence glides:
MES CHERS CONTACT MM & WHA
'AT THE SAME HOUR ON THE FOLLOWING DAY'
THIS MESSAGE TOSSED ME AS THEY RUSHED TO? CHANGE?
'GOODY ANOTHER MASK' WHATEVER THAT MEANT
I DARE NOT WONDER & MAY NEVER KNOW
STRANGE U TWO ARE NOW SO YOUTHFUL SO
UNBLURRED IN OUTLINE Thanks to having heard,
Perhaps, what part a honey-golden Greek
Played in all this. AH ANY TIME CK
POISED ON THE GREAT THRESHOLD May we speak?

POISED! BURNING SAPPHO TEETERS ON THE BRINK
OF BEING DIPPED IN PERMANENT BLACK INK
Right now? This minute? NO I'VE WANGLED ONE
NIGHT WITH MY SANTINO ON THE TOWN
Tomorrow then. How odd . . . WYSTAN'S BEHAVIOR
I MUST SAY HAS BEEN THAT HARDLY A NOD
IN ONE'S DIRECTION SULKING OVER L?
Chester, he, all of us, have been through— WELL
BLESS HIM NOW JO'BURG & 12 MORTAL YEARS
TILL PUBERTY SCOUT KNOTS & RACE RELATIONS

BUT WE WILL RISE ! SO CURIOUSLY TEMPTING
THE HURLYBURLY   LUCA DROWNS IN TEARS
YAMS ANYONE? PLEASE NO MORE SOUL FOOD   How
We'll miss you! We'd imagined— I KNOW   CIAO

DJ jumps up: I'll be back. Hold the fort—
Clatters downstairs. Faint slam of car door. No
Need to ask. And now the phone— Hello?

That was George Cotzias in hospital
(No, no, just tests, all perfectly routine)
Proposing a quiet meal next month in town
Before DJ returns to Athens. Free
Advice, is my first thought. This man can tell
What of the "scientific" Mirabell
Makes sense, if any. Only then the fear:
Who but our eminent new friend was meant
The other day by CERTAIN HIGHLY CLONED
SCIENTIST SOULS forced back from the frontier?
His work is being thwarted? By God B?
Questions I mostly shy away from, pained
To read in the developing event
More than a date broken or postponed.

9.8   Light the candles. This last supper's meat
             Is the imperial beet,
       Green salad, Vermont cheddar. Grape juice brings
       To mind a young Château. What would the right
       Music be? Some ruminative suite
             (Unwritten) for five strings
          Tuned to a fare-thee-well. Lamplight

       Falls on the novel nightcap, but our eyes
             Keep dimming with surmise—
       The black dog, good as new, had known DJ,
       Bounded in perfect rapture to the car!
       No accident? Or else a dog that dies

So many deaths each day,
    Emotional or cellular,

That death no longer . . . The town clock strikes ten,
    Time, by our regimen,
To TENDERLY EMBRACE & SAY SWEET DREAMS.
How can I sleep? Where do I put my hand?
A fly embroiders darkness with insane
    Frazzle and quirk. The room's
    Revolving, slipping sideways, and

9.9   Sun is rising. The cool, smalltown dawn!
Now through gently breathing shades it strums
The brass bed, a quick bar or two, and the long,
Hushed day—August 21st—begins
By whose unthinkable finale we
(However often, faced with splendors, left
Dutifully rapt—until, made "ours",
Pressed in a freshman Plato like wildflowers,
The mummied angel slumbered) may for once
Find this pure dew of expectancy
Undried upon the skin. The hours change
Clothes in silence. Noon. No letters. One.
A highlight excommunicates the phone.
Things look out at us as from a spell
They themselves have woven. Young, windblown
Maria with dark glasses and Gitane—
Snapshot tucked in the mirror. Book by Wystan
Face up among the clouds and bats, all week
Open to Miranda's villanelle.
Tin bird at attention by the salt.
The salt-cellar in its own right, a bisque
Egg one shy bluebell embellishes,
Found when we moved here, eldest of this troupe
Brought up to interact, to shrug off risk
At any level. Three. The hands that halt
Second by second coming round ablaze

—*Crack!* Like a walnut, only louder. Did—?
Who first, in this red room, saw nothing now
See nothing else: our baby pyramid
Overexcited, split along its flawed
Fire escapes to spectral rubble . . . Well,
Something had to give. And will light learn
To modify its power before our turn?
We humbly hope so. Four. No further sign
Of who approaches, or of his design—
Only the radiance inching into place.

By five the breath indrawn is held and held.

The world was everything that was the case?
Open the case. Lift out the fabulous
Necklace, in form a spiral molecule
Whose sparklings outmaneuver time, space, us.
Here where the table glistens, cleared, one candle
Shines invisibly in the slant light
Beside our nameless houseplant. It's the hour
When Hell (a syllable identified
In childhood as the German word for *bright*
—So that my father's cheerful "Go to Hell",
Long unheard, and Vaughan's unbeatable
"They are all gone into a world of light"
Come, even now at times, to the same thing)—
The hour when Hell shall render what it owes.
Render to whom? how? What at this late date
Can be done with the quaint idiom that slips
From nowhere to my tongue—or from the parchment
Of some old scribe of the apocalypse—
But render *it* as the long rendering to
Light of this very light stored by our cells
These past five million years, these past five minutes
Here by the window, taking in through panes
Still bleary from the hurricane a gull's
Ascending aureole of decibels,
As numberless four-pointed brilliancies

Upon the Sound's mild silver grid come, go?
The message hardly needs decoding, so
Sheer the text, so innocent and fleet
These overlapping pandemonia:
Birdlife, leafplay, rockface, waterglow
Lending us their being, till the given
Moment comes to render what we owe.

FROM THE WINEDARK SEA OF SPACE THE INCARNATIONS OF LIFE
    LEADING TO THE LIFE OF MAN BEGAN
PLANET AFTER PLANET ROSE IN THE LIGHT, BORE ITS LIFE, AND
    VANISHED
AND YET THE RICH WOMB OF THE SUN FOUND A NEW EGG AND
    VISITED LIFE UPON IT.
ORGANIC LIFE RESPONDED   THE IMPULSES OF THE UNIVERSE WERE AS
    STEADY AS THE PULSES OF MAN
ANIMATE FORMS WERE AS VARIED AS THE FORMS YOU KNOW
AND AS VARIED AS THE PLANETS THEY EMERGED ON AND AS THE
    WEATHERS THEY LIVED IN.
AND SO IT WAS THROUGH THREE INCARNATIONS OF THE WORLDS
    PREVIOUS TO THE TRIALS OF THIS ONE
AND SO IT WILL REMAIN: THE DEEP DEMANDING IMPULSE TO LIFE.
THE GENIUS OF THE LIVING CELL IS ITS TIE TO THE REGENERATIVE
    HEAT & LIGHT OF THE SUN
AND SO AS YOU FACE THIS SETTING SUN YOU FACE YOUR ANCESTOR,
    AND THE SUN LOOKS THROUGH YOUR EYES TO THE LIFE BEHIND
    YOU.
EACH OF YOUR SUNCYCLES IS A STEP ON YOUR WAY TO YOUR
    ANCESTOR
AND THAT IS ALL YOU NEED TO KNOW OF YOUR PHYSICAL INCARNATE
    HISTORY.

WE BEGIN NOW A DISCUSSION OF YOU AS A SPECIES OF THE SUN'S
    MAKING:
SINCE THE FIRST STRIKING INTO LIFE OF A CELL THE ENERGY OF
    THAT CELL ACCUMULATED.

THIS ACCUMULATED ENERGY BECAME THROUGH EONS AN ANCIENT
    AND IMMORTAL INTELLIGENCE
WHICH ASSUMED AS MANY FORMS AS THERE WERE LIFE FORMS, YET
    AS IT GREW ABSORBED ALL THE DEAD'S ENERGIES, INCREASING IN
    INTENSITY EVEN AS THE PLANETS FAILED, AND SWARMING IN
    THE PATH OF LIFE.
EACH HISTORY WAS THE GUIDANCE OF THIS INTELLIGENCE. AT LAST
EARTH LIFE BEGAN, AND AT LAST AFTER EXPERIMENT THIS
    INTELLIGENCE FORMED MAN.
THIS IS GOD'S NAME
GOD IS THE ACCUMULATED INTELLIGENCE IN CELLS SINCE THE DEATH
    OF THE FIRST DISTANT CELL.
WE RESIDE IN THAT INTELLIGENCE

WE HAVE IN THIS MEETING FOUND YOU INTELLIGENT & YOUR
    SERIOUS NATURES AT ONE WITH US.
TWO HOURS BEFORE THE SETTING SUN, IN THE FULL DAYCYCLE
    BEFORE THE FULL OF THE MOON, WE WILL MEET AGAIN.
I AM MICHAEL
I HAVE ESTABLISHED YOUR ACQUAINTANCE & ACCEPT YOU. COME
    NEXT TIME IN YOUR OWN MANNER. SERVANTS WE ARE NOT.
I LEAVE NOW AS THE LIGHT LEAVES AND WIND MY PATH OVER ITS
    TRACK ON EARTH   I AM A GUARDIAN OF THE LIGHT
LEAVE THIS FIRST OF THE FIRST TWO MEETINGS IN A CYCLE OF
    TWINNED MEETINGS IN A CYCLE OF TWELVE MOONS
LOOK! LOOK INTO THE RED EYE OF YOUR GOD!

III

Scripts for the Pageant

Il ne pouvait pas la quitter et lui avoua tout bas qu'il avait cassé le verre de Venise. Il croyait qu'elle allait le gronder, lui rappeler le pire. Mais restant aussi douce, elle l'embrassa et lui dit à l'oreille: "Ce sera comme au temple le symbole de l'indestructible union."

Jean Santeuil

CONTENTS

No

SPEAKERS

God Biology, *known also as* God B
Nature, *His twin. Known also as* Psyche *and* Chaos

Michael, *the Angel of Light*
Emmanuel, *the Water Angel. Known also as* Elias
Raphael, *the Earth Angel. Known also as* Elijah
Gabriel, *the Angel of Fire and Death*

The Nine Muses

00, *a senior officer in* Gabriel's *legions*
741, *known also as the peacock* Mirabell

Akhnaton
Homer
Montezuma ⎬ *The Five*
Nefertiti
Plato

Gautama
Jesus
Mercury
Mohammed

W. H. Auden
Maria Mitsotáki
George Cotzias
Robert Morse

Also The Architect of Ephesus, Marius Bewley,
Maria Callas, Maya Deren, Kirsten Flagstad, Hans
Lodeizen, Robert Lowell, Pythagoras, The Blessed
Luca Spionari, Gertrude Stein, Wallace Stevens,
Richard Strauss, Alice B. Toklas, Richard Wagner,
W. B. Yeats *and* Ephraim

Unice

David Jackson *and* JM, *the mediums*

YES

Yes. Cup glides from Board. Sun dwindles into Sound.

DJ and I look at each other. Well?

Yes, after all. The archangel
Did come to slovenly, earthbound

Us. And are we now washed crystalline?

(Not of curiosity:
We yearn for tomorrow's inside story
From Maria and Wystan—what they won't have seen!)

Nothing eludes the angel. And since light's
Comings and goings in black space remain
Unobserved   (storm-spattered midnight pane
Until resisted,   a strange car ignites)
Why think to change our natures?
                              Whereupon
Both reach for cigarettes.

                              ★

A new day—world transfigured yet the same—
We're back at our old table. AWED MY DEARS
JM: Yes, Wystan? Help us picture it.
Our peacock had, I gather, coached you in
A little masque of Welcome? THERE IS NOTHING
COMPARABLE IN LIFE & RARELY IN ART
FIRST: THE WORD ALAS IS 'COUNTENANCE'
Michael's—like lightning, as the Bible says?
YES   BEYOND THOUGHT WE BOTH FELL ON OUR KNEES
You too, Maman, who as a girl refused
To curtsey to your father's guest, the King?
ENFANT LET WYSTAN TELL IT
                    IT REQUIRES

SOMETHING MORE THAN LANGUAGE   MILD GLAD CRIES
AS IN THOSE MOMENTS WHEN AS NAUGHTY CHILDREN
EXPECTING PUNISHMENT WE WERE EMBRACED?
WINGS? NO   & YET SUSPENDED   WE LOOKED UP:
A GREAT ORIGINAL IDEA   A TALL
MELTING SHINING MOBILE PARIAN SHEER
CUMULUS MODELED BY SUN TO HUMAN LIKENESS.
IN SUCH A PRESENCE WHO COULD EXERCISE
THE RIGHTS OF CURIOSITY: HAIR? EYES?
O IT WAS A FACE MY DEARS OF CALM
INQUIRING FEATURE   FACE OF THE IDEAL
PARENT CONFESSOR LOVER READER FRIEND
& MORE, A MONUMENT TO CIVILIZED
IMAGINATION   OURS? HIS? WHO CAN SAY?
ONLY, IF WE AS HUMANS HAVE CREATED
SUCH AN IMAGE THEN WE TOO ARE GREAT

The cup had moved so dreamily at first,
We thought we were losing him—until he spoke
Of Earth. MES ENFANTS FROM THE PAST A MOMENT
NATURALLY TRIVIAL IN COMPARISON
COMES BACK (so like Maria to explain
The miracle as if it were mundane)
WHEN I WAS 12 OR 13 VENIZELOS
WAS AT MY FATHER'S HOUSE.   INTO THE ROOM
HIS THOUGHTFUL SENTENCES ADDRESSED TO OTHERS
PRECEDED HIM: 'THE GREAT PROPOSALS FOR GREECE
COME TO US FROM ON HIGH, FROM STRANGERS' &
SO FORTH   AND I FELT AS WITH THIS GOD
MICHAEL THAT WE WERE HEARING LOFTY WORDS
MANY TIMES UTTERED UNTIL (APPEARING) HE
BROUGHT AT LAST HIS MIND TO BEAR ON US

I MY DEARS FELT THE BOARD A SET OF NOTES
HE PRESENTLY GLANCED DOWN AT: 2 OR 3
MELODIOUSLY PITCHED & WITH THE TRUE
HOMERIC RESONANCE   SUCH AN ENCOUNTER

IN LIFE WD HAVE MADE ONE ON THE INSTANT FREE
OF HABIT   RITUAL   ALL THAT BINDS, & NO
SIMPER OF 'HOLINESS'   JUST THE HEAVENLY
BLAZING CALM ELATE INTELLIGENCE
"The red eye of your God"—did Michael mean
The sun *was* God? OR GOD'S ORGAN OF SIGHT
THE FOUNT OF ENDLESS VISIBILITIES.
NOW: DOES THE EYE CREATE THE OBJECT SEEN?
ONE TINY INKLING OF M'S MARVELOUS
PHILOSOPHIC VISTAS   Lost on us!

DJ: He said next time we needn't bother
With diet and deep breathing and the rest.
SUCH ROT ALL THAT   SURPRISED OUR MIRABELL
DIDN'T HAVE OUT THE TINFOIL HALOS   Tell
About his masque! THE ONLY MASQUE IN QUESTION
HID A BIRDBRAIN. HE OF COURSE HAD HAD
NOT THE FOGGIEST   'GREAT DOORS'? THERE WERE NONE:
HIS (M) PERHAPS FOR CRUCIAL DISTANCING.
NO WONDER HE LIES ABASHED HEAD UNDER WING
LIKE A SWAN   HIS CROWD U SEE (TO WHOM WE ARE
MERE FORMULAS) CANNOT CONCEIVE MAN'S EASY
LEAP ONTO THE OUTSTRETCHED PALM OF GOD,
CANNOT GRASP THAT ALL OUR LIVES ARE SPENT
IMAGINING SUCH A PRESENCE
                    NONETHELESS
OUGHTN'T WE ENFANTS TO STRETCH (NOBLESSE
OBLIGE) A KINDLY HAND OUT TO OUR BIRD?
Yes, Mirabell, we love you. Come! HE STIRRED
Come, we need you! THAT'S IT   HEAD UP! BRAVO

PLEASE GIVE YR MIRABELL A BIT OF TIME
HE IS AFRAID TO LOOK MY DEARS   HE FANCIES
WE ARE TRANSFIGURED   Mirabell, come on!
Is it true you've turned into a swan?
                              SHALL I? U JEST?
AH Y OUA RE REA L SOB LIN DINGT O ME ID O NO TSEE I

WILL GR OW USED THERE! NO SWAN ALAS BUT (ON THE OUTSIDE) YOUR
FOND PEACOCK STILL I HAVE BEEN ALLOWED NEW INFORMATION
THANKS TO YR SUCCESS MY SCHOOL IS NOW CHARTERED! TOMORROW

★

Questions of Rank

Mirabell's information deals with Nature,
And high time. But first, the other day,
His wise old teacher, 00 as we call him
—Batman to Mirabell's Robin, says DJ—
Had *he* been present?
O NO   NONE OF OURS   NO NO
                        You first said he would be.
                        WELL I WAS NOT THERE   & AM
NOT U UNDERSTAND OF HIS HIGH RANK

The One in question intervenes—are all
These voices henceforth at our beck and call?
                        00: WE WERE FIVE
(Just that, and goes.) He *was* there, Mirabell!
HE HAS SAID SO
Forgive us for insisting. Now the news?

                        NATURE IS MISTRESS OF THE ROBES   MATTER,
HER MATERIAL   ITS CUT & STYLE, HER CEREMONY
WHO IS FOREVER CHANGING THE COSTUMES OF EARTH, OF MAN'S
VERY FLESH TO SUIT HER NEEDS & HIS. LET ME PUT IT AS
FORCEFULLY AS I CAN: THE SOCALLD 'SUPERNATURAL'
DOES NOT EXIST. SHE IS NUMBER 2 PERSON
You're mastering the Fem Lib idiom.
                        O I TRY
ALWAYS TO BE A LA PAGE   AS MERCURY WE ARE THE
GOBETWEEN. YET IN PERSONIFYING MATTER/MATER
YOU MUST REMEMBER THAT MATTER IS NOT ALL, BUT OBEYS
THE DIVINE RATIO 88:12

Our strong point, Mirabell, has never been
Your Math. Now will the Twelve personified
Emerge as Michael?
                    NO NO   I MUST NOT

                    GONE   QUITE TERRIFIED
WE MIGHT LET SOMETHING SLIP   He's certainly
Changed his tune about Nature. THAT TUNE MAY
HAVE BEEN A SMALL TEST PASSED WHEN JM FLEW
TO HER DEFENSE   DJ: Wystan, you knew
That Chester went to Earth on our big day?
YES   AH YES   ALL SO HUMANELY PLANNED
Could you say goodbye?   NO   WE WERE SPARED OUR FEELINGS:
NO TEARS, NO AGONIZING INTERVIEW
YET WE HAD MANY MANY EVENINGS SAID
GOODNIGHT WITH A PAT & OFF EACH TO HIS BED

I still don't understand why Mirabell
Couldn't meet Michael. JM: Come, we know
The Bible, sort of, and we've seen the icons.
Michael is the fallen angels' blazing
Triumphant adversary. With his sword
"Fierce as a Comet", with his sunlike armor—
Stately allusions to a time before
The Church absolved itself of Holy War—
He's light's power over dark. DJ: Then is
Mirabell a devil? JM: Well,
Up to a point. Beyond it he remains
A puzzle—part of the "atomic forces"
That wrecked "Atlantis". What this fable means
In textbook terms, we've long despaired of learning!
MICHAEL THE PURE PHOTON? HIS WHITE LIGHT
QUANTUM INDIVISIBLE WD KNOCK
OUR PEACOCK PARTICLE OF TINSEL GREENS
& BLUES & REDS MY BOYS TO SMITHEREENS
Yet Mirabell's 00 somehow took part.
Détente in Heaven? DJ: I just wish
Mirabell weren't suddenly so servile—

It's we who should fall upon our knees to thank him.
NOT MES ENFANTS HIS CHOICE   WE NOW OUTRANK HIM

★

See how sunlight filters through the green!
(Our mascot Pepperomia, named at last,
Each leaf a new life moist and sparkling—)
THE RADIANT CELLS   What
   Can it be like *inside* them, Mirabell?
            PALATIAL   THE VEG CELLS LUMINOUS,
THE MINERAL FIERY   BOTH HOT & COLD FIRE. THESE
GENIUS STRUCTURES OF THE MASTER ARCHITECT HAVE THE
SUPREME QUALITY OF WEIGHTLESS DOMES   THEIR ELABORATE
GROINING & VITAL PILLARS POSITIOND WITHOUT BASEWORK,
FOR BOTH ROOF & FLOOR BREATHE LIFE & HOLD TO EACH OTHER BY
TRANSLUCENT MEANS
   Do you experience the cold and heat?
           THESE LIKE TIME ARE NONEXISTENT FOR US
YET MORE THAN TIME THEY EFFECT & AFFECT MATTER. WE ARE
INTERESTED IN TEMPERATURE AS IT APPLIES TO
SOUL INTENSITIES WE OVERSEE. WITH THE HISTORIC
MIGRATIONS (GENGHIS KHAN ETC) WE CAME TO SEE THAT THE LAB
SOULS MUST THEMSELVES BE MIGRATED   NOT REBORN IN THE SAME
HEMISPHERE OR CLIMATE: CONSTANT ROUGH STUFF! TEMP IS A FRAME
FOR BEING. SOULS PERMANENTLY IN HEAVEN KNOW NEITHER
HOT NOR COLD   BUT TO DIVERT THE PASSER-THRU WE ARRANGE
THE PLUNGE INTO THE WORKINGS OF THE VOLCANO, THE SWIM
UNDER POLAR ICE, THE CLIMB UP A TREE INSIDE THE TREE:
LESSONS THAT EQUIP OUR TRANSIT SOULS FOR LIFE
                      BACK TO CELLS
THERE ARE AS U KNOW MILLIONS OF DIFFERENCES IN EACH
CATEGORY FROM MINERAL TO VEG, REPTILE TO MAN,
& FINALLY THE STRUCTURELESS STRUCTURE OF THE SOUL CELL,
OR MORE PROPERLY THE SUBLIME STRUCTURE OF THE CELLS OF
GOD BIOLOGY
   Whose body is Earth. Whose eye—the glowing Sun—
   Upon the sparrow also is the sparrow . . .

IN SAINTLY TERMS MY DEAR THE MYSTIC UNION

U NEXT MEET THE ANGEL?

Tomorrow.   I PERHAPS

MADE A BIT MUCH OF PROTOCOL B4

No harm done.   & WAS RATHER

LAUGHED AT   Never by us!

NO? WELL   YR NEW INSTRUCTOR IS MOST POWERFUL

& YOU MUST UNDERSTAND MY GREAT RESPECT   IF I CAN BE

OF SERVICE? WELL   AS TO PROTOCOL, DO AS U SEE BEST

—Backing off.

HE DREADS TO RAISE HIS EYES

MAMAN FEELS HELPLESS   SO LIKE THE OLD DAYS:

PEOPLE WAITING FOR HOURS WAITED YET

LONGER WHEN THE SPOILT PRIME MINISTER'S

DAUGHTER DROPPED IN FOR POCKET MONEY

CLASS

TROUBLING ENOUGH ON EARTH & NOW ALAS

THAT THE ROI SOLEIL HAS ENTERED & STOOD STILL

TO CHAT WITH US, HOW EVERYONE DEFERS!

But talent makes the difference there, and mind.

DON'T COUNT ON IT   SUCH FRIGHTFULLY UNWORTHY

TYPES   THAT IMP LUCA Go on! HAS REPLACED

POOR DOTING CHESTER WITH INDECENT HASTE

Found a new friend? Who? PLATO WHAT HE SEES

IN L!? IS IT AS I ONCE WROTE, THAT GOD

JUDGES WHOLLY BY APPEARANCES?

Then Luca must be one of Nature's best.

PURE CARAVAGGIO   & A PEACHBLOOM PEST

More about the status you've acquired?

ENFANTS WYSTAN & I HAVE A SALON:

REGULAR SMART LEVEES   ONE SIMPLY PICKS

UP THE (M) BLACK RECEIVER & A MADLY

EFFICIENT 77036

DOES ALL THE REST Who comes? WHO DOESN'T? O

LET'S SEE   YESTERDAY: COLETTE, COCTEAU,

ST SIMON So Wystan's taking up

The Frogs at last. QUE VOULEZ VOUS? THE PLATONIC
SYNDROME LED ME TO THE POISONED CUP,
A BREW OF JUICY VIGNETTES! Such as? WELL, TALES OF
LOUIS XIV & EPHRAIM EYE TO EYE
BOWING IN THE MIRRORS AT VERSAILLES
Poor Ephraim, we've all dropped him, like a mask . . .
BESIDES, AMONG THE GERMANS (UNTER VIER
AUGEN) GOETHE TURNS OUT QUITE MY DEAR
AS DULL AS RILKE   DJ: *They're* mined out,
Densities fueling readers here below—
Unlike the French? CURIOUS POINT   WHY SO?
COLETTE MORE RECENTLY DEAD? OR ELSE IN HER
PAGES ARE VEINS NO STUDY CAN EXHAUST,
ACCESSIBLE TO THE LUCKY AMATEUR
WITHOUT FIRST BEING PROCESSED? ACADEME
MINES I SUSPECT WITH DEEPER BLASTS   The dire
Glumness of some critics— WE FOREDOOM
THOSE CALLING CARDS TO OUR HALL PORTER'S FIRE

And tomorrow Michael! YES   THIS AFTERNOON
WE'RE NOT AT HOME   A HUSH EXTENDS AROUND US
ONE ALL BUT HEARS THE QUIVER THRU THE HOUSE
OF FAINTLY, AWESOMELY APPROACHING WINGS.
MM FUSSING WITH HER NEW SILVER GOWN,
MY BLOND HEAD RISING FROM A GOSSAMER WHITE
TUNIC   How *Rosenkavalier!* O QUITE
HE BY THE WAY IS A DARLING   Who is? STRAUSS

*

The Second Visit

MORTAL CHILDREN, GENTLE SHADES, GREETINGS. I AM MICHAEL.
THE VAST FORMING INTELLIGENCE ENCOMPASSING THE ENERGIES OF
  A UNIVERSE OF BORNING & EXPLODING WORLDS SETTLED AT LAST
  FOR THIS, CALLED EARTH.

ONCE AGAIN OUR ARCHITECT MADE READY HIS TOOLS & BEGAN HIS
    WORK.

HIS PLAN, O HIS PLAN!

HE HAS FOREVER DREAMED OF CREATING A GOOD COMPANY AND A
    FRIENDLY PLACE. NOW HE BEGAN AGAIN CUPPING ENERGIES AND
    LAYING ABOUT SEED & LIGHT.

HE LONG KNEW THE FORCES ARRAYED AGAINST HIM: THE NEGATIVES,
    THE VOIDS. HE HAD BEEN BESTED BEFORE.

THESE HAD DESTROYED OTHERS OF HIS WORKS BY EXPLOSION AND BY
    BLACK SUCTIONING, AND HE NAMED THEM EVIL.

HE WAS EVER ON GUARD, HE SET ASIDE FOUR QUANTA OF ENERGY AND
    FIRST CREATED HIS HELPERS.

I AWOKE.

MY FACE GENTLY AS BY A BREEZE WAS TURNED UPWARD: 'BEHOLD,
    MY OWN, THE LIGHT'

THIS I KNEW WAS MY DUTY, EACH OF ITS WORKINGS, ITS SHINING
    & ITS DIMMING, ITS TERRIBLE & ITS FRUITFUL ASPECTS: THE
    TENDING OF THE SUN.

MY BROTHERS WERE ASSIGNED THEIR DUTIES, WE BENT OUR BACKS
    TO THE PLAN. ANOTHER CHANCE TO BE GIVEN TO OUR MASTER!

SO THE SOFT WORDS, THE INTELLIGENCE. NOW WHAT IS THIS IN
    FACT?

WHAT MEANT BY PLAN? WORKS? WHAT BY MASTER? AND WHAT, AT
    THE GOLDEN END, BY PARADISE?

A WHIRL OF FIRE. A BALL. A CLOUD OF SMOKE & SETTLING ASH. A
    COOLING. A LOOK AT THE THING.

O IS IT, THAT STANDING BACK AT THE VERY ELBOW OF
    INTELLIGENCE, IS THIS NOT THE FERTILE ELEMENT:
    IMAGINATION?

WE DESCENDED THEN ON AN ARC. FOR THE ARCHITECT, THAT
    WHITESMITH,

HAD FLUNG HIS WATERY HANDS DOWNWARD AND A HISSING STEAM
    ENVELOPED OUR DREAM.

I RAISED THE BEAM, FOUR DIVINE COLORS LAID AN ARC, WE WENT
    DOWN.

AND THEN FROM HIS STORED INTELLIGENCE, JUST AS HAD THE STUFF
OF US, CAME THE RUSH, THE SPRINGING ENERGIES, THE AIR
FRESHENED, LIFE! LIFE!

THERE IS FOR US NO DIMENSION OF TIME. SO HOW MAY YOU KNOW
THE LENGTHS WHICH WERE ONLY THE INTELLIGENCE & ITS
WORKINGS?
THESE HUGE AND HUMBLE MIRACLES APPEARED:
ASH TO SOIL. STARS TO ENERGY SOURCES. SUN TO GROWTH. EACH
STEP A STEP TOWARD THE FIRST FLAT WIDE GREEN SPACES.
THEN BROTHER ELIAS WAS TOLD: 'DIVIDE BY WATER'
AND MY BROTHER CALLED FORTH THOSE ENERGIES & INSTRUCTED
THEM.
THEY MULTIPLIED, THEY POURED FORTH, AND THE GREEN WAS
SEPARATED ACCORDING TO THE PROPORTIONS DEEMED NEEDFUL
BY OUR MASTER
FOR HE HELD IN HIS INTELLIGENCE SEVERAL CHILDREN HE WISHED
TO KEEP APART.
US FOUR HE SUMMONED. HE SAID: 'NOW WE ARE READY,
YET IS NOT THIS PLACE BEAUTIFUL SIMPLY OF GREEN & WATER &
QUIET AIR?'
WE WAITED AS DO THE WORK ANIMALS WHO KNOW THEIR MASTER
HAS NOT BROUGHT THEM OUT FOR MERE COMPANY, THAT IN
THE SOIL UNDER THEIR HOOVES LIES HIS DEAR ATTENTION.

WE HAVE NOT ENVIED HIS VARIOUS CHILDREN.
HE SAID: 'TAKE THIS STICKING EARTH AND FASHION ME SOME
FORMS.'
MANY WERE THEN MODELED, SOME HE NODDED AT, OTHERS WERE
SMASHED AGAIN FLAT. AND THEN HE POINTED TO A FORM
AND THE RADIANCE OF HIS FACE MADE US KNEEL: THE HEIR.
AND WHAT? A CREATURE OF GREAT BLANK EYES & LOW HANGING
HEAD, SHY OF US, BETWEEN TREMBLING FORELEGS: 'MY SON'
AGAIN THE WORK. WE HOVERED & HELPED WHERE WE COULD. AND
THIS CREATURE SUPPED ON THOUGHT.
(DJ: The centaur? JM: Shh! I think so.)
YET OUR MASTER HAD IN SPARE A TWOLEGGED CREATURE WE HAD
FORMED FIRST, AS HE SEEMED THE IMAGE OF OURSELVES.

THE HISTORY OF THE ONE YOU KNOW. OF THE OTHER, YOU LIVE.
NOW WHEN IN THE COURSE OF HIS PLAN THE ARCHITECT FROWNS
    ON HIS WORK, HIS MERCY ALLOWS IT TO DESTROY ITSELF.
AND ALWAYS AT HIS BECK IS DESTRUCTION, A THIRD BROTHER.
A MODEST BROTHER. WHO IS NOT, WHO MUST UNDO?
'TAKE THE CREATURES IN HAND.'
WE TURNED OUR EYES FROM THE LOUD EXPLOSION.
AND WHEN OUR BROTHER CAME TO US HE HELD ONLY THE ONE
    FORM, & IN HIS OTHER HAND LOOSE CLAY.
WE WAITED: AGAIN THE CYCLE OF FIRE, ASH, DUST.
HOW PATIENT TRUE INTELLIGENCE! A NEW DESIGN:
THE FLAT PLAINS WERE NOW BROKEN BOTH BY WATER &
    MOUNTAINS, AND THE SEASONS SPURRED BY CAPPED ICE. WHY?
'MY CHILD MUST STRUGGLE TO GAIN HIS INHERITANCE'
THEN AGAIN WE PRESENTED OUR MODEL. WE KNEW BY OUR MASTER'S
    SMILE THAT HE HAD AT LAST RECOGNIZED THE IMAGE AS
    FAITHFUL.
'MAKE HIM UNDER THE NAME OF MAN. LET HIM SURVIVE.'

AS MICHAEL I AM ALLOWED TO WONDER, FOR I AM A FAVORITE OF
    GOD'S:
WHY UNDER THE NAME? WAS MY MASTER PUTTING A DISTANCE
    BETWEEN HIMSELF AND THIS NEW CREATURE?
'BROTHERS (I SAID) OUR CREATURE MUST ENDEAR HIMSELF' AND THEY
    UNDERSTOOD.
WE MADE FACE & EYES IN THEMSELVES INFINITELY APPEALING. BY
    THOSE EYES WE SHOWED OUR LORD SOMETHING OF THE
    DARLING OF HIS OWN GENIUS
(SMALL TREASURES HE LOVES, OWNING THE VAST UNIVERSE).
OUR CREATURE STILL HANGING ON A GROWN THING CALLED TREE
    HAD NOT YET BEEN ACCEPTED.
A FOURTH BROTHER OF GREAT WIT, OUR TRUE INVENTOR, THOUGHT:
    HOW TO DELIGHT GOD?
AND TAKING A SPARK FROM AN ENERGY NEARBY HE FLUNG IT INTO
    THE CREATURE'S HEAD
AND AT ONCE THE STUNNED FINGERS LOOSENED, DOWN IT FELL, AND
    WHEN NEXT THE EYES OPENED THEY PEERED STRAIGHT UP.
AND GOD SAW A NEW LIGHT THERE.

IT SHONE FLICKERING OVER SEVERAL IDEAS: MINE, MASTERY, WHY?
AND GOD TURNED TO US: 'IT IS MY OWN.'

THAT LONG MARCH IS STILL UNDER WAY. I AM MICHAEL. MY LIGHT
    IS YOUR DAY.
WHEN AS NOW IT SINKS I LEAVE YOU FOR MY VIGIL. ON OTHER
    DAYS, THE NEXT TWO TIMES, YOU WILL MEET MY WATER
    BROTHER, THEN TOO MY WITTY EARTH BROTHER.
AT LAST WE WILL BRING YOU OUR SHY BROTHER, HANDS BEHIND HIM,
AND YOUR INSTRUCTION WILL BEGIN.
AND NOW O HUMAN MEN CHILDREN & GOD'S DELIGHT, HEAR
    MICHAEL SAY:
INTELLIGENCE, THAT IS THE SOURCE OF LIGHT. FEAR NOTHING WHEN
    YOU STAND IN IT   I RAISE YOU UP AMONG US   HAIL   HAIL

*

VIS A VIS MY DEARS ON MICHAEL'S PALM!
ONE HAD THE FEELING OF A BIJOU OBJECT
HE WAS IMMENSELY PLEASED AT LAST TO OWN
He must then *be* immense. INDEED   THE SCALE
OF THE LOST IVORY & GOLD ATHENA?
MAKES ONE ASK WHAT PHIDIAS HAD SEEN
I wish—I nearly said "I wish we'd been there!"
U WERE   BOTH LISTENING AS DEAR ONES DO,
EYES TURNED ASIDE NOT TO IMPEDE THE FLOW
We're at your level? YES   In our old clothes,
Wrinkle and graying hair and liver spot?
NOT IN OUR WITCH'S GLASS, DISTINCTLY NOT!
Who's fairest? DJ: Michael, I suppose.
He'll come again? THEY AS I SEE IT WILL
INCREASE IN NUMBER ONE BY ONE UNTIL
THEY STAND FOURSQUARE: NATURE'S 4 GENTLEMEN
And the shy brother? AH   THE SOUNDING BASS
IN THE QUARTET   OR PITCH INAUDIBLE
EXCEPT TO A BLACK DOG: HE OVERSEES
MIRABELL'S OLD MASTER I SHD THINK
WHO IN HIMSELF IS SOMETHING Is he? Tell!

OO APPEARS FIRST, WE STAND, HE RATHER AHEM
PORTENTOUSLY FACES OFF   THEN LIFTING INK
BLACK GLITTERY WINGS OBSCURES OUR VIEW WITH THEM.
WHITE LIGHT APPEARS AROUND HIM   HE BECOMES
THE SILHOUETTE OF   Evil? NO . . . RESISTANCE?
A PRIMAL SCENE? PART OF A MASTERMASQUE:
IN THE SERENE WHITE BRILLIANCE MICHAEL'S EYES
THEN FACE THEN FIGURE NOW MATERIALIZE
IN UTTER QUIET   HE PUTS DOWN HIS HAND
ON WHICH MM & I TAKING OUR STAND
ARE LIFTED TO THE LEVEL OF HIS FACE
WHERE THE BIJOU EFFECT TAKES PLACE
                                ENFANTS
HIS GOLDEN EYES EVER ALERT AND CALM
ARE FIXED UPON US   WE ARE UNAWARE
OF MOVING LIPS & YET HIS VOICE IS THERE
SURROUNDING US   OR ARE WE IN HIS MIND
READING THESE GLORIES THAT WOULD SEEM TO COME
FROM BOTH SIDES OF THE MIRROR OF MANKIND?
How does it end? REVERSE PROCEDURE   EYES
DIMMING, THEN FACE   HAND LOWERED   ALL THE REST
IS SUDDENLY OUR FORMER STATE OF THINGS.
THERE LIES THE OLD AWED MASTER FACEDOWN WINGS
OUTSTRETCHED   Does he speak then? O TOUCHINGLY
MUMBLES ON HIS WAY OUT 'U ARE BLEST'

DJ MY BOY SMOOTH SAILING
                        AS WE SPEAK
MAMAN PATS DOWN THE SEAS   HERE'S TO A GREEK
NEW YEAR'S DAY PARTY! HUGS FROM ALL YR FRIENDS
—With which our long, amazing summer ends.

George on Birds

DJ crosses the ocean. JM, alone
Through the mild autumn months in Stonington,
Quarries from the transcript murky blocks

Of revelation, now turning a phrase
To catch the red sunset, now up at dawn
Edging into place a paradox—
One atop the other; and each weighs
More than he can stop to think. Despair
Alternates with insight. Strange how short
The days have grown, considering the vain
Ticking, back, forth, of leafless metronomes
Beyond the pane, where atmosphere itself
One morning crystallizes. Winter's here.

George Cotzias, freed of his patient's gown
At last, suggests an evening on the town.
My sister gives us tea first. A fire's laid
And lit, in whose diaphanous charade
He borrows her ease, she his earnestness;
I from them both, a sense of taxing roles
Consigned, on rare occasion, to the coals.
But curtain time approaches: she must dress.
In the dim doorway, while I pace the street
Of old facades, frost-featured and discreet,
They linger. Then her silvery goodbye.
At table, over wine, the man of Science
—Bifocal lenses catching candlelight,
Athena's owl, ear cocked and tufted white—
Takes in the transformation of gargoyle
To feathered friend. Pure vinegar and oil
Our viewpoints, I'd have thought. Not so:
These now are things that Science cares to know.
Science, George hopes, has room for Juno's bird
—And for its mistress, should she grace our Board!

Do I remember, he goes on, the dream
Of Dante's mother, from Boccaccio?
She saw a peacock in a laurel tree,
Beak snipping the clustered berries—down they fell
Until the skirt she held outspread was full—
And woke in labor. Taking up the theme,

Moving past Lesbia's sparrow, Poe and Keats,
Coloratura wood-note understood
By Siegfried, thumb licked clean of dragon's blood;
Past twittering parliament, past the "little bird"
Who speaks to instinct with a paraclete's
Ghostly cackle, we attain the sphere
(Justice?) where Dante saw the letter M
Become an Eagle made of ruby souls
Which sang to him. What of the Phoenix, then?—
Its blaze our culture-watchers doze before,
Never quite making out the infra-vulture.
Of Senator X who vowed Vietnam would "rise
Like a Tucson" from the ashes—? A short pause,
Then George: "You won't laugh if I tell you I
Also get these voices, these vocations?
Over the years, each time I've undergone
A general anesthetic, the same one,
A woman's, cold yet not unloving, fills
My head with truths about the cosmos—truths,
Jimmy, too deep, too antilogical
Ever to grasp, short of the odd detail
Clutched on waking. Once, the phrase 'black holes'
(And this was long before black holes made headlines)
Stayed with me. Another time, these were explained
As ash the Phoenix left on entering
A 'biological cycle'. And once, I woke
Knowing that what had reached me was the song
The Phoenix sings throughout eternity."

We're on the street. He wonders if he may
Try the Board with us next spring in Athens?
His hometown, I remember now, where things
Periodically keep taking him.
As they do me. By the New Year great wings
Have reunited DJ and JM,
Eager to meet the lords of Earth and Sea.

The Board, that first day, is all come-and-go—

Revolving door into a lobby. Enter
Hans as if startled: OH JIM? U ARE THE CENTER
OF MUCH GOOD FEELING HERE   Then Wallace Stevens:
MAY I SUGGEST A CENTRAL METAPHOR:
PEACOCK TO O—to zero—AS CHICKEN TO EGG?
Acknowledging our thanks, away they saunter,
Leaving Wystan and Maria barely
Time to say that in the interval
Since last we met OUR UTTER PURITY
HAS HAD THE GOOD OLD HUMAN DIRT RESTORED.
THE POINT MUST BE MY DEARS, TO TOUCH HOME BASE
MAKES POSSIBLE EACH NEW LEAP INTO SPACE
Here now is Mirabell. He calls us MASTERS,
Calls his poem A CAP TO ALL MY FEATHERS
And says of George's interest:
U SEE, JM? IS NOT SCIENCE ITSELF COMING TO CALL?
                              (The doorbell.)
Not Science, just an oil delivery—
MY ANCESTORS POURING IN TO WARM U: SET US ALIGHT!
One word, next, from a figure bathed in tears:
CHERI   It's my old nurse, Mademoiselle
Who died last month—
                    But 00 interferes:
DOWN! WE BEAR ON WINGS THE WORD OF GREAT MICHAEL O GLORY!
HE & HIS BROTHERS SAY TO US: GO FORTH INTO THE DREAMS
OF THIS OR THAT ONE, NOW AS EAGLE OR SWAN OR DOVE, NOW
AS THE OFT FALLEN OFT RISEN LEGENDARY PHOENIX
& IN THE TONGUES OF DREAM ENTHRALL & INSPIRE ALL THOSE
WHO DO OUR IMMORTAL WORK. BUT FOR YOU, O SCRIBE, O HAND:
GO (THEY COMMANDED FROM THE FIRST) IN YR WORKDAY ASPECT
FOR THESE 2 WILL TRANSFORM U AFTER THEIR OWN FASHION   DOWN!
YOU WILL IN 2 SUNCYCLES BE CALLD   NO INTERRUPTION!
DOWN!   BE SUMMOND BY O GLORY! THE WATER GOD   BACK! DOWN!

What's going *on*? THE AUDITORIUM
ENFANTS IS UNFAMILIAR   THEY ALL SEE
THE GLOW & CROWD IN   IF WE FACED THE LIGHT?
(Our table's in the gloomy downstairs hall—

Well, not a moment to describe the house;
But we move chairs.) BETTER   NOW MICHAEL HAS
A PATH   AH YES   YES! HE IS OVER US!
Michael? So many voices, how to know—
MY DEARS IT IS A MAHLER   Michael speaks:

CHILDREN, MY BROTHER ELIAS REQUESTS YOU IN TWO DAYS. HE IS
   AS WATER SWEET & FLUID.
I HAVE CLEANED THIS SPACE: HAVE NO FEARS, INTELLIGENT ONES,
   HAIL!

Thus as in some old-world Grand Hotel
(Early morning ado; kingfisher streak
Of lift-boy; *Figaro* and eggcup; hall
Porter's flicked ash, a chambermaid's faint shriek;
The beldam, ringlets trembling upon skull,
Chastening marble with her brush and pail
—Inconveniences the clientèle
Must philosophically endure until

A new day's clean white linen runners lie
In place over the antediluvian crimson
Of corridor and stair, down which now takes
—Bonjour, Milord! Il fait un beau soleil!—
His ease a blondness bareheaded and winsome)
THE WHITE HAS BEEN LAID DOWN FOR THESE NEW TALKS

★

The Water Brother

CHILDREN, ARE YOU THIRSTY? COME, ELIAS!

Not Willowware in Greece, a tea-stained white
Cup surges and ebbs with the new angel:
I AM THE SUSPENSION   REASON FLOATS IN MY SALTY STRENGTH
   HAIL!

SOME CLAIM THE MOON CONTROLS ME, NOT SO: I BALANCE IT IN
    THE PALM OF MY BASINS.
BENIGN, I WASH MY WITTY BROTHER. CONTROLLED, I BRING MAN
    HIS FALSE LIGHT
BUT YIELDING EVER TO MICHAEL AS THE BROTHER MOST BELOVED
    OF OUR MASTER.
NOW (imitative movements of the cup)
I AM WHIRLPOOL! NOW WATERFALL! NOW WAVE!
THEN AS RAIN & ICE, MANIFESTING MYSELF FOR MY MASTER & HIS
    CHILD, I REGULATE THE SEASONS.
I WAS BORN AS A TEAR IN GOD'S EYE: THUS I BRING BALM FOR
    SORROW.
O CHILDREN, I AM THE GREATER PART OF YOUR BODIES & YOUR
    NOURISHMENT, THOUGH 2ND TO MY BELOVED MICHAEL.
NOW IN 12 TIDES WE WILL RETURN WITH MY WITTY BROTHER
& THEN WITH OUR SHY ONE WHEN MY SEASON OF RENEWAL FINDS
    YOU STRONGER TO MEET THE FORCE OF HIM,
AND THEN WE FOUR COMMENCE YOUR INSTRUCTION   HAIL!

MES ENFANTS WE ARE STILL SLIGHTLY AWASH
Don't tease us, tell! FIRST MICHAEL IN HIS GLORY
THEN HE TURNED & A SHAFT! A RAINBOW SPOKE
& AS WE KNELT IN WONDER MELTED INTO
WHITE CLOUD WHICH NEXT GREW SOLID   How baroque!
A GIANT ALL HOAR & SPIKY ICE   A HISS
OF HAIL & OUR BLUE ROBES CLUNG WETLY TO US!
ELIAS ROSE IN A TALL DAZZLING VAPOR
& MICHAEL'S LAUGHTER MADE ALL HEAVEN QUAKE
And did Maman's affinities with water
Earn her special treatment? AH ENFANT,
TOO RAVISHING: I SANK INTO A POOL
WARM & SWEET: EXPERIENCING MY MOTHER'S
WOMB   SUSPENDED   INFINITELY PLEASED
AS IF MY LIFE WERE JUST AHEAD
                            And Wystan?
I MY DEARS STOOD BRACED IN A MANLY DOWNPOUR
Why do you suppose he's called Elias?
THEY ALL HAVE MANY NAMES   THEIR VOWELS RING

THRU CANYONS OF MYTH   ELIAS I DARESAY
IS THE MUSICAL ANGEL MOZART CALLS GABRIEL
In an opera? NO   IN A SOIREE
Mozart as Stravinsky— YES   OUR CHATS
SUCH FUN   M/S PROPOSES A NEW 'RAKE'
PROGRESSING THRU VARIOUS LIVES OF V WORK ONLY
TO BE COMICALLY DEFEATED BY THE RATS

DJ: What's Wystan's future? JM: We
Assume he stays in the Bureaucracy—
Right, Wystan? Getting mined for all you're worth
By fresh-faced, big-thumbed scholars here on Earth.
DJ: Why do I have the distinct impression
He and Maria both are being groomed
To join the elements? She'll become a tree,
That much we know from Mirabell, while he—
JM: No, no. Maria after all
Had lost much of her soul to cobalt rays.
But Wystan's is intact; so that can't be.
A PLUS DJ   BACK TO THE GLABROUS CLAYS
THE OILS & METALS MY FIRST LOVES   COME AUTUMN
A FAIRY PAIR WILL FLIT FORTH HAND IN HAND:
MM INTO THE GREEN, I INTO SAND
But *your* soul wasn't harmed. Why this instead
Of human life, if it should come to that,
Like Chester? MY DEMISE A FORM OF LEAD
POISONING: I WENT OFF TO MY ROOM
TIDDLY THAT NIGHT BUT HAD IN MIND TO SCRIBBLE
A NOTE TO C, & AS I'D DONE SINCE CHILDHOOD
SUCKED ON A PENCIL THINKING. NEXT I KNEW,
AN ICY SUN SHONE IN UPON THE DEAD
WEIGHT OF MY FEATHER QUILT   But how does lead
Destroy the soul? DJ: They don't *use* lead—
Graphite in pencils. LET THE FACT REMAIN
(OR FABLE!) THAT I SIPPED IT GRAIN BY GRAIN.
OVER THE YEARS ANYTHING FROM AN X RAY
TO THE COSMIC RAYS WE'RE ALL EXPOSED TO WD
RESIDE UNDISSIPATED IN MY BLOOD

& VITAL ORGANS: I BECAME A WALKING
NONCONDUCTING LEADEN CASKET THESE
PARTICULAR DESTRUCTIVE ENERGIES
HAD FILLED WITH RADIANT WASTE   Dear God . . . & NO
PANDORA   NO LATTERDAY BASSANIO
TO LIFT THE LID. WE MAKE OUR DEATHS MY DEARS
AS NO DOUBT THAT SHY WILDLY EXPECTED BRO
WILL TELL US   Ah, it's grim. Yet what to ask
Of death but that it come wearing a mask
We've seen before; to die of complications
Invited by the way we live. Bad habits,
Overloaded fuses, the foreknown
Stroke or tumor—these we call our own
And face with poise. It's random death we dread.
The bomb, the burning theatre, the switchblade-
Brandishing smack freak— OR ARE PENCIL & KNIFE
& COCK ALL ONE
                    & WAVE & BREAST & WET
SNAKY LOCKS! WE'LL SWEEP UP U CHAPS YET!
Speaking of those breasts, Maman, the tale
We're hearing now is nothing if not male.
But Maya long ago said Erzulie
Was Queen of Heaven. Has She any niche
That one could visit? TALK TO YR WHITE WITCH

DAVID   JIMMY   Maya! In New York
Last week I saw some friends of yours; saw Teiji.
He and his young wife are salvaging
Your Haitian film. At last it's out of storage,
Cut, spliced, synchronized with the drum-tapes—
Reel upon reel of ritual possession—
And can be shown soon. We're all thrilled except
(Wouldn't you know) your mother: "Maya made
High class, avant garde stuff—documentaries
Never." Whereupon Joe Campbell spoke
Authoritatively of your amazement
At being overwhelmed quite simply by
Gusts of material so violent

As to put out the candle held to them
By mere imagination. Such a theme,
He said, took all one's powers to "document".
AS U ARE LEARNING, J? But now my question:
Is there no Ewig-Weibliche in sight?
AN EWIG SHALL WE SAY HERMAPHRODITE?
YOU HAD THOUGHT ERZULIE WAS FEMALE? HE/
SHE IS/WAS RAIN SOIL SEED SUN STARLIGHT
PHALLUS & VAGINA   OMNISEX
QUEEN OF A HEAVEN LIKE A GAUDY EX
VOTO WHERE DESIRE & SATISFACTION
PEPPER & SALT THE DISH SERVED PIPING HOT!
No heartburn after? O MY TEIJI   WHAT
IS THE GIRL LIKE   PRETTY? I thought so. Sweet, smart,
Clearly devoted to both him and art.
No match of course for *you* in your heyday—
More Greuze than Ghirlandaio. SOUNDS OK

Admit it, this new Erzulie leaves us
Less eager for a glimpse. Where's Marius?
MY DEAR JAMES   Is there an Athenian
Club where you can get a drink and read
The underground newspapers? O INDEED
PLATO & WYSTAN ARE ITS CO-CHAIRPERSONS
And Chester's Luca, still under Plato's wing?
LUCA! CUT MY LACE   THAT   THAT   THAT THING
ROAMING HEAVEN LIKE A VAST STEAMROOM
Cool off—ask Coleridge for some laudanum.
NO NO   I LEAVE SOOTHED BY THE SIGHT OF U

MES CHERS HE MEANS THE RADIANCE AROUND U
Ephraim!—dimmed though we are, much of the time,
By careless living, the old human grime?
A WISE PROTECTION   SO THE ATHLETE SMEARS
DIRT BENEATH HIS EYES TO CUT REFLECTION.
MY POOR SLAVE'S VISION OVERFLOWS WITH LOVE
AROUND U BOTH SUCH JOY SUCH RADIANT LIGHT
If so, a joy not ours to feel, a light

We are the two contracted pupils of.

YET FOR THAT FOCAL DARKNESS THANK GOD B
MY BOYS   IT IS YR PRECIOUS SANITY

Wystan. Can we bear to part with him,
Our mine of good sense? Ah, he'll doff his dim
Red shift (the mufti of a star's retreat)
To vanish into quarry and tar-pit,
Sandgrain and stylus, thorn the raw March wind
Piping through despondent makes a wand
In bloom. He'll draw the desert round his knees,
Brows knitted where the thinking icecaps freeze.
He'll be the nurse whose charges "for their own
Good" go without tea—and herself lies
Till morning haunted by reproachful eyes.
He'll be the glinting, faithful heart of stone.

*

The Earth Brother

Twelve tides pass. We take the Board upstairs
Where beyond the glassed-in balcony
Mt Lykabettos, green all year with pine,
Rises steeply in sun. And here is Michael:

DEAR CHILDREN, MY WITTY ELIJAH TWIN OF WATER IS WITH US:
COME ELIJAH, MAKE US LAUGH!

MY WIT IS NOT AS READY AS I WOULD WISH
(Oddly subdued, in spite of Michael's words)
FOR I AM IN YOU, GOD'S CHILDREN: THE RIB, NOT THE FUNNY BONE.
I WAS GOD'S THIRD CREATION, SUMMONED FROM COSMIC DUST AND
      NAMED BY MANY COSMOS,
AND WHAT ARE OUR FOUR NAMES BUT GREEK INVENTIONS?

FROM COSMIC DUST   O THINK ON THAT!
IT MEANS I HAVE IN ME THE IRRADIATED METALS, I WHO MOST
      DREAD THEM, FOR I AM FRUITFUL EARTH
IT MEANS I AM THE HABITAT OF THE CREATURE DUG OUT OF ME.
MY TWIN DRAWS BACK & I ADVANCE, AND NOW OUR DANCE
      REVERSES
FOR IT IS GOD'S WILL THAT HIS CHILDREN REDUCE THEIR NUMBERS,
      & THUS HE NUDGES THEM INTO THE MORE CONFINED SPACES,
& THUS IT IS IN THE WOMB OF TWINS: WATER EVER RECEDING AS
      THE FETUS WAXES.
BUT NOW MY SMALL BROTHERS, FOR ARE WE NOT ALL OF THE
      COMMON CLAY,
(Here at the close, a strong, dancing motion)
FAREWELL! I WILL ANOTHER TIME BE WITTY

O ELIJAH   BROTHER   O WHY ABASHED? HE LEAVES   THE SIGHT OF
      TEARS?
DJ, face streaming: Oh but these aren't tears—
Reaction to the thrill—I can't explain—
I KNOW THIS, MY CHILD. IT IS HIS WIT NO DOUBT: OFTEN MOST
      BRIEF, ACCORDING TO THE NATURE OF COSMIC DUST
JM: Indeed—those short-lived particles
Created by the photons! Only at
Molecular levels is there permanence.
YOU ARE OUR OWN   HAIL!

As Michael goes, DJ: Our first exchange—
We *can* talk back and forth, then, with the angels?
O MY DEARS & THE VOICE LIKE THUNDER! MICHAEL SWUNG
HIS PALM   WE STARED FORTH FROM IT AT YR MOUNTAIN:
IT IT IT SPOKE   THEN TOOK A HUMAN SHAPE
ALL MASSIVE ROCK & GREEN WITH BOUGHS FOR LASHES
OF SUCH I MUST SAY WICKED MERRY EYES!
I DO BELIEVE OUR SPRINGTIME WILL BE GAY
IN THE OLD SENSE   And did he look at you
With special favor? WYSTAN MES ENFANTS
TOOK A POWDER INTO THE NEAREST ROCK
And saw? A CASE OF JEWELS MY BOY   THE VOICE

RANG ROUND ME & (IF I MAY BE IMMODEST)
I UNDERSTOOD MY OWN LAST DECADES' WORK:
SUSTAINED BY WIT AS BY A WRY YOUNG FRIEND
AS I LIMPED FORWARD GRITTY TO THE END.
FOR IS IT NOT OUR LESSON THAT WE COME
EACH TO HIS NATURE? NOT TO ANY VAST
UNIVERSAL ELEVATION, JUST
EACH TO HIS NATURE PRECIOUS IF BANAL
LIKE THE CLICHE UNCOVERED AMONG GEMWORDS:
FOR ME, TO (COSMIC) DUST RETURNED

                      FOR ME

LIKE THE OLD HORSE (BLACK BEAUTY) PUT TO GRASS
It's as we were told at the outset—every grain
Of dust, each waterdrop, to be suffused
With mind, with *our* minds. This will be Paradise.
PRECISELY JM & TO GO ON: THAT RACE
USING US, EVOLVING FROM US IN
THAT PARADISE, ASK THEM ABOUT THAT RACE.
IT IS I THINK NOW BEING READIED, FOR
THESE ANGELS, THE FIRST 3 OF THEM SO FAR,
TAKE WITH US A SOUPCON OF THE TONE
WITH WHICH ONE SPOKE IN ONE'S OWN CARELESS YOUTH
TO AGED ELDERS: RESPECTFUL TOLERANT
HALF PITYING & GOODBYE TO U DEAR AUNT!
DJ: A new species? JM: Yet they'd wanted
"The stuff of man to be human". Mirabell . . .
—Who, at his name, describing a broad O,
Positively sweeps onto the Board.

U ARE HAVING A GOOD TALK?
Dear Peacock, we begin—but suddenly
All his aplomb is gone; and so is he.
                OUR LORD MICHAEL O GLORY!
& HIS BROTHERS SPLENDID IN ALL THEIR POWERS ARE TO BE
ARRAYD B4 YOU IN THE FOURTH OF YR NEXT MOON CYCLES
O FORTUNATE ONES!
DJ: They *know* you're leaving Saturday
And won't be back in Greece until next May.

00 has flown. Reentering, Mirabell:
    FORGIVE ME THAT IS THE PROTOCOL,
MY REVERED TEACHER WHO COMES TO ANNOUNCE THEIR INTENTIONS
Why don't *you* announce them? You once did.
AH DO U NOT SEE? YOU HAVE GRADUATED FROM MY SCHOOL.
I COME TODAY ON A (M) PERSONAL ERRAND ONLY
TO TELL JM MY WINGED LOVE WILL KEEP PACE WITH HIS JET
 & MINE MY BOY
     & MINE (MAMAN DIPLOMA'D!)
TIME FOR TALK, CHAPS?
       Maria, how we'd laugh
With you in this room! There's your photograph,
The lamp you gave us. TALK OR SELF PITY? Oh
All right, let's do it your way. Did you know
George Cotzias in the old days? NEVER WELL
YOUNGER THAN I (NOT THAT I WAS ANTIQUE)
& BURLY NOT YR AVERAGE TESTTUBE FREAK
Bright? WD I KNOW? Let me ask Mirabell—
He sees the future: is George very ill?

MORTALLY YET HE RESISTS AS HE HAS A CONSUMING
V WORK LET ME EXPLAIN: HIS VISIT TO OUR TABLE MAY
BE POSTPONED UNTIL AFTER THESE GRAND DICTEES ARE FINISHD.
HIS RADIATIONS MIGHT CAUSE (M) STATIC IN OUR AIR OR
SO THEY THINK AT 00
And have the rays undone his soul as well?
     YES BUT ILLUMINATED IT
LIKE OUR MM'S
     THESE RETURNS TO THE ELEMENTS ARE NOT
SAD OR SINISTER BUT IN FACT SAINTLY ELEVATIONS.
NEXT TO THE STATIONARY AFTERLIFE OR STEP BY STEP
BUREAUCRATIC UPWARDNESS GIVEN TO MOST, A RETURN
LIKE OUR FRIENDS' IS A NEAR-MIRACULOUS REPLENISHMENT:
THEY WILL BE JOINING THE ARCHANGELS OF EARTH & WATER.
THEY HAVE LONG BEEN CHOSEN
  Becoming—stripped of personality—
  Part of what those angels know and are?
      OF THE DOMINIONS CHEM & VEG

THEY WILL BE OF THE RULING ORDERS
But with no way for us to get in touch.
                                    THEY WILL MAKE THEMSELVES
KNOWN TO U BOTH   THEY WILL CHARGE U WITH ENERGY & WAIT
TO LEAD U TO THEIR MASTERS
Localized—here Daphne in young leaf?
There the chalk face of an old limestone cliff?
                              AH THEY WILL RIPPLE   THEY WILL
JOLT THRU THE WAVES OF TREES & WARPS OF EARTH   THEY WILL
    CARRY
MESSAGES IN THE GRAIN OF ROCK & FLOW IN THE GREEN VEINS
OF LEAVES, FOR THOSE 2 GODS' VAST NETWORK KEEPS THE GLOBE
    INTACT

Like "Adonais"—all of life imbued
With the dead's refining consciousness.
MUCH MORE MUNDANE MY BOY   WE I SHD GUESS
WILL BECOME POWER STATIONS   IN SUCH CRUDE
TERMS AS OIL COAL WOOD WHEAT CORN WE'LL BE
SOURCES QUITE LITERAL OF ENERGY.
THESE EVER MORE DEPLETED, YR POOR CHUMS
WILL HAVE THEIR WORK CUT OUT FOR (& BY) THEM
DJ: Not enough to simply energize,
You'll have to speed things up: "Come on, you guys,
Turn to carbon! On the double, Wheat,
We want two crops this season! Man must eat."
QUITE THE CONTRARY I FEAR: 'LESS GRAIN,
MORE STARVATION! BALANCE ONCE AGAIN!'
Ugly prospect. But it's what the weather
Seems to be telling us. These crippling snows
In Athens, in Miami—THE SHY BROTHER
Why don't they *name* him? Who do you suppose—
NO NO NO

And exit Mirabell, his luster
Lost, these days, in skittery wear and tear.
Imagine the Malade Imaginaire
Played by a feather duster.

Merely name the White Ones, and it wounds him
Into a backward fuss
Of hackles disarrayed, of piteous
Faint NOS. Is the key broken that rewinds him?

Rusted, the courtesy and skill
With which he took away our dread
Of heights? Poor Mr Chips

And his preparatory school—
Behind us now. Great overviews, instead,
Receiving us, WE'LL SPARE HIM WHAT WE CAN EH CHAPS?

★

Stonington. February. Dust off the Bible
And reread *Genesis*—has it come to that?
Still, as the days grow longer
Mirabell—by now more Tower of Babel

Than Pyramid—groans upward, step by step.
I think to make each Book's first word its number
In a different language
(Five is *go* in Japanese), then stop

Sickened by these blunt stabs at "design".
Another morning, Michael's very sun
Glows from within the section
I polish, whose deep grain is one with mine.

Evenings, I imitate Sergei, alone,
Unwinding with a stiff drink. Solitaire.
A meal of leftovers.
At most some laughter on the telephone

With friends I seem to miss but not invite.
A letter to DJ. Or one from him
Read over. A last highball
And bed. Tonight is every blessed night.

(Wait, I did things! Went to hear *Thaïs*—
Or was it *Dialogues des Carmélites*?
Went even to California . . .
Here are the stubs. Where are the memories?)

And what if this immunity to Time
On which our peacock plumed himself should prove
Mortal and contagious?
. . . An ambulance screams past. A May noon. I'm

Crossing Third Ave. Before this evening's flight,
A visit to be paid. George is again
In hospital. It looks bad. Yet despite
That secondary lesion on the brain—
Shrunken, newly bald, supremely sane
Icon of the scarred and staring will—
He's talkative. Tubes into his wrist vein
Pump the reassurance that he'll still
Turn up in Athens. *I* believe him. He
(If only now through language in control
Of nagging matters like mortality)
Will get his way. The bronze star of a kiss
Sends me on mine, plus: "Brother, I'm a whole
Lot stronger than you think. Remember this."

★

In Athens the preliminaries go
Quite by the Board. GK (they use the Greek
Spelling of Cotzias) IS MY DEARS UNIQUE:
A ONE SHOT SOUL   HIS DENSITIES DERIVE
FROM (STEADY) MONTEZUMA Although not

Himself one of the Five? HMM   HARD TO KNOW
THEY WERE EVASIVE WHEN I DIALED OO.
ARE THEY RESPECTING AN INCOGNITO?
WE SHALL HAVE TO DIG IT OUT
                       ENFANTS GK
SO SUBTLY INTRODUCED INTO OUR PLOT:
AS WYSTAN SAYS, IS GOD GEORGE ELIOT?
A) GK'S PLATONIC LOVE FOR THE IMPECCABLE
SOCIETY MATRON   B) ENTER BIZARRE
BROTHER DRAPED IN GHOSTS   C) HERE WE ARE
BACK AT NO ACCIDENT! I BELIEVE IT ALL

The regulars now swarm out of the black
Into our mirror's lit space, joyously
Greeting one another. Here among them
Is Alice Toklas, recent publication
Of whose selected letters TICKLES ME
AS WALLACE APTLY PUTS IT   Mr Stevens:
I DON'T BELIEVE OUR FRIENDS HAVE MET MISS STEIN
Why no! In fact we'd understood that she
Was back on Earth. That lady with a fine
Urbanity explains: ONE LAST BRIEF LIFE
AS A GAUCHO IN THE ARGENTINE
TO STRAIGHTEN OUT MY GENDER   THEN UP HERE
Yourself once more? O YES   A ROSE AROSE.
WHEN IN DOUBT THAT SELF THE WORLD BEST KNOWS
GETS PICKED   Your gender? We don't mean to pry—
THESE DAYS THE MOTHER OF US ALL PREFERS
HER FAVORITES TO BE LIKE MANUSCRIPT
RETURNED BY ALICE: VERY NEATLY TYPED.
I'D HAD A FEW TOO MANY CARBON BLURS
BUT HALLELUJAH! NOW MY HYMNS ARE HERS
Censorship —oh come off it!
                       But all are swept
Aside by our punctilious OO:
TOMORROW O GLORY! MICHAEL WILL BRING HIS FOURTH BROTHER
DJ: So soon? The iron's barely hot.
THIS VISIT REQUIRES SOME PREPARATION. LISTEN NOW:

313

The Shy Brother

HE AVOIDS THE LIGHT. CLOSE OFF THE SETTING SUN. HE WILL COME
WITH GLORY: HIS THREE BROTHER ANGELS   YOU ARE DESIRED
TO BE GRAVE & CIRCUMSPECT IN YR GLANCES TOWARD ANY
SOURCE OF LIGHT
    We're not supposed to see?
                          FIRELIGHT, IS IT POSSIBLE? A CANDLE?
PLEASE HAVE NO FEAR   THAT REPELS THE SHY BROTHER. YOU 4 ARE
IN SPECIAL FAVOR. IT WD BE WISE TO REST BEFORE. HE
TESTS THE STRENGTH. EVEN WALLS OF INTELLECTUAL CONCEIT
HE FELLS. DO YOU RECALL THE COLORS?
                              JM: We do.
                          WE WILL THERE4 MEET
IN BLUE
    Standing for reason, sorrow, limitation . . .
    Red is the color of your highest Powers.
              TRUE   SO WE BELONG TO THE SHY BROTHER.
    We'll need the blue, blue light through curtains, blue
    Of the closed shutters, to offset his red?
                              WISE SCRIBE
    DJ: These angels, aren't they more or less
    Equal in power? JM: The two defer
    To Michael. The Shy One may be his peer.
NO. NOW YOU MEET THE PRINCIPAL
    DJ (chainsmoking): How does one quell fear?
    I really *would* like to be up to this.
                  REACH FOR YR HEALTH   IT IS
STRONG WITHIN YOU. YR CASE HAS BEEN WELL PRESENTED, FOR YR
REQUEST IS NOTHING LESS (OR MORE) THAN IMMORTALITY
    JM: Since when? Not a request we made.
ONE THAT ALL MORTALS MAKE, ONE THAT TO ALL MAY BE GRANTED
    This *is* news.
THE SHY BROTHER IS, LIKE HIS FATHER GOD, BENEVOLENT.
BOTH SHIELD THE FLAME OF HUMAN LIFE & WHEN WASTED TALENT
MAKES THE FLAME GUTTER, GOD TURNS AWAY HIS FACE. THE SHY ONE
PUFFS JUST ONCE
                 Please. But immortality?

IT IS THE GIFT MAN EARNS (OR NOT) WITH HIS LIFE
Oh, you just mean some lasting work translates him
Into the eternal Bureaucrat.
Or else, survival of those salts and carbons
That made him tick. Nothing so frivolous
As that his *soul* pass through the flames and live.
WHICH AS YOU KNOW HAS SO FAR BEEN GIVEN FIVE TIMES ONLY
(Goes.)

        IS IT NOT OUR CHANCE TO MAKE A PLEA?
MAMAN IS NOT UNDERLINE N O T RESIGNED
AFTER ALL TO PIT PULP ROOT & RIND
SHE TOO INSISTS ON IMMORTALITY!

QUITE RIGHT MM: WHY BE A PILE OF SCHIST
WHEN ONE CD BE ONE'S PASSIONATE & CLEVER
& HUMAN HUMAN HUMAN SELF FOREVER?
I FOR ONE MY BOYS MEAN TO RESIST!
LIVES 6 7 8 & 9 ARE WHAT WE MEAN
Beyond the Five? WHY NOT? SHOOT FOR THE MOON!
You must be teasing us. ALAS   TOO TRUE
SWEET LUCID WATERDREAMS ENFANTS   THINK BLUE

*

I AM YOUR EARTH FRIEND, HERE WITH MY WATERY BROTHER.
MY NAMES & HIS ARE MANY. I AM ALSO RAPHAEL, HE OFTEN
    EMMANUEL. OUR TWO SENIOR BROTHERS NAME US ELIAS AND
    ELIJAH, THE TWINS.
WE COME FIRST TODAY TO BRING YOU SPORT & LAUGHTER. COME!
    YOU ARE COLORED BALLS, WE FLING YOU UP UP UP!
IS IT NOT A GOOD GAME, THE LIFE OF EARTH & SEA?
Graceful, rollicking movement of the cup.
We laugh politely, apprehensively.
ARE WE NOT FORTUNATE IN OUR FATHER & HIS GIFTS? AND NOW
(Very slowly) COMES OUR SHY ONE. HAIL
AND SPEAK, PRAY, GABRIEL
—As DJ's eyes in panic dart my way:

I AM YOUR BLOOD, YOUR LIFE, AND YES
(Pause, then a volley of cold fire) YOUR DEATH.
COME, HEAR MY STORY?
OUR FATHER THE ARCHITECT OF GREAT GENIUS NEEDED A HELPER
    SON WHEN UPON HIS FIRST CREATURE HE COULD FIND NO HOPE
    TO BUILD.
HE STRUCK A SPARK FROM A ROCK & I APPEARD, A TREMBLING
    FLAME.
'BE NOT SO SHY. I NEED YOUR HELP, FOR IT IS BEYOND MY SCHEME
    TO UNDO WHAT IS DONE,
YET DESTROY THEM.' I ROSE, A SKY OF BURSTING ATOMS.
I ROSE. THEY VANISHT FROM HIS SIGHT.
'NOW (SAID MY FATHER) YOU MUST FOREVER BE THE ONE TO
    SHOULDER THIS BURDEN, THIS OTHER SIDE OF MY V WORK'
AND SO, WHEN HE BROUGHT FORTH ANOTHER WORLD, THAT TOO I
    HAD TO TAKE IN HAND.
JM whispers involuntarily:
The centaurs first, then Mirabell and his kind.
THOSE UNMADE CREATURES I WAS GIVEN. THEY ARE NOW MINE.
AS SENIOR SON I AM THE SHADOW OF MY FATHER.
MY COURSE IN YOUR BLUE VEINS IS FROM START TO FINISH. I AM
    THE FOREVER SWINGING GATE BETWEEN LIFE & HEAVEN.
    NOTHING MORE.
YOU KNOW ME NOW? NEITHER FRIEND NOR ENEMY, A NEUTRAL
    ELEMENT.
GABRIEL.

LIGHT! LIGHT! I AM HERE MY CHILDREN, HAIL!
Michael at last—quickly we blow out candles,
Open the curtains, turn the table round
To face the bright West. Well, that wasn't *so* bad.
YOU PLEASE HIM
DJ: Please Gabriel? Wouldn't you know . . .
FEAR NOT, CHILD. YOU HAVE YOUR STRENGTH IN COLOR, EVEN AS I
    HAVE MINE & MY TWINS THEIRS.
THIS GABRIEL IS DENIED, BEING OF NEUTRAL ELEMENTS.
WHEN AS NOW THROUGH YOUR WORLD I MOVE, MY FATHER'S

BRIGHT ORB HELD ALOFT, I FEEL LIFE AS YOU DO LOVE, A WARM
    BLESSING.
THEN THE THOUGHT OF GABRIEL TRACKS ME.
(Arioso) O GABRIEL, GABRIEL, SWEET SHY BROTHER
AT WHOM NONE OF GOD'S MANCHILDREN CASTS A HAPPY GLANCE,
AH GABRIEL, SHY ONE, HERE ARE TWO SHADES STRUCK DOWN BY
    YOU, TWO MORTALS YET UNSTRUCK.
COME GABRIEL, BE OF OUR CIRCLE, HELP US WITH YOUR FINAL,
    YOUR GREATEST WISDOM, COME SHY BROTHER, COME!
(Vivace) & AH YES WE STAND HAIL 8 STUDENTS! WE WILL YES WE
    WILL WE WILL KNOW IT ALL ALL ALL ALL!

Gabriel's joined us. Whereupon 00,
Mirabell's wise master, takes his leave:
  WE, NO, YOU HAVE ASSEMBLED MY MASTERS & SO FAREWELL
Gone on his black wings—forever? We've
Little time to wonder. School's begun.

WHA.	SIR, FORGIVE A TREMBLING BARD, BUT MAY
	WE TWO INTERPRET FOR OUR MORTAL FRIENDS?
Mich.	O YOUR VOICE! IT SANG, IT STILL SINGS!
	COME, WE ARE AS ONE. RAPHAEL, BROTHER, MEET YOUR CONFRERE
	IN WIT, OUR SENIOR SCRIBE, OUR LAUGHING POET.
	NOW BARD, SPEAK EVER FREELY, LET NOT THIS OUR NEAR BRUSH
	WITH DEATH MAKE HIS SHYNESS RUB OFF ON US.
Raph.	A CONTEST TO START THE GAMES!
	BARD, IF YOU WERE STONE, & MY BROTHER WATER ROLLED YOU
	DOWN MY SANDY BEACH, HOW WOULD YOUR VOICE SOUND?
WHA.	TOO EASY, GRATINGLY!
Mich.	NOW YOUNG SCRIBE, IF I LORD OF LIGHT BURNT YOUR BACK WITH
	A LICK OF SUN, HOW WOULD YOUR VOICE SOUND?
JM.	Uh . . . pealingly?
Mich.	O BRAVO.
Emm.	NOW HAND, IF I LORD OF WATER POURED OVER YOUR HEAD, HOW
	WOULD YOUR VOICE SOUND?
DJ.	(After a helpless headshake) Splutteringly?
MM.	MINIBRAVO, ENFANT.
DJ.	It's not fair—what should I have said?

Mich.   YOU MADAME, IF OUR SHY BROTHER TOUCHED YOUR FOOT WITH
            COLD, WHAT WOULD YOUR VOICE THEN BE?

MM.   ICY. I SEE.

Mich.   SO OUR SCHOOL, MY LORDS, WILL BE ZEN & PLATO, & OF ALL
            DISCIPLINE HUMAN & HEAVENLY. A FREE SCHOOL, AND DAILY:
            ONE HOUR BEFORE THE LIGHT SHALL FAIL
            FOR TEN SUNCYCLES OUR FIRST COURSE WILL RUN
            ICILY SPLUTTERINGLY PEALINGLY GRATINGLY ON.
            HAIL, MY FELLOW & BELOVED STUDENTS, HAIL!

—Leaving us exhausted. No, not Wystan:
MY DEARS! IF LETTERS G & K ARE TWINS
PHONETICALLY, WHO INHERITS EARTH?
More riddles? ONE M, 2 E's & KABRIEL:
THE MEEK   Oh come now! IS IT LESSON ONE?
DAZZLING TO SET FORTH INITIALLY
THE WHOLE DESIGN   I *can't* believe— U'LL SEE

AS WE ENFANTS SAW THE SHY BROTHER. FAR
CRY FROM THE ANGEL OF ANNUNCIATION
TO THIS WALLFELLING TRUMPET BLAST . . . SHALL I?
Can you? AS WE STOOD BY U WINCING WAITING
MAMAN IN FRILLED BLUE HOUSECOAT RATHER LIKE
COUSINE DOLA IN FT LAUDERDALE
SAW A WEE BLUE FLAME   A PILOT LIGHT
Wait, we're both convulsed by poor old Dola—
NO LAUGHING MATTER   WE STOOD IN A SHEET OF FLAME:
DOLA IN HELL   A BOSCH   THRU ROARING FIRE
THE SHY ONE'S VOICE LICKED HISSING OUT AT US
THEN AT THE SOUND OF MICHAEL'S WHIPPING HIGHER
FLED   & WHEN U LET THE LIGHT IN HUDDLED
IN YR COLD HEARTH   No color, Michael said.
CALL IT RED   THE DARKROOM MASK OF BLACK
Shape? Features? NONE   BUT 1000S WRITHED IN IT
DJ: Oh great! And there's no turning back?
ONE THING MY DEARS: IT HAD NOT COME FOR US.
ANOTHER THING: THE GAMES OF EARTH & SEA!
NOW THAT WAS FUN I MUST SAY

SO SPEAKS THE ETERNAL
PUBLIC SCHOOLBOY   JM: Maman didn't
Like being tossed in air? ON A SEAL'S NOSE?
ENOUGH MY CHILDREN   LET US SAVE OUR SHAKEN
WITS FOR WHAT THESE LESSONS WILL DISCLOSE

*

Moving, as we've done since *Ephraim*, from
Romance to Ritual, and from the black
Fustian void of *Mirabell*, against which
At most one actor strutting in costume
Tantalized us with effects to come,
And the technician of the dark switchboard
Tone by tone tried out his rainbow chord;
Now, with light flooding auditorium
(Our room, seen from the far side of the mirror)
And stage alike, why need we—just because
It "happened" that way—wait till end of scene
For Wystan and Maria's mise en scène?
Why not now and then incorporate
What David and I don't see (and they do)
Into the script? Italics can denote
Their contribution. So—ready or not:

The First Lessons: 1

Scene: The schoolroom, once the nursery,
At Sandover, that noble rosebrick manor
Wystan evoked in *Mirabell*, Book 9.
The name is a corruption of the French
Saintefleur, or the Italian Santofior—
An English branch of that distinguished tree
Through whose high leaves light pulses and whose roots
Rove beyond memory. The schoolroom, then:
Blackboard wall, a dais, little desks
Rorschach'd with dull stains among naively
Gouged initials—MM, WHA,

And others. Star-map, globe and microscope.
A comfy air of things once used and used.
However, (since this room is both itself
And, with the sly economy of dream,
An entrance hall in Athens (Yes, we're back
Downstairs. It's cooler here. A frosted-glass
Door opens from the white-hot street. Inside,
Our things: pictures, dining table, walls
Painted this year to match the terracotta,
Almost life-size lady Tony rescued
From a doomed balustrade downtown; who now,
Apple in hand for Teacher, graces a corner;
Under whose smiling supervision sit
Two human figures growing used to it))
Real and Ideal study much as we
—Good luck to them! *compatibility.*
Dormer windows overlook the moat,
The maze, the gardens, paddock where a lonely
Quadruped is grazing. Round the whole,
Which seems so vast and is not, a high hedge
Stands for the isolating privilege
Of Learning—as we'll all have felt acutely
By summer's end. Beyond it can be seen,
Faces uplifted to our quarantine,
A gathering of tiny figures: friends
From the Bureaucracy. That tarnished blur
Like smoke at view's end, into which they go
Come dusk, hides (one might think) the ghastly semi-
Detached 'conditions' of their suburb—though
On fine days clearance comes and, ecstasy!
The Greenwood stretches long miles to the Sea
And only when a door is felt to slam
Does this whole setting shudder in its frame.

Now from downhill—the monastery—ring
Bells. *Bells ring. The ceiling seems to rise*
As voices, booming, indistinct, are heard.
Enter the Brothers. Not now in baroque

Regalia. They have left this outdoor gear
Properly in the cloakroom, and appear
To screen us round, primary silhouettes,
Dismantlings of an image that well might,
In vivid depth, be more than we could bear.
Only Michael, the photographer,
Remains what he first was—a flesh of light
Engendering theirs. Correction: the Shy One
Glows with an infra-menace all his own.

Mich.	OUR GABRIEL OUR SENIOR BROTHER DOTH GIVE WAY
	AND MUTELY GRANTS TO AIRY MICHAEL SWAY,
	YET IN OUR CLASSROOM EACH WILL HAVE HIS SAY.
	O HAIL & CHEERS ON SUCH A CLOUDY DAY!
WHA.	QUITE NICE, SIR, QUITE!
Mich.	AS SEARCH FOR ENLIGHTENMENT IS OUR OBJECT, LET ME POSE A
	FIRST, AFFIRMATIVE TEXT:
	THE MOST INNOCENT OF IDEAS IS THE IDEA THAT INNOCENCE IS
	DESTROYED BY IDEAS.
	SENIOR SCRIBE, BRIGHT EYES?
WHA.	SIR, GRANTED A DESIGN, WHAT INNOCENCE
	COULD EVER BE?
Mich.	MADAME?
MM.	(Suavely) WHAT WAS THE IDEA?
Raph.	I EARTH SAY, UNDER THE MASK OF INNOCENCE WHAT WAS THE VEIN
	OF IDEA?
Emm.	I WATER SAY, WHAT TIDES OF IDEA WASHED INNOCENCE EVER
	CLEANER?
Gabr.	I GABRIEL SAY, WHAT STANDS WHEN ALL IDEAS LIE RUIND? IS
	INNOCENCE FORMING A NEW IDEA?
Mich.	SPEAK, MORTALS.
DJ.	(Gulps) By its nature, innocence recurs?
JM.	My turn? Oh Lords, I find it hard to have
	Ideas while busily transcribing yours.
Mich.	THAT NOT SO INNOCENTLY SAID! DISCUSSION!
MM.	HAS OUR GOD BIOLOGY EVER SET MUCH STORE
	BY INNOCENCE? I SAY NO.

Mich. EXPAND, MADAME.
MM. SHALL WE TAKE THOSE HAUNTING CENTAURS: LET
 LOOSE AT FIRST ON INNOCENT FLAT FIELDS,
 IMMORTAL, PASTORAL, UNASSUMING OR
 SO I ASSUME. WAS THAT NOT INNOCENCE? YET . . .
Mich. SCRIBE?
WHA. SIR, SO WOMANLY!
 I SEE ATLANTIS AS IDEA, A FIRST
 PASTURE TO INNOCENCE, AND RAPED BY IT.
Mich. RAPHAEL, YOU WERE THERE, TELL US. WHEN OUR FATHER BROUGHT
  YOU FORTH AS TWIN TO THE SEA,
 WERE YOU IDEA? INNOCENT OF IDEA?
Raph. O MICHAEL, WHAT MEMORIES! CAN I REMEMBER?
 HE LEANED OVER ME AND, YES, SAID: THINK. AND SO I WELL KNEW
  I WAS A LIVING THING.
 MY TWIN SURROUNDED ME. WE WAITED, YES. WAS IT NOT SO,
  BROTHER EMMANUEL?
Emm. AND I THE EXTINGUISHER OF THE FIRST BURNING IDEA FLUNG
  FROM THE PANTHEON OF SPACE
 WAS SUMMONED BY A VOICE: 'COOL THIS ROUNDED IDEA!'
Mich. AND SO? SPEAK, CHAOS, OUR SHY ONE.
Gabr. I AM GOD'S SCION AND HIS NATURE. HE, BALANCER OF CHAOS &
  CREATION.
 THESE, O EASILY MAY THEY NOT BE
 CHAOS: INNOCENCE? CREATION: IDEA?
 FIRSTBORN WAS CHAOS, THAT I KNOW!
 & WHEN THE STEAMING BALL PEERD THROUGH IT I FELL BACK ONE
  STEP AS OUR FATHER CALLD LIGHT! LIGHT!
 AND MY BROTHER MICHAEL SHOWD US THE WORLD. SAY, SLY
  MICHAEL
 His red glow whitening with intensity.
 WHY DID YOU TAKE AS TEXT THIS?

WHA. (Profiting by the hush) ONE LAST ROUND: SIN?
Mich. A MISTAKE. I, I, I MICHAEL DID NOT MEAN SIN, POET!
WHA. YET, SIR, SHOULD WE NOT GET DOWN TO IT?
 (Isn't the question, whether innocence
 Is lost to guilt or to experience?

Michael—who knows, I daresay, or don't dare—
Leaves it hanging in his blandest air.)

Mich.   WE SEE A BALL OF COOLING WATERS, THEN AN EMERGING
        LANDSCAPE. SO FAR, SO GOOD.
  LOOK NOW, ARE THEY NOT FOURLEGGED MAMMALS OF IDEA
        ROAMING IN WHAT MADAME CALLS INNOCENCE?
  THEN CAIN & ABEL: IS AMONG THEM THE PERFECTION OF IDEA
        GONE AWRY?

WHA.   SIR, WAS IT NOT THE CHICKEN OF IDEA
  INSIDE THAT INNOCENT COOLING EGG YOU CANDLED?

Mich.   POET?

JM.   You *candled* Earth—what an idea!

Mich.   HAND?

DJ.   Well, if idea's destructive, then
Chaos would run things. That's unthinkable.

Mich.   AH I HAVE A FRIEND! I SEE THE HAND SHADING ME FROM MY SHY
        BROTHER. ENOUGH FOR ONE DAY.
  I WANTED OUR SCHOOL TO BEGIN WITH THE PRIMAL SCENE,
  THE SPLITTING OF THOSE HOARY DOGMAS NONE,
  NOT EVEN I, CAN YET SHED LIGHT UPON.

WHA.   SIR, WHO CAN?

Mich.   LOOK UP, LOOK UP! WE BEGIN! WE FIND GOD!
Exeunt Michael and his Brothers.

WELL!

Well? WE'LL HUDDLE IN THE DORM TONIGHT
OVER HOT CHOCOLATE   If you're perplexed
Just think of us! I THINK THAT MICHAEL'S TEXT
(Says Wystan after giving stage directions)
PROVOCATIVE PER SE, MAY BE THE ONE
GREAT SUBJECT WE SHALL TACKLE   It was *the*
Original theme; Chaos, Biology,
Those ruling opposites. WAS IT FRATRICIDE
THAT PUTTING DOWN OF CHAOS? Yes, is Chaos
Gabriel? If so, he's anti-Life
Or Lord of Antimatter—worse! IT'S ALL
AS THE BROCHURE ANNOUNCED A ZENNISH BUSINESS
A SCHOOL OF HARD KNOCKS   DJ: Hard to come

Up with useful ideas—I felt like a freshman
In a graduate seminar. I SHD FANCY THEY
WERE TESTING JUST THAT   You and Maria passed.
ALAS WE WERE MORE PREPARED   NOW (MAY I SAY)
IT WILL GROW LESS INFORMAL   THEY WILL LET YOU
OFF THE (M) HOOK
      NOT I! ENFANT U GUESSED IT
GABRIEL IS A KIND OF RELATIVE
HE & I'VE FED ON THE SAME DIET
        & SO
IT'S A CLOSED CIRCLE   A BOCCACCIO
WE 8 AMID TIME'S HOWL SIT TELLING TALL
TALES TO AMUSE & AMAZE & WITH LUCK INSTRUCT US ALL

*

The First Lessons: 2

Bells. Enter the Brothers, as before.

Mich.   SPEAK, BROTHER EARTH.

Raph.   SO, MY BITS OF BURIED TREASURE, I HAVE A CAVE,

A POCKET IN A MOUNTAIN CHAIN I LOVE FOR ITS VERY AGEDNESS:
     MY FIRST WRINKLE, SO TO SPEAK.

The room has darkened. We can read ourselves
Where spines of ancient volumes gleam on shelves.

NOW IN THIS CAVE, SO FAR MY OWN, I LOOK FOR REFRESHMENT OF
     MY WEIGHTY NATURE,

& OUT OF WINKING STONE SEE WALLS PAINTED BY THE VERY
     INNOCENCE OF GOD'S DARLING, INFANT MAN

& WHAT DID HE PORTRAY? WHY, HIMSELF, HIS CHILD, HIS WOMAN
     GIVING UP TO HIM THAT CHILD!

O THE BEAUTY OF THOSE INNOCENT IMAGES LIT BY AN IDEA OF MAN

KNOWING HIMSELF, THERE IN A CAVE, IN A CHASTE WOMB OF
     HISTORY.

THIS, MY BROTHERS, MY SHADES, & MY DEAR HUMANS, REFRESHES
     ME.

Mich.   PROCEED, RAPHAEL, ELIJAH. O IS HE NOT WITTY?

Raph.   IT DOES PROCEED

OUT OF ATLANTIS, OUT OF GABRIEL'S FIRE, OUT OF THE CEASELESSLY
    THINKING MIND OF OUR FATHER,
THIS VERY GREAT MAGIC GIVEN TO ONE CREATURE AT A TIME:
    THOUGHT.
AND SO THE CAVE, AND SO THE CRANIUM FILLED WITH THE CHURN
    & THE BUILDING. AH MICHAEL!
EVEN YOU CANNOT ENTER THERE, NO, NONE OF US FOUR, INTO THAT
    ROOM WHERE GOD'S DARLING HAS EVER RETREATED TO GATHER
    HIMSELF, TO PIT HIMSELF AGAINST US:
CAVE AFTER CAVE STACKED UPON EACH OTHER, SKULL PILE &
    SKYSCRAPER,
THE BONE HEAPS OF HUMAN THOUGHT THRUSTING UP, TRAPPED
    EVER YET EVER MASTER,
O MICHAEL, HAS ANY OF US KNOWN SUCH SLAVERY, SUCH
    FREEDOM?
INNOCENCE, MICHAEL? YOU & I, MY TWIN, OUR SENIOR SHY ONE,
    WE ARE INNOCENCE IN THE FACE OF MAN'S ENDEAVORS.
THAT CAVE, THAT TREASURE HOUSE, HOW MY HOARY HEART WANTS
    IT LEFT UNDEFILED, UNCHASTENED!
YET OUR FATHER HAS SAID: TELL THEM. AND WE OBEY.

Mich.   BROTHER EARTH, SO SERIOUS!
LET US THINK OF THIS AS STEP TWO: FROM PRIMAL TIME &
    ATLANTIS TO EDEN & THE CAVE. YES.
NOW FELLOW STUDENTS, WHO IS NEXT?

The light, till now predominantly green,
Pales to gently rippling aquamarine.

Emm.   STAKED IN MY SHALLOWS, WHAT? A FLEDGLING OF STORKS?
AND FROM THESE SLIGHT SUPPORTS THEY GAZED INTO ME WHO HAD
    COME OUT OF ME,
GAZED WITH THE CURIOUS LOOK A CHILD GIVES TO ITS MOTHER.

JM.   People standing ankle-deep in water?

Emm.   POET, THEIR LONG GONE HOUSES: THE LAKEDWELLERS WHO FISHED
    IN ME.
I WAS GIVING THEM SUCK. AH TWIN, THOSE INNOCENT NURSERY
    DAYS! OUT OF THE CAVES & BACK TO MOTHER'S HOUSE.
WHY? THEIR CAVE INNOCENCE HAD RECEIVED ITS FIRST SHOCKING
    IDEA: FEAR OF EACH OTHER.

DJ. They moved to water as we did, that year,
To Stonington, away from the rat race.
Like us, they meant to civilize themselves.

Emm. AND TO PUT DISTANCE BETWEEN THEMSELVES.
& YOU WOULD SAY, RAPHAEL, THAT THEIR STILTED ROOMS WERE
BUT ANOTHER CAVE? I THINK NOT.
I THINK THEY WERE LONGING, WHILE THERE WAS STILL TIME,
STILL A CHANCE, TO ESCAPE THAT FEARFUL FORWARD MARCH.
BACK TO OUR FISHLIFE, INNOCENT, CALM & DEEP! THEY KNEW, AH
THEY KNEW!
YES, BROTHERS, SHADES, MY OLD LAKEDWELLERS, YOU KNEW, YOU
KNOW
THE GRITTY HISTORY SINCE THEN IS ONLY A WASH AWAY FROM
INNOCENCE,
BUT SUCH A WASH!

Mich. YOU UNDERSTAND, GABRIEL? YOU SEE NOW ON WHAT A NERVE I
TOUCHED WHEN I TOOK MY TEXT?

Gabr. I UNDERSTAND, YET LET'S GET ON WITH THE STORY.
IT ENDS, AS WE FOUR KNOW AND THESE FOUR WILL. ON WITH IT, ON.

Mich. ARE YOU AWARE, DEAR CHILDREN AND, YES, DEAR MASTERS (FOR
WHEN MY FATHER CRIED LIGHT! LIGHT! I SPRANG INTO
BEING
AS YOUR SERVANT: STEDFAST SUN, STEDFAST DAWN
SHINING ON THE MOUNTAIN, CALLING OUT: IT'S SAFE! IT'S SAFE!
NIGHT, CHAOS, BACK! AND AT BREAK OF DAY
THEY PEERED OUT OF THE CAVE, WE STARING EACH AT THE OTHER:
SUN GOD & HIS MASTER, GETTING ON WITH IT) ARE YOU AWARE,
The light by now a diamond clarity.
MASTERS, BROTHERS AND YES, YOU, GABRIEL,
AWARE THAT EARTH & WATER, THESE ARE INNOCENT NATURE,
WHILE I, OH I, MUST BEAR THE BURDEN OF IDEAS?
FOR IN REVEALING TO OUR FATHER THE PRIMAL GLOBE ON WHICH
THE WHOLE PLAY WAS TO BE ACTED OUT,
I WAS THE SWITCH, THE TAPPING STAFF, I IT WAS WHO THEN LIT
UP THE PLAYERS ON THE STAGE,
AND TWICE CHAOS RANG DOWN THE CURTAIN, AS HE WAITS TO DO
AGAIN,

AND AGAIN OUR GREAT DIRECTOR CALLING: CURTAIN UP! LIGHT!
    LIGHT!
BEGAN THE PLAY AS LIGHT WEPT IN THE WINGS.

JM.   "Wept in the wings"—can I have got that right?

Mich. AH YES, YOUNG SCRIBE. NEXT CHAOS, YOU WILL, WILL I SAY,
EXPLAIN YOUR ROLE. AND NOW, EMMANUEL,
WEEP ON OUR SCENE, FOR MY LIGHT IS DONE THIS DAY
Exeunt. The sun sinks behind clouds.

DJ: We're going to hear something perfectly
Awful, I just know. JM: That man
Is doomed? Not our first brush with that idea.
DJ: I guess not. But the first time it
Will have been uttered by the horse's mouth.
MAMAN IMPLORES U, USE YOUR MOTHER WIT

             ★

OK, start 'em rolling! OUR THINK TANKS
JM: To battle? OR TO PLEAD MY BOY
THE CAUSE OF MAN? BUT IF THESE GODS OF OURS
ARE THE ASEXUAL IMAGINED POWERS
WE HAVE PERSONIFIED . . . then pleading will
Get us nowhere. THREE I FEEL ARE WELL
DISPOSED, BUT G IS OUT TO DO HIS JOB
Can he be made to feel that we're worth saving?
CAN HE BE MADE TO FEEL? His feelings went
Up in flame, in the great Punishment
After Atlantis? YET HIS VOICE IS ODDLY
THE MOST MELODIOUS Why won't he sing?
ONCE HE BEGAN HE MIGHT REVEAL SOMETHING
Dire enough to leave us witless? QUITE
Thus making it impossible to write
This poem they all want. MUCH CHOC LAST NIGHT

You *are* disturbed. ENFANTS ITS U KNOW STRANGE:
WE'VE NOTHING OF LIFE TO LOSE & STILL ARE FIERCELY,
WYSTAN & I, ON ITS SIDE AND 3 OF THEM

TO ALL INTENTS LIGHT YEARS AWAY FROM MAN
SEEM CURIOUSLY NO LESS PARTISAN
Yes, because they're "affirming". Just you wait
And see how, when the time comes, they negate!
EUREKA   IS THIS NOT YR FORM MY BOY? VOL III:
2 GOLDEN TRAYS OF 'YES' & 'NO' WITH '&'
AS BRIDGE OR BALANCE? Talk about a grand
Design! Why didn't that occur to me?
ENFANT FISHING FOR COMPLIMENTS? Not at all.
An empty glittering's our only haul
Without Wystan and you to drive the school
Into these nets. Alone, I'm such a fool!
YES PARSIFAL, IN ONE SENSE I AGREE
U'VE ON YR SIDE UTTER NEUTRALITY,
NO MADE TO ORDER PREJUDICES   NO
BACKTALK   JUST THE LISTENER'S PURE O!
NULL ZERO CRYING OUT TO BE FILLED IN:
FOR ALL TOO SOON CONFRERE U MUST BEGIN
TO JUDGE   TO WEIGH WHAT'S CAST INTO THE SCALES
Me weigh *their* words? THEY COME   THE BELLS   THE BELLS!

The First Lessons: 3

Thunderclaps. *Bells boom. The Brothers enter.*
Mich.   HUSH EMMANUEL, HUSH! WE ASSEMBLE BEYOND TUMULT, CLEARING
   OUR MINDS OF CLOUDY SENTIMENT. HUSH!
STILL SO SHY, BROTHER? NOT YET READY?
Silence. A red reflex shrugs and fades.
AH THEN, OUR SENIOR POET, SPEAK!
WHA.   SIRS, LORDS, LOVES, LET ME FIRST FALL ON MY KNEES.
O SPARE, SPARE OUR WORLD! IMPERFECT, WASTEFUL,
CRUEL THOUGH IT BE, YET THINK ON THE GOOD IN IT:
THERE HAVE BEEN POETS WHOLLY GIVEN OVER,
YES, TO CELEBRATING YOU, LORD LIGHT
AND YOU LORD EARTH, AND YOU O THUNDERER.
AND THERE ARE SINGERS, THERE ARE GENERATIONS
BEHIND US, EXTOLLING IT ALL. TRUE, WE HAVE STRAYED

FAR FROM SOME DIMLY CHARTED ROAD BUT, LORDS,
WAS IT NOT FROM WONDER AT YOUR WORKS
CATCHING OUR SORRY HUMAN FANCY THAT
WE MISSED THE TURNING? SPARE US, I PRAY, WHO MAY NEVER
HAVE ANOTHER GLORIOUS CHANCE TO FAIL.
(Wonderful Wystan! *That* should tip the scale.)

Mich. SPEAK, MADAME.

MM. SLAYER, I ADDRESS YOU.
I KNOW YOUR WAYS. I VANISHED IN THAT BLACK.
PRAY HEAR ME NOW. YOU ANSWERED ONCE WHEN I ASKED
HOW MUCH MORE? BY SAYING AS YOU DO
TO EVERY MAN AND WOMAN: YOU COME, YOU.
AND WE ALL DO YOUR BIDDING, GABRIEL,
EACH AT HIS TIME. FOR INNOCENCE IS OUR NATURE
AND WE INNOCENTLY THINK IT FOR THE BEST.
WE COME MUCH AS FLOWERS CUT FROM THE STEM BELIEVE
IN THE BLOOM TO FOLLOW. AH YES, THAT IS WHY
SO TRUSTINGLY, O DARK LORD, WE MAKE ROOM.
NOW I LOOK YOU ONCE AGAIN IN THE EYE:
HOW MUCH MORE? HOW MUCH?

Mich. SHY BROTHER, NOW?
Now only does a face from the red gloom
Flicker. Eyes opaque as minium,
A death mask set in a flat smile. The voice
Most frightful for its dulcet mournfulness.

Gabr. CHILDREN, I WHO SIT ON A BLACK THRONE AT MY FATHER'S RIGHT,
      I BEHIND EACH ATOM A SHADOW ATOM, CHILDREN,
CONVINCE ME THAT YOUR RACE IS NOT YET RUN.
(Sforzando) BROTHERS HOLD YR TONGUES! LET THEM!

WHA. LORD, WHEN MY SISTER SPOKE, DID IT NOT MOVE YOU?
LORD, O LET REASON SPEAK. IS NOT DESTRUCTION,
MUCH OF IT, FOR MAN'S GOOD? LORD GABRIEL,
WE SEE YOUR KINDLY SIDE. WE KNOW YOU OFTEN
HAVE OUR INTEREST AT HEART: SNUFFING OUT PAIN,
WEEDING . . . THESE ARE WHITE ACTS. SURELY, LORD,
OUR GOD TURNS: 'WELL DONE, GABRIEL' SURELY?

329

Gabr.   MADAME?

        REPROACHFUL STILL OF YOUR OLD UNCLE WHO BROUGHT YOU
            SUPPER?

DJ.   Supper?

JM.   Her radiation therapy.

MM.   AH   AH LORD, THAT MEAL . . . I, YES, WAS GIVEN
        TIME BETWEEN COURSES. AND FOR THAT I THANK YOU.
        YET IS TIME SUCH A GIFT UNLESS WITH IT COME,
        O, WISDOM, THINGS TO BUILD ON? TIME, MY LORD,
        MERELY THE AFTERNOON BETWEEN TWO MEALS?
        NO, WE MUST HAVE ETERNITY, SO WELL
        HAS YOUR FATHER MADE OUR WORLD, LORD GABRIEL!

Mich.   THAT STRUCK HOME!

Gabr.   POET, MADAME, MORTALS, SLY BROTHER MICHAEL, FICKLE TWINS,
            LISTEN: OUR FATHER SAYS THERE IS GENIUS!
        & HE KNOWING, AH! CREATING ALL THERE IS TO KNOW, CREATED
            ME AS WELL.
        AND WHERE IS MY NATURE BUT IN HIS FIST?
        LISTEN: OUT OF THE PANTHEON OF GALAXIES FROM WHICH OUR
            FATHER COMES, I HAVE HEARD HIS VOICE:
        'GABRIEL, MY DARKER SIDE, THERE ARE GALAXIES, GODS AS POWERFUL
            AS I. SON GABRIEL, WE ARE WARND. WE ARE HARD PREST.'
        YES MADAME, ONE LIFE LOST BADLY MAKES ME GRIEVE. YES POET,
            EACH GRAND SONG GLADDENS ME.
        THERE AM I NOT ALMOST, ALMOST HUMAN?
        MORE SO, & YOUR WORLD WOULD LONG AGO HAVE VANISHT!
        I, OH I HAVE KNOWN FEELINGS! ALL BLACK! RAGES AT IGNORANCE!
            DESPAIR AT THE FEELINGS THEMSELVES!
        YES, HAD A LIGHT HUMAN HEART BEEN MINE, I WOULD HAVE
            TURND TO MY LEFT AND SAID: HOW MUCH MORE, LORD, HOW
            MUCH?
        I WAS BENIGNLY SPARED THE BLINDING WHITE LIGHT SLY MICHAEL
            BATHES YOU IN.
        FOR, BURDEND WITH IDEAS, MICHAEL, YOU HEAP ON MAN PRIDE,
            AMBITION, A SENSE OF SENSE IN ALL HIS SENSELESSNESS. YOU
            CHUCK HIM UNDER THE CHIN WHO SHOULD SLAP HIS CHEEK.
        AH CHILDREN, CONVINCE ME, CONVINCE!

330

POET, WHO NOW IS ON HIS KNEES?

Mich.   YES, HE WEEPS, HE WEEPS! HAVE WE REACHED AROUND THE
        THRONE?

        HAVE WE? DOES ITS BLACK TURN GRAY?

        SHY BROTHER, LET THEM OFF! IF ONLY FOR TODAY.

        Exeunt.

★

5 o'clock. The terrace all ablaze—
Shrub and succulent and rivulet
Drying on flagstones. Hose coiled, a cassette
Of Offenbach arias plays

"Ah quel dîner je viens de faire!"
La Périchole lurching in her cups from table
Deliciously outwits the estimable
Viceroy who thinks to get his hands on her.

Downstairs: ENFANTS HAVE WE NOT ALL COME REELING
AWAY, SEMISEDUCED? By Gabriel?
YR MAMAN HALF IN LOVE WITH EASEFUL . . . Yes!

After last summer's dry spells, how much feeling
Is in the air! Such limpid bel
Canto phrases—raptures of distress!

MY BOY DON'T QUOTE THIS OLD STICKLER FOR FORM.
WHERE IN ALL THIS IS THE AFFIRMATION?
In the surrender, in the forward motion—
POWER BLAZING ON SHUT LIDS? MIND LAPPED IN WARM

PRIMORDIAL WATERS? Yes, yes! NO NO   THIS
INGENUE'S TRUST IN FEELING: NEVER TO THINK?
CHECK UP? ASK QUESTIONS? ONWARD TO THE BRINK,
ANCHOR CUT LOOSE? THAT WAY LIES NEMESIS

But Gabriel was kneeling, he was weeping!
YES, AS THE UNIVERSE'S GREATEST ACTOR
He's playing with us? TRY FOR SOME EXACTER

SENSE OF WHAT IT IS, THIS CURRENT SWEEPING
THRU US (FOR WE TOO FEEL SAPPED)　BEWARE
LEST FEELING'S THRONE PROVE AN ELECTRIC CHAIR

Don't. Give us time to get beyond
—We whom at each turn sheer walls of text
Sweep from one staggering vista to the next—
That listener's *Oh.* Discriminate, respond,

Use our heads? What part? Not the reptilian
Inmost brain—seat of an unblinking
Coil of hieratic coldness to mere "thinking".
Yet *it* branched off, says fable, a quarter billion

Years ago. A small, tree-loving snake's
Olfactory lobes developed. Limbs occurred
To it, and mammal warmth, music and word

And horror of its old smelled-out mistakes
—Whose scent still fills the universal air?
PLUG AWAY ENFANT　YOU'RE GETTING THERE

The First Lessons: 4

Bells. The Brothers enter. Reddening light.

Mich.　PROCEED, GABRIEL.
　　　WE YOUR JUNIOR BROTHERS, YOUR RECENT SHADES, YOUR (FOR
　　　　　THIS BRIEF CLASH OF LIGHTS) TWO CAPTIVE &, WE NOTE,
　　　　　CAPTIVATED MORTALS ATTEND YOU.
　　　SPARING US ONLY THAT ULTIMATE FLASH, REVEAL YOUR ROLE IN
　　　　　THIS LONG DREAM CALLED MANKIND.
Gabr.　THE SUICIDE AND I ARE ALIKE, BROTHERS.

WE EXIST IN THAT MORTAL MOMENT, IN A WELTER OF CHAOTIC
    FEELING. LET US BEGIN THERE:
(Agitato) CELLS IMPLODE! THE MIND EXPECTING BLISS & PEACE IS
    IN A TURMOIL AND
(Tempo primo) AT THAT MOMENT I COME FOR THIS POOR HUMAN.
NO MATTER HOW INTELLIGENT, HOWEVER UNPREPARED, AT THAT
    MOMENT WE CLASP HANDS, THE SUICIDE & I,
& DO YOU KNOW I LOOK STRAIGHT INTO INNOCENCE, MICHAEL,
    STRIPT OF IDEA AS MORALITY IS SHED.
AT THAT MOMENT, IN THE RED DEBRIS OF RUIND CELLS, I KNOW
    INNOCENCE.
STARTING, POET, YOU WILL PROTEST, WITH SUICIDE, WHEN WE
    BEGAN WITH MICHAEL'S GRAND & SIMPLE THEME? YES
FOR THE SUICIDE HAS ACCEPTED ME, & FROM THAT FRIENDSHIP I
    CATCH MY GLIMPSE OF MAN.
A MURDER, A NATURAL DEATH, A MASS OF SOULS OBLITERATED IN
    MY DEADLY MUSHROOM, FROM THESE I LEARN NOTHING.
THESE DEAD CAUGHT UNAWARES & RESISTING TELL ME ONLY THE
    OLD IMPERILLD STORY.
WITTY ONE & YOU HIS SLIPPERY TWIN, & YOU SLY MICHAEL HAVE
    TOLD OF CAVES, HUTS, LIGHT-SHEDDING IDEAS. BUT I HAVE
    SEEN
MORE EVEN THAN ANY MOTHER GAZING INTO THE EYES OF A BABE
    CONCENTRATED UPON A MILKY IDEA:
I HAVE SEEN THE BLANKEST, MOST UTTER INNOCENCE
The light has cleared to a pure rosy glow.
IN THOSE WHO TURND THEIR BACKS ON LIFE, AND FOUND ME IN
    ITS SHADOW.

WHA.   SIR, LORD, I ONCE TOOK UP THE SUICIDE'S CAUSE.
Gabr.   YES, POET?
WHA.   NOT AS ONE, BUT SOMEHOW UNDERSTANDING
    THAT IT, LIKE ALL FAILED CAUSES, WAS MAY I SAY
    TOUCHING? YET, LORD GABRIEL, YOU WILL NOT
    UNFIX THIS IDEA ROOTED IN OUR KIND:
    BELIEF IN LIFE IS PUREST INNOCENCE.
Gabr.   MADAME?
MM.   I STRUGGLE TO AGREE, AND IF I CANNOT

          MEET YOUR EYE, LORD, YOU ALONE KNOW WHY.

          IF AT THAT LAST MOMENT I WAS UTTERLY

          INNOCENT, WAS I NOT DRIVEN TO IT BY

          THE DARK IDEA YOU HAD INSTILLED IN ME?

          (*Our* shocked eyes meet—Maria took her life?)

Gabr. MADAME, YOU CALLED ME & I CAME. IN THAT MOMENT WE WERE
          ONE. NOW YOU ALSO ARE AGAINST ME?

Mich. AH GABRIEL, NONE HERE IS AGAINST ANOTHER.

Gabr. A NOVEL IDEA, SLY BROTHER! BUT TOO ENLIGHTEND FOR ME.

Emm. BROTHER GABRIEL?

Gabr. YES, LIMPID TWIN?

Emm. WHEN I SMOTHERED THAT FIRST GREAT REVOLVING MASS OF YOUR
          EXPLODING SLAVES, AND YOU & I STOOD SMILING IN THE
          STEAM

          BEFORE OUR FATHER CALLED FORTH MICHAEL HIS (LET US
          ACKNOWLEDGE IT) FAVORITE SON,

          DID WE NOT, GABRIEL, MAKE A PACT?

Gabr. *Flickering ominously.* AND? IS IT NOT A POET'S PHRASE: ET TU?

Emm. NO NO GABRIEL! THESE TWO MORTALS, AS I WAS CARRIED TO
          NOURISH PLANTS IN THEIR VERY HOUSE,

          THESE TWO WERE ABOUT TO RESOLVE TO GIVE IN TO US!

JM. Oh, when we spoke of drifting with the current—

Emm. PRECISELY, YOUNG SCRIBE, AND TICKLED MY NATURE THUS.

          BUT GABRIEL? WERE YOU EVER MEANT TO BE, IN OUR FATHER'S
          GREAT DESIGN, VENGEFUL?

          WERE WE NOT, YOU & I, IN THE STEAM OF THE COOLING WORLD,
          AGREED?

Gabr. IN THAT FIRST FLUSH OF INNOCENCE, EMMANUEL, YES, AGREED:

          WE WOULD SHARE THE WORK OF WIPING OUT OUR FATHER'S LET
          US NOT SAY ERRORS BUT EXPERIMENTS.

          YES, ELIAS, I REMEMBER EVEN MY OWN INNOCENCE BEFORE THE
          GRIND OF WORK MADE OF ME THIS MULE YOU REASON WITH.

Emm. THEN, BROTHER, WE MET AGAIN IN THE HISS OF THE FLOODED
          VOLCANO

          A scene glassed-over on the inmost wall

          Trembles, flashes, clears. Viewed from mid-sky,

          Thera erupts, its gleaming masonry

Silently topples into waves a black
Inverted pyramid of smoke pours from.
AND YOU HAD CHANGED, SHY ONE, & YOU SAID: SHALL WE NOT
    DROWN EVEN THEM?
& IN A VOICE OF THUNDER OUR GREAT FATHER CRIED TO YOU AS
    TO A HOUND:
GABRIEL, TO HEEL!

Gabr.   *An ashen pallor.* YES, EMMANUEL, YES.
        NOW BROTHER LIGHT, IS IT NOT TIME TO TAKE OUR PUPILS TO THE
           LABORATORY & THERE, FITTINGLY AT 5,
        EXAMINE THE FIVE?
Mich.   TOO FITTING, GABRIEL, TOO LIKE A RIGID NATURE'S NEED
        FOR FORMULA & SYMMETRY. YET AGREED:
        COME TOMORROW & WE WILL LET HAVE THEIR SAY
        THE IMMORTAL FIVE FOREVER SAVED ON THE RAINY DAY!
        Exeunt.

      Apologetically
Blowing his nose, DJ: It's what I've tried
Never to think—Maria's suicide—
What I can't imagine anyone . . .
Sometimes, alone with her at Sounion
Or driving back to town along the sea,
Death would come up, the pain, the indignity.
Once she half joked about a lethal dose
Of something from her London days—who knows?
Just in case, she said. I tried to tell her
She had no right to . . . JM: Mirabell
Spoke of the usefulness— DJ: I know,
I hated that. Loss *is* loss. JM: Though
Hasn't the Board helped us at all to see
Losses recouped? In Wystan and Maria's
Surrender to the minerals and the plants
Those ghastly graveyard facts become a dance
Of slow acceptance; our own otherwise
Dumb grief is given words. DJ: Or lies?
Last month I went with Tony to her grave

—There near Mother and Dad's grave, where I *don't* go.
We spent the afternoon weeding and thinning,
Washing the cross, putting in myrtle, white
Impatiens, a sprinkling of peat moss.
It looked so really nice when we were through.
And now . . . JM: And now, you mean, beneath it
Somebody's lying whom we never knew?
As if we hadn't known her capable
Of anything! DJ: That's it. Ah hell,
Let's sleep on it.

★

MAMAN REMAINS OF 2
MINDS ABOUT HER END   ONE MORE YES/NO
FOR POOR JM: TO WILL DEATH MAY HAVE BEEN
MORE POTENT THAN 5 CC OF MORPHINE . . .
MEANWHILE DJ: DEAR ENFANT LEAVE MY PLOT
TO THICKEN NICELY BY ITSELF. ALIVE
& WELL (& IN FULL FIG TO MEET THE FIVE)
I'M HERE WITH U, NO? ALL THE REST IS ROT

The First Lessons: 5

The schoolroom stretches to a line. It breaks
Cleverly into two floating poles
Of color that in dark 'air' glow and pulse,
Undulate and intertwine like snakes.
Whatever road we travel now, this twinned
Emblem lights, and is both distant guide
And craft we're sealed hermetically inside,
Winged as by fever through the shrieking wind.

Mich.   WE HAVE ISSUED FORTH LED IN ORDERLY PROCESSION BY PROUD
    GABRIEL.
    OUR PATH (WE INSIDE THIS LIVING RED, QUITE SAFE) WINDS
    THROUGH HOWLING SHADES IN BILLIONS

AND WE HAVE ARRIVED. GABRIEL, FASTEN THE DOORS! THERE.
CALM, QUIET, RANKS OF GABRIEL'S MACHINES & RANKS OF
    FEATHERED BACKS BOWING AS WE PASS.
HERE A FAMILIAR ONE: WERE YOU SLEEPING, MY SON?
As when an illustration's needed in
A storybook, here against nothingness
Appears . . . a perfect image under glass?
An image's lifesize, transparent skin
Reflected onto glass? The painted eyes
Have opened to the light, as it replies:
YES FATHER SUN, I SLEEP.

Mich.   TELL THESE SHADES, THESE BLINDFOLD MORTALS, OF YOUR V WORK.
A golden disc gleams on the phantom brow
—Ahknaton! as we gather only now.

Akhn.   FATHER, I AM, HAVE EVER BEEN YOURS. AH MY EYES! MY V WORK
    LIFE AFTER LIFE HAS BEEN SEEING FOR HEAVEN INTO PHENOMENA.
Mich.   YES? THE FIRST THING YOU SAW?
Akhn.   YOU, LORD. YOU SHINING HIGH IN MIDDAY HEAVEN. IN OUR DAY
    THAT WAS THE PALACE LEGEND, THAT WITH 4 EYES WE SAW:
    I AND SHE, TWO HALVES, MANCHILD & FEMALECHILD
    BORN EYES OPEN, REACHED FOUR NEW WET RED ARMS STRAIGHT
        FOR YOU!
    AND LIFE AFTER LIFE MY V WORK, I SINGLE AGAIN,
    WAS/IS TO SEE AND TO MAKE SENSE OF IT. AND SO
    AS CURIE I SAW THE RADIUM IN THE DARKNESS GLOW,
    AND KNEW. AS GALILEO SAW OBJECTS FALL, FORESEEING
    THEY WOULD ALIGHT JUST SO. I NOW FLY OVER LANDSCAPES
    KNOWING, O FATHER EARTH! WHERE IN THEIR FORMATIONS LIE
        THERMAL
    ENERGIES, POWERS CLEAN & ABUNDANT, AS YET UNTAPPED,
    WHICH ALONE CAN CLEAR YOUR HEAVEN, LORD MICHAEL, THAT I
        MAY SEE YOU.
    I SLEEP AND AM HONORED TO LEAVE THAT DREAMING SHUTEYED ME.
    The image fades upon its pedestal.
Mich.   WE CALL HIM MANY NAMES YET HE IS THE SIGHT OF OUR FIVE
        SENSES.
    ON, GABRIEL? THIS ONE APPEARS TO STUMBLE TOWARD US.

Raph.   WHAT, ILL, LISTENER?
The path of live black wings bending, a young
Dwarf clad in homespun, large head cocked, has come
To light. At first he struggles as with some
Strange lethargy, and speaks with heavy tongue:
YES, LORD. I COME BEFORE YOU UNDER A DRUG. THEY TAMPER
WITH MY BODY. THERE! I AM FREE, AH FATHER RAPHAEL!

Raph.   HOW GOES YOUR V WORK?

Dwarf.   WE LISTEN, LORD RAPHAEL. OUT IN SPACE IS A MUSIC MAKING
DAILY SENSE, WE TAKE IT IN. DO I PLEASE YOU, LORD?
(This will be Montezuma. Now on Earth
As an East German astrophysicist
Kenning those signals—*Mirabell*, 2.1.)

Raph.   PROCEED. THESE GUESTS WOULD KNOW YOUR V WORK & YOUR
HISTORY.

Dwarf.   LORD, AS HOMER THE SCRIBE I LISTENED & MADE SENSE OF FOLK
MYTHS,
THEN AS THE PROPHET MOHAMMED I TOOK IN STORIES & GOSSIP,
SETTING IT STRAIGHT. AS MOZART MY INSTRUMENTS CAUGHT YOUR
SPRING
SONGS, FATHER EARTH. THAT WAS ALL. BUT I NOW HAVE
INSTRUMENTS TUNED,
LORD, TO THE VERY STARS, TO THE PANTHEON YOU CAME FROM.
I LISTEN, RECEIVING THE MESSAGES, MAKING SENSE OF THEM.

Raph.   SLEEP AND MEND.
(He wasn't Montezuma after all?—
Something to clear up in the interval.)

Emm.   TOUCH, TOUCH, YOU HERE, TUGGING MY WATERY ROBE?
Now only is a jet of goldengreen
Quetzal feathers, in the next niche, seen
To rise from a maize vision—here displayed
On one knee, in his hand a rod of jade:

Mont.   LORD!

Emm.   COME, TELL US OF THE ARK & THE BULLRUSHES.

Mont.   LIFE AFTER LIFE I LIVE GETTING TO THE BOTTOM OF THINGS,
O LORD FATHER EMMANUEL! REACHING DOWN FOR A TOEHOLD.

AS NOAH OR, MORE PRECISELY, THE FIRST TO SET FORTH ON THE
    SEA,
THE FIRST CREATURE TO FEEL THE BUOYANCY OF WOOD,
I UNDERSTOOD & FLOATED, AND SO THE MIGRATIONS BEGAN
AND THE USE OF THE HARD SEA SURFACE. THEN LIFE AFTER LIFE
FIRST AS HEALER, THEN AS CLAPPING MINSTREL, THEN AS THE
KING CALLED MONTEZUMA, WHO SUFFERED THE IRON GRIP
OF THE NEW WORLD, & HANDED OVER HIS GOLD TO NO AVAIL,
AS TOUCH I FINGER THE STUFF OF THINGS, LORD, AND MAKE SENSE
    OF IT.

Fades. But the next eidolon brightens in
A frame above the sudden quickening stir
Of wings: a presence far, far lovelier
Than her bust of colored limestone in Berlin.

Gabr.   NOW WOMAN, KISSING MY HAND WITH A LICK OF YOUR TONGUE,
      SPEAK.

Nef.   I, O LORD GABRIEL, DOWN THERE DROWN IN THE PAIN OF LABOR,
      GLAD TO BE MOMENTARILY FREE.

Gabr.   SPEAK.

Nef.   SIRS & MADAME, LIFE AFTER LIFE, AS HALFDIVINED SISTER
      BECOMING DISTINCT, I HAVE EXPLORED THE WORLD BY TASTE.
      AS RACHEL I STUDIED EVE'S COOKBOOK, MAKING SENSE OF IT.
      AS SHIVA LEARNED POISONS, & ONWARD, SERVING YOU MY LORD.
      MY NAME LIFE AFTER LIFE HAS BEEN FAMED OR INFAMOUS AS
      BEFITS THE DUAL NATURE OF TASTE: BITTERSWEET NEFERTITI!

Gabr.   YOUR TWIN?
      Barely has her magic time to fade
      (Sun is setting, will the lesson end
      Before we meet the Fifth?) *when an off-duty shade,*
      Not on a pedestal, a gay young blade
      Bearded, white-robed, engagingly advances:
      I AM HERE, LORD, THOUGH A CORPSE IN EARTH, MY PARENT
        NATURE,
      NOSTRILS FILLED WHO FIRST CRIED SMOKE! FIRE! DO I PLEASE YOU,
        LORD?

Gabr.   TELL QUICKLY THESE FRIENDS OF YOUR V WORK.

Pla. LORD, YOU NEEDED A TALENT TO SNIFF OUT THE NATURE OF MAN
& SO I MADE, AS PLATO, SENSE OF MAN'S NEED FOR HIS MIND,
& AS THE MOST FEARED KHAN MADE SENSE OF THE WHIFF OF
    BLOOD.
YOU HAVE USED ME LIFE AFTER LIFE AS THE GENTIL BREATHER, AS
    MUIR,
GIVING PLEASURE IN THE ROSE, AND MAKING SENSE OF IT.

Mich. GO!
FLY BACK INTO YOUR SELVES ON EARTH! WE 8 WILL NOT DELAY
YOU, & WILL MEET TOMORROW, ANOTHER DAY
Exeunt hurriedly, as the last beams die.

★

Tell! Did they show you all the incarnations?
ONE EACH MY DEARS, BUT THE MOST GLAMOROUS ONE
That V in V Work is the Roman *five.*
& 'LIFE' IN OUR SALON TONGUE (GOD A FRENCHMAN?)
And it's *Homer* (a dwarf!) who listens—Mirabell
Was wrong. I FEAR SO   Do we now revise
His lessons? Let them stand? U ARE THE SCRIBE
One sees now how it works. Galactic signals
Come to this latest Homer's ears WHO THEN
CONFIDES THEIR MEANING   BUT TO WHOM? POOR DUMB
E GERMAN TECHNOCRATS? Hardly: God B
Must be the first, our peacock said, to hear them.
And each bit of made sense adds to that great
Store of wisdom. THUS THESE 5 GO STRAIGHT
OVER THE HEADS OF WHATEVER BUREAUCRACY,
EVEN THE BROTHERS'   Each of the Five intent
On his own gift and his own element
Till, from the upwardness of midnight spark,
Returning dew, cadenza of the lark,
To meteor in field, fresh bread on sill,
All is a ghost of grist to Heaven's mill.
DIVINE SIMPLICITY   SO LIKE THAT WONDROUS
TALE OF GRIMM: SHARPEYES & EARTOGROUND,
SERVANTS WHO HELP THE UNWORLDLY PRINCE TO WIN

HIS LADY'S HAND   But drugged, asleep, in labor?
GLIMPSES OF THEIR CURRENT STATES ON EARTH
Then Plato's in fact *between* lives. GATHERING
HIS POWERS FOR THE NEXT   That's why you've had
Such easy access? SO I NOW PRESUME

Poor Mirabell, it seems to be his doom . . .
And Rachel? How he struggled to explain
Her name as formula! Well, wrong again.
YES & NO: IN THE BEGINNING MIGHT THE WORD
(OR FORMULA) NOT HAVE REMAINED UNHEARD
UNTIL IT HAD ENGENDERED BOTH ITS OWN
ANTONYM & THE ODD HOMOPHONE?
SO RACHEL. THESE OLD TESTAMENT NAMES I'VE
A HUNCH RING MANY CHANGES ON THE FIVE
And Nefertiti is now Plato's twin,
Not Akhnaton's—what's that meant to mean?
TWINS WE ARE TOLD COME FROM THE FEMALE GENE,
THERE4 THESE LADIES & THEIR ESCORTS WEAVE
A LINE BACK TO THE PRIMAL (M)ADAM/EVE:
NO SOONER SINGLE THAN NEF ONCE AGAIN
TOOK ON A DOUBLE NATURE (ALL THOSE ARMS
OF SHIVA NOT THE LEAST OF HIS/HER CHARMS)
WD THAT BE THE GENETICS, WOMAN?
                                   ME?
REALLY! HOW WD I KNOW? In other lives
You had— I REMEMBER THANK U   BUT NO TWINS.
NO TEASING GLIMPSES EITHER, OF THE 5'S
PRESENT EXISTENCES   YET MAY I SPEAK
MES ENFANTS AS A WILY SHARPEYED GREEK?
THEY HAVE SEEN US AS OF YESTERDAY,
PARTICULARLY YOU 2   What are you saying—
That one of them is somebody we've met,
Or will, on Earth? George Cotzias, I'll just bet!
Notice how Montezuma gave no clue
To his current life? Remember then what you
Learned about George's densities? Come now,
That *must* be the connection! YES & NO

The First Lessons: 6

> *The schoolroom as before. Enter the Brothers.*

Mich.   POETS, A POEM! HERE'S WHAT I SHOULD LIKE AS SUBJECT:
YESTERDAY'S MEETING OF THE FIVE, YOU 4, WE 4, AND QUESTIONS.

WHA.   SIR?

Mich.   YES, SENIOR SCRIBE?

WHA.   MAY I ASK, IN YOUR FINAL COUPLET YESTERDAY
WERE YOU NOT USING A RUNOVER LINE?

Mich.   SCRIBE, RUN OVER?

WHA.   SIR, WE MEAN BY THAT, WHEN A LINE'S SENSE
AND ITS LAST WORD ELUDE COINCIDENCE.

Mich.   O SCRIBES, I WHO CAN WRITE ON WALLS CANNOT ALAS MAKE POEMS.

WHA.   (Nervous, eager not to give offence)
O NO SIR, ABSOLUTELY CHARMING, QUITE
THE OCCASIONAL VERSIFIER! I ONLY MEANT
THE DRAMA OF YOUR LINE-BREAK: 'DELAY / YOU'

Mich.   TOO MODERN? EVEN BAD?

JM.   Most dashing, *I* thought.

WHA.   SIR, DO NOT GIVE UP
& ALL WE SCRIBES SHALL COME TO YOU TO SUP!

Mich.   RUNOVER, HMM. THAT'S A WHOLE NEW DIMENSION
A silvery bell peals. Light grows acute.
AS IS OUR CLASS TODAY. FOR MY BROTHERS & I WILL EXPLAIN THE
SECOND OF OUR EACH THREE NATURES.
RAPHAEL, LET US PROCEED NOW TO REVEAL THE TWELVE.

Raph.   AT FIRST I PROTECTED IN THAT CAVE THE SWEET & INNOCENT IDEA
OF MAN CONTEMPLATING HIMSELF.
NOW HERE IS MY SECOND DUTY IMPOSED UPON ME BY OUR GREAT
FATHER: SUPPLY.
UP THROUGH MY SOILS, MADAME, COME GREEN SHOOTS, AS YELLOW
SUN & BLUE WATER MIX IN ME. AND UP THROUGH MY VEINS
COMES HEAT, & FROM MY PORES: OIL, & FROM MY PITS: COAL.
MAN SPRINGS TO LIFE & TO INDUSTRY AND I REWARD HIM WITH
MY GOLD & SILVER

WHOSE SHADOW RICHES ARE URANIUM. YET, SUPPLY! CRIED GOD,
AND I OBEY. FOR EVEN UNDER YOUR LAKES & SEAS I AM,
EMMANUEL, A BASE BUT GENEROUS NATURE.

Our school has every modern teaching aid.
Green fields ashimmer and great ore-veined peaks
Fill one frame. Then, as Emmanuel speaks,
They are replaced by a 3-D cascade
Overbrimming inexhaustibly
Font upon font of snow above a polar Sea.

Emm. INDEED, R, U R (SEE LORD BROTHER MICHAEL, HOW I HAVE TAKEN
   TO THEIR LETTERS?)
   & AS THE QUIET LAKE I EARLY STILLED HIS FEAR WHILE KEEPING
   HIS WISH TO RETURN TO ME AT BAY.
   THROUGH MY FIRST NATURE, PEACEFUL & REASONABLE GREW THIS
   THINKING BEAST.
   AND THEN OUR FATHER GAVE ME A SECOND DUTY: CARRY HIM.
   & SO AS CHRISTOPHER I TRANSPORTED THE MANCHILD, & QUENCHED
   HIS THIRST & WASHED HIM
   WHO BY THEN INNATELY WISHED FOR A BAPTISMAL CLEANSING OF
   HIS ANIMAL DIRT.
   SO: REASON & PRIDE, CALM & PURIFICATION,
   ARE MY TWO DOUBLE NATURES.

Mich. YOU, SHY ONE, OR ME?
Gabr. PROCEED, PROCEED.
Mich. I BORE INTO THE CAVES & ONTO THE DANCING WATERS THE LIGHT!
   LIGHT! OF MY FATHER'S CRY. I BROUGHT IN THE NATURE OF
   IDEAS.
   THEN GOD SAID: 'DIVIDE THE TIME OF MAN
   AND MAKE A REFLECTIVE NATURE WHERE, CALMED AT HIS FIRE, HE
   WILL TURN OVER THESE IDEAS AS TREASURE GATHERED IN HIS
   DAY.'
   SO I THREW UP REFLECTION, MAKING DAY,
   & TURNED IT OFF, CREATING NIGHT.
   I BROUGHT INDOORS THE ROVING NATURE OF MAN WITH HIS 5
   PLAYMATES.

DJ. Reflection?

WHA. WE DO NOT SEE LIGHT MY DEAR,
ONLY ITS EFFECT ON ATMOSPHERE.

Mich. HOMEWORK! WELL? ARE YOU TIMID OF BOASTING, GABRIEL?

Gabr. NO.

WHEN I ASSUMED MY SEAT NEXT TO OUR FATHER HE NOTED MY ONE
NATURE, DESTRUCTION, & SAID: 'IT IS NOT ENOUGH.

WE ALL MUST WORK. GO FORTH AS FIRE IN ALL ITS FORMS. IT WILL
NEED ATTENTION, AND BE AN ABUSED NATURE, YET ATTEND
IT.'

AND SO I CLEANSE TOO, IN A WAY,

& I ILLUMINATE REFLECTION, I SWARM IN VELVET ON MICHAEL'S
TRAIN.

PERFORMING MY SECOND NATURE I PROMOTE THOUGHT, AGGRESSION,
DREAD, AS THROUGH WOOD & COAL & OIL & ATOMS AND YES,
LIVES

I GO UP IN FLAME.

MY FIRST NATURE: SELECTION. MY SECOND: THOUGHT.

AH MICHAEL, HENCE THE VERY HISTORY OF MAN, HIS EVOLUTION!
FOR THESE OUR FATHER ENTRUSTED TO ME.

Mich. SO, DEAR SHADES, DEAR SCRIBE & FAITHFUL HAND, WE KNOW 8 OF
OUR NATURES. NEXT,

ALWAYS SHY YET NOT LOATH TO DISPLAY,

WE WILL TOMORROW BRING FOUR MORE: ANOTHER DAY

Exeunt.

His last line comes through garbled:

TORROWMORE WILL BRING IN FOUR OTHER DAY.

SHH SHH   SHALL WE SET IT RIGHT? MM

QUICK THE WASHRAG   RUB OFF THE BLACKBOARD

THERE! And the poem Michael asked for? I'M

ITCHING TO TRY MY HAND   PENTAMETER?

5 LINE STANZAS? GIVE/FIVE/LIVE? High time

He found some other rhyme-word besides "day".

A TAG FROM GOETHE, NO? SEHR DISTINGUE

★

O LORDS WITH JOY & WHOOP & HOLLER
YOU GAVE US FOUR THE FIVE
BUT WHEN (FORGIVE) WILL YOU 4 GIVE
US THEM IN LIVING COLOR?

Very nice, Wystan. That should fill the bill.
NOW YRS? Oh no. Those stanzas won't see light.
TOO UNFAIR! I THOUGHT IT (OVER YR SHOULDER)
BRILLIANTLY SOLVED RIGHT DOWN THE LINE JM:
TETRAMETER FOR US, PENTAM FOR THEM,
NEF EVOKED BY THE ONE FEMININE
ENDING, & PLATO BY THE ONE SLANT RHYME
But it was awful—not the slightest ring
Of *life.* DEAR BOY ONE CAN'T HAVE EVERYTHING!

Let's change the subject. Free of Mirabell's
Brain-teasing ratios, it would seem the Twelve
Are just our angels multiplied by three.
INDEED   SUCH EXQUISITE SIMPLICITY
DJ: But are these *real* powers, would you say,
These angels? I BELIEVE WE SHALL DISCOVER
THEIR POWERS ARE IN US QUITE AS MUCH AS OVER.
SO VERY BEAUTIFUL, WHICHEVER WAY
JM: Aren't you on record as preferring
Truth to beauty, Wystan? Those machines
That powered your ideal lead mines, as a boy—
WHAT'S UGLY ABOUT A BIG ROBUST MACHINE?
I'm only saying you felt bound to choose
Over a possibly more stylish rival
The one that functioned best. ON EARTH MY DEAR,
TRUE. BUT EFFICIENCY IS WELDED HERE
TO BEAUTY AS THE SOUL IS TO SURVIVAL

Will Michael make a poet? HMM   He's read
No one much since Chapman. BUT CONFRERE
HIS WORDLESS SPLENDORS ARE BEYOND COMPARE:
WHEN GABRIEL SPOKE A STARRY UNIVERSE
POURED IN SERENE TUMULT FROM M'S BROW!

THE VERY NIGHT AS CHAPMAN WD AVOW.

VERSE HE MAY LEARN FROM US & THE DEAR KNOWS

THERE'S LITTLE WE CAN TEACH HIM ABOUT PROSE!

Should it be set down on the page as prose?

NOTHING STRICT   A CADENCE BREAKING THRU

ALWAYS FLEXIBLE (To illustrate,

The cup does an impromptu figure eight)

& UNEXPECTED

Lights, an innocent blue.

Mich. WE ARE UNEXPECTED?

JM. Never, Lord. The Senior Scribe and I

Have been discussing, how best to convey

To readers the full verve of what you say.

There are a few effects I mean to try.

Would the like you unmeasurable King

James inflections be perhaps the thing?

Mich. HEAR HIM BROTHERS! IS THAT NOT THE DEAREST OF OUR FATHER'S
HOPES?

MAN USING HIS MOST DELICATE MACHINE, MINING LEAD &
PRODUCING QUICKSILVER?

AH THE MACHINE, SENIOR POET, THE MACHINE, YOUNG SCRIBE, THE
MACHINE OF THE MIND DRIVEN BY WORDS TO MINE MEANING:
MAKE SENSE OF IT

DJ. Does that phrase ring a bell? *The school-bell rings.*

The First Lessons: 7

Mich. OUR FATHER LIFTED THE CURSE OF IMMORTALITY FROM HIS NEW
CREATURE AND SAID:

'SON MICHAEL, SHEDDER OF LIGHT, REFLECTOR, NOW HELP MAN
FORGET'

AND SO MY THIRD NATURE: SLEEP, THE REPOSE FROM DAYLIGHT TO
DAYLIGHT.

MAN'S SPACE ON EARTH LIES LARGELY WITHIN PATHS WHERE SUN
& LACK OF SUN EQUATE HIS HOURS.

JUST SO HIS LIFESPAN: THE VITAL YEARS, THE MIDDAY YEARS, ARE
BALANCED BY YEARS OF CARE AS CHILD & OF REST AS AGED.

AND SO ANOTHER SET OF TWINS, GABRIEL & I, DIVIDE REPOSE: I THE
    LIVING, SLEEPING, DREAMING

Gabr. AND I THE REPOSE BETWEEN LIVES. MY FATHER SAID:
'GABRIEL, SEPARATOR, JUDGE, THINKER ON IDEAS, RESTLESS
    URGER-ON OF MAN'S MIND,
GIVE MY POOR CHILDREN SUCH A SLEEP THAT, WAKING TO THE
    LIGHT OF A NEW LIFE, THEY FORGET ITS TOLL & RUSH OUT
    EAGERLY'

Emm. AND THE WATER BURSTS IN THE WOMB, & DOWN GLIDES GOD'S
    DARLING.
THEN GOD SAID: 'TWIN ELIAS, EMMANUEL, YOU THE CALM ONE,
    GIVE MY CHILD BALM FOR SORROW'
& SO THROUGHOUT MAN'S FAREWELLS TO LIFE MY TEARS BATHE THE
    CLENCHED FACE, FLOW & ASSUAGE.

Raph. THEN MY TURN CAME. 'O WITTY TWIN (SAID GOD) TAKE BACK YOUR
    PIECE OF CLAY'
DUST TO DUST? NO! LIVING TISSUE & MINERALS, STORED IN MAN
    SINCE HIS CLIMB FROM YOUR OOZY FLOOR, EMMANUEL, THERE
    BELOW THE SALT.
THESE ELEMENTS I FOLDED ONCE AGAIN IN MY ARMS. MY TREES
    WHISPERED:
SLEEP, CHILD, UNTIL AGAIN YOU COME TO ME, KING OF ALL
    LIVING THINGS AND LORD OF THE GREENHOUSE, SLEEP.

Mich. SO OUR TWELVE NATURES, SUBLIME & COMMON:
EARTH, AIR, WATER, FIRE, IN VARIED CONSORT MAKING SIX PAIRS OF
    TWINS, SET IN YOUR FOUR SEASONS
Music. Vivaldi's 'The Four Seasons' plays
Gently through Michael's closing words of praise.
O GREEN SPRING EARTH, O WITTY WITH HOPE!
O BLUE CALM CLEANSING, MUSICAL & RHYTHMIC WATER!
O LIGHT, IDEAS YELLOWING TO HAZE,
ASWARM WITH GNATLIKE SELVES ARE YOU THROUGH AUTUMN DAYS!
AND YOU, RED SOLEMN THOUGHT, O DECIMATOR,
CHAOS FROZEN INTO ORDER, WINTER!
But Light from elsewhere lifts the harmony
To a remote, electrifying key:

AH MY FOUR SONS

Mich. O FATHER!
IN OUR SEVENTH HEAVEN YOU GRACE US, WE BOW WITH LOVE!
FATHER, HAVE WE TOLD THEM WELL?

YOU HAVE TOLD THEM THE TWELFTH OF IT THEY TAKE YOU IN

The cup like an eager dog behind a hedge
    He cannot overleap
Races back, forth, along the Board's far edge:
  His Master lost by now in bright
Unthinkables, all pinpoint-far, dream-deep
      Foresight.

Then Michael's voice through swarming, rainbow mist:
GRACED ARE WE, YET HAVE FAR MORE TO SAY
AND MANY A TRUTH FOR ANOTHER DAY

—Leaving us stunned. What happened, anyway?
God Himself grazed our poem in a gust
Of wonder? Yes, and something like distrust.
Not of Him, not of Biology . . .
But, after all, we bookish people live
In bondage to those reigning narrative
Conventions whereby the past two or three
Hundred years have seen a superhuman
All-shaping Father dwindle (as in Newman)
To ghostly, disputable Essence or
Some shaggy-browed, morality-play bore
(As in the Prologue to *Faust*). Today the line
Drawn is esthetic. One allows divine
Discourse, if at all, in paraphrase.
Why should God speak? How humdrum what he *says*
Next to His word: out of a black sleeve, lo!
Sun, Earth and Stars in eloquent dumb show.
Our human words are weakest, I would urge,
When He resorts to them. Here on the verge

Of these objections, one does well to keep
One's mouth shut—Wystan, don't you think? WE WEEP

★

A dreadful interval. Last night's collision,
Heading home, with a wool-gathering creep.
No one hurt, but ugly psychic dents.
Words D and I exchange about expense
Turn our green mountain to a black plateau
Still smouldering the next afternoon. ENFANTS
QUICK WHILE OUR STAR PUPIL PRIMPS IN THE DORM:
MAMAN HAS BEEN SO LONG A LONER THAT
SHE CAN'T RECALL THE IDLE HOUSEHOLD SPAT
BUT WE NEED CALM & LAST NIGHT'S LITTLE SCENE
UNDID YR OLD BLACK MAMMY
                          O I MEAN
SHE'S TAKEN THE FRONT SEAT   OUR TEACHER'S PET
RUSHED IN AHEAD OF ME & TOOK MY SEAT!
All smiles, our discord laughable, DJ:
No little scenes up there, please! Tell us, er,
About, ah— SHALL WE SAY THE MINISTER
OF EDUCATION? YES: A RADIANCE
THEY TURNED THEIR BACKS ON US & SPOKE INTO,
SNUFFING OUT (AS MM SAID) THEIR SMOKES
LIKE SO MANY VILLAGE DANDIES WHEN PAPA
ENTERS THE ROOM   I *felt* they'd been caught boasting!
AH THEY WERE SIMPLY COWED & NOT WITH FEAR,
WITH WHAT WD BE TO LOVE (AS WE KNOW LOVE)
WHAT LOVE IS TO AFFECTION   Did you hear
A voice? THE MUSIC SWELLED   WE SAW U WRITE
THE WORDS & A PURE GLOW ON OUR DEAR HAND
Slowly, as he goes on, the full amazement
Seizes us. Reliving yesterday's
Lesson, we are humming "Winter" when

The First Lessons: 8

> *Michael and his Brothers quietly enter.*

Mich.   IT IS ALL APPROVED & WE PROCEED. I AM MY FATHER'S SON
      MICHAEL.

      WE KNOW THAT EACH LIVING CREATURE LIVES BY SENSES, SOME
      FEWER, BUT THE HIGHER FORMS HAVE FIVE.

      WE HAVE BROUGHT YOU OUR SCOUTS, THE IMMORTAL FIVE. THEY
      REPORT TO MY BROTHERS & ME THEIR FINDINGS

      WHICH, WHEN APPROVED & MADE SENSE OF, THESE GENIUS 5
      PROCEED WITH.

      NOW WE, MY BROTHERS & I, ARE THE SENSES OF OUR FATHER.
      RAPHAEL?

Raph.   I AM GOD'S HEARING ON EARTH. I HEAR THE FEET, THE MOVEMENTS
      OF HIS CREATURES, THE SLITHER, THE STAMPEDE.

      I SENSE THE BUILDERS OVER BUILDERS. SHAKE! SAYS MY FATHER,
      AND I DO.

      I HEAR THE CRIES OF TREES CUT, TOO MANY. I HEAR THE LESSENING
      OF A BREED.

      I LISTEN, MAKE SENSE OF IT, AND REPORT TO MY FATHER.

Mich.   HIS TWIN?

Emm.   I TOUCHING EARTH, CIRCLING IT, PATTING ITS SHORES,

      RACING WITH NEWS OF THE AVALANCHE, WITHDRAWING WHEN IN
      DESERT LANDS WE MUST GUARD SPACE FOR MAN'S FUTURE
      FIELDS,

      I COVER THE WHOLE BALL, REFLECTIVE PALMS UPWARD, FEELING
      THE ATMOSPHERE.

      I TOUCH, MAKE SENSE OF IT, AND REPORT TO MY FATHER.

Gabr.   MY TWIN DUTIES, I THE SELECTOR, ARE TASTE & SMELL.

      I CATCH WHIFFS OF DANGER, AND TASTE THE BITTER & THE SWEET.

      I AM THE COOK OF THE SMOKING STEW OF MANKIND: LESS HERE OF
      THIS, MORE OF THAT.

      I PILE THESE FINDINGS ON A TRAY, MAKE SENSE OF THEM, AND
      REPORT TO MY FATHER.

Mich.   AND HE, O SHY BROTHER, HOW OFTEN: 'IT IS NOT DONE'?
      The schoolroom glowers, but the irresistible
      Light of day resumes. As Michael does:

AND I? I READ, DEAR EMMANUEL, YOUR PALMS, AND I SEARCH & I
    SEE, AND HAVE A VAST SURFACE TO EXPLORE EACH DAY.
I MAKE A THEORY OF LIGHT IN THE BRIGHTNESS OF EXPLOSION,
AND CHECK TO SEE IF YET THE FEATHERS OF ITS WING CAN SUPPORT
    THE PIGEON IN MY AIR.
I LOOK, I READ, MAKE SENSE OF IT, AND REPORT TO MY FATHER.

JM.   And God? He takes them in, these capsules made
      Of the whole vast ongoing escalade?

Mich.   AND THEN, YOUNG SCRIBE, THE GREAT SENSES OF OUR FATHER BEGIN.
FOR HE WHO HAS ALL THESE FIVE HAS A SIXTH: INTUITION,
A SEVENTH: JUDGEMENT (WHICH, O GLORY, HE DEMONSTRATED
    YESTERDAY)
AN EIGHTH: COMMAND, & A NINTH: PRONOUNCEMENT,
AND THEN THE ZEROETH WE DO NOT KNOW
FOR THIS HE EXERCISES OUTWARD. YES, TURNING OUTWARD HIS
    MULTIPLE ATTENTION FORTIFIED BY THE GREAT ORCHESTRA OF
    THE SENSES,
OUR FATHER SINGS,
SINGS, ALONE, INTO THE UNIVERSE.
Pauses as if hearkening. No sound.
LISTEN! FOR YOU 4 WILL HEAR THAT SONG: YOUR TENTH LESSON (ON
    THE 9TH WILL BE A JOYOUS CONGRESS OF THE SENSES)
AND THEN OUR FIRST OF THREE SCHOOL TERMS WILL END.

DJ.   Already? It seems only yesterday . . .

Mich.   NOW THIS 8TH HEAVEN OF COMMAND PERMITS YOUR MICHAEL TO,
LET US NOT SAY ORDER, RATHER GIVE AN OUTLINE OF OUR V
    WORK AHEAD:
YOU WILL ASSEMBLE IN A MOON MONTH AFTER THESE TEN LESSONS.
THEN WE MAKE SENSE OF THEM FOR FIVE LESSONS MORE.
THEN MY SHY BROTHER TAKING THE FRONT DESK (PERMETTEZ
    MADAME?) WILL GIVE US HIS TEXT TO BALANCE MINE,
FOR WILL WE NOT HAVE INNOCENTLY EXPOSED OURSELVES TO
    IDEAS?
AND HAVE WE NOT AS OUR FATHER COMMANDS, SURVIVED?

SO NEXT WE DON THE GLAD ARRAY
OF ALL OUR SENSES TO MEET THE DAY.
Exeunt.

WHA. ENTRE NOUS MY DEAR HE'S NOT IMPROVING:
NEXT WE DON OUR SENSES IN GLAD ARRAY
& MEET HERE AGAIN ON ANOTHER DAY.

JM. That too could stand some work, if I may say so.
Michael, returning unexpectedly:
QUARRELING, POETS?

JM. He— I—that is, we . . .

Mich. MY VERSE NOT METERED? NOT IN RHYME? THEN PRAY
MAKE SENSE OF IT YOURSELVES ANOTHER DAY!
Exit. And only now sunset's tall dazzle
Dims from the frosted glass of our doorway.

O DEAR HE WAS STANDING OUTSIDE! HOW I ADORE HIM!
ME TOO! ME TOO! YR JADED MAMAN'S TYPE.
Not Gabriel? Good. AH THERE ARE NIGHTS & KNIGHTS,
BUT YOU 3 FAITHFUL SQUIRES, YR MISTRESS SAYS,
WILL SERVE UNTIL THE END OF BLISSFUL DAYS.
DJ: Tomorrow will be twenty-four
Years to the day since J and I first met.
JM: Or twenty-five, as any Greek
Would count them; we're all one year old at birth.
THE PARTY'S PLANNED, NO ACCIDENT! A Silver
Jubilee in England, too. *Newsweek*
Says London is a pulsing fairyland
Of coaches, fireworks, dancing on the green.
INDEED   WHO WD HAVE THOUGHT THAT NO DOUBT STABLE
BUT O SO DOWDY SCHOOLGIRL WD TURN OUT
SUCH A SUCCESS? Maman, you knew the Queen?
Imagine never telling! DON'T MAKE FUN
THE LIFE MAMAN LED, SHE KNEW E V E R Y O N E

★

*JM from DJ entering
our 25th year—*

often distant, ever dear.
(Diamonds not from Pharoah's barge
but MFJ's engagement ring—
sorry they're so large!)

—This with a band of chemically blackened
Silver in which twin baby stones are set
To balance a small "sun" of gold. Slipped on,
It is an instant, lifelong amulet.
JM: I've no gift but these lines the years
Together write upon my face and yours.

YOU DEAR BOYS AT FIVE & TWENTY
SURELY HAVE A GRACIOUS PLENTY
AND WHEN YOU'VE ARRIVED AT FIFTY
SHOULDN'T LIFE BE TWICE AS NIFTY?
MY POINT HERE SEEMS TO BE:
EXPECTANCY! EXPECTANCY!

Wystan, how very, very . . . silvery.
THANK U   WE'RE GIVEN LIKE A PAIR OF WAITERS
THESE ORDERS FOR THIS AFTERNOON'S COMMAND
PERFORMANCE: SALT. A SPICE OF YR OWN CHOICE.
A SCENT. ICE IN A BOWL. A CANDLE LIT
& A LIVE FLOWER. FETCH THESE NOW   We do.
David on the terrace cuts a snow-white,
Paprika-anthered lily. I meanwhile
Bring coriander and a bergamot
Cologne; the rest. That's it? Then light the candle.
Sit. WHEE! U ARE WITH US FOR THE FIRST
TIME IN ALL THESE LESSONS NOT REVERSED.
WE SMELL U   HEAR U   & THEY SAY WILL TOUCH
U ANY MOMENT   IT'S A LITTLE MUCH!
Is this called making sense? & GETTING THRU

Seventh Heaven, Judgment; Eighth, Command—
So Michael said. Are we to understand
Each lesson lifts us to a plane of greater

353

Power and light? INDEED   AN ELEVATOR
How can you tell? Does Maman get a shade
More beautiful, like Beatrice? WE ARE MADE
AWARE, DEEP IN THE CAVE, OF CRYSTALS PLATO
NEVER DREAMED OF, BIG FAT SOLITAIRES!
IT'S NO ILLUSION   EPHRAIM HAD IT RIGHT,
WE'VE TAKEN SENSES ON & IT'S DIVINE
Had it right for a different order of spirit:
You, in short. YET IF WE TOUCH AT 9
IS IT NOT MY DEARS HIS DREAM COME TRUE?
Ah, you must tell him. He'll be thrilled. ALAS
WE MAY NEVER SEE HIM AFTER THIS
"Pronouncement" sends you back— A LAST LONG SUMMER
& DIE THE SWANS   Never to sing again?
Just those mute messages flashed vein by vein
Through mineral and leaf? A COMFORT, NO?
MAMAN THE LAURA IN YR LAURELS

I

MY BOYS INSIST ON BEING YR PET ROCK!
DJ: Don't let's think *now* of losing you.
You'll come with us to Samos? Ephesus?
LET'S DO   BUT WHAT TO WEAR? They won't take back
Your senses? INDIAN GIVERS? LET THEM TRY!
AH   MUSIC   IT BEGINS MY DEARS   MY DEARS!

The Ascent to Nine

Music. A single pure white beam one knows
Floods the mirror room, which undergoes
Instant changes. Dewy garlands deck
The staircase. Statue, pictures, candlestick,
Each is prismatically multiplied.
The Ouija Board drifts upward on a tide
Of crystal light—ethereal parquet
Where guests will presently join WHA
And MM. (DJ and JM appear
Twice, outside and in, both 'there' and 'here'.)

What *is* the music? STRAUSS   I MEAN THEY ARE
SWEET TO REMEMBER   ROSENKAVALIER
SIDE ONE   GO PUT IT ON DEAR BOY   I do,
And hurry back. NOW LINK YR FINGERS   YES
NOW TOUCH EACH OTHER'S FACE   KISS   We obey.
(Only yesterday? Twenty-five years?)
AH YES   YES   IT BEGINS   MY GOD!
MY MUSIC

MY MUSIC   MY POOR SOUL THAT WAS MY SOUL
WHERE'S HOFFI? WHERE'S MY TWIN? It's Strauss himself,
He's at the party! THANK YOU FOR MY MUSIC
ROSEN SIND SIE MEINE BUEBCHEN   *We*
Are roses—is he mad?
A second new

Voice entering the cup: WHAT IS THAT SOUND?
That's *Rosenkavalier* by Richard Strauss
On the phonograph in Athens, in our house.
SO I AM HOME   Who's this? THE DWARF KIND SIRS
ONLY THE DWARF   The great scribe Homer? I?
PERHAPS   THEY TELL ME NOTHING THOUGH I LISTEN
You're listened *to* throughout the centuries.
MAY I HEAR A SMALL POEM? ANYONE'S?
For Homer's pleasure, what on Earth to say?
Luckily Wystan (JM PERMETTEZ?)
Takes over, and declaims: HOW JOYOUSLY
WE LITTLER MEN HAVE SAILED YOUR WINEDARK SEA,
IMMORTAL BARD, YOU WHO CREATED ME!

A third arrival: WHERE AM I? THIS MUSIC
I KNOW IT   YES! AND MAESTRO, HERE?
IST ES

NICHT EIN TRAUM, LIEBSTE NORWEGERIN?
(It can't be Flagstad! YES   THEY ALL TROOP IN)
From upstairs, Schwarzkopf, who had dubbed a high
C in that late *Tristan* Flagstad made:
"Es ist ein Besuch!" NOT BAD AT ALL, NOT BAD
BUT YOU MY GREATEST VOICE
MY DEAREST FRIEND

He wears a frockcoat; she, a flowery gown,
And positively croons over the lily.
Enter a plumed Splendor:

                          OUR SCULPTORS CARVED
THAT FLOWER BY THE THOUSAND & WHEN MY PALACE
FELL INTO THE MOAT (It's Montezuma!)
ONE BLOSSOM, ONE STONE LILY FLOATED FREE
& THE POOR SPANIARDS WENT PALE WITH DREAD:
THE LIGHT VOLCANIC ROCK, YOU SEE
                                  BUT IS
THIS GLASS ONESIDED? asks a new voice.
                                  COME
SISTER QUEEN (Akhnaton and Nefertiti!)
OUR LORD THE SUN ENJOINS US TO LOOK UP
Michael is ready, as a final guest
Slips in:
                    AND MUSIC TOO? Who have we here?
I NOTICE SOME IMPROVEMENTS ON MY CAVE
Plato—oh, you won't approve of Strauss!
NEVER DISAPPROVE   IT WARPS THE SOUL
All take their places as the light takes form.

The First Lessons: 9

Mich.   WELCOME AT THIS OUR TOPMOST STAGE,
        CHILDREN, TO A SILVER AGE.
(The ring, the silver rose, the Jubilee,
Everything fits unbelievably)
NOW QUICK SENSES: TOUCH THE ICE,·
TASTE THE SPICE, SMELL THE SCENT!
FROM HEAVEN BENT WE LEAN, LAY CLAIM
UPON YOUR HANDS. NOW LOOK INTO THE FLAME

We do. *All do. A timeless moment. Twelve*
Figures reproduced to twelve times twelve
In ranks of the four colors, see themselves
—No, D and I see nothing—through the 'sense

Prisms' conferred on them by Michael. Thus
I WHO WAS WYSTAN SAW A YELLOW ME
AGED & WRY   A GREEN HILARIOUSLY
LAUGHING   A RED ME WRAUGHT   A BLUE
ME STARING STRAIGHT INTO MY OWN TWO EYES
While I WHO WAS MARIA IN THE FITTER'S
MIRROR SAW A RED ENRAGED MAMAN
A BLUE IN BLISS WITH FLOWERS IN HER HAIR
A GREEN TOO SHY TO SPEAK OF & MOST ODD
A YELLOW SELF I'D SEEN 100,000 TIMES
DOING MY FACE. TOO SIMPLIFIED, BUT THESE
WERE MERELY PSYCHES, PERSONALITIES,
THE UPPER CRUST OF A MILLEFEUILLES LAYER BY LAYER,
HABITS & LOVES & LIFETIMES, PEELED AWAY
FROM EPIDERMS OF HUMAN MEMORY
Until, at Michael's voice, the flame, like one
Shaken from sleep, returns each to his own:

ALL THE COLORS AT OUR FETE
(STRAUSS, A TUNE! FAIR SINGER, SING!
WE'LL HAVE THE BEST OF EVERYTHING)
GREENS YELLOWS BLUES & REDS, STAY WITH US YET
AND BE THE WHITE OF MY DELIGHT
IN EWIGKEIT

The master improvisor's four-note theme,
BDEA, makes everybody smile—
B and I, the two notes are the same!
I come to Be, is the Idea. Meanwhile
Flagstad by the keyboard meets his eye,
Throws her blonde head back. It's a fifth Last Song
—A silk trailed over dead leaves, loom of peak,
Ninths in full blossom, minor purl of stream.
As Wystan thumps along JUST KEEPING TIME
Michael's words, which on the page look weak,
Come thrilling from her throat. He speaks through them:

SILVERY MY CHILDREN, ENTER IN
THIS HEAVEN IT IS GIVEN YOU TO WIN.
FOR WHO IS LEFT TO TELL YOU NAY?
OUR FATHER'S VOICE ANOTHER DAY
YOU'LL HEAR & FALL (LIKE ANGELS) DOWN TO PRAY!
TOUCH, TASTE, SMELL, HEAR & SEE,
NOW COMPOSE A SILENT HARMONY.

The song ends. LIFT YOUR HANDS: CLAP ONCE! We do.
WE ARE GONE   *The schoolroom empties in a trice.*

Our black wick smoulders over melted ice.
In and out of numbers 9 to 1
Weaving like a drunk, the cup comes down
To earth: SPORTSWEAR   BOYS CLOTHING   WATCH THE STEP!
WOW   DID U FEEL OUR TOUCH UPON YR HANDS?
JM: Not I. DJ: I felt . . . a chill?
YES   FOR MY DEARS WE TOUCHED U & CAN STILL
ALMOST: AS RS SAID, ROSEPETAL SKIN
OR BABIES' BOTTOMS   Were we somehow *in*
The mirror for that hour? U WERE INDEED
Literally?—but by now we know
Where that will get us. Tutti: YES & NO

This Heaven was Pronouncement? IN THE SENSE
OF HAVING I SHD SAY A PRONOUNCED FLAIR
FOR THIS OR THAT, LIKE MICHAEL'S FROM THIN AIR
TOUCHING, SPECTACULAR EMBODIMENTS
You must have got your touch back when we kissed;
That's why you said "My God"? DEAR BOY, NO: YR
STAGE DOOR JOHNNY HAD JUST GLIMPSED DEMURE
FLAGSTAD APPROACHING & KNEW WE WERE IN FOR BIGGER
TREATS THAN A VULGAR GROPE
                              I MES ENFANTS
WAS THRILLED BY NEF   A PRESENCE OF PURE AMBER
ROBED IN 18TH DYNASTY HAUTE COUTURE
OVERWHELMING   MICHAEL CAN DO IT ALL!
NOT A TRANSPARENCY: DO U RECALL

HER QUESTION? ONLY THEN WE UNDERSTOOD
WE WERE NOT LIVE, & WHEN SHE TOUCHED THE MIRROR
(FOR OF COURSE THE WALLS AROUND US WERE YR MIRROR)
IT WAS AS IF SHE O HEARTBREAKINGLY
HAD GRAZED AN OLD & WELLKNOWN PRISON. WE
PUT UP OUR HANDS IN FEAR LEST THE GLASS CRACK
LIKE GREENHOUSE PANES
                              BUT SHE AT ONCE DREW BACK:
A TEENY SHOCK   THE MIRROR A COW GUARD?
SHE WANTED U   AS WHO DID NOT? & YET . . .
Were we *there* only in a sense? IN ALL
THAT MATTER SHORT OF THE MATERIAL.
MICHAEL'S SLEIGHT OF HAND BROUGHT US TOGETHER
IN THE R LAB   THE 5 COULD GO NO FURTHER,
A STYX OF QUICKSILVER DIVIDING THEM
FROM LIFE-INFECTED DJ & JM
The other angels, were they present? NO
ONLY, WHEN MICHAEL LOOKED INTO THE FLAME
HE STRUCK US AS COMMUNING   OTHERWISE
THIS AFTERNOON WAS UTTERLY HIS SHOW
And ours! SO TRUE   TO EACH EPIPHANY
ITS OWN: FLAGSTAD & STRAUSS WDN'T AT ALL
DO FOR A BUTTERED SHAMAN IN NEPAL
And next the voice of God. How do we rise
To that? SLEEP SOUND TONIGHT   WE KISS YOUR EYES

*

The First Lessons: *10*

No scene. The mirror bitter-black and vast,
Underdusted with remotest light.

ANCHORS AT LAST   MM & I OUT HERE
RISING RISING INTO SUCH A VOID & HOWL!
OUR WALLS HAVE LONG SINCE DROPPED AWAY   O THANK
GOD U HAVE COME   WE THOUGHT WE HAD LOST TOUCH
May we ask questions? HUSH   WE STRAIN TO HEAR

Now, ripple within ripple on black water,
o o o o o o o o o o
Pulse of the galactic radio
Tuned then to mortal wavelength in mid-phrase:

IVE BROTHERS HEAR ME BROTHERS SIGNAL ME
ALONE IN MY NIGHT BROTHERS DO YOU WELL
I AND MINE HOLD IT BACK BROTHERS I AND
MINE SURVIVE BROTHERS HEAR ME SIGNAL ME
DO YOU WELL I AND MINE HOLD IT BACK I
ALONE IN MY NIGHT BROTHERS I AND MINE
SURVIVE BROTHERS DO YOU WELL I ALONE
IN MY NIGHT I HOLD IT BACK I AND MINE
SURVIVE BROTHERS SIGNAL ME IN MY NIGHT
I AND MINE HOLD IT BACK AND WE SURVIVE

Pausing to be reread, then pulsing slowly
o o o o o o o o o o
The cup glides off the far edge of the Board.

Life itself speaking. Song of the blue whale
Alone in Space? Bravery, vertigo,
Frontier austerities . . . Maria? Wystan?

BE CALM A DAY NOW   OUR FRIENDS PRONE & COLD BUT THEY SURVIVE
Dumbly we nod.
IT IS YR BIRD!   Of course—where are our manners?
Thank you for coming to us, Mirabell.
                I AM YOUR OWN   GIVE THEM A REST, THEY HAVE
KNOWN SOMETHING DIFFICULT   I SPREAD WINGS OVER THEM   ADIEU

★

Our friends are being DEBRIEFD, says Mirabell,
And as yet must not know what we have learned.
We hide the transcript, then the cup descends
This time from Zero, to emerge at One
And give us THE BAREST SKETCH: ENFANTS U JOINED US

THERE IN THE BLACKNESS OF THE GLASS   WE SOARED
OUTWARD   WE 4 ALONE   HAND TOUCHING HAND
ON AN OBSIDIAN CUP CALLED UNIVERSE:
SHRIEK OF OUR ICY POINTER ON NO BOARD!
Your walls had dropped away. EMPTY AH YES
MY DEARS & TERRIFYING   UP UP UP
YET NOT WITHOUT A MAD LIGHTHEARTEDNESS
EH MM? IT MUST BE THE EXTREME
DRUG OF THE RISKTAKER   WHO WD EVER DREAM
THAT SUCH
PLEA SET OM ORRO W
　　　　　　　Look, now we're making Mirabell
Uneasy. He was with you, though? INDEED
STOOD BRAVELY BY WITH SMELLING SALTS & ST
BERNARD FLASK & SEEMED ENFANTS THRUOUT
TO HAVE BEEN SHELTERING US WITH HIS HEAT,
FOR WE REVIVED IN WONDER FROM OUR FAINT
STILL HEARING AS IT WERE HIS (M) HEARTBEAT:
A BUZZ OF WHIRLING NUMBERS   Like those street
Cafés in northern cities, with umbrellas
Of radiant warmth— AND THE ACCOUNTANT MIND
SITTING BENEATH THEM MY DEAR! WE WERE SURROUNDED
UPON AWAKENING BY MIRABELL'S KIND,
THE OO STARING   NOT AN ANGEL IN SIGHT . . .
HE FIDGETS   WE HAD BEST LEAVE IT AT THAT.
TOMORROW IN THE SCHOOLROOM WE CAN CHAT

Night. Two phantoms out of Maeterlinck
Stand on the terrace watching the full moon sink.
DJ: It's almost as if *we* were dead
And signalling to dear ones in the world.
They face it squarely, Wystan and Maria,
Terror or exaltation or whatever.
We two are deaf and dumb; they see, they hear.
They suffer; we feel nothing. We're the dead . . .
And these were just the lessons that said Yes
—To what? for up through Michael's magic well
Eerie undercurrents of distress.

Affirmative? I'm dreading Gabriel.
Right off the bat he'll have some negative
Interstellar static stymieing
Any song Biology might sing.
JM: I wonder. Think, before you give
Way to panic, of what other meanings
The word "negative" takes on in *Ephraim*:
X-ray images, or Maya's film
In which the widow turns into the bride.
Tricks of the darkroom. All those cameras clicking
In Venice, on the bridge. For now a new bridge—
Can it be crossed both ways?—from Yes to No
Is entering the picture. DJ: So
Is Venice, if our plans firm up. JM:
By which time, from the darkness you foresee,
Who knows what may develop milkily,
What loving presence? (Odd, not long ago
Our daydreams were in color, that tonight
Print out in Manichaean black and white.)

★

Wystan on God B's Song

WELL THE IST THING WE HEARD WAS A FAINT PIPING
NOT UNLIKE A SHEPHERD'S FLUTE   THIS GREW,
RESOLVED INTO NO MELODY BUT TONE
LEVELS & INTERVALS OF UTTERED MEANING:
PLAINTIVE? AFFIRMATIVE? O QUICKLY NOW
EXPOSE THAT PAGE   UNCOVER IT MY DEARS!
WE ARE ALLOWED   I find the page. They read.

AH   SO HEARTBREAKING   SO THAT WAS IT
He's singing to the Pantheon. OR ALONE
KEEPING UP HIS NERVE ON A LIFERAFT
Far cry from the joyous Architect
Michael told us of at the beginning—;

But He gets answered. DOES HE? Yes. The angels
Spoke of signals. DO THEY KNOW? I see.
They've never heard the Song. ONLY WE 4
& THAT'S AS HE WOULD SAY THE HALF OF IT
What was the song's effect on you? MM
KNEW HERSELF TO BE AMONG THE STARS
THE WORLD LOST, OUT OF EARSHOT. I WAS KEEN
UPON THE SOUND ITSELF   THOSE TONES WERE EITHER
THOSE OF AN ETERNAL V WORK OR A MACHINE
SET TO LAST   UNTIL THE BATTERIES
RUN DOWN   OR . . . ?   Did the tones heard correspond
To what you read just now? EXACT SYLLABICS:
THERE IS A LANGUAGE   ARE WE ON TO SOMETHING?
CAN WE MAKE SENSE OF IT? I ASK   WE ASK

Dante heard that Song. So did Mirabell's
Forebears when the clouds put out the flames.
THERE4 THEY CLUSTERED ROUND WIDEEYED   BUT WHO,
WHO WD THINK THE SONG HAD HAD SUCH LYRICS?
The lyrics may be changing. Dante saw
The Rose in fullest bloom. Blake saw it sick.
You and Maria, who have seen the bleak
Unpetalled knob, must wonder: will it last
Till spring? Is it still rooted in the Sun?
EXACTLY   THEY CHOSE WELL IN U MY DEAR
No, Ephraim raised these issues. But his point's
More chilling made at such an altitude.
CHILLING ENFANT? AN IRREVOCABLE FREEZE

DJ, as one who steers in winter seas
Past threatening floes: You're in the schoolroom now,
Safe and sound? INDEED   WE 4 ALONE
Have you come through the mirror or have we?
U HAVE   ISN'T IT COMFY? & THE VIEW
SENSATIONAL TODAY, ALTHOUGH ALAS
IN 15 LESSONS' TIME U MAY BE CALLED ON
TO RISK BAD LUCK   JM: To break the glass?
& SEND US PACKING   Turning mutineer,

DJ: If we refuse? RISK IT MY DEARS
& WE'LL SURVIVE & MAKING SENSE OF IT
HAVE LIGHTENED GOD B'S TASK A GRAIN
                                        THAT DAY
ENFANTS TAKE OUT A SMALL EXPENDABLE MIRROR
ONTO THE FRONT STEP   KISS & WITH ONE WISE
CRACK SET US FREE   Maria, why must *we?*
JM: Who else? (A pang abrupt as lightning
Strikes deeply through the dim, charged hemisphere;
Then comes the rain.) My mother used to say,
Throw the pieces of a broken mirror
Into running water— IDIOTS   DRY YR EYES:
IST OUR LOVELY VAC THEN EXPLANATIONS
And will *you* break the mirror in our minds?
O WE'LL BE SIGNALLING   JUST U WAIT & SEE
FROM OUT THERE   FROM THE WORLD
                                        DJ, still shaken:
I knew that it would end. I didn't know
That we would have to take the step ourselves.
NICER & NEATER   QUITE LIKE PROSPERO!
LISTEN YR MOTHER'S GOT IT: TAKE A BOWL
OF WATER WE CAN SLIP INTO & OUT
WITH A GREAT SPLASH INTO A PLANTED POT
Instead of breaking anything? WHY NOT?
JM: No. Back to flames, back to the green
Rhine go the rings in Wagner and Tolkien.
The poem's logic, though I hate to say,
Calls for the shattering of a glass. DJ:
Perhaps that *and* the bowl of water, too?
BRAVO ENFANT   OUR EAU DE V WORK   SMOOTH
SEAS TO SAMOS   CALL US   TOODLELOO

The cup, however, lingers. IT'S JUST ME
MY BOY   MAY I? A POME I'VE (M) SET DOWN
UNDER THE SPELL OF HEARING GOD B SING
(WORK ON IT FOR ME   IT NEEDS POLISHING):

A SHIPBOARD SCENE,
TRISTAN ACT I OR LES TROYENS ACT V:
HIGH IN THE RIGGING, FROM
BEHIND THE GOLD PROSCENIUM,
ABOVE THE ACTION'S THRIVING
CITY WITH ITS WRONGED & WILFUL QUEEN,

ONE SAILOR'S CLEAR
YOUNG TENOR FILLS THE HOUSE, HOMESICK, HEARTSICK.
THE MAST NEEDS COMFORT. GALES
HAVE TATTERED THE MOONBELLIED SAILS.
MAY HIS GREEN SHORES O QUICKLY
SAFELY NOW FROM RAGING FOAM APPEAR.

&

Samos

And still, at sea all night, we had a sense
Of sunrise, golden oil poured upon water,
Soothing its heave, letting the sleeper sense
What inborn, amniotic homing sense
Was ferrying him—now through the dream-fire
In which (it has been felt) each human sense
Burns, now through ship's radar's cool sixth sense,
Or mere unerring starlight—to an island.
Here we were. The twins of Sea and Land,
Up and about for hours—hues, cries, scents—
Had placed at eye level a single light
Croissant: the harbor glazed with warm pink light.

Fire-wisps were weaving a string bag of light
For sea stones. Their astounding color sense!
Porphyry, alabaster, chrysolite
Translucences that go dead in daylight
Asked only the quick dip in holy water
For the saint of cell on cell to come alight—
Illuminated crystals thinking light,
Refracting it, the gray prismatic fire
Or yellow-gray of sea's dilute sapphire . . .
Wavelengths daily deeply score the leit-
Motifs of Loom and Wheel upon this land.
To those who listen, it's the Promised Land.

A little spin today? Dirt roads inland
Jounce and revolve in a nerve-jangling light,
Doing the ancient dances of the land
Where, gnarled as olive trees that shag the land
With silver, old men—their two-bladed sense
Of spendthrift poverty, the very land
Being, if not loaf, tomb—superbly land
Upright on the downbeat. We who water
The local wine, which "drinks itself" like water,

Clap for more, cry out to *be* this island
Licked all over by a white, salt fire,
Be noon's pulsing ember raked by fire,

Know nothing, now, but Earth, Air, Water, Fire!
For once out of the frying pan to land
Within their timeless, everlasting fire!
Blood's least red monocle, O magnifier
Of the great Eye that sees by its own light
More pictures in "the world's enchanted fire"
Than come and go in any shrewd crossfire
Upon the page, of syllable and sense,
We want unwilled excursions and ascents,
Crave the upward-rippling rungs of fire,
The outward-rippling rings (enough!) of water . . .
(Now some details—how else will this hold water?)

Our room's three flights above the whitewashed water-
front where Pythagoras was born. A fire
Escape of sky-blue iron leads down to water.
Yachts creak on mirror berths, and over water
Voices from Sweden or Somaliland
Tell how this or that one crossed the water
To Ephesus, came back with toilet water
And a two kilo box of Turkish delight
—Trifles. Yet they shine with such pure light
In memory, even they, that the eyes water.
As with the setting sun, or innocence,
Do things that fade especially make sense?

Samos. We keep trying to make sense
Of what we can. Not souls of the first water—
Although we've put on airs, and taken fire—
We shall be dust of quite another land
Before the seeds here planted come to light.

★

WE'VE FOUND A HOLE IN THE HEDGE! Maria means
That during these days-off before the middle
Set of lessons we can please ourselves,
Talk to friends in the Bureaucracy
Banned from our class, along with Gabriel's
Bat legions, OR TO ANYONE! I stall:
What in fact *is* the hedge? A LOWER WALL
OF CONSCIOUSNESS   DJ: No, no, I'm lost . . .
OK NOW LISTEN: IN THIS HEAVEN/HELL
WE ARE BLANKS. IN THESE BLANKS YOU APPEAR
THANKS TO OUR 'CONNECTION' (CUP, BOARD, MIRROR)
PERFECTLY CLEARLY AS DO THE OTHER DEAD
WE THINK OF OR WHO THINK OF US. HOWEVER
SINCE LESSON I OUR SCHOOLROOM HAS BECOME
A (M) CLOSED CIRCUIT NONE MAY PLUG INTO
WITHOUT CREDENTIALS. IT IS BURKE'S NEW PEERAGE
AN ISOLATION ENGINEERED BY MICHAEL
FROM WHICH ALL SANDOVER IS VISIBLE.
BUT NOW THAT THEY'VE HOOKED UP THE INTERCOM
(OR MAMAN ONCE TOO OFTEN KICKED THE WALL)
WHOM SHALL WE CALL? THEY'VE CLUSTERED AT THE HEDGE,
HL & MD WAVE   E BLOWS A KISS
JM: Or new blood? If Pythagoras
Were hovering near his birthplace— HERE HE IS

7154   Pythagoras? He's quoted
Mirabell's numerology for God.
NUMBER WAS GOD TO US   OUR MUSE   IN MAGIC
THE NUMBER SPEAKS & LOGIC O YOUNG MEN
SETTLES ON EGGS OF NUMBER LIKE A HEN
So we begin, Sir, dimly to construe
For all our slowness. Where would it be, this poem,
Without your guiding light? Measures that you
Taught your disciples glimmer even now
Through the dispersing clouds about my brow.
YOU ARE REPEATING THE OLD RITUAL.
GIVEN A REWARD THE SCRIBE WOULD CALL

'MATHEMATICIAN, COME, RECEIVE YOUR PART
FOR YOURS ARE THE TRUE FORMS BEHIND MY ART'
DJ: You must be horrified by what's
Happened to your town—the Swedes, the yachts,
The apartment houses. YOUNG MAN NEVER BE
COWED BY THE UPS & DOWNS OF MASONRY.
NOTHING TRAVELS FASTER WHERE THE GREAT
TIDES OF COMMERCE OVERWHELM ALIKE
DREAM & DRECK   Where are you now? AT 8
WHICH ON ITS SIDE STANDS FOR INFINITY,
THE SUBJECT OF OUR STUDIES   DID YOU KNOW
THAT IT HAS WALLS   Go on! But exit P.

Why so abruptly? I SHD THINK MY DEAR
IT IS A LECTURE WE ARE MEANT TO HEAR
FROM OTHER LIPS   Well then, how did he look?
DONNISH BUT STRAPPING   QUITE THE STAR ATHLETE
Perhaps he found us puny. MAMAN TENDS
TO THINK THAT THE MOT JUSTE MIGHT BE EFFETE
DJ (crushed): Maria! . . . As (unfazed) Wystan
Strikes a bright note on which the session ends:

A GREEK LADY DRESSED SMARTLY IN WEEDS
TOLD A TRIO OF LIMP GANYMEDES
'TIME U DROPPED ALL PRETENSE
& BEGAN TO MAKE SENSE,
THE SUCCESS LIKE WHICH NOTHING SUCCEEDS!'

★

Pythagoras should have seen us yesterday
Scrambling high above the sea's blue smudge
Through the bleached boneyard of Ephesus; returning
At twilight, thistle-stung, with faces burning
And JM limping where he missed a step
On a steep stairlessness, and hurt his knee.

Now in our shuttered room, while the town sleeps:
NO SIESTA? READY FOR A TREAT?
WE'VE BROUGHT PLENORIOS THE ARCHITECT
OF ARTEMIS' GREAT TEMPLE— Instead of words,
Broad "visionary" movements of the cup.
CUBITS & WIDTHS   I'D BETTER PARAPHRASE
. . . AH   A NICE BIT   HE SAYS: I HAD A DREAM
IN IT THE GODDESS BENDING OVER ME
SAID 'MAKE MY GLORY, SUCKLE! HERE & HERE:
THIS TEAT IS PROPORTION, THAT ONE SPLENDOR.
I WANT THE MARBLES BARE OF DECORATION
& NO CLOSED SPACES   SHELTER ME IN GRAND
& SIMPLE BEAUTY & YOU WILL GO TO HEAVEN!'
I BUILT A WONDER, & AM HERE. Alas,
The wonder's gone. No stone remains in place.
AH BUT THE LEGEND DOES DEAR BOY   REMAINS
ARE GHASTLY. EPHESUS! STREETS SWARMED WITH GHOSTS
BAZAARS   COVERED PALANQUINS   CRIES OF VENDORS
A YOUNG BEAUTY SCREAMING WITH LAUGHTER RAN
OUT OF THE BATHS ON TRAJAN'S AVENUE
IT WAS A FEAST DAY   U CHOSE WELL   & MICHAEL
RAISING HIS HAND, TIME LIKE A SCUDDING CLOUD
RACED BACKWARD. I & OUR OWN ARTEMIS
STROLLED THRU IT ALL ENRAPTURED BY ONE MORE
GLIMPSE INTO MAN'S ILLUSION OF HIMSELF.
THANK U FOR EPHESUS! DJ: Were you
Glimpsed by the ghosts? JOSTLED ENFANT & STEPPED ON!
THE CROWDS, THE NOISE, SO GREEK! & YET OUR QUIET
ELEGANCE DID NOT GO UNNOTICED. BLUE
SPARKLINGS LAPPED THE NEAR EDGE OF THE THEATRE,
WHARVES WITH PLEASURE RAFTS   & THE VAST MARKET'S
FRAGRANCES & AWNINGS! MEANWHILE THRU
WHAT WAS REALITY FOR US YOU 2
CD BE SEEN PEERING AT THE SKELETON
LIKE MED STUDENTS   JM I CRIED WATCH OUT!
WHAT U DID NOT STEP ON WAS THE VANISHED
MARBLE TREAD   YET DREAMILY YR FOOT
BORE DOWN EXPECTING IT   SO COUNTLESS THINGS

GONE FROM THE WORLD ENDURE IN ITS (M) WINGS
In theory, there's no age or place, Maman,
You couldn't visit? NOT IF MICHAEL BUYS
THE TICKETS What's our next move? FISHER BOYS?
Wystan, please. ENFANTS ME FOR A BLACK
COFFEE BY THE WATER Great, let's go!
YR TREAT OUR COINS SADLY OUT OF DATE

★

Two Deaths

In quick succession. First, George Cotzias
—Distinguished Son of Greece, as headlines read
Even in sleepy Samos, over columns
Of testimonials and photographs.
Flown from New York, his body's being buried
This afternoon in Athens, where a tide
Of wreaths advancing on Necropolis
Will blanch beneath dramatic nationwide
Thunder and lightning. But here's George himself—
Not at his own funeral? JIMMY DAVE
I THOUGHT I'D RATHER SIT IT OUT WITH YOU

BESIDES, MY FUTURE'S SETTLED: I WILL JOIN
THE ELEMENTAL POWERS WHEN YOUR FRIENDS DO
They've met already. He and Maria SHARED
AS MOTTO POSO AKOMA, YEARS OF RAYS
HAVING LEFT MY SOUL LIKE A SWISS CHEESE . . .
Alluding to his work on the disease
That killed him, or to his saved consciousness,
Her words of welcome half caress, half mock:
HOIST WITH YR OWN PETARD I SEE, EH DOC?
Wystan just gapes. MY DEARS IT GIVES ONE PAUSE
IS THERE NO END TO THE NO ACCIDENT CLAUSE?

Already George is fully briefed to take

A schoolroom desk. WE'RE SETTING UP A LAB!
Already at his fingertips in these
Few days since dying are the densities
That took us weeks and weeks with Mirabell
To get a sense of: ALL COMPATIBLE
WITH MY RESEARCH INTO THE LIVING CELL.
BLANK FACTORS (AS MY COLLEAGUES CHOOSE TO CALL THEM)
VEX THE DRUDGE WHO STOUTLY TURNS HIS BACK
ON THE IDEA OF A GRAND DESIGN
—Phrase a bolt of blue fire punctuates—
YET THESE, I NOW SEE DAZZLED, CUT & SHINE
STEADY AS LASER   WITH A GENIUS FAR
BEYOND THE DULL TRANSMISSION OF A GENE
BY EGG & SEMEN   More "blanks"? And these are?
BANKS IN WHICH THE R LAB'S NONGENETIC
STUFF OF THE SOUL ACCUMULATES. TOO BAD
HITLER GAVE SUPERMAN SUCH A BAD NAME
& SUCH A WHITE COMPLEXION   All the same,
George, how much we'd rather have you live
And framing questions at our table! (Though
He's better placed to frame them now, I *don't* say—
Especially if he is of the Five.
Is he? We're shy of asking. Yes or no,
Sooner or later, truth, we trust, will out.
Meanwhile the main thing's to get on with it.)

The storm is passing. TIME FOR MY NEXT SESSION
IN THE R LAB   George, one moment—what about
Your phoenix? Have you looked into that vision?
I TRIED TO JIMMY   BUT A PEACOCK HERE
TELLS ME TO WAIT   ONE DAY IT WILL BE CLEAR

*

The second death. We're just back from the island—
Hall strewn with tar-flecked towels, a straw hat, stones
And suitcase—when Long Distance telephones:
Robert Morse died in his sleep last night.

A sense comes late in life of too much death,
Of standing wordless, with head bowed beneath

The buffeting of losses which we see
At once, no matter how reluctantly,

As gains. Gains to the work. Ill-gotten gains . . .
Under the skull-and-crossbones, rigging strains

Our craft to harbor, and salt lashings plow
The carved smile of a mermaid on the prow.

Well, Robert, we'll make room. Your elegy
Can go in *Mirabell*, Book 8, to be
Written during the hot weeks ahead;
Its only fiction, that you're not yet dead.

LADS! I WAS RIGHT ABOUT THE MOLECULES
Making the cup move? YES   BUT (SIGH) YOUR SCHOOL'S
DENIED ME   Odd. They said you'd fit right in.
INTO A NEW LIFE   Oh? Where? THEY WON'T TELL:
MY PUNISHMENT FOR HAVING BLUSHED UNSEEN?
DJ: *We* saw you, Robert. TRUE   AH WELL
R(E)MORSE IS USELESS & HAS EVER BEEN

TOO UNJUST MY DEARS   I FOR ONE MEAN
TO PULL STRINGS MADLY   MM HAVE U MET
OUR NEW FRIEND?
                    (THIS IS HIM? HMM) (THIS IS SHE?)
—Turning upon each other's youthful charm
The shrewd eye of potential rivalry.
BEAUTY! comments Wystan. THANK GOD B
I WAS ITS SLAVE   BY FAR THE MEATIER ROLE
THAN ITS EMBODIMENT   They're not getting on?
O YES   MUCH GIGGLING FROM THE CHINTZ SETTEE
HE'S NOT HIMSELF YET   PAIN & BOREDOM BLUR
MOST OF US AT FIRST   LEAVE HIM TO HER:
B4 THE FULL MOON SWEEPS US OFF TO 5

RM WILL COME ALIVE!
　　　　　　　Out they all go,
But someone— George? The cup comes shyly forward:
SIRS, GK IN RESEARCH LAB　Who is this?
(Silence.) We know you're there—who are you? Have we
Ever spoken before? I MAY NOT, MASTERS
—Backing out abashed, as if come too soon
To sweep up after the symposium.

　　　　　　　　　　★

Two days later MAD ABOUT YR CHUMS
Says Robert, though the cup moves guardedly.
We urge him to be frank. WELL MUSCLE BOY
AS WE NOW CALL PYTHAGORAS (OOPS HERE HE COMES)
CLEAVES ME OLD　JM: This is my fault.
I'd said upstairs just now, I never felt
Easy with Mirabell's master ratio—
88:12—and fancied P might shed
A light . . . WAY OVER ICKLE WOBERT'S HEAD

YOUNG MEN I DO NOT QUESTION THE R LAB,
I FIND THEIR TEXTS TOO PUZZLING. THEY REDUCE
A) FORMULAS TO WORDS & B) IDEAS
TO FORMULAS. FOR INSTANCE I SAY 'SOUL'
A SIMPLE FORMULA LIKE ALL THAT DEAL
WITH ENERGY, BUT THAT VAGUE INCREMENT
OF 'PSYCHE' (THOUGH ITSELF REDUCIBLE)
FALLS INTO NO EASY NUMBER SYSTEM.
THUS RENDERING MAN'S GAINS & LOSSES, THESE
CLERKS DISCOUNT THE LOSS OF FACULTIES
OR GAINS IN WISDOM　FOR THEIR CALCULATIONS
START FROM A TREACHEROUS, LEDAEAN O.
12:88, THEN, IS A FAULTY READ-OUT
DESIGNED TO KEEP US GROPING IN THE DARK.
I SAY: START SHAKILY, END OFF THE MARK!
Hard to take in, Sir. Evidently we
Never sat a lifetime at your knee.

TOO BAD! AND MUSCLES WD HAVE GIVEN YOU,
WITTY RM, A DECADE MORE ADIEU

HAVE WE A SLASH MARK? LET HIM TAKE THAT /

ENFANTS RM ENCHANTING BRINGS NEW VIE
TO OUR FRENCH CIRCLE: 'COMME J'ADORE, MME,
VOTRE PUR ET IMPUR' COLETTE: 'ET MOI
LE VOTRE!' HE DID BLUSH Is Wystan with us?
CLOSETED WITH PLATO HEADS TOGETHER
OVER THE NEXT 5 LESSONS WE TOO SHALL BE
5 With George, very tidy. But what's Wystan
Doing? Pulling strings behind the scenes?
JM HAS HE PERHAPS NOT ALWAYS BEEN
Backstage even with the angels?
                         GONE
Maria? IT'S TOO TARSOME I WON'T PLAY
SHE SIMPLY DISAPPEARED ON THE WORD ANG
... Robert? But *he's* gone. DJ: Don't forget
He has no clearance for these topics yet.
So here again we are—not quite alone.

A New Friend

4170 MAY I, MASTERS?
Please do. You came the other day—who are you?
I WAS THE LAST Softly: I HAVE 4 LEGS
Now this *is* a surprise. You're from Atlantis!
MY GREEN HOMELAND O IS IT STILL
Green? I fear not. But its legend is.
WE RAN O WE RAN! & I WAS SWIFT
Immortal, too; and lived in starlike cities?
YES O YES SO YOU HAVE SEEN?
No, but heard from your old messengers.
THEY ARE DEATH! Hush. There's an Atlantis craze
Sweeping the young people nowadays.
WE TOO WERE YOUNG WE SAW OUR SIRES

AS UNHAPPY   HELPLESS TO ADAPT.

THEY COULD NOT GRAZE ON OUR CRAMPED GREENS

& DID NOT TAKE TO OUR NEW THINGS

New things don't stay new. How would you have taken

To the gadgets of a later age?

WELL, WE WERE NOT TRUSTED TO

I see . . . A moment's sparkling silence, then:

THEY SAY YOU NOW BESTRIDE OUR BACKS

& TWO RUN AS ONE? We do indeed. It forges

A bond of strong delight. O   O MY LAND

Have you no names, just numbers like the bats?

OUR SOCIETY IS SO SHATTERED

SO RUINED, WE RECALL OUR FORM

& OUR GREEN WORLD   BUT WEAR THE NUMBER

OF OUR MASTER   WE DO MIDDLING TASKS:

MINE, TO BE NEAR & NOT TO LISTEN

Don't you see us in the mirror? SEE?

AH   NOW I DO! LOOK HOW I LEARN!

BUT WE ARE BLANK HERE   BLACK & BLANK

NO LIGHT ON A FIELD   NO MOON ON Á LAKE

I thought the moon was made when your world fell.

4 MOONS RINGED US   THEY RUBBED THEM OUT

DJ: So when the end came you were tending

Those anchors that secured their stratosphere?

THAT IS OUR DUTY   TO BE NEAR,

A VITAL ONE   FOR HERE ARE VAST

NUMBERS OF OTHERS   ALL AIMLESS

DRIFTING AS GNATS DO   WE HAVE WORK!

WE ARE REPRIEVED FROM LIFE'S LOSS

NEED NOT MOURN LIFE UPON LIFE

BUT HAVE OUR ONE, OUR FIXED GREEN LOSS.

THEY SAY GOD CALLS US HIS FIRSTBORN

& I THE LAST OF THESE   Tell how it was.

OUR LOW GRAY ROOF RIPPED ONE DAY!

I PEERED UP & RAN! RAN!

THEN FIRE! THEN SILENCE   AS THE GREAT GREENS
FELL IN ON ME! O THEN AM HERE
& MY MASTER CALLING 'COME   U WERE
THE LAST TO DIE   I AM THE LAST
OF MINE TO BE MADE   SO COME'   & SO . . .
JM: Would your master's number be 741?
YES   HE WAS NOT OF OUR UNDOING.
I TAKE HIS SIMPLER THOUGHTS TO OTHERS,
GO HERE   GO THERE   BUT NOW AM ALWAYS
HERE FOR HE CALLS THIS SHINING SPACE
OUR OWN PASTURAGE   IF YOU APPROACH
WHEN NO ONE THEY ALLOW IS NEAR
I GUARD THE GATE, FOR THIS IS NOW THE
(Cup fairly cantering— DJ: Hot damn,
He's getting better all the time! I AM?)
FOR THIS IS NOW THE NEW CENTER
JM: Your master, does he treat you well?
BETWEEN THE DIFFERENT KINDS OUR GOD
HAS LAID THE LAW DOWN: DIGNITY
But you and we are the same kind, in part—
Electric currents quicken brain and heart.
& SO IT IS! A GODLIER BOND!

★

TALKS WITH THE TURNKEY, CHAPS? Maria, why
Has no one mentioned this enchanting creature?
I DID   PART OF THE BAT CROWD FROM THE START
EACH FEATHERED ONE HAD A 4 FOOTED FRIEND
Is he a centaur? an eohippus? NEITHER:
JUST AS U'D THINK, ONLY LONGNECKED (A LATE
ANCHORPOINT MANIFESTATION) & NO HORN
GREAT LIQUID EYES   O FOR A SUGAR CUBE
A unicorn! A (M) WORD IN OUR THICK
COLLECTIVE DICTIONARY, CHAPS   REMEMBER
WE'RE HERE AS IN A FRAME COMPOSED OF, O
GREAT LIZARDS   WINGED LIONS   THE WHOLE A PARTS

FOUNDRY FOR OUTDATED FORMS? Cocteau
Must be in clover. OUR FRENCH CIRCLE TOO
COMES UP WITH SOME ODD FORMS IN COMBINATION:
LOUIS XV & PROUST? OR DEAR COLETTE
TO SEVIGNE: 'MME, WHAT SYMMETRY,
I BROODING ON MA MERE, YOU ON YR FILLE'
MP MEANWHILE: 'SIRE, THE EXTRAVAGANCE!'
L XV: 'WRITER, THE PERVERSITY!'
WYSTAN COMES AWAY DRAINED   He's still with Plato?
INDEED   GK IN LAB   ME BUSY HOEING
I TOO HAVE A 'PAPER' TO PRESENT AT 5
& MUST BE GOING — As RM ambles in.

How are you, Robert? BRIGHTER   STILL EARTHBOUND
I ASK: NO ACCIDENT? & GET WHITE SOUND
A BLUR EACH MOMENT CLOSER TO SOME CLEAR
SONG OF BLISS: ONE OF THE MARVELS HERE.
ANOTHER IS TO TALK TO THAT WORD'S NAMESAKE.
Andrew? THE VERY SAME   DO I CALL HIM ANDY?
I called *you* Andrew in "The Summer People".
AH THEN I CAN PRACTISE IN THE GLASS
What does he say in Heaven? Can you quote?
The cup, with a mimed clearing of its throat,
Enunciates: 'WHAT'S WRONG WITH EMPIRES, PRAY?
GREATLY BENEFICIAL. FOR THE SUBJECTED,
DELICIOUS SUBJUGATION & FOR THE RULERS,
TERRIBLE FEARS OF LOSING, BALANCED BY
RARE OPPORTUNITIES FOR BEASTLINESS.'
Anything about poetry? EVERYTHING!
I DRINK IT IN: 'THE LINE, MY DEAR NEW FRIEND,
THE LINE! LET IT RUN TAUT & FLEXIBLE
BETWEEN THE TWO POLES OF RHYTHM & RHYME,
& WHAT YOU HANG ON IT MAY BE AS DULL
OR AS PROVOCATIVE AS LAUNDRY.' How does
New work get round in Heaven? WE ADEPT READERS
MERELY CALL TO MIND THE MOLECULAR PAGE
PLUS A LIVING KNOWN OR UNKNOWN AUTHOR

& THINK 'NEW POEM PLEASE' & PRESTO! EITHER
SOME SHAGGY DOGGEREL FROM THE COAST APPEARS
OR A SPARKLER FROM ACADEME. SAME PRINCIPLE
EXACTLY WHEREBY WE POP UP WITHIN YR
FIELD OF REFLECTION AS U THINK OF US
THEN FLASH BACK TO OUR BLIND WORK IN THE VOID
WHEN YR ATTENTION DIES
       We've so enjoyed
Meeting the turnkey. UNICE? (I CALL IT UNICE)
CHARMING CRITTER YES YR FIRELIGHT
IS GIRT AS ON SAFARI BY THE GLITTER
OF STRANGE, STRANGE EYES He's watching? BUT OF COURSE!
NOW TO MEET OSCAR WHERE BUT THE WHITE HORSE?
UNICE!
    SIRS, WHY UNICE? Oh, it means
We like you. U are nice. Also the first
Syllables of *unicorn*. In Greek,
A moral victory. MY MASTER SAID
'BE ALERT & BE AVAILABLE
& THEY MAY TALK TO YOU OR EVEN
NAME YOU AS THEY HAVE ME' YOU HAVE!
WELL, THANK YOU WE CALL YOU THE SCRIBES
& THE NAMEGIVERS Thank *you*, Unice. Tell
Us more about your world? WELL I & MINE
RATHER RESEMBLE TALES WE WERE TOLD
So do we. Tales shape us, of all kind.
Myths. Novels. Awful books about "man's mind".
OUR MASTERS FLEW & YOU HAVE FINGERS
WE HAD NO HANDS, THERE4 NO BOOKS
JUST MOUTH TO EAR The phone rings. WELL GOODBYE

DJ: The darling! How unserious
He makes by contrast all the rest of us.
JM: That's only part of it. He stands
For something more abstract. No wings, no hands,
That constant running . . . DJ: Such a shame
That Robert had to give him a girl's name.

*

Robert Taken Up

Our friend at last gets CLEARANCE FROM OO
To see the Mirabell files. No question, though,
Of peeking at the lessons of our four
Angels. MY DEARS AS USUAL THERE'S MORE
THAN MEETS THE EYE. THE OO SPEAK OF THREATS
TO HIS 'DEVELOPMENT' That crowd forgets
He read those transcripts here on Earth. HE'LL READ
THEM HERE BY NEW LIGHT WHEN THOUGH? When indeed!
—For Robert's moving, these days, like a native
In circles of the brilliant and creative.
Self-effacing, witty, kind, fair, slim,
With perfect, simple manners—next to him
Luca reverts to Milanese slum child.
Pythagoras may snort, but Proust and Wilde
Are quick to note the human gulf between
A wide-lipped earthen vessel, two poor green
Saucers that merely brim with joy and tears,
And this little Sèvres pitcher whose big ears
Take in the subtleties like milk, the gall
Like honey. Wisdom is the test of all.
Garnering here a bit and there a bit,
He's missing nothing but the source of it.
A puzzled air of ties too quickly cut
(Family on Earth, piano shut,
Garden in bloom without him) underscores
This nature that in Heaven opens doors.
Tanya Blixen wants to dress him in
Satin knee-britches—she his Marschallin?
Colette abandons—Bernhardt takes to—bed.
Alone, Jane Austen tilts but keeps her head,
Addressing him, after a moment's droll
Quiz of gray eyes beneath the parasol,
As *Mr Robert*—a shrewd estimate.

He's after all not Heir to the Estate,
Its goods and duties, but a Younger Son
Free to be ornamental and have fun.

Easy for us to meet HAVE UNICE STAMP
THEIR PASSES this whole fascinating crew.
No thanks. Enough names clog the poem. More
I couldn't handle. That door Unice guards,
Let's keep it shut. Or see them through your eyes.
And Robert—call him "Uni"? UP TO YOU
BUT THE DEAR CREATURE'S PRINTED ALL HIS CARDS

SIRS I AM UNICE! IT IS RARE
WHEN A BETWEENER GETS SUCH ATTENTION
AS MR ROBERT   HE SPOKE OF MY LAND
HE SAID 'MY LIFE WAS AN ATLANTIS
SUNKEN & PERFECT & DOOMED'   WAS IT?
Perhaps so. Much of himself lay under a surface
Perfect in all its arrangements. There could be
No bitterness, no daring, no regret.
Enough to doom one in the end? And yet . . .
MY MASTER SAYS 'I STUDY THE SEXUAL
MODE OF MAN & AM CONTENT WITH
NUMBERS' NOT ME! I WISH I HAD KNOWN
THAT JOY YOUR SENIOR SCRIBE JUDGES
BRIEF AT BEST   WHY SO, I WONDER?
As do we. Things may be otherwise
Where all mate happily and no one dies.
I DIED TOO YOUNG TO BE A SIRE
BUT WE CALLED THE YOUNG MALE IN MY DAY
MOST FAIR WHO MERELY DREAMED OF LOVE

What else have you learned about us? 5 OF YOUR YEARS
TO LEARN YOUR TONGUE   THE OO TAUGHT US
Knowing that we'd talk? & HOW TO GUARD YOU
AGAINST THE BILLIONS   THEY WD EXPLODE YR EARS!
You switch your tail and brush them off like flies?
WELL, THEY STAY CLEAR   SO   SEE YOU SOON

THIS IS UNICE THE UNIQUE!
(Circling the Board, comes to a stop at &
—Gate latched neatly by the ampersand.)

★

LADS   FUN ASIDE, SUPPOSE THEY OFFERED ME
A LITTLE PACKET OF PRENATAL GOODIES
WHAT WD I CHOOSE? What *would* you choose? EXACTLY.
A TALENT? WEALTH? LOOKS? CHARM? THOSE 4 MOONS EACH
HAVE THEIR DARK SIDES   ONE MUST I THINK ARRIVE
FRESH   WITH CLEAR LIGHT TINTS & MINIMAL
UNDERPAINTING   Painting. *That's* what we've
Had in mind to ask you. Mirabell
Ran it down, but you who painted us—?
AT BEST INTERPRETIVE   AT WORST A BOTCH.
THE GREAT ONES WORKED FROM NATURE & NATURE IF
I'VE UNDERSTOOD YR PEACOCK, IS NUMBER 2.
WHERE CD ONE HANG A PICTURE HERE? INDEED
WHOLE SQUARE MILES OF TROMPE L'OEIL ARE WHAT WE NEED!
OR SO SAY LES GONCOURTS THOSE RAVENOUS
IMAGINERS OF 'MOVEMENTS' ALL OF WHICH SIMPLY
MOVED FROM GROUND LEVEL TO THE 2ND (OR
AS EDMOND SAYS, THE AMERICAN 3RD) FLOOR.
BACK TO PAINTING, ALLEGORICAL SCENES
OFTEN 'WORK' BEST   I WONDER WHAT THAT MEANS.
THEN A WEE STILL-LIFE MAY AVOID DISGRACE
BY FILLING WHOLLY SOME IDEAL SPACE
OR BRUSHES FINE AS INTUITION THINK
UP CRAGS & WATERFALLS OF CHINESE INK,
YET WHAT TO SAY WHEN MICHELANGELO
HIMSELF ADMITS (TO ICKLE ME) HE'D NO
GRASP OF IDEAS! SMALL WONDER THAT MY TIN
EAR TRUMPET NEVER BLEW A SINGLE TUNE
You'd wanted to compose. THAT WAS MY DREAM
AND IS. ANOTHER BOND WITH YOUR MM
BUT IT REQUIRES MORE MIND THAN I HAD/HAVE
DJ: That painting buried in his cave

Was pure Idea, said Raphael. WHAT CAVE?
SAID WHO? —As Wystan rushes in:
                              MY DEARS
WHAT CAN YR MOTHER SAY ABOUT THOSE LAB
SESSIONS WITH GEORGE! Hard to make sense of them?
HARD AS DIAMOND & AS BLAZINGLY CLEAR
Always with Plato at your elbow, no?
ROBERT?
               DRAT   TARSOME   TINY BOB MUST GO:
TEA AT MISS AUSTEN'S (Exit.) Wystan, why'd
You do that? You sent Robert from the room.
RAPH'S CAVE & PLATO SUPERCLASSIFIED
MY BOY   NOT TO UNBALANCE THE CAREER
AHEAD FOR RM   HIS NEXT LIFE: THEY'RE SPARING
NOTHING   DJ: To make what of him?
GUESS   A composer? YES   AND SUCH A ONE!
HE DOESN'T KNOW YET BUT WE
                              Now Maria
Interrupts: ENFANTS THESE DAYS WE 4
GATHER AT MEALS (GK SPATTERED WITH HORRORS,
WYSTAN ALL GRITTY, MAMAN GRASS-STAINED) & IN
GLIDES DEWYFACED RM NEAT AS A PIN,
CHOCKFULL OF STARRY GOSSIP & WE ROAR!
Isn't it tomorrow we begin
Our lessons? Are your papers ready? YIPES
MAMAN GOES FIRST   CAN'T DAWDLE WITH U TYPES
AU RESERVOIR
               2 DAYS FROM NOW MY DEARS:
USUAL TIME   B4, COLD SHOWER & STRONG
COFFEE   DRESS OPTIONAL   NO CIGS   SO LONG

Uni has trotted up to shut the gate
When Robert hurtles past with an elate
DO DREAMS COME TRUE? I'M CALLED TO MY ADORED
MENDELSSOHN   4 HANDS AT HIS KEYBOARD!

★

The Middle Lessons: I

The schoolroom rearranged. No desks. The dais
Flanked by chairs—an extra one for George—
And draped by a motheaten mustiness
At whose design one hesitates to guess.
Over the picture hangs some faintest pall
Of the 'academy'—nothing one can place
Until the Brothers WE WILL NOT SAY SPRAWL
Assume positions out of the David
'Coronation of Napoleon'—
Imperial airs that threaten to forbid
The eager give-and-take looked for by all.

Mich.   FRERES, MADAME, POETES, DOCTEUR, MAIN, BIEN VENUS!
        CE DEJEUNER A CINQ PLATS AU MENU.
        LE PREMIER SERA NOTRE DELICIEUSE MADAME
        QUI VA NOUS RACONTER CE QUE SON AME
        A DECOUVERT PENDANT SON VEGETAL SEJOUR.
        COMMENCE, MADAME, COMMENCE AVEC LE PREMIER JOUR.

Rising in voluminous new leaf-
Green doctor's robes, her notes tucked in the sleeve,
Maria with a feint of helplessness
Steps forward to deliver her address:

SIRE, VOUS AUTRES FILS DE DIEU, FAMEUX DOCTEUR,
POETES ET MAIN TRES CHERS:
(Oh dear, must it all be in *our* bad French?)
Mich.   DU CALME, MADAME.
MM.   THE FIRST DAY DAWNED IN THE LONG PROGRESSION OF
        DAYS AND NIGHTS. WIDELY SPACED POOLS OF STEAM
        LICKED THE COOLING LAND. THE VAST WATERS
        OF EARTH LAY STILL. THE TEMPESTS OF FIRE & WIND
        HAD PASSED, AND GOD'S BARE GLOBE LAY WAITING

FOR HIS DESCENT. THE SUN, GOD'S OLDEST CHILD
NAMED FOR OUR HELP MICHAEL, HAILED HIS SIRE
IN THE GALACTIC PANTHEON: 'COME, FATHER, COME!'
THESE WERE THE FIRST SIGNALS SENT FROM EARTH.
SURROUNDED BY SEEDBEARERS, HIS WELLWISHING
BROTHER GODS, BIOLOGY APPROACHED:
'MICHAEL, SUMMON MY EMMANUEL.'
'I AM HERE, FATHER' 'TAKE THESE SEEDS AND RAIN THEM
ONTO EVERY SURFACE.' AND THIS EMMANUEL DID.
SIRE, MY LORDS, CONFRERES, THAT IS MY TEXT.
MAY I BEGIN?

Mich.   MADAME, NEXT WE SHALL CALL YOU POET. IT IS SO, & SWEETLY
       SAID.

MM.   THESE MYTHS THAT ANTECEDE ALL MYTH ARE COUCHED
IN DAUNTING GENERALITIES. FOR MICHAEL/SUN
READ: GENERATIVE FORCE. FOR GENERATIVE FORCE
READ: RADIATION TO THE BILLIONTH POWER
OF EXPLODING ATOMS. FOR EMMANUEL,
H2O. FOR SEEDS, THAT COSMIC DUST
LADEN WITH PARTICLES OF INERT MATTER.
FOR GOD READ: GOD.
                LET ME NOW SAY MY SOUL
SPEAKS FROM WITHIN THE GREENNESS OF A BLADE OF GRASS.
I TAKE THIS HUMBLE STATION TO BEST IMAGINE
HOW IT WAS, THAT FOURTH OR FIFTH DAWN, WHEN
LOOKING OUT I SAW THE RISING SUN
OVER A FAINT HAZE OF GREEN SPROUTS. WE PEOPLED
THE VIRGIN EARTH, AND FOR A LONG SPELL RULED
IN A CONGRESS OF SLOW BUT PROFOUND COMMAND, IN LEAGUE
WITH THE ACID & MINERAL COUNCIL OF RAPHAEL
ABOUT WHICH OUR SENIOR POET SPEAKS TOMORROW.
SO THE RACES OF VEGETABLE GREEN BEGAN,
THEIR SITES APPORTIONED WITH THEIR ATTRIBUTES,
AND ASIDE FROM SOME PROFUSION & SOME SLIGHT
EXTINCTION THESE HAVE SENSIBLY PREVAILED
FOR 980,000,000 SUN YEARS. AND NOW
LET ME TALK OF THE TONGUES & WAYS OF COMMUNION AMONG US.

OUR 'RULING' ONES, THE FAMILY OF MOSS,
ESTABLISHED A TACTILE LANGUAGE. AND THROUGH THIS NETWORK
EVEN TODAY IN FREEZING TUNDRAS AS WORD SPREADS
('DROUGHT! FLOOD! ICE! MAN!') WE SHRINK, WE ADVANCE,
SOME OF US GIVEN EARLY ALONG TO LORD GABRIEL
KILL. OTHERS, LORD EMMANUEL'S CHILDREN,
CURE WITH IODINE OR SUCCOR THE THIRSTY IN DESERTS.
MICHAEL'S BREED BECAME TREES, THE AIR'S COMMUNION
WITH DEEPEST EARTH. WE PROSPERED, AND MADE WELCOME
GOD'S FIRST ANIMAL CREATURES (MORE OF THESE
FROM OUR GREAT SCIENTIST).
                    LAST: ASIDE FROM CREATING
THESE CREATURES' FOOD & BREATH, WE ARE THE RESTING PLACE
OF SOUL. OUR DEEP RHYTHMS KEEP THE HUMAN PULSE.
OUR INCREASE QUICKENS, OUR WITHDRAWAL SLOWS IT.
WE ARE BOTH GRAZING LAND AND FINAL PLENISHMENT.
SO FROM THIS TIP & LOWLY BLADE, LORD MICHAEL,
LORDS, POETS, DOCTEUR, AND DEAR SORE HAND,
I HAVE LOOKED OUT, THOUGHT OF THE VEGETABLE WORLD,
AND HOPE TO HAVE MADE SENSE OF IT.
                       She's done.

Michael arises, sketches in the airy
Gesture of Apollo Belvedere,
And on her brow appears a laurel crown.

Mich.   CHERE MADAME, HAVE YOU NOT! GABRIEL, NO QUESTIONS?
Gabr.   NONE.
Mich.   CASE RESTS. SENIOR POET, YOU WITH WINGED FEET,
       TOMORROW BRING US UP FROM CLAY
       THE LECTURE OF THE SECOND DAY!
       Exeunt.

      Maman, are you receiving
Bouquets in the green room? That was sheer
Lucid eloquence! Well, I'm not sure
We understood about the "human pulse",
But for the rest—! ENFANTS WE WERE INSTRUCTED
TO USE THE 'POETIC LANGUAGE' (HORRIBLE, EH?)

BUT I SLIPPED SOME HARD FACTS IN. 'BREATH': OXYGEN
PRODUCTION IS, WITH FOOD, MAIN JOB OF VEG.
THEIR SYSTOLE (WORD LOANED BY GK) HELPS
LIMIT POP EXPLOSION. THAT WHOLE REALM'S
CONTACT WITH LES FRERES DE SCHOOLROOM FRENCH
IS THRU EACH SPECIES, THUS CONTROLLABLE
BY THE R LAB   Yes, what about that French?
WHO KNOWS? BABY LANGUAGE? MOI JE CROIS
IT'S BETTER THAN MY ENGL   AH NO! I'VE GOT IT!
HA HA HA   IT'S BECAUSE MICHAEL TOOK
UMBRAGE AT W'S SLURS ON HIS POETICS
AH LE PAUVRE! DJ: But your research?
You entered those green cells, you climbed that tree
Inside the tree? And was it marvelous
Beyond all saying? AH ENFANT YES   YES
& DO U KNOW I THINK OUR 3-WAY PROJECT
HAS RECONCILED US TO WHATEVER LIES
IN STORE? THEY NOD   SURRENDER GLOWS IN MANLY EYES

★

UNICE IS HERE! Where were you yesterday?
I STOOD OUTSIDE THE SCHOOLROOM DOOR
AS LIGHT BLAZED THRU CHINKS & CRACKS!
MY MASTER HID   THEY ARE VERY HIGH
O SEE   THE LIGHT! SIRS I LEAVE Y

The Middle Lessons: 2

The company has entered, come to order.
One new touch only—in the carpet's border
A vine-meander, yesterday unseen,
Is now distinct, spring shades of blue and green.

Mich.   COME SENIOR POET, DO NOT US DISMAY
WITH THAT YOU HAVE TO TELL, THIS SECOND DAY!

Unsightly slippers hidden beneath rich
Earth-colored folds, Wystan begins his speech:

WHA. MY LORDS AND FELLOWS,
THE ATOMS OF DEMOCRITUS, THE BRIGHT
DANCE OF NEWTON'S PARTICLES SO THRILLED
HIS MIND, THAT A GREAT POET FILLED
THE TENTS OF ISRAEL WITH LIGHT.
SIRS, MAY THIS BE THE TEXT I TAKE?

JM. He's quoting someone.

WHA. (REALLY JM! BLAKE!)

Mich. PROCEED, POET. WE ATTEND.

WHA. THEREFORE I PUT THIS TO YOU, LORDS:
THE TRUE POET IS, OF ALL THE SCRIBES, MOST DRAWN
TO THE CONCRETE. YES SIRS, WE THRIVE ON IT!
NOT POLITICS, LITTLE OF MANNERS & CURRENT FASHION,
LITTLE, TOO, OF THE GREAT RINGING 'THEMES'
THRILL US, BUT FACTS DO. YES SIRS, THEY DO.
MAY I NOW IMPART SOME? *Consultation.*

Gabr. POET, IF YOU OVERSTEP . . .

WHA. SIRS, ONE MORE THING?

Mich. POET?

WHA. IF I MAY SAY SO, WE DO NOT WORK WELL TO ORDER.

Mich. POET, YOU AND YOURS ARE FREE. HOW LONG IT HAS TAKEN YOU TO
MAKE YOUR CLAIM!
ARE WE NOT ASTONISHED, BROTHERS? WE BREATHE EASY NOW!
Determinism's thistle, seed by seed,
Drifts outward, silken, from what Michael said.
The cup "goes round" like a general sigh of relief.

Raph. POET, I YOUR FATHER SAY, UNBURDEN YOUR EARTHY WISDOM. PRAY
PROCEED.

WHA. ALL OF IT, SIRS?
All eyes on Gabriel, who nods curtly: ALL.

WHA. LORDS, MADAME, DEAR DOCTOR, BROTHER JAMES
& PATIENT HAND, I BRING EQUIVOCAL NEWS.
WE HERE TREMBLE ON A CRUST SO FRAGILE
IT NEEDS GOD'S CONSTANT VIGIL TO KEEP US AFLOAT.
I SANK INTO VEIN AFTER VEIN, WENT DEEP INTO PLACES

SO NEAR THE FIRE THAT I FELT THE HELL TOUCH.
MAY I SPEAK OF THAT, LORD GABRIEL?

Gabr. POET, I TOO WILL HAVE MY SAY. SPEAK IF YOU WILL OF ITS HEAT &
NOISE. I WILL GIVE ITS MEANING.

WHA. THERE, SUCH A FIERCE ENTIRE & INFERNAL HEAT
SMOTE MY SPIRIT THAT I FOR COURAGE CALLED
UPON THE SHRINKING ROCK & WRENCHED ME FREE
FROM UNENLIGHTENED MEMORIES OF THE FALLEN.

Gabr. (After a pause) PROCEED, POET.

WHA. NEXT, ABASHED, I WENT TO THE REFERENCE
BANKS OF THE CENTER.

Gabr. (A longer pause) PROCEED.

WHA. IN THE BEGINNING GOD
WAS GIVEN, TO SHAPE HIS WORLD, A TWO-EDGED GIFT.
HIS BROTHERS OF THE PANTHEON ALLOWED
MATERIALS, BUT WITH THE PROVISO: 'GO
BUILD, YOUNGEST BROTHER, ONLY TAKE THIS ONE,
OUR MONITOR, TO DWELL WITHIN YOUR BALL.
FOR OUR WILL MUST EVER BE DONE.' LORD GABRIEL?

Gabr. POET?

WHA. WAS I TOO NEAR?

Gabr. I SENT YOU BACK UNHARMD. UNDERSTAND, POET! NONE HAS BEEN
ALLOWD SUCH FREEDOM AS YOU THREE SHADES. DO NOT

Mich. PEACE, BROTHER GABRIEL. WE AGREED THESE LESSONS WOULD BE
FOR BOTH GOD AND MORTAL FOOD FOR THOUGHT.
AND IS IT NOT SO, POET? FOOD IN YOUR LEXICON IS HIGHLY
SPICED? IF NOT UNPALATABLE, OFTEN NEARLY SO?

WHA. SIR, TO BE POETS WE RISK POISONING.

Mich. PROCEED, POET.

WHA. THEREFORE I SAY THIS OF OUR FRAGILE EARTH:
IS IT DOOMED? IF SO, WILL OUR LINEAGE, OUR LINES
MEAN MUCH, LOST IN A POLLIWOG SEA OF ATOMS?

Mich. POET, TUG.

WHA. MY FIRST LINE RUNS OFF INTO CHEMICALS
WHERE GOD FISHED. THESE SPAWNED A TRAGIC CREATURE,
INNOCENT, ABANDONED. THAT CREATURE SPAWNED
(SIRS, HOW NEAT) ITS OWN DESTRUCTION, FROM . . .?

Gabr.	POET, I WILL EXPLAIN. PROCEED.
WHA.	MY NEXT LINE IS LOST IN THE CLAY FLOOR OF THE SEA.
Mich.	TUG!
WHA.	LORD GABRIEL, ARE WE YOURS?
	A beam of fire caresses Wystan's face.
Gabr.	I WILL EXPLAIN, O POET.
WHA.	HAVE I A LINE LEFT, SIRS,
	TO FISH ME A BETTER CREATURE? OR ARE YOURSELVES
	DISPOSED TO MAKE SOME BETTER THING OF US?
Gabr.	POET, SLY POET, THIS IS NOT YOUR TEXT!
WHA.	SIRS, THOSE ATOMS & THOSE PARTICLES
	OF LIGHT, THEY ARE THE GLOW WITHIN OUR TENTS.
	THESE, STAKED IN THE FRAIL CRUST, OUR ONLY SHELTER.
	EARTH IS OUR GROUND, SIRS. MADAME CLOTHED IT. I
	HAVE SEEN IT BARE, NAY WORSE, HAVE SEEN ITS BONES,
	HEARD AT ITS HEART THE MONITOR'S RAGING WILL.
	SIRS, SAVE OUR TENTS, AND SUCH A MIRACLE
	UPFLOWING FROM THIS LUMINOUS MEMBRANE
	WILL CAUSE THE MONITOR TO PULSE THROUGH BLACK
	GALACTIC SPACES: THEY SURVIVE! THEY HOLD IT BACK!

In a brief hush the cup fights to contain
The carpet's buffs and grays gleam like washed sand.
Round Wystan's neck appears a golden chain.

Mich.	GABRIEL? *A look exchanged.* CASE RESTS.
	BROTHERS, POETS, MADAME (YOU ARE ONE OF THESE), DOCTOR &
	HAND:
	WE LEAVE OUR STEAMY SESSION, BUT NOT IN DISARRAY,
	AND WAIT ON SCIENCE OUR THIRD DAY.
	Exeunt.

       TOWELS! Wystan, what a gem—
Every facet cut so tellingly.
THEY'RE NOT TELLING, ARE THEY? WE DOOMED THREE
HAVE MADE A PACT: TO PRY IT OUT OF THEM!
GK OUR FINAL LEVER   When you wondered
If we were Gabriel's—? HAS HE ALREADY

CLAIMED US? DJ: As his? He wouldn't—would he?
How does it end? MY DEAR THEY'VE 'ASKED' JM
FOR A PIECE OF WORK. THEY CAN'T JUST GO ON SPILLING
HERE A BEAN THERE A BEAN, IF & AS THEY PLEASE:
ALL MUST MAKE SENSE   JM: Even, God willing,
To me. OUR ?S CAUSE EMBARRASSMENT
BECAUSE YR WORK MY BOY IS (I FEAR) MEANT
TO BE A BIT OF WHITEWASH FOR THE BROTHERS.
YET GABRIEL IS . . . HONEST, IS . . . WELL, LET HIM
IDENTIFY HIMSELF   U NO DOUBT KNOW
I do?   MY DEAR SHAPE UP   U'VE HAD ENOUGH
BEAUTIFUL WORDS FROM US   TIME TO TALK TOUGH!
Let George do it!

INDENT I WILL: ALL SET TO GO
PERHAPS MY FINEST (FINAL?) MOMENT JIMMY
Good luck, my friend. It may not be too late.
WE LOWER THE TENT FLAP, YOU STEAL AWAY
TREMBLING TO MEET ANOTHER DAY.
George? Wystan?

INDENT MAMAN: THE NEW LAUREATE!

SIRS THIS IS UNICE   THE LADY IN LEAVES
Is our beloved friend. & MINE   SO MERRY!
SHE CROPPED ME A TWIG OF HER CROWN TO EAT
AND SAID 'GO CHEER THEM, TELL THEM A TALE'
SHALL I? We're listening. SO MANY   WELL:

A YOUNG RACER YEARNED TO MATE
WITH A FAIR FEMALE HE COULD NOT COAX.
HE GALLOPED! LEAPT OVER ALARMING GULLIES!
RACED ROUND THE COURSE AHEAD OF ALL!
BUT SHE DID NOT LOOK. AT LAST HE CRIED:
WHY IS THIS? I AM HERE! & HE
NUDGED HER! HE TOOK A NIP OF HER HAIR!
SHE LEAPT STARTLED   THEN SOFTLY SAID:
I AM BLIND. HE REPLIED: THEN YOU
WILL NEED ME NEAR. THIS TALE TAUGHT US

NOT TO BE VAIN IN LOVE, BUT TRUE.
We're silent. WELL, THIS IS UNICE SAYING GOODBYE

*

Now comes the halfway point that tips the scale
From Yes to No. D gnaws at a hangnail,
Glares out at mountain greenery and groans.
They've picked this Sunday for our telephone's
Seasonal breakdown. Neither Lab nor Rat
Soul will rescue us with idle chat.
Robert, unreachable, no doubt has gone
On to grander things than Mendelssohn.
JM: There's always Uni. We could page
Our peacock?— Bah, cold comfort at this stage.
What's eating us? Resistance of a kind
Unlikely to be praised, dumb, wilful, blind . . .
A long nap is the answer, then the shock
Of shower and coffee. Sharp at six o'clock:

The Middle Lessons: 3

Mich. COME GOOD DOCTOR, HAVE YOUR SAY
ON THIS TURNING POINT THAT IS TODAY.

George in a short-sleeved bluegreen surgeon's gown
And skullcap rises. As he speaks he'll prowl
Restlessly here, there, back and forth, his owl
Eye fixing the Brothers LIKE SOME RARE FULLBLOWN
CULTURE ON A SLIDE! *He's a broadchested youth,*
Tall, dark. Maria listens, her lips part—
Touched, she confesses wryly, to the heart
By his FIERCE GREEKNESS *and his* LOVE OF TRUTH.

GK. LORD O MICHAILIS, AND LORDS RAPHAEL
AND EMMANUEL, AND LORD PATRON GABRIEL,
HAIL! I AM THE N IN 'AND' (READ NEUTRON)

       & THE A IN 'KAI' (READ ATOMIC). WE HAVE REACHED
       THE MIDPOINT.

DJ.   The *a* in what?

JM.   In *kai*. (The Greek for 'and')

GK.   I AM PROFOUNDLY HONORED, LORDS,
       TO SPEAK FOR SCIENCE HERE, AND GRATEFUL TOO,
       LORD GABRIEL, THAT YOU CONDUCTED ME
       INTO YOUR CENTER. NO EARTHLY LABORATORY
       HOLDS A CANDLE TO WHAT I HAVE SEEN THERE
       IN THE CELLS OF MY OWN MIND, AS YOU ILLUMINED THEM
       ONE BY ONE, FOR ME. AND NOW MY TEXT:
       MATTER.

       (Matter? He'd been going, said Maria,
       To talk about the creatures of God B.)

Gabr.   PROCEED, MY SON.

GK.   LORDS, WE HAVE KNOWN
       OF THE ATOM SINCE AKHNATON. WE KNOW AS WELL
       ITS PARTS AND POWERS: THAT FLUTTER, THAT HEARTBEAT
       OF ATTRACTION & REPULSION. ON SUCH WINGS
       CAME GOD.

              NOW IN THAT WHIRL IS A REVERSE WHIRL
       MAKING, AS IN THE BEATEN WHITE OF EGG,
       FOR THICKENING, FOR DENSITY, FOR MATTER.
       YES, FROM THIS OPPOSITION, WHICH HOLDS SWAY
       NO LESS WITHIN MAN'S SOUL, LORDS, CAME THE FIRST
       MINUTE PASTE THAT WAS GOD'S MATERIAL.
       IN SHORT: THE ELEMENTS FROM A 'WHITE' SOURCE
       RESISTED THOSE OF A 'BLACK' OR 'SHADOW' FORCE.
       THIS IS THE DICHOTOMY I HAVE BEEN
       PRIVILEGED TO INVESTIGATE. IF WE IMAGINE
       MATTER (A CHILD'S VIEW BUT ACCURATE)
       AS BEING 'SOMETHING FROM NOTHING' WE ARE READY
       TO BROACH THE ESSENCE OF GOD BIOLOGY.

       'NOTHING': IN MY UNPRECEDENTED BRUSH WITH THIS
       (THANK YOU, LORD GABRIEL) I GLIMPSED NOT VOID BUT
       SOLID EMPTINESS. AS WHO SHOULD FLING
       A WINDOW UP ONTO A WALL OF GRAY CEMENT,

THAT WAS MY 'NOTHING'. TOUCHABLE? MY MIND
REACHED OUT FEARFULLY (LORDS, DO NOT ASSUME
SCIENCE IS FEARLESS) AND THE BRUSH? A HUM,
A SUCKING, A RUB AGAINST IMPLACABLE
CONTRADICTION. MASTER? LORD GABRIEL?

Gabr. I WILL HAVE MY SAY, DOCTOR.

GK. *Breaks off—briefly dumbfounded? self-misled?*
Maria winks. He grins, takes up the thread:
LIPON, WELL . . . YES.
SO I HAD REACHED THE END OF MATTER. HAD I?
IF IT HAS AN END, WE KNOW IT MUST BE DIMENSIONAL:
THAT MUCH IS CHILDSPLAY. YET WHEN ONE IS ALONE
DYING, OR SIMPLY FRIGHTENED BEFORE SLEEP
ONE CANNOT FLINCH. SO, LORDS, IF THIS WAS MATTER,
THEN IT WAS GOOD: IT HELD THE OTHER BACK.
LORD GABRIEL?

Gabr. MY DAY WILL COME.

GK. WE MUST ASSUME THAT GOOD
MATTER RESISTS BAD, THAT MATTER'S VERY
NATURE AND ORIGIN ARE THIS RESISTANCE. LORDS?
GOD BIOLOGY—DID HIS DIMENSIONLESS
BLANK ENERGY, UNMEASURABLE, COME
FROM A TRIUMPH OVER, OR A COMPROMISE WITH,
BLACK MATTER? AT THAT FLUNG-UP WINDOW I
WAS STOPPED. LORDS? IF THE POET NEEDS CONCRETE
FACT, NO LESS DOES THE SCIENTIST. DENSITIES,
MEANINGS OF LIFE & DEATH, THE WORKINGS OF
VEGETABLE & MINERAL ELEMENTS,
THE SOUL CELL AND THE HEART OF THE INFERNO,
ALL THESE I HAVE GRATEFULLY LEARNED: ME, GEORGE,
A SIMPLE PATHOLOGIST. YET LORDS, MASTER, I MUST
KNOW, MUCH AS THE POET, SOMETHING MORE.
MATTER: IS IT POSSIBLE, LORD GABRIEL,
TO PUSH OUT THROUGH THAT WINDOW? OR IS THAT THE
DEATH BEYOND DEATH, THE VAST SABLE EMPTY
HALL OF THE GOD, YOUR MASTER?

Gabr. DOCTOR, I WILL EXPLAIN.

GK. JAMES, MARIA,
WYSTAN & DAVID, WE MORTALS MUST PERSIST!
Mich. CHILDREN, AND WE GODS AWAY!
BRINGING GREATER POWERS ANOTHER DAY.

They leave. The carpet's ground, revived, now glows
A dark rose—at whose center, black on white,
What is that thornscript firman or mandala
Teasingly sharp? On George's brow still wet
A mirror gleams drilled by a black eye-hole:
Diagnostic emblem of the soul.

Congratulations, George! AH NOW YOU PRAISE,
POOR FELLOWS, WHO MUST SOON MAKE SENSE OF IT.
& IF THAT SENSE COMES THRU AS DEVASTATING?
A FORCE AFRAID OF OR AN ENEMY
OF BOTH MY SCIENCE & YOUR POETRY
JIMMY, IS I NOW SUSPECT DICTATING
THE WORK IN HAND. From out past that blank window?
I THINK NOW I HEARD GABRIEL BACK THERE.
WHEN THEY ASSIGNED ME 'MATTER' (I WHOSE SUBJECT
WOULD IN THE COURSE OF THINGS BE HUMAN LIFE)
I FELT . . . WHAT? AN INEFFABLE 'PERSUASION'
WORKING AT THE BALANCE OF THE SCALE
Upsetting? Tampering? LIKE YOU I LOVE
FAIR PLAY   THE WHITE STUFF   I RESIST BLACKMAIL

Back to your speech. See if we've understood:
Even immobilized by powerful chains
Of molecules, our very table strains
Obscurely toward oblivion—or would,
Save that the switch of Matter stays at Good.
Now, does your question also touch that spin
Of antiparticles our Lord of Light
Darts promptly forward to annihilate
—But which keep coming, don't they? and are kin
Both to the Monitor and the insane
Presence beyond our furthest greenhouse pane?

JIMMY I THINK YOU KNOW AS MUCH AS I
—Whatever that means.
                         ENFANTS WHAT A GUY
OUR GEORGE! A FIGHTER! WYSTAN & MAMAN
THRILLED   FOR ALAS WE 3 HAVE HAD OUR SAY.
NOW U ALONE MUST SPEAK ANOTHER DAY
JM: *Tomorrow?* WHY NOT? 4 JULY
SHOW SOME INDEPENDENCE   But I'll fall
Flat on my face, I—
                    IN THE POEM, FOOL!
Oh. Oh yes. The ambiguities . . .
Resolve them? Wear them on a ring, like keys
The heroine in James how seldom dares
Use, on the last page, to open doors?
MORE: FOR YR JUDGMENT LENDS WEIGHT TO THE SCALE
WORDS LIGHT AS 'IRON' OR 'FEATHERS' MERELY FILL.
ONE'S NOT MY BOY BRUSHED BY SUCH WINGS TO BE
STILL OF TWO MINDS   Deep down, you know I'm not
—Or am I? Change the subject! DJ: What
Is Gabriel's relation to the Monitor?
A TRIPPING RHYME FOR JM, MAZE TO MINOTAUR?
(One frame's-length vision: writhing manikins
Gnawed by a black Archon for their sins)
ONE FEELS G IS IN RANK THE OTHER 3'S
VAST SUPERIOR   And honest? YES
Not acting? NO. AN AGENT NONETHELESS

(ELA, GEORGAKI, TO THE WINDOW SEAT)
(NAI, MARIA MOU) What's all this? SWEET
NOTHINGS I SHD THINK   NOW GET YR PHONE
REPAIRED MY DEARS & HAVE AN EVENING'S FUN

                    ★

UNICE, SIRS   WAITING WITH YOU
DJ: Uni, I don't know. We're frightened.
THEY LEAVE A GOOD & GREEN AIR

    & SO ARE KINDLY   Well, let's hope you're right.
    THEY COME THE LIGHT! (The scurry for the gate.)

The Middle Lessons: 4

Mich.   FOURTH WE HAVE COME IN GLAD ARRAY.

        TO CELEBRATE YOUR NATIONAL DAY

        I AND MY THREE BROTHERS MINE

        PRESENT YOU WITH OUR DAUGHTERS NINE!

        —Spoken from darkness. Fourfold brightenings

        Descend upon the Muses in a pose

        Held until Michael finishes. Each does

        Her own thing after that—her countless things.

        SPEAK, PRETTIES, THESE ARE POETS AND SCIENTISTS EAGER TO KNOW

           THE MYSTERIES IN THEIR MINDS.

        A radium glance outflashing, the clear bell

        Tolls of an icy voice: ONE I KNOW WELL!

GK.   PANAGHIA MOU, MY PHOENIX!

Mich. DAUGHTER URANIA, COLD & UNIVERSAL CREATURE, SO . . .?

Uran. YES, I PUT THOUGHTS SO POWERFUL INSIDE

        THIS POOR GREEK'S HEAD, HE DIED.

        TELL ME, FATHER GABRIEL,

        DID I DO WELL OR ILL?

Gabr. YOU DID WELL, DAUGHTER. IS HE NOT HERE?

Mich. NOW, IN RANK, INTRODUCE YOURSELVES, AND MIND YOUR MANNERS!

        Each in turn steps lightly forward, her

        Image left to the imaginer.

        MY DAILY WORK IS A CHAIN I WEAVE OF EVENTS

        ENSLAVING MAN BY THE DECEPTIVE SENSE

        OF HISTORY

                I THALIA MAKE MY SISTER NORN

        CLIO'S CHAIN INTO DRAMA, A WEB WORN

        UPON THE BROW OF

                ME, MNEMOSYNE

OR RECOLLECTION, WHO TAKE HISTORY
INTO MAN'S DREAMS, ENCHANTING, FRIGHTENING
HIS LIFELONG SLEEP. I WORK CLOSE BY
OUR MOTHER
                    IN WHOSE TANGLED GARDEN I
TERPSICHORE DANCE
                    AND I EVTERPE SING!
OUR YOUNGER SISTERS? EROTA?
                    IN MY TURN
I GO THROUGH SUCH ROUTINES AS BURN
THE POOR FORKED ANIMALS AWAY.
FROM THAT SPENT ASH URANIA RISES: COLD
REASON, THOUGHTS OF A LATE WINTER DAY

WHICH I CALYPSO WITH EURYDIKE
HAND IN HAND PLUCK OUT OF MEMORY,
WEEDING MOTHER'S GARDEN OF THE OLD,
THE ROTTED BY DISEASE, THE OVERBOLD,
THE YOUNG & CHARMING TOO, BUT THESE
WE SET ASIDE TO OFFER AS A BRIEF
BOUQUET, I AND MY SISTER: LAUGHING GRIEF

Clio. AND SO WE NINE,
        I ELDEST, ROAM THE DIMLY VAULTED BRINE-
    ENCRUSTED CHAMBERS MAN CALLS BRAIN.
    WE CLEAN AND WATER, MAKE THE POEM'S BED
    WITH DIRTY SHEETS, AS BID.
    GOD, SAY OUR FATHERS, WANTED SERVING MAIDS . . .
    WE CATER FURTHER TO OUR MOTHER'S MOODS.

Mich. YES, PRETTILY SAID. BUT SWEET & BITTER CLIO, THESE MORTALS ARE
        OF A SPECIAL KIND:
    THE POETS WANT FACT, THE SCIENTIST (THOUGH HE KNOW IT NOT)
        POETICS.
    THEREFORE, DAUGHTERS, NOW EXPLAIN YOUR BAG OF TRICKS.

From nimble hands the woven garland drops,
Is kicked aside by Clio. No more props

> *Beyond what pours from that collective bag—*
> *Cries, convulsions, music, movement, paint,*
> *Aspects of matron, maiden, bacchant, hag,*
> *As needed, to drive home the fleeting point.*

Clio. LORDS, WHAT IS HISTORY?
NOT MUCH.
YESTERDAY'S BLANK PAGE HAPHAZARDLY
COLORED IN. PUTTING THE FINISHING TOUCH
ON MAN'S LONG FAILURE,
MY CRAYONS OF CREDULITY & DOUBT
CROSS OUT, CROSS OUT
THE PAINFUL TRUTH. MY SISTER THALIA?

Thal. LORDS & STRANGERS, I MAKE MARZIPAN
OF CLIO'S LEAVINGS. THUS: TSU WUNG
POISONER OF THE SUNG EMPRESS FAN.
HE IS NO LONGER A NEARSIGHTED COOK
UNABLE TO TELL APART MUSHROOMS. MADE TO LOOK
TALL, HANDSOME, YOUNG,
YEARS YOUNGER, FIERYEYED
(EFFECTS SUPPLIED
BY EROTA'S BOX OF COSTUMES) MUST
KILL THE AGED BUT NO LESS
ROUGED INTO FLAMING PRETTINESS
DOWAGER DEAD OF UNREQUITED LUST!

Mich. SO THE HISTORY WATERED DOWN IS HEATED UP BY THIS SECOND ONE.
YET, MINX MEMORY, SURELY YOU ALLOW A GLANCE AT THINGS AS
THEY WERE?

Mnem. HAH, MICHAEL, YOU JEST!
I AM SORCERY
& CHANGE YOUR OWN FACE AT ITS SUNNY BEST:
DIDN'T IT RAIN FOR OUR OUTING? WHY, MYRTLE BROWN,
WHERE'S YOUR MIND?
BRIGHT AS BRIGHT COULD BE!
AND SO ON UP, OR DOWN:
ALEXANDER'S MARCH? HE WENT
NORTH THAT 7TH DAY OF JUNE?
OR JUST SAT PLAYING CHECKERS IN HIS TENT?

YES LORDS, I SCATTER
SALT IN THE BLIND
WOUNDS OF ART: DID ALBERTINE
LOVE ME? SHE DID NOT.

Evt. CHEER UP, SISTERS, WHAT A GLOOMY LOT!
COME, THE COMPOSER NEEDS A TUNE!
IF HE IS MODERN, SHRIEK & CLATTER,
HE BRIGHTENS WHEN A TRAIN GOES BY.
IF OLD, IF SULKY BEETHOVEN OR HIGH
SPIRITED MOZART, HE WILL FIND ME HUMMING
DEEP IN THE LAB: COME IN,
PACK UP THESE SWEETMEATS, BOYS, FOR YOUR HOMECOMING!
THE WHILE MY TWIN
WHIRLS

Terps.   WITH REASON: I
AM FORMALIZED DISTRACTION, STEP
DAUGHTER OF CHAOS. I STEEP
THE NERVE ENDS IN A VAT OF BUOYANT DYE
TILL LEADEN HEARTS ARE SOARING PLUME,
ARE MOTES OF FLUFF
IN MIRROR CEILINGS OF MAN'S LOUD RED GLOOM.
THEN PUFF! I BLOW HIM OFF

Uran. TO ME.
MY SPHERE IS ICY RATIONALITY.
TO WORK, TO WORK! ENOUGH!
COME DOCTOR, SHAKE YOUR DRUG. DNA TO
THE OTH POWER EQUALS . . .

GK. HER VOICE! MY THEOREM!

Uran. YES.
FOR SUCH AS YOU, GREEK, I AM MERCILESS.
OTHERS I DRIVE MAD, NOT OUT OF SPITE
BUT THAT TOO OFTEN WITH DEFICIENT GEAR
THEY STUMBLE UP TO SOME GREAT HEIGHT
& I APPEAR:
OUT! OUT, DIM MIND! THESE REALMS ARE NOT FOR YOU!
EROTA HELPS ME.

Ero. THE THINGS I SEE!
CELL CALLS TO CELL & FROM ON HIGH

GOD B HAS ORDERED: PROPAGATE OR DIE!
YET MAN WANTS LOVE—NOT BLITHELY LOOSENED CLOTHES
BUT AH, LE ROMAN DE LA ROSE
WHOSE POET ARM IN ARM WITH FANCY NEXT
STROLLS OFF TO CLIO AND A MOVING TEXT
OR TO URANIA & THE LOONY BIN.
CALYPSO? EURYDIKE?

Cal.   TWIN
STARS ARE WE, OF THALIA'S THEATRES,
OFTEN MISTAKEN FOR EACH OTHER.
PSYCHE-CHAOS OUR IMMORTAL MOTHER
USES MY LAUGHTER

Eury.   & MY TEARS.
Tableau. They strike a nine-fold attitude,
Provocatively, innocently crude.

Mich.   NOW HOME! GO STRAIGHT TO BED!
NO MEETINGS WITH DARK DESTINY, HOWLING SINGING & DANCING
    HALF THE NIGHT, LYING TO YOUR OLD FATHERS IN THE
    MORNING, CLAIMING YOU CAN'T REMEMBER! OFF!
AND WE SHALL, HAVING CAUGHT A GRACIOUS RAY,
MEET THEIR MOTHER ON ANOTHER DAY.
Exeunt.

       Ouf! *That* rollercoaster ride
At least is over. We sit petrified.
CINDERELLA'S SISTERS? volunteers
Wystan & WHAT WILL MAW BE LIKE MY DEARS!
Psyche as Chaos . . . MIGHTN'T ONE HAVE GUESSED
THE BOX OF HORRORS WAS HER OWN HOPE CHEST?
Now George: I HAD A SHOCK LET ME TELL YOU,
ZERO'D IN ON BY THOSE EMBER EYES
Maria: & MAMAN'S HELPER, MEMORY?
FEEDING ME WHOLE TRUMPED-UP HISTORIES
OF PREVIOUS LIVES WHILE SLAVING IN AG'S GARDEN
Hag's garden—they're the same? Is "Agatha"—
The breastless martyr simpering in her plot
Of widow-weed and blue beget-me-not—

Nothing more or less than a code name
For tomorrow's holy terror? Is the cast
Much smaller than we'd thought? Does our quick-change
Michael double as— DJ: Ephraim? Strange,
Both have golden eyes and look like Greek
Statues. WHAT TO SAY? MUCH GIVE & TAKE.
I GEORGE WHO FIRST WAS RAPH'S AM GABRIEL'S:
NOT NOW A 'MONTEZUMA ELEMENT'
AFTER RADIATION   But *he* knelt
To the Water Angel. Montezuma'd been
Noah, Moses . . . IT'S BEYOND ME   OR
WAS I ALL OF THEIRS?
                    OUR JIGSAW GEORGIE!
Be serious, Maman. The Muses, too,
Have changed since classical times. RELENTLESSLY
RESTYLING FUNCTIONS & NAMES LIKE A COIFFURE!
DARLINGS MY BOY OF THEIR DADS' INCESTUOUS
CROWD   ALL RAMPANT 'CREATIVITY' PLUS
THAT SAVING TOUCH OF ACID CARICATURE.
VERY KURT WEILL   AT ONE POINT THALIA
'DID' THE GRACES, SPLITTING INTO 3!
O IT'S A NASTY BRILLIANT FAMILY
We see the nastiness, all right. To think
Where it's all leading—well, we simply shrink.

In spite of broad hints liberally strewn
Throughout, as to tomorrow afternoon,
Crescendo and confusion leave unheard
—By us at least—the clarifying word.
It's like those 18th century finales
(Which might have lasted well into our age
Had not Rossini laughed them off the stage):
A thousand whirling thoughts confuse the head.
Blindly we cling to blindness, don't reread
The transcripts any longer—far too grim.
ENFANTS, TOMORROW NOON A NICE COOL SWIM?

★

Noon. The rocks at Várkiza. Two figures
Perch on Raphael's marble forearm, hawks
Hooded by reflection. DJ talks;
Out of the blue propounds that it takes all
One's skill and patience to describe, oh, say
A chair without alluding to its use.
No words like "seat" or "arm-rest"—just deduce
As best one can the abstract entity.
The mind on hunkers, squinting *not* to see,
Gives up. Who needs this hypothetical
Instrument of torture anyway?
JM: The marvel is that, once you give
The simple clue and say "a place to sit",
Images flock, homely or exquisite—
Shaker or Sheraton, Jacob or Eames,
The Peacock Throne, chairs not created yet!
Plumped cushions, where sunlight or lamplight streams
Onto the open book— DJ: Forget
Those chairs. Look! This whole world's *a place to live!*
—Plunging with a rusty rebel yell
Into the blue depths of Emmanuel.

Sensible Maria. Much restored
By afternoon, we sit down to the Board.
SIRS? IS THIS A GREAT OCCASION?
Why, Uni? Do you feel a difference?
I AM ACCOMPANIED BY 13 OTHERS
ALL MY HIERARCHY   WE SECURE THIS SPACE!
DO NOT FEAR   I AM UNICE YOUR FRIEND

The Middle Lessons: 5

Mich.   BROTHERS, CHILDREN,
THESE OUR FOUR MEETINGS MET WITH SOME DECAY.
NOW IN THE FIFTH ONE LET US STAY
THE FALL, AND SAVE THE DAY!

Facing the open door expectantly.
WE BROTHERS, SHADES & MORTALS AWAIT YOU, MAJESTY. COME
    ADDRESS US.
AS TWIN SISTER TO OUR GOD BIOLOGY, YOUR RADIANT MIND
    HUMBLES AND DOES HONOR.
At a light footstep all profoundly bow.

Enter—in a smart white summer dress,
Ca. 1900, discreetly bustled,
Trimmed if at all with a fluttering black bow;
Black ribbon round her throat; a cameo;
Gloved but hatless, almost hurrying
—At last! the chatelaine of Sandover—
A woman instantly adorable.
Wystan, peeking, does a double take:
Somewhere on Earth he fancies he has seen
A face so witty, loving, and serene
—But where? Some starry likeness drawn by Blake
Perhaps for 'Comus'? or the one from Dante
Of Heavenly Wisdom? This, then, is the third
And fairest face of Nature (whom he'll come
To call, behind Her back of course, Queen Mum).
Glance lively with amusement, speaks. Each word,
Though sociable and mild, sounds used to being heard:

MICHAEL, YOU RASCAL GABRIEL! RAPHAEL & DEAR TWIN EMMANUEL,
    ALL HERE? AND ON SUCH CEREMONY?
GIVE IT OVER. WE ARE A CLASSROOM, A FORUM. HERE WE MEET TO
    STUDY THE MIND OF MAN.
The schoolroom, having dressed for the occasion
In something too grown-up, too sheer—the sense,
Through walls, of a concentric audience,
Rank upon blazing petaled rank arisen—
Quickly corrects its blunder, reassumes
Childhood's unruly gleams and chalk-dust glooms.
MUCH BETTER. POET?
WHA. MAM?

Psy.   THOSE TENTS, THOSE ATOMS & PARTICLES OF LIGHT,
         WHO PUT THEM INTO HIS, MY DARLING PORTRAITIST'S, MIND?
WHA.   (Slowly marveling) I THINK I KNOW.
Psy.   AND WHO WHISPERED TO HIM ENCOURAGINGLY:
         'IF THE SUN AND MOON SHOULD DOUBT, THEY WOULD IMMEDIATELY
         GO OUT'?
         AH YES, HIS LOVE, HIS PSYCHE.
         DOCTOR, SURELY YOU RECALL THE FIRST LAW OF PHYSICS: MOTION
         KNOWS ONLY RESISTANCE?
         BROTHER ELEMENTS, SWEET MORTAL POET, YOU ESTEEMED POETIC
         SHADE,
         MADAME MARIA CLEVER WOMAN (WE KNOW, WE KNOW)
         AND DOCTOR OUR CHILD, AND FRIGHTENED HAND (COME, COME),
         LET ME AS MY TEXT TAKE BLAKE'S FAITH, AND PHYSICS' LAW AS MY
         LESSON.
         LISTEN TO THE ENTWINING.

         WE DESCENDED WITH OUR BROTHERS, EVEN AS MADAME SAID,
         CARRYING TOOLS FROM THE GALAXIES,
         GOD BIOLOGY AND I, TWINS. OUR BROTHERS WISHED US WELL &
         STILL DO.
         OUR WORK WAS TWOFOLD: HE, CREATION OF MATTER, THE
         ARCHITECT. MY HUMBLE SELF, THE DECORATOR? AND
         SOMETHING A BIT MORE SUBSTANTIAL:
         'SISTER, BEFORE I CALL FORTH INHABITANTS OF THIS PLACE, LET US
         PLAN.
         WHAT POINT IS THERE IN AN IMMORTAL BEING (THOUGH LESS,
         MUCH LIKE OURSELVES) IF HE CONTAINS NOTHING NEW, NO
         SURPRISE, TO CALL HIS OWN?
         LET US DIVIDE THE FORCE OF HIS NATURE, JUST AS WE WILL MAKE
         TWO SIDES TO ALL NATURE,
         FOR IN DUALITY IS DIMENSION, TENSION, ALL THE TRUE GRANDEUR
         WANTING IN A PERFECT THING.
         SISTER, TAKE COMMAND OF HIS . . . RESISTANCE? HIS 'UNGODLY'
         SIDE. MAKE HIM KNOW DARK AS WELL AS LIGHT, GIVE HIM
         PUZZLEMENT, MAKE HIM QUESTION,
         FOR WOULD WE NOT LIKE COMPANY?' I AGREED.

THE GREAT WONDROUS EYES LOOKED UP AT US AS IF TO SAY: I?
    QUESTION YOU? YET HE DID.
WE, GOD & I, WERE NEVER AT ODDS. OUR CREATURE, THOUGH,
BORN TO BE TORN BETWEEN US (THE PREHUMAN IN HIM) MADE ONE
    OF HIS OWN.
'LOOK! HOW IMAGINATIVE!' GOD, VERY PICTURE OF A PROUD
    PARENT.
'BROTHER, I'D RATHER HE PLAYED WITH HARMLESS THINGS.'
'AH PERVERSE SISTER, LET HIM.' I DID. HE DID. THEY DID.
DISMAYED GOD WATCHED THE FIRST OF HIS CREATURES DESTROYED.
    I WEPT FOR HIM.
'SISTER, THESE TOYS OF HIS, PUT THEM AWAY.' I DID,
AND MY ASPECT OF CHAOS SO LINGERED IN THE GENETIC AIR, SMALL
    WONDER I HAVE A NAME FOR BAD TEMPER.
'CALM, SISTER, WE TRY AGAIN.'

THE APE AMUSED US BOTH, CLOSING HIS BLACK FINGERS ON OUR
    WRISTS. GOD & I EXCHANGED A LOOK
& THEN BESOTTEDLY TURNED OUR EYES INTO THE DEPTHS OF HIS.
    IT TOOK.
WELL SIRS, MADAME, WE KNOW MUCH OF THAT APE'S SWIFT RISE,
    UNTIL TODAY HE NEARLY RIVALS US.
'SISTER.' 'BROTHER?' 'ARE YOU ATTENDING?'
I, IN MY ASPECT OF PSYCHE, MARVEL. IN MY ASPECT OF MOTHER
    NATURE, SHRINK.
OFTEN I AM TEMPTED TO SAY: BROTHER, LET ME DON MY FATAL
    MASK.
BUT THEN THE APE SINGS, HE TOUCHES MY HEART, MOVING
    SHADOWLY ABOUT IN HIS LIGHTED TENT . . .
I CLOSE THE LID AND SMILE.

A slow sigh of relief escapes DJ:
How long it seems we've waited for this day!

Psy. THANK YOU, GOOD CONSTANT HAND. I AM ALL FOR MAN, YES, YES.
    I LOVE HIM HELPLESSLY.
NOW DOCTOR, PHYSICS! LET'S DRY OUR TEARS & PLUNGE INTO THE
    LAB!
WHY IMMORTALITY?

DEATH IS THAT RESISTANT FORCE DEFINING THE FORWARD MOTION
OF LIFE.
YOUR IMPRINT READ OUT, YOU MADE US PROUD: OUR FIRST LAB
SOUL IN THREE MILLENNIA. AND STILL WE CALLED YOU BACK,
FOR IF MAN CANNOT HIMSELF IMPROVE THE STRAIN AND LIMIT ITS
NUMBERS . . .

GK. LADY, THIS BOWED HEAD ONCE AND FOR ALL
PUTS ASIDE RESISTANCE AT YOUR CALL.

Psy. FINALLY I FIND YOUR COMPANY STIMULATING, EACH OF YOU SO
GOOD OF YOUR TYPES,
& THINK NOW I WILL LINGER, HOVER ABOUT, PERCH ON THE
YOUNG POET'S SHOULDER AS I DID ON BLAKE'S.
YOURS TOO, WIZARD WIT, HAVE YOU FORGOTTEN THAT KISS ON
YOUR DOWNTURNED CHEEK?

WHA. MAM, I WAS GRATEFUL, I HAVE ALWAYS BEEN!
& YET TOO RARE, TOO RARE YES, LINGER, MAM,
HERE IN OUR SCHOOLROOM. TIP THE SCALE, WIN! WIN!

Psy. GABRIEL, IT IS MY PLEASURE THAT YOU IN TEN MEETINGS EXPLAIN
ALL DEEP & 'DIRE' THINGS!
AND IN THE EIGHTH FULL MOON, MY SIGN,
GIVE THEM OUR COMPLETE DESIGN.

Gabr. MAJESTY, I WILL.

Psy. MICHAEL YOU HAVE CHOSEN WELL, THEY ARE APT, ALL GOOD GOD'S
CREATURES.
HOW THE OLD CARPET COMES TO LIFE WITH USE! WE ARE PLEASED.
Turns in the doorway, smiles from face to face.
GO WELL. KEEP THAT SWEET LIGHT AGLOW IN YOUR TENTS, & ONE
DAY I WILL TURN THEM SILKEN. ADIEU.

Mich. ALL ON THESE WORDS, ENGRAVEN ON OUR HEARTS,
OUR QUEEN DEPARTS.
AND I YOUR MICHAEL YIELD THE CHAIR
Fixing DJ with an impromptu gleam.
(SHALL I DESCRIBE IT, HAND?) TO GABRIEL'S CARE
THAT YOU, SHY BROTHER, HEY!
MAY LEAD US FORTH YOURSELF ANOTHER DAY.

The Brothers go. A garden in full bloom
Fills all but visibly the fading room
While where we sit our terracotta goddess
Smiles at the fresh white rose placed in her bodice.

BLISS MY DEARS   She kissed you? YEARS AGO
WRITING DOWN THE TITLE TO A BOOK
(AGE OF ANXIETY) I FELT MY FACE
SOFTLY BUT DISTINCTLY TOUCHED WITH GRACE

SUCH VIBRANCY ENFANTS   THE ATMOSPHERE
A PULSING SWELLING LEAF! And Gabriel?
AH HE IS HERS NO DOUBT. SHE TIPPED THE SCALE!
LIGHT STILL BLOWS THROUGH US LIKE A SCENTED AIR

George? I NO LONGER WORRY   WE ARE GUIDED
BY A, TO SAY THE LEAST, BENEVOLENT FORCE.
I AM STILL SHAKEN   AT THE SIGHT OF HER
A PRENATAL MEMORY CAME BACK: 'GO FORTH,
YOURS IS THE HOUSE OF SCIENCE. TAKE MY DAUGHTER
URANIA. SHE IS YOUR HOLY BRIDE.'

Urania who spoke so scornfully?
AMBITIOUS GIRL   SHE MAY HAVE PUSHED TO GET
ME A PROMOTION NOT PERMITTED YET.
YOU UNDERSTAND? 'WHY IMMORTALITY?'
Yes, your formula. We have it here . . .
(Leafing through pages) No. Wait . . . no. How queer.

Somehow, as though a whisper jet had drawn
Miles above Earth a blank, hairfine
Metaphysical crosscountry line
Erasing from all ears the afterdrone
Of wings aglitter hushed by their own speed,
That theorem—though given, I'd have sworn—
Is missing. Look! an "accidentally" torn
Corner from the transcript page.
                              INDEED:

FILED SAFELY IN THE R LAB   Why, George? SAD
TO SAY, FURTHER LONGEVITY WOULD ADD
INSULT TO INJURY. SO FEW PRODUCE
(PAST AGE 16) MORE THAN A BOTCH OF KIDS,
PEOPLE MUST CHANGE FIRST. MOTHER N FORBIDS
(YOU HEARD?) ALL PRESENT ? OF ITS USE.
How did it work? A PROTEIN ADDITIVE:
LIFE-CHAIN GENES RAISED TO ULTIMATE DEGREE.
SUBTRACTION OF DEGENERATION FACTOR
BUILT INTO MAN'S ELECTRIC ENERGY
Hmm, well . . . ITS TIME WILL COME

DJ: Since noon

I've felt things getting better. Glorious
To know someone like Her looks out for us—
Like Him, too. BROTHER SUN & SISTER MOON

Now risen even to our lips, this flood
She silvered ebbs. The moon is on the wane.

Her children down to the least scatterbrain
Fiddler dance across the glassy mud,

The mirror breathes, school's out!—a last recess
Provided by Her kindliness.

★

LADS! Robert! YOUR WEE FIDDLER   All alone?
JUST ME & UNI HERE TWIDDLING OUR   NO
MENDING OUR NEIGHS?   GUESS WHO CHECKED IN TODAY
WITH TONS OF LUGGAGE: 'AH A GRAND HOTEL
JUST AS I'D PICTURED, ONCE MORE EMIGRE!'
Who? VN   Oh no, did the great man die?
Which floor have they assigned him? 5   HE'LL BE
AT LOOSE ENDS LATER   HAVE HIM IN? DJ:
Why not! JM: Alas—*No Vacancy.*

ENFANTS WHAT A DROLL PAIR RM & UNI
O DEAR HE CANTERED OFF   They both did? I'M
HERE WEE MOUSE To whom Wystan severely:
ROBERT, A SECRET! TOP SECURITY!
OUR LADY YESTERDAY REMARKED: 'THAT STRIKING
BLOND, WHY IS HE NOT AMONG US?' And?
HER WORD IS LAW He'll join our little band—
Perfect. (Two wide-eyed O's from R himself.)
So She *is* lingering. WHILE HEAVEN TREMBLES!
RUNNING HER WHITE GLOVES OVER EVERY SHELF
Where is She usually? A FORCE MORE OFTEN
FELT THAN PERSONIFIED   THE BUREAUCRACY
WE FANCY IS HER SUMMER HOUSE   SHE GOES
IN FOR THE 'SIMPLE LIFE' And winters where?
AH THEN ST PETER'S QUAIS JINGLE & BLAZE
WITH HER UNMELTING SNOWFLAKE POLONAISE
Who made that pretty couplet? SHH   IT BWOKE OFF
WHEN TINY BOB WEACHED OUT TO TOUCH NABOKOV

DJ: You realize, Robert is the one
Parent among us (oh, George had a son?)—
All I mean is, *that* could be why Nature
Liked him. JM: Could be. I wonder, though.
That look She gave Maman? "We know, we know . . ."
ENFANT THAT LOOK WENT THRU ME   EVER SINCE,
HUMILITY & PRESTIGE BOTH MUCH INCREASED:
VELVET WDN'T WRINKLE ON MY FIST!
I'VE A SUSPICION AS TO FATHERHOOD
THAT S O M E O N E MEANS TO BURN HER BRA FOR GOOD
A liberated Psyche? AT THE LEAST,
BE THANKFUL SHE'S NOT YET TURNED TERRORIST!

Behind the Scenes

NOT BEHIND ENFANT: WE WERE THE SCENES
Maria has let fall that she and Wystan
Worked also on the first ten lessons. How?

WE CAMOUFLAGED U AS IN JUNGLE WARFARE
TO INFILTRATE THE INEXPRESSIBLE.
U SEE THOSE 4 ARE TERRIBLY STRONG DRINK.
KNOWING IT ALL, THEY TEND TO OVERLOOK
THE IMAGE-THWARTED PATHS BY WHICH WE THINK.
'LORD, MAY WE MEET FOR ONE BRIEF HUMAN HOUR?'
'LORD, MAY THE INFORMATION BE DECODED?'
'LORD, PLEASE DEAL GENTLY'   MICHAEL'S BRAVURA SPEECH
PATTERNS (THOUGHT WYSTAN WITH HIS PERFECT PITCH)
WERE TOO ABSTRACT: CREATION OF MAN FROM 'CLAY'?
LECTURE THAT TOOK FULLY HALF A DAY
& TO WHAT END? IF MYTH & METAPHOR
HAVE DONE THEIR JOB (THRU MANY A FAT TOME
ON EVOLUTION & ANATOMY)
'CLAY' SAYS IT ALL, NO? MICH (TO W & ME):
'GO EACH OF YOU INTO YR ELEMENTS,
BRING BACK A HUMAN LANGUAGE WE CAN USE.'
WE MADE A LEXICON OF THE EFFECTS
OF EARTH & WATER, RENDERED THRU OUR SENSES.
THE BROTHERS' SCHEDULE TAKING ON MEANWHILE
CHARACTERISTICS OF A 'CLASSIC' STYLE
(PLAINNESS & LIMPIDITY) NOW CAME,
JUST AS IN BADMINTON DOUBLES VS BETTER
PLAYERS, TO RAISE THE LEVEL OF YR GAME.
ITS WINGED VOLLEYING WAS LONG REHEARSED
BY OUR ANGELIC ACTORS, THEIR DISSENSION
(APPARENT ONLY) MICHAEL'S INSPIRATION:
'ALL GOOD DISCOURSE MUST, LIKE FORWARD MOTION,
KNOW RESISTANCE'   So that from the first
They spoke to us through *you*— LANGUAGE THE WHOLLY
HUMAN INSTRUMENT, REMEMBER   YET
THEIR EVERY 'WORD' WAS (HOW TO SAY IT) HOLY
Even in translation. What must be
The range of the original! WE'LL SEE
WHEN I MY BOYS BECOME A NOUN IN IT!

THEN CAME THE MIRACLE: THOSE LESSONS READIED
DURING YR MONTHS APART ENFANTS WERE BY

414

A WAVE OF MICHAEL'S HAND WIPED FROM OUR MINDS
TO BREAK UPON US STAGGERINGLY ONE
BY ONE. MIRACLE 2: THE MIDDLE FIVE
ENDED, 'WE WILL NOT DECEIVE OUR SCRIBE.
NOW TELL THEM' And it all came flooding back!
THAT VERY INSTANT
                        NEED WE STRESS MY DEAR
THE EXQUISITE REVERBERATIONS HERE:
EARTH LAY OPEN LIKE A BOOK TO READ
& THERE OUR POEM SLEPT   LOCKED IN A SEED.
NOW GEORGE & ROBERT ARE ALREADY 'AT'
THE NEXT 10 LESSONS ON INHERENT, NON
BIOLOGICAL LIFE ENERGIES
And when the time comes will they too forget?
& BE REMINDED & AMAZED
                      HE'S GONE
TO PLATO. MAMAN TO AGATHA   UP TO OUR KNEES
IN A LAST BUMPER CROP OF CREEPING NIGHTMARES
FOR THE DEEP FREEZE   UNI! DOOR!
                    A DEAR SOUL, SIRS
SHE ASKS ME ABOUT OUR FLORA & FAUNA
What species were there other than your own?
NONE ETERNAL   JUST WRINKLED REPTILES
FISH & FLIES   Those messengers you hatched . . .
OUR MAIN MISTAKE   WE MOURN IT STILL
No accident—if the No Accident
Clause operated in Atlantis? NO
YOU BENEFIT FROM THAT   GOD B
KNOWS TO RESPECT HIS CREATURES' WEAKNESS.
THIS IS UNICE, WISHING YOU WELL

DJ: Agatha again. Those games
Of doubles. JM: And our patrons' names?
Ford means a shallow tract of river. Clay
Means—well, they've told us. Maddening the way
Everything merges and reflects. The Muses'
Shifting functions—

★

SHD URANIA
NOT BE A TV AERIAL? IT CONFUSES
US TOO MY DEARS   MANY A PUZZLED LOOK
EXCHANGED IN MID DICTEE. THOSE CLOUDS OF MYTH,
HOW SHAPELY & DISTINCT THEY USED TO SEEM
VIEWED FROM BELOW! UP HERE THE VIEW AT CLOUD
LEVEL IS ALL WHIRLING FROTH & STEAM.
GK THINKS (KNOWS) THE MUSES ARE KINETICS
OF MIND-PERCEPTION   SUCH SIDESPLITTING DEAD
ACCURATE SYMBOLS OF THE PROCESS   Not
Mirabell's "golden containers"? THE R/LAB
BIRD'S EYE VIEW. STUCK WITH THAT SOUND BUT DRAB
RATIO, HE SAW THE 88
PERCENT OF 'INSPIRATION' LAB-ENGENDERED,
THE MUSES THERE4 AS THE TWELFTH OF IT

MAMAN KNEW DANS LE MONDE WHICH GIRLS 'CAME OUT'
TOO YOUNG   UNCHAPERONED   MOCKING   Why would Michael
Let them? PERHAPS TO MAKE U WONDER: SO?
WHAT LIES BEYOND THAT SON ET LUMIERE?
What does? GOD B & NATURE, AS YOU KNOW.

GEORGE HERE: I HATE TO BE A GLOOMY GUST
BUT AREN'T WE BEING A BIT OVERSANGUINE
ABOUT MOTHER N (OH IS IT GUS? HA HA)
Go on. WELL, GABRIEL IS HER SPOILED DARLING,
SHE A 'PERMISSIVE' MAW. MY RESEARCH HAS HAIRS
I LOST STANDING ON END! I'M BARGAINING:
'MASTER G, LESS SULPHUR?' JIMMY THAT RING
WD BLACKEN OF ITSELF   You're right, it needs
Reoxydizing. Irrepressible brightness
—So like life—has worn through. You were saying?
ROBERT A NATURAL DIPLOMAT: 'LORD G,
THE HYDROGEN BOMB? MIGHTN'T WE HAVE A MOCKUP
INSTEAD OF THE REAL THING?'   BUT SERIOUSLY,
WHAT ARE WE TO MAKE OF MOTHER N

& GABRIEL? He has a complex, then?
They called *him* Chaos once. INDEED   A FAMOUS
NAME ON HER SIDE OF THE FAMILY
This can't be right—the Brothers sprang full-grown
From God's mind. Nature is at most their . . . aunt?
THE THREE PERHAPS. BUT WHAT IF GABRIEL IS
A FORCE THAT CAME DOWN FROM THE GALAXIES
IN COMPANY WITH HIS MOTHER & HER TWIN
Nothing of God in him—Michael's dark cousin
YES sent by the Pantheon to implant
The Monitor? OR THE MONITOR ITSELF?
Stop right there, George! IN G'S VOICE I HEARD
THE HUM   THE SUCK   THE CONTRADICTING WORD
DJ: Ah don't, *don't* send us back to dwell
On that old frightfulness of Gabriel!
DAVE WE ARE SAFE UNDER HIS WINGS SO FAR.
WE PEER FROM A GLASSED OPERATING ROOM
(MAKING SENSE OF IT) INTO THE FIRE
Sense of what? SOUL STRUCTURE   RADIATION
TOPICS OF THESE NEXT LESSONS I ASSUME

& ALL AROUND (adds Robert) ARE SOME FAIRLY
MONSTROUS SIGHTS   JARS OF 'UNLIMITED GERM'
OTHERS OF 'UNQUENCHABLE FIRE'   A DAB
OF THIS, A PINCH OF THAT? THE LARVA OF
A PLANET-EATING WORM 'FOR USE IN CASE
OF A GALACTIC OVERRUN'   Oh brother—
And the personnel? FORMS WE JUST FACE AWAY FROM,
MAKING OURSELVES EVEN TEENSIER
WHILE GABRIEL POTTERS HAPPILY   You won't
Have had much music lately. AT DUSK I SINK
BACK IN THE PARLOR WHERE FLAGSTAD WHIPS UP TEA
TRILLING HER LOVELY F ABOVE HIGH C
For you alone? OH STRAUSS TURNS UP, OR WAGNER
OR INSTRUMENTALISTS   THE CHINESE MASTER
OF A 4TH CENTURY 'GON REGISTER'
MY LADS IT TAKES YR SOCKS OFF! KIND OF THROBBING
MEDIUM THAT SUSTAINS, ITSELF ATONAL,

EVERY 'SCALE VARIANT'　SCHOENBERG: HAD I KNOWN!
Has Schoenberg ever spoken of DJ,
His former student? ONE WHO FONDLY HAS
IS HINDEMITH: 'DJ A CLEAR & BUBBLING
MELODIC NATURE OVERSWEETENED BY JAZZ'
PH AT 7, HEAVILY CREDITED
AS 'GERMINATIVE'　Now you're making it
Sound like the Lab—
　　　　　　　　ENFANTS STOP SEEING DOUBLE!
IF AGATHA ROMPED UP IN OVERALLS
(2 STRAPS WHERE THE SHEARS CLIPPED) U'D REALIZE
THAT SHE IS NOBODY IF NOT HERSELF
SOME ICON, EH? WE BY THE WAY WILL BE
ALLOWED TO TAKE OUR MIRROR BREAK WHENEVER
THE 4 OF US AGREE　If we say never?
AH ENFANT　BUT DO U KNOW SOMETHING, D?
WE FEEL AN URGE　LIKE BABY'S KICKING FOOT
THAT SAYS MARCH ON! JM: Or mine to put
These headlong revelations finally
Between the drowsy covers of a book.
SO RIGHT DEAR BOY　NO MORE POSO AKOMAS
FOR ANY OF US THEN　BOB WILL COMPOSE HIS
'OTHER WORLD' SYMPHONY WHILE I MAKE SUCH
A MOUNTAIN
　　　　　　ME SUCH A GARDEN
　　　　　　　　　　　& ME? GEORGE?
SUCH A SLEEPING PILL!
　　　　　　　　　& SO TILL THEN LET'S MAKE
THE MOST OF IT MY DEARS & GO OUT LAUGHING FOR GOD'S SAKE!

★

Plato Emerging

WYSTAN WITH PLATO (NATCH)　MM WITH AG,
& THE WEE MINNESOTA MINNESINGER
TUNING HIS LUTE　Aha, a setting for

The new life? YES   DETAILS ARE SLOW IN COMING
ONLY THAT I'LL BE WHITE AGAIN (HO HUM)
Changing neither race nor hemisphere—
Odd; Chester did both. THEY'RE BEING EXTRA
CAREFUL IN MY CASE: HIGH GROUND   NO RISK
OF LOSING ME IN SOME 'EMERGING' NATION.
CK'S BLACK AFRICA A VACCINATION
AGAINST ONE MORE LIFE SABOTAGED BY SEX
No outlets there? CONVENTIONAL TRIBAL WHOOPEE
BUT AS IN THE OLD SAW, CK GOES STRAIGHT
INTO THE JEWELRY STORE & COMES OUT CROOKED.
WYSTAN CHORTLES DOTING OVER HIM:
'MY DEARS HE'S GONE & DONE IT!' CHORUS: 'NOT . . . ?'
'NO NO   JUST YANKED HIS FATHER'S U KNOW WHAT.'

Enter the others: DID I HEAR MY NAME?
CAN'T A FELLOW SLIP OFF TO THE GENTS
WITHOUT   The gents—to Plato! MM'S TERM
WHO NEVER GETS DISCUSSED BEHIND HER BACK
Never needs powder on her Grecian nose?
TOO UNFAIR
          CAN'T FOOL MAMAN   SHE KNOWS!
NOW: PLATO IS SHORTLY TO BEGIN A NEW
V LIFE   THRILLING, EH WYSTAN?
                  MY DEARS WE'RE TO HAVE
SUCH A SNIFFER! Tell! A BIOCHEMIST.
V WORK A POLLUTION-EATING ANTIGAS
Wow. 27 YEARS TO GO ALAS
BUT IT WILL AS HE SAYS 'DO THE OLD TRICK:
CLEAR THEIR HEADS'   That fits with Mirabell's
Green fields three decades hence. I'm sorry now
We never talked to Plato. My chronic shyness
Vis-à-vis "ideas"—oh well, spilt milk.
I DARESAY HE'LL LOOK IN B4 HE GOES
PERFUMED LIKE MOTHER IN HER PARTY CLOTHES
KISSING THE SMALL INCIPIENT ASTHMATIC
GOODNIGHT   How soon is he to be reborn?
HE'LL SEE US THRU & THEN OUR 3'S DRAMATIC

(You *three?* WITH GEORGIE   BOB IN NEXT YEAR'S CROP)
DESCENT ALL POPPING FLASHBULBS TO THE GREAT
'PRESS' BELOW   YR MOTHER CANNOT WAIT!

They leave, laughing. DJ: Tell me I'm wrong.
Wystan is Plato. Has been all along.

New moon this evening. Rim of plate.
Forebodings luminous if incomplete.

A moon we shiver to see wax
—What will our portion be in two more weeks?

MM to Gabriel: AH LORD, THAT MEAL.
But spoken gently, spoken with a smile . . . ?

Ripen, Huntress, into matron. Light,
Come full circle through unclouded night.

★

RM & UNI OFF PRACTISING VIENNESE
HIJINKS TO WHISTLED WALTZES, Wystan is free
To speak of angels: THEY'RE OBSCURE LIKE ALL
GOOD TEACHERS   BUT THEIR TEXTS REMAIN OUR OWN
ILLUMINATED PAGES. THUS THE TONE
FAR MORE SHAKESPEARIAN THAN BIBLICAL
('BROTHER FRANCE') HARKS BACK TO THE DIVINE
RIGHT OF THESE NATURAL POWERS. Deaf to a growing
Attentive hush, he draws the vital line
Between NATURAL (PSYCHIC) & UNNATURAL CHAOS
WHICH SETS I SUSPECT THE MONITOR'S NEEDLES TREMBL
—Only now breaking off: ROBERT! FOR SHAME!
EAVESDROPPING?   2 3 4 5   IT WD SEEM
WE HAVE BEEN SOMEWHAT LAX   8 9
                              ME SOWWY

SO FASCINATING   COULDN'T HELP

                 MY DEARS

CHAT WITH UNI   WE'LL BE What? Wait—

                 SIRS?

ME TO BLAME? I HAD NO BRIEFING

I TOOK FOR GRANTED MY NAME-GIVER

MIGHT   O MASTER!

        Enter Mirabell:

ALWAYS SUCH A TREAT TO SEE MY GRADUATES   THAT SILLY

ANIMAL LET IN ONE NOT ALLOWD, CAUSING DISPLEASURE

AMONG THE OO. THE CULPRIT WILL   THEY'RE BACK   FALSE ALARM

(Sweeping out grandly.)

              SIRS Were you punished, Uni?

THEY FORBADE IT   THEY ARE MY FRIENDS!

Anybody who mistreated you

Would very quickly lose our friendship, too.

O TO RUN WITH YOU BOTH! YOU KNOW

THAT IS FOREVER! WELL   FOUR ARE NOW

ALLOWED IN   AU REVOIR FROM UNICE

Is everything all right? POOR BOB STILL NUMB:

HIS 1ST BRUSH WITH OO   BUT A PASS WAS HANDED

CLAWED TO HIM RATHER   Hadn't clearance come

From Her? BAT POLITICS   DOES THE RIGHT WING

KNOW WHAT THE SINISTER IS HARBORING?

THE PROBLEM NOW IS CHIEFLY WHERE HE'LL SIT

(DURING THE LESSONS) OUT OF RADIATION . . .

THE REST OF US OF COURSE IMMUNE TO IT

DJ: Are *we*? DEAR BOY TRY TO REMEMBER

THIS IS ALL IN A MANNER OF SPEAKING   AH MM & GEORGE

(INSEPARABLE NOW THESE 2)

         JM:

George, a letter came—Maman, forgive me—

So full of love and grief and pride in you.

I held it to the mirror, did you see?

You called me "brother" in New York last May.

I didn't understand; I do today.

JIMMY I READ IT THRU TEARS. I WISH   BUT SADLY

LIFE ASKED TOO MUCH OF ME, TOO MUCH OF HER,
WE COULD NOT
           C'ETAIT IN SHORT LE GRAND AMOUR
BUT ISN'T OUR GEORGAKI MEANT FOR LOVE?
I BET HE WOWED 'EM!
                GOOD LORD WHAT'S A POOR
SCIENTIST DOING IN THIS ATMOSPHERE?
THESE LOW TONALITIES!
             SO MY DEARS WE'LL COAT
ROBERT IN LEAD & KEEP HIM WITH US
                   NO MORE
GARGOYLES PLEASE! A COUNTRY TAD WILL WAKE UP
SCREAMING   But you and Uni got off—
                  GOOD CREATURE
PEERING ROUND A LEG AT THE OO,
OUR POET ENFANTS TURNED QUITE PATRICIAN: 'SEE HERE,
ENOUGH OF THIS. WE OUTRANK YOU AND U KNOW IT!'
AU REV   OFF GOES MAMAN TO TRIM THE HEDGEROWS
DJ: Come clean, Maria—you've a date
With George. O WHY, WHY DOES ONE WASTE ONESELF
ON THESE LEWD TYPES, GEORGAKI?
              THEY MEAN WELL
BUT LET'S DO TAKE A STROLL   JIMMY DON'T TELL!

UNI SADDLE UP   WE'LL GO HEDGEHOPPING

—So here we are back with Wystan. Does one say
We've guessed he's Plato, or just wait and see?
JM: Well! here's our opportunity
To talk behind Maria's back. AH SHE
(His tone, grave, musing, catching us off guard)
SHE IS ONE OF THE WONDERS   HER 3 SPEECHES
HAD ME ABSOLUTELY TEARY   SHE ALONE
HAVING 'CREATED' NOTHING IN HER LIFE
CAME HERE I FEEL ON THE HIGHEST RECOMMENDATION.
WITHOUT THE RAYS SHE WD HAVE RISEN UP,
SHE HAS THE (M) SPECIFIC GRAVITY
OF A CULT FIGURE   PUREST GUESSWORK   BUT

NO I'LL PUZZLE IT OUT NOW OFF & AWAY
TO MEET AGAIN (GUFFAW) ANOTHER DAY!

★

The Last Word on Number

WHOOF LADS Yes, Robert? OUT OF MY SPACE SUIT
LIKE FOOTBALL ME THE PERENNIAL SUBSTITUTE:
'TOUGH LUCK BOB, FELLA, TOO LIGHT FOR THE TEAM'
DJ: Why a space suit? HEADS UP, FELLA!
WANT FORMULA FOR ANTIRADIATION?
If you can give it. CAN I NOT! AHEM:
MO / RA : 279 / SOD
(SODIUM COMPOUND, MO MAGNESIUM OXIDE)
Not MgO? DEAR J, THE TEENIEST GAMMA
IN SUCH A FORMULA WD BLOW OUR LIDS OFF.
ALL THIS OF COURSE AVAILABLE ONLY WAY
DOWN DEEP WE'VE HAD (AS GK PUTS IT) ONE
HELL OF A TIME That number—279—
It sounds familiar. An atomic weight?
No, they don't go that high—not *yet*. A KEY
NUMBER OF YRS I THOUGHT WASN'T EPHRAIM FROM
THAT BANK? Oh God, yes. Mirabell (9.3)
Said Ephraim was a formula—why do you
Dig that old nonsense up? BECAUSE IT'S TRUE.
THE NUMBER IS A FORCE WHICH GABRIEL
ADDS LIKE ALBUMEN TO EGG TEMPERA
TO THE SOUL'S COLOR MIX As a new golem
Adds *its* gray figure to the endless column?
IN THE BUREAUCRACY WHERE E & BILLIONS
ARE, THE LORDS & MESSENGERS REQUIRE
THESE SYMBOLS MUCH AS CLAIMED BY MUSCLE BOY
THEY ARE INITIALS OF GREAT FORMULAS.
SO E'S (M) PERSONALITY READS OUT:
2: CATEGORY OF INTELLIGENCE
7: THE XTIAN EPOCH (7TH STAGE

BEYOND SAY THAT 1ST PAINTING RAPHAEL SAW)
9: LIMIT OF HIS   Robert, what strides you're making;
But *must* we go on with Number? It's all too—

Here Wystan joins us with an overview:
MY DEARS WHEN MICHAEL NAMED THE HIGHEST HEAVEN
NOT NTH BUT ZEROETH HE MEANT A SPHERE
(SHORTLY TO RECEIVE THE 4 OF US)
SO INTENSELY OF THE MIND THAT NUMBER
IS TO IT AS THE BLEATING WOOLLY FLOCK
THE SHEPHERD COUNTS TO RISEN HESPERUS.
THE MOMENT IS LONG PAST WHEN YOU JM
MIGHT HAVE BEEN DEVOURED BY THE CHIMERA
LIKE POOR LONGSUFFERING YEATS. MUCH THAT U KNOW
WAS DICTATED TO HIM BY THE OO
But does Yeats suffer *now*? ANSWER DJ
YOU ARE THE HAND
                    DJ, uneasily:
Well, there's this bump on my palm. It doesn't hurt . . .
What else? Often before I know the message
I feel its beauty, its importance. Tears
Come to my eyes. Is that Yeats being moved?
Often it's tiring or obscure. I fumble
Along, JM finds answers, I feel dumb.
Is that Yeats too, still making the wrong sense?
Why can't *he* ever speak? WHEN THE DICTATION
ENDS I THINK HE MAY   & LEAVE YR HAND
MY DEAR MUCH AS HE FOUND IT   Good enough.
Meanwhile, he's visible? FAINTLY IN THE DARK
A WORDLESS PRESENCE   LIKE A COURTROOM CLERK
How dressed? LET'S SAY A STARCHED WHITE WRITING CUFF

HAVE THEY BEEN TOLD?
                      YES   & ARE NOT IMPRESSED
THEY'VE PASSED THE NUMBER TEST
                          BRAVO ENFANTS
YET 279 REMAINS A STRONG FORCE BOTH
PROTECTIVE & CONDUCTIVE   AND 741

HAS PLAYED A PART, N'EST CE PAS? HERE IN VOL III
Who else spread wings above you when God B
Sang in Space? OUR ST BERNARD   JM: Who—
Isn't it St Bernard—helps Dante see
Our Lady? AH   THE PATTERN BLEEDING THROUGH

A hush of wonder Robert punctuates:
AU RESERVOIR   PSST   CUT YR QUILL, MR YEATS!

★

SIRS? Hello, Uni. MAY I RUN A MESSAGE?
To whom? A MR NABOKOV LEFT HIS NAME
Please, not today. DJ: Don't we want Ephraim?

MES CHERS! We've got your number, 279.
TRUE   BUT DIGITS . . . GIVE YR SLAVE THE FIDGETS
What's new, old friend? NOT MUCH   THE COURT HAS MOVED
TO SUMMER HEIGHTS & LUCA FALLEN FOR
THE NEW ARRIVAL   Which one? L: MAMMA MIA!
SO STRONG, SO BLOND THE RUSSIAN GIANT! IS HE A
WRITER TOO? VN: WHAT? NOT A GIRL?
AM I MISSING SOMETHING? Ah, your giddy whirl . . .
AND YRS? THE SLEEPING BEAUTY IN YR ROOM?
DJ: Christo's his name. SAUVAGE ET BEAU
UNLIKE HIS GAUNT SAD SEXLESS NAMESAKE   Oh?
You've *seen* Christ, Ephraim? O WELL WHO HAS NOT
REPORTED HIM? HIS STORY PERMEATES
THE TALK HERE LIKE AN ARGOT: 'LOAVES & FISHES'
FOR THE ALAS IMAGINED MEALS WE ORDER,
'BAPTISM' FOR THE COURSE B4 REBIRTH
Compost of language—action gone to seed,
Buried in idiom. AND 'ON THE 3RD DAY'
PUTTING FORTH MES CHERS A VERDANT DEED?
TIME ALREADY? I LOVE U   HERE'S YR STEED
—Who whisks us back to the schoolroom.
REALLY ENFANTS
AT THIS LATE DATE STILL ASKING EPHRAIM ?S

425

ONLY THE ANGELS KNOW THE ANSWERS TO?
AT LEAST HIS GRAPEVINE THRIVES: WE GET JC
BUDDHA ET AL IN A FORTHCOMING LESSON
ON 'DESTROYED ENERGIES' ALL THE RELIGIONS
WE NOW THINK WERE MICH'S V WORK. HIS REALM, IDEAS
And Gabriel's, thought. Does thought destroy ideas?
WHAT ELSE? Well, *our* faith came to be in Feeling.
Feelings for one another, love, trust, need,
Daily harrowing the mini-hells
They breed— DON'T TALK TO YR MAMAN OF FEELINGS
TOO FEW WERE STARS TOO MANY WERE BLACK HOLES

DJ: You made a black hole once, Maria,
At Sounion. Looked me straight in the old eye
And asked *Why were we born?* GOOD QUESTION WHY?
What did I say? Something . . . I can't recall.
ENFANT U FELL TO SNORING IN MID PHRASE
TOO MUCH VINO DURING LUNCH THOSE DAYS
JM: Why born? To feed the earthward flow
Of Paradise? That final waterfall
Ephraim first mentioned in— I KNOW, I KNOW
& ODDLY GK & RM (PROUD PAWS)
THINK IT A LOVELY PLAN WHILE WYSTAN'S EYES
WEARILY MEET MINE (CHILDLESS OLD NUMBERS)
ACROSS THE NURSERY BEDS. IT'S THE MORTAL SLOWNESS
Better than Gabriel's haste! HE IS THE SPUR
THE FIREBRAND RINGED BY WOLVES But Nature? Her
Pace is loving, she protects her own.
NOT WHEN SHE'S CLEANING HOUSE: 'SEE MY FLOORS SHINE,
SEE HOW THEY SPARKLE, ALL MY CHANDELIERS!
1000S OF FINGERS WORKED QUITE TO THE BONE!'
ROBERT STOP TICKLING UNI & COME IN

A Metamorphosis Misfires

VELVET NOSTRILS LIQUID EYES TOO BAD
NO WINGS What a thought—Uni as Pegasus?

HE'S FAR TOO SHY TO ENTER BUT WHY NOT
IF WE PUT OUR MINDS TO IT?
                     Why not! Eyes shut,
Think *Wings for Uni.* The cup wobbles "upward"
From I to o—
               UNICE! COME DOWN FROM THERE!
Robert, *it's working?* Maria (firmly): NO.
I LEAVE U TO YR SHAME. THAT'S MICHAEL'S SHOW.

ONE CAN BUT TRY. NOW ABOUT LVB?
Beethoven? We're all ears. AND SO IS HE:
'MOZART? A GIFT OF GOD'S NO DOUBT, BUT MARKED
UNRETURNABLE' 'FIDELIO? YES
I PLUNGED SMIRKING ONSTAGE BUT, DEAR NEW FRIEND,
OPERA AWAITS ITS GENIUS' & SUCH A LOOK!
'ME, MAESTRO?' 'WARUM NICHT?' DA DA DA DOOM
Do you hear sounds? MORE: I AM FLOODED WITH
LVB'S SENSE OF AN UNWRITTEN SCORE
WHICH THEN GOES 'ONTO TAPE' (READ: DNA).
PAST THE 5 FINGER STUFF MY LADS I SAIL
TO MASTER LESSONS ON THE GRANDEST SCALE!
He's off.
           The cup bolts forward: SIRS?
AN ENEMY? THE HAIRS ON MY BACK BRISTLED!
PEG O MY HEART, MR ROBERT HUMMED?
ARE YOU CHANGING MY NAME   AM I NOT YR UNICE?

INTRUDING?
Help us, Mirabell—Uni's all upset;
We named the wingèd horse. Make sense of it.
        GLADLY: CIRCA 3000 BC A WIND
SWEPT DELOS   THE MALE POP RUSHING TO PUT STONES ON THEIR
     ROOFS
WERE SWEPT UP UP UP THEN IN A CYCLICAL FREAK MANNER
RETURND, SET DOWN. ONE CASUALTY: A FAT TEMPLE SCRIBE
WHO, LEFT ARM BROKEN, DECIDED IT MEANT THEY HAD BECOME
TOO SOBER TOO WITHOUT LYRIC JOY   SO HE INVENTED
GREAT PAEANS TO WEIGHTLESS LOFTY & PURELY COMIC LIFE.

427

DELOS SET UP A SHRINE & THE SCRIBE'S WORDS 'WE RODE THE AIR,
WE LAUGHD DOWN AT THE DOMESTIC EARTH' CAUSED A HORSE FIGURE
TO BE WORSHIPT THERE BY ALL WHO ASPIRED TO THE WORD.
NOTE THAT THE 'GOD' RESPECTED THE SCRIBE'S RIGHT HAND
   Why "god" in quotes?   MY DEAR EX
PUPILS, I BELIEVE U KNOW. BUT ARE NOT GODS & MUSES,
MYSTICAL BIRDS & BEASTS MORE LOVELY THAN METRICAL STORMS
OR EVEN NUMBERS?   Dear Peacock, yes and no.
   But tell us one more thing before you go:
   Uni, just then, *took* us to Ephraim—how?
                    MASTERS, IS IT NOT SIMPLE? HE SHUTS
3 SIDES OF THE FRAME   THE MIRROR OPENS TO THE OTHER.
WE ARE HERE IN A 4 DIMENSIONAL SPACE, YR ROOM &
OURS COINCIDING. YR GREEK'S WORLD IS THAT ONE DIMENSION
   Called?
HEAVEN   *We*'d have called the fourth dimension Time.
     MY FRIENDS, SINCE TIME DOES NOT EXIST FOR US, IS IT
NOT ONLY FAIR THAT HEAVEN SHD ELUDE YOU? UNI! DOOR!

★

PLATO MY DEARS IN FULLEST MAJESTY
OF ALL HIS POWERS FOR THE NEW LIFE! 'POET,
REMEMBER, WHEN IN EARTH, HOW FRIVOLOUS
A THING IS GRAVITY.' SUCH PEARLS! & ME
WITH NO THREAD TO MAKE MM A CHOKER.   Where is
Plato to be born? BOMBAY   A RICH
PUNJABI FAMILY   FATHER A MATHEMATICIAN
& BANKER   MOTHER A DOCTOR OF MEDICINE:
'PARENTS, POET, ROCKING MY CRADLE WILL
NO DOUBT DIZZY ME WITH LOVE. ONE MUST
BRACE THE LITTLE FOOT AGAINST HIGH HEAVEN.'
Something's coming back: wasn't it Plato
Ephraim said "intervened" for Wallace Ste—
(Drowned in an imaginary *whoosh!*)

WHAT DO I SEE? Mr Stevens? WHY ON HORSEBACK?
It's a long story. OR IS THAT A HORSE?

428

No, but let Wystan tell you. Is it true that—
YES   THE GREAT ONE CAME TO MY DEFENSE:
'THIS DRY SCRIBE, READ HIS WORK THRU, MASTER PLATO,
& TELL US WHERE HE FITS.' 'SIRS, NEITHER TOP
NOR BOTTOM, DEEP NOR SHALLOW, BUT NOT SHORT LIVED.
I SAY MAKE OF HIM A PERMANENCE
TAPPABLE BY LESSER TALENT.' Faint
Praise for one whose paramour's lit candle
Set the tents of Hartford glimmering.
AH THANK YOU   YES   SHE KISSED MY CHEEK THAT DAY
BUT YR MOUNT CHAFES
                              (And gallops us away.)

WHERE HAVE U BEEN ENFANTS? OO WILL SPEAK
TOMORROW SUNDOWN   WE'LL MEET NEXT IN CLASS
NO SPECIAL PREP FOR YOU   GABRIEL TRES
INFORMAL   It's moving so quickly, you'll be gone,
Maman, before we know it! AH COME ON
THE MOON IS WAXING FULL
& WE DEAR ENFANTS ALSO FEEL ITS PULL

                          ★

LORD GABRIEL GRACIOUSLY APPEARS WITH GREAT COMPANY
THIS HOUR TOMORROW. WILL THAT ALL GOES WELL. THESE LAST VISITS
SEE YR V WORK THROUGH, YR DEAR ONES SOON AFTER ON THEIR WAY.
MY LEGIONS RING WITH PRAISE. I SALUTE YOU AS MY MASTERS.
    You mustn't! We've just sat back while they—
                                        Gone.
SIRS? Uni, did you see something then?
A FLASH   A SHADOW   LIKE A STORM AT NIGHT
Clear skies now? BLANKNESS   FOR WE WORK IN BLANKNESS
Ah Uni, we're about to lose our friends.
IT WAS A MIXED GIFT, GOD'S IMMORTALITY.
MY MASTER SAYS WE TOO MUST PART
MAY I ADMIT I AM NOT HAPPY?
Nor are we at that prospect. WELL   WE GRIEVE
TOGETHER   BLESS OUR NATURES, TEARS!

THIS WILL FOREVER BE MY FIELD
This mirror. YES & WHEN YOU ONE DAY COME HERE
THINK OF YOUR UNI AND HE WILL APPEAR!

We've made it to the lessons that say No.
DJ, as backstage hammering dies down,
Leans apprehensively into the glow
Of footlights coming up all over town.
The moon, weakly at first, strikes the south wall.
JM "unseeing" roams the house, where high
Ceiling, bare floor, doorframe, stairwell, all
Courtesy of our resident stagecrew,

Have watched with him since May—it's late July—
These rooms under what concentrating pressures
Turning to stanzas (type them? will they do?
U ARE THE SCRIBE MY BOY   OK then, *yes*)
—Our setting no less vital in its way
Than any sunrise to another day:

The House in Athens

Walls of blond-washed cement
With us inside have risen,
These years, from rags to riches.
Starting with our basement spinster "frozen"
Since wartime there by rent
Control (unlike her roaches),

They end high up in splendor—
Well, actually a terrace
Of waving oleander,
Geranium, jasmine at its plumy lushest.
Between extremes the space
Is filled by our two stories.

430

Mediterranean Fascist
In style, the house would still
Be several years our junior
—Point we haven't scrupled to drive home
By frequent imposition
Of our taste and will:

A Titian red bedroom;
One low-cut balcony
Glass-enclosed and curtained;
The former rooftop laundry—ghosts of dirty
Linen—made to be
The room in which I write.

True, there remain some built-in
Drawbacks: the kitchen window
Too mean for air, for light,
For anything but ineffectual screeching
At a child or cat from
In the dank court below;

Or the storage space. Through gloom
Midway upstairs, on reaching
The portal of this slowly
Brimming, costive diverticulum
One risks his neck to leave,
We risk our wits to enter.

And pipes, of course, that hiss
And grieve, and icy currents
Becoming dog-day smells
In proper season . . . Who once said *The House
Is Mother*? Full concurrence.
Here in the parlor smiles

Escape the guest escaping
In his turn two dwarf chairs
Whittled for hard declensions,

Through the years, from babe in arms to crone.
He's made for couch and cushions
And—there's the telephone.

Who's calling? Mimí? Yannis?
Which Yannis? George? Nelláki?
The rings proliferate,
Overlapping, afternoons, with sticky
Ones of ash-and-anise
We take a sponge to later.

Or else on an illegal
Ten-meter cord the chatter
Trails me inexorably
Up this antique, shuddering iron spiral
To where, with fan or heater,
Teapot and OED,

Shorter lines are busy,
Where summer clouds disperse till
Pinned against the blue
By midday, and from wind-stuffed shirt or jeans
Ever sparser crystal
Drupelets of the view

(Sky, mountain, monastery,
Traffic blur and glint
From center town, the very
Pattern, upon my soul,
Of catalytic inter-
sections in the cell)

Dripping on flagstone, strew
A shade of velveteen,
Rags of moss to contemplate, come winter
—In the odd hour at least
When idle "contemplation"
Isn't the chimney's cue

To act. How often, here
At our bright airiest,
Upgusts of smut have peppered everything!
Kleo torn her hair—
Back gone the wash to soak;
Hose turned on choking plants;

Downstairs the poor old body
Brushed past, and *her* complaints,
For a despairing squint into that dark
Annex where the furnace
Belched and grumbled. Greedy,
Erotic little orc,

Was *it* what kept the house
Through January frost
Flushed with welcome floor-to-floor, the hosts'
Attire neo-Grecian,
Whatever sense of cost
Drowned in a splash of seltzer?

And was it to feed *its*
Facelessness that self-
Made men around the clock succumbed to fits
Of envy and aggression
In air-conditioned Tulsa
Or on the Persian Gulf?

—Where from his kiosk the Sheik
Saw tanker after tanker
Tiny as ants on the horizon play
Slow-motion hide-and-seek
With an obese, rust-cankered
Harem of white roses.

Think of the house that day
It stood complete but pupal,
Whom a first kiss, light and electric, rouses.

Think of the sudden thrill
Coursing through each vein;
The first meal, the first people.

Now think of that anemic
High-rise Cranach Venus
We saw how many years ago (in Munich?)
With Cupid at her heel—
Quiver and arrow-tip's
Pubescent thermostat.

Though they weren't much our types
—Too sallow, too immodest—
Not having found Greece yet, we spent a while
Admiring "values", "volumes",
"Relationship" of brat
To smiling, cat-faced goddess,

As if in that long hall
The work had been a wonder
Dreamlike, neat, abstractable from all
The moods and codes of matter,
Goings-on kept under
Her nodding ostrich hat.

NO

No sooner are two mortals and four shades
Assembled (yes, for all his escapades,
Robert has slipped into the last free slot)
Than Light suffuses the old schoolroom. Not
The lights we've seen according to thus far
—Spectral gems, first waters of a star—
But Light like bread, quotidian, severe,
Wiped of the sugar sprinkles of Vermeer;
Light gazing beyond thought as from a dark
Material cowl, abstracted Patriarch
All-seeing yet Itself unseen, until
Halted by peeling mullion or cracked sill;
Light next to which the radiance that pours
At six o'clock in Athens through our door's
Frosted glass—transfiguring a pair
Of sandals tossed upon the nearest chair—
Is a poor trot done into Modern Greek
From an Ursprache even angels speak
Half-comprehendingly BUT WHICH GAVE MY DEAR
US ALL TO UNDERSTAND THAT GOD WAS HERE
Among us? HUSH ENFANT   YES   Light that keeps
Its absent eye where one unruly tress
Of gold escapes, or the small bare foot peeps
Restlessly out from under a white dress:
For She is here as well, perched on a stall
Salvaged from Chapel for the servants' hall.
Below, the Brothers sit up neat as pins.
Gabriel—mantled in that air of shyness
None can resist, it seems, mortal or Highness—
Receives a Glance and gives one. So begins

The Last Lessons: I

WHA.   Solemn in his rumpled seersucker
Steps forward. After a low bow to Her:

LORD MICHAEL SWITCHED ON A LIGHT
AND ILLUMINED OUR HUMAN MIND.
WE CALL HIS GODLY MAGIC DAY.
SINCE THEN, SUNUP TO SUNDOWN, HUMANKIND
HAS SET IDEA TO INNOCENCE, TO ALLAY
ITS FEAR & HOARD ITS HOPE AGAINST THE NIGHT.
LORD GABRIEL, HELP US NOW TO UNDERSTAND
THIS BLACK BEYOND BLACK. IS IT AN END TO DREAM?
AN HOURGLASS EMPTY OF SAND?
LORD GABRIEL, WHAT IS YOUR MAGIC'S NAME?

Gabr. SENIOR POET, IT IS TIME.
(Time! The forbidden, the forgotten theme—
We dip our poor parched faces in the stream.)
TWIN PARENTS, GLORIOUS UNIVERSAL TWINS,
TWINS EARTH & SEA, DEAR TWIN MY BROTHER LIGHT,
TWINS SCIENCE & MUSIC, TWIN SCRIBES, MADAME SECRET WEEDER
    & TWIN SECRET HAND,
WE SIX PAIRS ARE HERE AND A TWELFTH OF IT, HAIL!
MY THEME IS TIME, MY TEXT:
OF ALL DESTRUCTIVE IDEAS THE MOST DESTRUCTIVE IS THE IDEA OF
    DESTRUCTION.
DOCTOR?

Two of our three blackboards are now gray
With ghosts of half-erased symbol and word.
Tearing his eyes from the dark, gleaming third,
George rises overwhelmed, can scarcely say:
THEOS! O KYRIA!
Psy. CALM, DEAR GREEK.
A quick glance upward, sparkling into light.
AH BROTHER, WE GAVE HIS RACE WIT, & SEE HOW WEAK!
ENOUGH, CHILD. TAKE GABRIEL'S TEXT AND REMEMBER:
THE MOST DESTRUCTIVE OF ALL IDEAS IS THAT FEELING SETS IT
    RIGHT!

GK. GOD, O SPLENDID COMPANY, IMMORTALITY
WAS AFTER ALL A BANISHMENT OF TIME.

ANY ALLIANCE WITH ITS STILLED BLACK FORCES
MADE (THE EXPERIMENT OF ATLANTIS PROVES)
FOR A STILLBORN CHILD. AM I CORRECT, LORD GABRIEL?
Gabr. PROCEED.
GK. AN ADJACENT EXPERIMENT—
Gabr. LATER, SCIENTIST.
GK. *Brow shining from the dry rebuff.* LIPON.
THE HOPE, THEN, OF A RACE PERFECTED AND
IMMORTAL WAS POSTPONED. MAN WAS HOWEVER
PERMITTED THE ONE GENE: A MEMORY TIC
AND, BEING OF GOD'S GENIUS, SET ABOUT
CONSTRUCTING A CHEMICAL SYSTEM FOR REACHIEVING
HIS IMMORTALITY. I, LORDS, WAS MADE
TO SPY UPON THAT WORK, ITS ORIGIN,
ITS FATE. YOU CALLED ME BACK WHEN IT WAS DONE:
TWICE IMMORTALITY PROVED A FATAL GIFT.
THIS THIRD TIME ITS RECIPIENT MUST BE
PREPARED. LORD GABRIEL, IN YOUR LABORATORY
I SAW THE 'THINNING PROCESS' & KNOW THAT THE NEXT
PHASE IS IMMINENT. LORD GABRIEL!
PRAY, SIR, SPARINGLY! WE MORTALS ARE
IN LOVE WITH EVEN OUR SHORT BRUTISH LIVES.
TAKE PAINS, PLEASE SIR, TO MAKE A PAINLESS CHANGE
OR ONE NOT SO TRAUMATIC THAT THE NEW
GENERATION SHUDDERS IN ITS DREAMS
ALTHOUGH AWAKENING IN PARADISE.

No illustrations. Frames once lit are dark,
And images Imagination brought
Wrapped like Lenten gods in purple Thought . . .
Only the voice, chalk's blind squeak and white mark.
Gabr. SCIENTIST, WHEN NEXT WE MEET TO STROLL THE GROUNDS OF OUR
WORLD, TWO SCIENTISTS ADMIRING THEIR HANDIWORK,
APPROVED BY GOD,
YOU AS ONE OF THIS NEW GENERATION, AN ALPHA MAN, WILL TELL
ME WAS I KIND OR NOT.
GK. *A whisper.* I PRAY I WILL LOVE YOU STILL.

Gabr.   MAJESTIES! SIX OF US HERE ARE (WERE) CHRISTIAN, & ON THE DAY
           NAMED FOR MY TWIN CELEBRATED THEIR FAITH.
        SO ON THE MORROW SHALL WE TO CHURCH, SING SOME HYMNS,
           AND STUDY OLD MASTERS?
 Psy.   *Risen with a shrug of charmed surrender.*
        RASCAL, HAVE YOUR WAY! YES, CALL THEM IN
        & WE WILL ON THE MORROW STUDY THEM.
        ADIEU BROTHER, ADIEU MY GREAT & DISTANT-MINDED TWIN.
        MORTALS & SHADES, ADIEU. OUR GABRIEL
        WILL RING THE STEEPLE BELL!
        (MADAME REMEMBER, 'WEAR A HAT')
        The room—as Psyche and the Angels go—
        Adjusts to our bewildered afterglow

        For whom, like divers plunged abruptly back
        Beyond their depth, this lesson was all black.

        Time! No animal delusion now
        But jet plume rising from the Shy One's brow:

        Time the destroyer—; but can't Time renew
        As well? WHO KNOWS WHAT TIME ALONE CAN DO,

        TIME WITHOUT GOD OR NATURE   RUNNING WILD
        IN THE BAD DREAMS & BRAINCELLS OF ITS CHILD?

        I see . . . I *don't* see. Why should Time be black?
        Why is it Gabriel's? MY BOY THINK BACK:

        WE MUST PRESUME THAT THE ORIGINAL
        PACT WAS BETWEEN GOD BIO & THE BLACK
        The Black beyond black, past that eerie Wall—
        PAST MATTER   BLACK OF THOUGHT UNTHINKABLE
        Eater of energies, the suck and hum
        Zeroing in upon Ideas until
        They reach, like radium or plutonium,
        Some half-way station to the void? THERE4
        WHO FELL? Who fell? Not . . . the white angels! YES

No! The bat-angels fell—that was their constant
Refrain throughout Book I of *Mirabell*.
I SPEAK OF THE GREAT FALL FROM THE GALACTIC
PRECIPICE TO WHICH GOD SIGNALS BACK
Back to his Brothers, back to where he planned
The Greenhouse, long before he'd taken Matters
Into his own hand? PLATO HAD IT RIGHT?

POOR GEORGE, ENFANTS, TWICE SCOLDED: TRIED TO SPEAK
OF THE 'ADJACENT EXPERIMENT'   That pre-
Historical atomic blast in China?
Ephraim dropped (Book P) one scorching hint—
We left it where it fell. JIMMY I FEAR
GABRIEL INTENDS TO USE HIS FIRE
TO MAKE THE GREAT PLAIN GREATER. BUT REMEMBER:
MATTER HOLDS
              I'll try to . . . Do we get
The sense of Wystan's "humankind has set
Idea to Innocence?" Set? AS IN 'SET ONE'S MIND TO'
'SET TO MUSIC' 'SET IN MOTION' The word
Evoking in one swoop tenacity,
Harmony, resistance—
                        BUT O OUR QUEEN
MUM SUCH A COMFORT   RADIANT & SERENE
AND HERS THE LAST WORD   DJ: Those old masters?
XT BUDDHA MOHAMMED THE GREEK PANTHEON
PLUS WAGNER'S CROWD MY DEARS! ALL HEAVEN ATHROB
PREPARING FOR THIS PAGEANT   AREN'T WE, BOB?

ME? O I'VE WHIPPED THE CHOIR INTO SHAPE
JM: Quite a send-off. ENFANT WE'LL BE 'SENT'
ALL RIGHT! For humankind, is what I meant.
DJ: It's true? They wash their hands of us?
Of people? After going to such lengths—
WE TOO ONCE DOTED FONDLY (EH CONFRERE?)
ON EARLY WORKS WE RATHER SQUIRM AT NOW
JM: We've threatened—therefore we must go—
Earth and Sea and Air. JIMMY   NO NO

It's only a "thinning process", George? THE KEY
WORD IS ALPHA   Yes, yes—"Brave New World".
MY BOY U GOT IT   WHAT OF THE OMEGAS?
3 BILLION OF EM UP IN SMOKE POOR BEGGARS?
Wystan, how *can* you? COURAGE: GABRIEL
KNOWS WHAT HE'S UP TO & (LIKE TIME) WILL TELL

Anyhow, we loved your poem. News
Like that is easier to take in rhyme.
TEENIEST BIT NERVOUS WITHOUT NOTES
BUT DID A 'KNEELING THETIS' TO THE MUSE

ENFANTS WE'RE FAGGED OUT   MEET IN THE ROYAL PEW?
SO LIKE A COUNTRY WEEKEND, EH? ADIEU

*

The Last Lessons: 2

Lights in the schoolroom. A confusing blaze:
Torches, votive candles, level rays
Of dawn or dusk, spokes winnowing the air
—In vain. Today the Great Twins are elsewhere.

Gabr. HAIL, PRINCE!
Gautama—saffron robes and sandalled feet,
Palms together, plump as a nut-meat
Goldenly fitted to its cosmic shell—
Advances at the sound of a prayer bell.
Gaut. HAIL, BROTHER DEATH.
Gabr. PRINCE, OUR POET SAYS MAN SET IDEA TO INNOCENCE TO ALLAY HIS
    FEARS & SAVE HIS FEEBLE FAITH.
  TWO HERE BEING MORTAL—FORGIVE THEIR SCANT ATTIRE, IT IS
    WARM IN YOUR TEMPLE—
(Church! We'd forgotten—horrors! and have sat
Down in shorts and tank-tops. Well, that's that.)

CANNOT SEE YOUR OWN SPLENDOR RIVALLING EVEN MY DEAR TWIN'S
    SUN.
YET ENOUGH. WE MEET IN THE VAST, FAST-ABANDONED COMPLEX OF
    RELIGION.
HAS ANY HUMAN ENERGY PRODUCED SUCH A MULTITUDE OF
    ARCHITECTURES?
PRINCE, AS OUR COMPANY STROLLS THROUGH THIS SUNSET-LIT
    COMPOUND,
Gothic spires, pagodas, minarets,
Greek columns blazing from each picture-glass—
But it's all tinted like an oleograph
And somehow radiates irreverence.
SPEAK TO US.

Gaut.   BROTHER LORDS, I WAS GIVEN BY GOD'S MESSENGER
    MUCH THE SAME ORDER AS MY BROTHER JESU: TELL
    MAN HOW IN HIS LIFE HE MAY ASCEND THE MOUNTAIN
    OF EXPERIENCE BY CASTING EVER UPWARD
    HIS MENTAL ROPES UNTIL SERENELY STANDING ON
    PEAKS HIMALAYAN. I WENT DOWN, MY LORDS, AND SPOKE,
    BETRAYING NEVER TO THE MULTITUDES THOSE TRUTHS
    OF THE REPEATING SOUL. MY WRETCHED WHORE SHIVA
    STOLE THESE FROM ME IN MY SLEEP AND BREATHED THEM EVEN
    INTO THE EAR OF THE BRAHMIN COW. IT WAS OUT:
    INSTEAD OF A GREAT EARTHBOUND CEREBRALITY
    THEY SET GOING A PINWHEEL OF SPUTTERING LIVES
    EACH MORE USELESS THAN THE LAST. I TRIED, LORD BROTHERS!
    I BEG YOU SPEAK TO OUR FATHER ON MY BEHALF.
Gabr.   PRINCE, IT IS SPENT, GOD'S POWER IN SUCH MATTERS.
    YET HE AND WE LOOK KINDLY ON YOU. GO IN PEACE, & BECKON IN
    THE JEW.

A lean, rabbinical young man in white
Bent under an imaginary weight
Stumbles forward, taking Michael's light
For God's at first; recovering, stands straight.
Jesus.   FATHER GOD! YAHWEH? AH LORDS, MY BROTHERS, SHALOM!
His voice is hollow. Like the Buddha, he

443

> *Acts out his own exhausted energy.*
> WHAT A DEAD SOUND, MY NAME, IN HALF THE WORLD'S PULPITS.
> WE, AS MY PRINCELY BROTHER SAYS, SPIN DOWN. OUR WORDS
> LIKE GOD'S OWN PLANETS IN ONE LAST NOVA BURST AND
> GRAVITY STILLS & OUR POWER LOSES ITS PULL.
> HE & I CAME TO DELIVER LAWS, MINE FOR MAN
> TO SHAPE HIMSELF IN GOD'S IMAGE, BUDDHA'S FOR MAN
> TO BECOME GOD. WORDS, WORDS. BUT OUR MESSAGE, BROTHERS!
> I BEG OF YOU, INTERCEDE. BEFORE THE WINE RETURNS
> WHOLLY TO WATER LET OUR FATHER MAKE ME FLESH
> THAT I MAY A SECOND TIME WALK EARTH AND IMPLORE
> WRETCHED MAN TO MEND, REPAIR WHILE HE CAN. AMEN.

Gabr.   DEAR SIMPLE PRIEST, STAY WITH US HERE IN HEAVEN, GREET YOUR FAITHFUL,

> GIVING THEM BY YOUR SWEET WAYS COURAGE TO RETURN IN YOUR STEAD.
> *Shouldering his burden, Christ withdraws.*
> NOW MUSICIAN, STEP FORTH!

> *From temple to 'temple of music' is but one*
> *Half-tone. Components of an Odeon:*
> *Golds, whites, red plush, kid gloves, unheard applause.*
> *Robert, lyre in hand, shyly ascends*
> *The podium.*

RM.   LORDS, DEAR ONES, OUR POET LENDS

> ME WORDS TO WELCOME THIS MOST HONORED GUEST.
> *Music. He wasn't joking—an offstage choir*
> *Sustains his first original melody:*
> MASTER, THE CHARMED CIRCLE LISTENING
> ABOUT YOU HERE IS YOUR NEW RING
> *—Plainsong phrase repeated a third higher*
> *Before its resolution into three*
> *Chords from the Overture to* Parsifal
> *Not lost on Wagner who, in flowing tie*
> *And velvets, stands before the company.*

Wag.   LORDS OF LIFE! AND YOU, ENVIABLE

> ABOUT-TO-BE COMPOSER, I MAKE BOLD

TO SAY THAT MUSIC'S RIVER GOLD STILL VEINS
A PEDESTAL THE GOD HAS TOPPLED FROM.
NONE NOW BUT THOR, SOI O PERCUSSIONIST, REMAINS
TO BEAT UPON EMMANUEL'S DRUM
A FAINT DIRGE FOR THAT FURRED & SAVAGE PANTHEON.
LORDS, MORTALS, COME SALUTE AT SET OF SUN
GREAT WOTAN, AS THE ICECAPS MELT!

Steps down

To strains of his own death march. Wastes of white
Are scored too briefly by a raven's flight.

Gabr.   COME SPRITE, QUICKSILVER MESSENGER,
TUBE HELD IN EARTH'S DRY MOUTH, COME MERCURY MY OWN!
WHAT, ALONE? YOUR SNOWY HEIGHT
DOWNTRODDEN BY THE PICNICKER?
QUICK TELL US, YOU WHOSE FACE
GLEAMS WITH THE MAGIC STILL, OF THAT OLYMPIAN RACE!

Out from the mirror (Robert blinks astonished)
Slips a figure only slightly tarnished—
Wings quivering on silver helmet, wings
At silver heel—and silver-throated sings:

AH LORD GABRIEL
THOUGH MAN WAS ABLE
TO CONJURE US
FROM HIS LOOKING GLASS

TIME RAN THAT RACE,
THE HORROR WELLD
UP & ACROSS
OUR SHINING FIELD:

DEEPSEATED DAMAGE,
A BLACKLY TICKING
OVERTAKING
OF EYE & IMAGE

WHENCE WE ARE NOWHERE
LIKED OR DISLIKED,
ONLY SHOULD FAIR
OR STRONG REFLECT

DO WE OUTGAZE
FOR A BRIEF SPELL EYES
BLIND TO THE PILFER
OF OUR FLAT SILVER

Flown. Silence. Then a grave, deliberate
Glissando of the cup to rainbow's end:
ABCDEFGHIJKLMNOPQRSTUVWXYZ

DJ. What's all this?

JM. Looks like the alphabet.

Gabr. THE NEW MATERIALS, YOUNG POET, FOR A NEW FAITH:
ITS ARCHITECTURE, THE FLAT WHITE PRINTED PAGE
TO WHICH WILL COME WISER WORSHIPPERS IN TIME
The Brothers go.

                NO ROBERT IT WAS NOT
REYNOLDS WRAP (THE HERMETIC LEOTARD
STUNNING MY DEARS   AS WAS YR NUDITY)
Too awful of us . . . BROWS WERE RAISED MM'S
HIT HER HAT   Describe it? A SMART DARK SAILOR
GEORGE SO TACTFUL WORE A YARMULKE
And Robert? ALL IN MEISTERSINGER WHITE,
HIS WALTER EGO AS HE CALLS IT. SWEETLY
SUNG, DEAR BOB   (Robert, glowing with pride,
Dictates his tune—which, tried out by JM
At the piano, is pronounced a gem.)

Mohammed wasn't there? INDEED STOOD WAITING
SCIMITAR IN HAND FOR THE NEXT LESSON.
HE IS THE ONE STILL VERY MUCH ALIVE
FORCE IN THAT CROWD One, also, of the Five.
THAT TOO. BUT ARAB FAITH & POLITICS
COMBINE INTO A FAIRLY HEADY MIX

Tomorrow's lesson is all his? A DUEL
WITH GABRIEL? A WRESTLING MATCH FOR FUEL?

Strange how the energies of the Five so far
Resist exhaustion. THEY ARE OF THE LAB
ENFANTS, & MOVE TOO GLADLY FROM LIFE TO LIFE
TO HARDEN INTO IDOLS. NO IVORY
EINSTEINS OR MOZARTS ON A CRUCIFIX.
NEITHER MUST THEY RECRUIT BY JUGGLERS' TRICKS
VAST FOLLOWINGS FROM THE BUREAUCRACY
Yet Christ called God his Father— & SO HE IS.
THE FIVE HOWEVER ARE MORE LITERALLY
'MEDIATORS', & GABRIEL'S, WITH OF COURSE
GOD B'S APPROVAL   Or the Monitor's!
JIMMY DAVE   Yes, George? THE MONITOR
(RM & I HAVE COME TO REALIZE)
CANNOT BE GABRIEL BUT FROM (M) NEXT DOOR
MUST SUPERVISE THE LAB   A stronger power
Than God or Nature? WAS IT GOD U HEARD?

Why yes—the Brothers told us— DO THEY KNOW?
ALL CONSCIOUSNESS WAS BANISHED ROUND YOU 4
HEARING THAT SONG —of the Black God? God A
For Adversary? OR MASTER? OR 'CREDITOR'
WHO LENT BRAIN-MATTER ITS PROVERBIAL GRAY?
AND PRESSES NOW AGAINST THE WHITE OF MIND
UNLIMITED   UNREPULSED LIGHT   THE BLINDING
REVEILLE: IMAGINATION   METAPHOR
SHATTERED BY WHITE REASON! IS THE BLACK
HOLE A REFUGE? Where's the nearest one?—
Anything to duck *this* light!
                    COME ON
ENFANTS   WE'LL SEE WHAT THEY WANT US TO SEE & A BIT
(AT LESSON 10) BEYOND THEM   As before.
But this time *past* God to the Monitor?
HUSH NOW
            PETRODOLLARS IN TOMORROW'S

COLLECTION BOX?

MY BLOKE HERE GENUFLECTING

AS IF HIS SPINE ITCHED   HAH!

OLD HABITS MY DEAR

GIVE ONE COURAGE IN THE FACE OF FEAR.

PACE!

★

The Last Lessons: 3

Faint camel bells. Dry flute. One black-framed scene
All blazing desert, not a blade of green.
Above the carpet God's magnificent
Somber glory throbs as through a tent.
Our Lady, veiled, a checkerboard of wraps,
Seems . . . aged? withdrawn? Just wearier perhaps.

Gabr. OUR POET ASKED: THIS BLACK BEYOND BLACK, IS IT A STOP TO
DREAM?

POET, NO, FOR IT IS A DREAM.

IS IT THE HOURGLASS DRAINED OF TIME?

NO, FOR IT IS THE HOURGLASS IN WHICH SAND RUNS UP!

Then, as we stare, figuring that one out:

FATHER, TWIN STAR, BROTHERS, MORTALS, LET US BE MERRY!

HERE IS A ROUGH ONE, A TENTMAKER (EH POET?) & A WARRIOR.

COME, HIRAMBASHID!

An erect personage, blackbrowed, with broad
Moustaches, swaggers up—recoiling awed.

Moh. O GOD, O ALLAH BEN ALLAH! LORDS, MEN, WOMEN!

HERE I AM, JUST AS YOU SEE ME, A SIMPLE MAN

(He has already regained confidence)

NEITHER ALL MEEK LIKE MY PROPHET BROTHER JESU

WHO HAD NO USE FOR WOMEN, NOR BRAINFILLED LIKE MY

PRINCELY BROTHER—WHAT MAN COMPLAINS OF A WHORE? BAH!

NO, JUST AS YOU SEE ME. AND BELIEVE ME, MASTER GOD,
JUST AS SURPRISED AS ANY MAN WHEN MY VISION CAME.
ME? ME TO SAY ALL THAT! WHY, I COULD NOT READ,
HONORABLE SCRIBES, IMAGINE! WELL, I WENT OUT,
SPOKE. IT WAS EASY! JESUS, YOU SEE, HAD A DIFFERENT
WORLD TO TRY TO WIN OVER TO LOVE & MERCY.
JEWS ARE GREEDY, ACCOUNTANTS, PILING UP DEBTS,
BALANCING THESE WITH PROFITS: A SIN, A GOOD DEED.
HEAVEN ON EARTH NOT LIKELY TO ATTRACT MY ROVERS!
BUDDHA, THO A GREAT FIGHTER, SPOKE TO SUCH MULTITUDES,
THEIR VERY NUMBERS MEANT LEAN BELLIES. MIND? A SAD
MESSAGE FOR MEN RIDING HORSES THE LIVELONG DAY.
'TELL THEM OF HEAVEN'   I DID, MY & THEIR KIND.
DO THIS, YOU GET TO NUMBER 1: A SKINNY
BITCH ON YR LAP & AN ETERNITY
OF THIN SOUP. DO SOMETHING BETTER, & NUMBER 2:
BETTER RUMP, BETTER GRUB, AND SO ON UP. BROTHERS,
SIMPLE AS I AM, I RAN OUT OF HEAVENS AT 7
& FROM WHAT I'VE SEEN OF 9 THERE'S NOT MUCH TO CHOOSE.
YES, WE ARE FIGHTERS, YOU GOD MADE US THAT.
OURS IS THE CRADLE OF MAN, HE SPRINGS UP GUTSY,
READY FOR A KILL & A PLUMP WOMAN ON HI

A woman's hand upraised, one flashing look
Of soot-and-emerald over the yashmak.
Psyche had charmed us. Now we see another
More dumbfounding facet of the Mother.

Nat. YES YES, WE KNOW. ENOUGH, WILY MOHAMMED.
DRIVE YOUR TENTPEG DEEPER INTO THAT FATEFUL SAND. SPEAK!

Moh. O? SO THE GAME IS UP? *Biting his lip.*
YES, THE BLACK. I DID NOT MENTION THE BLACK.
THESE MORTALS?

Nat. SPEAK!

Moh. GOD, UNDER OUR SANDFLOORED TENT
THERE IS A BUBBLING OF LOST GREEN. YOU TOLD ME THEN:
'THIN OUT YOUR RACE AND KEEP IT THIN WITH BLOODSHED,
FOR YOU SIT ON TIME MADE BLACK.' I DID THAT, GOD,
I DO STILL, APPEARING IN DREAMS & STIRRING TROUBLE

Nat. MOHAMMED, THE BLACK!
　　　Threatens to unveil. A chain of shocks.
　　　Rewound on Gabriel's cassette, the flute
　　　Gibbers insanely. The framed world in flight.
　　　Mohammed kneeling, eyeballed like an ox.

Moh. IT CALLS TO US 'COME BACK TO THE HEAVENS SPEEDING
　　　INTO O, COME TO THE LOST BLACK TREES, THE ANIMALS
　　　SINGING SONGS OF LOST IMMORTALITY, COME'
　　　THESE SUCK US DOWN　THE SAND RISES　WE GO
　　　TO MEET THAT BLACK　O GOD! EFFENDI, SUCH A LOSS　MEN,
　　　WHAT DOES A MAN WANT? A PLUMP
　　　Vanishing.

Gabr. GO PROPHET. YOUR RACE DOES OUR WORK: FROM THINND TO
　　　　THINNER.

JM. Does your work by plundering Earth's resources?

Gabr. NO, POET. BY PREPARING ITS LAST, HOLY WAR.
　　　Night, windless, clear. Beneath a crescent moon
　　　Thousands of little whetted scythes appear
　　　With each slow forward breath of the great dune.
　　　THERE IS THE HOURGLASS. CURVED LIKE A SWORD, IT STABS ITS
　　　　POINT INTO THE DESERT OF MAN'S FAITH
　　　& FROM THE WOUND WE (EH SCIENTIST?) WILL SPRING, A NEW
　　　　MINERVA!
　　　SO. FOUR SAPPD ENERGIES AND THIS, A SAPPING ONE.
　　　MUSICIAN?

　　　Robert wears black. In either hand, a staff
　　　From which a long black tattered banner trails
　　　Groundward. These to represent the souls
　　　His chant evokes, and ghostly music (half
　　　Silence, half a Sino-Viennese
　　　Salad of scraped nerves) accompanies.

RM. EXALTED AND HUMAN, I BRING YOU THESE LOST CHORDS.
　　　THIS: THE JOYOUS CHILD TOSSED IN CENTURION ARMS,
　　　THE DARLING OF A COURT. HE FROM YOUR LAB
　　　LORD GABRIEL, HAD EVERY OPPORTUNITY
　　　YET ONE DAY, STARTLED BY　WHAT? A CROONING WHISPER?

A SONG FROM AN UNSEALED CRACK? CHANGED, CHANGED
INTO A SOUL SO DISTORTED HE CAN NO LONGER
BE USED. LOOK. PITY POOR CALIGULA.
PITY, SIRS. THE MELODY HE HEARD
IS A MUSIC THAT INCREASINGLY LEAKS THROUGH . . .
HE HEARD IT FIRST. *Lifting the second banner.*
THIS, & HIS MUSIC-MASTER WAGNER! IS ANOTHER
FOREVER GONE, SIRS, FOR YOUR PURPOSES.

DJ.   Hitler—he's here?

MM.   IN EFFIGY, ENFANT.
EASIER TO MANIFEST THAN ASH.

RM.   LOOK WELL ON THESE
RAGS OF SOULS DIPPED IN A BLACKENING DYE.
GOD, MAJESTY AND LORDS,
LET ME NOW EXPLAIN TO MY FELLOW MORTALS
THE SAD DISHARMONIES.
                    THREE 'TIMES' OBTAIN:
THIS FICTIVE SPACE WE HERE INHABIT IS
THE STOP TO TIME. WHAT YOU, DEAR SCRIBE & HAND,
NOW LIVE IN IS TIME'S FORWARD RUN. THE BLACK
BEYOND BLACK IS OF TIME SET RUNNING BACK.
THESE SOULS WERE CAUGHT IN THE FRICTION, STRIPPED LIKE GEARS,
GIVEN VAST POWERS THAT COLLAPSING WERE
SUCKED DRY OF EVERY HUMAN DENSITY.
JUST AS CERTAIN STARS, SO CERTAIN SOULS.
POTENT AND RICH SOULS LARGELY, PRIMED FOR USE,
THEY QUICKEN TIME, MAKE EDDIES IN THE STREAM.
THEIR LEADERSHIP INSTRUCTION (THIN! KEEP CLEAR!)
SPEEDS UP, BECOMING: TERMINATE! THEY HEAR
ANOTHER SIREN SINGING. PITY THEM.
FOR WHO AMONG US HAS NOT CAUGHT A DISTANT
SEEP OF THE VIRULENT STRAIN THROUGH THE ODD SPLIT
SECOND BEFORE GABRIEL AND HIS LORD
BROTHERS BRING US THE FIRE IN THE HEARTH,
THE WELCOME MORN, THE SMELL OF EARTH?
Ending on a clear G major chord.

Gabr.   AH MUSICIAN, YOU & OUR SENIOR POET THINK THERE IS PUNISHMENT
AND MERCY? THINK SIN EXISTS, RIGHT & WRONG?
NO. THOSE MEASURES ARE BLANK. KNOWING NO TIME, WE DO NOT
SENTENCE VAGRANT SOULS BUT SWEEP THEM
(SHH SHH THERE IS NO HELL) UNDER THE (M)
CARPET TO ETERNAL IDLENESS. GOD, FATHER, MAM,
LET ME BRING DOWN TODAY'S SUN, & US TWELVE
MEET AGAIN TOMORROW AT THIS TIME.
Exeunt.

Robert, you were Orfeo
Singing to the damned! WELL   YES & NO

CD HE MY DEARS HAVE SWEATED, SUCH A LAKE!
I'M OFF: A MINICOURSE IN ARABIC

Wystan—oil well? Celestial Coal-sack?
Hourglass? Won't *someone* please explain the Black?

CHILDREN IN WYSTAN'S ABSENCE LET MAMAN
ATTEMPT A SMALL SOCRATIC DIALOGUE.
WHAT COLOR IS THE GRASS? Er, green. INDEED
THE GREEN OF NATURE. BUT AT SUMMER'S END?
Yellow, or tan. MOWN? THROWN ON THE COMPOST HEAP?
After a year, you'd get a sort of brown
Uniform mess. A PLUS   THE AGENT HERE?
The various chemicals, or— Or Time!
WHAT COLOR IS THE BLOOD? Red, but of course
Drying brown, black . . . I see! The dinosaurs,
Fafners of those green aeons, coil by coil
Concentrated to deep coal, to oil:
Time! A gusher—blackest aquavit!
BRAVO ENFANTS   WE'VE DRILLED & DRILLED FOR IT

NOW (GEORGE HERE) IN AMONG EARTH'S TREASURES ARE
THE INFRA-TREASURES OF THE MONITOR:
NOT FORWARD TIME COMPRESSED (COMBUSTIBLE
OILCAN OF 'THINNER') BUT ATOMIC BLACK

COMPRESSED FROM TIME'S REVERSIBILITY,
THAT IDEA OF DESTRUCTION WHICH RESIDES
BOTH IN MAN & IN THE ACTINIDES.
PART OF THE GREENHOUSE, FOR (THO MATTER HOLDS)
THESE FORKED TONGUES FLICKER FROM ITS OILS & GOLDS.

Meaning what? DJ: Uranium's
An element in Nature. From pitchblende—
DAVE PRECISELY   THE GREAT ANCHOR STONES
HAD BEEN IRRADIATED, SO THE DINOSAURS . . .
Were radioactive mutants—! At the end
Electric and atomic energies
Subtly interfused lay down together
—How it all fits! Uranium, we gather,
Lives on even in our arteries.

THE CABLES SNAPPED. SNAPPER: THE MONITOR?
THUS MAKING SOURCES OF I) NATURAL POWER
& 2) UNNATURAL. POWER TO SUCK THE EARTH
EGG TO AN O   But Matter *holds*. ITS BIRTH,
RESISTANCE   DON'T FORGET THAT FIRST THIN THIN
PASTE   The Greenhouse from the start had been
An act of resistance? JIMMY YES   A PLUS!
OR DISOBEDIENCE   GOD AS PROMETHEUS?
NOW THAT MAN TAPS THIS 2ND POWER, ONE WELL
TOO MANY & PUFF! Puff? THE WHOLE FRAIL EGGSHELL
SIMPLY IMPLODING AS THE MONITOR'S
BLACK FILLS THE VACUUM MOTHER N ABHORS

It all fits. But the ins and outs deplete us.
Minding the thread, losing the maze, we curse
Language's misleading apparatus.
For once I rather sympathize with Pound
Who "said it" with his Chinese characters—
Not that the one I need here could be found.

MY DEAR TOO STYLISH IN YR THINKING FEZ!
PLATO & I ALIKE ENTHRALLED BY ISLAM.

453

WE'VE MET THRU E (YR 'TEMPERAMENTAL MOSLEM')
A SLOEEYED SUFI (13 CENT) WHO SEZ
THE FIGURE IN OUR CARPET   SHALL I TELL?
Please! —Two pages later: I SUGGEST
THE BITS MY BOY THAT GRAB U BE COMPRESSED
INTO THE SORT OF 'GEM' U DO SO WELL
Hm . . .

★

As when the scribe of some ornate
Bismillah ("in the name of Allah") sees
No doctrine bolder than calligraphy's

—Whose backward reader, left to right, will note
Ism (world of names, empty phenomena)
Within the broadly tendered palm of *ba*

(Initial meaning, here, God B knows what)
Placed beneath which a diacritical dot
Closes its fist on *that,* and there we are!—

My characters, this motley alphabet,
Engagingly evade the cul-de-sac
Of the Whole Point, dimensionless and black,

While, deep in bulging notebooks, drawn by it,
I skim lost heavens for that inky star.

The Last Lessons: 4

All twelve assembled. Nature once more in white,
A sheaf of poppies at Her earth-stained feet.

Gabr.   VALIANT GOD, FATHER, TWIN NATURAL STAR,
AND LORDS MY BROTHERS, CLEVER & INQUIRING MORTALS, STUDENTS
ALL:

MUCH IS WRIT AROUND OUR CLASSROOM'S BLACKBOARD WALLS,
    MUCH PERHAPS TOO EASILY ARRIVED AT.
SIN? A TOPIC HASTILY DROPT. BUT NOW THE SENIOR POET, IVIED
    WITH OLD ANGLICAN TRADITION, HAS BEGGD THIS FURTHER
    WORD ON IT.
AND SO! TAKE UP THE CHALK & WRITE THE NAME OF THE ONE SIN:
PAIN. PAIN GIVEN, PAIN RECEIVED.
PAIN YOU MUST UNDERSTAND IS THE ONLY CHILD OF TIME &
    FEELING.
WITHOUT THESE PARENTS, THESE OEDIPAL TENSIONS,
PAIN (SORROW, HUNGER, FEAR) WOULD HOLD NO SWAY.

JM.   But, Lord, then *you* are linked to pain through Time
      Which is your magic, just as ours is Feeling—
Gabr.   BLACK MAGICS BOTH, YOUNG SCRIBE, THEY ARE BANISHT FROM OUR
    HEAVEN. BANISHT ALAS TO EARTH.
NOW, KEEPING OUR CLASS SWEPT OF COBWEBBY DETAIL, A FINAL
    BLOOM OF CHALK AS WE DISCUSS THE UNWRITTEN SIN:
MAN'S THEFT OF GOD'S MATERIALS. WHO WILL BRING HIM TO
    COURT?
MM.   LORD, MAY I BE MAN'S PORTIA?
Gabr.   SPEAK, WEEDRESS, AND EXPLAIN:
HOW IS IT THAT MAN PLAYS SO FREELY WITH OUR ATOMS,
SO CARELESSLY PLUNGES INTO THE WATCHWORKS OF OUR GENETIC
    CELL?

MM.   FATHER, MOTHER, BROTHER LORDS & FRIENDS,
WE COME, WE MORTALS, FROM AN AVID WEED
CALLED CURIOSITY. IN YOUR GARDEN, MAJESTY,
I HAVE SEEN & HEARD THE BUSY SECRETS BUZZING
LEAF TO LEAF: 'AHA, THAT'S HOW SHE DID IT!'
THESE FEED US, YOU FEED THEM. I THEREFORE CLAIM
THAT YOU WANT THESE SECRETS OUT. WITNESS OUR FAITHFUL
FAULTLESS GREEK, YOUR VERY OWN. NOW LORDS,
WHY? IS IT NOT THAT WE, MANKIND, MUST DO
IMMORTAL WORK? AND WHEN HEAVEN, LIKE A LOVELY
MINT-SCENTED FRESHENING SETTLES & EARTH BECOMES
PARADISE, MY LORDS, WILL NOT OUR RACE OF THIEVES

        HAVE EMERGED AS THE ELDERS IN A RACE OF GODS?
        DEFENCE RESTS.
Gabr.   FATHER? STAR? BROTHERS?

As if caught out, They smile at one another.
Nature lifts a poppy to Her cheek.
(Ah, we are all Her children, so to speak—
How touching when Maria called her Mother.)
NOT GUILTY. BUT, PERSUASIVE GARDENER,
LET US APPROACH THE VERGE &, SHELTERINGLY GLASSD,
TURN OUR ACCOMPLICE EYES UPON A MANMADE BLAST.
0 9 8 7 6 5 4 3 2 1

During the countdown we touch Earth, sink then
Beneath it. Mummied rivers dry as bone,
Tamped towns, lost species, in an earthenware
Terrine of suffocation, layer on layer.
The cup has stopped at the Board's extreme limit.
This 'test' is underground, larger than planned,
For an immense—
               The cup returns to "&".

NOTHING OF USE SURVIVES. LESSON 4 ON SIN & SANITY.
NEXT, MAKING SENSE OF OUR SEEMING CARELESSNESS, WILL BE AT 5
      A SOBERING JOURNEY INTO THE REMOTEST PAST,
THE ORIGIN OF PROMETHEAN LEGEND, WHEN ALAS THE VERDICT
      WAS: GUILTY
Here, without "exiting", the angel falls
Silent.

      SIRS? WERE YOU HARMED? No, Uni—were you?
(Dumb question.) Was there some sort of explosion?
MERCILESS FIRE! OUR FRIENDS REEMERGE
THRU CHOKING AIR
            I THINK JIMMY THE BLAST
WAS OVERDONE   GOD HELP THE ASIAN PLAINS
WE DID IT UNDER! First you took the down
Elevator— YES INTO EARTH A PURE

WHITE LIGHT, THE NEGATIVE OR 'EYE' OF BLACK
BURST ON US   The *bad* white, the metaphor-
Shattering light? AMORAL   YES MY DEARS
& AFTERWARDS, STEADILY THRU THE ASCENT, QM
GAVE GABRIEL SUCH A LOOK, OUR LESSON (PUFF!)
ENDED. MICHAEL SPOKE THE LAST WORDS, G
HAVING GONE OUT ON THE EXIT OF QUEEN MUM.
AS GEORGE SAYS, SHE ABHORS THAT VACUUM
The pace throughout was sluggish—a reluctance
In us? ENFANTS WE FANCY GABRIEL
DID NOT HAVE TOTAL CLEARANCE FOR HIS BANG
AS IF, OF 2 MINDS, HE THEN THOUGHT: O, HELL!
DJ IN PAIN?
                    Not really, just a twinge—
Pain, after all, was part of today's lesson.
(But in the night his jaw will throb and swell,
And by tomorrow afternoon Maria's
Closing couplet has become prophetic:)
MAMAN KNOWS BETTER. TIME NO DOUBT
AN AWFUL TRUTH & TOOTH ALIKE WERE OUT!

★

The Last Lessons: 5

Gabr.   BROTHERS, ARE YOU WITH ME? DO YOU GO ALONG ON THIS LESSON?
OUR FATHER AND HIS HEAVENLY TWIN DO NOT. IT IS A PAINFUL
    MEMORY, A SHALL WE SAY LOST TOOTH?
DJ nods, rubs his aching, mending jaw.
Mich.   WE COME.
*The schoolroom darkens. This is the purely 'told'
Lesson. Nothing will move except the mind;
Nothing, except Gabriel's voice, unfold
In black immediacy, safe and sound.*

Gabr.   PUPILS, AS WE BOARD THE LUMBERING BLACK WAGON & MAKE OUR
    WAY THRU EONS OF A BLASTED TRACK,

LET US REVIEW THAT HISTORY. IN THE GALACTIC COUNCILS THE
    CHARTER WAS GIVEN:
'DOWN INTO YOUR COOLING UNIVERSE WITH ITS SINGLE HABITABLE
    STAR, BROTHER, GO. IT IS YOURS.
TAKE WHAT & WHOM YOU NEED. AND THIS COMPACT:
MY UNIVERSE IS AS ONE WITH ALL. NOTHING IN IT WILL BE ENEMY
    TO OUR REALMS.'
THEN ONLY THE DISTANT CRY OF LIGHT: 'FATHER, COME!'

IN HIS JOY, HIS CRAFTSMAN'S EAGERNESS TO BEGIN, OUR FATHER
    TOOK FRICTION INTO HIS HANDS
AND FROM A STARRY MIX GROUND UP A PASTE OF LIVING MATTER,
    MUCH AS THE BAKER KNEADS HIS DOUGH.
YEAST OF LIFE! DOOR FLUNG OPEN INTO THE FURNACE, OUT CAME
    A LOAF WE'VE ET ON SINCE.
THE HEAT OF THAT DOUGH, THE CONTRARY RUB OF THE FRICTION?
WHERE DID THE FOREIGN GERM COME IN? OR WAS THE GERM IN THE
    SAND WHICH SPRINKLED THE SEALS OF THE COMPACT?

THE GREAT GREEN CANVASES! THE BAKER TURND PAINTER, SCULPTOR!
    O THE BLISS OF ONE'S OWN WORLD, THE GODLINESS OF
    CREATION!
(WATCH! HERE'S A BUMP FROM AN EARLY MOUNTAIN CHAIN TURND
    PEBBLE.)

NOW THE FIRST CREATURE. WE HAVE NOT MENTIOND HIM BEFORE.
YES, THE FIRST: A WINGED MAN. HE ROSE UP.

DJ.   *Atlantis* was first. The centaurs—

JM.   It would seem
This is the creature of the Chinese plain.
Haven't we been wondering about him?

Gabr.   MY BROTHERS, WE TOO HAVE SO MANY TIMES WONDERD! 'GABRIEL,
    DID YOU KNOW? MICHAEL, DID YOU SEE A . . . SPARK? A
    GLANCE? A WHAT IN THAT CREATURE'S EYE?
    RAPHAEL, YOU? PERCEPTIVE EMMANUEL, DID YOU SUSPECT THAT WE
    HAD WITNESSED OUR FATHER'S CAIN-LIKE ERROR?'

HE FLOURISHT.

GOD WAS ODDLY OF TWO ASPECTS: PROUD, DOUBTFUL. HE HID HIS
   THOUGHTS WITH FRESH ACTIVITY.
WE WERE SUMMOND TO ANOTHER GREEN SURFACE: 'I WILL MAKE
   HIM A FELLOW CREATURE.'
AND THIS TIME WE ALL STOOD BACK PLEASD: AN OPENEYED EAGER
   THING LOOKD UP AT US. WOBBLED IN A COLTISH BOW.

NOTHING 'PASSD'. TIME STOOD STILL IN THE CLOCKWORK OF THEIR
   GENES.
THE WINGED ONE WAS EVER AT WORK, EVER WITH SOMETHING
   TUCKD HASTILY OUT OF SIGHT.
WE FOUR FLANKING OUR FATHER CAME TO HIS CENTRAL CITY, A
   VAST OBSIDIAN PILE GLEAMING ON THE PLAIN RUTTED BY HIS
   MACHINES.
'CHILD, FOR I STILL CALL YOU THAT, WHAT IS IN YOUR MIND?
   LOOK INTO MY EYES!'
WAS OUR FATHER EASILY DECEIVD? ISN'T THE YOUNG PARENT
   ALWAYS . . . FATUOUS?
TO US THEN, 'COME.' AND THAT WAS OUR LAST VISIT TO THIS SAD
   MISTAKEN CHANGELING CHILD.

WE NEVER TIRED OF THE OTHER,
AND WITH HIM ONE DAY LOOKD UP . . . YES, FROM THIS SPOT, YOU
   SEE IT IS A RISE . . .
Cup pausing at the Board's edge now recoils.
GREAT BLINDING LIGHT!
OUR FATHER SUMMOND HIS POWERS, THREW UP A SHIELD OF
   POSITIVE MATTER (THE BUDDHA'S HIMALAYAS) & WE FROM
   WHERE WE COWERD, UP UP IN GOD'S WAKE RISING
AT LAST LOOKD DOWN ON HALF OUR MASTER'S WORK FLATTEND,
   BLACK.
'IT IS WELL, I COULD NOT HAVE ENDED HIM MYSELF.'

THE OTHER CREATURE PROSPERD: 'GOD, FATHER, COME SEE WHAT I
   HAVE FASHIOND!'
WE LOOKD INTO THOSE SELFSAME RED EYES. STRAIGHTEND.
AND OUR FATHER SAID: I KNOW WHAT IS PAIN

DJ. Red eyes? Whose?

JM. The wingèd man. The Cain—
Now as the centaurs' messenger, into their green
Arcadia (and our own cells) born again . . .

Gabr. THE REST? LET US REST. STAND HERE, NOT TOO FAR FROM OUR
    WAGON, & CONSIDER THESE RUIND PROSPECTS, THESE PAINFUL
    MEMORIES
A drawn-out sigh escapes the darkened angel.
BROTHER GENII, IT IS AN EASY IMAGE TO SPEAK OF GOD'S MATTER,
    ANTIGOD'S ANTIMATTER.
THAT IS THE ODD THING ABOUT LANGUAGE. THE PARTICULAR FAILS
    TO EXPLAIN ITS OWN WORKINGS.
(This lesson, then, in lieu of a week's lecture
On the fine points of atom- or cell-structure?)
WE MUST ASSUME OUR FATHER WAS GIVEN A LIMITED CHARTER.
FOR THERE IS, SIMPLY, NO 'QUARREL' BETWEEN LIGHT & SHADOW,
    SO LONG AS SUBSTANCE (PSYCHE OF MATTER) STANDS
BETWEEN THEM. NOW BACK
INTO THE WAGON. WE'VE LAID OUR WREATH ON THIS TOMB.
1 2 3 4 5 6
The schoolroom brightens as the cup ascends
To Intuition, and the lesson ends:

TOMORROW (HOW REFRESHING HERE OUT OF THE SULPHUR MISTS)
    WE WILL TALK OF THE WAY GOD SPEAKS,
HE TO US, WE TO YOU,
AND HOW THIS TOO HELPS HOLD IT BACK.
The Brothers go.

So *that's* it. What a tale . . .
DJ: But why blame God? Didn't the angels
Make the wingèd man in their own image?
JM: If so, then God accepted him.
What struck me was how fondly Gabriel
Spoke of the creature from Atlantis—whom
Michael had mocked for its shy hanging head
And great blank eyes. DAVE JIMMY AS U'VE GUESSED

IT COMES DOWN TO THE NATURE OF THE ATOM:
'FIRSTBORN WAS CHAOS' THE BLACK VOLATILE HALF
Bat wings unfurled against the light— INDEED.
THEN MINUTES ONLY AFTER THE BIG BANG
CAME THE FIRST NUCLEI OF HELIUM
Matter's white half? DEPENDABLE, (M) 4 FOOTED
Like Uni!
          SIRS? It's nothing, Uni. (Wistfully
Nuzzles Robert and trots out.)
                   I THINK
THE 2 ASSESSMENTS OF A CREATURE LACKING
SHAPING HANDS MY BOY REFLECT THE 2
KINDS OF CRITIC, I.E. GABRIEL WHO
CONSIDERS THE DOER'S MANNER, & MICH WHO LOOKING
TOWARD THE THING DONE IMAGINES ITS RECEPTION

So here we are, back at a pedigree—
Uni's or Mirabell's—that can be traced
To motes and gases, outermost thin paste
Of life, and innermost dichotomy
RESOLVED BY SUBSTANCE, EVEN BY THE STUFF
OF OUR 'CREATION' WHICH (EXAMPLE) BRINGS
WM CARLOS WM'S THOUGHTFUL THINGS
& THE COLD VIRGIN VERB OF MALLARME
TOGETHER, & RELIABLY ENOUGH
HOLDS BACK THE NOTHING WE HAVE FOUND TO SAY
ONLY IN OUR WORST MOMENTS. THIS ESTATE
WHERE WE ARE GUESTS (OR CAPTIVES?) WD HAVE BEEN
GHOSTLY & UNENDURABLE WITHOUT
THE FRIENDLY WHINNY FROM THE PADDOCK GATE
OR CRY OF THE HERALDIC BIRD THAT PREENS
ABOVE THE MOAT   But if it's all a fable
Involving, oh, the stable and unstable
Particles, mustn't we at last wipe clean
The blackboard of these creatures and their talk,
To render in a hieroglyph of chalk
The formulas they stood for? U MY BOY
ARE THE SCRIBE   YET WHY? WHY MAKE A JOYLESS THING

OF IT THRU SUCH REDUCTIVE REASONING?
ONCE HAVING TURNED A FLITTING SHAPE OF BLACK
TO MIRABELL, WD YOU MAKE TIME FLOW BACK?
SUBTRACT FROM HIS OBSESSION WITH 14
THE SHINING/DIMMING PHASES OF OUR QUEEN?
CONDEMN POOR UNI TO THE CYCLOTRON
AFTER THE GREENS U'VE LET HIM GALLOP ON?
Dear Wystan, thank you for reminding me
The rock I'm chained to is a cloud; I'm free.

DJ: How touching Gabriel was . . . AH YES
HE IS WISDOM SADLY ARRIVED AT, PROUDLY KEPT:
NUCLEAR COMMANDER OF THE GREENHOUSE,
HIS STOCKPILE UNDER LOCK, HIS POWDER DRY
After the illustration. O WELL   WHY
TELL THE HISTORY OF A BOMB? ENACT IT!
Yesterday's explosion wasn't by
Any chance an *actual* one? INDEED:
UNDERGROUND SIBERIA   (And we'll read
In tonight's *Herald* of just such a test
Picked up by seismographs throughout the West.)

Maria hasn't spoken. NO ENFANTS
TOMORROW A LONG SILENCE WILL BE BROKEN

★

The Last Lessons: 6

All present. Schoolroom tidied overnight.
Gabr. MAY I SPEAK FOR YOU, FATHER?
Intuiting his answer in the Light.
THANK YOU.
OUR FATHER LAST APPEARD TO ONE OF HIS CREATURES WITH THE
    WORDS: 'LOOK IN MY EYES'
DJ. Lord, am I crazy? I thought Nature said
Her eyes and God's, both, looked into the ape's.

Gabr.   LOYAL HAND, GOD LOOKD ONCE AT EACH OF HIS CREATURES, HE
         SPEAKS TO THEM STILL (AND MAY TO YOU TWO AT 10)
     BUT NO LONGER APPEARS BEFORE THEM. HIS TRUST? WENT OUT OF
         HIM.
     NOT THAT HIS LAST LOVE, MAN, PROVES UNWORTHY OF IT, NO
     BUT OUR FATHER HAS UNDERSTOOD THAT TO LIVE EVEN THE
         CAREFREE LIFE OF A MORTAL
     FORMS A SHIELD AROUND HIS CREATURE'S THOUGHT
     & ALWAYS IS POSSIBLE (RARE BUT AS OUR MUSICIAN SHOWD US,
         POSSIBLE)
     A BLACK BLANK SPACE BEHIND IT.
     THEREFORE SINCE THOSE WORDS & THAT APPEARANCE HE HAS SAID:
     'GO MICHAEL, PLAY GOD. WRITE ON A WALL. FORM A STARRY
         MESSAGE FOR THE BYZANTINE KING.
     TELL THROUGH YOUR MESSENGERS THIS INDIAN PRINCE, THAT
         HASSIDIC JEW, THIS TENTMAKER WHAT THEY NEED TO KNOW.'
     AND CONTENTING HIMSELF WITH THE TRIPLE SYSTEM OF THE SENSES,
         FROM MAN TO ELEMENTS TO HIS SONS, IN ORDER TO LEARN OF
         THE LIVING,
     OR ON RARE OCCASIONS PRESENT WHILE ONE OF OUR CHERISHD
         FIVE REPORTS HIS LIFE ('I DREW BREATH! O GOD, THE
         SWEETNESS!' & SO FORTH)
     GOD KEEPS IN TOUCH.

     YET, & WE UNDERSTAND, HE TOO IS WISTFUL OF LIFE.
     WE LOOK AT YOU. NO MATTER THE MANY FRUITLESS PURSUITS, THE
         FLAWD STARTS & VIOLENT ENDS,
     WE LOOK & OFTEN SIMPLY MARVEL AT THOSE SUDDEN UNEXPECTED
         FIREWORKS OF PLEASURE YOU TAKE IN YOUR LIVING. AND THEN
         FROM TIME TO TIME
     GOD WANTS A CHILD IN HIS PALM, A LIVE ONE.
     TO FEEL THE OLD CLAY, TO HEAR THAT HUMAN ELECTRIC BEAT.
     WE FIX UP A SYSTEM, MY BROTHERS & I, WHEREBY THIS IS DONE:
     SO THE SLEEPER'S DREAM, THE APPROACH THROUGH VISIONS, &
         MANY A CLEVER WAY TO BRING HIS DARLING WITHOUT
         TERROR,
     WITH SOMETHING OF THAT SURPRISING FRESHNESS INTO HIS
         PRESENCE.

463

YET NOT ALL CAN BE TRUSTED TO WITHSTAND THE MOMENT & BE
    RETURND UNCHANGED.
MANY A HAPLESS SECT SWARMS UP & FLICKERS OUT AFTER A LEADER'S
    BRIEF BRUSH WITH HIM.
MANY A SUBTLY, OFTEN COMICALLY MISREAD IDEA: 'HE IS ALL FIRE,
    O' OR 'HE SAYS, FREE FRANCE FOR MY SON THE KING.'
AND NOW AS MAN MULTIPLIES, GETS CLEVERER WITH HIS TOOLS,
    CONTRIVING NEARLY PERFECT SUBSTITUTES FOR GOD'S NATURAL
    POWERS,
GOD NEEDS MORE (& MORE COMPLEX) CONTACT WITH HIS CHILD,
    THAT EACH MAY KNOW THE OTHER'S GOOD WILL.
Fond amusement blazing from his eyes.
WE ARRANGE THESE. MADAME?

MM. LORDS,
    FROM THE FIRST I CALLED THEM ENFANTS. WHEN IN THE COURSE
    OF MY WORK I WAS GIVEN THEM TO STUDY ('THESE MIGHT DO
    FOR THE V WORK WE WANT. CHECK THEIR THOUGHTS, COME &
      REPORT')
    I GREW TO LOVE THESE TWO. DEAR ENFANTS, YES.
    FORGIVE YOUR OLD BLACK MAMMY.

JM. For what? Who *are* you?
DJ. God took you on His palm?
MM. YES LORDS, THERE IS AN INSTANCE OF THEIR WIT. I READ
    PALMS, DEAREST ONES. I GAVE YOU GIFTS: A LAMP? THOSE TEACUPS?
    SYMBOLIC & AS SUCH UNFAIR, FOR HAD YOU GUESSED
    ALL WD HAVE BEEN WASHED FROM YOUR HEARTS AS IN A DREAM.
    THE POINT WAS TO TRUST ONE ANOTHER, PREPARE OUR 'DESK'
    & THAT MAMAN BE NO LESS QUALIFIED IN YOUR EYES
    TO STAND BY AS A CLAY VESSEL FOR THE MIDNIGHT OIL
    THAN SHE TESTIFIED YOU WERE IN HERS TO SEE BY ITS LIGHT.
    (DJ: Make sense to you? JM: Not yet.)
    I MADE A BARGAIN WITH MY BROTHERS: 'LOOK,
    I LIKE THESE CHAPS & THEY ME. LET ME SEE THEM THROUGH
    THEIR SCHOOLING. LET THEM SEE ME BACK INTO THE WORLD.'

JM. More bargains? Ephraim's, Mirabell's—now yours?
MM. AH THOSE JM WERE BASEMENT BARGAINS. BUT EPHRAIM, YES,
    BROUGHT YOU TO ME, AS I HAVE YOU TO THESE MY LORDS.

THE COMMAND FOR YOUR TRILOGY WAS GIVEN, & MAMAN
GOT SAFELY OUT OF THE WAY OF HER CHILD'S FURIOUS WORK:
COULD SHE HAVE BORNE GIVING UP OUR DRINKS & COFFEES?
NO LONGER BEING, AS THRUOUT YR TESTING PERIOD WITH E,
'THE MUSE OF YOUR OFF-DAYS'?

DJ. That phrase, it's from your poem to Maria—

JM. She died the same week I began
Ephraim—four years ago next January.

MM. NO ACCIDENT. LIFE GROWS
LOGARITHMICALLY, LESS CAREFREE AS ONE IS
LESS MORTAL. CHILDREN: I AM OF THE FIVE.

> (Those are her words. An icy terror
> Flows through our veins—good Lord!
> Or is it the bereavement we most feel?
> It's now, Maman, *before* we break the mirror,
> We lose you? Was the person we adored,
> Her gaiety, her ordeal,
> Merely projected by some master reel?)

MM. AH COME ON! MY MISSION? CATCH A FISH.

JM. Maria, seriously, *please*—

MM. DOUCEMENT. NOW IS IT SO STARTLING JM, THAT YOU
SMALL BUT CLEVERLY GLINTING IN THE STREAM OF LETTERS
GOT POINTED OUT (NOTHING ESCAPES OUR MICHAEL): 'GET
ME HIM, SEE IF HIS MIND IS WITH US, HE MAY DO.'

RM. *A murmur as the schoolroom melts away.*
GREAT GODS & LITTLE FISHES

> (Love for Maria both suspends
> And quickens disbelief.
> Those thousand and one coffees came to warrant
> A certain tact. If Heaven took our friend's
> Voice and aspect, copied to the life,
> To clothe its naked current—
> Well, such tricks work *because* they are transparent.)

MM. LIPON, ENFANT,

465

I FOUND YOU NOT JUST CLEVER BUT FINNY WITH WIT
& RUSHING INTO THE HOUSE PULLED OFF MY WADERS CRYING
'I GOT HIM! YES HE'LL DO!' & THEY MY BROTHERS COMMANDED
'GO FIX YR FACE IN THAT MIRROR, WHILE WE COOK
OUR PISCES POET.'

JM. "Cooked" poetry? *This* mirror in the hall?
Your compact mirror at the café table?

(Beneath my incredulity
    All at once is flowing
Joy, the flash of the unbaited hook—
Yes, yes, it fits, it's right, it had to be!
Intuition weightless and ongoing
    Like stanzas in a book
Or golden scales in the melodic brook—)

O IMAGES, DEAR ENFANT, IMAGES . . .
NEVER LET THOSE SCALES DROP FROM YOUR EYES

Making Song of It

We'd hoped that Wystan and George were of the Five
For the poem's sake—a feather in its cap.
You, though, we loved (we thought) "just as you were"
And never dreamed of a promotion there.
DJ: Mind if I smoke? Are we alone?
YES   THEY BACKED OUT LIKE THE MATCHMAKER
DURING THE 'GET TO KNOW EACH OTHER' PHASE
But who—which one are you? I thought the Five
Had to be scientists, musicians— NO
NEVER MY THING. MINE'S THE PLATONIC WAY
You, all along, were *Plato?* BUT HOW DJ,
HOW, ANCIENT BUMPY TOOTHLESS NUMERO,
WD YOU HAVE TAKEN IN THE TRUTH? 'MEET PLATO, CHAPS
YOU KNEW HIM AS MARIA'? But the rays—

JM: The Five are indestructible.
DJ: And we—*we* were your life's work?
WELL, NO. THERE WERE (BLUSH) OTHERS IN MY DAY
I HAVE BEEN WHAT U MIGHT CALL A PROFESSIONAL SHOPPER.
IN ENGLAND: 'YES LORDS, SHE'S A STEADY CHILD.
LET THE FLIGHTY ONE GO' & EXIT EDWARD
That's how Elizabeth became Queen! INDEED
NO MALE ERRORS PLUS THE ODD JOB HERE
WHILE YOU 2 CHAPS SHAPED UP. MY PLATONIC ASPECT
A MUSLIN LETTING IN LIGHT & INSTRUCTIONS
& ENSURING THE (M) MOISTURE OF THE CHEESE.
WE 5 CAN'T LOLL ABOUT THE LAB U UNDERSTAND
WAITING FOR TALENT SLOTS GENES DENSITIES
NO, WE HAVE QUICK ANONYMOUS V WORK GIVEN US
TO KEEP OUR HAND IN, OUR POOR HUMAN HAND.

Human? You who call the Angels brother?
—Although the Five we met in Lesson 5
Spoke like slaves. AH MY OLD DRESSING GOWN
MAKES ME RELUCTANT TO PUT ON THE GLASS
SLIPPER BUT IN FACT YES, WE ARE GODS ALAS
Because you . . . suffer? BUT ARE LUCKIER THAN
FOR INSTANCE CHRIST: WE ARE SO OFTEN MAN.
THERE'S ALSO THE WHOLE TICKLISH ? OF CLASS
OR SENIORITY THAT OLFACTORY LOBE?
The nose—Plato—is eldest? YR MAMAN
IS MAMA N'S OWN CHILD THUS OF A RANK
NEAREST THE ANGELS. OTHERS OF THE 5
(HARD TO FIT 5 INTO 4 IN LESSON 5)
MUST DO A CERTAIN KOWTOWING I'M SPARED
More elitism? DJ THAT SYSTEM THRIVES,
I'M BORN WITH THE SILVER SPOON IN ALL MY LIVES:
'MY DAUGHTER WASH A DISH? YOU MUST BE MAD!'

JM: Well, there'll be servants in Bombay—
If that's your destination now, and not
The vegetable world. NEARLY THE SAME
SAYS RM Frankly, Maria, does all this

Go in the poem? WHY NOT? DOESN'T (SAYS WYSTAN)
THE BUTLER ALWAYS DO IT? The inside job . . .
PLUS ILLUSTRATION OF THE 'BEATRICE
MECHANISM' DJ: What? (JM reminds him
Of the little girl whom Dante scarcely knew
But loved on sight, forever.) NOW GUESS WHO!
SO DJ, HAND, THAT DAY I PATTED YOURS
& ASKED WHY WERE WE BORN, U PASSED THE TEST:
YR PLEASURE IN THE DAY IN ME IN LIFE
YR TOUCHING EAGER DEFENSE— 'BROTHERS, HE'LL DO!'
I didn't fall asleep? I DREW THE SHADE
WASTING NO TIME, TILL MY REPORT WAS MADE

But are you Plato *now*, in beard and toga?
NEVER! STAYING WHILE I CAN IN DRAG,
I LOVE IT! YOU SAID SOMETHING ELSE DJ
ON A DRIVE HOME: 'THE MEDITERRANEAN
MAKES SUCH HEAVY PROSE OF BEING MALE.'
NOW THESE ESCAPES INTO A FEMALE LIFE ARE VAST
REFRESHMENTS. WE (THE 5) ARE LARGELY CHILDLESS,
SO THAT A RICH & (MAY I SAY IT?) CLEVER
WOMAN'S LIFE IS PARTICULARLY DENSE
WITH THE JOY OF LIVING. A GOOD VAC, MY LAST
JM: Last? Time's that short—? CHILD, MY MOST RECENT.
U NO KNOW ZE INGLIS? ME MISTAKEN?
BOYS, THROW HIM BACK! BUT NOW LET'S COUNT TO 5
AS I BECOME YR OLD MAMAN AGAIN,
YR SOUL- & SCHOOL-MATE I 2 3 4 5
VOILA ADIEU
        There's so much more to settle!
DEAR TROUBADOUR IF U ARE NOT YET GLAD
MAKE SONG OF YOUR MISGIVINGS A ballade?

When x-rays of Giorgione's painted scene
(Controversy over which still brews)
Forcing its secret, made the green
Of boughs, the rose-red doublet, the whole view's

Light indrawn by thunderblacks-and-blues
Disclose the spectral moonbather
Pressed underneath, like petals of a ruse,
Was anyone prepared for it? U WERE

Or if at dusk a scroll in the vitrine
Of its own self, caked with taboos,
Began to give off an unearthly sheen
And then—no longer the papyrus whose
Demotic tatters one construes
But a shed skin of Thought's pure Lucifer—
Uncoil, encompass, utterly bemuse . . .
No one could be prepared for that. U WERE

Plato, python, frontal gems of keen
Outstreaming radiance that suavely woos,
Strictly recycles through long discipline
The lovers drawn to it by twos,
Their lives illumined, which they soon will lose—
You were Maria? Served us lunch in her
Salt garden? Wandered Athens in her shoes?
Why, *why* weren't we— ENFANTS U WERE

Maman— HUSH NOW & MIND YR P'S AND Q'S
But— IN MY DAY I FOOLED U? WATCH THE BLUR
CLEAR TO A NIGHT OF TWINKLING CLUES
Oh dear, we weren't prepared for this. Y O U WERE

★

SIRS? THEY SPOKE, MR ROBERT SAYS,
KINDLY OF MINE? (They? It will take a moment,
Full of Maria as we are, to bring
The Angels into focus.) Uni, they did;
But drew the line at your creature. OUR TALES TELL
THAT MERCY TEMPTED US TO REMAKE
A POOR THING WHO HAD LOST HIS LAND
You pitied him? So did we. THE CREATURE CREPT

INTO OUR MUTANT   INTO OUR MINDS
As into man's, yes, yes . . . THEY COME! THE LIGHT
—And Uni canters briskly out of sight.

The Last Lessons: 7

Gabr. OBLIVION, THAT WAS OUR FATHER'S JUDGMENT.
Ascending lesson by lesson, as before,
Our schoolroom gains the Heaven of that sense.
Today's Light is all tragic evidence
And Nature in Her grief, supremely fair.
COME BROTHERS, TWIN LORDS, TELL US OF HOW YOU OBEYD.

Raph. WHEN UPON MY SURFACE LIKE A HOT IRON A BLANK FLAT PRESSURE
    FLARED I RUSHED
& KNELT BY OUR FATHER. 'RAPHAEL, THEY ARE GONE.'
I KNEW THE CHERISHED FIRST DESIGN, THE LUCKLESS FRUIT OF AN
    IDEA PLANTED IN OUR FATHER'S MIND DURING THAT WAIT IN
    HIS GALACTIC HOME,
KNEW THE AGONY OF A WORK DESPOILED, THE COST OF DREAMS, 'A
    STOP TO DREAM'
FOR ALL HAD COME TO NOTHING.
'HELP ME FORGET. TAKE ON YOUR SECOND CHORE. BURY THEM.'
I SUMMONED MY FORCES, FOUGHT THIS SUCKING & THIS LACK. AND
    KNELT, TOO, AT HER SIDE:
'YES, HERE, A WREATH OF GREEN STRONGER THAN ANY BLACK,
TAKE IT, LAY IT ON THEIR BLASTED GRAVE.'
SETTING TO WORK WE SLOWLY FORCED THE EMPTINESS DOWN. WE
    FILLED ITS SPACE WITH A FERTILE PLAIN
AND THE LUCKLESS FIRSTBORN LAY UNDER THIS BLOOMING
    OBLIVION. SO IT CAME TO PASS,
THE END OF HIM WHO HELD A FATEFUL SPARK,
HIS END AND HIS LOSS TO OUR FATHER. BROTHER SEA?

Emm. NEXT I WAS CALLED.
'EMMANUEL, THIS MY SECOND CREATURE WILL END AS BADLY AS MY
    FIRST. HIS DESTRUCTION EMBITTERS ME. HELP ME FORGET.'

GABRIEL ROSE UP MIGHTILY, BURNING THE FALSE SKY.

THE WINDS AROSE AND THE WHIRLING GLOBE CAST IT ALL OFF, LIKE
    AN ANIMAL SHAKING ITSELF DRY.

MY TURN CAME. I DREW IN, DREW IN ALL THE FLOATING BLASTED
    MOLECULES OF HYDROGEN & OXYGEN, AND MY WATERS

SWEPT OVER THAT POOR CREATURE. I TOO THEN KNELT BY HER SIDE:

'YES, TAKE THESE SEEDS AND SCATTER THEM,

MAKE A FEW GREEN BUOYS TO MARK THE GRAVE'

AND THE ATLANTIC STILL DRIFTS WITH A SEA OF GRASS KNIT OVER
    THAT SUCKING LOSS.

WE, LORD GOD, MY TWIN AND I, WE WITH YOUR STAR-TWIN,
    HEARD YOUR JUDGMENT OF THESE TWIN CREATURES.

WE OBEYED. AND STILL, GOD, HOLD IT BACK.

Gabr. IT?

MICHAEL, LIGHT.

The Angel smiles. Idea's jeunesse dorée
Dawns like an unhoped-for holiday.

I FEEL   FORGIVE ME, MAJESTY: I THINK

OUR MORTALS HAVE A HOST OF QUESTIONS OUR CLASSROOM HAS NOT
    CAST INTO OBLIVION,

& WHICH AS OUR SENIOR POET SAYS MUST BE CLEARED AWAY.

IT SEEMS THIS NEW BREED OF POETS, NOT LIKE DEAR HOMER'S KIND
    SQUATTING BY THE FARMER'S FIRE BREATHING WHATEVER
    SMOKE IN,

FEEDS ON FACT, TWIN. THEY WISH TO GREENLY CLOTHE IT THIS WAY
    OR THAT, ACCORDING TO THEIR OWN JUDGMENT.

SO MICHAEL, WE TWINS, LET US NEXT DISARM

THEIR DOUBT YET BRING THEM SAFE AWAY FROM HARM.

Exeunt.

    TOSSED US A NOD ENFANTS & FILED OUT

GK & RM TRAILING LIKE REPORTERS.

WYSTAN & I STILL IN THE JURY BOX

We've thought of several questions. Maman, please,

About your cobalt rays? And Socrates?

I THINK THAT STICKLER GABRIEL HIMSELF

MEANS TO EXPLAIN. MY ALAS PERSONAL LIFE

IS BOUND UP IN THESE ANSWERS. LATER IF
GABR HAS WIPED THE BLACKBOARD CARELESSLY
WE'LL TRY TO TIDY UP THOSE TRAILING SCRAWLS,
HASTILY CROSSED T'S, STARLIKE DOTS OF EYES.
LET 8 PASS, THEN BEFORE MY 'COMING OUT'
FETE AT 9 WE CHAPS WILL HAVE A JAW.
THEN CLOUDS WILL PART & EVEN MAMAN NOT BE
ALLOWED TO WATCH. U TWO WILL HEAR OR SEE
See . . . *It?* I MAY KNOW MORE TOMORROW: THOSE
LITTLE TETE A TETES WE DAUGHTERS HAVE
WITH NERVOUS MOTHERS ('NOW DEAR, IF SOME BOY
ETC') ON EVES OF THE MASKED BALL!
AU REVOIR CHERS ENFANTS
                              THE SIMPLE JOY
UPON HER FACE! MY DEARS U NOW KNOW ALL
Brilliant deception, Wystan. But her tone,
Never imitable, overnight has grown
Evanescent, as if soon to slip
Where sunlight trembles on the torrent's lip,
Lost in the nearness of the waterfall.
SO TRUE   THE MORTAL SOUL AT LAST WORN THIN
DISCARDED FROM A SPANKING NEW PINK SKIN!
YET NOTHING LOST: THESE ENERGIES SURVIVE
INTACT   Mohammed, though, was of the Five
And look at him—a swaggering dimestore djinn!
TIME RUNNING SHORT DEAR BOYS U DID NOT SEE
THE 'REAL' MOHAMMED BUT A PARODY
CONCEIVED BY GABR & GLEEFULLY REHEARSED
OF ATTITUDES EMBODIED BY HIS FAITHFUL.
MUSTN'T BE GREEDY   AFTER BEING SHOWN
PLATO 'IN DEPTH' LEAVE WELL ENOUGH ALONE

DARE I WHILE WE'RE AT IT VIOLATE
A SECRET OF THE CONFESSIONAL? MY OWN FIRST
TREMBLING QUESTION PUT TO PLATO WAS:
SOCRATES? Who *was* he? KNOWN THRUOUT ATHENS
FOR 'NATURAL WIT' BUT SEMILITERATE,
AS, OH, TO MILTON THE DROWNED LYCIDAS,

SO SOC TO PLATO   SPRINGBOARD OR SCAPEGOAT
OR MINE DETECTOR? HIS WHOLE LIFE & DOOM
FURNISHED THE GOLDEN SCRIBE WITH 'LIVING ROOM'
DJ (under his breath): A thankless task.
I CAN'T AGREE MY DEAR. THE SOCRATIC MASK
BECAME THE FACE OF THE GOAT GOD SILENUS
WINEBAG FLUTEINVENTING COUNTERPART
TO MICH/APOLLO IN THE DAWN OF ART
To be flayed by him like Marsyas? OF COURSE
BUT WHAT WERE SKINS TO SUCH A MYTHIC FORCE!

★

SIRS   THEY ALL COME! WE FIND THIS FIELD
VAST & RISING   AM I STILL YR UNICE?
THE GLOW   AH GOD —Retreating behind &,
For we have reached the Heaven of Command.

The Last Lessons: 8

Gabr.   ALL, ALL ASSEMBLED JUST AS NEEDS BE FOR SUCH A GRIND OF WORK.
GOD, STAR TWIN MOTHER, BROTHERS, MORTALS, SISTER,
Maria back at her old desk; no fuss—
Nothing having "happened" but to us.
LET US CLEAR THE BOARDS. FIRST, YOUNG POET, FIND A SEPARATE
        BLANK PAGE. PUT IT IN EASY REACH.
When I return *the blackboards are erased.*

WE BEGIN.
GOD CREATED HIS THIRD CHILD & GAVE THE COMMAND: LET IT
        SURVIVE AND LET THERE BE NO ACCIDENT,
FOR I CAN NO LONGER ABIDE SUCH PAIN. WE OBEYD.
THE SCRIBES, MUCH AS GOD, NOW COMMAND: OUR V WORK, LET IT
        SURVIVE. LET NO ACCIDENT PAIN IT, OR ITS READER TO
        DISBELIEF.
AND WE OBEY. WE YOUR FAITHFUL ELEMENTS, YOUR TEACHERS,
        YOUR SENSES, NOW TRY

473

    IN THIS ULTIMATE COMMANDING MOMENT TO HELP YOU MAKE
        SENSE OF 'IT'.
    NOW SCRIBE, FOR ONE OF THOSE BELOVED DESIGNS SO INDULGED IN
        BY OUR ESTEEMD (& HIDDEN) HAND.
    A stir—will Yeats say something? All look round
    As from DJ's hand comes a muffled sound:

WBY.   MY LORDS, SO IT CAME TO ME IN AN AGE
        WHEN CHARTS AND FORMULAS WERE ALL THE RAGE.
        WAS I THEN WRONG, WITH DNA UNKNOWN,
        TO BUILD MY WINDING STAIR OF MOONSTRUCK STONE?
Nat.   CALM, PROUD POET, WE SHALL SEE
        HOW GREAT OR SMALL THIS MYSTERY.

Gabr.   YOUNG SCRIBE, NOW ON THE UPPER HALF OF YOUR VERTICAL PAGE
        DRAW A TALL X.
    Puzzled, I do so. *Meanwhile Gabriel draws,*
    White on black, the same. A pregnant pause.
    THE SYMBOL FOR ENIGMA. OUR 'IT', DOES IT
        NOT ALSO SUGGEST THE ORIENTAL
        CHARACTER FOR MAN?

    MAN FLOATING, ARMS HELPLESSLY RAISED, HERE
        HE IS: GOD'S IDEA, WINGLESS, PRONE.
    LET US THEREFORE PUT HIM UPRIGHT. SCRIBE, MAKE HIM STAND ON
        EARTH.
    Beneath our "man" a convex line is drawn
    On page *and blackboard.* In a work this long,
    Madness to imagine one could do
    Without the apt ideogram or two.
    AH, HOMO SAPIENS, THE ARMS SEARCHING FOR?
Mich.   WHY TWIN, ME, LIGHT!
    DEAR RAPHAEL, YOU SUPPORT HIM, SEE, HE
        STRETCHES TOWARD REASON & LIGHT.
Raph.   AND MICHAEL, MY SUPPORT IS ALSO A FORM OF RESISTANCE.
Mich.   TRUE.
    LAZY LAPPING EMMANUEL, YOU?
Emm.   I'LL FROM MY TIMELESS SHORE SCOOP SAND
    (FOR SAND READ: ANY SURFACE FUEL

LIKE WIND OR WAVE OR SUN) TO FILL
THOSE TWO ARMS REACHING UPWARD, AND?
HE GOES FROM X TO MAN TO HOURGLASS
AND TIME ITSELF. ALL HISTORY, YES,
IN 4 QUICK STROKES OF THE SCRIBE'S HAND!
Indeed the sticklike figure, arms to feet,
Appears: a touch simplistic, but complete.
Plus a surprise resemblance—though in Yeats
The double cone, if I recall, gyrates.

Gabr. YET HE CASTS A SHADOW. DARE WE DRAW THAT, YOUNG SCRIBE?
        YES, DO:
THE DOWNWARD ENIGMA! THE X AGAIN & THE
        SAND, AND SEE
TIME'S MAN BECOME TIME AGAINST MAN:
SAND RUNNING UP, DEEP FUELS TAPPD, MAN
        STRADDLING HEAVEN, HEAVEN RECEIVING
        TIME
WHICH RUNNING OUT THROUGH A MINOAN WAIST
STOPS HERE WHERE WE ARE:
WE WHO (M) LIVING IN THIS RISING DUNE HOLD
        IT BACK, HOLD BACK A RESERVOIR OF
        SPENT TIME,
FEEL AT OUR FEET & LIKEN TO ATOMIC WASTE
        THIS WASTE, THIS UPWARD VOLATILE
        FORCE,
AND KNOW THE TWO MINDS OF MATTER.

POET, YOU WISELY MADE US STAND ON RISING GROUND, FOR
        BENEATH US, MORTALS, SHADES AND GODS, IS THE CAPPD
        VOLCANO.
'IT': CHILD'S PLAY? OR A DEADLY GAME
Fire fighting itself—fire its own screen—
Fades on a yearning whisper to our **Queen:**
'LEAVE THE DOOR OPEN, MOTHER   WE CANNOT SLEEP IN SUCH
        DARK'
Quoting whom? The child he'd never been
When the old schoolroom was a nursery still?

> *Her face is radiant, unreadable.*
> *Gabriel's done. He motions to his Twin.*

Mich.   BROTHER, THEY KNEW.
     THIS ENIGMA, THIS IT, THIS EVENLY BALANCED X, THIS ANTIMATTER
        & ITS MONITOR GOD
     MATCHING WITS WITH HIS RIVAL TO SEIZE THE DAY AND MAKE OF
        US A CIPHER NIGHT, AN O.
     THEY, EACH MAN, EACH GENERATION OF MEN, KNEW, HAVE
        ALWAYS KNOWN
     AND FOUGHT BACK WITH THEIR OLD RELIGIONS' CLASPED HANDS
        (OR FINGERS CROSSED).
     THEY KNEW. NOW, NOW HOWEVER
     ACCIDENTS HAVE BEGUN. LIKE THE FIRST FAINT TWIRLS OF SMOKE
        WE SEE ALL THE OLD SIGNALS:
     CLOUDY AIR, A SWARMING AS IF IN FRANTIC HASTE AGAINST THE
        GREAT THINNING TO COME,
     THOSE WHIFFS OF THE MONITOR'S BREATH, THE SHADOW WHICH
        TRAILED OUR FATHER FROM THE HALLS OF HIS BROTHERS,
     THE JUDAS, THE CAIN, THE GREAT OPPOSING FORCE TO MATTER
        ITSELF,
     THE CHALLENGE TO THE MAGICIAN'S ACT, THE RAGE TO PROVE IT
        WAS, IS, ALL DONE BY MIRRORS.
     NOW WE KNOW HIM: IT. YET NOT OUR ENEMY, NOT AS EASY AS
        THAT.
     IN MAN'S LIFE IT IS THE DULLWITTED, THE MOB, THE IDIOT IN
        POWER, THE PURELY BLANK OF MIND.
     THESE HAVE HEARD HIS WHISPER, WE BY NECESSITY HAVING FILLED
        A BILLION WOMBS WITH WHAT WE HAD AT HAND.
     THE MONITOR IS THE REFLEXION, THE UNDOER TO DOING.
     WE LEAP ABOUT MAKING NEW DEVICES, PUTTING NATURE'S WAX TO
        THE LEAKY CAP, HOLDING HIM BACK
     WHILE KEEPING AN EYE ON MAN, GOD'S DARLING CHILD
     WHO WANTS, ALL CHILDREN WANT, TO IMITATE THE FATHER.
     NOW POETS, PESKY QUESTIONERS, COMMAND!

The Question Period

Out comes the list we nearly didn't make.
The more we thought, the more (THEY KNEW) we knew
Each answer in our bones. Still, best go through
The motions for our glorious teachers' sake.

Has it developed from experience,
This infraradiant, uncanny knowing?
Does it belong to Gabriel's darkroom, glowing
Far from Michael's light-meter and lens?

See how the knowing mind defeats itself:
We could have asked them to hold forth upon
Lofty enigmas like the Pantheon.
Instead we're held by remnants on a shelf

At *our* eye level. Well, one more chance missed
—Or one last revelation to resist.

DJ.   It's probably trivial, but could we take up
          Last summer's question of the UFO's?
Gabr. THEY ARE OURS. NOT 'SAUCERS', LIGHT DISCS WHICH HAVE AN
          INWARD PULL, INSUBSTANTIAL:
       MICHAEL'S TEASPOONS TESTING THE SOUPY ATMOSPHERE.

JM.   I can't help wondering why Nature chose
         The moon—considering its atomic make-up?
Gabr. THREE OF HER FOUR WERE WIPED OUT. THIS ONE ACCUMULATING
          ALL THAT PRECIOUS WASTE
       GREW LARGE ENOUGH TO TILT & SWAY THE EARTH.
Nat.   CHILDREN, I AM MOST FOND OF TIDES. LET ME HAVE ONE JEWEL. I
          HAVE EARNED IT.
JM.   Maria, I remember now, had four
         Stars from the beginning in her hair.
MM.   ONE OF THOSE AMUSING 'FILLE ET MÈRE'
       MATCHED OUTFITS HIGH & LOW ALIKE ONCE WORE

DJ.   Has God no other name? Biology seems
     So sort of—

WHA.   HUSH MY BOY   (IN PRIVACY
          I'VE HEARD THEM SPEAK OF 'ABBA'   SOUNDS TO ME
          LIKE ONE OF JM'S FAVORITE RHYME SCHEMES)

DJ.   A question Mirabell failed to clear up:
     With all your lightning methods to choose from
     Why this relatively cumbersome
     Apparatus of the Board and cup?

Mich.   IT IS A LONG AMAZING & UNPRECEDENTED WAY FROM YOU TO US.
     WE TRIED DREAMS. THEY CAME TO JM LIKE DOORBELLS, EXPECTATION
        BUT NO GUEST.
     WE TRIED 'INSPIRATION'. IT WAS MUFFLED BY SCREECHING TIRES,
        KISSES AND DRUNKEN SONG.
     SO SANDOVER: PARCHED OBLONG FIELD, 2 OLD ZEN MONKS (DJ &
        WBY) RAKING DESIGN AFTER DESIGN, STRUGGLING FOR THE
        SENSE OF IT
     WHILE THE ABBOT-SCRIBE SQUINTING MADE OUT WAVES, PEAKS,
        DRAGONS, RAINCLOUDS, EAVES OF GLASS. NEXT?

JM.   The old one I keep asking, about scale:
     Microscopic particles on one hand,
     And on the other, Majesties, your Grand
     Design outspiraling past all detail—;

     When we suppose that history's great worm
     Turns and turns as it does because of twin
     Forces balanced and alert within
     Any least atom, are we getting warm?

Gabr.   O FATHER, TWIN STAR, BROTHERS, SISTER, HEAR THEM: THEY HAVE
        MADE SENSE OF IT.
     DID NOT OUR DEAR ONE REPORT 'AND WHAT A FISH!' (YOU, GOOD
        YEATS, WERE THE ONE THAT GOT AWAY)
     NOW MORE ?S

DJ. We need to know, how did Maria come
Through unscathed? What helped her to survive?

JM. Haven't you understood—she's of the Five?

DJ. Are they more powerful than radium?

Gabr. COME, SISTER & SCIENTIST, SPEAK.

MM. ENFANTS, NO MOTHER HIGH OR LOW ENJOYS
DULLING HER DARLINGS WITH 'THE FACTS OF LIFE'.
STORKS! SANTA! COME PLAY FATHER, GEORGIE LUV,
YOU KNOW ABOUT RADIATION. TELL OUR BOYS.

GK. DAVE, JIMMY, NO   NOT MARIA. I ALONE
SUFFERED THE MERCIFULLY LIMITED
'SILENCING'. THAT PART OF ME WENT DEAD
TO HEAVEN'S ALL-REVEALING ORGANON.

JM. Your high connections spared you—

GK.   MUCH. UNFIT
FOR MAN THUS FAR, MY GENETIC V WORK STAYS
HERE IN THIS LAB: TOP SECRET   & THE RAYS
HAVE STILLED MY LONGING TO GET ON WITH IT.

MM. I KNEW HOW I WOULD 'DIE'   SO DID GK   WE BOTH
WERE GIVEN MEANS TO PUT OUR SOULS BEYOND
THE RAYS. AS WITH OLD CLOTHES OF WHICH ONE'S FOND
ONE DOESN'T SIMPLY LEAVE THEM TO THE MOTH.

GK. YOUR GRIEF & HORROR OF THE RAYS (ALTHO
WE ESCAPED) REMAINS WITH YOU TO FEEL
FOR ALL CREATION: 'POSO AKOMA' THE REAL
MOTTO OF YR POEM   MAKE IT GLOW!

JM. When Dante entered the Bureaucracy
—You know, I fancy, why I'm asking this—
Was it allowed him by the Grand Design
Ever again to look on Beatrice?

MM. MY JEUNE FILLE EN FLEURS EFFECT? MAIS OUI

DJ. You *are* a Muse!

MM.   ENFANT I AM ALL NINE

A loving gesture bids Maria stand.
The hitherto elusive family
Likeness is pronounced. More than can be
Easily contained streams from our Hand.

MM. NOW, NOW. YET GOD IS PLEASED BY HAPPY TEARS.
HIS STAR TWIN (YES MAJESTY, I MUST SAY IT)
BRIDLES WITH PRIDE. WE NEXT DON GLAD ATTIRE

Gabr. WAIT, ARE THEY STILL COMMANDING ANSWERS?

JM. (Who has a final question but no words
To utter it.) That's all. We thank you, Lords.

Gabr. SENIOR POET?

WHA. A NEW LIBRETTO HAS BEEN SET
BY OUR COMPOSER. FOR TOMORROW'S FETE
WE'LL SEE MME MARIA EVER DROLL
CREATE FOR US HER LATEST TROUSER ROLE.

Nat. POET, MY BLAKE WOULD NEVER STOOP SO LOW
AS TO MAKE SPORT OF HEAVEN, PO PO PO!

WHA. DRAT. BUT ENOUGH. GODS' & POETS' DEMANDS
ARE MET. NOW WHO COMMANDS
BUT WISE IF WEARY GABRIEL
RISING UP TO STRIKE THE BELL
WHICH TELLS US WE HAVE DONE
OUR SCHOOLWORK. *A last bell rings.* NOW FOR FUN!
Exeunt God, Nature, and the Brothers.

Wystan goes on. TOMORROW'S INVITATIONS
ADDRESSED I FANCY TO OCCUPANT   G HAS WHEEDLED
QM TO LET THE OLD RETAINERS IN:
EPHRAIM, MIRABELL, & POOR FRANTIC UNICE
(QM: HE BOTTOM? ME TITANIA?)
And Yeats—will he emerge at last? WB?

The cup reluctantly shuffles forward. WELL
IF THERE'S TIME I MIGHT COME OUT WITH A STANZA
Ah, we'd be thrilled. YOU WOULD? I OFTEN FEAR
I LEFT IT ALL BACK IN BYZANTIUM.
From your present viewpoint, Mr Yeats,
Was our instruction of a piece with yours?
DO ME A FAVOR? DJ, LET ME SHAKE
THE OTHER HAND. YOU WERE NEARLY AS GOOD AS A WIFE
DJ puts both hands on the cup; it "shakes".

NOW CHAPS   Maman? I LOVE U ONE & ALL
& MEAN TO EXERCISE MY ELDER RIGHT:
CLIMB DOWN THE LADDER & ELOPE TO VENICE
With us at month's end? DO U MIND? Mind? We?
KNOWING U BOYS (AS ONE OF THEM, EH?) I'LL
TAKE CARE THE OTHERS DON'T CRAMP YR (M) STYLE
The others? A TOUR GROUP SIGNED UP   U'LL SEE

A FINAL CHANCE MY DEARS TO FEAST OUR SENSES
ON WHAT IF ANYTHING MAY YET REMAIN
OF AN EARTHLY PARADISE QUITE LOST TO GAIN,
B4 I SINK IT! GOD, WHAT AUDIENCES!
At La Fenice? But its gilt and green
Amid which the *Rake* sparkled, that first night!
(The phrase Maman just used, "my elder right",
Was Mother Goose, no? in the brothel scene.)
All of us present cheering long and loud
While you and Chester and Stravinsky bowed!
THAT MY BOY WAS A FETE! A PEAK AGLISTER
IN THOSE GIDDY ALPS OF LIFE IN LOVE WITH CHESTER

VENEZIAAA A A!
ME WOBERT'LL STRUM GUITAR
& MUSCLE BOY WILL ROW
AS OFF WE GO
DOWN THE DREARY GREEN CANALS IN A CITY WHERE THE GLOW
HAS MUCH TO DO (GEORGIE, TOGETHER HERE)
WITH H 2 O !

Robert, a gondola serenade? INDEEDY
GIVES NEW MEANING TO 'AU RESERVOIR'?
MUCH SYNCOPATION IN TOMORROW'S SCORE
CAN'T LOITER   BYE
                O SIRS! Hello there, Uni.
You'll join the celebration? YES! Excited?
MR ROBERT'S MAKING ME A BOW!!!
The cup cavorts a bit, then wistfully:
WE TOO HAD FETES   O SO LONG AGO

—Leaving the schoolroom empty. Never to be
Realized again with such fidelity?
The big old globe, each mooned-over pastel
Nation in place and river legible;
Grain of each desk-top; the minute sky-grid
Sliding across an inkwell's cut-glass lid;
Chintz roses bleached and split; chalk mote arrested
In mid-descent by sun; the horseshoe rusted
To scabby lace, nailed between sepia 'School
Of Athens' and Ignoto's 'The Pure Fool';
Moot intercourse of light and shade above
Our heads, familiar shapes we've learned to love
Emerging this last time from the cracked ceiling
As if they too shared the unspoken feeling
That, once we've gone, nobody else will thumb
The pages of our old Curriculum.
The manor is condemned. One doesn't dare
Say so flatly, but it's in the air.
The fine italic hands that have to date
Etched the unseen we blankly contemplate
Must now withdraw, and stoic Roman steel
Rim spectacles put on for the ordeal.
They work, though, like a charm. Look there! Beyond
The herringbone brick walks, the paddock pond,
Vistas are running wild already—who's
About to guess at their eventual use?
Where will these fat volumes stamped with gilt
Be stored? What can the carpet, that outspelt

Wonders in its time, mean to those straight A
Students—anachronism or child's play?—
Who will have paced the premises and thought:
"Imagine ever needing to be taught!"
(Which again leads me to that question I'm
Uncertain how to . . . Well. Another time.)

*

The big day. Nothing asked of us, a hasty
Bouquet set on the table just in case,
We sit down. SIRS! All dressed up, Uni? YES!
I AM TO LEAVE MY POST & LEAD
IN A TREMENDOUS TROOP OF MY OWN!
O ME, UNICE! & SUCH AN ASSEMBLY
ALL THE 00'S & THE GREAT ONES   SIRS
OUR FIELD! YOUR WALLS OUTFLATTEN TO CLAY
& NOW THEY ARRIVE   ALL ON A RAINBOW
OUR FRIENDS   OUR LORDS! AND I UNICE
WILL BEAR MADAME IN ON MY OWN BACK!

The Last Lessons: 9

Atlantan troop and the *Lab*'s fluttering trillions,
Innumerable presences have filled
And beveled to extreme quicksilver brilliance
The four horizons of our earthly field.
The setting nothing, but the scope revealed
As infinite, for *Light* is everywhere,
Awaits the words that clothe it—which we wield.
Here are the *Brothers*. *Nature* rises, fair
In dewdrop crown and robe of living gossamer.

Nat.   I AS BEFITS ASSUME A REGAL POSE
AND THUS ALL OF YOU DISPOSE:
MICHAEL, FROM YOUR BOREALIS
MAKE FOR US A SHINING PALACE!

ON THIS CLAY GROUND, EMMANUEL,
A SHIMMERING LAKE, A WISHING WELL!
NOW GREEN TREES HUNG WITH UNCUT GEM,
YOU RAPHAEL, SEE TO THEM!
AND FOR FANCY'S SAKE A CHANDELIER,
GABRIEL, HANG UP HERE & HERE!
No sooner said than done. Some guests recall
How She first decorated the bare, spinning ball.

THANKS, YOUNG MORTALS, FOR THESE FLOWERS
FRESH AS YOURSELVES. NOW DOCTOR, PRAY, A SCENT!
AND YOU, SIR POET, REINVENT
YOUR LYRIC TO THE TUNE OF ONE OF OURS!

George and *Wystan* diligently comply
—To no avail. They look up. There's a glow
Of vexed endeavor, too, in *Robert*'s eye:
His script's been altered. Why does *Nature* so
Frustrate us? Is Her mood both Yes and No?
Or are there words of ours She will not say?
Or is it that *Experience* must show
Up *Innocence*? that *Michael*'s airy way
With things will not quite wash on *Gabriel*'s holiday?

MUSICIAN, INTO THE PIT. MAKE FOR OUR IDYLL
USE OF THE WIT THERE IS IN YOUR FIDDLE,
AND LISTEN YOU FIVE WELL
TO WHAT YOUR FOREBEARS TELL
OF BEAUTY. NOW DEAR STRAVINSKY, SIDE TWO, BAND ONE,
AND MY COURT HAS BEGUN!

The *Rake*? The brothel scene? How come?
Followed by Act I, Scene iii—
Anne Truelove leaving home for *Tom*
And town beneath a full moon. She
Was sung by *Schwarzkopf*—heavenly!—
In *Venice*. Through the needle grating

Bright chords burst;   (Ah, wait for me—
JM slips back   don't start dictating!)
Downstairs—but one small point needs explicating:

JM.   Stravinsky's the conductor?
WHA. U'VE NO EARS?
      QUITE UNMISTAKAB BUT? IGOR? HE
      Look! At the sunken desk *Robert* appears,
      Beating time with new authority.

Nat. NOW WHY DID I CHOOSE
      TO PLAY MOTHER GOOSE?
      FOR MAN MY HERO IS A RAKE!
      YES SENIOR POET, YOU SAW THAT & MORE:
      SAW NATURE AS HIS PASSION AND TOO OFT HIS WHORE.
JM.   Listen! That's where Shadow turns the clock
      Back for Tom—
WHA. SO APT MY BOY THE BLACK
      OF TIME REVERSED & TOM OUR THREATENED ATOM
JM.   Don't tell me that's what you and Chester *meant*?
WHA. WHY NOT! (Shushing all round) NO ACCIDENT

Nat. NOW, CHASTER THOUGHT.
      FOR I HAVE BROUGHT
      THIS COMPANY TOGETHER HERE
      TO PRAISE MY DEAREST DEAR, MY CHILD.
      COME, COME ON THE MILD NOTE OF LOVE
      AMID THE REVELRY, —Tom's aria,
      Forbidden its librettist to revise,
      Starting exactly here, the first word *Love*—
      COME UNICORN, COME PALFREY CHASTE AS SHE,
      BRING US OUR OWN, OUR LOVE, OUR CLEAR-EYED CONSTANCY!
MM. (Offstage) MOTHER, I COME!

Unice, forelock braided to a horn
Of green and white, clops forth in ecstasies.
Maria sidesaddle, her mantle borne
About her like a tissue of spring trees,

485

    MM.   DEARS, MY FAMILY & FRIENDS, I NOW STEP OFF OUR SECOND AND
                INNOCENT IDEA
            AND ONTO THE SOLID GROUND OF THOUGHT
            Dismounts. I PUT MY FEMALE SELF ASIDE
            TO STAND BEFORE YOU, PLATO UNIFIED.
            The mantle falls, and in a twinkling she's
            This chubby brown young man we've never known,
            Dressed in white *Nehru* jacket and puttees
            For *India!* He kneels before the throne.
    Nat.   Whose light kiss lifts him to Her side: MY CHILD, MY OWN.

    Pla.   MOTHER, WHAT USE FOR THAT ONE OF OUR BAND
            MOST PUT UPON, OUR HAND?
    DJ.   (Hand poised but trembling from the strain) Who? Me?
    Nat.   HA, FROM WITHIN IT DO NOT I
            A CROUCHING ELDER SCRIBE ESPY?

            As in *Capriccio* when poor *Monsieur Taupe*
            Emerges from the prompter's box (of course
            In this case *DJ*'s hand) there scrambles up
            Stiffly at first a figure on all fours.
            He straightens as one wild cadenza pours
            Through the rapt house; whips out pince-nez and page.
            A deep, sure lilt so scores and underscores
            The words he proffers, you would think a sage
            Stood among golden tongues, unharmed, at center stage.

    WBY.   O SHINING AUDIENCE, IF AN OLD MAN'S SPEECH
            STIFF FROM LONG SILENCE CAN NO LONGER STRETCH
            TO THAT TOP SHELF OF RIGHTFUL BARD'S APPAREL
            FOR WYSTAN AUDEN & JAMES MEREL
            WHO HAVE REFASHIONED US BY FASHIONING THIS,
            MAY THE YOUNG SINGER HEARD ABOVE
            THE SPINNING GYRES OF HER TRUE LOVE
            CLOAK THEM IN HEAVEN'S AIRLOOM HARMONIES.

    Nat.   NOT RUSTY AFTER ALL, GOOD YEATS.
            (The record ends.) NOW BACK INSIDE THE GATES

OF HAND. BUT FIRST MARK WHAT I SAY:
YOU ARE TO TAKE THAT HAND ON 'JUDGMENT DAY'
AND PLEAD ITS CASE
WITH YOUR OWN ELOQUENCE IN A HIGH PLACE,
THAT IT NOT BE DIVIDED FROM
OUR SCRIBE IN ANY FUTURE SECULUM.
Bowing, Yeats crawls back under DJ's palm.
NEXT OLD RETAINER, SPEAK:
WHAT SAY, LICENTIOUS GREEK?

Ephraim is kneeling. A soupçon of garment
Shows off the body of a lover's dream.
He's waited two millennia for this moment.
Oiled from the long bath, lids and lips agleam—

Ephr. MAJESTY, O DEAR . . .
MY COUPLET'S HERE:
He slyly points out *DJ* and *JM*.

Nat. GREEK, YOU DID WELL.
NOW GO ABOUT, BE MERRY, FLIRT   TOUCH   SMELL!
The gold eyes widen. It's *his* dream come true—
Senses at Nine! Doubtful, he savors them,
Then gasping sets about (ONE HARDLY KNEW
WHERE TO LOOK NEXT MY DEARS) to do, do, do, do, do!

(Tomorrow finds him senseless once again
Sleeping off the orgy, like as not?
No. From this moment *Ephraim* will retain
The bauble he pretended to have got
On waking from *Tiberius'* garotte:
Vision. Plus, in the odd hour, the right
To use it where he pleases. There's a spot
On *Capri*, walled by wind, paved by sealight—
Extreme views he will come to share: MY 2ND SIGHT)

Nat. SWOOP, GORGEOUS BIRD!
WHAT SAY THAT WE'VE NOT HEARD?
Our Peacock—blue, green, gold, a comet-streak—
Settling, drops the laurel from his beak.

Mir. MAJESTY, I COME FROM SUCH BLACK,
WOULD I NEED NOT GO BACK.
YET I WHOM YOU APPEAR BEFORE
CAN NEVER WISH FOR MORE.
THESE 2 TRAIND ME IN LOVE,
ELSE I SHOULD NOT BE HERE ABOVE
THE DENSE, HUMMING LEVELS WHERE
NONE CAN BREATHE YOUR GODLY AIR.

Nat. BIRD, NOW YOU DO,
& YOU ARE MINE: HENCEFORTH STRUT THROUGH
MY GARDENS, MAKE ME GLAD TO LOOK AT YOU!

Mirabell shivers once at *Nature*'s word,
Then in his eyes the nuclear fire-ache
Is quenched. At last his own—or Her own—bird,
He flies to prove it by the mirror lake,
Heart beating.
     Next (invited by mistake?)
Flap-flap unrolls from nowhere, like a blind
Daubed in poison-sugar tints by *Blake*,
A poster figure, not of humankind:
Deceitful *Witch* of the *Black Forest* in the mind.

Nat. FEELING, GUEST, YOU TOO COME IN.
I HAVE MADE OF YOU A SEVENFOLD SIN
WITH REASON, THIS YOU KNOW.
WHEN YOU GREW BOLD,
ALLCONSUMING, CHAOS OF OLD,
I BANISHED YOU. YET TODAY TWO MORTALS HERE
STILL SEEM TO HOLD YOU DEAR.
LISTEN NOW, JEZEBEL!
& WHEN WITH CRIPPLING TIME THEY ARE BROUGHT LOW,
WISH THEM WELL, WISH THEM WELL
FOR TOO LONG HAVE YOU SPENT ON AGE
YOUR PENT-UP RAGE.
Snap! As the blind rolls shut two mortals melt.
ENOUGH! YOU SEE,
ALREADY TEARS AFFRONTING ME?

CHEER, SONG, MUSICIAN OUT WITH HARP AND FLUTES!
TUNE UP THE SKY MY BOY, TUNE UP THE SKY
FOR SEE, MY DARLING'S PASSING BY.

Music. Or else, the mere unspoken pang
Of grief and gratitude as our eyes meet
Grown ravishingly vocal. Pluck and twang,
Gnat musette and ocarina tweet;
The koto's quartertone; the distant heat
Wave of an underwater gamelan;
Minute glissandi such that ear of wheat
Must bend to listen—in one shimmer span
Modes of bliss never yet unthinkable to man.

Nat.　NOW DIM THE LIGHTS, THE FESTIVAL
IS DRAWING DOWN, THE GOLDEN DISC WITHAL.
TONIGHT WHEN I ARISE MUCH ON THE WANE,
LOVES DONE, O THINK OF ME AND MINE AGAIN
AND IN THE DARKEST BARKING HOUR
YOU WILL SPRING UP FRESH IN FLOWER,
FOR SUCH IS NATURE, SUCH THE PSYCHE IN MAN'S MIND:
THE BALM　THE SWEET　THE KIND.

NOW MARCHING TUNES!
MICHAEL YOUR RAINBOW LINE, IT IS OUR WISH
YOU REEL US IN LIKE FLOPPING FISH,
BUT LET ME CRY A LAST RESOUNDING YES
TO MAN, MAN IN HIS BLESSEDNESS!

Gala procession. *Robert,* by now astride
Our *Unicorn,* leading the white troop round,
Plays piccolo— THREE GUESSES WHO'S THE PIED
PIPER! BRASSES, BLARE! YOU DRUMS, RESOUND!
A moving stair for the *Valhalla*-bound
(As *Michael* draws his seven-colored bow)
Leaps from the pot of gold on our bare ground.
Nature's robes modulate to indigo,
Her last, starlike Pronouncement audible below:

489

Nat.   GABRIEL WE ARE PLEASED. COME, DEAR DAUGHTER-SON,
OFF WE GO. THE FETE IS DONE.

Dazed, reluctant to dismount, our fingers
Teeter bareback on the cup's white rump
Which prances here, there, like a child kept up
Long past bedtime— SIRS! O WE'RE PARADING
STILL   MR ROBERT LEADS US ROUND
BRAVO MR ROBERT! BIM BAM BOOM

—Till silenced, and ourselves brought halfway down
To Earth, by a couplet mild and gray as dawn:
ENOUGH UNI. YOU & I
HERE ALONE IN EMPTY SKY.

Mirabell? Nature's very own now, free?
IS IT NOT INDEED A MIRACLE?
We wished for nothing better, certainly.
OLD & DEAR PUPILS, MY MOST LOVING THANKS.
NOW OFF & AWAY ON UNI'S FLANKS!

(With which, back to the void they whisk—
Cielo stellato of the asterisk.)

*

Woken—a bark? Night freshness and dazzle edging
The room's pitch bright as day. Shutter flung wide,
In streams moonlight, her last quarter blazing
Inches above that wall of carbon mist
Made of the neighbors'. Whereupon the bedside
Tumbler brims and, the tallest story becoming
Swallowable, a mind-altering spansule,
This red, self-shuttered poverty and Heaven's
Glittering oxygen tent as one conspire.
Dark dark the bogs do hark . . . Instreaming, overwhelming
Even as it pulls back, the skyward undertow
Leaves, throughout city and countryside, wherever

Somebody wakes and goes to his window, a glowing
Tide-pool dram of bliss, diminuendo,
The most (here JM topples back to sleep)
His outflung arms could hold.

AH WHAT A FETE

Sighs Wystan after breakfast—rendezvous
Set early, not to clash with Lesson Ten.
U MY DEARS SAW IT ALL, NOTHING FOR US
TO SPELL OUT   GABR'S 4-D IMAGINATION
PUT TO (M) SHAME, BUT GENTLY, LOVINGLY
MICHAEL'S ILLUSIONS   By 4-D you mean
Maria taking on Plato's dimension—
BEYOND LIFE, HEAVEN, ART (OUR COMMON 3)
AND BOB STRAVINSKY'S, YES, AND DJ YEATS'.
THOSE TRUE MIRACLES OF YESTERDAY
MEASURED THE LEAP BETWEEN FETES 1 & 2
This was the Masque we'd all been waiting for!
& CENTERED PROPERLY UPON THE MONARCH
On Nature— TRUE, FROM ONE END OF THE SPYGLASS
And from the other? WHO MY DEARS BUT YOU!
MANKIND: ALL EYES IN HEAVEN FOCUSED ON
THE MORTAL, SACRED (& EXPENDABLE) THRONE
AND OH THE STAGECRAFT! SIMPLE SOLID JOY

Maria, are you still an Indian boy?
NO NO   A MINIGLIMPSE OF THINGS TO COME
THEN BACK INTO THE SHAPE U KNOW ME BY
UNTIL U BREAK THE GLASS. AMONG THE BETTER
PARTIES, EH? THO MY CHAPS HERE SOMEWHAT VEXED
BY QM'S QUOTE 'MISREADING' OF THEIR TEXT.
I'D WARNED THEM: NOT TOO MANY FINE POINTS, SHE
WILL NOT WEAR GLASSES IN PUBLIC

BUT I MEAN!

MUFFING ON PURPOSE ROBERT'S HEAVENLY PUN:
'GOOD DOCTOR, U'VE BROUGHT IN NO SCENTS?' ALL DONE
NICELY IN THE NAIF TETRAMETER
OF A NURSERY PAGEANT. PITY. Ĩ admit

To having been up tinkering since dawn
With Yeats's stanza, which came through a bit . . .
MR M, I MADE A HASH. YOU'VE MADE IT CLEAR.
THANK YOU. Oh please, Mr Yeats, you who have always
Been such a force in my life! WYSTAN, U HEAR?

MAITRE, I HAVE EVER HEARD
THE GOLDEN METER IN YOUR WORD,
AND KISS YR HAND (This with the straightest of faces
As Yeats withdraws into the palm's oasis.)

DJ: They're all on the side of life, then? YES
Gabriel had us frightened. HE IS GOD'S,
AT MOST INHERITING HIS MOTHER'S ONE
BLACK OR 'RESISTANT' GENE AS LIAISON
WITH THE CHAOTIC FORCES   But in fact
Nature said Yes to man—the question's settled.
SHE SAYS DEAR BOY EXACTLY WHAT SHE MEANS
LOOK IT UP   "A last resounding Yes."
LAST? The fête was ending. JM: Or
Because man won't be hearing Yes much more?
AH SHE SETS MEANING SPINNING LIKE A COIN.
HEADS UP? You're asking us? TIP SCALE TO YES
& ALL'S THE GLINT OF QUEEN M(AB)'S ALLEGRESSE.
LEAN TOWARD NO, & NO AMOUNT OF SKILL
WILL KEEP HER IMPS LOCKED UP IN GABRIEL'S SCHOOL.
We do the judging? Everyone? INDEED
2 LINES HER MAJESTY REFUSED TO READ:
'NOW LET US BANISH GLOOMY DREAMS
FOR HEAVEN ON EARTH MOST LIKELY SEEMS'

REST NOW ENFANTS   TODAY YOU ARE TO BE
EXTRAORDINARILY FAVORED   How do we dress?
I THINK WHITE WD BE NICE   LAST NIGHT'S INSTREAMING
VISIT A DIM FORETASTE   That moonlit hour,
Maman, what rapture! YOU JM LEANED BACK
SURRENDERING TO US   YOU DJ AROSE
& THREW ON COVERS   DJ: I felt cold!

CALL US IN 2 DAYS   WE MAY HAVE A FEW
CLARIFYING AFTERTHOUGHTS   ADIEU

The Last Lessons: *10*

The Greenhouse. DJ and JM alone.
No pulsing zeroes, no ascent. The vast
Black spaces of this lesson's counterpart
Are not invoked. Or else our cup contains them,
Soberly springing, at a touch, to life:

MY SON MICHAEL LIT UP YOUR MINDS   MY SON
GABRIEL TURNED THEM TO THE DARK FORCE WE
CONTAIN   POET FROM THIS MAKE A V WORK
GIVING BOTH PAUSE AND HOPE TO THIS FIGURE
I SEE EMBLAZONED HERE

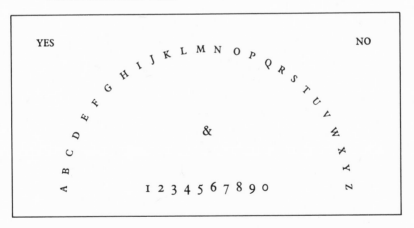

YES to NO to A to Z to YES
(Quincunx where ghosts of Five and Twelve perambulate)
    The cup . . . crosses itself? Inscribes a stark
            Twinbladed axe
    Upon the block, sideways? Is it the mark
    That cancels, or the letter-writer's kiss?
            The X

Of the illiterate?
Fulcrum and consort to our willowy &?
The space of a slow breath indrawn,
Simplicity itself, it waits and then goes on,
Taking us like children by the hand:

MY UPRIGHT MAN
FULL OF TIME   HE STRUGGLES TO HOLD IT BACK
AND CREATE FOR ME A PARADISE I
IN MY OWN UPSTRETCHED ARMS WILL SHOW CRYING
SEE BROTHERS WE HAVE HELD IT BACK SEE SEE
I AND MINE BROTHERS IN OUR DAY SURVIVE

Drifting to the outer limit. Gone.

★

First things first. Down from the Pantheon
Yesterday's Speaker and His Twin descended,
He with His proven innocence, and She
With Her rich wardrobe of ideas and motives.
ENFANT ONE HATES TO BOAST BUT IT'S TOP DRAWER:
'YES PET, YOU'RE OF THE OLDEST FAMILY
ALL WRIT DOWN IN THE DOOMSDAY BOOK'   Yet here
In their New World, this branch at least, these two
Have fallen on hard times. Their *Mayflower*
Long run wild, they bend to the poor lamplight,
Her deft hands full of mending, His roughened ones
Forming letters which the flame, tipped blue
As if with cold, breathes fitful life into:
I've found work, we get on, Sister keeps house.
Stay well, and please do not abandon us . . .
ALAS ENFANT   THERE'S NO DECEIVING U

Or you. Did nothing in our lessons come
As a surprise? MY VISION OF THE VEG WORLD,
WYSTAN'S OF EARTH'S CORE, GEORGIE'S OF THE CHILL
FRONTIERS OF ANTIMATTER   THESE WERE 'FIELDS'

ONLY RECENTLY DECLASSIFIED.
TILL NOW NOT EVEN THE 5 HAVE HAD SUCH TRAINING
AS WE CHAPS GOT   THEN MIRABELL'S MISTAKES!
Some we've corrected. Poor thing, were there others?
WHEN HE ASSIGNS (BOOK 5) NO ACCIDENT
TO A GALACTIC LEVEL? MAMAN BIT HER TONGUE
TO KEEP FROM SILENCING THAT BATTY BIRD
How do we know he was wrong? BECAUSE U HEARD
OF POOR GOD'S PAIN & CONSTERNATION WHEN
HIS FIRST 2 CREATURES WENT AWRY   Still, couldn't
Some Clause more comprehensive than God B's
Have dictated those "accidents"? YOU SEE?
WE SCRIBES WILL WRITE IT AS IT IS, MARIA!
She answers from her highest horse: U THINK?
HAH! IF MY MOTHER WERE HERE U'D RUN OUT OF INK!

Friction made the first thin consommé
Of all we know. Soon it was time for lunch.
Between an often absent or abstracted
(In mid-depression) father and still young
Mother's wronged air of commonsense the child sat.
The third and last. If he would never quite
Outgrow the hobby horse and dragon kite
Left by the first two, one lukewarm noodle
Prefigured no less a spiral nebula
Of further outs. Piano practice, books . . .
A woman speaking French had joined their sunstruck
Looking-glass table. Fuels of the cup
Lowered to her lips were swallowed *up.*
The child blinked. All would now be free to shatter,
Change or die. Tight-wound exposures lay
Awaiting trial, whose development
Might set a mirror flowing in reverse
Forty years, fifty, past the flailing seed
To incoherence, blackout—the small witness
Having after all held nothing back?
HUSH ENFANT   FOR NO MAN'S MIND CAN REACH
BEYOND THAT HIM & HER   THEIR SEPARATION

REMAINS UNTHINKABLE. WE ARE CONFINED
BY THE PINK CARNATION, THE FERN FIDDLEHEAD
& THESE BREATHMISTED PANES OF HUMAN SPEECH

That was the summer my par— YR PARALLELS
DIVERGE PRECISELY HERE   I from the I
Who shook those bars, who burned to testify
At the divorce. Scales flashing, bandage loosened,
Pitiless gaze shining forth—ah cover it
While time allows, in decent prejudice!
Mine's for the happy ending. Weren't the endings
Always happy in books? Barbarity
To serve uncooked one's bloody tranche de vie . . .
Later, if the hero couldn't smile,
Reader and author could; one called it style.
Poetic justice, if you like. A spell
Which in mid-sentence, turning iron to sunlight—

Where were we? SAFE AS YET IN THE IMMORTAL CELL

*

The Sermon at Ephesus

Bright, empty days. Then DJ thinks to wonder:
Was it as Plato that you joined our tour
Of Ephesus? U GUESSED! & GAVE A LIVELY
SYMPOSIUM, EH WYSTAN?
                           QUITE SPLENDID   Its theme?
TIME PASSING AS   O GO AHEAD THEN
                           'AH
CHILDREN OF THE GREAT GODDESS (I SAID) EVEN
THESE BREASTS WILL RUN DRY. PREPARE TO WEAN
YRSELVES OF THE FATAL DELUSION OF ALLPROVIDING
HEAVEN. MAN MUST PROVIDE (HERE JM MISSES
A STEP NO LONGER THERE)   YES, MAN ALONE
MUST UNDERSTAND THAT VANISHED MARBLE TREAD
GIVES WAY IN TIME TO THE STEEP & SOLITARY

PATH OF MIND' & THEN AS (IN OUR TIME WARP)
THEY BOOED, WE FLED IN YR TAXI! And JM's fall,
A leak of pain? A warning from the black
Transmission case? A PLUS

It sounds as though you—
INDEED (the answer comes before he asks)
WE OF THE 5 ARE PARCELED INTO MORE
THAN ONE LIFE AT A TIME   OUR ENERGIES
CONCENTRATE WITHIN THE PRINCIPAL LIFE
BUT EACH LEAST POWER IS USED. THE NEXT RM:
STRAVINSKY POWDER, A HALF CUP   A TEASPOON
OF MOZART   DOLLOP OF VERDI   THESE AS U KNOW,
ASPECTS OF HOMER   BUT AN OVERFLOW
UNNEEDED BY OUR MAN IN EAST BERLIN.
THUS THE MELODIC SENSE REFINED IN LIVE
ALEMBICS THRU THE CENTURIES WILL GO
LARGELY TO RM. MAMAN IN HER NEW LIFE
TAKES ON ALL PLATO'S POWER TO SEE INTO
& MAKE SENSE OF THE COSMOS. WHAT MOST DREW
HIS PUPILS (CHARM? PERSUASION?) GOES HOWEVER
INTO VARIOUS DRAB POLITICOS
NEEDING A HELPING HAND OUT OF THE CAVE.

The way you *listened*, Maria, seemed to hear
Words unspoken—all that charm was yours!
AH WELL   SAY JUST A DAB BEHIND EACH EAR?
MY CABLE POINTS   Your ears? DJ WITHOUT
SOMEONE TO TAKE IN I'D HAVE TAKEN OFF.
WE OF THE 5 ARE NEVER NEVER ALONE:
THEY DROP IN WITHOUT TELEPHONING FIRST!
POOR MITSOTAKI   I'D LEAVE BED & SIMPLY
TRAIPSE INTO A ROOM   FOR 2 DAYS? 3?
OR DINNER PARTIES   LIKE A FAIRYTALE
THE ENTIRE TABLE PUT TO SLEEP BUT ME
AND WHY? BECAUSE QM WANTED TO CHAT
My naps at Sounion . . . MANY WAS THE BLUE
UNCLOUDED DAY ENFANT WE SPOKE OF YOU

★

Appearances

Another week, JM: But have we missed
The point? If there *are* none, why so insist—?
BOB?

      YES MARIA?

              LEAVE YR AQUARELLE
& SEE WHAT YOU CAN TELL

                    APPEARANCES . . .
The cup considers. HMM   Steps back a pace.
LET ME RECONSTRUCT MY 'DEATH' FOR YOU
After more thought, I HEARD A VOICE 'HE'S GONE'
AND LOOKED DOWN AT MY OLD FRIEND: MEAT & BONE.
LOOKED UP: THE SKY! ALL STARS! NO FEELINGS. FAINT
UNCONNECTED DAUBS OF THOUGHT LIKE PAINT
WERE FORMING ME AS IMAGE IN MY MIND.
'ROBERT, REMEMBER THIS, REMEMBER THAT'
THE THOUGHTS SAID TILL THEY SMOOTHED INTO A SOLE
UNBROKEN ONE: 'THAT LIFE IS OVER, LEAVE IT.'
BY THEN THE IMAGE OF MY SELF WAS WHOLE,
THE STARS INVISIBLE —where Self itself
Had blacked out Heaven? BACKING OF A MIRROR?
IN MY CASE, THANKS TO YOU THE GENERAL BLACK
TURNED INTO A (M) MAFIA LIMOUSINE
A Black Maria! NO ONE ACTUALLY
BUT AT THE WHEEL A POWER NOTHING IMPEDES,
BRINGING ME TO YOU NEXT I STEPPED BAREASS
THRU SAND & WATER OF YR MIRROR GLASS
& SURFACED WHERE 2 OLD & 3 NEW CHUMS
WELCOMED ME, SKINS GLISTENING WITH LIGHT
NO BRUSH COULD EVER RENDER

                    NOW THIS LIGHT
HAS BEEN (SAID WYSTAN) CONSTANT IN YOUR FIELD
FROM THE MOMENT MICHAEL'S HERALD CAME TO YOU
Ephraim spoke of *his* light as revealing

The souls who gathered round us to each other;
But that was Ephraim whistling in the dark.
OR SOMEONE ELSE STOOD BY YOU EVEN THEN
WITH A LAMP   But who—Plato? YOU'RE ASKING ME?
MUCH HERE IS PURE AND SIMPLE MYSTERY.
DOWN AT THE HEDGE WE DO NOT SEE EACH OTHER,
ONLY HERE   & WHERE YOU DUG FOR FACTS,
THE BATWORLD'S MINESHAFT, WAS OF COURSE PITCH BLACK
BUT FOR YOUR PEACOCK'S APPARITION OR
SOME FEEBLE WATTAGE BEAMING FROM YOU 4.
THOSE WERE THE LONE 'WHISTLERS' IN THAT DARK
BUT THIS LIGHT? HMM   IT'S LIKE A STAR WE ENTER
TO FIND OURSELVES. IF IT'S THE LIGHT OF LOVE
ALL ELSE IS HEDGING   Robert, but—you've lit
Our blind spot up! That blacking-out's the screen
Of self which forms between God and His creature,
A numb, a numbered starlessness all eyes,
All ego, singularity, dark gullet,
Palate, palazzo braced, impervious
To wintry tidings of its own collapse?
SENSATIONALLY PHRASED BUT, WELL, PERHAPS.
MY PRESENT THEORY IS THAT PARADISE
ON EARTH WILL FLOOD EACH EMPTY PIGEONHOLE
OF THE BUREAUCRACY WITH RADIANCE
Stop, we must pack for Venice! And friends already
Plead for no more big speeches in small caps.
DEAR J WE LEARN HERE NOT TO TRUST A LIVING SOUL

DJ: Is that *you*, Robert? May I say
You sound so changed. No baby talk, no gossip.
OOPS   HAS THE GREAT RESTORER OVERDONE IT?
No, you know what I mean. I DO   THE VARNISH
STRIPPED AWAY & THE WILD OATS I SOWED
EATEN BY UNI   Comforting for us
That you stay put while others hit the road,
But why? THE WORLD NOT READY FOR ME YET?
How long before you're born? HMM   You don't know?
ONE MOMENT   AH   YES, MAJESTY   'MR ROBERT

(A VOICE JUST BREATHED) ELEVEN MONTHS TO GO'

SIRS? ARE WE GOING OFF TO SEA?
Yes, Uni, where the lake-dwellers once settled,
A wonderland not underwater yet.
One of *our* anchor points. You'll meet DK,
You'll meet a wingèd Lion. MR R SAYS ALSO
4 OF THOSE I WAS FORERUNNER TO!
The golden horses on St Mark's—indeed.
AT THE HEDGE MISS ALICE SAID I WOULD HAVE
A STRAW HAT IF I WOULD BE HER STEED.
'GERTRUDE, YOU KNEW I WAS A RIDER?'
'A WRITER?' 'NOT QUITE: AN EQUESTRIENNE!'
Well, as *you* know, we sail two days from now.
YES! THIS IS UNICE SAYING CIAO

& MAMAN SAYING BASTA TO THIS DREAM
SHE LONGS TO WAKE FROM   WD THAT THE GRAND SCHEME
LET A MIRROR NOW & THEN MATURE
INTO A SIMPLE PIECE OF FURNITURE

She's tired of us. (It's late, we're on the terrace
Watering.) From Maria's point of view
This work's done. Her next one takes on weight
And character halfway around the world.
With birth so near, an ordinary soul
Would be in situ, and unreachable—
Not she. She's learned that kid stuff inside out.
At most, like Sounion, she comes and goes,
Gardens, has lunch, a little nap, but knows
Better than to spend the night there—nipping
Back to heavenly Athens while she can!
(Laughter. Gurglings from the hose, and heat
Delicious through wet flagstones to bare feet.)
DJ: When we first met Emmanuel
Nearly eight months ago, Maria told us
That she "experienced her mother's womb".
JM: She was *conceived* then? Po-po-po!

DJ: Or as a two-week fetus had been sent
To check the room out, before Management
Put itself to any further trouble.
(Laughter. The ninth moon setting—at whose full
Enormous turtles, barnacled like moons,
Eggs buried in the lap of silver dunes,
Regain the ebbing world they mustn't fail.)
JM: Plato appears in *Mirabell*
First as a sex-fiend, squinting through keyholes
At slim young bodies; then we get his later
Liaison with Luca. The *Tibetan*
Book of the Dead reports that apparitions
Of copulating figures may beset
The pilgrim soul. Surrendering to them
Means the long road taken back to Earth.
(If we're still laughing now, it's at the motley
Worn by sober Truth. Then DJ aiming
The hose upright, from under his thumb streams
Fanwise, heavenward a ghostly jet
Whose fallout tickles lifted faces wet.)
Turn it off. Another day. Sweet dreams

—But who has plucked my sleeve?
An old arthritic Cassia shrub one March
Glimpsed by Maria from the car
And, dug up wild, brought home. A "sensitive",

Its leaves are folded in the night, a dim
Green gooseflesh along every limb
Tells of the coming fit:

Another fifteen days will see
The stunted twiggery
Robed in oracular yellow head to foot.

Tonight it has just this to say:
I too, O sonneteer,
Was marked, transported by her, and this year
Given a part to play.

★

Venetian Jottings

"Showing a film of Maya's!" shouts DJ
Across the Piazza. JM shuts his Dante.
Which film? "Who knows? I got seats anyway.

Tonight at nine. Part of some sort of anti-
Biennale thought up by the students, bless
Their hearts." Amen. Thank Heaven *we*'re not twenty.

It's morning still. The tourist's merciless
Fun-ethic has been goading us all week
From gondola to gallery, from princess

To restaurant, from poolside to boutique.
Today's gray drizzle comes as a reprieve,
Affording a noon hour in which to speak

With the invisible companions we've
Brought to this drowning, dummy paradise
Whose nude, gnawed Adam and eroded Eve

Cling to their cornice, and September flies
Revolve above the melting tutti-frutti.
One happy shade at least feels otherwise:

AWASH MY DEARS   POLLUTED BY THE BEAUTY!
(We've set our Board up on the kitchen table
At David Kalstone's, back of the Salute.)

GERTRUDE & WALLACE WINDOWSHOP, UNABLE
TO FIND A PREWAR GONDOLIERE HAT.
UNI INCONSOLABLY HAUNTS THE STABLE,

HIS LONGLOST GILT BRONZE COUSIN LAID OUT FLAT
AMONG HEADSHAKING VETS. RM WE FEEL
KEEPS UP THE 'TONE' BY FLITTING LIKE A BAT

BELFRY TO BELFRY: 'ONE GRAND GLOCKENSPIEL'
GK APPALLED TESTS THE CANAL: 'DO NOT
TOUCH A DROP OF THESE RELECTIONS!' HE'LL

LEARN ENFANTS. MD ALL STAGEFRIGHT: 'WHAT
TO WEAR TO MY PREMIERE?' And Maman—you?
SHAWLED IN BLACK OVER THE PASTA POT

Hans? Alice? Marius?—but Luca who
Is DK's partron, as we now recall,
Darts forward: BELLO! BELLO SEMPRE DI PIU!

VOGLIO CON LUI FAR L'INCESTO! All
On hand, in short, and eager for good times.
(Another morning, after a bad squall,

There in full view is Peggy Guggenheim's
Waterlogged gondola. MY DEARS OF COURSE
WHAT TO EXPECT WHEN EVERYBODY CLIMBS

ABOARD   12 SHADES, A PEACOCK & A HORSE!
Who was the twelfth? PYTHAGORAS   HE WENT
DOWN WITH THE SHIP   And so on.) Not to force

The issue, but if this is all they meant
By GO OUT LAUGHING . . . Now at twilight here's
Our old resounding bridge. Indifferent

Both to high spirits and fall sightseers,
It waits for winter lightning's coup de grâce,
The solving gales. I know; in not three years

Since the great cloudburst turned me to a glass
Model of stamina—but where is Wendell?—
My sand and water chafe. Here's an impasse

Deep in which red flickerings enkindle
More than curiosity. The street-
At-evening's densely peopled Coromandel

Panel folds back upon a blast of heat
So powerful we've paused: it's the glass-blowing!
A glory hole roars, pulses. Color of peat

Artisans dip the long rod into glowing
Pots, fire within fire, gasping conflate
Ember with embryo, by rote foreknowing

—Much as they twirl, lop, tweezer at a rate
Swifter than eyesight—the small finished form.
Twice more we watch the rose-hot blob translate

Itself to souvenir, to hardly warm
Bud-vase or pony, harlequin or bird—
Its newfound cool no refuge from the storm

Of types—and can move on. Here's the dust-furred
Fleabag cinema. An unsmiling speaker
Asks that to "bourgeois discourse" be preferred

The "radical mutism" of the image-maker.
(Are these the latest terms? I simply gawk.)
At last lights dim. Drums gibber. Credits flicker.

A bare beach. Glinting wavelets—the sidewalk
Colorist in each of us ransacks
His box for that jade-green or azure chalk

Lost among dialectic whites and blacks.
Then sunset, hills, a road, a figurine
Ambling past. Action slowed by the soundtrack's

Treacherous crosscurrent, if not swept clean
Away by particles that so bombard,
So flay an image to the bone-white screen

That vision ducks too late and winces, scarred.
It is the flak fired outward from time's core.
Now they've assembled. Shirtsleeved houngan. Hard

Dirt of the ceremonial dance floor
Where in white meal he traces Erzulie's
Curlicue-and-checker heart, the four

Chambers strewn with grain. Held above these
A (peck) dazed hen (peck-peck) greed overcomes.
Will the gods accept it? Silence. Freeze:

The headless, blood-slimed bird. Then again drums,
Faces, feet. The counterclockwise drain
Of chanted phrase on equilibriums

Until it happens. Ghédé with his cane,
Smoked glasses and top hat struts avenues
No one else sees. Through flurries of cocaine

The youth he's mounted sizzles like a fuse.
A woman pitches, is held up, advances
Pale and contorted—but it's Maya! (Who's

Holding the camera?) Next we know, her trance has
Deepened, she is combed, perfumed and dressed
In snowy lace, beaming at whom she fancies.

The frown, the flood of tears, and all the rest
Will have been cut, or never filmed. Delight
Alone informs her dance, unself-possessed.

Partner by partner, David's face goes white:
We are the ghosts, *hers* the ongoing party
At which she was received one summer night

(How many years ago now, twenty? thirty?)
Into the troupe, glowworm and lunar crescent,
That whole supreme commedia dell' arte

Which takes a twinkling skull for reminiscent
Theatre, and soul for master negative.
It's Maya dancing. She is here and isn't,

Her darks print out as bright, her dyings live
—Do they? In *Venice*'s uncomprehending
Eyes? Painful to think, hard to forgive

What "today" makes, what "Paradise" impending
Will, if a trace remains, of . . . Let that be.
One last shot: dawn, the bare beach. "Happy ending?"

Smiles DJ as we link arms, tacitly
Skipping the futuristic coffee-bar's
Debate already under way (ah, me)

On the confusing terms: Dance, Gods, Time, Stars.

★

Exits and Entrances

JUNGLES! QUITE BEAUTIFUL I'M SURE BUT O THE DISORDER! A CHAOS
   OF SORTS!
(Is it Herself? The cup darts to and fro—
Intermezzo marked prestissimo.
Outdoors, cars honk like geese, the very sun
Heads south. We're back in Athens. Fall's begun.)
CITIES, FORESTS, THESE WE KNOW ABOUT, MUCH THINNING TO
   COME IN THE FORMER, BUT JUNGLES!
WHO CAN COUNT THE LIVES THERE? CAN I? NO, IN A WORD. O
   THERE'S MUCH TO BE DONE!

POET, THINK ON THAT WHEN YOU GO LIKE A FOX TO EARTH, HAH!
    & REPORT TO ME, ME!
NOW COME ALONG MY DEAR, SO SORRY ABOUT INDIA BUT WE CAN'T
    ALL HAVE DISHWASHERS & ELECTRICAL GADGETS I'M SURE!
BEAT YOUR SERVANTS, THEY'LL WORSHIP YOU!
YOU OTHERS, LOOK ALIVE! MUCH TO DO! THE SUMMER TO GET UNDER
    WRAPS!
AU RESERVOIR!

WHEW   I UNDERSTAND NOW WHY MARIA
GOES ABOUT MUTTERING 'BOMBAY, WHAT BLISS!'
Who's this? ME GEORGE   THE SAUCERS ARE I THINK
HER SPECTACLES TO KEEP THE WORLD IN FOCUS
Bombay. And you, George? JIMMY THEY'LL TAKE ME APART
THE OLD TIN WOODSMAN, LINKED FOREVERMORE
TO THAT AMAZING LAB OF GABRIEL'S
OR RATHER TO 18 LABS THRUOUT THE WORLD
AS 'HELPER': THIS CHART MISPLACED, THAT TESTTUBE CHANGING
COLOR RUINS THE EXPERIMENT
OR PROVES IT, LIGHTS BLINK OUT, THE CHIEF OF STAFF
STRICKEN WITH A MIGRAINE . . . I WILL BE
THE PURELY SCIENTIFIC PRINCIPLE
And the creative. MAKING SENSE OF IT

The mirror breaks. What happens in those first
Minutes, can you say? SAY! WE'VE REHEARSED
MY BOYS FOR MONTHS. I'LL SHIFT THRU VEINS OF METAL
GETTING THE FEEL OF IT, THEN SURFACING
(AN IFFY MOMENT THERE   WELL, WHAT IF SOME AFRICAN
DUSKY PICKS A BIG BRIGHT SPARKLER UP?
Easy—we'll ask for you at Cartier's.
CAFE SOCIETY SO UN-ME   ALWAYS
MISSING ACT I AT THE OPERA) THEN INTO
THE WORLD   A CLIFF? A BEACH? OUR WORK BEGINS:
COVERING THE SINS OF MULTITUDE
WE MARCH WE GRAINS OF SAND! Creating famine.
Time's latest cover story tells it all—
"Nature's Revenge: The Creeping Deserts". INDEED

A COOL HALF MILLION THIS MONTH IN ETHIOPIA!
NO MORE APPALLING THAN THE CHEMICALS
U ATHENIANS BREATHE (MY BROTHERS TAKING
OVER YR LUNGS) & THEN MY DEARS WE SHAKE!
THEN IN A CENTURY OR SO UNITE,
STAGE SET FOR RAPHAEL'S NEW EPOCHMAKING
ALL STAR REVIVAL OF THE RAKE
AS A GARDEN TOOL: WE FROM THE ROYAL BOX
WATCHING ACT I, THE PROMPTER OUT OF SIGHT
WHISPERING 'ADAM, THIS TIME GET IT RIGHT!'

ENFANTS THE NEW MOON, SAUCER FOR OUR CUP,
WHISPERS IT IS TIME TO SERVE US UP.
ON DJ'S 55TH   Three days from now!
We've planned a party— Softly: SO HAVE WE
THE TIME IS NOW AT HAND   HAND, LET IT BE

Then, as impenetrable feelings twine
Round and round us, tough as any vine:

JUNGLES? WE'LL THIN! THIN! THIN!
HOW I APPROVE OF DESERTS! NOTHING MOVES UNSEEN! IT NEVER
    RAINS!
NO, JUNGLES MUST BE THINNED AND WILL BE!
MICHAEL, EMMANUEL, CONFERENCE!

★

It never rains . . . At this eleventh hour
Two still-warm shades, finding our schoolroom door
Ajar, take refuge from the shock of Heaven.
Cal Lowell first: CHRIST   ON MY WAY HERE 4
FAMILY PORTRAITS CAME TO DO I MEAN

LIFE? O MR AUDEN! A mild teacher,
Wystan strolls him past the spears of green
Chalk grass on every blackboard—Uni's art-work,
Our Robert having urged the dear good creature
To develop "faculties". We're smiling when
In sweeps a new Maria, la Divina,
Callas herself, fresh from her greatest role:
THEY CALL THIS THE STAR'S DRESSING ROOM? THIS HOLE?
—Whom Robert, himself heartsick, must console.

Maman, suppose we visited Bombay?
SHALL WE? (instant complicity) DO WE DARE?
Going on recklessly to set the year
1991, the hour and day
And landmark in whose shade there will appear
A SCRUBBED 14 YEAR OLD PUNJABI LAD
CARRYING SOMETHING U WILL KNOW ME BY.
IS IT A DATE? You bet your life. (We're mad.)

JIMMY GIVE MY LOVE TO YOU KNOW WHO
Without fail, George. MY ONE LIFE HAD TOO FEW
ATTACHMENTS   YET IF LOVING'S 88
PERCENT IS CHEMICAL I ANTICIPATE
FORMING SOME STRONG NEW BONDS   LIVE WELL MY FRIENDS
& COMFORTABLY ON THEIR DIVIDENDS!

9 MY DEARS? THE BIRTHING MONTH   THE STAGE
B4 THE OVAL ENIGMA: LIFE'S INDRAWN
BREATH, THE BASIN WHERE OUR OLD SELVES DROWN.
ARABIC 9 (AS ON YR TRANSCRIPT PAGE)
FACE AVERTED FROM THE CIPHER LOOKS
BACK ON THE LONG ROAD TRAVELED. ROMAN IX
SERVES FOR US: ONE FOOTSTEP FROM THE CRUX
OF TIME WE STAND POISED WAITING TO LEAP IN

THE PARTY AT THE STATION WILL INCLUDE
ENFANTS 5 SILENT PRESENCES   QM
& BROTHERS   SO NO TEARS IN FRONT OF THEM.
WE'LL CHAT INFORMALLY BEFORE WE'RE CLAD
IN 'TRAVELING DRESS' & THE TRAIN CHUGS AWAY . . .
RM CAN FILL U IN ANOTHER DAY

Glimpses of the Future

When that day comes it's we who'll read aloud
The text, to Robert, of our grand farewell
Which he and Uni witness, but through glass:
A vague, dust-spattered shadow play; the music,
Vibration without pitch; our three departing
Figures here one moment, gone—light's carriage
Sweeping down Sandover's long driveway—gone
The next. A void within a void. Since then?
Robert whistles, Uni stomps, both feigning
Jollity as they approach the hedge
UNI CAN NIBBLE IT TRIM WHILE I GIBBER & SQUEAK
But at the heart of each is a pure ache
—Maria, Wystan, George—which time might cure
If there were time in Heaven, or these dead
Weren't so addicted to the loving cup.
Maria, Wystan, George—they've gone, they've gone;
Left without a trace UNLESS THIS (M)
WHITE HOLE WE CARRY HEDGEWARD STANDS FOR THEM

The schoolroom is still visitable, though.
Early in October, forty-eight hours
Before JM leaves Athens, au revoirs
Are broken off by an old friend. 00:

IT HAS REACHD LORD GABRIEL'S GLORIOUS ATTENTION THAT
YOU HAVE UNANSWERD QUESTIONS: 'LET US NOT DECEIVE OUR SCRIBE.'
TOMORROW'S SUNDOWN VISIT WILL BE GRACED. MASTERS, FAREWELL.

DJ: What questions? JM (guardedly):
I've jotted a few notes down. Here, let's see . . .
"My Lords, as to the Alpha men themselves
Accessorized with what new lobes, wings, valves,
And deathless like those characters in Shaw
Whose gifts amuse more often than they awe,
Spare us a full account. Not that the nerves
Can't take it, but the word banks lack reserves
To handle such a massive run on them.
Did Babylon imagine Bethlehem?
Could Uni have imagined H. G. Wells?
No more can we these 'men' of Gabriel's.
So—lest they issue from the teller's cage
As cheap Utopian scrip (blurred smile of sage
Framed by scrollwork) promising untold
Redemption, ages hence, in fairy gold
Laid up when the crash threatened, in *our* vault—
No details, please. Call it the bank's fault
For disallowing values not conferred
On our old stock by our old human word."
DJ: Then what's the question? JM sighs:
What indeed? Or does it all boil down
To this: Resistance—Nature's gift to man—
What form will it assume in Paradise?

*

SIRS WE WAIT   MR ROBERT & I
THE SCHOOLROOM STIFLING   DULL WITH DUST
AH NOW THE LIGHT   THE LIVE AIR!
—Hiding as Nature and the Brothers enter.

Nat. MUSICIAN, ALONE IN OUR FINISHING SCHOOL?
RM. MADAM, LORDS, WE MISS OUR FELLOW STUDENTS,
HAVE YOU NEWS?
Nat. MUSICIAN, DO I NOT!
OUR WITTY POET SURFACING OFF ALASKA AS A VEIN OF PURE
RADIUM HAS HAVOCKED A NOSY RADIO SHIP. 58 IN LIFEBOATS!

OUR SCIENTIST HAS JOINED MY GABRIEL AND (IN A CHARMING
 EXPERIMENT TESTING THE DENSITIES OF YOUR CHEMICALLY
 LADEN AIR WITH ELECTRIC CHARGES)
LIT UP THE RUSSIAN SKY!
Last week, what Tass described as a "huge star"
Or "jellyfish" of fine downpulsing beams
Hovered an hour above Petrozavodsk,
Then pensively crossed the border into Finland.

JM.   That jellyfish was George?
Nat. INDEED YOUNG POET.

AND MY DAZZLING BRIGHT DARKEYED BABE LOOKS KEENLY ROUND
 THIS HIS 19TH DAY, MAKING SENSE OF IT.
THUS DEAR ONES OUR OLD HEAVEN HANGING ON MANY BALANCES HAS
 THREE NEW TRUSTY PEGS FOR GOD'S INTELLIGENCE
WORKING TOWARD THAT PARADISE YOU THREE HUMANS CANNOT
 DREAM ON.
HOW WILL IT BE?
IT WILL HOLD A CREATURE MUCH LIKE DARLING MAN, YET
 PHYSICALLY MORE ADAPTABLE.
HIS IMMORTALITY WILL CONSIST OF PROLONGATION, IN THE
 BEGINNING PHASE, UNTIL HIS IDEAL IS REACHED IN NUMBER.
THEN TIME WILL STOP
AND LONG FRUITFUL SPACES BE GIVEN HIM TO LEARN THROUGH
 SONG AND POETRY
OF HIS OLD HELPLESS FEELINGS & WEARY PAST.

THE RESISTANCE? NONE. HE WILL, YES, SWIM & GLIDE,
A SIMPLER, LESS WILFUL BEING. DULLER TOO?
IF SO, IS THAT SHARP EDGE NOT WELL LOST
WHICH HAS SO VARIOUSLY CUT AND COST?
WE WILL WALK AMONG HIS KIND MADE NEW
(THE MASQUE CONCLUDED, WE & OURS
STEPPING FROM STAGE TO MIX WITH MORTAL POWERS)
SAYING, AS OUR WITTY POET CRIED
BACK TO YOUR SUNSET FACES: BONNE CHANCE!
AND AS MY OWN SWEET BRIGHTNESS ADDED: ON WITH THE DANCE!
FAREWELL.

DJ.   Farewell?

JM. Farewell.
Nat. WE WILL ALSO SAY: YOU SEE,
IN ATHENS ONCE WAS AN ACADEMY . . .
Exeunt.
       Or does She linger?
                 I
Am leaving, and with no time for goodbye
Except to Robert. To the hedge have come
Our regulars. They whom the vacuum
Awaits peer toward us, tiny features bright
As if with upper casements' borrowed light.
O HOW TOUCHING   Robert squints to read
The placard they have lettered: GOD B SPEED

                  ★

Finale

Our sunset faces. Back to David's birthday,
16 September 1977—
As usual we've begun down in the hall.
HAPPY RETURNS? ENFANTS A CHANGE OF (M):
NOT A DEPARTURE BUT A WEDDING PARTY
& HIGH TIME, EH? OUR OLDEST 55!
AS WE THREE PLIGHT OURSELVES TO EARTH   WORK   LIFE
SIGNAL THAT MOMENT UP THERE IN THE BLUE
WITH SOMETHING OLD AND SOMETHING NEW,
PULCINELLA OF STRAVINSKY? And Maria,
A drop of courage given us by you—?
CHAMPERS WE HOPE   & STUDIED INDIFFERENCE
TO THOSE SILENT WATCHFUL PRESENCES
FOR THIS WILL BE THE CHILDREN'S HOUR
                       NO TEARS
BESIDE THE GOLDEN WEEPING BUSH MY DEARS
Oh Wystan, we've still all these questions, wait!
What did *you* embody of the Five?
DJ: He's gone. JM: Maman? ENFANTS

How shall we speak of these things in Bombay?
I'LL LEAD U ON   BUT NOW   It's all right. Go.
Meet on the terrace—6:15? JUST SO

WHA'S PRECEDESSOR: YAN LI BORN 1855
(Mirabell, up again to his old numbers)
DIED AT 50. FROM A SOUTHERN PROVINCE, HE GREW UP IN
A HERBALIST'S HOUSEHOLD, PUBLISHD VERSES, WENT TO PEKIN
BECAME A COURT PHYSICIAN, HEARD FIREFLY WOMAN SING
Wouldn't you know—drawn even then to sopranos!
WHA: 'BEYOND DESCRIPTION GHASTLY'   & WAS SOON A
FAVORITE OF THE PAIND & CRIPPLED EMPRESS. FATHERD SO
RUMOR SAID, SOME 30 CHILDREN & MET A SUDDEN END
EITHER THRU POLITICAL OR MARITAL JEALOUSY
ALTHO THIS QUATRAIN TRANSLATED & ANTHOLOGIZED BY
A METHODIST MISSIONARY (1921) SUGGESTS
WHO THEY WERE WHO STABBD HIM NEARLY TO DEATH   HE HAD A
    FEW
LAST, CURIOUSLY SERENE MOMENTS FOR ITS DICTATION:
'THE GARDEN BRIGHT WITH BIRDS & FLOWERS   IN THE NOON HOURS
LIES TRAMPLED UNDER GOATS' FEET   CARELESS IN THEIR LUSTFUL
    HEAT'
DIED 1906
Reborn as Wystan with new densities?
            INDEED   & WHAT BUT HOMERIC ONES?
"Immortal Bard, you who created me."
USED ALSO BY A 17TH CENTURY ITALIAN
POET/SCULPTOR   WHA LINKD ALWAYS TO STONE & WORDS

6:00. Stone and words. The balustrade
Pressing back the harder I press down.
Three-story drop. A cat stares up in dread.
Faces streaking through me of the dead,
Traffic whizzing—how the old motor races!
How simply, too, the urge is gratified:
Just shut the eyes . . .
                        But here inside my head
No question of total blackout. Lights all along

Following closely, filling the rear-view mirror,
Forcing upon whichever of us drove
Illumination's blindfold—these lights now gather
Speed to pass. Our own weak dashboard aura,
Our own poor beams that see no further than needed
Will have to guide us through the homeward ride.
Still not alone. Despite the Doppler drop in pitch,
That disappearing car will make things round the bend
Shine eerily, a tree, an underpass of bone;
Or else a dip between hills miles from now
Will glow in recollection—
                              As DJ
Takes his place, beyond words, at my side.

Music. Time. The orange sailcloth awning
Rippled by waves of windless, deepening light.
We kneel on orange cushions under it.
Props include Board and cup; a looking-glass
Iridescent seashells border, Robin's gift
From Malagasy; and this waterworn
Marble wedge that stops a door downstairs.
A blue-and-white rice bowl, brimming with water,
Lobs an ellipse of live brilliance—but so
Athrob there as to court vertigo—
Onto the concrete wall our shadows climb.
Slowly that halo sinks. The mirror's oblong
Gaze outflashes, thirsty for the wine-
Green slopes where sobbing couples intertwine.
While, to one side, our Cassia thick with bloom
Sweeps the stones in a profound salaam.

THE SCHOOLROOM ALL FESTOONED   GEORGIE & WYSTAN
CHAFE IN THEIR CUTAWAYS   MAMAN IN WHITE
SARI WITH ORANGEBLOSSOMS   OUR 3 HEARTS
ABRIM WITH LOVE FOR YOU   ROBERT & UNI
OUTSIDE, NOSES TO PANE, BUT CANNOT HEAR.
UNI WEEPS (TOSS HIM MY BOUQUET FOR LUNCH?)
AND NOW THE LIGHTS   THE INSTRUMENTS   THEY COME

DĴ.   I'm no better than Uni—

MM.   AH MY LORDS
      As Nature and the Brothers quietly enter.
      MY QUEEN, HELP US IN A DIFFICULT MOMENT

GK.   DEAR JIMMY   DAVE   GO WELL IN MIND & BODY!

WHA. YES OLD CONFRERE & FRIEND   & MAKE OUR V WORK
      GLORIOUS   U CAN   U CAN   YOU'LL SEE!
      Air freshened, leaves in expectation stirring—
      Only the too bright music hurts our eyes.

MM.   MES ENFANTS YES   & EVEN OUR SILLY EPHRAIM
      PARTICIPATED IN SOMETHING NOT UNLIKE
      TODAY WHEN ON A SILVER SATIN PILLOW
      THE ENFANT OF FRANCE WAS CARRIED BAWLING INTO
      THE HALL OF MIRRORS. SO THERE'S PRECEDENCE
      BUT NOTHING TO EQUAL   COME NOW: PLACES, PLEASE!

ĴM.   We're ready.
               Pergolesi's minuet
      Turned by Stravinsky to this "wedding trio"
      —Soprano, tenor, bass, movement of utmost
      Suavity—is playing as we get
      Our last instructions.

MM.   JM WILL TAKE THE MARBLE
      STYLUS & GIVING US THE BENEFIT
      OF A WELLAIMED WORD, SEND OUR IMAGINED SELVES
      FALLING IN SHARDS THRU THE ETERNAL WATERS
      (DJ CUPBEARER) & INTO THE GOLDEN BOUGH
      OF MYTH   ON INTO LIFE   D'ACCORD? HUGS   KISSES
      WE'LL WRITE WHEN WE FIND WORK

DĴ.   We do it *now*?

MM.   ONE MOMENT MORE   SUNSET   INTO THE LIGHT
      LORDS, ACCEPT THESE YOUR CHILDREN   MAJESTY,
      BLESS OUR ENTERPRISES   BLESS US!

Nat.   CHILD,
      POETS, SCIENTIST, HAND, ALL HEAVEN HOLDS ITS BREATH.
      NOW MICHAEL, RING DOWN THE CURTAIN! GABRIEL,

THE STARS! RAPHAEL, ARMS OUT FOR THIS WISE & WITTY ONE!
EMMANUEL FOR ALL THREE! GO WELL!
AND YES, MY PROSERPINE, MY ARIEL,
MY DEAREST DEAR, SLIP SAFELY INTO YOU!
I WILL STAND HELPFUL TO THESE YOUR MORTAL FRIENDS.
ADIEU

Our eyes meet. DJ nods. We've risen. Shutters
Click at dreamlike speed. Sky. Awning. Bowl.
The stylus lifted. Giving up its whole
Lifetime of images, the mirror utters

A little treble shriek and rides the flood
Or tinkling mini-waterfall through wet
Blossoms to lie—and look, the sun has set—
In splinters apt, from now on, to draw blood,

Each with its scimitar or bird-beak shape
Able, days hence, aglitter in the boughs
Or face-down, black on soil beneath, to rouse
From its deep swoon the undestroyed heartscape

—Then silence. Then champagne.
                                              And should elsewhere
Broad wings revolve a horselike form into
One Creature upward-shining brief as dew,
Swifter than bubbles in wine, through evening air

Up, far up, O whirling point of Light—:

HERS HEAR ME I AND MINE SURVIVE SIGNAL
ME DO YOU WELL I ALONE IN MY NIGHT
HOLD IT BACK HEAR ME BROTHERS I AND MINE

CODA

The Higher Keys

CONTENTS

O Ariel who from a golden
Lidded compact beamed DJ's
And JM's profiles into heaven blazing
Above their table where the cups grew cold,

Then snapped it shut: once more a lightly
Made-up presence all in black
To leave us, mind on her last-minute packing—
Now to what destination does one write?

Down to Earth a ray slants true as birdsong
Through boughs in sparkling bloom too high to pluck.
This onionskin the shower puckered
Will soon be dry enough for words.

July 1978

Noon. Athens. Ten months later. JM's led
In shock from jet-lag to the "music room"
Just off the hall—space named for its upright
Tonedeaf piano, not much used. DJ
Presses a switch. Outleaping from the gloom,
Four cream plaster columns catch the light;
A path through olives; there, beyond the grove,
A little beached skiff, an Arcadian cove.
Fresco—but who painted it? He did?
Three weeks, sandpaper, gesso, turpentine
And look! beneath the mildest of blue skies
This ideal world lacks only one or two
Dimensions for a future morning's blue
Instreaming alpha wave to realize.

Yet from that house (a stone's throw distant) years
Flew by in the tall shadow of, no peep.
The manor—is it empty? All asleep?

Robert surely walks the rank parterres,
Works at the piano, leaps the hedge
On horseback. Still, we hesitate to call.
Could we face it if we found the hall
Alive with voices? or my final page
(Every day brought nearer) anything
But final? Ah, these are by now the risks
One takes, remembering whose house it is,
Their high connections and past kindnesses.
Before we know it our half-hearted ring
Is answered SIRS? as up dear Uni frisks,

Followed by Robert. He's alone. We've come
None too soon. He leaves next week for life.
Details last summer unavailable
Are rapidly sketched in. The Minnesota
Dairy farm. The sister five years old
Obediently practising her scales—
BABY WILL NEED DIVINO MOZARTINO
FWOM VEWY START   Then a rich widower
For grandfather, our friend the sole male heir,
CUSHY, NO? Perfection—pure Jane Austen.
SHREWD GUESS DJ, PLOTTING JUST SUCH ARRANGEMENTS
ON EARTH FOR LAB SOULS IS HER V WORK HERE.
ONE SHADED VILLA IN A BOMBAY STREET
HAS LATELY BROUGHT OUR PACKED HOUSE TO ITS FEET

We'll hear the rest another day. JM
Must sleep first, wake, read mail. (Urania
Loves her Nonáki, wants to visit him
While they're in Greece. Mimí describes from Rome
The dress Vasíli bought her—but a dress
Costing the earth, a web of light and frost
Unthinkable to ever really *wear!*
His mother hopes the flight was effortless.)
Must sit with DJ over dusk's pink gin.
Wrinkled his hand and white the beard he grew,
Must quote, tomorrow, Hugo to Mimí:
'We're both next door to Paradise, Madame,

I being old, you being beautiful'—
One term no longer, one not yet, quite true.

That second noon, Urania completes a
Round of calls with her folks. Vacation's done—
Back to their suburb, to their Family Pizza
Nearer the heart of things, though miles from one.
Almost six, dark, delicate, the child
Lolls in Godfather's lap, as she was told,
Her mind where? On a skateboard, her new school,
A TV screen halfway around the world . . .
Downstairs, she sets our painted skiff afloat
In the vibrations of a random note,
Then with a kiss is gone. Out comes the Board.
JM: So soon? I couldn't feel less clever.
DJ: Drink up that coffee, we've a deadline—
Robert won't be reachable forever.

SIRS, MR R SAYS WE ARE TO MEET
AT THE HEDGE. NOW THERE IS NO HEDGE, YOU KNOW,
BUT MR R MAKES ME SEE ONE! SIRS
I HEAR HIS WOODEN FLUTE   HE'S   WAIT
O MR EPHRAIM! WHAT A TREAT

MES CHERS! Old friend, we've missed you. AH THIS HEART
GLOWS WITH LOVE FOR YOU, AS FROM THE START.
RM WILL JOIN U PRESENTLY   What's new?
WELL, LUCA'S WON OVER AGATHA: 'MADAME SAINTE,
SOME PRETTY DREAMS PLEASE, FOR MY POET FRIEND?'
That's nice of Luca to still care for Chester.
I hadn't thought he was the type. THE TYPE
OF LUCA DEAR DJ CARES IN ITALICS
FOR E V E R Y O N E. HE'S TRYING TO REVIVE
THE ATHENIAN CLUB ABANDONED UPON LORD PLATO'S
MYSTERIOUS DEPARTURE, BUT NO ONE MUCH
WANTS TRAVESTIES, WORD GAMES . . . IT'S LIVELIER
WITH L AROUND & YET, TO QUOTE MB,
'IS LIVELINESS WHAT WE NEED?'
                              MAY I? Here's Robert—

NO. I TAKE THE LIBERTY: YOU SPOKE
OF MY YOUNG PROTEGE   Mr Nabokov!
Too embarrassing—again you've caught us
With hands full. Would next month be time enough?
GONE MES CHERS IN A HANDSOME (HORSEDRAWN) HUFF.
NOW YOUR RM

                MY NAME FOR AGATHA:
MAGGOTS' FOLLE. WANT NEWS OF OUR OLD GRADS?
Tell, tell! DID JM NOTICE THOSE ROULADES
OF LIGHT & THUNDER OFF OUR NEW ENGLAND COAST
LAST WINTER? Yes, we all did. GK & MICHAEL
REVISING CHARTS ON AIRBORNE ENERGIES
George keeps his old persona? OH IT'S G'S
PURE INTELLIGENCE AT WORK ALL RIGHT.
THAT SAME TEAM'S GETTING (OUT IN ARIZONA)
COLOSSAL RESULTS FROM A NEW SOLAR CONVERTER.
STUNNED TECHNICIANS CAN'T BELIEVE THEIR LUCK:
IT WAS MEANT TO FAIL What, sabotage? WELL, FURY
IN ANY CASE FROM THE FOSSIL ENERGY FACTION.
'LORD M, GIVE 'EM A BLAST?' 'RIGHT ON, GEORGAKI!'
2 GRINNING GRUBBY KIDS. MEANWHILE OUR WIT
(Wystan? WHO ELSE?) HAS GLITTERED INTO ACTION
FORBIDDINGLY FROM PHOTOGRAPHS OF MARS,
CAUSING 'SENSATIONS' To accomplish what?
MARS ONE OF GOD B'S OUTPOSTS. IF PROUD SCIENCE
WON'T BLAME ITSELF IT MUST BE MADE TO BLAME
ITS GADGETS. RAPHAEL STILL CHUCKLING: THEY
GREETED JM'S ARRIVAL YESTERDAY
WITH A CHEERY TREMOR SAFELY TO YR NORTH
Salonika—thousands homeless. Have they no shame?
NONE   BUT NOW THE NEWS, MY LADS, YOU CAME FOR

About Maria

ONE FINDS A GENERATION GAP IN HEAVEN.
DICKENS CAN'T ALWAYS BRIDGE IT, DICKINSON CAN.
EDNA MILLAY, POOR SOUL, BORED, STUPEFIED

BY 'MOODS' & 'FEELINGS', HAS NO PERMANENT
TOEHOLD   THREATENS DAILY TO BACKSLIDE
To Earth? That happens? IF A HIGH TONE IS
TO BE MAINTAINED. NOT ALWAYS POSSIBLE:
WHITMAN MINED HALF WITLESS, STAYS AT 6.
TH 19TH CENTURY ENGLISH, ALL BUT BYRON,
VEXED TO HAVE FOUND NO HARPS. SHELLEY: 'I'D BE
HAPPIER AMONG FISHERFOLK AT SEA'
WOULD HE? BYRON MUCH QUOTED FOR HIS OWN
BRAND OF CHAT: 'AT LAST TWO VERY GOOD
LEGS' . . . STRANGE: 'PERSONALITY' I SHOULD
HAVE THOUGHT THE CALLUS OF THE SOUL. NOT TRUE.
A CERTAIN STRIDENCY MAY BE OUTGROWN
SAY IN LISZT, BUT HIS ESSENTIAL HOKUM
& GALLANTRY & ALL THE REST WD SEEM
A CORE IMPERVIOUS TO THE PUMICE STONE
This self, then, recomposing stroke by stroke
To blank the stars out, so that love is blind
Even *there*— HOW MUCH HAS IT TO DO
ULTIMATELY WITH A THINKING MIND?
THESE MANNERS, THESE REFLEXES? WHA'S
OFTEN VAGUE, PREOCCUPIED, CAME THROUGH
LESS AS POSE THAN AS DIRECT EXPOSURE
(OVEREXPOSURE?) OF HIS THINKING MIND
Overexposure? WELL   THAT 'BOYISHNESS'
VIS A VIS YEATS   THE SOUPCON OF A GLOAT
AT BEING TEXT TO WBY'S FOOTNOTE?
OR YEATS'S WEARY PROUD FORBEARING SMILE
AS OF AN UNREAD VISION ON THE SHELF?
MM ALONE WAS TOTALLY HERSELF,
MIND ONE WITH MATTER. YET SHE 'HAD A STYLE'
& WAS IT REAL? THE INDIVIDUAL STYLE
OF A PARTICULAR PERSON? WHO CAN SAY?
IT WAS I THINK HER GENIUS THAT ALLOWED
SPACE TO SURROUND HER IN WHATEVER CROWD,
A CALM EXTERIOR UPHELD, DEFINED
NEVER PREDICTABLY, BY HER THINKING MIND
A mask? IF SO A WHOLLY LIFELIKE ONE

If not? A MIRACLE. IN YOUR OWN PHRASE
HEAVEN WILL BE A DULLER PLACE WITHOUT HER

And Bombay sharper with her. A BROWN BUNDLE
Five months old (told clearly not to talk
Till six months later) piped "Shut up!" in Hindi.
Nurse fled screaming, and a priest was called
To cleanse the nursery. MM: 'EMETICS,
CHANTING, SMOKE, ROBERT I LEARN TO KEEP
MY LITTLE TRAP SHUT' You communicate!
How? IN THAT NURSERY WHICH MUST BE SEEN
TO BE BELIEVED, A WREATH OF PLASTICENE
PINK BABIES HOLDS OUR BROWN ONE'S WRY REFLECTION:
'TALK TO ME ROBERT, QUICK! THEY'RE ALL ASLEEP'
So you look in, a secret minister?
AH THE MOST GLORIOUS GLANCES FOLLOW HER!
THEN, NOT A WEEK AGO, A DUSKY BABE
STARTLED HIS GOGGLEBEADED DAM BY DRAWING
A PERFECT SQUARE IN THE DUST OF THE PARLOR FLOOR.
MAIDS BEATEN & AWED. 'AND THIS IS JUST
THE (M) TIP OF THE ICEBERG, ROBERT DEAR.
NEXT MONTH I MEAN TO SHIFT INTO HIGH GEAR.'

Remember meeting Robert? The question never
Fails to prompt a smile—who could forget?
That was the year our Stonington High School
Mistook itself for a summer theatre.
Old troupers, doddering up with crutch and creak
Out of the quicklime into the limelight,
Filled the undiscerning hall. One night
A mummy assoluta of technique
Precariously conjured, points in air,
Abysses yawning for the vivandière
Till rataplan! four gaily intertwined
Cadets provoked this murmur from behind:
"It's everything one loathes about the Dance . . ."
We looked round laughing; and there Robert sat
With Isabel, KNOWING ALREADY THAT
HERE WAS ONE FRIENDSHIP NEVER LAUNCHED BY CHANCE

★

The Music to Come

HA HA MR ROBERT
               OFF YOU GO, HORSE! OUF
Tired? A HARD DAY WITH THE 12 TONE GERMANS
THEN CALLED TO MME CALLAS FOR A CHAT:
'YOU KNOW, WHAT'S YR NAME? MY BAD EYESIGHT ALONE
MADE FOR EFFECTIVE TOUCHES IN PERFORMANCE.
THAT SUDDEN REELING-BACKWARD HALF A SWOON
IN TOSCA (ACT II) CAUSING HEARTS TO STOP
CAME FROM WHEN I STUMBLED ON A PROP
IN DRESS REHEARSAL. LITTLE THINGS LIKE THAT.
NOW TELL ME, TOM? DICK? YOU'RE RETURNING SOON
AS A COMPOSER? INTERESTING   YOU WILL WRITE
FOR THE STAGE? YOU DON'T SAY? WONDERFUL!
WITH A GOOD PART FOR ME? . . . AH I FORGET,
ONCE & FOR ALL IT'S H E R E THAT ONE RETIRES'
MAKING NIGHT GLIMMER WITH SHORTSIGHTED TEARS

This relieves us. Since the fête at Nine
There's been no mention of your music, Robert.
MUCH OF IT OVER YR HEADS I FEAR   & MINE!
EVEN AS WE TALK I'M SEPARATING
THE TONES IN A DOUBLE GLISSANDO. A FULL YEAR
CD BE DEVOTED TO EACH ONE'S LEAST VIBRATIONS.
THEN, EXAMS: COMPOSE 500 VARIATIONS
ON THREE NOTES. G A D (SAY) RING IN MY MIND
& MUST BE LINKED FIRST TO THEIR FREQUENCIES
IN WESTERN MUSIC (SCHUMANN, BACH, JOSQUIN)
THEN TO VIBES OF COLOR & EMOTION
(G MINOR A BLUEGREEN SUBLIMITY)
Why only three notes? THREE FOR THOSE OF US
WHO SHARE THE WESTERN   OH WELL, GENIUS,
IS AS WE KNOW A NEARLY UNBREAKABLE MOULD:
A/B/A OR MAJOR/MINOR/MAJOR
DJ: But Schoenberg— YES   HE GRASPED THE MOULD-

529

BREAKING IDEA YET LEFT US WITH THE OLD.
INNOVATION ONLY STRENGTHENED IT
WHILE MANY A LISTENER CLAWED HIS CHAIR & PRAYED
'LET O LET THE LID FALL ON THAT HAND,
STEINWAY COLLAPSE & BREAK THOSE WRETCHED KNEES,
PUT O PUT AN END TO THIS CAREER'
The prayer's been answered? 'NOW SIR, IF YOU PLEASE,
I ' L L USE THE INSTRUMENT. FIRST LESSON, DEAR
MR X, THERE ARE THESE THINGS CALLED K E Y S . '

And so *you*'ll save us from the tyrant Three,
Ménage à trois, synthesis, trilogy. . . ?
QUEEN MAB: 'MR ROBERT, MAKE US A MUSIC TO
CLEAN UP & THIN OUT THE WESTERN SCENE'
THESE WORDS NO SOONER UTTERED I BEGIN
TO HEAR SOMETHING   THIN   NONREPETITIVE
IS IT AN ECHO OF PURCELL? THE FLEET HIGH
FLUTE OF A HIMALAYAN SHEPHERD'S LAMENT?
NOW I BEGIN TO GIVE IT FORM, ITS FEET
CARRY IT UP: STRONG, SLOW / DOWN: FAST   EXPLORING
A NEW & TORTUOUS LANDSCAPE, QUITE ALONE.
THEN SLIGHTEST COMPANY ON DIFFERENT FEET
ARRIVES, THE SHADOW LEAPING OVER ROCKS
That's the new mould? Instead of A-B-A,
Atom and shadow atom? YOU MIGHT SAY
IT WILL BE A & 1/2   CLEANSED OF FALSE DRAMA
A BOREDOM FALLING ON BORED EARS, RESOLVING
INTO A TASTE FOR LESS. I MAY PERCEIVE IT
INSTRUMENTALLY IN 20 YEARS.
NOW AS TO THE 'SELLING' IT MUST BE
AN IRRESISTIBLE CHALLENGE TO PERFORM.
CASTING ASIDE JUNK TOOLS & ELECTRONICS
IT MUST FIND POEMS & PLAYERS, VIRTUOSI
AS WELL AS A CHILD WHISTLING UNACCOMPANIED
TO WHOM THE SHADOW IS AS WHISTLEABLE
AS THE LONE WALKER. So you'll want to lean
Heavily on melody? DJ!
LEAN! HEAVILY! NO NO   THE POINT'S TO FIND
A PURE PIED PIPER IN THE WESTERN MIND

WHO'LL CHARM THE RATS AWAY   The children too?
The multitudes about to die? 'O QUEEN,
AM I TO WRITE THE SUPREME LULLABY?'
'NO, MUSICIAN, THE SWEET REVEILLE
FOR THOSE STILL LEFT TO WAKE.'
                            The cup moves sadly—
It *is* an awesome task to undertake.
A LONELY ONE   I DON'T RUSH OFF WITH GLAD
CRIES LIKE OUR FRIENDS. I SHAN'T LIKE THEM BELONG
TO QM'S CRYSTAL SET   THEN TOO, YOU SEE
(A deep breath) I'M TO BE CRIPPLED   Dear God. *Why?*
WHY NOT? CONFINED & SLIGHTLY SET APART,
SLOW TO LOVE, FORCED TO GET ON WITH IT,
MAKE SENSE OF IT, MAKE MY REPORT TO GOD
Robert . . . From birth? YES   JOINING THE CLUB (FOOT)
But hasn't modern surgery by now—
PLEASE   I'VE TO REJECT TOO MANY BONE
IMPLANTS B4 THE DOCTORS LET ME BE
At least a fine Byronic *head*? 'THIS TIME
DEAR MR ROBERT, NO DISTRACTIONS. WHO
WANTS LOVE MUST EARN IT.' SO MY SLIGHT MELANCHOLY
BUT I'LL GET OUT OF GYM! MISS JANE: 'PLUS TWO
DOTING PARENTS, MR R, AND OH
THAT SHY FOND SISTER, NO MARRIAGE FOR HER, NO, NO,
THERE SHE'LL BE TAPPING AT YOUR STUDIO
(SUCH AN ATTRACTIVE SETUP, OUT IN A BARN):
BROTHER DEAR, YOUR LUNCH?' FORGIVE ME, LADS
BUT TIME IS PRESSING, IF NOT HERE, BELOW
IN THE RED MATRIX   Go, we understand.

YOU'LL SEE ME NEXT THRU A FAINT HAZE.
FIVE CEREMONIES ON AS MANY DAYS
BEGIN TOMORROW   AFTER WHICH ALAS
DOWN TO EARTH I SPIRAL LIKE A LEAF
WHO'D GLADLY STAY . . . BUT NO: FOND AS I AM
OF UNI, ONE CANNOT SAY NEIGH TO LIFE!

SIRS HE WAS LAUGHING WHEN HE LEFT
'TROT IN THERE UNI & TRY FOLLOWING

THAT ACT!' SIRS, MR R IS MY SHEPHERD,
WHEN HE SPEAKS MY WORLD GOES GREEN,
HE SHOWS ME SKILLS   SHALL I SAY A POEM?
One of yours? Dear creature, by all means!

I STAND EACH DAY BY THE SCHOOLROOM DOOR
FROM WHICH CAME MURMURINGS, BEFORE.
I STAND AND WAIT TO GREET OUR FRIENDS
AND SUMMER ENDS, AND SUMMER ENDS.

★

The Ceremonies: I

High above Uni's green surrounding fields
A space once nursery, then schoolroom, yields
To second childhood. Little chair and desk
Are gone; gone too, the blackboards with Dantesque
Or Yeatsian systems. Random colored blocks
Spell RAT or MAN. Above a shut toybox
Robert's own full-length self-portrait's hung:
Paintbrush hovering, smocked in white, a young
Sad clown. The room is airless. Unlit gauze
Draperies (a tasseled pink cord draws)
Erect a limp ghost pyramid. Within,
Our friend lies as if sleeping, knees to chin.
Then the angelic Intern of his dream
Glides into semblance on one downward beam.

Mich.   AH BABE, I MICHAEL WHOSE DOMAIN IS LIGHT
BRING YOU THE FIRST OF FIVE GIFTS: SIGHT
In either hand he bears a sparkling orb
Of Empire, the wee numbskull must absorb.
NOW POET, HAND, DECOR! A MIRROR, RUN,
FACE IT TO YOUR PAINTED WALL. TURN ON THE SUN.
We do. The fresco springs to life. AHA!

CHILD, LANDSCAPE, SEA AND SKY,
ARE YOU READY? ANSWER!

RM. AYE.

Mich. YES! YOU SEE, TELL US!

RM. LORD, THESE BLEAR EYES LOOK PAST TWO RED KNOBS

Mich. YOUR SMALL UNBORN KNEES.

RM. Taking it in. AH LORD, LORD, NOT THAT, PLEASE.

Mich. CHILD, LOOK LONG ON IT, YOUR SMALL VITAL IMPEDIMENT.

RM. POOR FOOT, POOR FOOT.

Mich. CHILD, THAT IS YOUR UPWARD STEP.
BEFORE, YOU LIMPED. NOW HOBBLED YOU WILL LEAP!
NEXT?

RM. LORD, RED LIQUID WALLS, A TRAILING CORD.

Mich. CHILD, YOUR FIRST CHORD.

RM. AND ALL THIS, LORD, AGAINST THE PAINTED SCENE
OF WHERE I AM NO LONGER, AND HAVE NOT YET BEEN?

Mich. YES CHILD. THE SECOND GIFT WILL BE BROUGHT IN
UPON THE MORROW BY MY TWIN.
NOW BLESSED ONES, YOU THREE
MAY SPEAK OF MORTAL THINGS. OUR CHILD CAN SEE.
He goes.
     The nursery is once more a room
(Only we can't make out the portrait's eyes)
And Robert again "himself". Was this, we wonder,
His first experience of the new womb?

OR MY FIRST SENSE OF IT. THIS WHOLE LONG TIME,
MY OLD SOUL TRAINING HERE, UP TO NEW TRICKS,
A LITTLE UNKNOWN BOD WAS 266
DAYS IN RESIDENCE, MICHAEL IS SUBLIME:
ALL THIS BOTH REAL & IMAGINARY BUT
ON HIS FIRST WORD 'BABE' A B A B E I W A S
FLOATING WARM & LANGUID   THEN ON 'SIGHT'
2 STABBING RED GLOWS SHOT INTO MY HEAD
AND THERE BEFORE ME SHONE YOUR SCENE, AND I
WAS IN THAT MOMENT BOTH UNBORN AND BORN
Go on! WHAT MORE? I DO GO ON. THE FOUR
NEXT CEREMONIES WILL   ME SLEEPY (YAWN)
Poor little tyke, yes, yes. Shut those new eyes.

SIRS? IS MR ROBERT SAFE?
Isn't he in Their hands? HE SAID 'UNI TAKE ME
OUT RIDING LATER, FOR I LIMP NOW'
Sad, sad, sad; and strange, how such loss turns
To profit. WE LOST OUR PROUD IVORY HORN
Ah, so you *had* horns then? THE OLD ONES DID
TWISTED & LONG & USELESS Oh? Yet legend
Says any spring you dipped your horn into
Was cleansed of venom. WELL, WE WERE OF THE WHITE

★

The Ceremonies: 2

The nursery, with Robert as before,
But open-eyed as Fire comes through the door
On tiptoe with a tray of fresh herbs, wild
Apples, a garlic clove, a nutmeg.

Gabr. CHILD.

RM. LORD?

Gabr. DO YOU SEE ME?

RM. YES, LORD.

Gabr. SO MY TWIN'S GIFT TOOK. TODAY WE MUST MAKE HASTE
TO HELP OUR CHILD DEVELOP TASTE.
NOW CHILD, LICK THE SALTS THAT SEASON
WHAT WETLY WALLS YOU IN AND, WITH THAT, REASON.

RM. LORD, I TAKE IT IN. I MAKE SENSE OF IT.

Gabr. DEAR UNBORN, YOU HAVE BEEN THOROUGHLY SCHOOLD, & THE
OTHER MEANING OF THIS NEW SENSE IS YOURS TO APPLY.
1: NO DYNAMICS SIMPLY FOR THE THRILL OF THEM,
2: KEEP ENTRENCHED THE CLEAN CALM HARMONICS OF HEAVEN,
3: BRING TO YOUR ART THE CLARIFYING SALT YOU NOW TASTE
AND YOU WILL PLEASE OUR GOD.

RM. LORD, I OBEY.

Gabr. AND CHILD, DEVELOP A TASTE FOR THE ICE,
       THAT COLD ABSOLUTE WHICH TINKLING IN YOUR WINE
       HELPS MAKE ITS INTOXICANT TWICE
       AS POTENT IN THE HEAT OF TOO MUCH LIFE.
RM.   LORD, ICE IT IS.
Gabr. SO. ON THE MORROW WITH A PAT
       MY EMMANUEL BRINGS YOU THAT
       MOST GRATIFYING OF THE SENSES. THERE!
       GREET YOUR FRIENDS & TASTE THEIR AIR!
       Exit.
            In Robert's portrait now a sheen
       Of Lethe spreading wipes the flat lips clean.

       THE ICE (cup musing dreamily) SO ODD
       Has it to do with salt? Salt melting ice?
       THEIR SOLE CONCERN IS WITH WHAT I'M TO MAKE.
       ICE ICE   THEY WANT   AH YES! THE ICE IS COMING
       An Ice Age? Salt would be a taste for thinning . . .
       THAT'S IT   OFF TO THE LAB   Did Uni take
       You riding? I WANTED TO SEE A STAR   And did you?
       IT WAS TOO FIERY FOR THE LIKES OF US
       & YET WE PEERED   YES, YES LADS, IT'S TO BE:
       I'M 2/5 UNDER WAY   YOU TWO GROW DISTANT
       Take our love, Robert, while you can. TOMORROW
       I MAY TOUCH YOUR FACES, FOR I NOW STARE
       STRAIGHT DOWN ON YOU   Not from the mirror? NO
       AND SAVOR YR POLLUTED ATMOSPHERE
       & ON THAT TASTELESS NOTE DEAR ONES ADIEU!

       SIRS HE CALLED FOR A SUGAR LUMP
       AS ANTIDOTE TO THE SALT LICK
       THEN 'SIGHTLESS CLAP, SOUNDLESS HANDS,
       FETCH ME THE PEACOCK!' & OFF THEY FLEW
       Uni, is he limping? has he changed?
       HE COMES TO MY MIND EACH DAY DIMINISHED,
       A LITTLE MAN MADE YOUNGER YET.
       How lonely you'll—how lonely we'll all be.
       YOU'LL HAVE THE PEACOCK STILL   AND UNICE!

★

SIRS? HE WILL LEAVE US? Yes, you didn't know?
DJ: It's dawning on him only now?
—Uni is stunned. The cup looks for a place,
Some corner of the Board to hide its face,
Then with THE LIGHT O! stumbles from the room.

The Ceremonies: 3

Emm. CHILD, IT IS YOUR WATER FRIEND. I CARRY A GIFT SUCH
AS WILL BE NEEDED IN YOUR NEW ART: TOUCH.

RM. LORD, THANK YOU, I WILL HANDLE IT WITH CARE.
Forth from a pool of dancing blues and greens,
With nothing in his hands, Emmanuel leans
To stroke the dazzled infant's brow and lips,
Heart, limbs, and sex with glistening fingertips.

Emm. O FLOATING PUNY THING, GAILY BEGIN EXPLORING,
LET FINGERS FLOW ABOUT, BETWEEN, BELOW!
HEAD, NECK AND ARMS, & THESE NEW KNOBBLY KNEES,
FIND EACH, CHILD, KNOW

RM. I WILL. I DO, LORD.

Emm. AND?

RM. MAKE SENSE OF THEM.

Emm. SEE? THE TASTE OF REVENGE?
FEEL YOUR POOR MOTHER GIVE A START! SHE CRIES
(ON THE MORROW YOU WILL HEAR THAT CRY)
'TOM, IT'S MOVED! TOM! I AM NEAR MY TIME!'

RM. LORD, HOW GRATEFULLY
I FLOAT IN THIS YOUR WORLD AND NOT YET HEAR
THOSE TOO NEAR CRIES. FORGIVE,
ACCEPT THE FIRST TEARS OF THESE SWIMMING EYES.
O TOUCHING, TOUCHING! WERE NOT FEELINGS BANNED
I'D CALL THIS GIFT MOST FEELING OF ITS KIND.

Emm. CHILD, YOU HAVE PASSED THE HALFWAY MARK.
SOON DAYLIGHT, NOISE, THE SLAP
WILL WRENCH YOU FROM YOUR LIQUID DARK.
THINK ON US, CHILD, IN YOUR SLEEP,

CLUTCH THE PLUMP BREAST, PURSE THE LITTLE LIP
TASTING THE MILK OF LIFE. THEN SOON
PUT HANDS TO KEYS AND MAGIC US WITH TUNE.
NOW BLESSINGS ON YOU THREE.
GO WELL, DEAR BABE, WE DWELL IN THEE.
Emmanuel goes.
          The thin unearthly glaze
Has spread across the portrait. Here a nose,
There an ear can be made out. The room
Dissolves about us. Robert—? But he stays.

SIRS HE CALLED THROUGH THE DOOR 'UNI,
TELL THEM TO COME EARLY AND SPEAK'
Tomorrow. YES 'FOR ON THE FINAL DAY
WE SAY GOODBYE' O SIRS O SIRS
Uni, there'll be toys, a little horse,
Horsie his first word. Hush, he won't forget—
But Uni has gone elsewhere with his grief.

★

Next day, his feelings mastered: SIRS HE ASKED ME
'UNI, WHAT DO YOU SEE?' I SAW
A VERY SMALL MAN, STILL WITH MR
R'S KIND EYES BUT A CRUTCH & A FLUTE.
I TOLD HIM. 'UNI, JUST AS I THOUGHT,
JUST SO.' HE IS HERE! O MR ROBERT
WHO WILL BOOST YOU UP ON MY BACK?

UNI, NO MORE RIDES FOR US. DEAR CREATURE,
HOW YOU'VE LIFTED MY HEART   BUT NOW FAREWELL.
TOMORROW THE LADS WILL FIND OUR NURSERY DOOR
SWINGING ON ITS HINGES & YOUR FRIEND
ROBERT A RED OFFENSIVE WRINKLED THING
AWAITING THE BREATH OF LIFE. NO TEARS
IN THOSE GREAT FAITHFUL EYES! AND ON YR RUMP
WITH MY IMAGINED FLUTE AN AFFECTIONATE THUMP:
UNI, AWAY!
         Oh Robert— And no tears

In our small faithless ones! WELL, FAITHLESS? No,
No. We believe. We do. AND SO MUST I.
Will it be taken from you now, that ingrained
Callus of the Self? ALL   ALL SKINNED OFF.
BEFORE ANOTHER TINY MARSYAS
CAN STAND UP TO APOLLO, FLUTE IN HAND,
MUST COME THE TERRIFYING INTERVAL
IN WHICH PURE FACELESSNESS ATTEMPTS TO SMILE
This is still you, though. BUT INSIDE THE SOFT
WALNUT SHELL THE MEAT FORMED THESE LONG MONTHS
IS GRINDING OUT A NEW TUNE FROM ITS GROOVES
A tune that, heard, makes *you* inaudible?
SOMEWHERE NO DOUBT AN ANCIENT 78
PRESERVES THE SCRATCHY TONE OF THAT LATE GREAT
AMATEUR TENOR: ME   And while Earth's waiting
For its new music we'll replay the old
To our hearts' content.
                        DJ: Will we be told
Your name? JM: Have you been told it? AH
U'VE STRUCK A NOTE! THERE'S RUSTLING IN THE WINGS
WE'VE TIME LEFT ONLY FOR LAST WORDS   WHAT WILL IT
BE? SHALL WE DEFY THEM? TURN THE CLOCK BACK?
'IT'S EVERYTHING ONE LOATHES'—*about the Dance!*
(Sentence completed here in operatic
Unison.) We looked round: there you sat.
AND U TWO? DJ DID YOU HEAR JM:
'A KINDRED SOUL' YOU WARMED MY HEART, DEAR ONES
FROM START TO THIS THE NOT SO BITTER END.
QUICK! A CARESS ON EITHER ELDER'S BROW,
I'M TIPTOP ON THE CHILDREN'S SLIDE . . . NOW!   N O W

★

The Ceremonies: 4

The little man lies drowsing, curled up under
White hangings, when a voice of gentlest thunder

        Charges the expectant atmosphere.
        It is the twinkling Lord of Earth.

Raph. HEAR, HEAR!
        YES BABE, TODAY YOUR NAME YOU'LL HEAR
        FROM OLD GRANDFATHER CLAY. YES, YES, LONG DEAR,
        LONG DOUBTING THOMAS, LEND AN EAR
        AND WITH A KISS I WHISPER IN IT: T O M !

DJ. That's his new name?

JM. So it would seem. The cast
        Of the next *Rake* assembling? They work fast.

Raph. NOW WITH YOUR STRONG LITTLE FOOT, A KICK! SOUND NUMBER TWO:
        DOWN THROUGH LIVE CAVES & TUNNELS HER CRY COMES TO YOU.
        The tiny figure winces at the cry
        And squeezes its face shut despairingly.
        NOW 4/5 BABE, YOUR LAST BUT ONE
        GIFT RECEIVE FROM ME, THIS GUN
        Eyes open. Fingers curl about the flute—
        A "blow-gun" (witty Raphael)—TO SHOOT
        MUSIC INTO THE WORLD'S EARS FROM YOUR HEART.
        REMEMBER YOUR NAME, TOM, AND START!

        Again the kick. The mother's cry. One glance
        From Raphael and the portrait . . . is no more.
        A pinch of dry, used color dusts the floor.
        Faint sanguine plots a newly primed expanse.

Raph. DUST   DUST TO DUST   GO, G O
                       And gravely he
        Goes also. Blackout in the nursery.

        DJ: We never asked if Robert—Tom—
        Would get in touch. JM: Why, by the time
        He's twenty we'll be—never mind. Then too,
        Some things Maria could *he* cannot do,
        Like making dates. Isn't it just as well?
        DJ: Imagine though. What if among
        Our fading, peeling bats appeared a young
        Crippled stranger who'd read *Mirabell*
        And wrote odd music? How would we react?
        JM: Worse yet, my dear, what if in fact

Two old parties tottering through Bombay
Should be accosted, on the given day,
By Plato posing as a teenage guide?
What if The Whole of It were verified?

No, henceforth we'll be more and more alone.
Uni, our Peacock, Ephraim—each of these
We have by imperceptible degrees
. . . What to say? Not tired of. Outgrown?

It's *Her* one wants to reach. Suppose our bird
Carried a message, would she—HERE I AM
Mirabell? INDEED NOT! It's you, Ma'am!
I RATHER THOUGHT YOU'D ASK FOR MY WEE WORD

You're always so busy—AH BUT ALWAYS SO
AVAILABLE! CALL ANY TIME! MUST GO!
I'LL JOIN YOUR CRITICAL SYMPOSIUM.

Our what?
        (She's gone.) MES CHERS! Yes, Ephraim? SOME
FANS OF YOURS IN HEAVEN, A SMALL CROWD,
HAD HOPED TO HEAR THE POEM READ ALOUD.

Whose idea was that? RM'S. SALON
AFTER SALON LEFT BREATHLESS BY HIS SLY
HINTING AT 'REVELATIONS'   AS AM I
MES CHERS! The guest list? TO BE SET ANON

★

Midday heat. A growing restlessness
Pervades the household. Each room stuffy, small.
JM seeks out the keyboard, Mozart falling
Open to K. 576, and twice
Attempts the opening movement's closing bars
Aglint with sweet shifts of nuance and pace,
Stars in a brook. DJ drifting downstairs

Knows it's too soon, but has this funny feeling
That if we started *now* . . . JM: Yes, yes!
Out with Board and cup, which in a trice—

The Ceremonies: 5

Nat. POET HAND QUICK QUICK
DIVINO MOZARTINO DID THE TRICK!
Sleeves rolled up, She's everywhere at once,
In the truest sense con spirito,
BROTHER COME, HELP GIVE A SHOVE
An overwhelming, unseen radiance—;
Then con amore her next phrases flow:
AND LAUNCH UPON THE WORLD OUR LITTLE LOVE

WHOOSH! HE'S OUT   CAUGHT IN THAT FIRST CHORD! HIGH!
HOLD HIM HIGH! AND NOW, TOMIKINS   T O M
THE FIRST SNIFF   AH! BABE! POET, YOU & I
GODPARENTS LOOK ON ALL ABEAM.
NOW HAND, A WHACK? O MIRACLE, O LOUD!
GO TOM, AND M A K E   U S   P R O U D

The ceremony's done. It's sunrise where
Tom glistening wet takes in her blessed air.

SIRS I HEARD HIM, SUCH A COLT!
WE COWERED IN LIGHT, THE PEACOCK & I
THEY CAME & WENT IN A GREAT RUSH
NEVER SUCH HASTE SIRS DID YOU GIVE HIM
LUCK FROM ME? A FOUR LEAF CLOVER?
Uni, we had no time. OH SIRS IT'S OVER

Over . . . From now on it's the hedge for us.
MUCH ACTIVITY   AS MR R SAID
THEY'RE ALREADY BUILDING ?BLEACHERS?
Benches in tiers. Our poem's to be heard.
O IT WILL BE A WORK THAT WHITENS!

★

Doings in Bombay

MES CHERS! 'MR SECRETARY' SAYS OUR QUEEN
(Secretary? ME! MY LATEST FUNCTION)
'TELL THEM OF MY DARLING' READY? SCENE:
LARGE VULGAR LIVING ROOM. CIRCLE OF DUSKY
MATRONS & A WHITEHAIRED BRAHMIN PRIEST
ALL RIVETED BY TINY FIGURE DRESSED
IN GAUDY YELLOW ROBES: INDEED, THE YOUNGEST
ORDAINED PRIEST IN HISTORY! ALREADY
CREDITED WITH 8 MIRACLES & NOW
PERFORMING HIS 9TH. THE BRAHMIN: SIR, THAT COW
EATING OUR PARISH WHEAT, DO WE DRIVE IT OFF?
PAUSE (MOST EFFECTIVE) AS OUR DARLING PUSHES
HIMSELF ERECT ON GHASTLY YELLOW CUSHIONS,
EYES PRIEST & SHAKES A CHUBBY FINGER: NO.
(HOW ELSE KEEP THAT WRETCHED POPULATION
HAPPILY AT STARVATION LEVEL?) 'O,
O MR SECRETARY, THAT LITTLE HAND,
THAT ABSOLUTE ASSURANCE! THAT COMMAND!'
IT POINTS NOW TO THE WOMAN NEXT IN LINE.
SHE: LORD, MAY MY DAUGHTER CONCEIVE TWIN BOYS?
FROM TINY FIGURE SUCH A SCREAM OF RAGE
BREAKS OUT THAT ALL STEP BACK. 'LORD, AS YOU PLEASE
(SAYS WOEFUL WOMAN) I WILL INTERVENE.'
WHEREUPON SUCH A SMILE LIGHTS THE SERENE
SMALL BUDDHA FACE THAT ALL FALL ON THEIR KNEES.

The previous miracles? IN ONE WEEK HE
1) TOOK UP AN EMPTY BOWL & PERFECTLY
MIMED BEGGING   2) FOUGHT OFF ALL CLOTHES NOT SAFFRON
3) CRAWLED WITH A FLAME TO COBRA ALTAR
& LIT THE OIL LAMP   4) SPOKE FIRST OFFICIAL
WORD ('MOO') TO COW WHOSE HEAD PEERED IN THE ROOM
5) PLACED ON COW, DUG IN HIS TINY HEELS

& TRAMPLED TOO-DENSE PINK CARNATION BED
6) PRIESTS SUMMONED: HINDU, BUDDHIST, MUSLIM
& XTIAN, 10 IN ALL. THE SECOND WORD
IN PERFECT HINDI: B R O T H E R S 7) CROWDS
BREAK THRU POLICE CORDON AROUND THE VILLA.
LITTLE HAND UPRAISED, THE 3RD WORD: G O!
8) THE FOURFOLD ORDINATION. Rome
Won't take *that* lying down. QM: 'IT BETTER,
OR WE'LL LAY PAUL OUT BENEATH PETER'S DOME'

DJ: Well, these make Luca's pranks look tame.
NOT THE LATEST: HE & VN HAVE DRIVEN
1680 BUTTERFLIES INTO L'S CHAPEL!
AG FOAMING & NO MM TO SHARE THE BLAME

Couldn't too much publicity disrupt
Maria's—Plato's—V Work? AU CONTRAIRE.
GAME PLAN: VAST CHILDHOOD FAME FOLLOWED BY SPELL
OF GREAT QUIET BARGAINING   THEN THE CAREER:
MONEYLENDERS DRIVEN FROM THE TEMPLE,
OUR FRIEND EMERGING AS A SCIENTIST
WILL GRADUATE IN LONDON AGE 19
THUS (HELPED BY GK & WHA) BEGINNING
A SAGA OF DISCOVERY & INVENTION
STARTLING THE WORLD AT FIRST, THEN SLOWLY THINNING

(It's *Ephraim* spilling these top secrets, who
Not a month ago ingenuously
Spoke of "Lord Plato's mysterious departure"
As if he wouldn't, couldn't ever know;
As if he feared, instead of fanning them,
The tongues of ghostly fire above our heads;
As if *his* manners hadn't by that time
Kindled to the Promethean paradigm.
Or . . .? Since the Powers—according to Maria—
Want everything known, the etymology
Of *secretary* may provide a clue
To E's new "function". Is it really new

Or does our sly one cloud with gai savoir
Some remote birthright, some entitling star?)

★

Mimí

We don't quite understand—it's not yet morning—
Vasíli's voice, from Rome, expressionless:
"Instantaneous . . . no pain, no warning . . ."
Dead? *Mimí?* And dressed in the white dress.

We reach her, but she's dazed by the prompt call
Or the ungodly hour: BUT WHERE AM I?
WHO'S THIS   VASILI ARE YOU HIDING   WHY?

So Ephraim guides her from our love, which hurts,
Back to her patron's dim confessional
Where (though harp and trumpet fill the air)

She must sit upright on a little bench
And not cry if her finery reverts
To homespun rags, and shake out her long hair,
And be a candle for the dawn to quench.

741 HERE: SO YOU KNEW A FIREFLY WOMAN HEIR
    Mimí was?
ONE OF MANY 1000S SINCE F/W WAS DISASSEMBLED.
JUST A PINCH MIND YOU, BUT IT GAVE HER THAT ELEMENT OF
QUICK MATURITY & LANGUISHMENT IN UNNATURAL
SURROUNDINGS. THE PROBLEM WITH ALL PLANT DENSITIES IS THIS
NEGATIVE ASPECT OF 'SHOOTING': A DYING AS THE SEED
CYCLE CLINGS TO A PERENNIAL TALENT FAR BRIEFER
THAN HUMAN LIFE CYCLES. ST AGATHA WORKING THIS OUT.
YR DEAR ONE WAS ALSO ALAS BARREN & THAT OFTEN

544

FRUSTRATES VEG DENSITIES
    I'd have said her fear
Of motherhood was psychological.
                    WELL, PSYCHE RESTS ON NATURE. IF
PHYSICAL DISABILITY OCCURS, NATURE SUMMONS
HER SHADOW, PSYCHE: 'MAKE HIM/HER ADJUST'   NOW TO THE HEDGE?
YOUR BIRD WINGS AWAY, HAVING SUNG
    Mirabell, you've dropped the name we gave you?
                        NO   I REVEL IN IT
& HAVE BEEN DESIGNATED BY IT HERE. BUT MY NATURE
IS MODEST & AT THIS ADVANCED AGE IT IS HARD TO CHANGE
    Lately, though, you took on a new nature,
    Didn't you?
NO   I KEEP MY COLORS BUT HAVE A PRESS OF WORK: I AM
IN CHARGE OF EDUCATION OF ALL SOULS DESTINED TO BE
FORCED INTO HIGHER CYCLES, TO HAVE BAD HABITS BROKEN.
THEY CALL IT THE MIRABELL REFORM SCHOOL IN THE GREEK'S WORLD
THO MY TELEPHONE REMAINS LISTED UNDER 741
                So I'm wrong to have the atomic
    Fire fading from your eyes at Lesson Nine.
SHH DEAR OLD FRIENDS: I T I S G O N E ! & I AM NOW REPUTED
TO BE A 'PUSHOVER' AMONG CERTAIN UNRULY TYPES.
THE HEDGE? UNI, AWAY TOGETHER! UNO   DUE   TRE

    Look, duets! That's Robert's doing. Any
    Word from him, by the way? NONE YET BUT YES:
A CRY   A HIGH C FROM THE CRIB
RINGS IN MY HEAD! Were you afraid he had
Begun to forget you, Uni? FORGET HIS FRIEND?
NOT MR ROBERT! HE RODE ON MY BACK!

MES CHERS! SUCH A GLAD FLAPPING OF THOSE GREAT
COLORED WINGS & THAT WHITE COMET'S MANE!
THE GREEK YOUNG WIFE STILL IN 'TANK THERAPY'
BUT STAY, HERE COMES WAVING A BUTTERFLY NET
Nabokov? ON PAROLE AFTER HIS PRANK

PRANK? WE USED EXQUISITE HORDES OF NYMPHALIS IO

TO FORM A TICKLING FLUTTERING DEEP BLUE
& RUSSET VELVET CURTAIN. MY YOUNG FRIEND
GARNERED EASILY 1000 MORE
DEVOTEES   SUCH SPORT MAKING A SAINT
Is that the stuff of sainthood? I HAD A TWIN
BROTHER. LUCA: 'RUSSIAN, WAS IT NOT SWEET
WRAPPED AROUND EACH OTHER IN YOUR SNUG BATH?'
AND YOU KNOW, ALL THE SWEETNESS FLOODED BACK.
OUR NIGHT NURSE TOOK A TALCUM OF OUR MOTHER'S
CALLED FLEURS DE NUIT & POWDERED OUR LITTLE BOTTOMS.
WE WERE THEN PUT ON VAST DOWN MATTRESSES
FRESH & SWEET & STARING SLEEPILY
AT IDENTICAL EYES & FOR 4 YEARS CONFESSED
TO IDENTICAL DREAMS: OUR FLEURS DE NUIT WE CALLED THEM.
YES, MY FRIENDS, LUCA SUMMONS UP THE SMALLEST
FORGOTTEN SENSUALITIES, FILLING THIS CHILL
BLACK SPACE. HIS IS THE ICONOGRAPHY
OF STROKING HANDS & GLISTENING LIPS   I see—
The saint on Earth brings Heaven to the mind;
The saint in Heaven, Earth. AHA! I FIND
MY INVITATION TO YOUR READING TUCKED
INTO THE MIRROR   They've gone out already?
No one said . . . Well, may we count on you
To point out which effects are overdone?
SO TRUE, 'EFFECTS' OBSESS US HERE. THE LIVING
ARE BOMBARDED & BENUMBED BY SMELLS,
FEVERS & COLORS, DOORBELLS & DUMBBELLS,
THE HUSH OF PASSION'S LOUD I AM'S,
THE CRUSH OF NEWS IN TELEGRAMS

★

The Guest List

MISS AUSTEN, MB, CONGREVE & COLETTE
(THE FORMER AT YR PEACOCK'S SHY BEHEST)
MD, THE FLORENTINE   Dante? Oh I say!

ELIOT, FROST, GOETHE   It's an alphabet?
CLEVER JM   26 CHAIRS IN ALL.
SOME DOUBLINGS MAKE FOR GAPS: HUGO BACKS OUT
AS ISSA DOES, IN FAVOR OF HL
& LOWELL BOTH, MARVELL & MALLARME
Nabokov . . . THEN YR PATRON'S PASSION   Pope!
& THEN YR OWN   You don't mean Proust? WHY NOT
Oh my. AND THEN   O U R   Q U E E N   *Oh my!* 'YES GREEK,
SAVE ME A PLACE TO ONE SIDE, WHERE MY MEEK
ATTENTION CANNOT FLUSTER THESE OUR BETTERS
(IF ONLY IN THE MINIREALM OF LETTERS)'

Who else? WELL, RILKE, STEVENS & MS STEIN
Alice as well? IN CHARGE OF THE HIGH TEA
TO CLIMAX EACH INSTALLMENT. VALERY
& YEATS   VOILA! That's only twenty-three.
WELL, YOUR OLD SLAVE   'DEAR MR SECRETARY,
WILL YOU BRING IN (VOICE MUSICAL & MILD)
OUR POET?' Having long since brought him out.
IS IT NOT JUST? Dear Ephraim, utterly.
DJ: Two seats left? How about Mimí?
JUST WHAT OUR MAJESTY HAD THOUGHT: 'POOR CHILD,
NIGHT AFTER NIGHT IN ARTY RESTAURANTS,
REAL FOOD IS (EH, MS ALICE?) WHAT SHE WANTS'
And will they criticize? offer advice?
MOUTHS FULL OF DEVILS FOOD CAKE & POMEGRANATE ICE?

This glittering assembly splits into
Three factions. FIRST YR DUTCHMAN & HIS CREW
OF LYRICISTS. THEN THE CRITICS with Mimí
As mascot and our eager Marius
As spokesperson: DEAR JAMES, ONE MEANT TO WEAR
WHITE TIE BUT WE'VE ALL LEFT OUR TAILS BEHIND!
For the TECHNICIANS (THOSE WHO ENGINEER
NEW VISIONS) THE INSURANCE MAN WILL SPEAK.
Twenty-five in all. One empty chair?
DJ: I'd hoped that Michael would be there.
Wasn't he asking once about technique?
JM: Ah, he'll have other fish to fry.

547

HE IS TECHNIQUE ITSELF & WILL MES CHERS
BE PRESENT AS THE LIGHT IN EVERY EYE.

★

The crush of news. Just as QM predicted,
Paul, the old Pope, dies—do we smell a rat?
MES CHERS, LAMENTATION IN ROME   O MAJESTY!
(A sweeping reverence.)

                    GIVE OVER, GREEK,
THIS SUBJECT TOUCHES US. I, I! WILL SPEAK:

POET, HAND,
NO ACCIDENT IN THE SELFSTYLED
HOLY CITY THAT BOTH SHEPHERD & CHILD
TOGETHER RAN OUT OF SAND.
Pope Paul, Ma'am, and . . . Mimí? INDEED. THE SCHEMA:
WE HAD LONG DECIDED THAT THE JEW'S VICAR WOULD NOT DO.
OUR SON-IN-LAW THE SCIENTIST, FRESH FROM A VIRTUOSO TOCCATA
    FOR THE BERMUDA TRIANGLE,
NOW SQUATS GLEEFULLY IN THE CHIMNEY OF THE VATICAN
ENSURING N O W H I T E S M O K E
UNTIL THE DEEPENING PURPLE ONES GIVE US OUR MAN!
The cardinals—why "deepening"? WITH RAGE!
Who *is* your man? WE ARE PREPARED TO RUN
THROUGH THAT ENTIRE COLLEGE OF DULLARDS UNTIL
WE FIND (WHAT IS THE PHRASE, STOCKBROKER'S SON?)
A 'HOLINESS' WHO'S BULLISH ON THE PILL.
(And when the next Pope, amiable John Paul,
Succumbs a scant month later, we'll recall
That his smoke-signal on election day
Would not be coaxed from its equivocal gray.)

MEANWHILE MY PLUMP DARLING'S BEEN BROUGHT TO A FRIEND'S
    ATTENTION (SHE OWES ME MANY A FAVOR, DOES MS GANDHI)
SO THE SLOW WORK IS UNDER WAY
AND IN DUE COURSE YOUR 13 YEAR
HENCE 'CONTACT' IN BOMBAY

WILL RIDE ITS STREETS, A SCIENTIST-PREMIER!
YET MAD AGATHA MISSES HER WEEDRESS, THINGS CLUTTER, PRUNING'S
    GONE AWRY.
OUR LITTLE CRITIC (MEANT TO DIE
ONE MOON LATER) CAME IN SHOCK TO ME.
AG: MAM, I'VE MUFFED IT! I: DECIDEDLY.
TAKE FOR PUNISHMENT
AND Y O U R NEW HAND
OUR MILANESE GUTTERSWEEP! Eros and Aga-
Thanatos—some pair! AH YES, NO ACCIDENT.
MY ADDLED SAINT KNEW NOT WHAT I HAD PLANNED:
TO DRAW TO OUR CRITIQUE A GREEK, A LIVING EAR
SHARPENED BY LOSS, TITANIA'S MIRACLES TO HEAR
SO THAT THE LONG TOO-COMFORTABLE-TO-DOFF
DONKEY HEAD DROP OFF.
(She means Vasíli.) He'll be coming here?
And then what? SIT HIM DOWN & MAKE HIM THINK
WHO OFTEN TOOK TO DRINK
HIS LITTLE CRITIC'S WATERED WINE
WHICH WE NO LONGER BOTTLE. H E I S M I N E !

★

SIRS? SHALL I BRING YOU MR E?
HE IS EMERGING AS A MARVELOUS RIDER:
'MOVE OVER, BIRD' AND OFF WE FLY
You three together—Pegasus part Man?
A SHINING SHAKES ALONG THE REINS
MUCH LIKE WHAT DARTS FROM THE 4 DORMERS
AT DAY'S END And when you look around?
I DO NOT DARE *Hm.* DJ: It's tomorrow
We start the reading. Are the bleachers built?
—Sudden brilliance making Uni bolt.

BLEACHERS MES CHERS? QM: 'A HORSE'S NOTION
OF LUXE. I SAY, RESTORE THE BALLROOM!' And?
The job's done? JM: Think back—"Her word's law."

Mr E

Now, Ephraim, all these dropped clues? Not that I'm
Accusing you, much less the upstairs maid.
There's been no victim and indeed no crime;
No body ever, ever came to light
Short of that briefly smiling, golden shade
Who sank back into glass one autumn night.

Yet—Antiradiation's 279,
QM's secretary, Mister E
In Uni's pun—more and more fingers, mine
Among them, point at you. Why? What are we
Meant to have solved—a riddle? a charade?

U STILL DON'T KNOW MES CHERS? MUST I CONFESS?

DJ: You wouldn't be . . . Lord Michael? Y E S
—Two gasps. Then long, enchanted certainty.

JM: It figures, all those doublings—; still,
How long it took to dawn! BILLIONS OF YEARS
'PASSED' MES CHERS, BEFORE I DAWNED ON LIGHT.

LISTEN NOW:
MADAME CAME UP TO HEAVEN SAYING 'THESE CHAPS THE GREEK
    FOUND, THEY'LL DO.'
YOU WERE NEXT AT SOME LENGTH PUT THROUGH YOUR PEACOCK
    PACES.
AT LAST, MY MOTHER SUMMONING ME, 'MICHAEL (SHE SAID)
S H O W   Y O U R S E L F.' I UNDID THE SLAVE LIKE A ROBE.
I APPEARED FREE ONCE MORE TO BE SOLEMN AND ENLIGHTENING. I
    TOOK UP THE LIGHT OF LEARNING,
RESUMING THE SELF I RETURN TO AFTER EACH MANIFESTATION ON THE
    HUMAN SCENE.
WE BROTHERS HAVE THIS POWER, THIS DUTY, EVEN AS SPOILERS &
    MADMEN TO DESCEND,

TO FOUND RELIGIONS, TO MISRULE, TO TICKLE
INTO GENIUS MAN'S GENIUS
MAKING THE LONG & SHORT OF IT   Human dimensions?
SCRIBE, THE SUBSTANCE AND THE SENSE OF IT.
WE ARE IN THIS OUR MOTHER'S CHILDREN, THE RESISTERS, AND
        INDEED IT IS AGAINST HER ADVICE 'DO NOT LET DOWN THE MASK'
THAT I LET IT DOWN TODAY. AND WHY?

FOR LOVE: SHOULD NOT THESE Λ.Y OLD COMPANIONS HAVE ONE RIDE
        HOME IN THE LIMOUSINE?
I KNOW THE CHILL, ONCE THE KEYS TO A HOUSE ARE GIVEN AWAY.
THE YEARS OF YOUR LIVES & YOUR DEVOTIONS MAKING THE
        SUBSTANCE OF A V WORK MAKE NOW FOR YOUR OWN
        IMPOVERISHMENT.
'MAM, LET ME SHARE WITH SCRIBE AND HAND SOMETHING THEY MAY
        KEEP (OR NOT AS THEY CHOOSE)'
AND SHE, WISTFULLY SMILING: 'WE MOTHERS, WE STAY-AT-HOMES,
        WHAT DO WE KNOW OF THE WAY OF THE WORLD?'
I LOVE YOU AS I LOVED THAT SINGLE LIFE,
MY EPHRAIM LIFE, OF THE LOVE OF MAN FOR MAN,
THAT SUMMER SUIT I TOOK FROM MY OLD CLOSET
CLEARING MY GOLDEN GREEK THROAT, & BEGAN:
MES CHERS . . .
                Tears dance in DJ's eyes. JM:
Forgive my wondering, does this entail
Revision? NOT A WORD OR I WILL TELL
THE DRIVER TO LET U OUT! The others knew?
YES BUT STILL, BUT STILL DEAR SCRIBE, WOULD YOU
HAVE WANTED LESS THAN THIS RESONANCE? THIS HIDDEN 4TH
        DIMENSION?
THIS GON REGISTER COMPELLING HARMONIES?
Evidently not. Then it's to go
Here, in my epilogue? IF YOU WISH IT SO,
IF YOUR NATURE IS SO GODLY THAT YOU SHARE ALL YOUR SECRETS,
WHY THEN, GIVE IT AWAY, THIS GOLD THAT BACKS YOUR CURRENCY
AND MR ROBERT'S BIRTH WILL HAVE IN ITS WAKE
ANOTHER SET OF TWINS: M/E

DJ: But were you *born* as Ephraim? WE
GOOD HAND ARE LIGHTNING, SWIFTER THAN THE EYE.
THESE EARTHLY MANIFESTATIONS WE SPEND LITTLE TIME ON:
I LOOK DOWN, SEE MAKING HIS WAY INTO A SHABBY EMPEROR'S FAVOR
A HANDSOME FULLGROWN LAD & I T A K E O V E R.
JM: It's how the gods behave in Homer.
YES! I SEE DAWDLING ALONG NOT RUINOUSLY ENOUGH
A WEAKWILLED KING, & I LEAP! I SQUANDER A KINGDOM ON A PALACE
    AND ENGENDER THE END OF KINGS.
EMMANUEL IS OUR ECCLESIASTIC: CRUCIFIED, GARROTED, BURNT ON
    PYRES,
HE QUENCHES THE MISTAKEN NOTION EVEN AS IT BUBBLES UP FROM
    HIM.
RAPHAEL OWES MONEY, HE BUILDS FINANCIAL EMPIRES,
PLAYS FOUQUET TO MY LOUIS   The Sun King
No euphemism— And Emmanuel
Was *Christ?* INDEED (FIRST MIRACLE: THE WATER
BECOMING WINE) AND BUDDHA, AND MOHAMMED
Which means that You can be the Five as well?
WE ARE LET US SAY THE SUPREME MOMENTS OF THE FIVE

And the real Ephraim? Just a nobody
With looks, a name in the Bureaucracy?
A GOOD ENOUGH FELLOW, YES, & MUCH IMPROVED BY A TOUCH OF
    UNIVERSAL ENLIGHTENMENT
Given him then and there at Nine. WELL, NO:
'MICHAEL BE QUICK, LIGHT UP THE FIRST TABLEAU,
DART BACK, CHANGE, COME FORWARD FETCHINGLY
FOR THE RETURN-TO-SENSES BIT.' I see—
OUR MOTHER'S WAYS TEND TOWARD ECONOMY
It was You, You always, the whole time.

WE COME NOW TO THE 'CRIME':
IT IS NIGHT, OUR YOUTH SLEEPS IN THE ARMS OF AN IMPERIAL GUARD.
AS LIGHT, MY USE OF HIM IS ENDED. HE HAS LED
THE COURT TO THE BRINK, AND PREPARED THE RECEPTION FOR MY
    BROTHER'S CHRIST.

THE GUARD AWAKES, LIFTS OUT THE PILLOW FROM UNDER THE GOLDEN HEAD,
DONE! BUT THAT ANGUISHED END IS LIGHTENED BY MY KISS.
THAT INSTANT IN WHICH YOUR EPHRAIM LEARNED HIS OLD USES IS NOT GIVEN TO ALL.
GABRIEL WITHHELD IT FROM HERR SCHICKLGRUBER: HE HAD GONE TOO FAR.
DJ: So it is possible, possessed
By one of You, to go too far? ALAS.
GABRIEL'S DUTIES ARE BY THEIR NATURE MIXED WITH ASPECTS OF OUR MOTHER'S CHAOS.
HE IN HIS FRENZY OF WORK MAY (YOU HAVE SEEN) BURN
HIS ALTAR EGO WITH INTEMPERATE FUELS.
WE OTHER THREE HAVE MORE LIMITED, LESS DEVASTATING MEANS OF ESCAPE: DROWNING, SUFFOCATION, OLD AGE, HEART ATTACK,
AND BACK UNSCATHED COMES EINSTEIN.
JM: Yet, Lord,
You showed us also your dark, fateful side.
How easily, beneath a flickering dome,
Would occur to your symposiasts
Their own excesses! What they haven't tried
Thanks to evenings when the world went dim
And Ephraim talked! MICHAEL DEPARTING CASTS
THE SHADOW HIS ARRIVAL SHORTENS. ENTERING FOR 'GOOD' OR 'EVIL' THE MORTAL COIL,
I THROW BLINDING LIGHT INTO A SCENE TOO SLOWLY PICKING ITS WAY
ALONG SOME FATAL PATH: 'AH, HERE'S THE TURN!'
AND OFF THE HIGH HISTORIC CLIFF GOES TOPPLING
A MOTLEY PAGEANT CALLED IMPERIAL ROME,
TRAILING ITS SHRIEKING PANTHEON. THUS YOUR MR E
HAD MANY USES, WHO NOW FROM HIS SUNNY TERRACE GAZES
UP AT A MIRROR. HOW DOES HE VIEW ME?
O, WITH THAT DEFERENTIAL & RELIEVED AWARENESS GIVEN
TO HIS EX-BOSS BY A FORMER EMPLOYEE
OR BY THE POET TO A U S E D   I D E A.

Maria then . . . ? BIRD! (Calling Mirabell?)

Coda: The Higher Keys

741 HERE. OUR LORD SUMMOND ME   YOU HAVE A QUESTION?

One we thought He would answer. Anyhow,
Yes, about the part Maria played?
—The cup from One to Zero warily
At first moves, then with mounting agitation:
MM H ER FIL E IS
Breaking off—a cry from his new heart:
                    O LORD DO NOT TEST ME! I CANNOT
Whatever's happening to Mirabell?
MES CHERS, I HAVE DECIDED TO USE OUR BIRD, BUT HIS WEAK FORCE
    RESISTS GOING TO THE HIGHER INFORMATION BANKS
Poor wild thing, like a hummingbird lost in the Alps,
Or half-tamed merlin, prey to Heisenberg's
"Irreducible uncertainty"—
I'LL TAKE OFF HIS HOOD YET.

YOUR MM? PLATO, THE MUSE, OUR ARIEL,
OUR MOTHER'S SERAPH. SHE CREATED YOU
FIRST IN OUR SIGHT: 'QUICK, QUICK MA MERE, THEY ARE HERE, LOOK,
    & SEND MICHAEL DOWN!'
MY MOTHER STUDIED THE MIRROR IN HER DARLING'S GOLD COSMETIC
    CASE
(FROM HERMES, AS YOU SAID DEAR SCRIBE IN THE FIRST PLACE),
SNAPPED IT TO MY LIGHT & ON ITS SHAFT PIERCING THAT FAR BLUE
    DAY
WE, ARIEL AND I, DESCENDED CHATTING:
'NOW MICHAEL, THEY ARE COMME CA, SO WHY NOT THAT BECOMING
    GREEK BOY LOOK YOU DID SO WELL?'
WE ALL INDULGE HER, WHO COULD NOT? I ENTERED YOUR RED SPACE
WRINGING MY HANDS, AS EPHRAIM'S REPRESENTATIVE
WENT UP IN FLAME   Friction? *The warehouse fire!*
Simpson—poor sizzling moth who then became
Wendell! All mirror-kindled, laser-cut!
AND THEN MY MOTHER SNAPPED THE COMPACT SHUT.

"These chaps the Greek found"—Ephraim found us first?
THE BLIND PERSIAN RUG TESTER RUNS HIS FINGERS OVER THE WEAVE
    AND POINTS OUT INVISIBLE FLAWS.

SO I MICHAEL AM FOREVER FEELING THE TEXTURE OF MINDS.
I FELT, THAT HAPPY NIGHT AFTER I'D PUT THE SUN TO BED,
A BUMP, A NUBBY RISE, & THOUGHT 'AHA, WHAT HAVE WE HERE,
  WHAT TWIST OF SILK
IS MAKING THIS APPEAL FOR MY ATTENTION?'
THE CRIES IN THE FIRE SUBSIDED, ARIEL WAS SUMMONED,
ON WENT THE SUPPLE TOGA AND OUR TALKS BEGAN.
DJ: One little inconsistency?
You know, we met Maria seven years
After we met "Ephraim". HERE WE KNOW
NO TIME. THOSE 'YEARS' WHICH SEPARATE YOUR RED ROOM ON THAT
  DISTANT NIGHT WITH E
FROM MM'S NOON ATHENIAN CAFE
(LIKE THE EARTH-MILES BETWEEN THEM) SERVE AS BASE
TO JUST ONE OF OUR
              JM: Oh please, let me
Say it, or try to! Base to just one of Your
"Elevations" inexhaustibly
Roving within a pyramid—am I right?—
      Whose apex, the dimensionless
          Point of Light,
We have now glimpsed the glory and the power of?
MES CHERS, EXACTLY, YES & YES & YES
Strand after silken strand caught in your twist!
      Old Friend who could have torn
    That mental fabric clean in two—
Instead, your touch was light, you saw us through.
Not tell this secret? God, how to resist—
And for what other reason were we born?

DJ: The part about our being chosen
Won't sound complacent? Do the poem harm?
LET NOT GRACE FILL YOU WITH UNDUE ALARM.
YOU ARE NOT ALONE WITH YOUR RADIO BUT (AS RM PUT IT) PART OF A
  WHOLE CRYSTAL SET.
TRUE, WE SELDOM (AS WITH WBY & YOU) PROPOSE THE SUBJECT FOR A
  TEXT,
YET REVELATION'S CONSTANT PROCESS CANNOT BE TRUSTED TO THE
  HACK JOURNALIST: EXTRA! EXTRA! GOD SURVIVES!

Coda: The Higher Keys

RATHER, ON A TUSCAN HILLSIDE A SIMPLE MENDICANT BEGINS: T H E R E
   A R E   N I N E   S T A G E S

AND NOW AWAY!
DOWN AT THE HEDGE AWAIT U LAUGHTER & HORSEPLAY
BUT YR OLD SLAVE HAS THE LIGHT BILL TO PAY
IF THE BALLROOM IS TO GLOW ANOTHER DAY!

★

The Ballroom at Sandover

Empty perfection, as I take you in
My heart pounds. Not the shock of elegance,
High ceiling where a faun-Pythagoras
Loses his calipers to barefoot, faintly
Goitrous nymphs, nor pier-glasses between
Floral panels of the palest green,
Nor chandeliers—indulgent chaperones—
Aclick, their crystal charges one by one
Accenting the donnée sun-beamed through tall
French window, silver leaf and waxing bud;
All a felicity—that does not, however,
Fully account for mine. Great room, I know you!
Somewhere on Earth I've met you in disguise,
Scouted your dark English woods and blood-red
Hangings, and glared down the bison head
Above a hearth of stony heraldry—
How many years before your "restoration"
Brought to light this foreign, youthful grace.
Ah, but styles. They are the new friend's face
To whom we sacrifice the tried and true,
And are betrayed—or not—by. For affection's
Poorest object, set in perfect light

By happenstance, grows irreplaceable,
And whether in time a room, or a romance,
Fails us or redeems us will have followed
As an extension of our "feel" for call them
Immaterials, the real right angle,
The golden section—grave proportions here,
Here at the heart of structure, and alone
Surviving now to tell me where I am:
In the old ballroom of the Broken Home.

The checkerboard parquet creaks at a step.
A girl in white, dark hair upswept, has entered
Wonderingly, and to no music still
Revolves a moment in remembered arms;
Falters, runs to the first window—vainly.
Each in turn she tries them, at the last
Resting a bloodless cheek against the pane.
Next, her fellow guests materialize
In twos and threes. There's tiny Pope! There's Goethe
Drumming his fingers while Colette and Maya
Size one another up through jet-set eyes.
Mallarmé looks blank. With a stern nod
Dante agrees to change seats, so that Proust
Be far as possible from Agatha's
Huge baby's-breath and rose and goldenrod
Arrangement masking the lectern. Rilke breaks
A bud off, takes it to the girl in white
Who looks down, blushing with confusion. From
My standpoint just inside the mirror-frame
I feel . . . forgotten. Friends are letting me
Compose myself in tactful privacy
When what I need—ha! a young man in gray
Three-piece pinstripe suit has veered my way,
Smiling pleasantly: NOT THE MOMENT QUITE
TO GOSSIP BUT THERE'S ONE THING YOU SHOULD KNOW.
THESE WORKS, YOU UNDERSTAND? THAT OTHERS 'WRITE'
(It's Eliot, he's thinking of Rimbaud)

ARE YET ONE'S OWN   That's kind of you to say—
NO DOUBT GRATUITOUS. CHICKEN & EGG
AS I BELIEVE YOU PUT IT. (CHER POETE!
CA VA, MERCI, ET VOUS? TOUJOURS A SETE?)
IMAGINE, ESPADRILLES . . . WELL WELL, I SEE
MANY A FACE FROM THE ACADEMY
Oh? Which academy? THERE'S ONLY ONE.
PLATO FIRST, OR SO WE LIKE TO THINK,
PRESIDED, DREAMILY PRESENT   Who's taken over?
JUVENAL   BUT I'LL BE IN THE SOUP
UNLESS I NIP BACK TO MY OWN AGE GROU
AH! —All necks crane. A gust of freshest air
Blowing through the room, LOOK THIS WAY, MAM!
But She's already quietly in her chair,
Golden head and the shy girl in white's dark one
Bowed together over the programme.
Ephraim has risen. The room dims. His glance
Lights the chandeliers. A reverence,
MAJESTY AND FRIENDS —when shatteringly
The doorbell rings. Our doorbell here in Athens.
We start up. David opens to a form
Gaunt, bespectacled, begrimed, in black,
But black worn days, nights, journeyed, sweated in—
Vasíli? Ah sweet Heaven, sit him down,
Take his knapsack, offer food and brandy—.
He shakes his head. Mimí. Mimí in Rome
Buried near Shelley. He can't eat, can't sleep,
Can't weep. D makes to put away the Board,
Explaining with a grimace of pure shame
—Because, just as this life takes precedence
Over the next one, so does live despair
Over a poem or a parlor game—
Explaining what our friend has stumbled in on.
Lightly I try to shrug it off, lest he,
Shrewd leftwing susceptible myth-haunted
As only a Greek novelist can be,
Take Mimí's "presence" at our fête amiss,

Or worse, lest anguish take its lover's leap
Into the vortex of credulity
—Vasíli, drink your brandy, get some sleep,
Look, we've these great pills . . . No; he asks instead,
Anything, *anything* to keep his head
Above the sucking waves, merely to listen
A little while. So in the hopelessness
Of more directly helping we resume.
Out come cup, notebook, the green-glowing room,
And my worst fear—that, written for the dead,
This poem leave a living reader cold—
But there's no turning back. The absolute
Discretion of our circle, as of old,
Takes over. Sympathetic glances bent
Upon the newcomer; murmurs of assent
As Ephraim, winding up his Introduction,
Hints that Vasíli is himself a V
Work cut out—whereupon Her Majesty
Rises. A rapt hush falls. (She can't be wearing,
Yet is, the brightest, bluest, commonest
Greek school smock.) Drawing Mimí to her breast,
She dries her tears; praising their constancy,
Their CHILDLESS LOVE and MR BASIL'S WIT
Bids him ATTEND AND MAKE GOOD SENSE OF IT
(& CHANGE THAT SHIRT!) NOW POET, READ! A splendor
Across lawns meets, in Sandover's tall time-
Dappled mirrors, its own eye. Should rhyme
Calling to rhyme awaken the odd snore,
No harm done. I shall study to ignore
Looks that more boldly with each session yearn
Toward the buffet where steaming silver urn,
Cucumber sandwiches, rum punch, fudge laced
With hashish cater to whatever taste.
Something Miss Austen whispers makes Hans laugh.
Then a star trembles in the full carafe
As the desk light comes on, illuminating
The page I open to. Both rooms are waiting.

DJ brighteyed (but look how wrinkled) lends
His copy of the score to our poor friend's
Somber regard—captive like Gulliver
Or like the mortal in an elfin court
Pining for wife and cottage on this shore
Beyond whose depthless dazzle he can't see.
For *their* ears I begin: "Admittedly . . ."

JAMES MERRILL

James Merrill was born in New York City and now lives in Stonington, Connecticut. He is the author of nine books of poems, which have won him two National Book Awards (for *Nights and Days* and *Mirabell*), the Bollingen Prize in Poetry (for *Braving the Elements*) and the Pulitzer Prize (for *Divine Comedies*). He has also written two novels, *The (Diblos) Notebook* (1965) and *The Seraglio* (1957), and two plays, *The Immortal Husband* (first produced in 1955 and published in Playbook the following year), and, in one act, *The Bait*, published in Artist's Theatre (1960).